1 MONTH OF
FREE
READING

at

www.ForgottenBooks.com

By purchasing this book you are
eligible for one month membership to
ForgottenBooks.com, giving you
unlimited access to our entire
collection of over 1,000,000 titles via
our web site and mobile apps.

To claim your free month visit:

www.forgottenbooks.com/free923627

ISBN 978-0-260-03350-5
PIBN 10923627

REPORTS

OF

CASES ARGUED AND DECIDED

IN THE

CIRCUIT COURT OF THE UNITED STATES,

FOR THE

SEVENTH CIRCUIT.

BY JOHN McLEAN,

CIRCUIT JUDGE.

VOLUME VI.

CINCINNATI:
H. W. DERBY & CO., PUBLISHERS,
1856.

WRIGHTSON & CO., PRINTERS.
CINCINNATI, OHIO.

JUDGES,

WHOSE DECISIONS ARE REPORTED IN THIS VOLUME.

JOHN McLEAN,

ASSOCIATE JUSTICE OF THE SUPREME COURT OF THE UNITED STATES AND JUDGE OF THE SEVENTH CIRCUIT.

Hon. ROSS WILKINS,

DISTRICT JUDGE FOR MICHIGAN.

Hon. H. H. LEAVITT,

DISTRICT JUDGE FOR OHIO.

92033

TABLE OF CASES.

THE FARMERS' LOAN AND TRUST COMPANY OF NEW YORK,
v.
DOUGLASS McKINNEY.

If testimony be admitted without objection, and no motion is made to withdraw it from the jury, it will afford no ground for a new trial.

Under a law of Michigan, a conveyance of land within it is valid, if the deed be executed in any other State, according to the laws of such State.

Under a quit claim deed from one who has no title, a subsequently acquired title, will not enure to the benefit of the grantee. But under a warranty such a title would enure, by way of estoppel.

A deed of quit claim made before, but acknowledged subsequently, to the date of the title of the grantor, would, under certain circumstances, be good.

This, on the supposition that the transaction was bona-fide, the intention being to make a valid deed.

When the first deed was made, the land may be presumed to have been paid for, to the government, the patent only being necessary to give the legal title.

When the defendant against whom the judgment was entered, had no notice, and that appears from the proceeding, the judgment is a nullity.

But where there was due notice, or an appearance of the defendant, no other error in the proceedings can make the judgment a nullity.

Any other error may be ground for a reversal of the judgment, but it is not void.

Mr. *Clark* for the plaintiff.
Mr. *Howard* for defendant.

The Farmers' Loan and Trust Company of N. Y. *v.* Douglass McKinney.

OPINION OF THE COURT.

This is a motion to set aside the verdict of the jury on several points made at the trial, some of which were reserved.

The action was an ejectment, to recover the possession of eighty acres of land in the State of Michigan. A patent for the land was issued the 5th of June, 1837, to Daniel Hudson. A quit claim deed was executed by Hudson to Samuel T. Gaines for the land, the 25th of September, 1836, which was acknowledged the 31st of December, 1852. And on the 28th of September, 1836, Hudson, by his Attorney in fact J. Wright Gordon, conveyed the tract of land to Gaines by a deed of warranty. This deed was duly acknowledged on the same day it was signed, and recorded in the proper county, on the 17th of November following.

The power of attorney under which the above conveyance was made was executed by Hudson and wife, in the State of New York, on the 26th of August, 1836, and was acknowledged on the following day, before a Supreme Court Commissioner of the said State. It was received for record in the proper county in Michigan, on the 26th of November, 1836, and was recorded by the Register.

A mortgage on the land was duly executed by Gaines, to secure the payment of a sum of money to Ketchum, who assigned the same, in the State of New York, to the plaintiff, a corporation under the laws of New York, and doing business in that State, to secure the payment of a loan of money to him by the plaintiff.

The debt not being paid, a bill was filed by the bank to foreclose the mortgage, in the Circuit Court of the United States, within the district of Michigan; and by its decision, the foreclosure was decreed, and the land was sold to the bank, at public sale, by a Master in chancery, who was directed to sell it, and a deed in due form was made by him to the bank. And this action is brought to recover the possession of the same.

The quit claim deed is objected to, as having been executed by Hudson, before he received the patent from the Government, and that under such a deed, the subsequently acquired title by Hudson did not enure to the benefit of his grantee. It is true, where a deed of quit claim has been made for land, to which the grantor has no title, a subsequently acquired title cannot operate to make good the quit claim. Such a deed can only transfer the title of the grantor at the time it was executed. If the first deed had contained a warranty, it would have operated by way of estoppel to make it effectual.

But the quit claim deed was not wholly incorperative. It appears from the patent, that full payment had been made by Hudson, to the United States, for the land, under the Acts of Congress, so that he had at least an equitable right to the land, and that, by the quit claim deed, passed to the purchaser.

That deed was acknowledged by Hudson long after he obtained the patent, and it may be a matter of doubt whether such an acknowledgment, after having parted with the equity, does not give effect to the deed from that time.

But it appears that three days after the execution of the quit claim deed, the Attorney in fact of Hudson, executed a deed of warranty for the land to Gaines, which was duly acknowledged and recorded. The objection to this deed is, that the power, under which it was made, was defectively executed, and consequently was not valid.

The power had but one witness, and, it is insisted that the law of Michigan, under which it was executed, requires two. When this power was offered in evidence there was no objection made to its admission.

Unless an objection be made to evidence when offered, it will be presumed to be admitted by consent. And if no motion is made to withdraw it from the jury, during the trial, the objection will not be heard on a motion for a new trial.

But if this point were open on this motion, it could not be

sustained. The Territorial Act of Michigan of the 12th of April, 1827, provides, that deeds for lands in the Territory, when executed in any other Territory or State, "shall be acknowledged and proved and certified, according to, and in conformity with, the laws and usages of the Territory, State or Country, in which such deeds or conveyances were acknowledged or proved," such deeds are declared valid in law, the same as if executed in the Territory of Michigan in pursuance of its laws; which deeds shall be recorded, &c.

The power of attorney objected to was executed in the State of New York in pursuance of its laws. Two witnesses are not required by the law of that State to a deed; and it was duly acknowledged before a commissioner, who has power to take such acknowledgments. Under the above statute this deed, as a part of the conveyance, has the same validity as if executed in Michigan, conformably to law.

The power of attorney authorized Gordon to sell the lands of Hudson, in the State of Michigan, as was done in the above instance. The deed executed under the power contained a warranty which caused the title, subsequently acquired by Hudson, to enure to the benefit of his prior grantee.

But it is objected that the plaintiff, being a corporation in the State of New York, cannot hold land in the State of Michigan. By the second section of the Act of 1836, amendatory of the original charter, the plaintiff was authorized to take trusts, and to loan money on bonds and mortgages, &c.

As a general principle it is admitted, that no corporate functions can be communicated to an association of men, which they can claim a right to exercise, beyond the limits of the State in which their powers are given. But there are some things which a corporation may do in other States, as a matter of comity. In the *Bank of Augusta* v. *Earle*, 13 Peters 520, it is said—" It is well settled, that by the law of comity among nations, a corporation created by one sovereignty is permitted to make contracts in another, and to sue in its courts; and that the same law of comity prevails among the several sovereignties of this Union." But this comity may be prohibited by a settled course of policy of the State or by statute. Until this shall be done, however, the comity is presumed to exist in the several States of the Union.

By the common law an alien can take lands by purchase, though not by descent; in other words, he may take by the act of the party, but not by operation of law. Nor is there any distinction whether the alien claims by grant or devise. Co. Litt. 2. 6. It is said the alien has capacity to take, but not to hold lands, and that lands so taken may be seized into the hands of the sovereign. But until the lands are so seized, the alien has complete dominion over them. He is a good tenant of the freehold in a precipe, on a common recovery. 4 Leon. 84; Golds 6, 102; 10 Mad. 125. And the alien may convey to a purchaser. *Sheafe.* v. *O'Neil*, 1. Mass. Rep. 256. Coke Litt. 52 6, would seem to be contrary, but his meaning may be, that the alien may convey a defeasible estate, which may be devested on office found. *Fairfax's Devisee* v. *Hunter's Lessee*, 7 Cranch 603. This rule coincides with the Jus Gentium. Vattel. 6, 2; ch. 8, sec. 112, 114; Grotius Lib. 2, ch. 6, sec. 16.

It seems to be a settled principle, that a title acquired by an alien by purchase, is not devested until office found. The devestiture requires some notorious act from which it may appear that the free-hold is in another. 1 Bac. Abr. alien 6, 133; Page's Case 5, Co. 22. Even after office found, the king is not adjudged in possession, unless the possession be vacant. He must enter or seize by his officer. In *Doe ex dem. Governeur's Heirs* v. *Robertson et al.*, 11 Wheat. 332, it was held, that "An alien may take real property, by grant, whether from the State or a private citizen, and may hold the same until

his title is devested by an inquest of office, or some equivalent proceeding."

By the Act of 31st of March, 1827, aliens were authorized
to purchase lands in the Territory of Michigan, the same as
citizens. The reference to aliens, in this respect, was made,
therefore, on the ground that there was some analogy between
them and the corporations of other States. In *Leazure* v.
Hillegas, 7 Sergt. & Rawle 313; *Baird* v. *The Bank of
Washington*, 11 Sergt. & Rawle 418; the case of an alien is
considered as analogous to that of a corporation.

By an Act of the State of Pennsylvania, of the 6th of
April, 1833, relative to the escheats of lands held by corporations, without the license of the commonwealth, etc., it is
declared that no corporation, either of this state or of any
other state, though lawfully incorporated, can in any case
purchase lands within this state, without incurring the forfeiture of said lands to the commonwealth, unless such
purchase be sanctioned and authorized by an Act of the legislature. By this Act the corporations of other states, in
regard to the purchase of lands in the state, are placed on
the same footing as corporations of the State of Pennsylvania; and the Supreme Court of that state, in the case of
Leazure v. Hillegas, 7 Binney, 313, as to the right of the
Bank of North America to purchase, hold, and convey the
lands in question, held, " that the right of a corporation, in
this respect, was like an alien, who has power to take, but
not to hold lands: and that although the land thus held by
an alien, may be subject to forfeiture after office found, yet
until some act is done by the government, according to its
own laws, to vest the estate in itself, it remains in the alien,
who may convey it to a purchaser; but he can convey no
estate which is not defeasible by the commonwealth." And
this doctrine was sanctioned by the Supreme Court of the
United States, in the case of *Runyan* y. the *Lessee of Coster,
et al.*, 14 Peters, 131.

In Michigan no law or policy of the State is shown, which prohibits corporations from purchasing lands in the State, and it is presumed that no such law, as in the State of Pennsylvania, exists in Michigan. It would seem, therefore, that the corporation of another State, as the Farmers' Loan and Trust Company, which by its charter is authorized to loan money on mortgages, may take a mortgage on lands in Michigan, there being no prohibitory law or policy of that State on the subject. And if such a security may be taken legally, it may be made available in the ordinary legal mode in such cases.

It would seem that the principle which applies to aliens, in regard to the purchase of lands, should more strongly apply to corporations. They are constituted by associations of citizens, who, for the convenience of business, assume a name which, under the sanction of law, is binding on the individuals concerned. This artificial being, to use technical language, possesses all the qualities of a natural person, so far as regards the object of the corporation. And that such a legal organization, having the right to loan money on mortgages, without restriction of territory, should have a right to take mortgages wherever its loans are made, would seem to be a matter of course. And this may be safely assumed, where there is no prohibition. And where there are no laws of escheat, it may well be doubted, whether the land may not be conveyed to a purchaser, by the corporation, by an indefeasible title.

The argument is not used beyond the necessity of converting the mortgaged estate into money, to satisfy the debt. This would carry out the transaction of the loan by both parties, and thus far, we think, may be legally done, subject to the comity of the State. This is no more the exercise of corporate powers, than in bringing a suit and by due process securing the fruits of the judgment.

But it is contended that the decree, on the equity side of

the court, for the foreclosure of the mortgage and sale of the premises, is a nullity, the court having no jurisdiction.

In the case of *Sheldon et al.* v. *Sill*, 8 How. 448, the court held that where the mortgagor, a citizen of Michigan, assigned the mortgage to a citizen of the State of New York, the court could not take jurisdiction on a bill filed to foreclose the mortgage, as the assignment was within the 11th section of the judiciary act, which prohibits the assignee from suing in the federal courts on an assigned instrument, where the assignor could not sue, in the same court.

And it is alleged that from the face of the proceedings it appears in the case now before us, that the assignor of the mortgage was a citizen of Michigan, and therefore that his assignee could not sue in the Circuit Court. And the case of *Williamson et al.* v. *Berry*, 8 How. 541, is cited. That was a case involving the right of the Chancellor, under the Acts of New York, to make an order, authorizing Clark to convey a part of certain devised premises, in satisfaction of his debts. That case turned upon a construction of the acts referred to, under the decisions of the State, and the Supreme Court held the Chancellor had not the power. That decision, therefore, can have no direct application to the case under consideration. Mr. Justice Wayne, in giving the opinion of the Court, referred to the decisions of the State, very properly, as having a bearing on the case; but it is supposed that some of those decisions have gone too far, in permitting a record to be contradicted on the question of jurisdiction.

There can be no doubt, however, that where the party had no regular notice, against whom the judgment or decree was entered, and there was no waiver of notice, by an appearance, that the judgment may be treated as a nullity. But it by no means follows, that where a judgment is erroneous, and might be reversed on a writ of error, that it can be so treated.

It is a matter in this case of some nicety, as in all others, where the question arises, between what is void and what is voidable, by an appropriate procedure. The principal difficulty arises from a want of precision in the language of Judges who have acted on this question, where a judgment is brought collaterally before the court. In such a case there can be no doubt, if from the record it appears the defendant had no notice, the judgment entered against him is absolutely void.

The jurisdiction must always appear in the proceedings of inferior courts where jurisdiction is limited; but the jurisdiction will be presumed, in a case before a court, where jurisdiction is general. It is true that the Circuit Court of the United States exercises a limited jurisdiction, but still, it has been held by the Supreme Court, that it is not an inferior court, in the above sense, so as to make void its judgments, for want of jurisdiction, though they may be reversible.

In the case of *Kempe's Lessee* v. *Kennedy et al.*, 5 Cranch 173, Chief Justice Marshall said—"The Courts of the United States are all of limited jurisdiction, and their proceedings are erroneous, if the jurisdiction be not shown upon them. Judgments rendered in such cases may certainly be reversed, but this Court is not prepared to say that they are absolute nullities, which may be totally disregarded." And in the case of the *United States* v. *Nourse*, 9 Peters 28, the Chief Justice says—" It is a rule to which no exception is recollected, that the judgment of a Court of competent jurisdiction, while unreversed, concludes the subject matter as between the same parties."

In *Voorhees* v. *the Bank of the United States*, 10 Peters 449, the Court say, " The errors of the Court, however apparent, can be examined only by an appellate power." And they say, " The line which separates error in judgment from the usurpation of power is very definite; and is precisely that which denotes the cases where a judgment or decree is reversible only by an appellate court, or may be declared a nullity collaterally, when it is offered in evidence in an action concerning the matter adjudicated, or purporting to have been so. In the one case, it is a record importing absolute verity; in the other, mere waste paper."

In *Simms* and *Wise* v. *Slacum*, 3 Cranch 300, the Court say, "The judgments of a Court of competent jurisdiction, though obtained by fraud, have never been considered absolutely void."

In the case of *McCormick* v. *Sullivant*, 10 Wheaton 192, it is said, "The reason assigned by the replication, why that decree cannot operate as a bar, is that the proceedings in that suit do not show that the parties to it, plaintiffs and defendants, were citizens of different States, and that, consequently, the suit was *coram non judice*, and the decree void. But this reason," the court say, "proceeds upon an incorrect view of the character and jurisdiction of the inferior courts of the United States. They are all of limited jurisdiction; but they are not on that account, inferior courts, in the technical sense of those words, whose judgments, taken alone, are to be disregarded. If the jurisdiction be not alleged in the proceedings, their judgments and decrees are erroneous, and may, upon a writ of error, or appeal, be reversed for that cause. But they are not absolute nullities."

The above cases would seem to be conclusive on this point. If all judgments in the federal circuit courts were to be held as nullities, where the jurisdiction is not alleged, no one can tell the extent of mischief which might result. If they are nullities, no titles under such judgments, or other rights, would be available. A want of the proper allegation of citizenship of the parties, is often the result of inattention, in cases where no defences are made. The decisions above stated, are wise, as they protect substantial interests from a mere technicality.

Where the citizenship of the parties is not averred in the pleading, there is a want of jurisdiction as palpably as the face of the papers can present. No presumption can be drawn to supply the want of this averment. A court of errors on a writ of error, would necessarily reverse for want of jurisdiction in such a case. And if, as the counsel allege, it does appear that the assignment of the mortgage in the case under consideration, was made by a citizen of Michigan, that cannot affect the character of the decree. It may be reversed on error or appeal, but the judgment is not a nullity.

The judgment of the Circuit Court may be treated as a nullity, when the party, against whom the judgment or decree was entered, had no notice of the suit. But the judgment or decree cannot be so treated when the parties are before the Court, on account of any omission or error on the face of the proceedings. This would seem to be the true distinction in such cases. If the proceedings could be examined, to ascertain when an error had intervened which would be fatal to the jurisdiction, all judgments would be declared a nullity, which might be reversed, for want of jurisdiction, on a writ of error or on appeal. No Court can sanction such a principle of judicial action.

For the reasons above stated, the motion for a new trial is overruled, and judgment must be entered in the case.

ALICE FRASER v. CHARLES WELLER ET AL.

The ancient forms of the action of ejectment having been modified by the statute of Michigan, and a new mode provided, that mode must be pursued.

Special pleas in this mode are not allowed. A demurrer, on this ground, must be sustained to a special plea. The statute gives a second trial, as a matter of course, if the motion be made to set aside the first judgment within three years.

A new trial thus granted, which vacates the judgment, the party cannot bring a new suit in this Court. Having sought the special remedy under the statute, in the State Court, he cannot abandon it.

Mr. ———, for plaintiff.
Mr. *Hawkins* for defendant.

OPINION OF THE COURT.

This is an action of ejectment. In addition to the general issue, Weller, the defendant, pleaded that the grantor of the plaintiff had heretofore instituted an action of ejectment against the defendant for the same premises, in which a trial was had, and a judgment rendered for the defendant in the State Court.

To this plea the plaintiff replied, that the said judgment had been set aside and a new trial granted.

The defendant demurred to this replication; and assigned as cause of demurrer, that the revised statutes of 1846 abolished the ancient forms in the action of ejectment, and authorized a statutory action; and that by section 35 it is declared that the judgment in the action should be conclusive. But that the 36th section authorized the Court to grant a new trial, under certain circumstances, and declared that not more than two new trials shall be granted.

The statute provides that the defendant, in the action of ejectment, may demúr, or plead the general issue and give special matter in evidence. No special pleas, therefore, can be allowed. The demurrer to the plea is, therefore, sustained.

The Court intimated that the special remedy given by the statute must be pursued. The first judgment in ejectment is final, unless within three years a motion is made to set aside the judgment, and the costs of the first trial are paid. This motion was made within the time limited, and the costs were paid, so that the judgment was vacated, under the statute.

And the question arises whether under such circumstances, the suit may be brought in this Court. If the first judgment had not been set aside, under the statute, it would have been final. It was set aside without cause, on the motion being made within the time limited. The judgment was vacated under the statute, which was a part of the proceeding authorized; this being done, the party is not at liberty to resort to this tribunal. It would be a fraud upon the law.

For aught that appears, the first judgment could not have been set aside, except under the provisions of the statute. This remedy having been claimed under the statute, the party is bound to go on with another trial. Having set aside the bar to another suit, he does so, under an obligation to pursue the special remedy under the statute. He cannot claim the remedy in part, to his advantage, and then abandon it to the injury of the other party.

———

MATTHEWS v. LYALL.

The defendant being an alien, and being sued before the State Court of Oakland County, filed a petition at the first term to remove the cause into the Circuit Court of the United States. Bond was given, to which there was no objection, and it appeared that the matter in dispute exceeded the sum of five hundred dollars.

The State Court refused to permit the removal. This Court held, that the requisites of the Act of Congress having been complied with in this case, the State Court had no right to deny the removal. The law declares, that, under such circumstances, the State Court shall proceed no further in the case. And the Supreme Court have held, that all subsequent proceedings in the State Court are *coram non judice*. 16 Peters 101.

But in this case, the complainant dismissed his bill. This we suppose he had a right to do, whether the cause be considered in the State Court, or in this Court.

———

KETCHUM v. DRIGGS & CARGILL.

A demurrer, to a bill praying an injunction, must be decided, before a motion for the injunction can be heard.

A defective allegation of citizenship is a good ground of demurrer.

The Court gave leave to amend the bill, and also time to the defendant to put in a voluntary answer, and file affidavits.

Mr. *Campbell* for complainant.
Mr. *Davidson* for defendant.

OPINION OF THE COURT.

This is a bill praying an injunction, to which a demurrer was filed. The demurrer of course must be decided, before a motion for the injunction can be heard.

There is no sufficient averment of the citizenship of the complainant, and this being apparent on the face of the bill, the demurrer is sustained. Leave was given to amend the bill.

The Court gave time to the defendant to put in a voluntary answer, and to file affidavits.

HALSEY *v.* HURD ET AL.

A plea in abatement is not a waiver of process. The plea may be abandoned, and a motion to quash the writ for a defective service, may be substituted. Where there has been no personal service, the requisites of the statute which are in place of it, must be strictly complied with.

Messrs. *Howard* and *Wendall* for plaintiff.
Mr. *Frazer* for defendant.

OPINION OF THE COURT.

A motion is made to set aside the process in this case, on the ground that it has not been properly served.

The endorsement on the writ is "copy left at defendant's place of business." The law requires, personal service or a copy left "at defendant's usual place of abode." A plea to this effect being filed, it is abandoned, and the motion is substituted.

It is objected, that defendant by filing the plea appeared in the case, and that he cannot, under such circumstances, abandon the plea. But the Court held, that a plea in abatement by the party is not an appearance which constitutes a waiver of process, and also that the service was defective. Where a personal service of process is not made, the requisites of the statute substituted for it, must be strictly complied with. The copy should have been left at the residence of the defendant, and not at his place of business.

———

LYELL v. MAYNARD.

A certified copy of a patent, by the Recorder of a county, is not evidence, as the law does not require the patent to be recorded in the county.

Davidson and *Halbrook* for plaintiff.
Campbell, Hawkins and *Morgan* for defendant.

OPINION OF THE COURT.

This is an action of ejectment. To sustain the right of the plaintiff, a certified copy of the patent was offered for the land in controversy, which was objected to, as the law did not require patents emanating from the general government to be recorded.

The Court held that the copy was not evidence certified by the recorder of a county, as there was no law requiring the patent to be recorded in the county, or declaring that such a copy should be evidence. Patents are recorded in the general land office, and a certified copy from that office is evidence.

JOHN WILKINSON ET AL. v. CHARTER YALE ET AL.

The Courts of the United States can take jurisdiction, where property has been fraudulently conveyed to defeat creditors, and proceed under a State statute, where a judgment has been obtained, and execution has been returned no property.

And this proceeding may be had where the judgment was entered, and execution issued, in the State Court.

And the same proceeding may be had in the State Court, on a judgment obtained in this Court.

Under the statute, judgment and execution are required. Many authorities require this on general principles.

But execution can never be required, on general principles, where at law the property cannot be reached.

A proceeding in a State Court by attachment, where a garnishee is summoned, cannot be set up in bar or abatement to a creditor's bill.

Under a statute of Michigan, the procedure against a garnishee takes place after judgment against the defendant.

Until this, the procedure against the garnishee, under the statute of Michigan, is not a suit.

Partners cannot distribute among themselves any part of the stock in trade, to the prejudice of creditors. But when a distribution is made with the assent of the creditors, the act is not fraudulent.

Wells and *Cook* for complainant.
Campbell for defendant.

OPINION OF THE COURT.

This is in effect a creditor's bill. A judgment was obtained in the State Court of Michigan, for a sum exceeding five hundred dollars. An execution was issued, which was returned, no property real or personal to be found. And the complainants allege that the defendants have conveyed their property so that it cannot be reached by an execution. The bill asks a discovery and relief.

The defendants admit the obtainment of the judgment. They have no knowledge of the issuing of the execution or of the alleged proceedings thereon. They admit the judg-

ment remains unsatisfied. Defendant Bronson believes Yale
& Atherton have no property, real or personal. He admits
that the 27th of November, 1849, they assigned to him all
the notes and accounts then due to them as the firm of Ches-
ter Yale & Co., and all moneys on hand, and stoves not yet
in possession, upon trust to pay creditors, &c. And he
denies that the assignment was colorable or fraudulent, but
that it was made and received in good faith.

Bronson denies that the property is held, as charged, in
trust for Yale & Atherton, except the payment of two hundred dollars to Yale. He alleges, that at the time defendant
received said assignment, W. A. Cook was present as counsel for
complainants, and defendant understood he was acting for
them, and he expressed his entire assent to the same.

That the debts stated in said list as owing by Yale &
Atherton, to Rathburn & Co., and to Jewit & Root, were paid
prior to the assignment; and he has since ascertained that the
debt to Pratt & Co., is $530.75. Defendant has collected of
the demands assigned about $500, and has paid to Yale $100,
and to the creditors of Yale & Atherton $129 before injunc-
tion, and the balance remains in his hands, out of which he
claims to retain a compensation for his services and expenses.

That of the sum so paid to creditors, $15 was to complain-
ant, to apply on the debt for which said judgment was rendered. That some weeks before such payment, defendant
exhibited to said complainant, William Wilkinson, said
assignment and schedules, and fully explained the same, and
he expressed his concurrence therein; and the $15 were paid
to him at his particular request. That after this, and the
previous assent through Cook, it is insisted the complainants
have no right to disaffirm the same.

That 16th April, 1850, complainants garnisheed defendant
Bronson in the suit in which judgment was rendered. That
said proceedings are still pending in the County State Court,
involving the same matters, as in this suit which remain unde-

2a.

termined; defendant therefore insists that complainants have not exhausted their remedy at law, &c.

The first question made is, whether the Court can take jurisdiction in the case. In *Lanmon et al.* v. *Clark*, 4 McLean 18, it was held, a creditor's bill could be filed in this Court. The judgment in that case was rendered in this Court; but on the same principle, relief may be given, where the judgment was given in a State Court. Under the Statute of Michigan, the judgment must be shown, and the return of the execution, of no property, as a basis for proceedings; and it cannot be material whether such judgment and execution be shown in the Federal or State Court. The facts are sufficiently established by the record of either court. And we suppose a State Court could proceed in the same manner on a judgment and execution in the Federal Court. The basis of the procedure is the fraud alleged, or trust, which can only be reached effectually in a Court of Chancery.

A deposition was offered and objected to, because it does not appear by whom the deposition was written, or by what means it came into the hands of the Clerk.

When a deposition is taken, under the Act of Congress, in the absence of the other party, and without notice, great strictness is required. It must appear that the deponent, or the Magistrate before whom it was taken, wrote the deposition; but the case before us, was, where the deposition was taken under a rule of Court, as in State practice, and not under the Act of Congress, the same degree of strictness is not, therefore, required. We think, that *prima facie*, the deposition may be received, subject to any proof showing unfairness or fraud. It is insisted that the proceeding against Bronson, as garnishee, is a bar to this procedure.

By the Act of Michigan of the 28th of March, 1849, in the 13 Sec., it is provided, that in any action before a Justice of the Peace, &c., if the plaintiff or his agent shall make affidavit that he has good reason to believe, and does believe, that any one has money or effects in his hands, or under his control, or that such person is in debt to such defendant, the Justice shall issue a summons, and require such person to answer under oath, the matters alleged in the affidavit; and from the service of such summons on the garnishee, he shall be liable for the effects of the defendant in his hands. And it is declared that from the service of a summons, the suit against the garnishee shall be deemed as commenced. After the examination of the garnishee, the cause as to him, shall be continued until the final judgment against defendant.

After the final judgment, the justice, on request, shall issue a summons against the garnishee, to show cause why a judgment should not be rendered against him. And the plaintiff may declare against him in *trover*. And the 20th Section provides, that no suit shall be maintained or recovery had by such plaintiff against the garnishee for the amount of money sworn to, proved or admitted to be due from such garnishee to defendant, or for the property or value thereof, while the original suit is pending.

Although the statute declares the suit shall be considered as pending, from the time the garnishee is summoned, yet, it is clear, that until after the judgment in the original case is obtained, according to the 20th Section, no suit can be maintained against him. The first proceeding, therefore, against the garnishee, must be regarded in the light of a witness, except that from the time he is first summoned, he is held liable for the assets in his hands. Until after the judgment, the procedure against the garnishee cannot be considered as a suit pending, which can be set up in abatement of the present bill.

The next inquiry is, whether the assignment was void as against creditors.

In the case of *Fox et al.*, v. *Willis et al.* 1 Michigan Rep. 321, it was held, "That a deed fraudulent as to creditors, is not void but voidable; and can be avoided only by a judgment

creditor, or one claiming under him, who has taken out execution, and levied on the property fraudulently conveyed."
"Where a debtor conveyed property in trust for creditors,
which conveyance was fraudulent as to creditors, and afterwards gave a mortgage on a part of the same property to a
creditor, who was aware of the previous conveyance, for the
payment of a judgment the creditor had against him, it was
held that the mortgagee, though a judgment creditor, inasmuch as he had not taken out execution on his judgment, and
levied on the land fraudulently conveyed, could not call in
question the validity of the prior conveyance; and that he
was not protected against it as a purchaser for a valuable
consideration." 2 John. Ch. 189; 10 Pick. 413; 2 Kent's
Com. 533; 4 John. Ch. 529; 11 Wheat. 78; 4 John. Ch. 672.

The above cases are ruled, or some of them, upon the
ground that judgment and execution are essential, before the
party can ask relief in a Court of Chancery. But in the case
of *Hadden* v. *Spader*, 20 John. 569, it was held, that this
doctrine is not sustainable. That in case of stocks and other
property which cannot be reached by execution, a judgment
and execution are not necessary. This is undoubtedly the
reasonable doctrine, and it is applicable to all cases of trusts,
where a proceeding at law cannot reach the property.

In the answer of Bronson, he says, that he fully explained
to the Wilkinsons the nature of the assignment, as to the
amount reserved for Yale; and the receipt for $15 shows it
was received, as a part of the dividend. Received February
15th, 1850, of H. O. Bronson, fifteen dollars to apply on
demand against Yale & Co., signed Wilkinson & Co.

Choate, a witness, states, that before the assignment was
made, he told Mr. Cook, counsel for the plaintiffs, that Ches-
ter Yale, one of the partners, was to be preferred as a
creditor of about two hundred dollars, in consequence of his
having paid more capital than his partners, Atherton & Co.,
when he expressed himself gratified with the arrangement.

Samuel Higby, says, that fifty dollars were paid to Mr. Cook, with the understanding that it should be considered a part of the assets, and should be included in any dividends that should be made to said complainants.

Austin Blair, of counsel for defendants, explained to Cook the nature of the assignment agreed upon. Witness waived the injunction as to the payment of the fifty dollars, being attorney in the case, on the declaration of Mr. Cook, that if he would do so, he would receive it, as from the assignee, and would account for it out of the dividend they should be entitled to receive.

It is true, the partnership funds invested cannot be withdrawn and distributed among the partners, so as to equalize the sums advanced by each, to the prejudice of the creditors; but in this case the distribution seems to have been made with the acquiescence of the complainants and their counsel. That the complainants were fully apprised of the claims against the company, and of the claims and property assigned to the defendants, which they assented to, and that they, through their counsel, received certain sums in part of the dividends to be distributed. Under these circumstances, we think the assignment cannot be considered fraudulent. The bill is therefore dismissed at the costs of the complainant.

BENEDICT v. MAYNARD & MORGAN.

Under a rule of Court, if the signature of the parts to the instrument on which the action is brought, is denied by plea, the plea must be sworn to, or the signature is admitted.

A motion to make the affidavit, when the cause is called for trial, refused.

The affidavit should be made at the time the plea is filed.

The instrument being admitted, by the pleading, it may be read, as it appears upon its face.

Messrs. *Barstow & Lockwood*, for plaintiff.

Messrs. *Hawkins, Fraser & Emmons*, for defendants.

Benedict *v.* Maynard & Morgan.

OPINION OF THE COURT.

This action is brought on a covenant to pay money. On the cause being called, a motion was made by defendants to add an affidavit, denying their signatures, which was opposed by the plaintiff's counsel.

The court overruled the motion. The affidavit should have accompanied the plea when filed. To permit it now to be filed, would be a surprise on the plaintiff; he alleges his witnesses, by whom the instrument can be proved, have not been summoned, as the execution of the instrument was not denied.

The instrument being offered in evidence, objection to it was made, that there was a variance between it and the one stated in the declaration, in this; that Maynard in the instrument, appears to have signed it as President; the word President appears to have been stricken out. The oyer gives the signature without the designation of President. It was also objected that the instrument was drawn for several individuals who have not executed it.

The signatures, as they appear on the face of the instrument, are admitted by the pleading.

. If the defendants desired to take advantage of any defect of execution, they should have pleaded *non est factum*, and filed, with the plea, an affidavit of its truth. The word president being stricken out, the court will presume, from the admission of the pleading, that it was so stricken out, at or before it was signed.

The plaintiff proposed to read the declaration and oyer, and not produce the original instrument; but the court said it was unnecessary: the original instrument was admitted by the pleading, and the instrument was truly set forth in the declaration, and copy of the instrument annexed to it.

With the assent of the parties, the jury found a verdict for $9000. Judgment.

HORATIO G. WALCOTT *v.* JOHN ALMY AND WIFE.

Conveyances executed, under whatever pretences, by an individual insolvent or unable to pay his debts, will be held prima facie void in the hands of the grantee against creditors, especially when the grantee has knowledge of the facts.

Where the consideration passed from the grantor to the grantee, with the view of covering the property, by a conveyance to the wife of the grantor, it is a strong circumstance to show fraud.

Messrs. *Davidson & Holbrook*, for complainants.
Mr. *T. B. Church*, for defendants.

OPINION OF THE COURT.

This is a bill filed to aid an execution at law which has been levied on certain property, charged to have been fraudulently conveyed to defeat the claims of creditors.

The proof clearly shows that at the time the deed to Mrs. Morse was executed by John Almy, he was in embarrassed circumstances, and unable to pay his debts. In addition to the fact proved by the witnesses, the defendant, by his letters to the complainant, admitted his insolvency.

There can be no doubt that a deed executed under such circumstances, known to the grantee, who was the sister of his wife, on the pretence that he was indebted to the estate of Mr. Morse, deceased, with the intent of reserving it from the grantor's creditors, is void.

The consideration stated in the deeds to Mrs. Almy, for there were more than one, was paid by John Almy, and he thereby became the equitable owner.

Neither love nor affection, nor a gift, can support a deed, given fraudulently, though a moneyed consideration be named in it. 1 Story's Eq. 393, sec. 353.

The conveyance by John Almy to Frances Morse, was fraudulent and without consideration, as the grantor was unable to pay his debts at the time. The testimony of Mrs. Lester, late Mrs. Morse, contradicts the facts stated in the answer. The consideration of the deed of Mrs. Morse to Mrs. Almy, they being sisters, was for her support, and money furnished by John Almy; and he collected the rents for the house, which he did not occupy, and rendered no account of the same. And the defendants and Mrs. Morse continued to occupy the other house, from the time the conveyance was executed.

Under the circumstances, we cannot doubt, the conveyances were executed to protect the property from the claims of Almy's creditors, and that they were fraudulent.

The court, therefore, order the execution to issue, and so much of the property to be sold as shall be necessary to satisfy the judgment on which the execution was issued and levied.

MEWSTER v. SPALDING.

Where a record of a judgment of a state court is offered in evidence, in the circuit court, sitting within the same state, the certificate of the clerk and seal of the court is a sufficient authentication.

Such an authentication, it is supposed, would be good in the state courts of the same state; and if so, it is good in this court.

The judges of the supreme court are presumed to know the laws of the respective states, as their jurisdiction extends throughout the United States.

In Michigan, although imprisonment for debt is abolished, yet where a debtor acts fraudulently, or is about so to act, he may be arrested. And after such an arrest, the sheriff, if he permit him to escape, is liable to an action for an escape.

And such an action may be brought in this court.

Messrs. *Frazer & Davidson*, for the plaintiff.
Messrs. *Hawkin & Jocelin*, for defendants.

OPINION OF THE COURT.

This is an action against the sheriff of Washtenaw county, for an escape. A record was offered in evidence of a judgment obtained in that county, before a state court, against the defendant, who, it is alleged, was in the legal custody of the sheriff, and from whose custody he was permitted to escape; for which this action was brought.

The record was objected to, because it was only certified under the seal of the court, by the clerk, but had not the certificate of the presiding judge, that the record, etc., "was in due form."

By the Act of Congress, of the 26th of May, 1790, it is provided, "that the acts of the legislatures of the several states shall be authenticated by having the seal of their respective states affixed thereto; that the records and judicial proceedings of the courts of any state, shall be proved or admitted in any other court of the United States, by the attestation of the clerk, and the seal of the court annexed, if there be a seal, together with a certificate of the judge, chief justice, or presiding magistrate, as the case may be, that the said attestation is in due form."

It is supposed that judgments of the state courts as well as its legislative action, are required to have the above authentication, when used as evidence in another state. When used within the state, the published statutes are evidence, and so, it would seem, are the judgments regularly certified by the clerk under the seal of the court. It can hardly be necessary for a state judge to certify to another state judge, when each knows officially what is "the due form" required. And if such a certificate of the presiding or chief justice be not necessary to make the record evidence in a court of the state where rendered, the same rule is applicable in this court.

It has been held by the Supreme Court, that as its jurisdiction extends throughout the United States, the judges of that court are presumed to know the laws of the respective states. They require no authentication of the laws of the states, as above provided, but act on them from their own knowledge, or from the published statutes. And on the same principle, they take cognizance of the courts of each state organized under its laws, and of the jurisdictions they exercise. This being the case, the necessity of the certificate of the judge, as to the "due form" of a state court record, is not very apparent. It would be objectionable, to those of the profession who look more to form than substance. But, however this may be, we admit the record objected to without the certificate of the judge, as it is the record of a court of the State of Michigan.

It is also objected that the arrest in this case was made under a special statute of the state, partaking to some extent, of a criminal procedure, of which this court cannot take jurisdiction.

The procedure took place under the Revised Statutes of 1846, entitled "an act for the punishment of fraudulent debtors." The 1 Sec. declares that no person shall be imprisoned for debt, except as follows. The plaintiff may apply for a warrant to arrest the defendant, and the warrant may be issued on the affidavit of the plaintiff or some other person, that the debt is due, and that the defendant is "about to remove to defraud his creditors, or that he has property which he refuses to apply to the payment, or that he has disposed, or is about to do so, of his property to defraud his creditors, or that defendant fraudulently incurred the obligation sued on ; and upon proof to the satisfaction of the officer called on to issue the warrant, he shall issue it."

On the warrant, the defendant being arrested is brought before the officer, where the defendant may controvert the facts alleged, on which the warrant was issued. On this examination, if the officer finds the allegation true, he may commit the defendant, unless he shall pay the debt, give security, or enter into bond to assign in thirty days his property for the benefit of his creditors, and if committed, the defendant remains in custody until final judgment shall be rendered in his favor, or until he has assigned his property or obtained his discharge under the insolvent laws.

The commitment having been made under the above statute, it is charged the sheriff suffered him to escape.

No objection is perceived to the jurisdiction of this court. The proceeding, under the Statute, is not criminal. It gives a remedy against a fraudulent debtor, and in the action now before us, we have to inquire whether the defendant in the action before the State Court, was legally in custody. To prove this the warrant must be produced, or its loss must be shown, to authorize secondary proof of its contents.

The warrant is not produced, and some evidence has been offered of its loss. The warrant was issued by Judge Lane, who, on examination, committed the defendant. Shortly after this, Judge Lane died. A copy of the warrant appears to be contained in the recognizance entered into by the defendant, to appear and answer the allegations of fraud; but to make this evidence the original must be shown to have been lost. A file of the Judge's papers, found in his office, has been examined, but the original warrant was not found in it. The other papers of the Judge have not been examined, and this is essential to the reception of secondary proof.

A non suit was suffered by the plaintiff, which the court, on motion, set aside, on the payment of costs.

PRATT ET AL. *v.* WILLARD & SWEET.

This action was brought on a promissory note, no affidavit by defendants, denying their signatures, having been filed. A question to the court was made, whether the partnership of the plaintiffs must be proved. The court held that such proof was not necessary. The note was given to the plaintiffs as partners, and the defendants, by not filing an affidavit, have admitted their signatures, under the rule of court, and such admission extends to the facts which appear on the face of the note. Therefore proof of the partnership of plaintiffs is unnecessary.

Mr. *Walker*, for plaintiffs.
Messrs. *Backus* & *Harbaugh*, for defendants.

UNITED STATES *v.* SCHULER.

The indictment charged the defendant with being employed in "removing from lands of the United States, at the mouth of the River Muskegon, in the County of Ottawa, and District of Michigan, a large amount of timber, to wit: one hundred thousand shingles and twenty cords of shingle bolts."

I. The Court held this description too vague and uncertain. That the *locality* of the trespass was inseparably connected with the offense, and the *particular section* or *quarter section of the Public Domain must be stated, so as to protect the defendant from another trial,* for the same offense, more particularly described according to the designations of the public survey. That the question was not one of jurisdiction; but pertained to the Statutory description of the offense.

II. That the United States, as a great land proprietor, had the public lands officially surveyed, platted and designated, by fixed ranges, townships, sections, and quarter sections. These divisions were of record, and notorious, and the defendant was entitled to such a particular description that he might be apprised of what trespass he was called upon to defend. The mouth of Muskegon might embrace more or less of the land of the United States, and comprehend townships or counties. The being "employed in removing timber from the lands of the United States," had reference to the well known and legally designated parts of the Public Survey, by which the National Domain, other than that reserved, was purchased and sold.

III. The Statute under which the indictment was found, constitutes part of the Land Law of the United States, and was designed for the protection and the preservation of both classes of the National Domain by severe penalties. The term "other land" in the Statute, has reference to its surveyed divisions, and contemplates the lands known and described in the public surveys as distinct from those reserved for Naval purposes. The one was held for a special object; the other, by various enactments as Trustee for subsequent purchasers.

United States *v.* Schuler.

IV. The term "other lands" being general, and the intention manifestly requiring a specific application, in order to charge the particular offense, a particular description was necessary as to place. The general language, "Lands of the United States," not sufficient, as descriptive of the offense.

V. The term "timber" in the Statute, signifies, the standing and the felled trees prepared for transportation to a vessel or saw-mill, such as saw logs, or lumber in bulk; but does not embrace any article manufactured from the tree, as shingles or boards. The trees are those, the wood of which is generally used in ship and house building.

VI. It is not necessary in an indictment for removal, to allege that the timber was removed from the land on which it was grown or from which it was cut. But it must be stated that it was removed from the lands of the United States, specially described according to the public survey.

VII. The allegation that the defendant knowingly committed the act, is unnecessary.

Mr. Hand, District Attorney.

OPINION OF JUDGE WILKINS.

This Indictment contains two counts. The first charges the defendant with "*being employed*," and the second with "*aiding and assisting*" in removing "timber from lands of the United States."

The description of the offense is in these words. "That George Schuler, late of the village of Muskegon, in the County of Ottawa, on the 20th of June, 1853, *at the mouth of the river Muskegon aforesaid*, was employed in removing *from lands of the United States*, a *large amount of timber*, to wit: *one hundred thousand shingles* and *twenty cords of shingle bolts*, the property of the United States, of the value of one thousand dollars."

The description in the second count, is in the same words, with the exception as "to aiding and assisting in removing," instead of being employed to remove.

The act of Congress of March 2d, 1831, entitled "an act to provide for the punishment of offenses committed in cutting, destroying, or removing live-oak and other timber or trees reserved for Naval purposes"—defines the offense as follows:

"If any person shall cut, or be employed in cutting, or shall remove or be employed in removing, or aid and assist in removing any live oak or red cedar trees, or other timber, from lands of the United States, with intent to export, dispose of, use, or employ the same in any manner whatsoever, other than for the use of the Navy of the United States, the person so offending, on conviction thereof, shall, for every such offense, pay a fine not less than triple the value of the tree or trees, or timber so cut, destroyed, or removed, and be imprisoned not exceeding twelve months."

Several reasons are assigned as causes of demurrer. We will notice them in the order in which they have been presented in the argument.

1st. It is objected that the offense is not described in either count with sufficient certainty and precision. This objection, especially, has reference to the locality of the trespass. It is not charged that the timber was removed from *any designated portion* of the public domain. The language is general, "from lands of the United States at the mouth of the River Muskegon aforesaid."

Where the *locus in quo* is so inseparably connected with the offense,—as in this statutory trespass upon the public lands,—such a description should be given, as would certainly protect the defendant from *a second trial* for the same offense, in which the indictment contained a more particular description as to township, range, section, or quarter section of land from which the logs were actually removed. It is not necessary to specify any of the political divisions of the State, merely as *indicative of the jurisdiction of this Court*. It is sufficient to allege, that the trespass was committed within the district.

Such an allegation is all that is necessary in most of the cases triable in the United States Court. But this act of Congress, (being part of the land law of the United States,) in the creation of this offense, had reference both to the Naval Reservation and the *surveyed lands* of the National Domain, *with the intention of preserving* the timber on them from destruction, by the imposition of severe penalties. And the principal divisions and sub-divisions of the public surveys, being specially directed by Statute, and of public record and notoriety, are unquestionably intended by the Statutory language " *other lands of the United States,*" in contradistinction to "the lands reserved." The usual fiction of "breaking the close" in actions or indictments, for trespass upon lands, or the necessary description in ejectment, is not designative of jurisdiction, but essentially descriptive of the *particular* property of the plaintiff on or concerning which the offense has been committed. The principle of the fiction is applicable to the indictment. The United States as a great land proprietor, for their preservation, protection, and sale, has had the public lands officially surveyed, and by various agencies and functionaries has had platted off and designated by fixed boundaries and sections, the National Domain.

A description, then, omitting the material averment of the particular division from whence the timber was removed, is too vague and uncertain. A removal from a body of water, is not a removal from land. Such would not answer in an action for civil damages, much less then, in an indictment, which should be specially descriptive of the offense charged. An individual owning several parcels of land in the same township and county, must specify in his action, with distinguishing certainty, which one of his farms has been injured by the trespass for which he seeks reparation. It would not do, to describe the same generally as by county or townships, where such description would not specify, and *where specification was necessary.* The *mouth* of a river may embrace for many miles land on either side, and the land adjacent may comprehend more townships than one, it may be more or less extensive, and the lands on its banks or borders be varied as to ownership. In a case then, so seriously involving character, property, and personal liberty, the defendant is entitled to a more specific accusation.   The River Muskegon may water, and the County of Ottawa may comprehend a large extent of country, and such averment is no notice to a defendant, as to what *particular tract* of the lands of the United States, he is called upon to defend.   It might as well be "the United States lands" in the County of Ottawa, or the "United States lands in the District of Michigan."   No doubt, other lands are held in the County, and at the mouth of the River by individual owners, and so far, such description might generally distinguish the government lands from those entered at private sale.   But the patent or deed, to an individual, of government lands, describes his purchase by the well known returns of survey, and the marks on the ground, and that which remains unsold is as well known and as easily ascertained.   The defendant therefore should be apprised by the indictment of the particular subdivision to which the alleged offense attaches.   It is not a question of jurisdiction that the venue settles, but a matter of essential description.

A part of the statutory definition of the offense: material to be proved, and therefore material to be averred.

1. *Stat. at Large*, 465.   1. *Chitty's Pleadings*, 234.
4. "   "   "   472.   *Cowper*, 682.
5. *Hill*, 401.   3. *Greenleaf E.*, 12.
8. *Blackford*, 193.   1. *Baldwin, U. S.*, vs. *Wilson.*

The case of Wilson in Baldwin's Reports does not conflict with this view.   The offense was robbing the U. S. Mail in the eastern district of Pennsylvania.   Not necessary to prove and therefore unnecessary to aver particular locality, as essentially connected with the crime.   But here the offense is not the destruction or removal of timber on wild land, not merely the removal of timber, belonging to the United

United States v. Schuler.

States, but the destruction or removal of timber *on* and *from* the lands of the United States, and (with reference to prior enactments) *from the surveyed lands* of the United States.

II. But it is urged by the Government, that the description of the offense is of sufficient certainty, because such description is in the *very words of the statute.*

The words of the statute are, *"employed in removing any live oak, or red cedar trees, or other timber, from any other lands of the United States."*

The lands of the United States other than those designated and reserved for naval purposes, constitute the premises from which the timber is removed, being employed in which, comprises the offense defined in the statute. What, then, are the essential words of the statute? Certainly those which signify *the act,* such as "employed in removing;" also its specific character *"other timber,"* and also the place where the act was done, viz: *"on other lands."*

By following, then, the precise words of the Statute, is the offense so described as to apprise the defendant with sufficient certainty of the particular matter with which he is charged?

If so, the description is sufficient, being in the words of the Statute. But, if otherwise, if there be obscurity and uncertainty, the description is *not* sufficient, although the Statute is followed *in totis verbis.*

Such is the rule in 12th Wheaton, in the case of Gooding, the governing case. Mr. Justice Story, who gave the opinion of the Court, says:

"That where an indictment follows the language of the creative Statute, it is as certain as the Statute, and *in general* such certainty is sufficient;" but he further remarks, "There are cases where *more particularity* is required, either from the obvious intention of the Legislature, or from the *application of known principles of law.* Courts have thought such certainty not unreasonable or inconvenient," but "calculated to put the plea of *autre fois acquit*, or *convict*, fairly within the power of the defendant." "The course has been," observes the Court, "to leave every class of cases to be decided very much upon its own peculiar circumstances."

The case of Mills, in 7th Peters, does not conflict with this general rule and exception. And those cited from McLean, Mason and Gallison, would not modify, even if considered in conflict.

This Court takes the law from the Supreme Court of the United States, and if the point in controversy has been *there* adjudicated and settled, it is unnecessary to waste time or strength in protracted commentary upon either English or State authorities.

Ita lex scripta est,—the authority is conclusive,—*so* is the law, and the "*stare decisis*" of the Supreme Court is mandatory. This case then establishes this rule, viz. :—

That in Statutory offenses the description of the Statute is to be followed, except where more particularity is required from its "*obvious intention*, and the application of known principles of law." Cases may arise,—cases have arisen,—where it would not be safe for the pleader to follow the Statute; as for instance, where the Statute uses general terms, which manifestly require a specific application, in order legally to charge the particular offense.

Now, what is the obvious intention of the Statute of March 2nd, 1831, providing for the punishment of offenses, committed in cutting, destroying, or removing live-oak and *other timber*, or trees reserved for Naval purposes?

Its title and history exhibit its object.—The provisions of the prior Statute, exclusively protecting lands reserved from sale for Naval purposes, were by this act extended to other lands, and measurably to other timber, than live-oak or red cedar. Protection and preservation of the *surveyed* landed Dominion of the United States—whether North or South, whether growing timber or not ;—preservation from spoliation of the surveyed lands, and keeping them, as ordained by Nature, *attractive to purchasers*, was the sole object and spirit of this amended and extended law. This is obvious from the consideration that the Naval Reservation and the *unsurveyed lands*, are not dedicated either to settlement or sale. Within the Territorial limits of the United States, and acquired by treaty from the Indians, *the unsurveyed Dominion* await legislative action, the further fostering care of the Government, and the progress of population, in order to be appropriately redeemed from the obscurity and helplessness of the wilderness.

Conceived, but not born—in embryo, but not legally in existence, they await the breath of law, to give them legal being and ensure them legal protection. The Land law, for *the punishment of this description of trespass*, does not embrace the unsurveyed tracts of the public land. They may need such legislation, but it is not yet given. When the act of 1831 was passed, the revenue arising from the Land sales, formed a prominent item in the Treasury, and was an important object of national solicitude. Its annual increase by salutary legislation—holding forth inducements to the settler and purchaser, and its collection, were the leading motives of the land legislation for many years preceeding.

The Government did not seek the preservation of the timber growing on its lands (with the single exception of the Naval Reservation,) with the motive of enhancing their value for ornament, or special use, or speculation, but singly with the view of inducing speedy sale and settlement, and preserving for the purchaser, at Government price, the lands as they stood. If the evil then to be remedied by the Statute was the spoliation of the surveyed lands; and the remedy to be applied the preservation, by sufficient penalties, of its valuable timber—if regard is to be had to this manifest intention, certainly, cutting timber on the surveyed United States lands, must necessarily be described with reference to their legal notorious divisions and subdivisions, indicated in Statutes *pari materia*, and of public record. It is true, that cutting timber on lands of the United States is the offense, *in the words of the Statute.* But such description would not indicate on what part of the lands of the United States the trespass was committed. And as the lands of the United States are divided and subdivided—by official surveys and plats—the description required by the Statute, and the "application of known principles of law" demand that the indictment should conform to a statutory designation, exhibiting the Range, Township, Section, and Quarter Section, on which the trespass was committed. This is not inconvenient, certainly. This is not, certainly, unreasonable,—this *is* certainly calculated to "put the plea of former acquittal or conviction fairly within the power of the defendant." Should the defendant be acquitted, on a charge describing the cutting, or removing, on lands of the United States, at the mouth of a river, in a certain County and District, and be subsequently indicted for the same offense, describing the Range, Township, Section, and Quarter Section, to what purpose could the record of the first case be evidence? The first description did not necessarily include or cover the latter, and without testimony establishing the fact, it could not be inferred. In the Post Office Case, the offense defined was embezzling and secreting, and not stealing the particular enclosure. The breach of official trust was the offense. The descriptive words of the Statute are all that are necessary. The name of the Bank, or the genuineness of the note, is only necessary as to corroborative evidence, and may or may not be used in the indictment. The article of value, if stated, is proved by the note taken; but the fact itself is not essential to establish the offense of embezzlement, neither is it necessary to describe the letter by its superscription.

This Statute itself, illustrates the point in consideration. For cutting down, or removing Naval timber, it would not be sufficient to state merely that the act was on lands of the United States; but on *specific* and *reserved* lands. So here; cutting on lands of the United States would embrace the extent of the venue or jurisdiction, and leave the defendant on a wide sea, without chart or compass, to direct him to what particular trespass he must apply his defense. The Court considers that the Land Law of the United States furnishes the chart, and that the Government must observe it in these prosecutions.

III. But it is further objected to the sufficiency of this indictment, that it does not describe any offense whatever. The words of the Statute are, "being employed in removing timber."

In the Indictment, the word "*timber*" is used with a *videlicit*, explaining it to mean "shingles and shingle-bolts." This explanation is material, for without it, no charge is specially expressed. Timber is a generic term.

The question then arises as to the interpretation of the word Timber. However the word may be used in common intercourse, or whatever construction has heretofore judicially been given to it, in connection with other legislation, this Court will be guided and controlled by the *manifest intention of the Legislature in its use,* and the object of the Act of Congress. Unless the contrary clearly appears from the context, it will be presumed that the word was employed in its ordinary popular sense. It is not the interpretation of an artistic or technical word, or a word of equivocal meaning. It is a word in common use, and has an enlarged or restricted sense, according to the connection in which it is employed. Keeping in view the spirit of the Statute, the evil which it designed to prevent, and the remedy intended, looking to this and other Statutes on the same subject, such an interpretation must be given to the word as will effect, and not defeat, the Legislative will. As a generic term, it properly signifies, only such trees as are *used in building*—either ships or dwellings. *2nd Black.* 281 : 1st *Crabbe's Real Property*, *Section* 20. *2nd Burrell's Dict., Title, Timber.*

But its signification is not limited to *Trees :* it applies to the *wood*, or the particular form which the tree assumes when no longer growing or standing in the ground. Strictly speaking, a tree is that which is growing or standing in the ground whether alive or dead. There are dead and live trees, both standing. But when the trunk is severed from the root, and felled to the earth, it is no longer, properly speaking, a tree. It becomes *timber* or lumber, according to the use to which it can be applied. A forest of standing trees, if they can be appropriated to building, is called well timbered land, but loses that designation, if swept to the earth by a tornado.

The Legislature is presumed to be acquainted with the varied use of the word, and to have employed it in the Statute, in an enlarged or a restrictive sense, according to its connection with the subject matter; thus, when used in the Act of 1817, in the *plural* number, "red cedar timber," it signifies " standing or growing trees," and when in the 4th section, (prohibiting its exportation,) it is used in the *singular* number, "timber," it evidently applies only to the *tree cut down*, and prepared for transportation in ships. So that in the same Act, according to its association, does it bear two different significations; one, enlarged—embracing the trees of the forest, as standing; and the other a restricted, special meaning, applying only to the use to which the wood can be appropriated. And in the Act of Congress under consideration, the same varied use is made of the word. When the cutting is prohibited, it is synonymous with trees: " Cutting any *other* timber on—" i. e., felling them to the earth;— when removal is prohibited, removing any other timber "*from*," it is applicable to the restricted sense of the *trees* being felled to the earth, and prepared by the labor of man, on the ground where cut for transportation ; and where the Statute embodies both significations in the phrase "other timber, standing, growing and being." "Standing and growing" mean when alive as trees, erect in the earth; and "being" is applicable to their character, cut and ready for use.

That this distinction exists in the Statute, and was in the contemplation of the Legislature, seems evident from the use of the term in the second section, wherein the *timber cut* is used with reference to its being taken on board of a vessel. If cut, it was no longer a tree; if to be taken on board of a vessel, it is no longer a tree. Trees are not transported in vessels from place to place; but timber is, and dropping the word tree, in this section, and using the word "timber"—in connection with "red cedar and live oak cut,"—leaves no doubt in my mind, in regard to the legislative use of the word in the first section, prohibiting the being "employed in removing any live oak or red cedar trees or *other* timber." In this connection it is employed to signify the felled trees, prepared for use and transportation, and embraces the various uses to which timber can be appropriated, either in ship or house building—whether pine logs, square pine timber, or any other form in which the cut trees are prepared, either for the saw mill or transportation. It was not the intention of the Act of Congress, to punish the removal of any article MANUFACTURED from the timber cut upon the public lands; such as *masts, bowsprits, oars, breakers, casks, boards, tubs, buckets, barrows* or *hand-spikes;* or, to pursue the felled tree as timber further than such preparation of the wood *as was necessary for its transportation to the saw mill, or other place of manufacture.* Beyond such purpose the article became transmuted. Its nature and use changed. *It was no longer timber.* Its character as timber ceased when the labor of the lumberer ceased, and the art of the manufacturer commenced. When the article is once perfected for immediate use, it is only known by its appropriate name; and is no more timber than bread is flour, or flour, wheat, or mutton, sheep,—or beef, oxen;—and such also, are shingles, made of pine timber, because they are perfected by man's art for immediate use. We do not say that a dwelling is *timbered*, but shingled.

Timber logs or timber bolts are brought from the woodland and converted at the saw mill into boards, or scantling, or laths, or shingles; and the latter has a well known and fixed meaning, known to the Legislature, and certainly never meant by their term "*timber*," in the Act of 1831. It is true that "fat oxen" are provision and munitions of war, according to case cited from *2nd Peters*: there, the genus "provision" covers the species "oxen." But "provision" is not fat oxen—it may consist in something else; and here timber, as a genus, by no means includes a *manufactured article*, which does not bear to it the relation of a species. Timber is the genus of the various trees dedicated by custom to a particular use—such as the pine, the ash, the oak, the cedar, and the chestnut; but certainly not to the articles manufactured therefrom, or otherwise a frame building might be considered a species of timber. But to make the antecedent terms in the Statute limit the word to *their* specific character as trees, would be unnecessary repetition, and clearly defeat the object in view of inhibiting the principal evil designed to be prevented, viz., the illicit commerce between the cutters and those who traded in timber cut.

Such was the object of the Act of 1817, and with a like view the provisions of the law were extended to the whole surveyed National Domain. The question, then, is not as to the popular meaning of the word, considered as trees growing, or as hewn logs *in transitu* to the saw mill; but its statutory signification; not its lexicographic, but *its signification in the Statute*, and how it is here legislatively employed.

And should such a construction be now given, as to confine the penalty for removal of trees, as such, the Act would defeat itself. If applicable to trees only, the preservation of Naval Timber so earnestly desired by the Government, would be

extremely precarious ; and if the word is used in its enlarged
sense as to Naval timber, it must have the same meaning
when applied to other lands than Naval lands.

But it is further assigned as a cause of demurrer, that more
of the counts for removing timber, aver that it was removed
from lands on which it was *grown* and *cut down*. The charge
is that the defendant was employed in removing from lands
of the *United States*.

Now, if the indictment contains the proper averment specifying the lands by township, range, section, and quarter
section, this statement would clearly indicate the character
of the lands from which the timber was removed; and keeping the object of the Statute in view, and interpreting the
term "*lands*" as employed in the Statute, to refer *exclusively*
to the surveyed National Domain, held forth by the Government for entry and sale, in contradistinction to other real
estate belonging to the General Government, such as Dock-
yards and Arsenals, we must hold the charge contained in
the indictment to be sufficient.

Taking timber from the United States Arsenal, without
permission, may or may not be a felony, according to the
circumstances which surround the act; but it is not the offense
described in this Statute. Neither is it necessary to aver in
the indictment that the timber was removed from the *particular section* of the United States lands *where it was grown and
cut*. Such a fact need not be proved, to support the specific
accusation that the timber was removed from specific lands.
The Statute, with a view to preserve the lands from being
despoiled, has prohibited not only the cutting down, but the
removal. The offenses are distinct. As to the former, such
proof is necessarily connected with the cutting; for how
could the charge be maintained, without the other fact being
established, that the trees were growing or standing when
felled? But to remove that which has been already cut down
from section to section, and across section lines, either direct
to the mill, or to an adjacent stream for floating, is another

and a distinct offense, to be established by evidence showing the removal to be from that part of the public domain described.

One offender may cut the timber, another may convey it across the section lines to a place of embarkation on the water, and if eventually removed from the United States lands appropriately described, the offense of removal, or being engaged in removing, is fully made out. That the timber was not the timber of the United States is a matter of issue. But as Mr. Justice Story observes in the oft-cited case of Gooding, the charge is " *the precise language of the Statute.*" " *Employed in removing timber from the lands of the United States,*" communicates to the accused a definite accusation, by which he cannot be misled, and is unequivocally stated, so as to apprise him of the offense charged and what he is to defend. Here the particularity required as to the *locus in quo* is not necessary; and the ruling of the Supreme Court in the case of Gooding is directly applicable.

Another exception is taken to the form of the indictment apparently involving the *intention*, with which the alleged criminal act was committed. It is not stated in the indictment that the act was knowingly committed.

The Statute does not require such an averment. If the defendant was employed as charged, he must have known the character in which he acted, and the business about which he was engaged. Besides, the offense described in the 2d section of the law clearly shows the intention of the Legislature, that, in the case of freighting a vessel with this *timber*, the guilty knowledge must be established against the owner or captain; while such proof is *not* required in the offenses described in the 1st section, but the fact will be presumed, leaving to the defense to rebut such presumption by evidence showing mistake, ignorance of the section lines, and that the trespass was committed under the well-grounded belief that the timber removed was timber removed from other lands than those of the United States.

It may be otherwise as to the omission of such terms as would exhibit the unlawfulness of the act, but that point is held under advisement and until further argument, as it is involved in the motion in arrest of judgment in the case of Thompson.

I have thus carefully considered the points presented in the unusually protracted argument as to the validity of these indictments. It is much to be regretted that demurrers were not interposed at an earlier period, before jurors and witnesses were brought to attend this court. Not only would it have been expedient for the interests of the Government, but more satisfactory to the court called upon to decide grave questions of law, during the progress of its session, with a jury, and parties, and witnesses awaiting its action. Such should not be the case, and where causes of a criminal character are hereafter continued from one term to another, with the opportunity in the interval of presenting the law involved by demurrer, the court will not permit while a jury is in attendance, the objections to the indictment in this form to be discussed, but will compel defendants to proceed to trial, and reserve for the action of the court, after verdict, all considerations involving the construction of statutes, or the sufficiency of the pleading.

In the case of George Schuler and Paul H. Howard, the demurrer is sustained.

Baptist Missionary Union *v.* Israel Turner.

Where an injunction has been applied for to stay proceedings at law in a bill to quiet title, on the ground that the remedy at law was not adequate; a notice by the complainant that he will insist on the trial at law, is necessary, so that the witnesses by the plaintiff at law may be summoned.

Frazer & Davidson, for Plaintiff.

Patterson, Vanamringe & Gould, for Defendant.

OPINION OF THE COURT.

This is an action of ejectment where a bill has been filed to stay proceedings by injunction and quiet title on the ground that there was not adequate relief at law. The bill in chancery was continued at the last term with leave to amend. It is now insisted that the case at law shall be tried.

The plaintiff's counsel at law contends that without notice from the complainant in equity they cannot be ruled to a trial. The court held, a notice was necessary, as the party could not know that the complainant in equity would not insist on a hearing; that until notice, the plaintiff at law could not be expected to have his witnesses brought before the court.

WM. W. WEED v. ARMSTRONG KELLOGG ET AL.

The deposition of a witness, who is at the place where the court is held, if objected to, cannot be read if the witness be able to attend the court.

The confessions of a silent partner, not known in the proceedings, may be given in evidence.

Messrs. *Hunt & Newberry*, for plaintiff.
Messrs. *Frazer, Davidson, Holbrook & Lathrop*, for def't.

OPINION OF THE COURT.

This action was brought on a promissory note for $2092.01, payable at Oliver Lee's Bank, at Buffalo, three months after date. The defendants pleaded,

1. The general issue of *non assumpsit*.

2. That Smart was an accommodation indorser, at the request of Geisse & Kellogg, and signed the note which was paid 1 November, 1849.

3. That the note in the first and second counts of the amended declaration, was owned and in possession of

Elias Weed & Co., which firm was composed of plaintiff and Elias. Weed, of Buffalo in the state of New-York, and that heretofore, to wit, on the day and year last aforesaid at, &c. defendants delivered a large quantity of flour, to wit, one thousand barrels of great value, to wit, of the value of $8000, in full payment of said promise and assumptions in the first and second counts of the declaration, which flour was accepted to be applied as aforesaid.

4. That the note in the first and second counts of the amended declaration, heretofore, to wit, on the 26th day of Sep., 1849, was possessed by the firm of E. Weed & Co., (of which firm the plaintiff was the company,) and that whilst E. Weed & Co. so held and possessed said note, Asher L. Kellogg, one of the defendants, of the firm of James A. Armstrong & Co., shipped and consigned a large quantity of flour, to wit, one thousand barrels, of the value of $4000, with directions to apply and appropriate a sufficient amount of the avails to pay the note.

In his replication plaintiff says, defendant did not pay the sums of money in the first and second counts, or any part thereof, as alleged. That the said Elias Weed & Co. did not receive or accept the said thousand barrels of flour to be applied in payment, &c. To the plea of Smart, he says, that no part of the sum claimed in flour as alleged, was received.

The jury being sworn, a deposition of Mr. Sibly was then offered in evidence, which was objected to, as the witness was then in Detroit. The court held the deposition could not be read, if the witness were able to attend the trial.

Mr. Sibly states that in the spring of 1849, he was clerk for defendants. He left their employment, and was afterwards agent for the plaintiff, who lived in Detroit. In 1848-9, a contract was made by defendants with plaintiff, for the delivery of 500 bbls. of flour, to be delivered at Buffalo to plaintiff, who was engaged in the forwarding business at that place. Near the close of the spring of 1849, a second contract was made for another lot of 500 barrels of flour made at the Ceresco mills. This flour was not sent. The money was paid by Rockafellow or Weed as agent. This payment was made on the second contract, to be delivered on the opening of the navigation.

Plaintiffs refused to take any flour except from a certain mill. A note was given to deliver the flour, or return the advance. After harvest in 1849, all the flour made by the Ceresco mills was sent to plaintiff to pay the notes due.

Mr. Sanger, cashier of the Utica Bank, says, 'the note was received in bank and discounted, which had been given by Rockafellow.

Mr. Reed's deposition states, he knows the note was paid by a check, but farther he knows nothing, except from the books of the bank.

Mr. Weed was offered as a witness to prove the admissions of Elias Weed, which was objected to. The court observed, the pleas allege Elias Weed to be a partner in this note, with William Weed. His admissions, being a partner, though not named on the docket, are admissible to show the discharge of the said note, during the existence of the partnership. The witness stated that Elias Weed was a partner, having an equal interest in the note. In a conversation with him he admitted the note had been discharged, and should have been delivered up.

Nonsuit was suffered.

UNITED STATES V. PETER DARTON.

1. Under the act of 1831, for the punishment of offenses in cutting and removing timber from the United States lands, the rule of proof is fixed by the Statute. The Government must prove the cutting on the lands specified: the defendant may rebut the same, by showing circumstances of ignorance as to the section lines or mistake.

2. The proof must correspond with the charge—cutting oak is not cutting pine timber.

United States *v.* Peter Darton.

3. The proof of the act places the burden of explanation on the defendant. From an unlawful act an unlawful intent will be inferred.

4. A reasonable doubt is that which relates either to the character or the force of the testimony, and not a mere conjecture.

District Attorney of the United States, for plaintiff.

OPINION OF JUDGE WILKINS.

The defendant was tried on an indictment charging him with removing and cutting timber on Government lands. The testimony showed that his father owned a mill seat and various tracts of land, in the vicinage of the lands described in the indictment; that he resided at the mill, as the agent of his father, who lived in Chicago, and was under instructions to avoid cutting on the Government lands; that a number of trees were cut by mistake across the lines, which were subsequently ascertained by actual survey, the defendant accompanying the surveyor, and showing the corner posts; and when he ascertained that he had cut over his lines, he wrote to his father, and caused the quarter section on which the timber was cut to be entered at the Land-office, the certificate of which was given in evidence.

It was contended on the part of the Government—

1st. That circumstances showing ignorance and mistake, if believed by the jury, constituted no defense.

2d. That a *subsequent* entry of the lands was no defense.

Messrs. *Frazer & Hand*, for the United States.
Messrs. *Gray & Van Arman*, for the defendant.

CHARGE OF THE COURT.

The Prisoner at the bar, Peter Darton, whose true deliverance between him and the United States, *you* are obligated by your solemn oaths to make, according to the evidence given you *in* court, is charged with timber *cutting* and timber *removing* on and from the lands of the United States. The particular offense is created by, and defined and described in, the Statutes of the United States.

The Act of March 2d, 1831, by its 2d section, constitutes three general classes of offenses, with their respective accessorial subdivisions.

The Court will enumerate them in their order, that you may be better enabled to understand the particular offense *now* under consideration.

The *first* is—The *cutting* and *removing* Naval timber, specifically named *red cedar* and *live oak*, on lands specially selected and reserved by the Government, or aiding in such acts, or wantonly destroying on such lands, such Naval timber.

By a previous enactment of Congress, of the first of March, 1817, entitled "an act," making reservation of certain public lands "to supply timber for Naval purposes," it was made the duty of the Secretary of the Navy, under the direction of the President of the United States, to cause such vacant and unappropriated public lands, as produced the live oak and red cedar timbers, to be explored, and to select such tracts as, according to his judgment, were necessary to furnish the Navy of the United States, a sufficient supply of Naval timber.

It was then declared an offense, punishable by fine and imprisonment, for any person to cut *any timber* on such reserved tracts, *without authority to do so by order of a competent officer.*

At the same time it was declared criminal to cut, or remove or be employed in removing, the Naval timber specified, with intent to dispose of the same for transportation, from the same description of the Public Lands.

Such, with other measures of a penal character, and with the avowed design of preserving a supply of timber for the United States Navy, were the salutary provisions of the Statute of 1817.

But the Government was the proprietor of other lands, on which grew other timber, valuable in a great degree for other

purposes than ship building. Much of these lands were surveyed by and under National Authority, and by various Statutory
enactments were opened to settlements, and offered at a *fixed*
price, which could neither be augmented nor lessened by demand.

The policy of these Statutes was two-fold:—1st. The
speedy settlement of the public domain; and thereby converting the wilderness into a garden, and by the acquisition
of a revenue from the public sales. In furtherance of both
objects, it was desirable, that the lands should be so far protected from spoliation, as to encourage emigration, and induce
settlement and sale.

Moreover, it was discovered that the protection afforded by
the act of 1817, was not sufficiently extensive as to Naval
timber growing elsewhere, than on the reservations; and the
public lands in the north and south-west, being repeatedly
stripped of valuable house timber, by lawless trespassers,
the National Legislature was moved to amend and enlarge the
provisions of the Act of 1817, by those of 1831, embracing
other lands, than the reserved lands, Naval timber on *other*
lands, and *other* timber than Naval timber on the unreserved
public lands of the United States. Thus originated the
other two classes as designated in the 1st section of the last
Act,—namely:

2d. The offense of cutting Naval timber on other lands, &c.

3d. The offense of cutting or removing, &c., *other* timber
than Naval timber on *other* lands than Naval lands, with the
intent to *export,* dispose of, use, or employ the same *in any
manner whatsoever, other than for the use of the Navy of
the United States.* This last, comprehends the charges set
forth in this indictment, which contains four counts. The
1st is for cutting 3000 pine trees, at township 12, north of
range 17 west and township 12, north of range 16 west,
on section 13 of township 12, north of range 17 west, on section 13, township 12 North of range 17 west, and on
section 13 of township 12, north of range 16 west, in the

County of Oceana and State of Michigan. *The second count,* is for aiding and assisting in the trespass specified in the first. *The 3d,* is for *removing* 5000 timber logs from the premises described, and with the intent stated. And *the 4th count,* is for aiding in the last act described, or being employed in the same. To these charges, the defendant has plead not guilty—denying the cutting and the removing in every form and shape, in which the same is charged. Before any application of the law to the facts of this case—the court will briefly detain your attention on two prominent propositions involved:

1st. What must be proved by the Government, in order to sustain the prosecution.

2d. What must be proved by the defendant, in case the Government has made a case to warrant a conviction, as matter of complete exculpation.

What must be proved by the Government. The rule of proof is fixed by the Statute. The offense is cutting or removing timber from Government lands, with the evil intent described.

The fact then, must be fully established by conclusive proof, that timber of the kind described was cut by the defendant, or by his procurement: and that the same was cut on the township, and section, and range, specially set forth. Cutting *other* timber, than that charged, will not suffice. If pine trees, or pine logs are charged, proof of oak or hickory will not do. And so also, if the cutting is on *other* lands, the proof will not do. The defendant must be acquitted.

But, gentlemen, if the specific Act of cutting or removing is proved,—the guilty—the unlawful intent will be presumed. From an unlawful act an unlawful intent will be inferred. The Statute declares the act criminal. Proof of the commission of the act, raises the presumption of a guilty knowledge and a guilty intention. If poison be given, the malicious intent will be inferred, and need not be proved.

But this presumption may be rebutted, by the evidence of circumstances, showing a lawful intention. This applies to all crimes. To felony and to misdemeanor. An evil intent is an essential ingredient of every crime. And the Statute does not contemplate the punishment of the innocent. An unlawful act with a lawful intention, is not criminal.

With this view, the law declares one intent which exculpates in express terms, viz.; the intent to appropriate the timber cut to the use of the Navy of the United States. Nevertheless this does not exclude a defense based upon circumstances, clearly showing that no tresspass was designed by the defendant. Understand this—the Government must prove two prominent facts. The CUTTING, *and the premises where cut.* If such proof corresponds with the allegations of the indictment, and there is no explanatory proof rebutting an unlawful intention, your verdict must be guilty.

But otherwise, after such proof on the part of the Government, if the defendant clearly shows that a mistake was committed by the defendant himself, or, by the hands under his direction, in regard to the lines of survey, if proof be furnished, satisfactory to the Jury, that the defendant owned timber lands in the vicinage, or, was the agent of the owner, and that the section corners and quarter posts, as designative of the public survey, *were such*, that a mistake might be committed, as to the lines separating the private entry, from the unsold lands, and that the trespass charged was *thus* committed, without the design of cutting on the Government lands. If such be the conclusive character of the defendant's evidence, the inference of a guilty intention is removed, and an acquittal is his right under the benign provisions of the criminal law.

For it is a blessed and an unquestionable truth — a maxim not to be controverted—that the Government of the United States seeks not the conviction or punishment of an innocent man. *Conviction,* not recovery, is the important word; punishment, not recompense, the great object sought by the prosecution. Damages are recoverable by civil action. Reparation for injury, relief, and not a penalty.

Now, the United States, as a great land proprietor, is not inhibited the usual civil remedy allowed to and provided for all, for any loss or injury sustained. The courts of justice are opened to the civil actions of the Government as to those of an individual. But there is a vast difference in the rule of judgment between the civil action and the criminal verdict. In the former, the proof of the injury and its extent, calls justly for the rendition of appropriate damages; and the plea of ignorance or mistake, or an innocent intention, availeth not. The injury is done, the ignorant trespasser must repair the loss. So with the Government. Its landed dominion is under the protection of the general law, independent of the Statute of 1831. The action of trespass is an action to which the Government may resort, and under which it may recover damages to the full extent of the injury sustained.

And, a conviction and punishment of a defendant, for a a trespass, under the act of 1831, would not protect under a civil action for the injury sustained. Neither would a judgment, on the latter remedy, be a sufficient plea of defense under the indictment.

Wherefore, then, exclude from consideration in *this* species of criminal prosecution, the proof which negates an unlawful intention, or shows a clear mistake, or such ignorance as establishes beyond all doubt an intention other than that of cutting or removing the Government timber?

The Court, then, has no hesitation in giving you this instruction:

That if you believe, from the evidence given you in court, that the defendant cut timber on the lands in question, through a misapprehension at the time as to the lines which separated the Government lands from those of his father, whose agent he was, and that he *then* acted under a mistake, believing that the premises where the timber was cut, were those of his father, and not the public lands, your duty is to

ACQUIT. What, then, has been proved upon this issue ? This is for your *exclusive* deliberation. It is your province, your sole province, to settle what facts have been proved. The Court cannot, with judicial propriety, interfere with *you* in the discharge of *this* duty. *Your* opinion as to the facts, is that which must compose your verdict. The opinion of the Judge is not your opinion, and should not be made the foundation of your opinion.

And, furthermore, your verdict is the opinion of each and every one of you. Such is the peculiar and emphatic injunction of a juror's oath. Your conscience cannot repose with ease either upon what your fellow-juror or the judge may think, as to the facts, no more than the Judge can safely rely, at all times, upon the doctrines urged by able, learned and upright counsel. The inquiry, then, comes back to yourselves—what has been proved? Much difficulty, honestly felt by jurors in endeavoring to bring their minds into accord, arises from their omission to ascertain, in the first place, the facts upon which they are *all* agreed. On retiring, it is usually propounded, Is the party Guilty, or is he not guilty—a question of a general character, including a response to many particulars which together make up guilt; but upon which a vote is taken, without any antecedent settlement of material facts. Whereas, if *these* are in the first place made the subject of careful deliberation, comparison and determination, no inconvenient protraction or disagreement would, in many cases, occur. It is your duty to examine, and weigh, and sift the testimony. It is your duty *so* to inquire, as to be ready to give a reason to your own consciences of the faith that is in you. *You* cannot *jump* satisfactorily at conclusions in so important a matter as a verdict in a criminal case. Enquire, then, in your own minds, *now*, even now, what facts are conceded, or what are proved, and what are the subject of conflict? Did the defendant cut pine trees on the Government land specified? Is this so, there is no contest about the title to the premises. They are the Government lands acquired from the Indians, by the treaty of Washington.

There *is no contest* about the ownership and occupancy of the lands in the immediate vicinage. The father of the defendant was their owner, and of a mill seat for the manufacture of lumber, on an adjoining section. There *is no contest* about the residence of the defendant, and the relation he bore to the management of the mill and the lands. He was his father's servant, clothed with a special power, and under direction to cut no timber from the Government lands. *There is no question* as to the roads leading to and from the mill, and the purpose for which those roads were used— bringing timber to the mills. *There is no question* but what timber, to a great extent, was cut by some persons on sections 13 and 18. *There is no question* but what the 40 acre lots on S. W. quarter of section 18, and N. E. quarter of section 13, were used for the purpose of supplying the mill; and that the timber cut by the defendant's direction, was *not only cut upon these* 40 *acres*, but also across the lines, and on the lands of the Government adjacent.

Reaching this point, then, you have got to the remaining inquiry, mainly affecting the guilt or innocence of the defendant. Was *this* cutting done by him, and the hands under him, under a mistake, and a well-grounded ignorance of the lines which separated his father's land from that of the Government. The principal witness for the Government is Mr. Bean, who *visited*, observed and surveyed the premises, by direction of the Government agent, entrusted with the care of the Government timber in this District. The defendant showed him the quarter post on the township line, or section line, and accompanied him the whole day in running the section lines. No controversy in relation to these facts, and none, of course, in relation to what the witness observed, that much timber appeared to be cut on parts of sections 13 and 18.

During *this* survey, the defendant admitted that he had cut some of the timber, but claimed the propriatory intercession of the witness, because he had shown him the post, and aided him in ascertaining the lines.   Such is the alleged admission of the defendant, and its force and extent rests upon the credit you give to the witness, by whom it is established, and *all* that defendant said at the time must be taken together as one and an entire admission.   There is, in addition to the charge of cutting, a count for the removal.

If the defendant admitted he cut the timber, and you are satisfied that he had the management of the mill, and that the timber was removed to the mill, his admission will cover both charges.

In every criminal accusation reasonable doubt should materially sway the mind, in favor of the accused. This principle is of higher origin than human laws.   It should govern in social life.   It must control in Judicial Tribunals.

Wherefore condemn—if the mind hesitates as to guilt? But the suggestion of merciful conjecture, is not the reasonable doubt, contemplated by the law.   The doubt of the juror, consistent with his reason, is that which relates either to the character or the force of the testimony.   The test is, is or is not such a fact fully proved?   If yea, are the witnesses by which it is established, worthy of belief?   If yea, all doubt vanishes, and there remains no basis on which the reason can rest.

Sometimes a witness may be unimpeached as to general character, and may be uncontradicted either by others, or be perfectly consistent in his statement; and yet, from his deportment on the witness' stand, render himself unworthy of credit.

A hesitating or confused manner, or a studied narrative of which a jury may judge from all that accompanies the delivery of the testimony, will justly cast a shade of doubt upon it all. Of *this*, however, the jury alone, unaided either by the Court or the Counsel, must decide for themselves. *And* certainly where two witnesses contradict each other as to a particular fact, and one exhibits a frank and unbiassed manner; and the other is confused, hesitating, and evidently biassed,—the reliance of the jury can with more safety be given to the first, while they reject entirely the last.

It is another matter altogether, where discrepancies are fairly established in the narrative of the witness. Where he states in his examination in chief, a fact, which he contradicts in his cross-examination; or where he conceals the whole of a matter, which is afterward extracted by cross-interrogation, such discrepancy, or such conduct, if clearly apparent to the jury, should lead to the rejection of the testimony.

The jury found a verdict of Guilty; and the Court sentenced the defendant to one day's imprisonment, and fifty dollars fine.

UNITED STATES *v.* THOMPSON.

1. The Caption or Title is no part of the presentment of the Grand Jury, and may be amended after verdict as a clerical error.

2. Not necessary, in an indictment for cutting timber, to state the class of lands from which the trees were cut.

3. Such a description as shows the accused the offense with which he is charged, is sufficient.

4. Where a Statute creates an offense, and the indictment charges the same in the precise words of the Statute, it is unnecessary to prefix to the charging words, the word "unlawful," or any other word showing a wrongful intention.

Mr. *Hand, Dist. Atty. United States,* and Mr. *Frazer* for United States.

Van Arman & Walker & Lathrop for the defendant.

Motion in arrest of Judgment.

OPINION OF JUDGE WILKINS.

Several reasons are assigned for the arrest of the Judgment of the Court, comprising various objections to the indictment.

The 1st objection is, as to what is technically termed the *caption*, or that the Court is not properly entitled.

We consider that this objection has been long settled, both in England and in this country.

Forming no part of the indictment or presentment of the Grand Jury, being in fact no more than the clerical endorsement of the record, unnecessary as giving information to the accused, it is only matter of astonishment, that such a technical exception should *now* be gravely argued in Court. In the language of Lord Mansfield, in 1st Saunders, and which has been adopted by the most reliable American cases, it is only a copy of the style of the Court at which the indictment is found, and is amendable at *any time* before removed to a higher court. And, if the objection could now be entertained, so as to defeat Justice, it would be giving judicial weight to technical exceptions—calling loudly for legislative interposition. Moreover, there is no great fault to be found in *this* caption. The Court is in fact properly entitled.

"District Court of the United States." The other words, in relation to "Seventh Circuit," may be treated as surplusage, without any formal amendment.

The 2nd objection is, that the indictment, in its description of the offense, does not specify the class of lands on which the trespass was committed, so as to distinguish between the lands reserved and those not reserved for naval purposes. This was unnecessary. The Act of 1817, based upon the provision of law for the preservation of ship timber for the use of the Navy of the United States,—contemplated only the punishment of cutting Naval timber—where the same was cut and removed without authority.

The Act of 1831 was designed to extend the efficacious and salutary provisions of the first Act,—to all the public lands,—and to all timber, whether naval or otherwise. Under either Statute, the Secretary of the Navy could authorize an agent to cut and remove any timber from any of the lands of the United States, whether reserved or not. Such is the import of the closing language of the 1st Section of the Act of 1831, creating these offenses. "Other than for the use of the Navy of the United States."

Therefore, the allegation negativing the fact, that timber was cut "other than for the use of the Navy of the United States," is sufficient to describe the offense charged. What is the object of the general rule in criminal pleading, requiring a specific and succinct description of the offense, but that the accused may be apprised of what he is accused, by such a clear and intelligible description that he cannot be misled, but may know what charge he is called upon to meet? The old beaten paths of the Common Law, so much the subject of humorous comment, during the argument, had this principle as their foundation; although many of the old decisions, by too great an observance of technical terms, favored the escape of the guilty. But modern ruling is more consistent with common sense, and the safe administration of justice. All that is required now, is embraced within two simple principles.

1. Charge the offense as defined or described in the law.

2. Describe it intelligently, as to manner, time and place.

Such is the description as contained in this indictment. The Statute declares the act of "cutting any live oak or red cedar 'or other timber,' from any lands of the United States, with intent to export, *use* or employ the same in any manner whatsoever, other than for the use of the Navy of the United States," *a misdemeanor:*—I say a misdemeanor—although the term is not employed, but is implied; as the individual so doing is treated as an offender, and punished, on conviction, with fine and imprisonment. This indictment describes the offense in the precise words of the Statute—thus—"that the said William Thompson, DID, on the 1st of October, 1853, at the county, and township, and range, and section, specially described, a certain close of the United States; viz., the township, and range, and section aforesaid, broke and entered; and certain timber, viz., 5,000 pine trees—there standing and growing, and being on the said lands of the United States,—cause to be cut, felled and prostrated, *with intent*, the said timber, then and there to use and employ in another manner than for the use of the Navy of the United States, to wit,—for his own private use, &c."

It is difficult for the Court to conceive what other language could better describe the offense; or, wherefore there should be an additional showing, that the lands so specifically described, according to the public survey, had not been, and were not reserved for Naval purposes. The Legislature, by positive enactment, declares *that* act a crime, which before was but a civil trespass: the act itself was prior to this period unlawful, but not punishable by indictment; and the Statute now describes the characteristics of the offense which it creates and punishes—they are two.

1. Cutting timber on the Public Lands.

2. Cutting with the *intent* designated.

It is true, that the whole scope and spirit of the Land Laws of the United States, especially the provisions enacted since 1831, encourage and invite actual settlement on the public domain, and bestow upon the settler or pre-emptor certain privileges upon certain prescribed terms. But this invitation is not to trespassers or squatters, nor is there, even in the recent legislation of Congress, any provision countenancing the cutting of timber on the lands of the United States, for the private profit of the cutter, or, for his own use, beyond that which might indicate an intention of pre-emption, which

must be consummated within a *brief period*, or the cutter is
deemed a trespasser *ab initio*.

I am clearly of opinion, then, that *this* exception is not
well taken, that no such classification is necessary, and that
it is sufficient to allege the trespass, as in this indictment, by
the particular township, range or section.

The next objection, and which embraces substantially the
4th and 5th is, that there is no act set forth, from which the
law will presume a "criminal intent."

I copy the precise words of the exception. The argument
took a wider range ; but, in determining the validity of the
objection, the Court will consider the suggestions made as
applicable to the particular exception. It is urged, that the
description of the offense is defective, because there is no
term employed showing a wrongful act or criminal intention.
In support of the proposition, it is insisted that the Statute
of 1831, being part of one general system of legislation,
designed to punish as criminals, *only* those who wrongfully
entered the public lands, and wrongfully cut timber thereon,
and wrongfully removed the same after it was cut. That
antecedent to the enactment, cutting timber on the public
lands, was not wrongful or unlawful; and that the offense
under this act must be so described. The Court has already,
on three different occasions, fully commented on this Statute,
and given to its provisions a judicial construction. These
views need not now be recapitulated.

The position is well taken, that the Act of 1831 is part of
a general system ; that all the land legislation, *pari materia*,
may be considered *one* law, that there are benign provisions
encouraging settlement, and contra-distinguishing the pre-
emptor, the *bona fide* settler, from the lawless trespasser ;
that the former may, for the manifest purposes which are
consistent with his settlement and contemplated pre-emption
entry, cut such timber as corresponds with *his* supposed legal
immunity ; and furthermore, that a wrongful intention is

essential to constitute any act a crime. To all these propositions, the Court most cordially assents. But they are not involved in the exception taken to this indictment. An unlawful act is alleged; and consequently an unlawful intention will be presumed, on the proof of such unlawful act. Prove the allegata, and the intention is established, to be rebutted by the defense.

This principle is as old as the criminal law. The act of homicide implies malice, because the act is proof of the intent.

But, it is urged that a manifest distinction exists in this respect, between *mala prohibita* and *mala per se.* That distinction the Court fully recognizes.

But its applicability to the point in question, is not so clearly apprehended. An evil, prohibited, merely, is not that act which was an evil *before* prohibition; but that which is made an evil only by legislation.

If a trespass upon the public lands, and destroying the valuable timber, was never an evil or an offense until the Act of 1831, then there would be some weight in the argument; but such was not the case, for although the act was not before punishable by indictment, yet, it was in itself a wrongful, yea, an immoral act, an evil of itself, and for which the trespasser was answerable in damages recoverable by civil action. It is true, the intention to enter a pre-emption claim, vests certain privileges, and within their scope, the party may freely act, without being amenable to this Statute; yet, the existence of such an inchoate right, a mere *privilege*, not a consummated right, which could be perfected at the option of the party, is only available as matter of defense, and must be shown by proof only within the knowledge and power of the defendant.

It is matter of defense, then, and not matter of pleading, and need not be anticipated by the prosecution. The indictment alleges, in the very words of the Statute, the wrongful act, which it prohibits; and describes the offense with *all* the

certainty of the Statute itself. What more particularity can
be required; what "obvious intention" has been disregarded;
and what "known principle of law" would demand greater
nicety? To prefix the words "unlawfully or knowingly" to
the charging terms, would not serve any purpose favorable to
the defendant; it would give him no clearer notice of the
offense. His act of cutting or removing, was either lawful or
unlawful, according to the circumstances attending the transaction. If he cut, as a pre-emptor, he can shew it; if he
removed, he can shew it. Wherefore, then, does substantial
justice require the insertion of these words? The known
principles of law do not require it, nor does the Statute, in
its spirit or purview, demand it. Such is no part of the
Statutory description of the offense.

Upon this point the law has been long, and to my mind,
clearly settled, by an unruffled current of authority, both in
England and in this country, from Bacon's Abridgement to
Sumner's Reports, and Wharton and Blackford but copy
the old rule, tread in the old well beaten path of the common
law, which is common sense and substantial justice. Bacon
says: "Where the act itself is unlawful the law infers an evil
intent."

Story says: "Where it is not required by the State, it
need not be averred; and Mr. Justice McLean, in his opinion
in the case of Lancaster, does not express a different ruling,
or warrant the interpretation that has been given to his
language.

The Court holds then, that this exception is not well taken.
Setting forth the Act prohibited in the words of the Statute,
is all that is required; and on the proof of such act, the law
will infer a criminal intent. Motion to arrest, refused.

CIRCUIT COURT OF THE UNITED STATES.

EBER B. WARD AND SAMUEL WARD *v.* THE PROPELLER A. ROSSITER.

IN ADMIRALTY.

A Steamer, in entering the Harbor of Chicago in the night, at a speed of three and a half to four miles an hour, while another Steamer was in the act of turning, just above a bend in the river, came in collision with the latter, at that moment lying across the river.

The former was in fault, and was liable for the damages done. The river was full of craft, and the speed of the Steamer was too great under the circumstances.

If a Steamer, owing to any cause, cannot see its way clear before it, in entering a harbor in the night, it is its duty to stop.

Mr. *Shumway*, for libellant.
Mr. *Goodrich*, for claimant.

OPINION OF JUDGE DRUMMOND.

On the 27th of August, 1851, the Steamer St. Louis had returned from her nightly trip from New Buffalo to Chicago, and had entered the river and passed a little above her wharf to wind. It was about three o'clock in the morning. There was no regular place at that time for Steamers to turn. They winded where they could, though there was a place—the excavation—where it was more convenient and wider than at other places. The St. Louis was in the act of turning, lying across the river, (then two hundred and six feet wide only at that place, the St. Louis being one hundred and ninety-five feet long;) when the Rossiter came into the harbor at a speed of three and a half to four miles an hour. In turning the bend of the river, not far from the ferry, a little more than seven hundred feet from the spot where the St. Louis was winding, the Rossiter encountered a thick smoke, coming across the river from the ruins of Haddock & Norton's warehouse, then recently destroyed by fire, which prevented those on board, as they allege, from seeing the St. Louis, though the people of the latter assert that they could easily distinguish the Rossiter. The Rossiter blew her whistle as she came up the river. The St. Louis had all necessary lights. The Rossiter was hailed as she approached, but without avail, as she immediately struck the St. Louis and caused damage to the amount of $258,61. It was a clear star-light night.

These are the material facts in the case.

There can be no doubt that the Rossiter was in fault, and liable for the injury done. If those on board of the Propeller could not see their way clear, owing to the smoke, it was their duty to proceed with extreme caution, especially as they were approaching a bend in the river. It is a rule of universal application, that a Steamer in entering a harbor at night, crowded with craft as the Chicago river was at that time, shall be held to the greatest diligence and circumspection, and if owing to fog, smoke, or other cause, they cannot see their way before them, it is their duty to stop, or at least proceed with such slowness that they can stop at a moment's notice. It will not do for Steamers to proceed at haphazard, and trust to chance to go clear. If they cannot see the way they must stop till they can. I have repeatedly been called upon to investigate cases which have originated from the recklessness with which Steamers enter the Harbor of Chicago, as well in the daytime as in the night. They must be more careful and vigilant than they have been, or, clearly understood, they will have to answer in damages for the consequences.

A decree will be entered against the claimant and his sureties for the sum of $258,61 and costs.

THE UNITED STATES v. WILLIAM PRENTICE ET AL.

In a suit brought by the United States against the marshal and his sureties, on his bond for the recovery of moneys collected in divers executions, issued at the suit of the United States, the defendants attempted to set off the items of an account, contained in a Treasury transcript, which had been disallowed; but which transcript reserved a balance due the Government, over and above such items, without including any of the moneys claimed in this suit. It was held that the set off could not be allowed.

It makes no difference that the marshal might be able to plead the statute of limitation to a suit brought for such balance.

When a debtor has a set off equally applicable to the demands against him, the Court will apply it according to the equity between the parties.

Besides, the marshal had presented this account to meet another claim of the Government not included in this suit.

The Statute of the State can have no influence on this question: it depends upon the Act of Congress.

There is no law of Congress regulating set off in suits against officers; but several statutes imply that set off may be allowed.

Mr. *Williams*, *D. A.*, for the plaintiffs.

Messrs. *Lincoln & Logan*, for defendant.

OPINION OF JUDGE DRUMMOND.

This is an action brought by the plaintiffs against Prentice and his sureties, for the recovery of moneys which the former had received upon sundry executions in favor of the United States, and which had come to his hands as marshal. The declaration only counts upon breaches of the bond, because the marshal has collected money which he never paid over.

5a

After the plaintiffs had introduced the various executions which are mentioned in the declaration, with the endorsements made on them by the marshal, the defendants offered an account of the items which they claimed as a set off in this suit, amounting to the sum of fourteen hundred dollars, and then offered a transcript from the Treasury Department, to show that the items claimed as a set off were disallowed. The defendants insisted it was competent evidence for that purpose. By agreement, the whole transcript was admitted subject to the opinion of the Court upon the effect to be given to it. The transcript shows a balance of more than two thousand dollars against the marshal, so that if the $1400 were allowed as a set off in this case, there would still be, according to the transcript, a balance of more than $600 due the Government.

I am of the opinion that the account cannot be allowed as a set off, in this case.

The Government has not seen fit to sue the marshal on the account which contains these disallowed items, but has brought suit for money collected on divers executions. The Government can properly object to this account in this suit, because it was presented by the marshal as a charge against the Government, in another claim with which the subject matter of this suit has no concern. The defendants insist upon the set off here; because to the other claim, if suit is brought, they purpose pleading the statute of limitation. But this ground will not help them in this case. It would seem to be inequitable to suffer the defendants to avail themselves of an account which shows that so far from there being any set off for claims against the Government, there is a balance against the marshal, independent of the amount in controversy here.

Where a debtor has a set off equally applicable to two demands against him, he cannot select on which of the demands he will apply it; but the Court will apply it according to the equity between the parties. See *Tallmadge* v. *Fish-*

kill Iron Co., 4 *Barbour S. C. R.* 392, which was a suit in equity, and which cites *Collins* v. *Allen,* 12 *Wendell R.* 356, which was a suit at law, where a party had two claims—a note and an account—against a man, and transferred the note over-due, he holding claims against the man sufficient to meet a set off which was attempted to be put in in a suit on the trans-ferred note. It was held, it was not a good set off in that suit.

But here there is great reason for saying that the marshal himself elected to apply the account offered, as a set off to another claim of the Government against him, different from the one in suit here. And it would be manifestly unjust to allow him now to withdraw this account from that claim, because it may be barred by the 4th section of the Act of 10th of April, 1806.

The Statute of the State can have no influence on this question. It is something which depends entirely upon the Acts of Congress. No State law can affect the question of set off, in suits by the Government against its officers, because the rule on the subject must be uniform throughout the United States. *The United States* v. *Robeson,* 9 *Peters R.* 328. The Courts have frequently allowed claims as set off against the Government, which were not strictly legal, provided they were due *ex equo et bono. The United States* v. *McDaniel,* 7 *Peters R.* 1.

It is to be regretted that there is no Act of Congress regu-lating set off in suits brought by the Government. There are, however, various acts, such as the 3rd and 4th sections of the Act of March 3rd, 1797,—1 *Stat. at L.* 514, and others,—which imply that set off may be allowed.

Being of opinion that the defendants are not equitably entitled to the set off they claim, the judgment must be for the plaintiffs.

ADAM W. THAXTER *v.* REUBEN HATCH ET AL.

Where a mortgage was executed in Massachusetts to secure the payment of promissory notes also made there, for land in Illinois; and the payer of the note, then a citizen of Massachusetts, assigned them to the plaintiff, and continued to reside in that State till after cause of action had occurred on the notes; but before suit brought, the payer moved to Illinois, and at the time of the commencement of the suit was a citizen of Illinois. *Held* that the case was within the 11th section of the Judiciary Act of 1789, and that the Court had no jurisdiction.

When the Courts of the United States once acquire jurisdiction, by virtue of the citizenship of the· parties, it cannot be ousted by a change of residence; but this applies only where jurisdiction has vested by a suit.

The limitation in the 11th section of the Judiciary Act is confined to the time when the suit is commenced.

Messrs. *Grimshaw & Williams, D. A.,* for plaintiff.
Messrs. *Hay & Browning,* for defendants.

OPINION OF JUDGE DRUMMOND.

This is a bill to foreclose a mortgage given by Reuben Hatch and James Wilson on some land in Pike County, to John Preston. The mortgage was executed to secure some promissory notes, part of the purchase money of the land. They were made payable to Preston, who assigned them to the plaintiff. At the time of the assignment, both Preston and the plaintiff were citizens of Massachusetts. When the suit was brought, Preston had ceased to reside in Massachusetts, and· had become a citizen of Illinois. The mortgage itself had never in form been assigned by Preston to the plaintiff, and the only right of the plaintiff was founded on the fact that the note had been duly endorsed to him. It is objected, that under this state of facts the Court has no jurisdiction of the case.

In the 11th section of the Judicial Act of 1789, there is the following clause: " Nor shall any District or Circuit Court have cognizance of any suit to recover the contents of any promissory note, or other clause in action in favor of an assignee, unless a suit might have been presented in such Court to recover the said contents, if no assignment had been made, except in cases of foreign bills of exchange."

Whatever doubts may have heretofore existed on the subject, the case of *Sheldon* v. *Sill*, 8 *Howard R.* 441, decides that the kind of contract upon which this action is brought, is a chose in action or promissory note, within the meaning of this Act of Congress. But was a case of bond, secured by mortgage. This is a case of promissory notes secured by mortgage. The plaintiff is therefore an assignee of a chose in action, and the only question is whether within the meaning of the act a suit might have been prosecuted if no assignment had been made. In the case referred to, the citizenship of the parties remained the same; the contract was made in the State where the suit was brought, and between citizens of that State. Here, the contract was made in Massachusetts, and Preston, when he assigned the notes, was a citizen of that State; and it is insisted that inasmuch as a suit could at one time have been brought by Preston, he could not by his own act deprive the plaintiff of the right to sue in the Courts of the United States, that right existing at the time of the assignment. The question is, what is the limitation of the restriction? Is it general, or is it confined to *the time* of the commencement of the suit? It is true that at one time a suit might have been prosecuted if no assignment had been made; but before any suit was brought, the assignor became a citizen of Illinois, and consequently he could not have brought suit there if no assignment had been made, because the controversy would not have been between citizens of different States.

It has been uniformly held, that when the Courts of the United States have once acquired jurisdiction, by virtue of the citizenship of the parties, it cannot be ousted by a change of residence; but as I understand this rule, it only applies when jurisdiction has actually vested by the commencement of a suit. There can be no doubt, that as a general rule, the jurisdiction depends upon the character of the parties at the time the suit is brought; and this is the only inquiry for the Court in these cases. And I think the same rule must be adopted in this case. The limitation is confined to the time when the suit is commenced. *Morgan* v. *Morgan,* 2 *Wheaton* 290; *Mollan* v. *Torrance,* 9 *Wheaton* 587; *Dunn* v. *Clarke,* 8 *Peters* 1; *Clarke* v. *Matthewson,* 12 *Peters* 171.

The bill must accordingly be dismissed for want of jurisdiction.

THE COLUMBUS INSURANCE COMPANY *v.* THE PEORIA BRIDGE ASSOCIATION. ·

The principles declared in the *Columbus Insurance Company* v. *Curtinius et al. ante*—again affirmed—that the River Illinois is free to all the citizens of the United States. But the Legislature had no power to authorize the construction of a bridge which would be a material obstruction to its navigation, nor to declare that a bridge, with a draw of a particular width, was not an obstruction.

The true construction of the 2nd section of the Act of the Legislature of Illinois, of the 26th of January, 1847, is, that a space of seventy-five feet, fairly and substantially embracing the principal channel of the river, must be left open, estimating with reference to its course.

The right of the free navigation of the Illinois, is consistent with the right of the State to construct bridges, provided they do not materially obstruct the navigation. They exist together, and neither can be permitted to destroy or essentially impair the other.

The authority to construct a bridge across a navigable stream, should be so exercised as to interfere as little as possible with the free navigation of the river.

Every bridge may in one sense be said to be an obstruction; but that delay or risk which is inseparable from the thing which the State has the power to create, does not make it an obstruction in law.

The State is to determine when, where, and under what circumstances a bridge shall be constructed; and as a general thing, no third party can question the authority of the State in this respect.

If the bridge was an obstruction, the plaintiff cannot recover for the injury, if there was carelessness and negligence in the management of the boat injured.

OPINION OF JUDGE DRUMMOND.

This is the same case reported *ante*—the present defendant being substituted by agreement for the former defendants. After the decision of the Court upon the demurrer, the defendants had leave to amend their pleas, and in their new pleadings traversed the averment in the declaration that the bridge, as constructed, was a material obstruction to the navigation of the river. Issue was joined upon the pleas, and the case was submitted to a jury.

It appears by the evidence that the Steamer Falcon, on the 22d of March, 1849, having several boats in tow, among which was the canal boat Troy, loaded with wheat, was descending the Illinois river; and in attempting to pass through the piers of the bridge constructed at Peoria, the canal boat struck one of the piers, was stove and sunk, and the cargo lost. The plaintiffs, having a policy of Insurance on the canal boat and cargo, paid it, and brought this suit to recover the amount. There were only two questions made in the case;—the first was whether the bridge was a material obstruction to the navigation of the river; and the second, whether the boat had been managed with competent skill. A large number of witnesses were examined on these points, and there was some conflict in the evidence.

The case was argued by Mr. Lincoln and Mr. Chumasero for the plaintiff, and by Mr. Logan, Mr. Powell, and Mr. Peters for the defendant.

CHARGE OF THE COURT TO THE JURY.

From an examination of the subject in this case, at a former term, I came to the conclusion which I now repeat to you, that the River Illinois is a navigable stream, free to all the citizens of the United States, and the State could not authorize the construction of a bridge which would be a material obstruction to its navigation, and if you believe from the evidence, that the defendant has placed such obstruction in the river, then no exemption can be claimed by virtue of such obstruction. Whether it is a material obstruction or not, is a question of fact to be determined by the jury, upon a consideration of all the evidence in the case.

Some evidence has been given, which it is insisted proves that the bridge has not been constructed in accordance with the Act of the Legislature of 1847. It is for you to determine upon the evidence, whether it has been constructed as required by that Act. If it has not been so built, then, of course, the defendant cannot claim any protection by virtue of it.

The true construction of the second section of the Act of 26th of January, 1847, is, that the defendant was obliged to have a space of seventy-five feet, fairly and substantially embracing the principal channel; and if, for any purpose, the bridge was run irregularly across the channel, that was not a compliance with the Act, unless the seventy-five feet were left open, *across* the channel, estimating with reference to its curve. The defendant was not authorized to place any pier *in* the principal channel, but that must be left open, unless it was more than seventy-five feet wide, and in that event the usual channel for the passage of river craft should be left open.

The Legislature had no power to declare that a bridge constructed with a draw of a certain width, was not a material obstruction to the navigation of the river; and if the jury is satisfied from the evidence, that the defendant has complied with the Act of 1847, still that does not determine the question whether or not it was an obstruction.

The right of free navigation of the Illinois, is not inconsistent with the right of the State to provide means of crossing the river by bridges, or otherwise, when the wants of the public require them, provided such bridges do not essentially injure the navigation of the river. It must be considered as settled, that the right to a free navigation of our Western Rivers, and the right of the State to adopt those means of crossing them which the skill and ingenuity of man have devised, as both are equally important, are co-existent, and neither can be permitted to destroy or essentially impair the other.

The authority to construct a bridge across a navigable river, being in the State, it should be exercised in such a manner as, while it gives full effect to the power itself, it should interfere as little as possible with the other right—that of free navigation; and this is the true test whether a particular structure is such an obstruction as is contrary to law.

The State having the power, the State itself, or if delegated to a corporation, the corporation, as a general thing, is exclusively to judge of the time, place and circumstances which were to give it exercise, and if it seems to the State that the necessities of the community call for its exercise, no third party can question the propriety of it, unless under peculiar circumstances, which do not appear to exist in this case.

Every bridge—unless, indeed, one suspended over a river so as to be above all vessels and water craft—may, in one sense, be said to be an obstruction; but that delay or risk which is inseparable from the existence of the thing which the State has the power to create, does not make it an obstruction in contemplation of law. The necessity is the justification, and for such delay or risk the law will not give a right of action.

These are principles which I had occasion to announce in an investigation which was recently made at Chicago, upon a bill filed by certain parties, to prevent the erection of a bridge across the Chicago river, and they embody my views of the law upon this branch of the case.

The jury are to take into consideration all the facts and circumstances which are in evidence before them—the character of the river itself, the trade upon it, the craft navigating it, and are to judge whether the piers placed by the defendant were a material obstruction. It is almost impossible to do anything more than to lay down general rules, to guide the minds of the jury upon this part of the case. It is in the nature of the subject that no precise and absolute rule can be given to the jury in this case, to enable them to determine whether this particular bridge was an obstruction, because it is the province of the jury to apply the law to the facts, and their conclusions will be influenced by the view they may take of the facts. It may be clear that a supposed bridge is an obstruction and that another is not; but between the two there may be infinite degrees of difference one way or the other, and it may be, and often is, hard to decide where the line of division is, as a matter of fact.

If the jury are satisfied from the evidence that the bridge was not a material obstruction to the navigator, then from what has already been said, they will infer it was such a bridge as the State was authorized to erect, or cause to be erected; and the defendant is not liable for any damage sustained by the plaintiff.

If the jury still believe the bridge was a material obstruction, then it is their duty to enquire into the circumstances attending the collision of the boat against the pier. In such case, if there was any want of ordinary care, skill or diligence on the part of those navigating the steamer or canal boat, the defendant is not liable.

The plaintiff cannot recover from the defendant, solely on the ground that an obstruction had been placed in the river. Admitting the defendant had obstructed the river, a party cannot, by carelessly or wantonly running his boat against such obstruction, hold the defendant liable, if the boat was sunk. The law will not compensate for carelessness or wantonness like that; for such an obstruction the law would furnish a remedy in another way.

The law does not require that there should be extraordinary care or skill—in the case supposed—on the part of those navigating the steamer and canal boat. An error of judgment would not prevent the plaintiff from recovering, unless it was an error involving a want of care, skill or diligence. If they used the usual degree of care, skill and diligence, that was sufficient: the question is not whether the steamer by going in a different channel might not possibly have avoided the danger; but whether ordinary skill was exercised. To determine this, it is proper for the jury to take into consideration the unusual stage of the river, the submersion of the pivot pier, the carrying away of the superstructure, and all the other facts proved, such as the manner of fastening the canal boat to the steamer, &c.

It is the duty, undoubtedly, of persons owning boats navigating the river, to employ competent agents in the management of their boats, as captains, engineers, pilots, &c.; and if any damage be sustained in consequence of an omission in this respect, they must bear the loss.

The jury are to take the opinions of the witnesses as to the bridge being an obstruction, and as to the manner in which the steamer and canal boat were managed; simply as *opinions* of men of *experience* to inform their judgments, not as absolutely binding them. The jury may from their own conclusions on these points form the whole testimony. In this part of the case, of course, much more reliance ought to be placed on particular facts which establish a conclusion, than on the mere opinions of others.

The canal boat and cargo were abandoned to the plaintiff, and was sold, and the proceeds received; if the jury shall find for the plaintiff, the measure of damages is the amount paid by the plaintiff, with interest from the time of payment, deducting the amount received as the proceeds of the boat and cargo.

The jury, after being kept together a long time, were unable to agree, and by consent of parties were discharged; and the suit was finally compromised.

Edwin Hunt v. The Propeller Cleveland.

IN ADMIRALTY.

Several casks of hardware were shipped at Ogdensburg for Chicago. The casks were opened and examined at Chicago, and the hardware was found damaged. During the voyage, the Propeller encountered a storm, and shipped water and leaked. No positive proof was given as to how the damage was done. The bill of lading promised to deliver the merchandise in good order, the dangers of navigation only excepted. The vessel was tight, staunch and well manned at the time of shipment.

The damage being shown, it devolved on the carrier to establish it was within the exception of the bill of lading.

He has shown facts from which this can fairly be inferred.

The shipper has not proved that the damage could have been avoided by the exercise of reasonable care and skill. The carrier is therefore not liable.

It is a useful and proper precaution for a master of a vessel to note a protest at the first port of his arrival, after an accident, but it is not an indispensable duty.

Mr. *Stickney*, for libellant.
Mr. *Waite*, for claimant.

OPINION OF JUDGE DRUMMOND.

On the 8th of October, 1851, were shipped on the Propeller Cleveland, at Ogdensburg, New York, several casks of hardware, for Chicago, belonging to the libellant. On the arrival of the Propeller at Chicago, on the 1st of November, when the casks were opened and examined, it was ascertained that the hardware had been wet and damaged to an amount varying from three to five per cent., according to the kind of goods. The libel alleges that this damage was sustained in consequence of the carelessness and unskilfulness of the carrier. The claimants, in their answer, insist that the injury was the result of the dangers of the sea, and was unavoidable. The bill of lading states that the merchandise was shipped in good order and condition, and was to be delivered in like good order and condition—*the dangers of navigation only excepted.* The sole question in the case is whether the damage was within the exception in the bill of lading.

The proof is that the vessel was tight, staunch, well manned and equipped in every respect.

The injury being established, it is incumbent on the carrier to show that it was caused by the dangers of navigation, and if it appear it was the consequence of such dangers, then it devolves upon the shipper to make out that the damage might have been avoided by the exercise of reasonable care and skill on the part of the carrier. *Clark* v. *Barnwell*, 12 *Howard R.* 272.

Apply these principles to the facts in this case. The casks were stowed in the after part of the forward hold, which was a proper and safe place for that kind of merchandise. The Propeller had a cargo of various goods, for Cleveland, Sheboygan, Port Washington, Milwaukee, Racine, Southport and Chicago. Nothing of importance occurred till the 16th of October, when being off Saginaw Bay, the cylinder of one of the engines broke, and other damage was done which compelled the vessel to return to St. Clair to repair. The engine was repaired and they left St. Clair on the 21st. After leaving St. Clair, and passing Point of Barques, about midnight of that day they were met with a very severe gale from the West. The sea made a clean breach over the vessel, washed things from the promenade deck, stove in the larboard gangway, which caused her to ship a considerable quantity of water which went through the hatch-way into the fire-hold, and to leak. All hands were immediately called and set to pumping. The Propeller was put head to the wind and worked up under the lea of the land. At the end of about four hours labor, they succeeded in freeing her from the water, and she did not afterwards leak more than usual. The gangway had been well and securely fastened. They had heavy weather the remainder of the voyage, but nothing further occurred of any moment. The witnesses who testify to these facts are the captain, the engineer, the clerk and the mate. There is no contradictory testimony. They all concur in the belief, that whatever damage was done to the hardware was in this gale of wind, and that no human skill or prudence could have prevented it.

It seems fairly to be inferred from the proofs, that the damage was caused by the gale of wind, which resulted in wetting the merchandise, either by leakage of the vessel or by shipping water. The damage is thus shown to be caused by the dangers of navigation. It follows, that the shipper must establish negligence or want of skill in the carrier. It must not be matter of doubt merely, but it shall clearly appear there was a want of proper care, skill or diligence. Now, in this case, the Court must be satisfied, notwithstanding the statements of the witnesses that there was proper care and skill, that there was not. It is certainly true that the Court is not bound by the mere statements of the witnesses on this point; but facts must appear from which the Court is able to infer there was a want of due care on the part of those who had the management of the Propeller. There is nothing in the facts shown, to warrant such a conclusion. The testimony comes from those on board of the vessel, and this should lead to great caution in receiving it. Any considerable experience in this class of cases teaches us to scrutinize closely everything that may be said. But the testimony cannot, obviously, come from any other source. We must endeavor to draw just conclusions from it, making all due allowance for the influences which may be supposed to affect the minds and memory of the witnesses.

Some stress was laid on the circumstance of there having been no protest noted until the arrival of the vessel in Chicago, notwithstanding she stopped at various places before her arrival at that port.

It is a useful and proper precaution for a master of a vessel to note a protest on his arrival at the first port—when it is in his power to do so—in all cases where any accident has occurred, or any injury been sustained, or any possibility thereof; but it is not an indispensable duty, without which the carrier cannot be relieved from liability. It is always highly desirable that a statement should be made of all the circumstances attending any casualty or accident on ship board, while the facts are fresh in the mind, and before controversy has sprung up in relation to them. Still, if it be omitted, it operates against the carrier only by throwing a cloud over the transaction—at most, by casting something of suspicion on the affair. It cannot be said that the omission of the carrier shall throw upon him all the consequences of negligence in a clear case of none in fact. It may well have its effect in a doubtful case, but not in one where there is nothing to cause the mind to hesitate in its conclusion. *Abbott on Shipping*, 497 (side paging 380.) 9 *Leigh's R.* 54. *Conkling's Admiralty*, 684, *&c. Senat* v. *Porter*, 7 *T. R.* 158. *Arnould on Insurance*, 1337. *The Emma*, 2 *W. Robinson R.* 315.

There was a protest noted and properly extended on the arrival of the Propeller at Chicago, but it has not been introduced. No objection has been taken on that point by the libellant. It is said to be lost or mislaid. I think it is reasonable to conclude under the circumstances of this case, if it were here it would shed no new light upon the subject of this controversy.

The libel must be dismissed with costs.

ANN W. TIBBATTS, *v.* LEO TIBBATTS.

Tibbatts and wife entered into a contract with defendant, by which he was put in possession of a large farm, containing stock of various kinds to be managed by him, one third of the profits to be his, the other two thirds to be paid to the other party.

Soon after entering into the possession, he, Tibbatts, sold the stock on the farm, and the implements of agriculture, and leased the farm, reserving to himself the homestead and a small part of the ground.

The defendant became insolvent and unable to pay the money he had received on the sale of the property.

. The Court held, that this was an entire abandonment of the contract, and that the wife of Tibbatts, who owned the land, might claim the possession of it. By the contract, Leo Tibbatts, was to have the sole management of the farm, &c., which was a special trust and confidence, he could not transfer to another. Any modification of the written contract Tibbatts may have made to the injury of his wife, and to which she gave no consent, did not bind her after his death.

The contract was decreed to be cancelled and the possession of the premises to be restored to the complainant.

Messrs. *Swayne and Gwynne,* for complainants.
Mr. *Andrews,* for defendant.

OPINION OF THE COURT.

This is a bill in chancery praying, for the reasons stated, that a certain lease or contract in relation to the occupancy and management of a certain farm, by the defendant, should be set aside, and the possession of the same decreed to the complainant.

The contract was entered into between John W. Tabbatts, and Ann Tibbatts, his wife, on the 2d day of August, 1851, with Leo Tibbatts, the defendant. They leased unto Leo Tibbatts until the first day of March, 1862, a certain tract of land or stock farm, situated and lying in the County of Union, and State of Ohio, containing between eleven and twelve hundred acres; and in consideration of the covenants hereinafter made and expressed on the part of the said Leo, covenant and bind themselves, their heirs, executors, administrators and assigns, that the said Leo shall hold, use and occupy, the said farm and tract of land, for and during the term aforesaid without let or hindrance, under the following covenant and condition, viz:—"the said Leo is to pay no rents during the term of this lease." Second, he is to manage and conduct the business and operations of said farm, in accordance with his own judgment, without being subject to the dictation or direction of any one else. Third, the stock, implements of husbandry, and other utensils appertaining to farming purposes, now on said farm, are to be fairly valued by disinterested persons, chosen mutually by the parties interested in this agreement, and at the end or termination of this lease, are to be accounted back in equal value. Fourth, Leo is to have one third, and John W. Tibbatts and Ann Tibbatts, two thirds of the nett profits that may be made or accrue by the same. Fifth, the current expenses of the farm and the cattle too, are to be paid out of the general stock funds of the concern." But the real estate tax of the farm is to be paid by John W. Tibbatts. Sixth, on any advances made by either of the parties to this lease, the concern is to allow an interest at the rate of six per cent. per annum.

Seventh, the said Leo is to keep correct and regular book accounts of all the transactions of the farm; accounts of the receipts and expenditures of the same, which are at any time,

6a

whenever desired to be subject to the inspection of John W. Tibbatts, and Ann, his wife." Eighth, in case of the death of Leo Tibbatts, during the term of this lease, John W. Tibbatts and Ann, his wife, are to have peaceable possession of the premises."

The character of the above paper is a controverted point, by the counsel in the case. On the part of the plaintiff's counsel, it is argued, that the agreement is an article of copartnership, while on the other side, it is insisted that it is a lease.

It is a matter of some nicety to draw the line between the agency and a copartnership. A stipulated sum to be paid out of the profits of the partnership, would not constitute, technically, an individual a partner, although his agreement would bring him substantially within some of the leading principles which constitute a partnership.

It is not necessary to constitute a partnership, that each individual should contribute to the capital equally, or indeed that a partner should advance any portion of the capital. He may agree to contribute his labor in the management of the concern, which is sufficient to make him a partner, if he be a sharer in the profits and loss. Partnership, says Fourier, is formed by a contract, by which one person or partnership agrees to furnish another person or partnership, to whom it is furnished, in his or their own name or firm, on condition of receiving a share in the profits, in proportion determined by the contract, and of being liable to losses and expenses, to the amount furnished, and no more."

This definition covers the contract before us. Tibbatts and wife furnished the farm, the stock and farming utensils, and Leo Tibbatts is to manage the farm and pay to Tibbatts and wife two thirds of the profits. And books are to be kept of the farming transactions, which are to be open to the inspection of the other party. The stock is to be valued, and on the termination of the contract, it is to be accounted for in value, and peaceable possession of the land is to be given up. Here the distribution is to be made of the profits, which subject all the parties to loss, as there can be no distribution, if there be no profits. If advances be made by either party, he is to receive from the concern, six per cent. on such advances. The current expense of the farm was to be paid by Leo, and the tax on the cattle. The tax on the land, Tibbatts and his wife were to pay. Leo was to manage the farm according to his own judgment, and not under the dictation of Tibbatts and wife. This would be a singular provision in a lease for eleven years; but if a partnership was intended, it would be a very proper and necessary stipulation in behalf of Leo, whose labor and skill were secured, for the management of the farm.

An agreement to lease improved ground, for a certain part of the product is common, and in such a case the lessor receives only his proportion of the profits. But under such a contract the lessee would be bound to use reasonable diligence in planting or sowing his crop; but there would be no such liability under the above contract; as Leo Tibbatts was to exercise his own judgment, and not act under the dictation of Tibbatts and wife. Here was a trust and confidence reposed in Leo, which he could not transfer to any other person. And this is not affected by the fact that Leo might be less competent than any one he might substitute in his place.

But this contract did not relate to the management of the farm only, but included a large amount of live stock of various descriptions. These constituted a part of the capital furnished, and from which a profit was expected, as well as from the culture of the land. Indeed, it may be supposed, that the products of the fields, whether of pasturage or grains, would be used in feeding the stock and preparing it for market. This whole operation is different from an ordinary lease of ground, whether the rent be paid by a part of the product or in money. It is stipulated in the contract, that no rent should be paid. John W. Tibbatts was a lawyer, and could not but have known the significance of this provision. At the close of the contract, the farming utensils and the stock, in the language used, "are to be accounted back in equal value."

A suggestion is made that a feme covert cannot form a copartnership. There can be no doubt, that with her husband she may enter into a partnership, as stipulated in the above contract—she having an interest in the capital.

Looking at the nature of the above contract and the language used by the parties, there is less difficulty in considering it a partnership agreement, than a mere lease for the term specified, paying rent. It provides, that in the event of the death of Leo Tibbatts, the contract should terminate. This is an unusual provision in a lease, but the principle applies to all cases of partnership, whether stipulated in the agreement or not.

But let us consider the contract in this case as a lease, and see what must be the legal result from the facts.

The intention of the parties is shown to be, from the language of this instrument, to derive a profit from the farm, not by the ordinary culture of grains, but as a stock farm. The contract was signed the 2d day of August, 1851, and about the 1st of May, 1852, Leo Tibbatts made, to Eliphas Burnham, assessor, under oath, a return of the following stock, and its estimated value. Ten horses, seventy cattle, seven mules and asses, three hundred sheep, seventy five hogs, making an aggregate value of nineteen hundred dollars.

It is evident from the amount of stock on the farm, the parties looked to that as the principal source of profit, although the contract contains no special provision on the subject ; this view is strengthened from the fact that in the agreement the farm is called a stock farm, and that there is no stipulation in it, that Tibbatts and wife should be paid their proportion of the profits of the farm in agricultural products, or in the increase of the stock ; the inference therefore is, that the distribution of the profits should be in money. It appears, too, from the depositions of persons residing in the neighborhood of the farm, that stock raising is the business of those who own large farms. This enables the farmers to realize a larger profit from their farms, with less labor, than any other kind of culture. And this farm is spoken of, as well adapted for a stock farm. James Taylor, son of the ancestor of complainant and the brother of Mrs. Tibbatts, says, that this farm was managed on the shares for his father for some years before his death, and that it yielded to him, as he thinks, about a thousand dollars per annum.

Leo Tibbatts, it appears, took possession of the farm in August, 1851, and during the ensuing spring he commenced selling the stock on the farm. In July, 1852, John W. Tibbatts died, and Leo continued the sales of the stock until all was disposed of. To Daniel Watson he sold stock to the amount of seventeen hundred dollars, and the residue he sold to other persons. In the year 1853 the assessor's return shows that Leo had but one horse, valued at twenty five dollars.

In 1853, Leo Tibbatts rented the farm, reserving the dwelling house and grounds around it, &c., to Daniel Watson, for seven hundred dollars, and for the year 1854 for one thousand dollars, the payment of which is acknowledged. This lease expires on the 1st of March, 1855.

No rent has been paid or offered to be paid to John W. Tibbatts in his life time, nor to his widow, since his decease. And it is alleged in the bill, that Leo Tibbatts is insolvent, and utterly unable to carry on the farm under the contract.

On the above facts the complainant's counsel contend, that Leo Tibbatts has abandoned the contract, and that the consideration on which it was entered into, has failed.

Several excuses are set up in the answer, for the sale of the stock, &c., and proof has been introduced to sustain the answer.

It is alleged, that the stock was poor, and not such as

would be most profitable on the farm, and that it was sold with the consent of John W. Tibbatts. And in regard to the money received from the stock, it is stated, that it was applied in part payment of a debt due by the estate of John W. Tibbatts to Leo, the defendant, for personal services, and otherwise, amounting to the sum of $6,383.56; in which account certain credits are entered, amounting to the sum of $4,420.31, leaving a balance due to Leo of $1,963.25. In this account credit is given for the stock on the farm, sold to Watson and other persons.

It is averred, that the object in selling the stock, was to replace it by stock of a better quality, which would be more profitable to the parties concerned.

Another reason assigned is, that in April, 1853, the complainant commenced an action of ejectment to recover possession of the farm; and that the prosecution of that suit, rendered it necessary for him to lease the farm to Watson, as the best disposition that could be made of it, for the parties interested. And defendant avers it to be his intention to carry out the contract, and proposes to give security for the payment of any rent that has accrued, or that may become due, which the court may order.

In his will, the father of the complainant, gave the farm in question to his daughter, Ann W. Tibbatts, "to have and to hold the same during her natural life, and to enjoy the rents and profits thereof for her separate, sole and exclusive use and benefit, and for the use and benefit of no other person." In this devise it is clear that the testator intended to vest this land in his daughter exclusively, and not subject to the will or control of her husband.

But it may be admitted that uniting with her husband as she did, in the written contract respecting this stock farm, it may be treated as a valid instrument; whether it be denominated an article of copartnership or a lease. But a Court, in considering the agreement as the one or the other of these

instruments, cannot disregard the parties to it, and the circumstances under which it was made. Whilst the wife of
Tibbatts should be considered bound to the full extent of the
instrument, her interests should be protected, from any arrangement beyond the written agreement, which her husband
may have made with his brother, to her injury. Her obligations so far as they exist, arise out of the written contract.

The contract was made in relation to the farm and the
stock as they existed at the time. And it was in reference
to this state of things, that the complainant was induced to
sign the agreement. In it nothing was said as to selling the
stock, to purchase other and better stock. Nothing is said
in the contract in regard to such a sale or purchase, or how the
funds were to be procured. From the circumstances of the
parties and their relation to each other, there is nothing from
which such a presumption can arise. The contract embraced
the stock, the farming utensils and the land. Besides, if the
object in selling the stock, as alleged by the defendant, was,
to supply its place by purchasing better stock, why were not
the proceeds of the sale so applied? But not only the stock
was sold, but the farming implements also, which seem to
have been limited, as the sum for which they sold was set
down at thirty dollars. The farm also was leased by the
defendant for two years as above stated.

These acts by him evinced a determination, as it would
seem, rather to profit by the possession he had, than in good
faith to carry out the contract. He was bound not to assign
the indenture without the consent of Tibbatts and wife in
writing.

It is probable that the land was leased in consequence of
the step taken by the complainant to get possession of the
premises. In the lease for 1854 it is stated, that the rent
was paid. This is rather an extraordinary circumstance, as
it is not supposed to be usual to pay a money rent in advance.

In regard to the amount presented against the estate of

John W. Tibbatts, which not only covers the proceeds of the
sale of the stock, but leaves a large balance due to the defendant, it is singular that it was never presented to the administrator of Tibbatts, though public notice was given to all
who had claims on the estate to present them for adjustment.
Tibbatts had been dead some two or three years before this
account seems to have been made out, and the administrator
had no knowledge of it.   It is proved, that Leo Tibbatts was
some years in the service of his brother as clerk, at a thousand dollars a year, but it is hardly probable that he could
have had no occasion to call for his salary during that time,
for the support of himself and family.   Some of the witnesses,
well acquainted with the defendant at Newport, when these
services were rendered, are under the impression, that the
defendant was largely indebted to his brother.   This account
it seems was never known to the administrator of Tibbatts
until the present emergency, which is a circumstance sug-
gestive of doubts as to its validity.   But however this may be,
the question of law, arising on the facts is not affected by it.

By selling the stock and leasing the ground, the defendant
has not only disregarded the contract, but has disabled himself from carrying it into effect.   The lessee of the defendant of course must receive compensation for his labor and
care, so that the rent paid by him to the defendant, should
be paid to the complainant.   On what principle, under the
facts, could the defendant claim a part of this rent?   He was
entitled to but one third of the profits and those or a greater
proportion, are paid to Watson, who has been substituted by
the defendant for himself.

If the husband consented to the sale of the stock, it was to
the prejudice of his wife; and after his decease, the contract
having been materially altered, she was under no obligation
to continue it.   To make the farm a stock farm, as it was
when the defendant entered into the possession of it, a large
outlay would be required, which the complainant may not be

able to afford, and which is foreign to the contract and to the understanding of the parties.

Under the circumstances, I think the defendant has utterly disregarded the contract and abandoned it, and the proposal to give security cannot avail him, as he has forfeited the confidence of the complainant by an entire disregard of the obligations of the contract, and of her interests in particular. If the contract constituted a partnership, the death of John W. Tibbatts dissolved it; and if the contract be considered a lease, the sale of the personal property, and the leasing of the farm, and the inability of the defendant to restore the farm to its former condition, by which means only the profit contemplated by the complainant can be realized, releases her from obligation to continue the defendant in possession of the premises. The Court will therefore decree that the contract shall be delivered up and cancelled, and that the defendant relinquish the possession of the premises on the first day of March next, and on failure to do so, that a writ of possession shall be issued to the marshal, commanding him to turn the defendant out, and put the complainant into the possession. And in the mean time, the defendant is enjoined from committing any waste or injury to the farm, or any part of the improvement or timber on the same. And an account was ordered.

___

The United States *v.* Alpheus Poage.

The defendant was intimately associated with the individual, who stole the letter containing a hundred dollar bank bill and a promissory note for eighty-two dollars. But he proved himself to be a man of irreproachable character and of high intelligence, by witnesses of undoubted respectability.

This would seem to be sufficient to protect him from suspicion, where no other fact is proved to implicate him.

He was formerly acquainted with Coyle in Virginia, who was, probably, the guilty party; and this may account for their intimacy.

Mr. *Morton,* for the United States, Dist. Attorney.

Mr. *Pendleton,* for the defendant.

CHARGE OF THE COURT.

This is an indictment against the defendant, charging him
with stealing from the mail, a certain letter, written by Nesbat, and directed to George H. Calvert, Cincinnati, which
contained a bank bill for one hundred dollars and a promissory note for eighty-two dollars.

Mr. Nesbat being sworn states, that he lives in Kentucky,
at the Dry Ridge post-office; that on the 6th of January
last, the above letter was written by him, and directed to
George H. Calvert, containing a hundred dollar note, and his
own promissory note for eighty-two dollars. On the 11th of
the same month, the - note was presented to witness for payment by a young man at his residence, with whom defendant
was in company. The boy appeared to be fifteen or sixteen
years of age, who said he was connected with an insurance
company, and was sent out to collect. The note he said had
been received from Mr. Calvert. Witness paid the note in
cash, except each took a pair of gloves from his store. The
note appeared to have been endorsed by George H. Calvert.

The witness lives thirty-four miles from Cincinnati, and the
letter must have reached the city the day it was mailed. Two
letters were sent in the same post bill. Witness thinks the
words of the boy were, "we are connected with an Insurance
Company." The name of the young man or boy was James
C. Adams. On examination, the witness found the post bill
in the Cincinnati post office.

Henry G. Galt, a clerk in the post office, opened the
packet, at the Cincinnati post office, which contained the post
bill and the two letters.

Calvert, to whom it was directed, never received it.

Mr. Suffield, who works for Calvert, receives his letters
from the post office, and did not receive this one.

Mr. Jackson, kept the Farmer's Hotel in Covington last
January. On the 11th of that month, defendant boarded

with witness. On the night of the 10th of January, Coyle staid at his house, and registered his name Adams. He had been once before at the house of witness. Heard him say that he was acquainted with Poage in Virginia. They lodged in the same room the night of the 10th, and the next day they went to the country together in a buggy. On the 12th they returned at about ten o'clock.

Mr. Beal, states, that on the 10th of January, he met Mr. Poage early in the morning, who helped witness make a fire, and remained until about 12 o'clock. After some time Poage and the boy came together to the house, at between one and two o'clock. The boy showed a note, and said he had traded a galvanized watch for it, and that if he did not collect the note he would not lose much. The witness identifies the note. When he saw it, it was not endorsed, and he observed to the boy, without the endorsement of Calvert he could not collect the note. The boy soon went out to get the note endorsed, and when he returned, he said that he had met the man, who endorsed it.

Mr. Brown, says he first saw defendant at Cabell County, Virginia, and found him fifteen miles beyond Guyandotte. The defendant said that he had known Coyle at Staunton, but had not seen him for some time before he met him at Cincinnati. He said Coyle was in the printing office. Here the evidence of the prosecution closed.

Mr. Moore, a citizen of Virginia, was acquainted with the defendant, near Staunton, Virginia. He was then engaged as engineer on a Railroad, and was a man of good character and respectably connected.

Mr. Harrill, from the same neighborhood, spoke of the excellent character of the defendant, and that he was employed as an engineer on a Railroad.

Messrs. Walker, Wilson and Marcus all testified to the good character of the defendant in Virginia, where he was engaged in most respectable employments.

Some of the above witnesses had been members of the Virginia Legislature, and all of them had the appearance of gentlemen, and were intelligent.

The Court observed to the jury, there can be no doubt, from the evidence, that the letter which contained the bank bill and the promissory note of Nesbat was stolen, and from the fact that Coyle had possession of the note and collected it, under false pretenses, he would be presumed to be the guilty person, if now on his trial. The only evidence against the defendant is, that he was associated with Coyle when he collected the note, and received a pair of gloves in the way of change. The association with Coyle before they rode out to Nesbat's and afterwards, lodging in the same room on the night of the 10th of January, was enough to excite suspicion against him. But his good character, being sustained by most respectable witnesses in Virginia, where the defendant was reared and respectably employed, should exonerate him from mere suspicion, founded on such circumstances. Good character can seldom fail to protect an individual from suspicion. A man of intelligence and reputable standing in society, is not likely to indulge in crime, or to do anything which shall forfeit his good name.

If the defendant had participated with Coyle in stealing the letter, he would without doubt have suggested to him, that the note must be endorsed, to enable him to collect it. If he was acquainted with Coyle in Virginia, their intimacy may be accounted for, without presuming any participation of the defendant in the crime charged. And you cannot find the defendant guilty, unless you shall find he participated in stealing the letter. The case is left with you, gentlemen, not doubting, that after deliberately weighing the testimony, you will come to a just conclusion.

Verdict of the jury, not guilty.

COOPER *v.* ROBERTS.

Fraud may be shown in procuring a patent at law, as the execution of a deed, being executed fraudulently, may be avoided at law.

But in neither case can fraud be alleged and proved at law except, in the issuing of the patent or of the other, in the execution of the instrument.

Under a compact with a State to give to it section 16, unless it shall be sold or otherwise disposed of, Congress have a right to reserve all mineral lands, and if section sixteen contains mineral land, a section may be given, as provided in the compact, as contiguous to section sixteen as may be.

The right to a particular tract, under the grant, did not exist until a survey was made, and if the section should be found to contain minerals, it is appropriated, by a general law reserving all such lands before survey, and another section for school lands must be selected.

The power of reserving lands for mines or salt springs, has uniformly been exercised by Congress, notwithstanding the compact that section sixteen shall be given for schools, and other lands have been substituted for it. This is within the compact.

Doubts may exist whether the State of Michigan could sell the school lands without the consent of Congress, as they were given in trust to the State, for school purposes.

Messrs. *Vinton & Howard*, for plaintiff.
Messrs. *Smith & Campbell*, for defendant.

OPINION OF THE COURT.

This is an action of ejectment, to recover the possession of one hundred and sixty acres of land claimed by the plaintiff, and of which the defendant is alleged to be in possession.

The plaintiff claims under a patent from the State of Michigan, on a public sale. It was agreed that the land in controversy was advertised by the Commissioner of the State Land Office, four weeks; that pursuant to the notice, Alfred Williams, for the sum of two thousand five hundred dollars, became the purchaser; that at the time of the sale he paid six hundred and forty dollars in part, and that afterwards he paid the full amount of the purchase money, and received the State Land Commissioner's certificate, which entitled him to a patent, and that in pursuance of the certificate the patent was issued to him.

It is also admitted, that on the 19th of May, 1852, Williams, for the nominal consideration of ten thousand dollars, sold and conveyed the land by a quit claim deed to the plaintiff. The patent was in evidence, and also the deed from Williams to Cooper.

In the compact made between the United States and Michigan, on its admission as a State into the Union, it is provided that, "Section numbered 16 should be reserved for schools, in every township of the public lands within the State; and where such section has been sold or otherwise disposed of, other lands equivalent thereto, and as contiguous as may be, shall be granted to the State for the use of schools."

By an Act of 1844, the State of Michigan established a land office, and appointed a Commissioner, &c. And the same act provided that the "Commissioner shall have the general charge and supervision of all lands belonging to the State, or which hereafter may become its property; and also all lands in which the State has an interest, or which may be held in trust by the State for any purpose mentioned in this title, and may superintend, lease, sell and dispose of the same in such manner as shall be directed by law."

By a subsequent Act, the Michigan Legislature provided, that, "The minimum of the unsold and unimproved school lands shall be four dollars per acre; but no lands shall be otherwise sold until they shall once have been offered at public auction. Twenty-five per centum was required to be paid at the time of purchase; and a certificate of the purchase was to be made out by the Commissioner, describing the land, price, and the terms of payment, &c. And if any sale should be made by mistake, or not in accordance with law, or obtained by fraud, the same shall be void. On the presentation of the certificate of purchase, given by the Commissioner, the Secretary of State was required to issue a patent.

The defendants alleged that the above patent was fraudulently procured; and witnesses were called to establish the fraud.

To this evidence the plaintiff objected, that fraud could not be shown. But the Court held, that fraud at law might be shown in the execution of a deed, or in the procurement of a patent, as well at law as in chancery; but that at law the fraud was limited to the execution of the instrument, and no matter behind that transaction was admissible as evidence to show fraud.

Mr. Gibson, who is deputy Secretary of State, filled up the patent, the Governor having signed in blank. At the time, Governor Barry was not at the Seat of Government, and Mr. Gibson states that the patent was issued according to usage.

Mr. Williams, the patentee, states, that the purchase was made by Bacon, in the name of the witness, without his knowledge or assent. In another instance a similar act was done by Bacon, and in that case as in this, he executed a quit claim deed. The consideration named in the deed to the plaintiff, was nominal, so far as the witness was concerned. By the 57th section of the Act of 1844, the legal assignee of a purchaser at the sale, is vested with the same rights as the original purchaser. Evidence was offered, to show that Bacon, who was substantially the purchaser, knew that the school section contained a valuable mine, and deceived the Commissioner, &c. But the Court held this was a question between the State and the purchaser.

1. The defendant's title consisted in the assignment of a miner's lease, dated 1845.

2. In a patent from the United States, dated 9th of April, 1852, reserving any right the State might have as school land. The reservation in the patent was, "any right which the State of Michigan may have in and to the East half of the North-east quarter, and the East half of the South-east quarter of section sixteen in town fifty, under or by virtue of the provisions of the Act of 23d June, 1836."

The patent to the defendant was issued under the Act of Congress, 1st March 1847, which was an Act "to provide for the sale of mineral lands in the State of Michigan."

The second section of this Act requires, "that the Secretary of the Treasury shall cause a geological examination and survey of the lands embraced in said district, to be made and reported to the Commissioner of the general land office. And the President is hereby authorized to cause such of said lands as may contain copper, lead, or other valuable ores, to be exposed to sale, giving six months' notice of the time and places, &c., showing the number and localities of the mines known, the probability of discovering others, the qualities of the ores," &c. "And all the lands embraced in said district, not reported as aforesaid, shall be sold in the same manner as other lands are sold under acts now in force for the sale of the public lands, excepting and reserving from such sales section sixteen in each township for the use of schools, and such reservation as the President shall deem necessary for public use."

The third section provides, "that all those persons who are in possession, by actual occupancy, of any portion of the district described in the first section of this Act, under authority of a lease from the Secretary of War, for the pur-

pose of mining thereon, and who have fully complied with
all the conditions and stipulations of said lease, may enter
and purchase the same at any time during the continuance of
such lease, to the extent of such lease, and no less, by paying
to the United States therefor at the rate of two dollars and
fifty cents per acre. Provided, that said entry and purchase
shall be made to include the original survey of such lease, as
near as may be, conforming to the lines of the public surveys
of sections and subdivisions thereof. And all those persons
who are in possession by actual occupancy, of any of said
lands, for mining purposes, under authority of a written permit from the Secretary of War, and who have visible land-
marks and muniments as boundaries thereon, and who have in
other respects complied with the conditions and stipulations
contained in such permit, may enter and purchase the same,
to the extent of the tract selected by them, and reported to
the Secretary of War, as required by said permit and no less,
in the same manner as those who held under leases, and at
the same price:" Provided such entry and purchase be made
before the day said land shall be offered for sale by order of the
President ; and in the same section, all who were in actual
occupancy of mines before the law, and had paid rents, were
authorized to purchase, &c.

The fourth section provides, that all mineral lands shall
be offered for sale in quarter sections, and no bid shall be
received at a less rate than five dollars per acre.

The jury will observe that by the second section of the
above Act, the Secretary of the Treasury is to cause to be
made a geological survey of the entire land district, in which
shall be specially noted the extent and quality of the mines,
and the distance from market. All lands not reported to
be mineral lands, excepting a reservation of number sixteen
for schools, and such other reservations as the President
might make, were directed to be sold on six months notice.
And by the third section, rights of pre-emption were given

7a

to all those who held leases from the Secretary of War for mining purposes, who had complied with their leases, so that they were permitted to purchase at any time during their leases, at two dollars and fifty cents per acre; and such purchase was required to be made to the extent of the lease. Also, a right of purchase was given to those who were in possession by permit—provided the purchase was made before sale by order of the President.

And also, the right of purchase was given to all who were in actual occupancy of mines, before the passage of the Act, and who had paid rents.

By the fourth section, all mineral lands, not occupied as above, were required to be sold in quarter sections, at not less than five dollars per acre; but not to embrace outstanding leases.

It is proper here to consider the effect of the above Act of 1847.

It withholds the mineral lands from sale under the general law. This is clear from the geological survey in which mineral lands were to be noted, the express provision that such lands should not be advertised and sold as the other lands, the pre-emption rights given to all who were in possession of mines, and the different prices at which such lands were permitted to be entered, without being offered at public auction. All the other lands, except section sixteen, which was reserved for school purposes, were to be sold. And lands not occupied nor claimed, on which there were mines, were not to be sold under five dollars per acre.

If the mineral lands were withdrawn from the operation of the general law; if a different appropriation of them was made by the Act of 1847, the sale to the defendants is a matter between them and the Government.

And here a question arises whether Congress had power to dispose of section sixteen, as was done under this Act. There is no controversy as to the fact, that a part of the school section is included in the patent of the defendant, which is referred to in his patent. And it is proved that the mine of the defendant, under the license, occupies a part of section sixteen—that from twelve to twenty thousand dollars have been expended on it, and one of the witnesses says, the mine is very rich, and worth two hundred thousand dollars.

It must be observed that section sixteen, for school purposes, is not an absolute grant to the State. It was impossible to locate the grant until the surveys were made: there was this uncertainty on the subject; and to avoid any embarrassment arising out of this uncertainty, or the exercise of the powers of Congress, it was provided, that where such section had been sold or otherwise disposed of, other lands equivalent thereto, and as contiguous as may be, shall be granted to the State for the use of schools. This left Congress free to exercise its discretion in selling or reserving section sixteen. The grant is fulfilled literally by giving any other section as near to section sixteen as may be practicable.

By the Act of 1847, all mineral land in the land district was reserved for special disposition. Now, the only objection to this reservation is, that it interfered with section sixteen previously reserved for schools. The answer to this is, that section sixteen was not given absolutely for school purposes; but only on condition that such section, when ascertained, should not have been sold or otherwise disposed of. This refers to the location of the tract by the surveys. But before this is ascertained, the mining lands within the district are not only reserved from the mass of the other lands, but an absolute right of pre-emption is given to those who occupy the mining lands, for mining purposes. The sale is made to them absolutely, if the land be embraced in the lease, and the terms of the lease have been complied with.

The lease is proved in this case, and the rents have been punctually paid. All the conditions required to make the right absolute, if claimed, with the further condition that the miner shall purchase all the lands included in his lease, have been performed. And there seems to be no ground on which this purchase can be defeated, except by the prior vested right of the State to the school section. And it appears that no such right was vested in the State. It had a claim to a section, under the circumstances, as near to the section numbered sixteen as practicable.

Aside from the sale of this school section there is no hardship in the case, as the State receives what the United States were bound to give, and the State agreed to receive. In this view the sale was prematurely made, for the reservation of mining lands, had disposed of a part of section sixteen, which must have been known to the purchaser, from the fact that large and expensive mining works had been constructed on the land, which were in operation at the time of the purchase and for years before, of which the purchaser is presumed to have had notice. The geological surveys too, which were filed in the General Land Office at Washington, and in the Land Office of the United States, in Michigan, which gave a description of the mineral lands in the district, might have been examined. The purchaser of this section from the State had at least the means of knowledge, and this is notice. But, this is not a question, gentlemen of the jury, which turns on notice. It is simply a question of power in the United States, to reserve the mineral lands and give a pre-emption right, as has been done in this case. Of this, as a matter of law, there would seem to be little doubt.

It has been long the policy of the United States to reserve mineral lands, salt springs, &c. Under the Act of 8th May, 1786, the first Act that authorized the sale of public lands, salt springs were reserved. The Act of the 30th April, 1802, to authorize the people of the Eastern division of the Northwestern Territory to form a State, contained the above provision in relation to section sixteen. An Act of Congress, 3rd March, 1803, provided, that the sections heretofore reserved for the use of schools, in lieu of section sixteen, as have been otherwise disposed of, shall be selected by the Secretary of the Treasury, out of unappropriated reserved sections most contiguous.

Indiana and Illinois had the same reservation in regard to section sixteen. And by the Act of 3rd of March, 1807, mines in Indiana, then including Illinois, were reserved, and it was declared that all grants for the same should be void.

This being the course of the Government, it would seem that the power in Congress to reserve the mineral lands in question cannot be doubted; and if you find, gentlemen, that the land now claimed by the plaintiff is, with the mineral land, claimed by the defendant, first under a license and now under a patent, you will find the defendant not guilty.

There is another question in the case which has not been pressed in the argument, and that is, the power of the State of Michigan to sell the school lands. They were held in trust by the State, and unless the donor, the Government of the United States, should assent to the change in the trust fund, it is difficult to say that the State may sell and convey the lands. A trust must be executed in good faith, under the conditions of the donor. The United States, so far as appears in this case, have not assented to the sale, nor have they declared in what way the land shall be used for school purposes. Had the intention been that these lands should be sold, would not some act have so provided. In giving the lands, the most natural inference would seem to be, that a revenue from the use of the lands was designed, rather than a sale of them. A sale exhausts the fund, and the proceeds become mixed up with the funds of the State, and in the course of events, may be lost sight of. If all the school lands in the State have been sold, this question is of great interest to the State, as it would affect titles to a very large amount of property, and also the policy of the State in the application of the proceeds of the school lands. Verdict for defendant.

Exceptions were taken to the points ruled, and the case is now in the Supreme Court on a writ of error, and if the judgment shall be reversed, it will relieve the Circuit Court from a painful responsibility.

HALSEY & HALSEY v. J. L. HURD ET AL.

Where a contract was made for the purchase of a quantity of wheat at Detroit, to be delivered in the spring, on the opening of navigation, parol proof is admissible to show at what time payment was to be made.

This does not vary the written agreement nor contradict it, as by the agreement no time of payment was specified. Where it was agreed that the money should be transmitted through the express, the delays to which that conveyance was subjected, by the badness of the roads, is within the agreement.

On a failure to deliver an article, at the time specified, the purchaser may claim, as damages, the difference between the contract price of the article purchased, at the time the delivery was to be made, and the current price of the article at the time and place of the delivery.

Messrs. *Howard & Mandell*, for plaintiffs.
Mr. *Frazer*, for defendants.

OPINION OF THE COURT.

The partnership of the plaintiffs, and also that of the defendants, is admitted. The action is brought on a contract to deliver wheat. It is dated the 30th of January, 1852, at Detroit, and is as follows:—Mr. R. & H. Halsey, Bo't of J. L. Hurd & Co., the following lots of pure white Michigan wheat, first quality, sound and merchantable, to be delivered free on board vessel on opening of navigation.

Five thousand bushels at 72 cents,	- -	$3,600 00
Five thousand bushels at 73 cents,	-	- 3,675 00
		$7,275 00

Received on account of the above $100, signed,

J. L. HURD & Co.

Samuel Lewis, a witness, was present at an interview between the plaintiffs and Stewart, one of the defendants. The bill for the 10,000 bushels of wheat was in the hand writing of Stewart. Halsey told Stewart that he had come prepared to pay for the wheat; Stewart said that he should not, and did not intend to deliver it; Halsey said he had the money in the hands of Lewis & Graves, of Detroit; Stewart said he had not the wheat. Navigation was then open. Before the navigation was open, Halsey said to Stewart that the money was in the hands of the above firm. It was received by them the 13th of February, and they retained it until the middle of July.

The defendants' counsel asked the witness what time the money was to be paid. This was objected to, as changing the legal effect of the contract. That by the legal effect of the contract, the wheat was to be paid for when it was delivered; and that parol evidence is inadmissible to change the terms of the contract, or in any respect to vary the legal effect of it. But the Court said that the evidence offered did not alter, in any respect, the written terms of the contract; that the time of payment was not specified, and in such case the construction would be, that the payment was to be made when the article was delivered. But this was an inference of law, which the agreement of the parties might vary, by fixing a different time for payment. That on such contracts it was customary to advance the money, in order that the seller might purchase the article on better terms. And this not being a part of the written contract, may be proved by parol. It does not, in the sense of the books, contradict or vary the written agreement.

If the time of payment be stated in the written agreement, and the vendor give further time for payment, and it be made within the extended time, it constitutes a good defense.

In the *Susquehanna Bridge Co.,* v. *Evans & Evans,* 4 *Washington's C.C. R.* 480; the judge says, "the reasons which forbid the admission of parol evidence to alter or explain written agreements. and other instruments, do not apply to those contracts implied by operation of law, such as that which the law implies with respect to the endorser of a note of hand.

In *Hill* v. *Ely*, 5 *Sergt. & R.* 362; it is held, parol evidence is admissible in a suit by the endorsee against the endorser of a note endorsed in blank, to show that at the time of the endorsement the endorsee received it under an agreement, that he should not have recourse upon it against the endorser. In *Battles* v. *Fobes*, 21 *Pick.* 239, parol evidence was held admissible to prove the time at which a specialty was actually executed, contrary to the date. In *Bradley* v. *Washington Steam Packet*, 13 *Peters* 99, the Court held, " that in giving effect to a written contract by applying it to its proper subject matter, extrinsic evidence may be admitted to prove the circumstances under which it was made ; whenever without the aid of such evidence, such application could not be made in the particular case.

In *Davenport* v. *Mason*, 15 *Mass.* 85, it is said, "parol evidence may be admitted to establish an independent fact, or to prove a collateral agreement incidentally connected with the stipulations of a deed or other contract. In *United State* v. *Leffler*, 11 *Peters* 86; it was held that a surety, in a joint and several bond may show that he signed it on condition that others, besides those whose names are to it, would execute it, and that their signatures were not procured.

Lewis, a witness, said, at the time the contract was made, it was agreed that the money should be paid as soon as it could be forwarded by express, and the defendant said that a few days would make no difference.

Mr. Fargo, agent of the express at the above time, states, that the travel of the express was then by land, and it was from seven to nine days, and sometimes longer, in travelling from Buffalo by Cleveland to Detroit. The money was received by Lewis on the 13th of February.

Some four or five days before the money was received, Stewart called on Lewis for the money, who informed him it was expected daily; and on calling again two or three days afterwards, saying he had some notes to pay in bank, witness offered to loan the money to him, which he declined. After this the witness met Stewart in the street, and proposed to advance him the money on Railroad certificates, that the wheat was in the warehouse; but Stewart refused, saying, he had bought wheat in the interior; but as Halsey had failed to advance the money, he would not comply with the contract.

From the time the contract was made, to the receipt of the money by Lewis, thirteen or fourteen days elapsed, which exceeded by four or five days the time within which the money was expected to be transmitted from Ithaca. The navigation of the Lake opened from the 10th to the 15th of May.

Several witnesses proved the price of wheat, at Detroit, at the time the navigation opened.

There was some discrepancy in the statement of one or two witnesses called by the defendant, and the witnesses of the plaintiff.

The Court instructed the jury that from the parol evidence, the defendants agreed to the mode of payment stipulated, through the express, the defendants observing a few days would make no difference. After the contract, Halsey was to return to Ithaca, in New York, his place of residence, and from which the money was to be transmitted to Mr. Lewis, his agent at Detroit. It was supposed that this could be accomplished in some seven or eight days. But it was thirteen or fourteen days before the money was actually received. In the month of February it was shown, that the road the express travelled, in many places was almost impassable, and that it was liable to be delayed by high waters and various casualties.

If it appear, gentlemen, from the evidence, that there was no delay on the part of Halsey, but that he forwarded the money by the express, as he agreed to do; and the delay was principally, if not entirely, owing to the badness of the road travelled by the express, he is not chargeable with any laches, which would discharge the defendants from the obligations of their contract. In consenting to receive the money through the express, it is reasonable to say that they incurred the chance of a short delay, which amounted to no more than a few days, and which they said would make no difference.

That the defendants were desirous of avoiding their contract is manifest, from the fact that at the time navigation opened, wheat was somewhat higher than the prices stipulated in the contract. The money was ready for the defendants, three months before the navigation opened, which would seem to be a reasonable time within which to make their purchases. If you are satisfied, gentlemen, that the plaintiffs have substantially complied with their agreement, they are entitled to recover the damages they have sustained, by reason of the failure of the defendants. These damages arise from the fact, that at the opening of navigation, when the wheat was to be delivered, it bore a higher price, at Detroit, than the price stipulated to be paid in the contract. This difference, together with the hundred dollars advanced by the plaintiff, at the time of the contract, with the interest thereon, will form your verdict, if you find for the plaintiff.

The jury found for the plaintiff $520.

ABBE & COLT v. ROOD & ROOD.

When an agent exceeds his powers in the adjustment of a controversy, his principals, in a reasonable time, after a knowledge of it, should repudiate it.

If this be not done, the principals may become bound.

Abbe & Colt *v.* Rood & Rood.

If an agent entered into an arrangement, notifying the debtor that he would submit it to the creditor for his ratification, unless he shall ratify it, there is no binding obligation.

When witnesses contradict each other in a material fact, a jury will consider which of the witnesses, from the circumstances connected with the transaction, would be most likely to know and recollect the facts.

A witness who swears that a certain thing was said or done, is entitled to greater weight than a witness who said he did not hear the remark or witness the act.

The one is positive, the other negative; and both may be true, on the supposition that the first witness swears truly.

Mr. *Lathrop,* for the plaintiffs.

Messrs. *Vandyke & Grey,* for defendants.

OPINION OF THE COURT.

This action is brought on two promissory notes. The signatures on both notes were erased, and they were offered in evidence without proof of their execution, as by the pleading they were not denied. But the Court held that the notes could not be read without accounting for the erasures.

A witness was called, who stated that the notes were sent to him as also the account, as counsel, for collection. Being unwell, he sent the notes to Matthews & Taft, counsel at Niles. At that time, the signatures to the notes were not erased.

On this evidence, the notes and the account, were again offered in evidence. The account was receipted, and, as before stated, the signatures of the notes were erased. But the Court refused to admit them, because it was not shown under what circumstances the signatures were erased, and the receipt of the account given.

A deposition was then read, showing that a settlement was made, and that the defendants agreed to pay fifty cents on the dollar; that on this agreement being entered into, the signatures on the notes were erased and the account was receipted.

The agent Smith, alleged, that the counsel at Niles, never having been so instructed, had no power, as counsel, to compromise on the payment of a part of the debt. And this is undoubtedly the true view. Counsel may refer suit to arbitrators, but they have no power to discharge the debt on the payment of a part of it, unless specially authorized.

Smith, the agent, was dissatisfied with the compromise, as the payment of the notes of the defendants was not secured. He proposed to take one-half the debt on certain payments, and to retain these notes until half of their amount was paid. The defendants refused to sign the agreement. This suit was then brought.

Mr. Smith, agent of the plaintiffs, was called as a witness, he being contradicted by another witness. Objection being made, the Court said, the witness might be examined as to any matter of explanation; but that he could not be called to re-affirm what at first he stated.

The counsel for the plaintiffs contended that the defendants knew that Smith acted as agent, and must have known that if he went beyond his authority he could not bind his principal. And that the acceptance of a security for a less sum would not discharge a debt for a larger amount. This principle is undoubted, unless the agent acts under a special authority.—5 *East* 230; 10 *Adolphus & Ellis*, 121. A payment of a part, and an acquittance under seal in full satisfaction of the whole is sufficient, as the deed amounts to an acquittance. Accord and satisfaction cannot be pleaded unless executed. As an accord there must be an acceptance, 7 *Black.* 582.

The Court instructed the jury, that if the principal have knowledge of the agent's acts and do not repudiate them in a reasonable time, they will stand. If the contract be repudiated, the parties must be placed in the condition in which they stood before it was entered into; the notes given on the compromise should have been returned.

Where an agent does an unauthorized act, as the compromise of a debt, and the acts of compromise are known to the principal, who makes no objection, this acquiescence will bind him. *Story on Agency*, 255 Section. This presumption of the acquiescence of the principal does not arise, unless it be shown that he had full knowledge of the transaction.

It is laid down in many authorities, that money or notes for a less sum discharges the debt, if received in payment. 1 *Smith's Leading Cases* 391—3 and 4. 15 *Meeson & Welsby* 22–31, it was held, that negotiable notes may be pleaded in payment, when given in payment of a larger amount.

The original agreement of compromise was as follows :— Whereas, H. W. Rood & Co., of Niles, Michigan, being indebted to Messrs. Gilbert, Prentiss & Tuttle, of New York, in the sum of $1245,57; and they are also indebted to Messrs. Abbe & Colt of said city, in the sum of $1263,54; and also to the late firm of Colgate, Abbott & Co., in the sum of $2111,56; and, whereas, the said Roods being unable to pay the sum in full, I have agreed in behalf of said firm to settle and compromise said debts, for fifty cents on the dollar, twenty per cent thereof, N. P. Stuart agrees to pay in cash, for which I have taken his note, payable in thirty days, at the Michigan State Bank of Detroit, with interest; and the balance of thirty per cent. said Roods are to give other notes in equal parts payable in one, two and three years, with interest. If said twenty per cent. be paid, and they give their notes for the balance as above, then I agree to deliver up to them the notes for the said sums above specified, and the fifty per cent. to be in full therefor. Dated at Toledo, Nov. 10th, 1852, signed by E. J. Smith, who put also the other signatures to the agreement, all in his hand writing.

The notes were forwarded to Mather & Taft, lawyers of Niles, for collection, and they made the above arrangement, which Smith repudiated, having given them, as he alleges, no authority to make. The notes taken by Mather & Taft were returned to them by Smith.

Mr. Smith states, that when he entered into this writing he informed the debtors that he was not authorized to make it; but that he would enter into it, and see whether his principals would sanction it.

Mr. Stuart, witness called by the defendants, stated that he heard no reservation made by Smith, as to any want of authority; and that he was present when the arrangement was made.

As these witnesses contradict each other, gentlemen, you are to judge of their credibility. And in doing this, they being respectable persons, you will consider who had the best opportunity of knowing what transpired at the time of the supposed compromise. And in this view it must be admitted, that Smith had a better opportunity of knowing and consequently of recollecting the facts which transpired.

He was the agent of the principals, and he entered into the compromise; and he swears that he informed the parties that he was not authorized to make it, but would submit it to his principals for their approval. This condition was not heard by Mr. Stuart. The statement of the one witness is, that a fact did transpire, and of the other, that he did not hear the condition stated. The one is positive, the other negative. Now, where the witnesses are equally respectable, and one swears positively to a fact, and the other negatively, that he did not hear the condition, the weight of evidence will be with the one who affirms the fact, as his statement may be true and the statement of the other also; for though the condition was spoken of, the other witness may not have heard it.

On the supposition that the statement of Smith be true, and the jury should so find, then their enquiry will be, did the principals repudiate the agreement of their agent, within a reasonable time after they came to a full knowledge of it.

Abbe & Colt *v.* Rood & Rood.

The jury will first enquire whether the agreement set up in defense was made by competent authority. The agent who made it, says he had no such authority. The paper purporting to contain the agreement is all in the hand writing of Smith, and he received Stuart's check for $940 as part performance of the agreement. This check was payable some thirty days or more after its date. Under this paper, it is presumed that Mathers and Taft made the arangement or compromise with the defendants. This paper did not authorize these counsel to make the adjustment. But Smith offered to confirm the compromise, if the defendants would consent that the original notes should remain in his hands. When first informed of the compromise, Smith objected to it, returned the new notes given and the agreement.

Upon the whole, gentlemen, if you shall find that Smith was not authorized to make the compromise, as he has sworn, and also that his principals were dissatisfied with it, and that this fact was made known to the defendants, it will be your duty to find for the plaintiff on the original causes of action, and assess their damages accordingly. The jury found for the plaintiffs—for the original notes and interest—and also on the accounts.

As the plaintiffs recovered on the original ground of action, and not under the compromise, the money paid by Stuart in part performance of the compromise, should be returned to him, by Smith, the agent, unless it shall be made to appear, that the money so paid is the money of the defendants. And the Court orders that no execution shall be issued on the judgment, until said sum of money shall be returned to Stuart, or satisfactory proof adduced that it is the money of the defendants; and if so shown, it should be entered as a credit on the judgment.

COOK & COOK *v.* THE COMMISSIONERS OF HAMILTON CO.

This case, by agreement of the parties, was heard at Chambers, by Judge McLean.

By the Act of 1851, the Commissioners of Hamilton County were authorised to construct all such suitable buildings for the said County, upon the old Court House lot, in Cincinnati, upon such plan and of such materials as to them shall seem proper, under which they made a contract to build a Court House which covered the entire lot referred to.

In the same contract the contractors agreed to build a Jail, on such lot, within certain limits, as the Legislature might authorise.

Although the law contemplated all the buildings for the County should be placed on the Court House lot, yet the contract for building the Jail on another lot is not illegal, on the condition expressed.

It is made valid and binding by the sanction of the Legislature. The contract to build the Court House and the Jail, were separate and distinct, although included in the same instrument. The provision that both buildings should be erected on the same lot, is explained by a subsequent provision, that another lot should be procured for the Jail.

To justify the party in putting an end to a contract, the contractor must in effect abandon it, or refuse to carry out the plan or act in bad faith, so as to show that he does not or cannot complete it within the time limited.

Where there is not in the law an express limitation to the power given to do a certain thing, an inference cannot be made or sustained, which will defeat the object of the law.

Where two hundred thousand dollars were appropriated to construct County buildings, which must cost three times that sum, the appropriation imposes no limitation as to expenditures.

Messrs. *Fox & Pugh*, for the plaintiffs.
Messrs. *Gholson & Groesbeck*, for defendants.

OPINION OF THE COURT.

This action was upon articles of agreement, dated 15th July, 1851, in which the plaintiffs agree with the defendants to build a Court House and Jail for Hamilton County, in Cincinnati, on the Court House lot, according to the requisition of plans and sections thereof drawn, and specifications thereof made out, from number one to seventeen, by Josiah Rogers, architect, and which are referred to and made a part of the contract.

And the plaintiffs agreed to build, in a good and workmanlike manner, agreeably to the said plan, &c. And it was agreed that the said Court House building and Jail, are to be erected on the old Court House lot at the corner of Main and Court Streets, now in use, as at present understood; but should the Commissioners of Hamilton County, at the next session of the Legislature, obtain permission to build the said Jail in the rear of, or adjoining the said Court House lot, or on any other lot in Cincinnati, East of Main Street, West of Broadway, and South of Fourteenth Street; then and in that case, the said party of the second part agrees to erect and build said Jail in the rear of or adjoining to the said Court House, or on any other lot in the above limits, at the same price and without any additional charge.

The plans of the buildings are not furnished, but it is admitted that both of them cannot be put on the Court House lot. The stipulated price for the Court House was the sum $468,732 55, for the Jail $226,520 74.

Ten thousand dollars were to be advanced on the contract, and the building was to be commenced immediately.

The defendants craved oyer and pleaded,

1. *Non est factum.*

2. That the plaintiff did not begin the work and progress, with all reasonable speed, towards the erecting, building and finishing said Court House, &c.

8a

3. This plea merely negatives the averment of the declaration, as to the commencement and prosecution of the work; not alleging specially in what particulars the plaintiffs failed.

4. The fourth plea states, that by an Act of the General Assembly 28, January 7th, 1851, it was enacted as follows :— That Richard H. Cox, John Patton and David A. Black, Commissioners of Hamilton County, are hereby authorized to erect all such suitable and necessary public buildings for the said county, upon the place or lot of ground now known as the old Court House property, in the city of Cincinnati, upon such plan, and of such materials as to them shall seem proper.

The entire Act is set out in the plea, and it is averred that the Court House lot is 190 feet square, and no more; and that the size of the lot was known to the plaintiffs and defendants to be not of sufficient capacity to admit of the construction of the Court House and Jail thereon.

That at and before the contract was entered into, it was fraudulently agreed between the Commissioners and plaintiffs, that only the Court House should be constructed on the said lot, without reference to the location of the Jail, and that plaintiffs should be secured in the profits in said agreement, for the construction of a Jail in another place, when authority should be obtained. And that the agreement, &c., was contrary to the statute aforesaid and in fraud thereof.

To the fourth plea a special demurrer was filed, and to the others, except the first one, demurrers were also filed.

The buildings were to be constructed under the direction of Rogers, the Architect, who had power to vary the plan and dismiss the plaintiffs.

The second plea is defective. It merely negatives the averment in the declaration, without stating facts which show the failure of the plaintiffs.

The declaration avers that the work was commenced on the day the agreement bears date. Could an issue be made

upon that fact, which would bar the action? Suppose the
work was commenced on the second, third or tenth day after
the date of the agreement, would such a failure constitute a
bar?   To bar the action on such ground, it would be essential that notice should be given to the plaintiffs before they
were dismissed from the work. This notice was not given,
but they went on with the work for three months or more
without complaint. This is a sufficient answer to the allegation as to the commencement of the work.

But it is alleged the plaintiffs did not prosecute the work
as he was bound by the contract to do. The work was to
be done "with all reasonable speed, to be completed by the
first of May, 1855." And the plaintiffs were dismissed for
not so prosecuting the work.

To constitute a bar to the action on the ground stated,
facts must be alleged in the plea which amount to an abandonment of the contract, or, at least, which show the plaintiffs were acting in bad faith, and this too, after notice given,
unless the work had been in fact abandoned.

It does not appear from the plea, that the superintendent
of the work complained of its progress, nor that the defendants did so, until they dismissed the plaintiffs. The progress, as well as the manner of the work, was under the care
of the superintendent. He was the agent of the defendants,
expressly made so by the contract, and they had no power to
vary the contract, in this respect, without the consent of the
plaintiffs.

At the time of their dismissal, the plaintiffs had more than
three years within which to comply with their contract; and who
could undertake to determine that the buildings might not be
completed within this time? There is no complaint that the
plaintiffs did not conform to the directions of the architect;
and unless in this respect they had failed, or had abandoned
the contract, or had by their misconduct shown bad faith,
and a determination not to perform it, the defendants had no

power to put an end to it. And if either of these causes existed, it was essential to state the fact in the plea. But the plea contains no such averment, and in the absence of it there can be no justification or excuse for the acts of the defendants, in the dismissal of the plaintiffs from their work. The acts of the defendants, therefore, must be considered as arbitrary and inexcusable. The demurrer to this plea is sustained.

The fourth plea was the one chiefly relied on in the argument. It was contended, first, that the contract was an impracticable one, as the Court House and Jail could not be placed upon the Court House lot, as the Court House covered the entire lot; and, second, that the Commissioners had no power to build the Jail on any other lot.

It is admitted that the new buildings, as planned, covered the entire Court House lot. The Act of 1851, does not specify the Court House and Jail as the buildings to be erected on the Court House lot, but "all such suitable and necessary public buildings for the county." The plan of the buildings was left to the discretion of the Commissioners; and the one they adopted would accommodate all the officers of the county, clerks of the different courts, commissioners, etc., and the different courts. This was certainly a judicious plan, as it carried out the intent of the law, as far as practicable, on the space of ground allotted for the county buildings.

It was found that it was impracticable to construct, on the same ground, the jail. The contiguity of the courts and the county officers, promoted the public convenience, and facilitated the dispatch of the public business. And in this respect, it was immaterial whether the Jail was on the Court House lot or adjacent to it. It is, therefore, clear that the Commissioners acted wisely, in adopting the plan for the Court House.

There is admitted to be some inconsistency in contracting to build the Court House and Jail on the same ground which was covered by the Court House; but the agreement in relation to the structure of the Jail is consistent in the latter part of the article, which refers to the procurement of a lot for it, within certain prescribed limits. This gives consistency to the entire agreement. The plans for the Court House and Jail were distinct, and the price for each was specified in the contract. There was no confusion or uncertainty in the contract. It is, therefore, not an impracticable contract. Whether it be a legal one will be considered. The ground in the argument assumed is, that the contract is void, on the ground that it is impossible. Now, it may be admitted, that in cases where an individual engaged to do an impracticable or impossible thing, the contract is void and cannot be enforced. But to make out this position, the counsel consider the Act of 1851 as a part of the agreement; and that both buildings must occupy the same space. As before remarked, the law does not say what kind of buildings, as Court House and Jail, but "suitable buildings for the county." That every part of the Court House contains suitable and necessary buildings for the county, will not be controverted. And as all the suitable buildings for the county could not be constructed on the lot designated, it is not conceived why the Jail should not have been constructed on some other lot. It is more conveniently separated from the Court House than any other of the county buildings could be. That the Jail was intended to be included in the law of 1851, as a suitable and necessary county building, is admitted; still, as all such buildings could not be built on the lot, the Commissioners exercised a proper discretion in building the Court House on it. It does not come within the class of contracts referred to. The contract may be executed, if it be legal, and, therefore, is not an impossible contract.

But is it a legal contract? I think it is. The part which relates to the Jail is not an absolute agreement. The Jail is to be built according to the plans referred to, and for the price stipulated, if the Legislature shall sanction it. This proposes to do nothing against the law or its policy. It is valid, on condition that the Legislature shall legalize it. So far, then, from this agreement being against law, it expressly provides that the law-making power shall sanction it. And when this is done, the proceeding is as legal as if the law had authorized the contract.

A case similar in principle to this came before the Circuit Court, in the *Columbus, Piqua & Indiana Railroad Company* v. *Indianapolis & Bellefontaine Railroad Co.,* 5 *McLean,* 453. The Ohio Company entered into a contract to have the guage of their road the same as that of the Indiana road, which would be in violation of the Act of Ohio, that required the guage of all railroads to be of a different width. The court say, "an objection is made to the legality of the contract to build the Ohio part of the road, as the guage is in violation of the Ohio Statute."

"To this it is answered, in argument, that the defendants cannot take advantage of the objection, as it is a matter which rests between the State and the complainants, and that the State only can raise this objection." I am not prepared to say that any party who is called upon specifically to execute a contract, may not set up the illegality of that contract as being against an express Statute. But the answer to the objection is, "that although the contract was made, it was made with reference to a future execution of its conditions, when the modification of the law of Ohio should be obtained, which removed the objection. And, in fact, it appears that the construction of the road, by laying down the rails, was not commenced until long after the passage of the amended Act by the Legislature of Ohio. The law, therefore, was not violated under the contract, nor was it intended to be violated."

The plea in bar is defective, and, consequently the demurrer to it is sustained.

But there is a fifth plea, on which one of the counsel in defense principally relies. It is as follows: "That at the time of making the contract it was agreed that the Commissioners should, under the provisions of the above Act, sell and negotiate bonds to a large amount, to wit, the sum of two hundred thousand dollars, to make the payments under the agreements. That no other means existed or could be legally used in payment. And defendants aver the agreement was entered into without any reference to said bonds, with intent and purpose as a shift and device to violate and defeat the said Act, and evade the restrictions thereof, whereby the agreement is void in law.

To this plea a special demurrer was filed, assigning causes of demurrer.

1. That the plea is double and argumentative.

2. That in effect it is the general issue.

3. That it is not capable of being traversed or tried.

The statements in the plea are not very explicit, but its object seems to be, to allege that the agreement is void, because the limitation of the Act of 1851 was disregarded.

There is no express limitation in this regard, nor can one be implied, unless it be that two hundred thousand dollars only were appropriated.

In all public works, either by the federal or state governments, it is not usual to appropriate, when the work will require several years for its completion, more than a small part of the necessary expenditure. Any other course, especially where the money must be borrowed, would be a wasteful expenditure.

By the Act, the Commissioners were authorized to "erect all such suitable and necessary public buildings for the said county, etc., of such materials and upon such plan, as to them shall seem proper." From this provision it is clear that the buildings were to be constructed under the discretion of the Commissioners, which is inconsistent with the supposition that they were to be limited in their expenditure to two hundred thousand dollars. Every practical man must see that the buildings required to be constructed would cost more than three times that sum. In the absence of any express limitation, so unreasonable an inference as would defeat the object of the law, cannot be made nor sustained.

· It is insisted that a limitation necessarily arises from the limited powers of the Commissioners, to impose a tax on the people of the county to meet the expenditure incurred by them. These limitations operate on ordinary expenditures, and a tax must be imposed by the Commissioners to meet the expenditures. But the question of the legality of the contract raised in this case, is to be considered under the Act of 1851, which authorized the contract; and it would seem from its provisions, the Commissioners, in making this contract, did not exceed their powers. The Act is under the special law, and not under any general provisions in the Statutes, regulating the general duties of the Commissioners.

The demurrer to this plea is, therefore, sustained.

After the judgment of the Court was given, it was agreed by the Counsel on both sides, that they would go to a trial of this case on the general issue, and that this last point should be considered as open for examination under the general issue.

THE UNITED STATES *v.* NICHOLAS SHULTS.

An individual is liable to punishment, when he can discriminate a right from a wrong act.

And this can be best ascertained, not by any theory as to the mind, but by the acts of the party.

The concealment of the offense, an endeavor to elude the officers of justice by an escape, a judicious use of the money stolen, all show a knowledge of the offense.

And this is the point to be ascertained, when insanity is set up as a defense.

Mr. *Morton*, District Attorney, for the United States.
Messrs. *Carrington & Haber*, for defendant.

OPINION OF THE COURT.

This is an indictment against the defendant, charging him, while employed in carrying the mail of the United States, on a horse route, with the abstraction of certain letters, which contained bank notes and other articles of value. Plea not guilty—jury sworn.

John Keller, who is post master at Mount Ephraim post office, Noble County, in Ohio, states that defendant carried the mail from Sarahsville, in Noble County, to Washington in Guernsey County, a distance of twenty miles. In June, latter part, or first of July, witness mailed two letters for California, which were forwarded to the distributing office at Wheeling or Cleveland, directed to Nicewall. The envelope was returned to witness as being found in the road more than a month after it was mailed. The second letter was reported to have been found on defendant's route. Another letter was found on the same route, which had been mailed on the 6th or 7th of June.

Mr. Chance says, there must have been two violations of the mail while defendant carried it, which was about a week. Witness found a letter on the route on Friday after defendant commenced carrying the mail on the route. Another letter was found on the route which must have passed through the office of witness.

Mr. Forman is post master at Senecaville. He designates a letter picked up on the route; another letter found on the road must have been a letter forwarded in the mail.

Other witnesses proved that other letters were found on the route, which had been mailed by the post masters on the route, and which from their face purported to have contained money.

William Young, saw defendant first of June, and received from him a debt of sixty or seventy dollars. He had a watch, and witness asked him how he got so much money; he replied that he had sold a colt for sixty dollars. Witness exchanged with him ten dollars, giving silver for paper; next day he came and bought thirty dollars in gold from witness.

Mr. Renderneck, arrested the defendant near Marietta, in a wood boat, at which time he admitted that he had taken from the mail seventy-six dollars.

Several witnesses were examined to show mental imbecility in the defendant, so as to be incapable of committing a crime; and his defense rested on this ground.

Several medical gentlemen were examined, who differed somewhat in their opinions, some of them stating that in their view he was not a proper subject of punishment.

In the charge to the jury, the Court said, there seems to be no doubt that during the short time the defendant carried the mail, he repeatedly violated it by abstracting letters from it. This is established by the numerous letters picked up on or near the route, which had been mailed at one of the post offices on the route, or were carried on it; and by the confession of the defendant that he had taken from the mail seventy-six dollars. He was destitute of money before he was employed as carrier, after which it appears he had money to a considerable amount. All this evidence is uncontradicted, and the only ground of defense is, mental imbecility.

This defense has often been made, and much has been said and written upon the subject. Nothing is more common than for medical men to differ as to the fact of insanity, which should exculpate an individual from punishment. Where the insanity is in a degree which destroys the reasoning faculty, there can be no difference of opinion amongst professional men or jurors. But where the individual is subject to occasional aberrations of mind, or where the mind seems to be under peculiar excitement and error on a particular subject, as is often the case, and rational on other subjects, or where the individual reasons illogically and strangely, which brings him to results in action which violate the laws; in all these cases, and others which might be enumerated, a close investigation is required, and a wise discrimination should be exercised.

In such cases, the important fact to be ascertained is, whether the person charged can discriminate between right and wrong. If he be unable to do this, he is not a proper subject of punishment. And this fact can be best ascertained, not by any medical theory, but by the acts of the individual himself. Every person who commits a crime reasons badly. The propensity to steal in some persons is hard to resist. Where the moral development is weak and the passion of acquisitiveness strong, it will often prevail. This, in one sense, may be evidence of a partial insanity, but still the person is a proper subject of punishment. And there is no other test on this point, except the knowledge of the individual between right and wrong. And this knowledge is best ascertained by the acts of the individual in the commission of the offense, and subsequently.

Does the individual commit the offense by embracing the most favorable opportunity, in the absence of witnesses, and under circumstances likely to avoid detection. And if he

steal money does he account for the possession of it in an
honest way. And does he, under an apprehension of an
arrest, endeavor to elude the officers of the law. All this
conduces to show a knowledge that he had not only done
wrong, but that he was liable to punishment.

The defendant in this case accounted for the amount of
money he had in possession by saying, he received it as the
price of a colt. He changed the notes he had for gold and
silver, knowing that the notes might not be current at the
places to which he might go. Or he might fear that the
notes might be identified, by those who forwarded them in the
mail. On either supposition it showed a sound reflection on
the consequence of his acts should he be arrested. He
absconded, and was arrested several miles from home, on his
way to the West. He was found in a close room of a boat,
the door of which was locked; and it is proved that when he
came to the boat the previous evening, he engaged the room
and requested that the door should not be opened to any one.
This shows an apprehension that he would be pursued, and a
desire to escape the pursuit.

These acts would seem to be unmistakable evidence of a
sense of guilt, and a desire to escape punishment. He acted
under a motive which usually influences culprits. When
carrying the mail, on a suggestion being made to him that
he might steal from the mail, the penitentiary immediately
occurred to his mind. He bought and sold articles, and
evidenced in such matters, no deficiency of mind. He knew
the value of money and understood the matter of exchange,
and the uncurrency in remote parts of bank notes.

Upon the whole, gentlemen, if you think from the evidence
in the case, that the defendant in violating the mail knew he
was doing wrong, and that he was liable to be punished for
the act, he is a proper subject for punishment. It is true he
did not conceal the letters he took from the mail, but left
many of them scattered along the road he traveled, which

shows a great want of caution, still, if the other qualities of his mind were in such rational exercise as to enable him to discriminate right from wrong, you will find him guilty.

The jury found the defendant guilty, and the Court sentenced him to ten years in the penitentiary.

LESSEE OF BUCKLEY'S HEIRS v. ISAAC CARLTON.

Under the Territorial Government, the copy of a deed recorded is, *prima facie* evidence of its execution.

But this presumption may be rebutted by facts or circumstances.

Where the acts of the grantor are inconsistent with the presumption that the deed was delivered, they may be shown as weighing with the jury against such presumption.

All such presumptions gain strength against the deed, where there has been no possession under it for half a century, no claim asserted to nor taxes paid on the land. And where the party claims bona fide, having been in possession many years, under a conveyance, such possession is greatly strengthened by the lapse of time, and the adverse claim is necessarily weakened, as the title of the person in possession is made stronger.

Messrs. *Hunter & Smyth*, for plaintiffs.
Messrs. *Vinton & Nye*, for defendant.

OPINION OF THE COURT.

This is an action of ejectment brought to recover one hundred acres, lot No. 297, and one-third of one hundred acres, lot 298, east part—shares in the Ohio company's purchase.

The patent was issued to Rufus Putnam, Francis Manassah, Robert Oliver and Griffen Green in trust. A conveyance by the trustees to John S. Dexter, the 12th of May, 1792, included the land in controversy. The same land was conveyed by Dexter to Loomis, the 10th April, 1798, and Loomis conveyed to Roger Buckley the same land the 30th of July, 1799.

This deed was recorded, and a certified copy is offered in evidence, without any other proof of its execution.

The copy was objected to, as evidence, until proof that the original deed was lost. It is admitted that a notice was served on the plaintiff's counsel to produce the original.

The Court held, that under the recording act of Ohio, the copy was admissible as *prima facie* evidence of the existence of the deed, which evidence was liable to be rebutted, as regards the delivery of the deed, by the acts of the parties to the deed, and those who claim under it, which may be inconsistent with the presumption of a delivery. And the Court held that the plaintiffs, under the notice, were bound to deliver the original deed if in their possession or within their control. On this head the Court instructed the jury,

1. That the original deed was presumed to be in the possession of the ancestor of the plaintiffs, who is proved to have lived twenty years after the date of the deed; and that its non-production, was a circumstance which the jury might consider, there being no evidence of its loss, to raise some doubt whether the deed was delivered to the grantee.

2. The Court also instructed the jury, that as no claim under the deed by Buckley in his life time, nor by the plaintiffs, until the lapse of more than half a century from the date of the deed, the jury might consider the fact as conducing to show, in connection with the fact that Buckley was the father-in-law of Loomis, that the deed might not have been delivered.

3. The Court further instructed the jury that the admissions of one of the lessors of the plaintiffs, that she had no knowledge of the claim until 1850, when N. Ward, Esq., of Marietta, informed her, was also a fact to be considered by the jury, in relation to the delivery of the deed.

4. The jury were further instructed that the facts of Loomis having been forced into bankruptcy, by his creditors, a short time after the date of this deed, when this claim of lands in

the Ohio Company's purchase was placed upon his schedule as his property, under the bankrupt law, which schedule was sworn to be true, by the bankrupt, as the law required, were facts to be considered by the jury, as conducing to show the deed was never delivered to Buckley.

5. The jury were also instructed that the facts that the said lands had been duly assigned by Loomis to commissioners under the bankrupt law of 1800, and by the commissioners in bankruptcy to the assignees of Loomis, and by them were publicly 'sold as a part of the bankrupt's effects, might be considered as conducing to show the deed, to Buckley, was invalid. That the facts on which the above instructions were given, were admitted as evidence rebutting the presumption that the deed had been delivered, from the fact of its having been recorded. But if the deed had been executed and delivered bona fide, no subsequent act of the grantor could impair its validity.

6. The Court instructed the jury that if they find the deed of Loomis was made to defeat the claims of his creditors, that under the bankrupt law, the claim of the defendant, under the assignees in bankruptcy, is valid.

7. That the transfer of the commissioners in bankruptcy to the assignees, constitute a part of the proceedings in bankruptcy, and was valid under the Act of Congress. That the provisions of the Act, which required the deed to the assignees, to be executed and recorded under the laws of the place where the land was situated, refer to estates in tail, which the bankrupt could bar, by a common recovery, and not to the title of defendants.

8. That the description of the land in the schedule of Loomis, must be taken in connection with the muniment of title, which Loomis, under the bankrupt law, was required to surrender, and which gives to the land a sufficient description to make it certain.

9. That where there has been a long and an uninterrupted possession, as that which has been had by the defendant, under a bona fide claim of title, presumptions are favorable to such title. And that under such circumstances, the plaintiffs, if they recover, must recover on their strict legal rights. No possession of the premises has been had by the plaintiffs, no taxes have been paid by them on the land, and no claim to the land has been set up by them for half a century.

The facts on which the foregoing instructions were given to the jury, were brought before the Court and jury.

The jury returned a verdict for the defendant.

THE UNITED STATES v. TANNER.

If a letter written to a certain individual was intended for the person to whom it was directed, and also for another person; and such other person is authorised by the writer to take the letter out of the post office and read it, by so taking out and reading the letter, there is no violation of the post office law.

The person who writes a letter has a right to control its use, as it is his property.

The writer of a letter is entitled to an injunction to restrain the improper use of the letter, by the person to whom it is directed.

Mr. *Morton*, District Attorney, for plaintiffs.
Messrs. *Swayne & Barber*, for defendants.

OPINION OF THE COURT.

This is an indictment against the defendant, for taking a letter from the post office at Toledo, in Ohio, addressed to another person, with the view to pry into the secrets of such person. There is also a count for opening the letter.

Works Blum, lived in Toledo four years. In 1853, witness was in Toledo, went to Cleveland from Toledo, beginning of September. He expected a letter at Toledo, from St. Louis, after he left.   In eight days he received the letter at Cleveland.   Witness says the letter had been opened by Tanner, but witness never authorized him to open the letter, when he received it from the post office.   The witness never authorized the defendant to take the letter out of the post office.   On complaint being made by witness, defendant was arrested, but was discharged by the committing magistrate.   Mr. Young advised witness to pursue the case further.

Mr. Snatcher saw the letter in the hands of his sister, who brought it to the house of witness.   Defendant, when before the Commissioner, admitted that he took the letter out of the post office.

DEFENDANT'S WITNESSES.

Mr. Jamner, is acquainted with Blum, and with Myers the writer of the letter: they both lived with witness.   Myers and defendant talked about a letter to be written by Myers.

Judge Fitch stated, that Myers, the writer of the letter, before he left Toledo, said he would write a letter to Blum, for both defendant and Blum.   Several witnesses proved the good character of the defendant.

The Court instructed the jury that the writer of the letter had a right to control the use of it, it being his property; and that if they shall be satisfied the letter was written with the view that the defendant should read it, as well as the person to whom it was directed, the defendant is not guilty of a crime in taking the letter out of the post office, and opening it. Although the letter was directed to Blum, if Myers before writing it requested the defendant, or authorized him, to take the letter out of the office and read it, he had a right to do so, and the defendant is guilty of no violation of the post office law.   Parties may correspond under assumed names, without any violation of law.

The jury found the defendant not guilty.

9a

THE UNITED STATES *v*. THE CITY BANK.

No bank, under the Sub-Treasury law, can become a depository of the public money.

The Law prohibits such a deposit, and inflicts a severe penalty on the public officer who makes it.

But a State Bank may engage with the Secretary of the Treasury to transmit a draft to New Orleans or elsewhere.

This does not render a deposit necessary.

The same draft received by the bank may be transmitted, or having the specie at the place, the bank may draw on it and pay the Treasury at New Orleans.

This accommodates both parties, without expense.

Where the money of the Government is improperly placed in a bank, the illegality of the transaction is no bar to a recovery.

The agents of the Government do not bind the Government, when their powers are transcended.

The money, in such a case, would be received wrongfully, and without any authority from the assent of the Government.

It could be recovered by the Government, if not on the contract, on the general counts.

And in such a case the writing would be evidence to charge the bank.

Messrs. *Ewing, Corwine & Morton*, District Attorney for plaintiffs.

Messrs. *Stanbery, Swan & Andrews*, for defendant.

OPINION OF THE COURT.

This action is brought by the United States to recover one hundred thousand dollars from the City Bank, which were received by it under a contract to convey the same from New York to New Orleans.

The first count in the declaration charges " that on the first of November, 1850, the City Bank of Columbus contracted with the United States to transfer the sum of one hundred thousand dollars, monies of the plaintiffs, from New York to New Orleans, to be deposited in the Treasury of the United States at that place, by the first of January, 1851; and the said defendant, then and there, received the said sum, and promised to transmit and deliver the same to the Treasury of the plaintiff in New Orleans, etc. And that the said defendant did not transfer the said sum of money by the 1st of January, 1851, nor at any other time, but converted the said sum of money to its own use.

To this count a general demurrer has been filed.

On the argument of the demurrer, it was insisted by the counsel for defendant, that the contract was void, as against the policy and the provisions of the Act of Congress, of August 6th, 1846, to provide "for the collection, safe keeping, transfer and disbursement of the public revenue." 9 Minot's United States Laws, 59.

ARGUMENT OF COUNSEL.

"This Act requires all receipts and expenditures of the Government to be made in coin or Treasury notes. Section 18.

"It declares certain rooms in the Treasury building at Washington, in the mint at Philadelphia and New Orleans, and in the Custom Houses of Boston, New York, Charleston, and St. Louis, to be the Treasury of the United States; and provides for the appointment of four Assistant Treasurers, at the four last-named places. Sections 2, 3, 4, 5.

"Sec. 6 requires all public officers to keep safely, without *depositing in banks*, etc., all public money, till the same is ordered to be transferred or paid out; and when orders for *transfer* are made, to *make such transfers.*

"Sec. 10 authorizes Secretary of Treasury "to transfer" the monies in the hands of any depository to the Treasury, or to any other depository, as the safety of the monies, or the convenience of the public service, may require.

"Sec. 13 allows to public officers all necessary expenses for safe keeping, *transferring*, and disbursing public monies.

"Sec. 16. That all officers, and *other persons*, charged by this or any other Act, with the safe keeping, *transfer*, or disbursement of the public monies, are required to keep an entry of each sum received, and of each payment or *transfer*.

And if any one of the said officers 'shall use, loan, exchange,' or '*deposit in any bank*,' any public money 'entrusted to him for safe keeping, disbursement, *transfer*, or any other purpose, every such act shall be deemed an embezzlement, punishable by indictment, imprisonment from 6 months to 10 years, and to fine equal to the sum embezzled. And the provisions of this Act shall be construed to extend 'to *all persons* charged with the safe keeping, *transfer*, or disbursement of the public monies,' whether such persons be indicted as receivers or depositaries of the same; and the refusal of *such* person, whether *in* or *out* of office, to pay any draft, etc., for any public money, no matter in *what capacity* received, or to transfer or disburse any such money, shall be *prima facie* an embezzlement.

" It is manifest that the intention of this Act is to divorce the Government from the banks, and to prohibit all bank agency in its fiscal arrangements. It prohibits all public officers from so much as using a bank as a *place of deposit*, and it declares that the *deposit* in a bank of monies entrusted to a public officer, or other person, for safe keeping or *transfer*, shall be construed an embezzlement.

" In the face of those provisions, it is absurd to say that a bank may be an agent to make a transfer, or that the contract of a bank for such a purpose is valid.

" The act of transferring the money involves a receipt and *custody* of the money, and its transportation to the place of delivery. For the time being the entire control of the money is in the person charged with the transfer.

" Such a custody or control over public money by a bank is contrary to the policy of this Act, which proceeds on the idea of its insecurity.

" The simple act of depositing money, whilst in a course of transfer in a bank, is declared to be an embezzlement, and amounts to a high offense. If a bank cannot be used by a person charged with a transfer, so much as a place of temporary deposit or safe keeping—if that is forbidden by such a severe penalty—how can it be argued that the entire custody and control of the money, its receipt, transportation, and delivery, may be lawfully entrusted to such an agency?

" It may be very well maintained that this law considers the business of *transfer* as an *official* business, just as much as the receipt and safe keeping of the money. The 6th sec. requires the public officers to *make the transfer.*

" The 13th sec. allows to officers all necessary expenses for *transferring.*

" It is only in the 16th sec. that any provision appears which indicates that *other persons* than public officers can be charged with the business of transfer; but this provision applies as well to the safe keeping and disbursement (by other persons) of the public monies, as to their transfer, and these acts— i. e., the safe keeping and disbursement, are clearly official acts. It is difficult to imagine how a private individual can be charged with the safe keeping and disbursement of public money. It is also provided that all persons charged with any of these duties, is to make *an entry* of every payment or *transfer.* This carries the idea of official duty, the keeping of office books and accounts. So also does the last clause of the section, which provides that it shall apply as well to persons *in* as *out* of office. Persons out of office are clearly those who have been *in* office, but whose term of office has ceased in some way before their official duties were closed, and, therefore, for the finishing of their official duties, they are treated as officers, though denominated " other persons."

" But if the Act is capable of being so construed as to allow this business of transfer to be matter of individual employment and private enterprise, and there were nothing in the act which, as matter of public policy, would prevent the employment of a bank as a transfer agent; yet, on another ground, a bank could not be so employed.

" The only guards provided in the Act for the safe keeping, transfer and disbursement of the public monies, are these two—the official bond of the public officer, which secures the performance of the duty *civiliter*, and the prosecution for embezzlement, which secures it *criminaliter*. In one, if not in both these modes, the public treasure must always be secured. If the business of transfer can only be entrusted to an officer, then the security is in both modes; but if a person, other than an officer, can be so employed, then the security, the only sort provided, is the liability to a prosecution.

" A corporation, such as a bank, cannot be prosecuted in the mode provided by this Act. It does not come within the purview of the law as a *person* capable of undertaking the duty of *transfer*, for the reason that it cannot be made liable to the provisions of the Act intended to enforce and secure the performance of the duty.

" Nor can it be claimed that the public is secured under such a contract with the corporation, by the liability of the individual members or servants of the corporation, to a criminal prosecution. It is the corporation which makes the contract, and which is entrusted with the money, not the individual members or servants of the corporate body.

" ' Whenever a corporation makes a contract, it is the contract of the legal entity; of the artificial being created by the charter; and not the contract of the individual members.' *Bank of Augusta* v. *Earle*, 13 *Peters*, 587.

" The City Bank not capable of making this contract.

" The terms of the contract, as they are expressed, bind the bank to *transfer* $100,000 of the public money from New York to New Orleans, to be deposited in the Treasury of New Orleans, by the 1st of January, 1851, free of charge.

" It is clear from the whole scope of the Sub-Treasury Act, that a *transfer* of public money from one depository to another, involves simply the transportation of the money *in specie*, i. e., of the very money. It is in the nature of a bailment, a contract to carry and safely deliver the identical money entrusted to the agent.

"Every one knows that such was understood to be the meaning of this law, and that one great objection to the law, was the unnecessary cost of transporting coin between distant points, when transfers by means of drafts or bills of exchange would be so cheaply and readily made. Notwithstanding these objections, the law was so framed as to exclude all such paper or bank facilities, and there has been an annual appropriation to meet these extraordinary expenses. Vid. appro. Act of 1849, 9 Stat., p. 363. $15,000.

"The use, loan, investment, or *exchange* of public money for other funds, is expressly forbidden, as to all officers or persons entrusted with it for safe keeping or *transfer*, (sec. 16). This being the nature of the contract, we maintain that this bank had no capacity to make it.

"The City Bank is a corporation chartered by the State of Ohio, which, in addition to the ordinary incidents of a corporation, is expressly limited by its charter as follows:

"'To loan money, buy, sell, and discount bills of exchange, notes, and all other written evidences of debt, receive deposits, buy and sell gold and silver coin, and bullion, collect and pay over money, and transact all other business properly appertaining to banking.' 43, Ohio Stat., p. 44, sec. 51.

"It is too clear for argument, that such a transaction as this does not come within any of the enumerated powers. It is not a loan of money, a buying, selling, or discounting, a deposit, a purchase, or a sale of coin, or a collection and paying over of money. Nor does it come under the general provision of business properly appertaining to banking; for it is certainly no proper banking business to transport bullion or any other commodity, either for hire, or as in this contract, without charge. It is simply a bailment, a contract to carry and safely deliver, without any use of the thing. That the subject matter of the contract is coin, or money, does not make it any more a banking business than if it were corn or any other specific article.

" The only plausible ground on which such a contract could be put as properly appertaining to banking, would be to suppose that the bank might receive and use the coin in New York, and by means of drafts or bills of exchange, effect the payment of a like sum in other coin at New Orleans, and so have the incidental benefit in the rate of exchange, or otherwise, between funds at New York or New Orleans. That would, in effect, be a dealing in coin or in exchange. But such a dealing is expressly forbidden to persons entrusted with the transfer of the public money. It can neither be bought, sold, or exchanged. It must be kept without use, and transferred without use, and cannot, in any way, or by any device, be made the subject of dealing or traffic, by individuals, or, most emphatically, by banks.

" The foregoing points arise on demurrer to the first count of the declaration, which sets up a contract with the bank."

The entire written argument by the Counsel for the Bank is given, in order that the strength of the grounds assumed may be shown.

Many of the arguments, in behalf of the defendant, are admitted. It was, no doubt, intended by the Sub-Treasury Act, as it is usually called, to separate the moneyed action of the Government from the banks. Although the bank of the United States had for nearly twenty years acted as the fiscal agent of the Government, transmitting and paying public money at all points in the Union, when required, without loss or expense, the bank was rendered unpopular, and the deposits were withdrawn from it, and temporarily, state banks and other places were used for deposits, until the Sub-Treasury law was passed. This change has caused a heavy charge on the Treasury, besides the losses that have been incurred;

but it has been sustained until this time, by the popular voice.

No deposit of public money can be made by a public functionary in a state bank, without a violation of the Sub-Treasury Act. And it may be admitted that the Act speaks of the Sub-Treasury officers, as making transfers of public monies, when ordered by the Secretary of the Treasury. These transfers to disbursing agents are not necessarily to be made in specie. The 20th section of the Sub-Treasury Act provides, " That no exchange of funds shall be made by any disbursing officers or agents of the Government, of any grade or denomination whatsoever, or connected with any branch of the public service, other than an exchange for gold and silver; and every such disbursing officer, when the means for his disbursements are furnished to him in gold and silver, shall make his payments in the money so furnished; or when those means are furnished to him in drafts, shall cause those drafts to be presented at their place of payment, and properly paid according to the law; and he shall make his payments in the money so received for the drafts furnished, unless, in either case, he can exchange the means in his hands for gold and silver at par."

From the above provision, drafts were authorized to be transmitted in making disbursements, and these drafts may be exchanged for gold and silver.

There is no prohibition in the Act against the employment, as an agent to transmit funds, either an individual banker or a bank. And it is believed that under the present system bankers have frequently been employed to transmit the funds of the Government, from one part of the country to another. During the war with Mexico, and for some time after its termination, the heavy disbursements were necessarily made at the West. New York, from its large importations, was the principal depository of the Government; it was therefore necessary to transmit money from New York, where it was received, to New Orleans and other places in the West, where it was to be disbursed. Drafts on New York will readily command specie at New Orleans.

Now, the Secretary of the Treasury, it appears from the declaration, being desirous to transmit one hundred thousand dollars from New York to New Orleans, draws a draft for that amount on the Sub-Treasurer of New York, which is received by the defendant, under an agreement to pay it into the Sub-Treasury at New Orleans. The very draft received by the defendant, may be transmitted to New Orleans, and there exchanged for specie, or the defendant, having specie at New Orleans, may draw on it in behalf of the Sub-Treasurer in New Orleans, in payment for the New York draft. Such a transaction would be the safest, the most expeditious, and the least expensive mode, of remitting the money.

No one can be so competent as the Secretary of the Treasury to direct these exchanges, as he necessarily has a knowledge of the fiscal action of the Government, including all places of deposit, and the amount of disbursements necessary at different points. That this may be done by the Secretary, under the law, is clear.

But it is argued that the City Bank, by its charter, has no power to transmit coin from one point to another. That it might as well undertake the transportation of corn or anything else, which not being within the charter, would not bind the bank. But this does not meet the question. The question is not as to the transmission of coin, or any other commodity; but the City Bank is authorized to deal in bills of exchange. Of this there can be no doubt.

The bank has power, as declared in its charter, "to loan money, buy, sell and discount bills of exchange, notes, and all other written evidences of debt." This is ample for the purposes of this case. Having funds in New Orleans, or the means of making a deposit there, the bill in question may be supposed to have been received by the bank, to meet obligations incurred in New York, or to constitute a fund there on which drafts may be drawn. This, in effect, is a mere exchange of a fund in New Orleans, for a deposit of the same amount in New York. By this transaction the Government is accommodated without expense, and also the bank.

There are numerous cases, where two persons enter into a contract in fraud of the law, and against its policy, the rights of no third party being involved, in which neither a Court of Chancery nor of law will give relief as between the contracting parties. He who has gained an advantage will not be required to account, as the wages of iniquity are not adjustable at law or in chancery. But this rule does not hold, where the Government is a party. The agents through whom the Government acts, possess a limited authority, which, if transcended by them, does not bind the Government. The contract or writing in such a case would be evidence of the receipt of the money, and having come into the possession of it without right, the illegality of the transaction would be no bar to a recovery. The possession of the bank would be wrongful, and without the assent of the Government. And in such a case the contract would charge the bank, if not on a special on a general count in assumpsit. And the stockholders of the bank, having received the money through their agents, would be legally bound to refund it.

But in the present case there was no illegality, as the contract with the bank was not a deposit of money, but a matter of exchange, which both parties might enter into.

The demurrer is, therefore, overruled.

THE UNITED STATES v. CHENOWETH ET AL.

The Act of 30th August, 1852, which prohibits the shipment of gunpowder and other ignitible articles on board of Steamboats, punishes by fine or imprisonment, for putting up such articles for shipment, except they be put up and marked as required, or for shipping the same.

An individual who has not put up the articles, is not liable for shipping the same, if the articles have not been actually shipped on board of the vessel.

Mr. *Morton*, District Attorney, for the United States.
Mr. *Taft*, for the defendants.

OPINION OF THE COURT.

This is an indictment against the defendants for shipping gunpowder, in violation of the Act of Congress of the 30th August, 1852. By the 8th sec. of that Act, gunpowder and other materials which ignite by friction, are required to be packed in a particular manner, and distinctly marked on the outside with a description of the articles; and any one who shall pack or put up for shipment any of the above articles, or shall ship the same, except as above provided, shall be deemed guilty of a misdemeanor and punished by fine or imprisonment, &c.

The defendants having pleaded not guilty, a jury was sworn, &c.

A. H. Bayless, a witness, stated that three casks containing kegs, which he supposed to be gunpowder, were deposited on the wharf of Cincinnati, for shipment on the —— day of ——, 1853. The dray tickets represented the casks to contain merchandise. The head of one of the hogsheads was out, and witness saw kegs which he supposed contained gunpowder.

Capt. Halderman states, that in November last he went to the wharf, and found at the landing three bacon hogsheads, marked R. R., Florence, Alabama. He had the head taken out of the third hogshead, and found they contained powder. A man by the name of Ross said he had shipped them, and on being told it was contrary to law, said he was not aware of it, and that he had been in the habit of shipping powder.

The kegs which contained the powder were of the usual size, and contained each about twenty-five pounds. Each cask contained from seven to ten kegs. The defendants were engaged in the commission and forwarding business. Ross said the hogsheads had been carried to the Steamboat "Royal Arch."

Robert Kennedy, says he was clerk to the St. Louis mail boat, that the hogsheads were marked as containing oil cake, he received the hogsheads the evening before from defendants. In rolling the hogsheads to put them on board the steamer, the head fell out of one of them. Capt. Pearce spoke to one of defendants, who had the head put in.

Thomas Gwynne; the witness drives a powder wagon; he hauled the casks from the powder house. Saw when the head came out, the hogsheads contained kegs of gunpowder.

Capt. Pearce, saw the cask with the head out, and saw that it contained kegs of gunpowder. A motion was made to overrule the evidence, but the Court refused to take the evidence from the jury.

It appeared that the hogsheads had been forwarded to the defendants for shipment in the ordinary course of their business; and there was no evidence to show that they had any knowledge of the contents. The hogsheads appeared to have been used for pork or bacon hams, from the marks which they bore.

The Court instructed the jury that there being no evidence to show that the defendants had packed the gunpowder for shipment, in violation of the Act of Congress, they could only be convicted, under the Act, for shipping the article.

It does not appear that defendants had any knowledge that the casks were brought from the powder house, from which a presumption might arise that they had knowledge of their contents, but if such a presumption could be raised, it would not go to convict the defendants of packing the powder. This being the case, the jury will enquire whether the articles were shipped. The words of the law are "if any one shall put up for shipment, on board of any such vessel, except as before directed, or shall ship the same," he shall be deemed guilty, &c. The articles were not shipped by the defendants, although they were brought to the wharf for that purpose. Before the hogsheads were actually shipped on board the vessel, the head of one of them was taken out, and the gunpowder was discovered, which prevented the shipment of them within the meaning of the law.

It is admitted that the shipment of gunpowder or other articles specified, as prohibited by the Act, should be punished; as such act endangers the lives of passengers and the property on board, as well as the boat itself. But however aggravated the act, no one should be convicted, unless it be shown he is guilty of the offense within the Statute. The jury found the defendants not guilty.

JOHN W. WOOLSEY v. GEORGE C. DODGE, TREASURER, AND THE DIRECTORS OF THE COMMERCIAL BANK OF CLEVELAND.

The tax law of 1852, against banks, incorporated under the Act of 1845, having been declared to be unconstitutional, it can afford no justification to the Treasurer of the County in collecting the tax.

A citizen of Connecticut, being a stockholder, may file his bill for an injunction against the collection of the tax, making the Directors of the bank defendants, which will enable the Court to give relief, the same as if the Directors were plaintiffs.

A remedy by injunction will be given where there is no adequate relief by law.

A continual grievance will be enjoined.

An action of trespass is not an adequate remedy for the bank, when its funds are annually and unlawfully abstracted.

The State cannot be sued; its officer may not be responsible.

The credit of the bank is impaired.

The Courts of the Union follow the rule of construction of State Statutes, established by the Supreme Court of the United States.

The Supreme Court of the United States, under the Federal Constitution, give the rule of construction of that instrument.

Mr. *Ewing*, for the complainant.

Mr. *Spaulding*, for the defendant.

J. W. Woolsey *v.* G. C. Dodge, Treas., & Direct's of Com. Bank of Cleveland.

OPINION OF THE COURT.

The complainant, a citizen of Connecticut, filed his bill, representing, substantially, that he is a stockholder in the " Commercial Bank of Cleveland," to the amount of thirty shares of stock, which are worth forty per cent. above par, making an aggregate value of four thousand two hundred dollars; that an illegal and unconstitutional tax has been imposed on said bank exceeding eleven thousand dollars, and to the injury of the complainant more than five hundred dollars; and the bill alleges that the continuance of the tax will impair and substantially destroy the franchises of the bank.

And the complainant alleges that orders have been given to the defendant, who is Treasurer of Cuyahoga County, to proceed to collect the tax, under the tax law of 1852, which authorizes the defendant, if the tax shall not be paid on demand on notice being given, to enter the vaults of the bank by force, and take therefrom the amount of the tax in gold and silver coin, &c. And the complainant avers if the tax be levied and paid over to the State, he is without remedy, as the State cannot be sued, and that his recourse on the Treasurer would be inadequate, &c. He therefore prays that an injunction may be granted, there being no adequate remedy at law. There are many other averments in the bill which it is unnecessary to state.

The defendant demurs to the bill on the ground that there is no jurisdiction.

Two positions are assumed in the argument against the jurisdiction of the Court.

1. "That the charter of the bank contains a provision, that its affairs shall be managed by the Directors."

2. That "upon any other hypothesis, than an abuse of the trust by the Directors, a Court of Equity has no jurisdiction."

The authorities referred to in support of the above positions are undoubtedly law, but they are considered as having no application to the case before us. This is not a writ against the bank. No relief against it is prayed for in the bill. The Directors are made parties, having an interest in the matter not hostile to the complainant, but in accordance with his interest, in order that, the Directors being named on the record, the entire interest of the bank may be protected from the illegal exaction threatened.

This is a common proceeding in chancery, which in its decree protects the rights of parties on the record, whether named as complainants or defendants. In 1 *Story's Equity*, 680, it is said, "In equity, it is sufficient that all parties in interest are before the Court as plaintiffs or as defendants; and they need not, as at law, in such a case, be on opposite sides of the record." And in 2 *Story's Equity*, 742, he says, "In Courts of Equity, persons having very different and even opposite interests, are often made parties defendants." And in *Boone* v. *Chiles*, 10 *Peters*, 177, the Court say, "It is within the undoubted powers of a Court of Equity to decree between co-defendants, on evidence between plaintiffs and defendants." So in 2 *Sch.* and *Lef.*, 712.

In the case of *Piatt* v. *Oliver et al.*; 3 *McLean*, 27, the complainant being a citizen of Kentucky, filed his bill against Oliver and others, praying a decree against them, and also made defendants several other persons whose interests rested on the same grounds, as the rights asserted by the complainant; and the Circuit Court decreed, as between the parties defendants on the record, who, being citizens of Ohio, could not be made complainants, and that case being carried to the Supreme Court, the decree was affirmed, 3 *Howard*, 333.

No further reference to authorities on this point can be necessary. It is sustained in the reports, and in elementary treatises.

Has the complainant made a case in his bill, which gives

jurisdiction to the Court? He alleges that he has an interest in the bank, exceeding four thousand dollars; that an illegal tax has been laid on the bank exceeding eleven thousand dollars, and to his injury more than five hundred dollars; and that the collection of the tax will impair, if not destroy the franchise of the bank. The 60th section of the charter is relied on as containing a contract, that the bank should not be taxed more than six per cent. upon its dividends, which tax the bank has heretofore paid, and is now ready to pay to the Treasurer of State.

The complainant also alleges, if the tax demanded be paid over to the defendant he would not be responsible, and if by him paid to the State, he would be without remedy, as the State cannot be sued.

It has recently been held, by the Supreme Court of the United States, that the law under which this tax was imposed impairs the contract made by the State in the 60th section of the bank charter of 1845, and that the law was passed in violation of the Constitution of the United States, and is consequently void.

It has been suggested, rather than argued, by the counsel in this case, that the adoption of the new Constitution, which took effect the first day of September, 1851, contained provisions, in regard to taxation, inconsistent with the 60th section of the Act of 1845, and that consequently, that Act was modified by the Constitution. I say this was rather suggested than argued, as I would not do so great an injustice to the counsel, as to suppose that any one of his learning and ability could bring himself to the conclusion that the Constitution of the State is not a law of the State. It is indeed the fundamental and paramount law of the State; but it is only a law of the State, and the Constitution of the United States declares that "no State shall pass any bill of attainder, *ex post facto* law, or law impairing the obligation of contracts," &c., and the Supreme Court of the United States at its last

10a

term, having before it, by writ of error, the judgment of the
Supreme Court of Ohio, enforcing the tax law against banks,
reversed the judgment, on the ground that the tax law which
imposed higher tax on the banks incorporated under the Act
of 1845, than six per cent. on their dividends, impaired the
obligation of the contract in regard to taxation, contained in
the 60th section of that law.

That the Supreme Court of the Union had jurisdiction of
the case in which the above judgment was pronounced, is not
controverted, and it is equally clear that the decision is final
and conclusive.

If indeed a State, by calling a convention, could modify or
abrogate any part of the Federal Constitution, that great
palladium of our rights would be of no value. The founders
of this Government were too wise and patriotic to countenance
such a principle in the fundamental law of the Union. Such
a power, it is believed, has never been asserted by any
authority entitled to respect.

In the case of *Osborn* v. *The Bank of the United States*,
9 *Wheat*. 868, which was a case in several of its aspects
similar to the one before us, the Supreme Court say, the Act
of Ohio "is repugnant to a law of the United States, made
in pursuance of the Constitution, and therefore void. The
counsel for the appellants are too intelligent, and have too
much self respect, to pretend that a void Act can afford any
protection to the officers who execute it."

There is no axiom of the law better established than this.
A void law can afford no justification to any one who acts
under it; and he who shall attempt to collect the illegal tax,
under the law referred to, will be a trespasser. He will proceed, it is true, under the color of law, an act standing on the
Statute book, but a void act. If he open the vaults of the
bank by force, and abstract a portion of its specie, under a
pretense of collecting the tax, he, though the Treasurer of the
County, will stand without justification or excuse. He has no

more right to do this than any other person, who can set up no pretense of authority.

And this trespass is to be repeated annually. What a spectacle! What a spectacle to a law-abiding people! Is there no preventive remedy? What stronger ground than this can be imagined for an injunction? The action of trespass comes too late. The State cannot be sued. Its officer may be insolvent. At best, such a remedy is wholly inadequate. The money of the bank is annually abstracted, its credit shaken, and for years the money may not be recovered. It would be a mockery of justice as well as of law, to say to the bank, your only remedy is by an action of trespass.

It is a settled principle in chancery, that an injunction will be granted against a single trespass, if in its nature, it would be irremediable at law. But the case before us is a trespass to be repeated so long as the act laying the tax shall remain unrepealed. And there can be no question, that a collection of the tax after the decision of the Supreme Court, declaring the tax law void, will be continued until the law shall be repealed. This will in effect, not only disregard the highest judicial authority, on the question involved, in the Union; but it will nullify the Constitution of the United States, which is declared to be the Supreme Law of the Union.

This remark is not only justified but called for as two applications for injunctions have been made against the collection of the illegal tax at the present term. In the bill it is stated that orders have been given to the Treasurers of the Counties in which these banks are situated to proceed, under the law, to collect the tax. And this is to be done, if the tax be not paid on demand, by what, in common parlance, is called the crowbar operation. In all the bills praying for injunctions in these cases, the complainants state that the banks have offered to pay the legal tax under their charter, and are ready, at any time, to pay it.

In the case of Osborn above stated, the Supreme Court say, "The Circuit Court of the United States have jurisdiction of a bill brought by the Bank of the United States, for the purpose of protecting the Bank in the exercise of its franchises, which are threatened to be invaded, under the unconstitutional laws of a State; and as the State itself cannot, according to the eleventh amendment of the Constitution, be made a party defendant to the suit, it may be maintained against the officers and agents of the State, who are entrusted with the execution of such laws."

And the Court further say, "In the case at Bar, the tribunal established by the Constitution for the purpose of deciding ultimately, in all cases of this description, had solemnly determined that a State law imposing a tax on the Bank of the United States, was unconstitutional and void, before the wrong was committed for which the suit was brought." "We think then," the Court say, "there is no error in the decree of the Circuit Court of the District of Ohio, so far as it directs restitution" of the money taken unlawfully from the Bank.

The Court say in effect, as stated in the synopsis of the case, "A State cannot tax the Bank of the United States, and any attempt on the part of its agents and officers to enforce the collection of such tax against the property of the bank, may be restrained by injunction from the Circuit Court.

It is said that the tax on the Bank of the United States was intended to destroy its franchises. The exaction on each of the two branches of that bank, was the sum of fifty thousand dollars, while the illegal tax on the Commercial Bank of Cleveland was about eleven thousand dollars. This is a difference in degree, rather than in principle. But the Court say a tax on the Bank of the United States is illegal, and may be injoined by the Circuit Court.

Is not the tax complained of by the Commercial Bank of Cleveland illegal, and may it not be injoined? What higher and more conclusive authority than this can be cited in favor of this remedy by injunction.

In the case of *Pennsylvania* v. *The Wheeling Bridge Co.*, 13 *Howard*, 567; the Court say in reference to granting injunctions, "there must be such an injury, as from its nature is not susceptible of being adequately compensated by damages at law, or such as, from its continuance or permanent mischief, must occasion a constantly recurring grievance, which cannot otherwise be prevented than by an injunction." The character of the trespass threatened and complained of, is not only an annually recurring grievance, but if continued must be fatal to the bank. The tax, and the penalty for non-payment, together with the costs of collection, would impair the credit and destroy the usefulness of any bank.

It has been stated that the mode of giving jurisdiction in this case is merely colorable; or in other words, that it is a fraud upon the law. Is this so? The second section of the third article of the Constitution declares, that the judicial power shall extend to controversies "between citizens of different States."

The framers of the Federal Constitution were wise and sagacious men. They were profoundly acquainted with human nature in its individual and aggregate action. They were instructed in no ordinary school; and in nothing was their sagacity more eminently shown, than in establishing a judicial power to carry out and maintain the federal powers, and provide against the effects of local excitement. For these purposes were the Courts of the United States chiefly established. An option is given to citizens of other States than those in which suits are brought, to sue in the Courts of the Union.

The complainant is a citizen of Connecticut. He has stock in the bank, which he apprehends will be forcibly and unlawfully seized and abstracted. And if so seized, for the reasons stated in his bill, the law will afford to him no adequate means of redress. Under such circumstances, is he guilty of a legal fraud, or of claiming a colorable right only, by suing in the Circuit Court? He claims the exercise of a Constitutional right, to sue in this Court. And if a suit thus brought, makes the Directors of the bank defendants in the suit, and being parties on the record, brings the bank within the relief prayed, the fault is in the law, rather than in the complainant, and the reproach, therefore, should not be thrown on him.

This Court brings into a State no novel principles. It administers the law of the State. In giving effect to the Statutes of the State, where there is no conflict with the Federal Constitution, the Courts of the Union follow implicitly the rule established by the Supreme Court of the State. This is done, not on the ground of authority, but of policy. It would be injurious to the citizens of a State, to have two rules of property. Such a course, by the Courts of the Union, would produce unfortunate conflicts and encourage litigation. To avoid this, as a matter of policy, the Courts of the United States follow the State Courts, in the construction of their Statutes.

So far has this been carried, that the Supreme Court of the United States has reversed its own decision, made in accordance with the State decisions, in order to conform to a change of decision in the Supreme Court of the State, in the construction of its Statutes; and I trust that no circumstances will ever induce the Supreme Court of the Union to reverse this course of decision.

There are but few cases in which, under the Federal Constitution, the Supreme Court of the Union establishes the rule of construction for the State Courts. Where one such case occurs, there are more than five hundred cases where the Courts of the Union follow the State Courts.

If individuals and Courts shall disregard judicial authority, and carry out their own peculiar views of our Constitution and Laws, the harmony of our system of government must be destroyed, and the law of force must become the arbiter of rights.

We think that there is jurisdiction in the case before us, and that the injunction has been rightfully granted, and that it should be made, so far as the illegal tax is demanded, perpetual. The demurrer is overruled.

DISTRICT COURT OF THE UNITED STATES.

~~~~~~~~~~~~~

IN ADMIRALTY.

FASHION v. WARDS.

1. In case of a collision between a steamer and sail-vessel, in which the owners of the former libel the latter, the libellants must not only show fault in the latter, but all precautionary measures on their own part, to avoid the danger to which she was exposed.

2. Allegations in pleading are *admissions* by the pleader, and need no proof, unless denied and put in issue: and as against the pleader, will always be taken as matter conceded.

3. A witness swearing that he *thought* a particular order was given, and to his *belief* that it was obeyed, is not contradicted by testimony positively averring that such an order was not given.

4. The testimony of a witness should not be rejected, because in a hurried conversation, immediately after the collision, he gave a different statement as to a particular fact from that positively sworn to in Court.

5. The protest of the captain and crew, made the morning after the collision, when admitted in evidence, may be considered as evidence corroborative of the testimony of the witnesses in Court, when, as to all material facts, they correspond.

6. Doubtful words in a Statute, if not scientific or technical, are to be interpreted according to their familiar use and acceptation. The phrase *"going off large"* is nautical, and signifies having the wind free on either tack.

7. Since the introduction of steam in the propulsion of vessels, the rule of navigation has been enlarged, and steamers are required to use all their power and care, under all circumstances, to keep clear of sailing vessels. The former CAN be controlled and guided by human skill; the latter are governed by the wind.

8. Every precaution must be taken by a steamer to avoid a collision with a sail-vessel, and the timely slackening of her speed is a necessary precaution *at night*, when passing through a fleet of sail-vessels anchored at the mouth of a river. Under such circumstances a mere conformity with the rules of navigation will not excuse the steamer.

9. A rate of speed in steamers which, under the circumstances, necessarily endangers the property of others, is unjustifiable, and makes the owners responsible for the consequences.

Messrs. *Van Dyke, Gray, & Frazer*, for respondents.

Messrs. *Emmons & Newberg*, for libellants.

OPINION OF THE COURT BY JUDGE WILKINS.

This is a case of collision between a steamer and a brig, at the mouth of the river Detroit. The libellants were the owners of the steamer Pacific, and exhibited in their bill the following allegations, viz.: "That the said steamboat, of the burthen of 500 tons and better, on the 26th of May, 1853, sailed from the port of Detroit with a large load of passengers and a small cargo of merchandise, on a voyage to the port of Cleveland, in the state of Ohio. That, in the evening, when *about a mile and three quarters* below the port of Malden, and about *three quarters of a mile below* the Malden Light-house, and near the mouth of the river, while running her usual track, and ONLY *at the rate of* FIVE MILES AN HOUR, *because the night was* DARK, *without a moon*, and thus *being impossible to distinguish* a vessel *at more than about twice the length of the said steamboat distant;* and, furthermore, because the master of the steamboat *thus slowed the speed of the said steamboat, in order to pass* A VESSEL *about* FIVE OR SIX HUNDRED FEET *above the brig Fashion;* the master being on watch and on the look-out, descried a small light ahead, and soon discovered a vessel approaching the steamer he commanded, DEAD AHEAD and apparently about *three hundred feet distant*, which was but *twice the length of the said steamboat*. That as soon as he discovered the said brig Fashion thus approaching the steamer, he ordered his helm to be put 'hard aport,' designed to pass to her right, and leave her on his larboard side. That the helm of the steamer was accordingly put 'hard aport,' and *so kept* until the said steamboat had lapped her bow upon said vessel about twenty or thirty feet; and that when he perceived the Fashion was about to strike the steamer, he ordered his helm 'hard a starboard,' in order to throw his stern off and avoid a collision, which was accordingly done, but the said brig struck the said steamboat with her bow about midships, carrying away the wheel-house, the kitchen, and pantry, with its crockery and furniture, and also the wheel beams, deck frames, pillar block, and breaking the wheel of the said steamboat."

The libel further exhibits, that at the time the light of the Fashion was first seen, the steamer Pacific "carried a bright light at the top of her pilot house, a red light on her larboard side front of the wheel house, and a green light on her starboard side opposite the red; and that the said lights remained in their positions burning, when the brig struck the steamer, and that they could easily have been seen from the Fashion for a long time before, and in season for her to have avoided a collision."

It is further alleged in the libel, that "when the Fashion was *first seen,* she was so near the Canada shore, that the steamer could not safely pass between her and the shore; that when first discovered by the Pacific, she was sufficiently near for those on the steamer to see *her exact course,* and that her bow pointed from the Canada shore towards the middle of the river: that, *when the Pacific was nearing her, and about to pass her on the right, instead of hugging the said shore,* or *putting her helm to larboard, as she was bound to do,* or, instead of keeping on her course; *she omitted to do either,* but *put her helm to the starboard, and thereby throwing her bow out from the shore, across the track of the steamer, and by reason whereof the collision occurred;* that the orders 'to starboard' were distinctly heard given on board of the brig, and that, in obedience thereto, she bore out from the shore across the track of the steamboat, until just as the bow of the brig was about to strike the steamer, when the order was given 'to potr her helm and bear away,' which was too late to avoid the collision."

After thus succinctly narrating the circumstances attending, and the immediate cause producing the collision, (which, as the libel was prepared and filed within *four days* after the events described, and when the facts were then fresh in the memory of the Captain of the steamer and his crew, may be fairly considered as *their* view of the *facts* at the *time*) the libel proceeds to confirm this view of the transaction, by the recital of the admission of the Captain of the brig, that his vessel was *in fact* starboarded, as thus represented; and that the collision was consequently occasioned by the carelessness and mismanagement of the Captain and crew of the Fashion, in *not putting her helm* to the larboard, or otherwise continuing her course up the river on the Canada side of the channel.

The respondents deny that the collision was occasioned by the fault of the brig; but directly charge the same to the carelessness and mismanagement of the steamer, averring that it was occasioned by the steamer's attempting to cross the bows of the said brig, when she should have continued her course and gone to the starboard. They further deny, that the brig was pursuing a course *upward near the Canada shore;* and aver, that the brig, being on a voyage from the port of Buffalo to Chicago, entered the mouth of the River Detroit, from Lake Erie, about 8½ o'clock in the evening of the day when the collision occurred. That having set the compass to give their vessel a bearing *N. by E.*, they pursued a course up the river *west of mid channel*, direct for the Bow Blan Light House. That they continued such course without material variation; that on entering the mouth of the river, *all their crew*, ten in number, were summoned upon deck, and stationed at the braces and other suitable places so as easily to manage the vessel in case of emergency. That she was staunch, strong, well manned and equipped. That she had a signal lamp burning and suspended over the pilot house, visible to those approaching. That in addition thereto, a man with a large globe lamp was stationed forward of the railing. That when she was two-and-a-half miles up the river, and a quarter of a mile from the light house, and about half-a-mile from the Canada shore, her master, who was on the look out, discerned the light of the Pacific coming down the river about half-a-mile off. That both the lights of the steamer were then visible, and continued so, until she approached to within 40 or 50 rods of the brig, when the larboard light disappeared and continued so until within 20 rods. That at *this* time she was from 2 to 3 points to the starboard of the said brig's bow, and was then pursuing a course which would have carried her some 15 rods to the starboard, and prevented the collision. That there was an abundance of room *then* between the brig and the Canada shore for the steamer to pass with entire freedom and safety, the river being about 2 miles wide in that locality : That the said steamer *here* suddenly changed her course, and her larboard light again appeared. That the Fashion was then sailing up the river at the rate of a mile and a half an hour, and on the same course with which she had entered, and that her course was not altered until a collision with the Pacific appeared inevitable, at which time her helm was ordered a port to ease off the blow of the steamer. That within a minute after the re-appearance of the larboard light of the Pacific, she ran across the course of the brig, striking her larboard bow, carrying away her jib-boom, bowsprit, and breaking through her larboard bow. That the speed of the said steamer was, at the time, in full motion and unchecked. The respondents, therefore, fully deny that the collision complained of, could have been avoided by the brig Fashion, but affirm that it was caused by the sudden and improper change made in the course of the steamer. They deny further, putting the helm of the brig to the starboard, and aver that she only changed her course at the time, in the direction and to the extent and for the purpose previously stated; and further affirm that no order to starboard was given by the master or any one on board of said brig, and that no collision would have occurred, had the Pacific kept her course to the Canada shore, or stopped her engine when the danger first became apparent.

The issue of *fact*, thus presented by those allegations of the respective parties, comprehend therefore, the affirmation of the libellants that the collision was caused by the unskillful starboarding of the Fashion, when the vessels approached each other; and the denial of the same by the respondents. But assuming the fact to be according to the statement of the libel, and that such an order was given and obeyed by the brig, it by no means exonerates the steamer from fault, and attaches responsibility to the respondents, unless the alleged consequence of such order was *solely* attributable to such alleged false movement of the brig. The libellants must show that their vessel performed the duty which devolved upon her under the existing circumstances, in adopting all precautionary measures to avoid the danger to which she was exposed. They are not only called upon to establish fault in the respondents, but, *to prove* ordinary care and diligence on their own part. At the moment a collision is apprehended to be inevitable, an injudicious order, given in the excitement and alarm of the moment, is not to be considered as the *only cause*, even if deemed a fault, should the antecedent negligence and conduct of the one party, have placed the other in a situation where there was no time for judicious action. *8th Law Rep.* 275, 12 *How.* 461.

Hence the enquiry of the Court embraces the consideration of other facts, than those composing the issue specified in the libel and answer. The pleadings admitting a collision, the principal enquiry is, whether it was the result of inevitable accident, beyond the control of human care and skill, or, if not, which vessel was in fault; or, were both in such fault as would call for an equitable apportionment of the damages. It was clearly *not* an event caused by a sudden storm, or, any such *vis major* as caused the vessels to be driven against each other, and which human foresight could not have prevented. Yet, if there can be no fault found by the testimony on either side, it will nevertheless be considered as an inevitable accident. The steamer was on her usual evening trip to Cleveland, Ohio, and the brig on her voyage to Chicago, had entered the mouth of the Detroit river, in the vicinage of which and within the range of a mile of the light house, a fleet of 50 or 60 sail vessels, bound upward, were detained by unfavorable weather. In the language of Captain Shepherd, of "the Hope,"

"The vessels were so thick in the channel, and the night so dark, that it was a difficult matter for a steamer to steer safely through them, and required the greatest precaution."

The testimony, which is principally applicable to the other points involved, is not only voluminous, but greatly contradictory. This is necessarily incidental to all cases of this description. The witnesses, usually the crews of the colliding vessels, are not at all times the most reliable; and, viewing the leading incidents from different and ever varying positions, a correspondence in their testimony cannot always be expected. With much care and attention, I have laboriously examined and studied the facts in the case, and will not undertake to reconcile the marked discrepancy in the evidence. Certain prominent facts are free from all doubt, and *on them* mainly will the decision of this Court depend. Other facts are left in uncertainty, by the witnesses on the one side contradicting each other on material points, widely differing in matters of judgment, as to time, place, distance, and the character of the night; and all of them, almost with one accord, positively affirming the leading fact in the controversy, which is *flatly*, and as positively denied by all the witnesses on the other side.

Before we proceed, however, to an examination of this testimony, it would be well to notice *four very material facts*, placed on the record of the case by the libel.

Allegations in pleading, are *admissions* by the pleader, and need no proof, unless denied and put in issue; and as against the pleader, will always be taken as matter conceded. These facts are,

1. The night of the collision *was very dark*, and so dark as to be impossible to distinguish objects at more than twice the distance of the Pacific.

2. The *speed of the Pacific* was *slackened* to *five miles an hour*, in order to pass a vessel about five or six hundred feet *above* the brig Fashion.

3. Captain Goodsell, of the steamer, *first* discovered the brig Fashion approaching the Pacific *dead ahead* and *at the time* about 300 *feet off*.

4. That as soon as he discovered the Fashion, *thus* approaching his vessel and at *this distance*, 300 feet, he first ordered his helm "*hard aport*" and kept her so, *until she lapped her bow upon the brig about* 20 *or* 30 *feet;* and then, perceiving that the Fashion was about to strike the steamer, he ordered his helm "hard a starboard," in order to throw his stern off, *which was done*, and *then* the collision occurred.

I. The first proposition presented by the pleadings and the proofs is, was the collision the result of the fault, or the unskillful conduct of the officers and crew of the Fashion?

It is argued on the part of the libellants, that the Fashion, in her onward course up the river, closely hugged the Canada side of the channel; that she was on this course when first seen from the Pacific, that she continued on this course until nearly opposite to, although somewhat below, a house on the Canada shore designated as the Elliot House, and stated by

Mr. Elliot to be "about 60 feet below the Light House." That the Pacific, having a minute before slackened her speed, to avoid a collision with the vessels lying in front of the Light House, was slowly proceeding onward in mid channel, when the Fashion, suddenly changing her course for the American side, recklessly crossed the track of the steamer, and by unskillfully putting her helm to the starboard, rendered a collision unavoidable. Such a state of facts, if sustained by proof of every precautionary measure taken by the steamer to pass in safety, (would certainly fully exonerate the steamer,) and render the respondents liable to the amount of the damage incurred.

Is such a view of the case maintained by the preponderance of the evidence? *I think not.* While no two of the crew of the Pacific agree as to the relative position of the Fashion to the Hope and to the Canada side; and Smith Holt, *the wheels-man*, locates the Hope "*in mid-channel, tailing towards Canada;*" while Noble, the clerk, says, "she *seemed* to be coming up the Eastern shore, and *did not alter her course until a minute before the collision;*" while Elliot swears "that the point of collision was further off in the stream and near the middle of the channel; while Goodsell states that he could not doubt as to the position of the vessel, and that her course was up the river on the Canada side, and about 250 *feet from the shore;* and in cross-examination, invalidating the strength of this testimony, by swearing, *that the collision occurred half-a-mile below the Island*, and consequently locating the Hope at a greater distance from the Canada side, and the Light House, than the same is fixed by Shepperd and Dumont; while such glaring discrepancy weakens the position of the libellants in this respect. The Captain, the *two* mates, the *helmsman* and *seamen*, numbering nine in all, and constituting the entire crew of the Fashion, clearly, unitedly and emphatically testify to her course from opposite Bar Point upward, west of mid-channel in a specified direct bearing for the Light

House. And in this they are mainly supported by Wolf of the Walbridge, and Marshal Capron of the Blossom, the one following and the latter preceding the Fashion in the same course, and passing unobstructed up the stream to the Light House Point, between the Hope and the so called American side, shortly before the collision, the crash of which was heard distinctly on her decks.

If, *then*, taking the Canada side of the channel, and continuing in the same until the moment of collision, and putting the helm at that crisis to the starboard, thereby suddenly turning her bow to the left and across the river, *is* the fault of the Fashion, I cannot, from all the consideration I have given the evidence, *so find the fact.*

The libellants' witnesses by no means agree with each other as to *hearing* the order " to starboard," or from what quarter it proceeded; and those of them who testify to such a fact, are *positively* contradicted by the Captain and the entire crew of the Fashion, who must have heard such an order had the same been given, and must have been conversant of the fact had such an order been obeyed by the vessel. *They could not be mistaken,* while it is probable that those on board the steamer were so, hearing such a shout from the Walbridge, and from the appearance of the Fashion in "easing off her main sheet." If the fact was so, and such an order was given and obeyed, the Captain, the mates, the helmsman, and the seamen of the Fashion have *knowingly* and *corruptly* sworn to a falsehood, material in this controversy, and which would require of this Court, so believing the fact, to direct their *recognizance to respond to a criminal* accusation. Not so in regard to Goodsell, Fish, Dumont, Noble, and the wheelsman, Holt. There is a mental reservation, or a cautious modification in *their* testimony, which, however morally inexcusable if the fact was otherwise, would be protection of them on an indictment for perjury. *Thinking* such an order was given on board the Fashion, and believing the brig them

11a

swinging to the left, is not an oath contradictory to the fact, that no such order *was* given, and that no starboarding nautically considered ever occurred.

Captain Goodsell says, in his testimony in chief:—"I heard them on board the *brig* sing out starboard, and then 'hard starboard,' and *saw* the *Fashion* swing towards our vessel ;" and in cross-examination, he says, "I *think* she put her helm *to starboard*, when we put our helm *to port*." All this may be consistent with the fact that the Fashion was *not* put to the starboard. *Fish* did *not* hear the order to starboard, but says, "the Fashion *seemed* to be *swinging* towards us, after Goodsell gave the order 'to port,' and *then* it was too late for either vessel to have avoided a collision;" corresponding with the statement. of Kennedy Andrews, "that the Fashion, *at the time*, eased her main sheets," which would appear to those on the steamer, as- if she was starboarding. Dumont says "that he heard the order 'to starboard,' but the Fashion was so close, that he could'nt say whether she swung or not." Noble says, "the Fashion *seemed* to be coming up on the Canada side ; heard the order 'hard a port' on the steamer, and observed an alteration in the course of the Fashion towards us, and immediately the collision occurred." And Holt says, "I *think* the Fashion luffed up just before the collision, and changed her course, heard the order 'to starboard,' but can't say the sound came from the Fashion."

All of which testimony amounts not to the weight of a spider's thread, when contrasted with the unequivocal denial of the fact by nine witnesses, who *best knew* of the circumstance, if it occurred, and still more so when taken in connection with the testimony of Wolf, that he, *immediately* before the collision, gave such an order on board of the Warbridge, whose position was directly astern of the Fashion. And were I to accept the equivocal affirmation of the libellant's witnesses on *this* point, thus explained by the order given on the Walbridge, and reject the positive and direct denial of the respondent's witnesses, I should give a preponderance to *doubt* over certainty, and establish a new rule of evidence for the discovery of truth.

I am obliged, therefore, to say, that my examination of the evidence, in regard to this very serious conflict between the witnesses, has led me irresistibly to the conclusion, that *no such order was given on board the Fashion*, and *therein she was not in fault.*

Heretofore I have considered the course and conduct of the Fashion, principally with the light shed thereon, by the crew of the steamer. *Their* testimony certainly does not make out the case, as exhibited in the libel. Nor is much strength superadded thereto by Simonea and Guiteau; the latter of whom, by his conduct on the stand, did not commend his oath to the favorable regard of the Court. We will presently consider the weight to which their evidence is entitled, with reference to the object for which it was offered.

During the recess of the day, when the libellants closed their testimony in chief, my mind was impressed with the conviction that they had not presented a case so free from doubt, as to warrant a decree in their favor. With that conviction, I was disposed to stop the further investigation; but, conceiving that the examination of the crew of the Fashion might lead either to an amicable adjustment by the parties, or to a decree on the basis that the real facts of the case were inscrutable, I permitted the hearing to proceed.

But the testimony of the respondents gives an entirely different view of the transaction, and, if worthy of credence, completely exonerates them from all liability, leaving only for the determination of the Court, the credibility of the witnesses who testify to the facts. It establishes that the brig Fashion was on the right course, as confirmed by Captain Willoughby, bearing from off Bar Point North by East, and heading for the Light-house; that that course was kept without variation, except in passing the Walbridge, and the shoal which made out from the head of the Island; that she was properly manned; that she had a proper look-out; that she used extraordinary precautions to escape a collision with other vessels; that she added to the usual lights required by the law, the captain placing a man with a globe lamp outside of the railing; that, with the wind lightly freshening from the West, she crept up the stream at less than two miles an hour; that every man of her crew was at his post; and that she made no injudicious movement whatever, continuing on her course until colliding with the Pacific.

Such is the substance of the testimony of Captain McKee, corroborated in every important particular by *Andrews, Salmon, Rogers, Flack, Mason, Sheely,* and others.

How has it been impeached?

I must confess I place but little reliance upon the mathematical argument, or that which has been adduced to show the inconsistency of *this* testimony with natural truth. Such argument is based upon a misapprehension of the testimony as to the position of the *other* vessels; for displace the Hope a few rods further West or South, or farther from the Lighthouse, (*localities* about which all the witnesses for libellants greatly differ, and no two agree,) locate the Deer further up or down, and change but a few feet the witness Elliot, and the whole argument as to the place of collision falls to the ground. It requires but a little variation in the lines drawn upon the chart to demonstrate this. Besides, if the witnesses locating these objects (no one of which can be safely considered as a fixed object but Elliot's House and the Island Light,) had satisfactorily agreed in relation to the same, which is not the case, it would only amount to the testimony of *three* witnesses hypothetically contradicting that of nine; for Capron and Wolf, in this respect, sustain the crew of the Fashion, who place the point of collision below the Hope, and some 80 rods off, and the course of the Fashion *at the time* westward, or more towards the American side of the channel.

Neither can I accede to the opinion that, because Chart B., drawn by Mr. Compeau, represents a straight line from the point of starting, near Bar Point, to the Light-house; and these witnesses testified to *its* accuracy, as representing the mouth of the river, and the course and position of the vessels in its vicinage, that, *therefore*, they swore to such a straight line as the course of the Fashion, which would consequently be' inconsistent with keeping the light constantly in view over their larboard bow, when steering by the compass North by East. Their testimony was in substance, " That having *fixed* the compass, and taken the bearing North by East in starting up the river, their course was made direct for the Light-house, sailing or heading direct for it, until coming near the shoals, when they sheered off a little to avoid them, and *resuming again their course by the Light.*" In the language of the captain, " when the Light bore North by East, we kept away, steering *directly for the Light.*" In pursuing this course, it is true, the Fashion would be continually nearing the eastern side of the channel as she advanced up the stream, because, as Captain Willoughby testified, "the Canada shore protrudes more westwardly, and the channel contracts as we approach the mouth of the river, and as the point of starting *was more or less west of the Light-house.* And here I must say that a careful examination of the testimony has corrected the mistake under which I labored for a short time during the able argument of the Counsel of the libellants ; that, in this respect, the testimony of McKee and his crew was as to an impossibility, and therefore, so to be considered. But, on review, I find instead of "keeping the light bearing a little over the larboard bow," the testimony is, that they kept the position of the Fashion directly ahead for the light, as is fully and intelligently explained by Andrews, the first mate, saying :

" We kept away *till we opened* Bois Blanc Light, a little
on our larboard bow, and *then*, that is, after this, *steered* by
the light and compass, the man at the wheel going by the
light."

And Flake, the helmsman, swearing " that he kept his eye
on the light, and kept it as right ahead as he could see."

I was very careful in noting the testimony as given by
McKee, Andrews, Flake, and their companions, as to the
course of the vessel, reading over repeatedly to them what I
had written ere they closed their testimony, that I might
not afterwards be misled; and I am satisfied their testimony
is not obnoxious to the objection which has just been considered.

But, it is furthermore urged, that McKee should at least
be discredited, because, as is charged in the libel, he stated
on the following day, when he arrived at Detroit, " That his
vessel was starboarded," and that such a statement differs
from the testimony he has delivered in Court.

That he told a different story on the occasion alluded to,
is not so clearly established. The conversation he had with
Mr. Thompson and others was a hurried one, just as he had
landed, and when on his way to telegraph the owners; and it
was an easy matter for them, under the circumstances, to
have misunderstood the purport of his language, or, for him
unintentionally to have let fall a word, that did not technically convey his meaning.

Thompson, Montgomery, Fish and McDonald decline testi-
fying to his using the term starboard, while only Murray and
Goodsell, of the eight that were present, swear positively that
such was his language. Goodsell had preceeded him to
Detroit, and given his version of the transaction, and yet the
same remarkable want of coincidence between this witness
and the 1st mate Fish, which distinguished their testimony as
to the relative position of the vessels, and their conduct at
the period of collision, characterizes *their* testimony as to the

strong point of *this* conversation. Goodsell swears positively that *he said* " he gave the order and starboarded his vessel," While Fish "will not be so positive about the word starboard being uttered," but, *that he said* "he *thought* that the Pacific would go between him and the Canada shore,-and that he *headed* a little for the American shore, and gave her a wide berth on the Canada side;" which is not materially variant from McKee's testimony on the stand. The witness Thompson, however, places this matter of impeachment, I have no doubt, in its true light, as it occurred; and giving to his version its proper weight, it would not justify the entire rejection of McKee's testimony, *on the ground* taken by the libellants. With the change of one word, his narration of the transaction to Mr. Thompson is but an epitome of his testimony in Court, as I have recorded the same. He said to Thompson, "He saw the Pacific descending the river, he watched her to see her course, she seemed to change some as she approached, shutting out and opening her lights:" from all of which he, McKee, concluded she was going to take the Canada side, and he, willing to give her a wide berth, "*put* to the American shore."

But, that he told another story, is *successfully rebutted* by the *protest*, which, *if not competent evidence* as to any fact it contains, is at least evidence, that *he* and his whole crew, the morning after this conversation on the dock, entertained *the same opinions*, and narrated succinctly the *same* facts, to which they have testified in Court; and so far raises the probability that the witnesses thus impeaching the memory or integrity of McKee, were clearly mistaken as to his meaning, if not as to his language. Where a witness is sought to be impeached in this manner, by a *number of others*, it would be more satisfactory if those others could agree among themselves, or, that the memory of each had caught and retained at least the convicting word of the reported conversation.

Moreover, the rejection of his testimony would in this case

amount to nothing, it would not weaken the preponderance, as the *same* facts are testified to by Andrews, Sheely, Flack, and the others; and if McKee has sworn falsely, they all have sworn falsely; and not only so, but their moral turpitude is magnified beyond the one offense of perjury to a corrupt combination deliberately to swear, by whole-cloth manufacture, to a tissue of falsehoods, to the injury of the libellants, a supposition too monstrous for judicial confidence. McKee might have a 'motive, in self-protection, as between him and the owners; but it is hard to imagine how his crew could be brought to such a stage of crime, without the appliance of the usual incentives to human action. The intelligent, demonstrative and conclusive evidence of Kennedy Andrews, was in all particulars corroborative of McKee; and Flack, the helmsman, was as direct as to the same facts as either, and my confidence in both of them, as witnesses, has not been impaired. The great point of controversy, in the impeachment of Captain McKee, is as to the course he ran, and the necessity he was under to order his helm a-starboard. If he was on the Canada shore, such necessity may be conceived possible; but, if on the other hand, he was on the American side of mid-channel, such an order would only tend to put his vessel unnecessarily more in that direction. Now, that Mc Kee is right, is confirmed by a portion of the testimony of the libellants.

Let a line be drawn through the river, from the starting place off Bar Point upwards, equi-distant from both sides of the channel. Call the same *mid*-channel.

Now, according to the testimony of Noble, and Smith Holt, the wheelsman, the Hope *lay in mid-channel*, tailing, or with her stern towards the Canada side : Noble saying, "the Hope lay in mid-channel, and as we rounded her, we left her on our starboard side." The *bow* of the Hope, then would of course be pointed to the American side. But Shepherd says, "that the Pacific, in passing, *rounded the Hope.*" In doing so, *her stern* would of course tail or turn several points to the *Canada* shore, and consequently her bow-sprit *across mid-channel*, would *directly point down the river westward*, towards the American shore. But Fish swears that the collision took place 35 or 40 rods below the Hope; and Goodsell, that the Fashion was dead ahead, and consequently that distance in a line, drawn from and along her bow westward, places beyond controversy, according to the testimony of these four witnesses of the libellants, the point of collision on the American side of the channel; and therefore sustains McKee in the testimony he has given.

Thus disposing of this branch of the case, we are called upon to decide a two-fold objection which arises from the testimony of the respondents: viz.,

1. That the Fashion being on her larboard tack, as is contended, she did not display the signal light as required by the 5th sec. of the Act of Congress of 1849.

2. That the ignorance of Captain McKee, as to the new regulations in regard to navigation by steamers, exhibits such a want of seamanship, as to prove that the Fashion was not well manned.

Apart from the consideration, that the display of an enormous light, is not made either by the libel or the evidence, the cause of the collision, I am by no means satisfied that *this* objection is well taken under the provision of the Statute.

The language of the 5th sec. of the Act of 1849 is as follows: "During the night, vessels on the *starboard tack* shall show a red light; vessels on the *larboard tack*, a green light; and vessels *going off large*, or *before the wind*, or at *anchor*, a white light."

It would seem from the use of the conjunction "or," in the last branch of the sentence, that legislation designed to contra-distinguish "*going off large*" from sailing "before the wind," and to direct the display of the white light under three contingencies. If so, the phrase, "before the wind,"

cannot be considered as definatory of "going off large."
What then was meant by the latter contingency?

Doubtful words in a Statute, if not scientific or technical,
are to be interpreted according to their familiar acceptation.
But the words here are all *technical*, and have a *nautical
meaning* in the science of Navigation, with which, in the
interpretation of a Statute, it is presumed Courts of Justice
are acquainted. No experts need be called on to interpret
the Law. Many terms and phrases are used in our Law
Books and Reports in Admiralty, that are not in common
use out of that jurisdiction. Booms, and pawl bits, and cat
heads, and braces, and aft, and abaft, and larboard, and starboard occupy a prominence in Admiralty, and are all, in legal
supposition at least, known to the Court. So in regard to
the phrase under consideration; its definition is the interpretation of the Statute.

Congress designed to provide *three* signal lights, for five
contingencies, and "going off large," and being "before the
wind," and "at anchor" in the river, of a dark night, *presenting a similar peril* to approaching vessels ahead, have assigned them the same signal light as a warning. "Going off
large" is having the wind free on either tack, properly
termed a vessel "off large," because it is in her power to
take a course to either side—starboard or larboard—proceed
straight forward on her course, or return back to her anchorage, or to the point from which she started. In other language, she is free to the wind. She is not bound, but like
a discharged debtor under the old insolvent system, who
being at large, is at liberty to leave, as a free man, his prison bounds, and go whithersoever he will.

Was such the condition of the Fashion? McKee testifies,
"that the wind on entering the river was W. S. W.—that
at first it was very light, and scarcely sufficient to take them
up the river, and that he had everything arranged to let go
her anchor. But it soon blew a little stronger, and kept

us moving slowly on our course." And Fish and Dumont both say, that when they first discovered her, " they could not tell whether she was at anchor or not." And Andrews says, " that they had a board her larboard tacks; " and he and his companions, all testify, that the course of the brig was direct, without any change of helm or sails, and free to the breeze. Moreover, McKee swears, " that he had the *regular signal light burning* on the ' pawl bit,' " which, being the *white light*, and taken in connection with the evidence already quoted, shows that she was " going off large," with the wind on her larboard.

Being, then, a vessel " off large," on a larboard tack, or, to use the phrase of Judge Nelson, in 10th Howard, " having on board her larboard tacks," she was not in fault in displaying, in such a contingency, her *white light* from the pawl bit.

2. Neither can the second objection, as to the brig not being well manned, be considered as of any force, unless the catastrophe can be fairly attributed to the ignorance of Captain McKee of the rules and regulations adopted by the Board of Inspectors, under the 29th Sec. of the Act of 1852. The Act itself, in its various provisions, is only applicable to vessels propelled in whole or in part by steam; and no special provision is made for promulging these "rules and regulations" to be observed by steamers, beyond "furnishing to each steamer two printed copies, to be kept in conspicuous places." The law did not go into operation, except as to the appointment and qualification of Inspectors, and the licencing of pilots and engineers, until the 15th of January last; and there being no proof of these regulations being promulged until after the opening of spring navigation, the notice of the existence of such new rules, and, therefore, the knowledge of the consequent change as to lights, was limited to steam vessels. Excepting the application of the old maxim, that ignorance of the law is no excuse, it is not easily apprehended,

how the ignorance of the captain of the brig as to these regulations, can be seriously deemed bad seamanship. Besides, he made no movement whatever founded upon his belief, that the old regulations were still in force. He, his two mates, and his helmsman, swear, that they fixed their course and took their heading near two miles below, and kept it, without deviation, until the collision.

Such, then, being the preponderance of the testimony, I am constrained to determine, that I find no fault in the Fashion; because I find no material discrepancy in the evidence sustaining the defense—but much difference, both as to fact and opinion, between the witnesses called to sustain the libel. Neither am I able to say that McKee and his crew were mistaken or deceived as to the course and movements of the brig; but, on the other hand, if that to which they have testified be untrue, in the main or in any important particular, I must declare they are guilty of wilful and corrupt perjury, and should not be permitted to escape with impunity.

Our next inquiry is, whether or not the collision occurred in consequence of, or can properly be attributed to the negligence or misconduct of the Steamer Pacific. And this inquiry is necessary, in order to determine the question of *inevitable accident.*

The rule is well settled in cases of this description, that the libelants must not only show, that the collision was occasioned by the fault of the opposite party, but also, that ordinary care and diligence were used on their own part to avoid it. A *failure in either respect* will dismiss the libel.

The law imposes the burden of proof on them, with one single exception; and that is where the libellants establish misconduct or negligence on the part of the respondents's vessel, the burden of proof is partially shifted, requiring them to show that such *fault* DID NOT cause the collision. As is observed by Mr. Justice Nelson, in *Newton* v. *Stebbins,* 10 Howard, 605 :

"If every proper precautionary measure was carefully and
timely taken by the steamer to pass the sloop Hamlet in safety,
and the accident happened *solely* in consequence of the mismanagement and unskillfulness of the officer in charge of *that*
vessel; then the damage can only be attributed to his own
inattention and want of skill, and not to the steamer."
Otherwise, if the steamer was in fault, *Vide*, as to similar
ruling, *Clapp* v. *Young*, III. Law Report, 8; and 5 How., 465.

In this last case, Mr. Justice Wayne, by whom the opinion
of the Superior Court was delivered, emphatically observes
that—

"In cases of collision, where the one vessel is *clearly*
proved to have neglected a duty imposed by law, she will be
held responsible for all losses, unless it *also* appears that the
collision was *not* caused by such neglect."

Another rule has been likewise well settled in Admiralty,
both in England and in this country, and that is, "That a
vessel having the wind free is obliged to get out of the way
of a vessel close-hauled, and the burden of proof is on the
former to show the exercise of all care and skill to prevent
a collision. Vide 8 Hag., 214; 2 Dodson, 83 and 86; 1
Conklin, 305. *St. John* v. *Paine & al.* 10 How., 581.

Since the introduction and application of steam in the propulsion of vessels, this rule has been so construed and enlarged as to require from steamers the use of *all* their power,
under all circumstances, to keep clear of sailing vessels, and
for this reason, that their impetus being controlled by human
skill, they are considered as vessels navigating with a fair
wind, or (in the language of Judge Nelson, in 10 Howard)
"GOING OFF LARGE," and, therefore, bound to give way to
sailing vessels beating to the windward on either tack. Vide
the cases of *The Perth*, 3 Hag., 414; *The Shannon*, 2 Hag.,
173; *The James Watt.*, 2 Rob., 277; *The Birkenhead*,
3 Rob., 82. These four cases, taken from recent English
Admiralty Reports, in their application, strongly illustrate

the rule as to steamers. In the first, the *steamer* Perth ran foul of the libellants' brig, while she was running at the rate of TWELVE miles an hour, in a dense fog, and in *a track frequented by coasters.* THE BRIG WAS NOT DISCOVERED UNTIL THE STEAMER WAS CLOSE UPON HER. The order to port helm was immediately given, but NO ORDER TO STOP THE ENGINES. The *only* question with the Court was, "*had the steamer done* ALL *in her power to avoid the collision?* and it was held that, *considering the fog,* and that the *track was frequented by coasters,* she ought to have reduced her speed at least one-half, or to six miles an hour ; and that such precaution was due to the safety of other vessels; the Trinity masters declaring that, from their own experience, a steamer could be stopped in a little more than her own length. Here, then, the fault was that of the steamer, in not slackening her speed one-half in passing through the fog, and also in neglecting to stop her engine on first discovering the brig.

In the 2d case,—which is that of the Shannon, and was also the case of a steamer and a sail vessel, the Court held—that, although the Shannon made out a clear case *of a compliance on her part* with *the rules of navigation,* and proved that the sail vessel was navigating in violation of the same;—yet, as the former *received her impetus from steam,* and discovered the latter ascending the river *five miles off*—she *should* have been then under her master's control, and was therefore bound to give way, and *in not doing so,* was at fault—and decreed to suffer the loss which had accrued :—and this on the principle, that the steamer did not use *all* the necessary precaution.

The 3d case is that of the steamer James Watt, which collided with the schooner Perseverance, while the latter was ascending and the former descending the river on a dark night. The master of the Watt, *being in doubt* what course the schooner would take, put her helm to port when the collision occurred. It was held, that the Watt *was bound,* under the circumstances, (*stress being laid on the doubt of the Captain as to what course the schooner was in,*) instead of porting his helm, to have SLACKENED his speed, *until the course and situation of the other vessel* were discoverable, and then to have acted according to circumstances.

In the other case, that of Birkenhead, it was held, that although the watch on board were justified in an erroneous belief, occasioned by the darkness of the night as to the character and position of the Brig with which the Birkenhead collided; yet, that the proper precaution was not taken on board of the steamer, by reversing her engine in time, and *keeping it so* until the fact was ascertained, whether or not the brig could be passed on either side.

These cases, and others of a kindred character in the English Admirality, have been specially cited and recognized as law, and their principles adopted by the Supreme Court of the United States. 10th How. 584. The general rule is thereby established, that in all cases of collision between a sail vessel and a steamer, the latter will not be exonerated from liability, unless on proof that *every precautionary measure* was adopted by her to avoid a collision. And timely slackening the speed, is deemed a necessary precaution. A mere conformity to the rules of navigation will not excuse; neither can she under such circumstances, attach responsibility to the sail vessel, on showing *her fault*, in non-conformity to such rules, unless such fault and non-conformity, and not the steamer's want of the utmost care, was the sole cause of the accident.

Steamers invoke a power in navigation, highly advantageous to trade and commerce, but at the same time perilous to other vessels, unless managed with the greatest care, and the most constant vigilance. Greater than the winds, and not so capricious, this power is ever under the guidance of experience and skill; and in their greatest speed steamers can be almost instantly stopped, by stopping their engines, or their course, "though they be so great, easily turned about, with a very small helm, whithersoever the governor listeth."

The law therefore, in tender regard to human life and property, will not sanction the use of this power, however convenient to the public, to the destruction of the rights and interests of others.

In St. John vs. Payn, 10th How'd, Judge Nelson in delivering the opinion of the Supreme Court, and approvingly citing the Perth and the Shannon, declares:

"The obligation of steamers to avoid a collision, extends further than sail vessels, because they possess a power not belonging to the latter, even with a *fair wind*, the Captain having the steamer ever under his command, both by altering the helm, AND by *stopping the Engines*." "Greater caution and vigilance therefore will be exacted of them, and, as a general rule, when meeting a sail vessel, whether close-hauled or with a free wind, the steamer must adopt *such precautions* as will avoid collision."

The rule is imperative. *The steamer must do* ALL *in her power*. Any omission of a duty, under the exigency, will make her owners liable for the consequences.

In Newton vs. Stebbins, 10th How'd 606, the same Judge, announcing the opinion of the Court, again declares:

"The steamer was greatly to blame in not having slackened her speed, (she then running from eight to ten miles an hour,) as she approached the fleet of River Craft. It is manifest to common sense, says the Supreme Court, that *this* rate of speed, under such circumstances, exposed the other vessels to unreasonable and unnecessary peril, and WE *adopt* the remark of the Court in the case of the Rose (2d W. Rob. 8); "That it may be a matter of convenience that steamers should proceed with great rapidity, but they will not be justified in such rapidity, to the injury of others." And in the case of Genesee Chief; 12th How'd 563, Chief Justice Taney observes:

"A steamer, having the command of her own course and her own speed, it is her duty to pass an approaching vessel at such distance, as to avoid all danger where she has room; and if the water is narrow, her speed should be so checked, as to accomplish the same purpose." The Supreme Court of the U. S., then, have gone to the fullest extent of the English authorities, and in adopting the language of the Court in the Rose, have also adopted the principle which governed that case, viz., that a rate of speed in steamers, which under the circumstances, necessarily endangers the property of others, is unjustifiable, and makes the owners responsible for the consequences.

In the case of the Rose, the night was dark and hazy, she had her lights burning, the sail vessel had none, and no vessel could be discerned at a greater distance than a quarter of a mile; and at the time of the collision the steamer was running at the rate of *ten or eleven miles* an hour; under such circumstances, and *based upon the speed of the Rose,* was the remark made by the Court, as approvingly cited in *Newton* vs. *Stebbins.* Time, place and circumstances, therefore, are all to be carefully considered and weighed, in the formation of a judgment as to what would constitute a legitimate speed in case of a collision. It would vary under different vicissitudes. Full speed would not be improper in an open lake, with a wide berth in day light: or, in navigating a river clear to observation and free from obstruction: while, on the other hand the greatest caution and the utmost care is essentially requisite at night, on a narrow channel, frequented by other vessels, and especially where a number *are known* to be anchored, or detained by stress of weather. Under such circumstances, a steamer is obligated by the law, either to stop her engine, in order to ascertain her course, or, slowly to feel her way, under no greater power of steam than that which is barely necessary for steerage purposes; and any greater rate,

12a

even where the peril is imminent, and has been foreseen, would be unjustifiable.

Moreover, in the last case cited, that of the Genessee Chief, the Supreme Court has established a rule, that must govern in all such cases. It presents a simple alternative to steamers in meeting sail vessels, by declaring, that they must "pass approaching vessels at a *safe distance* if possible; or, if not possible, they must stop their further progress until the difficulty be obviated."

Such a rule then, being authoritatively given by our highest Judicial Tribunal, our duty is to apply it to the facts of this case; and in doing so, a two-fold inquiry is presented, which we will briefly discuss:

1st. Was the speed of the Pacific, at the time and under the circumstances of the collision, such as to amount to a fault occasioning the accident?

2d. Was there space for her to have passed on the Canada or American side of the channel, and thereby have avoided the Fashion?

Were it not for the great discrepancy in the testimony of the Officers and Crew of the Pacific, as to the question of speed, the Court would have very little difficulty in fixing the fact. For *their* testimony on *that* point, especially that of the Engineer Hickey, is more reliable, than the testimony of the other witnesses, who were not on board of the steamer. With all of them, except the Engineer, it would be but a matter of opinion, and with him, *it is knowledge* derived from experience and observation of his machinery and the revolutions of his wheels. The Libel fixes the speed at *five miles* an hour and no doubt the Proctor in drawing his Bill, obtained this fact from that source; then fresh in the recollection of the party. The testimony adduced on the part of the *libelants*, varies from *four to seven* miles; while that of the respondents runs up from *seven to fifteen* miles an hour. Sheppard stood on the Brig Hope, and noticed the vessels *passing* and *thinks* the speed of the steamer between *six* and *seven* miles; but I am of opinion that the *satisfactory* preponderance, is with the *officers of the steamer*, who should be best conversant of the fact, and better qualified to form a right judgment, while one of them *could know* the fact, if he thought proper to have directed his attention at the time to the subject.

There can be no doubt, that until she was abreast of the VIRAGO, her speed was as usual, about *fifteen* miles an hour; and that THEN, *for the first time, observing the peril to which she was exposed*, she checked her speed, and, in the intervening space between that vessel and *the Hope*, (they being a quarter of a mile apart) the steamer was carefully worked BY HAND, and not by steam, the connection between her paddle wheels and machinery being suspended; and hooked on again as she rounded the Hope, and *not* a minute before the accident.

Her speed, therefore, between the Virago and the point of collision, becomes the important question. Anterior to *this*, there could be no fault in her full speed, as it endangered not the property of others; and she was not obligated to check or change until the necessity was apparent, when, abreast of the Virago, the captain and the mate first discovered their vicinage to the fleet of sail vessels, and observed the brig ascending half a mile off.

Our attention, therefore, is limited to the testimony as to her speed in that space.

Captain Goodsell swears:

" On passing the Virago, we checked our speed, by backing and reversing the engine; and at the time of the collision, the Pacific *was passing the land* at the rate of *four or five miles an hour*, the current being there *four miles an hour.*

Gooley, the captain of the Virago, swears:

" That he heard the bell ring to stop the engine, when the Pacific passed the Virago."

Hickey, the engineer, on whom I most rely, swears:

"Between the Virago and the Hope, the steamer was passing the land at the rate of FIVE miles an hour, *with a current of four miles.* Her speed had been checked a few minutes before the collision took place. The engine was *stopped* and backed, and I worked her very slow by hand, with *no greater motion than a good steerage way, making but seven or eight revolutions of the wheel.* Before she was checked, she was running at the rate of fourteen or fifteen miles an hour. Hooked on, just before the crash, and stopped the engine at the same time. Her engine speed but one mile."

FISH, the mate who had the temporary command, swears:

"When we got near the Virago, I ordered the engine reversed and backed, almost stopping her headway; and her speed did not exceed four miles an hour from that time till the collision," including the current.

Dumont, second mate, swears:

"On nearing the Virago, we reversed our engine, and slackened our speed from three to five revolutions, and continued so until the collision. Passing the land at four miles an hour, and about a mile an hour was sufficient steerage way."

Considering the official position occupied by these witnesses, the one captain, *who ought to know;* his two mates, *who had every opportunity of knowing;* and the engineer, whose especial function was to direct the machinery, so as to attain with safety a certain power as to speed, all of whom had ability and experience to form a correct judgment, and all concurring that the speed did not exceed, including the current, five miles *an hour;* and the fact is satisfactorily settled, that her impetus at the time did not exceed more than what was necessary for *steerage purposes.* For if the current was four miles, some motion of the machinery was necessary, to enable the wheelsman to guide the ship, and move her through the perils by which she was surrounded.

All agree that the night was dark—no moon or star light—and objects but dimly discerned at a few rods distance. Her duty then was to move cautiously, *not to return*, but to feel her way in her downward progress, and without absolutely anchoring in the stream. She must exercise some power to enable her to avoid a collision. I do not question the integrity of these witnesses, and I confide in their ability to give a reliable estimate as to this *very important point*. Had the testimony been otherwise, had the speed exceeded that which was merely necessary as steerage power, had her officers neglected the precaution of reversing her engine and stopping her headway, when off the Virago, and when they were first apprised of the peril ahead, the steamer would have been grossly in fault, and under no pretense could claim the protection of this Court.

The next question is, whether there was room for her to have passed on either side of the Hope.

Here there is great discrepancy in the testimony. While the crew of the Fashion testify positively that there was such an open space on the Canada side, and there is no doubt but what other steamers passed both, shortly before and shortly after the collision, and while the Blossom reached the Light-house on the American channel; yet Goodsell and Fish, with whom the responsibility of navigating the steamer chiefly rested, testify that the latter channel was blocked up, and that although there was open space on the Canada side, yet there was danger of running aground. From this discrepancy, as to this point, I am not able to declare the *course* of the steamer a fault. How much soever we know the fact now, yet, at the time, either passage seemed hazardous to the officers of the steamer. I am of opinion, therefore, that the collision was an inevitable accident, resulting from the darkness of the night, and is not attributable to the fault of either party. Both, from the preponderance of the testimony, did all in their power, all that was called for under the circumstances; both vessels were properly manned and skilfully managed, and both used every precaution that could be used under the circumstances to escape the catastrophe which occurred.

Under such circumstances, the settled rule in the United States is the rule of the Admiralty in England, and not the rule which prevails among the maritime states of the Continent of Europe. That rule has not merely been cited and recognized by the Supreme Court of the United States, as by Woodbury, Justice, in *Waring* v. *Clark*, but expressly adopted and directly applied. Vide. 1 Howard's Reports, 28 and 30; 5 How., 508, and 14 How., 538.

In the last case, that of *Stairback* v. *Rae*, after citing the English and the two preceding American cases, and the Continental Rule, Judge Nelson, who delivered the *unanimous* opinion of the Supreme Court, says as follows:

"We think it more just and equitable, and more consistent with sound principles, that where the loss happens from a collision which is the result of inevitable accident, without the negligence or fault of either party, that *each should bear his own loss.*

"There seems no good reason for charging one of the vessels with a share of a loss resulting from a common calamity beyond that happening to herself, when she is without fault, and, therefore, in no just sense, is responsible for it."

This reverses the New England decision, and the libel, therefore, must be dismissed with costs.

THE UNITED STATES *v.* ERASTUS POTTER.

1. Where, in the opinion of the Court, the evidence preponderates in favor of the verdict, the Court will not set it aside on the ground of testimony subsequently submitted, impeaching the credibility of *one* of the witnesses.

2. Where a cause has been closed at the evening of adjournment, and the parties agree to a *sealed verdict,* and the jury come in with a sealed verdict, to which all their names are appended, the Court will not permit the jury to be interrogated as to their finding, but will order each juror to be asked, whether or not the sealed verdict is or is not his verdict; and on every juror replying that it is, will direct it to be recorded as such.

Hand, for United States.
Lathrop & Van Arman, for defendant.

OPINION OF THE COURT BY JUDGE WILKINS.

Five reasons are placed on record, why the Court should grant a new trial.

The four first were not pressed in the argument, and are certainly not founded either in law or in the facts of the case.

That the Court erred in refusing parol testimony of that which was matter of record by *law,* and which was in the power of the defendant to produce, might well be abandoned, when well considered.

That the verdict was against the evidence of the case, or without evidence.

But I do not yield my assent to the proposition that either of these counts are essentially defective. It is conceded that the prosecutor cannot, in the same count, charge different offenses in the alternative, as, for instance, that the defendant did this, *or* did that, because, in pronouncing judgment, there would be no certainty in the finding of the jury, and consequently no basis of record for the sentence of the Court.

But I am inclined to question the construction of the Statute, which makes two offenses, where but *one* was evidently contemplated. The Statute declares cutting, or procuring to be cut, one offense, i. e., cutting, on the principle that the procurer is the doer; aiding *or* assisting one offense, as he who aids is of identity with him who assists; and removing er procuring to be removed, another offense. A count for aiding *or* assisting, would certainly not be defective, because aiding *is* assisting, and assisting *is* aiding. And so, in contemplation of law, he who procures or causes the cutting, is of identity as to the offense with the actual cutter, as, by the subsequent language, the latter is an offender, under the appellation of "being employed in cutting." But it is unnecessary to consume time on this particular exception, as the third count is, in the opinion of the Court, entirely unexceptionable.

Motion to arrest overruled.

KIEF AND LONG v. THE STEAMER LONDON.

1. The sixth section of the Act of Congress of 1790 confers power on the Judge or Justice to issue summary process in the cases specified; and the Court will not look beyond the certificate of such officer for the authority of the clerk to issue the process prescribed; but such certificate must show on its face that the Commissioner had authority to act.

Two seamen, being discharged from the steamer London, at the Port of Detroit, made oath before a United States Commissioner, of the amoun t due them as wages, who certified the same to the District Clerk; on which a summons was issued, directed to the master of the vessel, to show cause why proceedings should not be forthwith instituted against the vessel.

The principal objection to the process was, that the certificate upon which it was based did not state the residence of the District Judge, or that he was absent from his residence in the city of Detroit, where the Admiralty Court was held.

Sidney D. Miller, for libellants.
Hunt & Newberry, for respondent.

OPINION OF THE COURT BY JUDGE WILKINS.

A motion is made, on the part of the claimants of said vessel, to quash the writ issued in this case, and all subsequent proceedings, on seven distinct grounds set forth in the application.

The process was issued by the Clerk of the District Court against the vessel, on the certificate of a Commissioner of said Court, stating that there existed sufficient cause of complaint, on behalf of complainants, on which to found Admiralty process, under the summary provisions of the sixth section of the act of 1790, (first Statute at large).

The first six exceptions taken, embrace objections to the regularity of the proceedings before the Commissioner, the service of the summons, and the *sufficiency* of the case made before that officer, as the basis of the certificate.

Into these matters the Court will not inquire. The Statute clothes the Judge or Justice with power in the premises, and this Court will not look beyond the certificate, as conferring authority on its clerk to issue the process.

But although the Court will not look *beyond*, it will look *at* the certificate, in order to ascertain whether the exigency specified in the Statute existed; or, in other words, whether there was a statutory authority for the process.

The object of the law is the speedy adjustment and recovery of seamen's wages, and at the same time prevent vexatious litigation. With this view, the Statute provides, that "if the wages be not paid within a specified period, or any *dispute shall arise in regard thereto*, it shall be lawful for the *Judge of the District* wherein the vessel is moored, to issue a summons for the master to appear before him, and show cause why proceedings should not be forthwith instituted against the vessel, according to the course of Admiralty Courts, for the recovery of the wages due." But the Statute further provides, "that in case the residence of the Judge of the District be more than three miles from the place, or he be absent from his place of residence, then, in *such case*, any State Magistrate or United States Commissioner may issue such summons, take temporary cognizance of the complaint, and *certify*, if the amount be not settled, the subject matter to the District Clerk, as the foundation of process in behalf of the seamen."

Such certificate must be in compliance with the Statute, or else it is no foundation for the action of the clerk. It must state the residence of the Judge of the district, and if that be more than three miles from the place, or he is absent from his residence at the time the proceedings are instituted before the magistrate, the proceedings are regular.

As the certificate is the only paper placed of record in this Court, as the basis of proceedings here, it must show on its face, that the State Magistrate or the Commissioner had authority to act.

Such is not the character of this certificate, and the writ is set aside, and the subsequent proceedings.

IN ARREST OF JUDGMENT.

THE UNITED STATES v. ERASTUS POTTER.

1. Where an indictment contains several counts, one of which is good, the judgment will not be arrested, although the other three are bad.

2. It is not charging an offense in the alternative, where the language describes the *same* offense. Cutting, or causing to be cut, is one offense by the Statute of 1831.

Hand, for United States.
Lathrop, for defendant.

OPINION OF THE COURT BY JUDGE WILKINS.

The reasons set forth in this case, why the judgment should be arrested, are the same as in Thompson's case, with this exception, that it is further objected to this indictment, that three of the four counts charge the offense in the alternative.

The third count, which charges the defendant with taking and removing timber, is unobjectionable, and will sustain the indictment, as the verdict is general. If one of several counts in an indictment is good, on a general verdict the judgment cannot be arrested. Such is the ruling in the courts of the United States.

It was given in evidence, that the defendant built a shanty on the corner of lot No. 23, described in the indictment; that he was on the sections cutting; that he admitted to one Alexander Johnston, when on his way up to the place where the timber was cut, in the month of February, 1852, "that he was going up a-logging;" that one Dobbin was hired by him to move his tools, with which the timber had been cut and removed; that logs, numbering more than 800, were cut; that defendant hired men to bring or haul them to the river; that he claimed them as his; and that they were cut from the lands described in the indictment.

Such being the evidence of Johnston, Dobbin, Bean, and Risdon, how is it possible for the Court to entertain, for one moment, the proposition that there was no evidence to sustain the verdict.

There was evidence submitted by the defendant, that he was in the employment of one McNeel, who owned lands adjoining, and that the cutting on the Government lands was through ignorance and by mistake; and the Court charged the jury that if they believed such to be the case, they should acquit.

Mr. Samuel Potter, the brother of the defendant, was the only witness to this point, and, it seems, the jury did not believe the defense in this respect sustained.

The Court entertains no doubt whatever, but what the jury were right, in the preponderance they gave to the evidence. But if I thought otherwise, I could not interfere. The jury had *all* the facts fully before them, and they had the right to credit or discredit the witnesses, and give such weight to the testimony as they believed it fairly entitled to. In such a case, the rules of law and the purposes of justice, do not call for the interposition of the Court.

A court is not authorized in setting aside the verdict of a jury, unless in a clear case of wrong, and where manifest injustice will be done, by sustaining the verdict of the jury. It is not how the Judge considers the testimony, or the impression in his mind, that had he been on the jury, he would have found a different verdict, that should lead to the granting of a new trial. The two departments of trial are distinct. The province of the jury should not be ruthlessly invaded; and, unless he is satisfied from a careful examination of all the evidence, *that the verdict cannot be right*, it should not be disturbed by the Judge.

Another ground is urged, based upon the affidavit of the defendant, stating that, "when the jury came in with a sealed verdict, it was opened and read: that something was then said between the Court and counsel, as to the effect of the verdict's specifying on what count or counts, they found the defendant guilty. That one of the jury said in open court, and before the verdict was recorded in substance, 'that the jury had spoken of *that*, but had not acted upon it, or come to any conclusion whether he was guilty upon one or all of said counts.'" With this affidavit, by no means accurate or corresponding with the recollection of the Court, is there a sufficient foundation laid for a new trial? The case had been given to the jury in the evening, and the defendant assented that they might seal their verdict, and bring it in in the morning. They did so, and on the opening of the Court, the jury being present in their seats, and being called over by the clerk, the sealed verdict was handed in, signed by each juror; saying "that they found the defendant guilty in manner and form as he stands charged in the indictment, and assessed the damages at $83." After the clerk had read it, one of

Kampshall v. Goodman et al.

the counsel for the defendant, addressing the Court, desired to know whether the jury applied their verdict to *all* the counts or any one count in particular. This remark elicited the opposition and comment of the District Attorney; when one of the jurors observing that they had not considered a finding on each count necessary, the Court stopped any further altercation by directing the verdict to be recorded *as written out* and signed by the jury, the paper itself to be filed for further reference; and on the application of defendant's counsel, the jury to be polled. The record shows the result.

"And the jurors aforesaid, being each separately INTERROGATED by THE COURT, whether the foregoing verdict is his verdict as it stands recorded, each for himself separately answers, that it is."

What more is necessary? Where is there room to doubt the action of the jury? Is it not their verdict, twice solemnly assented to by them in open court; once by their names recorded by each in his own hand-writing, and filed on record; and again as solemnly in the presence of the defendant, proclaimed by each juror, as his separate act, and as such, recorded on the Journal of the Court?

Wherefore should such a verdict be set aside? For irregularity? Whose? It was no error of the jury in writing out their verdict, and if they had changed their minds since that act, it was competent to retract or express such change, when specially interrogated by the Court. That they adhered to their written opinion was not error.

New trial refused.

KAMPSHALL *v.* GOODMAN ET AL.

There are two modes by which an action may be revised, after the Statute has barred it.

1. A clear and an unconditional acknowledgment of the debt, from which the law implies a promise to pay.

2. If the acknowledgment be conditional, the liability attaches, under the conditions.

3. But if the acknowledgment be connected with any condition which shows there was no intention to pay the debt, it does not take the case out of the Statute. The action must be on the new promise, the indebtment is considered a sufficient consideration to support the promise.

But the remedy is on the new promise. If the acknowledgment of the debt, be coupled with a proposition to pay it, partly in money and partly in property, the payment can only be enforced as the terms propose. The original debt is not revived, and it is considered only as affording a good consideration on the new promise.

Messrs. Lathrop & Porter for plaintiffs.
Messrs. Terry & Howard for defendant.

OPINION OF THE COURT.

This action is brought on four promissory notes, dated 16th May, 1835, payable at different times; one for five hundred dollars, and the other three for one thousand dollars each; signed by Lowell Goodman, E. S. Goodman, and A. A. Goodman. Lowell Goodman, the father of the other two, being dead, and also E. S. Goodman, process was served on A. A. Goodman, the defendant.

The defendant pleaded the Statute of Limitations, to which the plaintiff replied that, the defendant promised within six years, &c.

The case turns on the new promise. All the notes were admitted in evidence, from which it appears the Statute has run against them, so as to bar a recovery, unless under the plea, a new promise be shown.

The action in assumpsit must be brought, under the act of limitations, within six years after the right of action accrues; but the 13th Section provides, that "in actions founded upon contract, express or implied, no acknowledgment or promise shall be evidence of a continuing contract, whereby to take a case out of the provisions of this chapter, or to deprive any party of the benefit thereof, unless such acknowledgment or promise be made or contained by or in some writing, signed by the party to be charged thereby."

Angell on Limitations accurately and succinctly states the rule to be in this country and in England, as ascertained from decided cases : 1. That a debt barred by the " Statute of limitations, may be revived by a new promise. 2. That such new promise may either be an express promise, or an implied one. 3. That the latter is created by a clear and unqualified acknowledgment of the debt. 4. That if the acknowledgment be accompanied by such qualifying expressions or circumstances, as repel the idea of an intention or contract to pay, no implied promise is created."

The letter on which the new promise is founded, reads as follows: "Mount Clement, May 30th, 1847. Dear Sir : I take the liberty of writing you at this time, more especially for the purpose of obtaining a receipt for the $300 I sent you in October, 1845, in a draft on Buffalo, or one of the notes, should there be one of that amount. The receipt I wish to be given to me as administrator of L. Goodman's estate, which I hope you will forward me soon. It is necessary for me to have a receipt for the $300.

"My only brother was drowned in Detroit last fall. Afflictions have been multiplied upon me in various ways for the last few years, and that old demand of yours on my father's estate, is a subject of no little anxiety. I think (I) could raise some cash to pay you on a month's notice, provided you would take the Willoughby house and lot in Ohio to settle up the whole demand. The house and lot were appraised at $1,333, and $300 I have paid, and I can get from our Cleveland debt $500, which is all we shall probably get; and I can borrow $500 more in cash, provided I can settle the whole demand and give a mortgage on what is left us of the rest of the property, for the $500 we loan. That will make $2,633. The small lot in Ohio was set off for mother, and the house and lot are free from any encumbrance..

"I should be obliged to have some time to raise the cash, and get an order to sell, from the Court in Ohio, to make the conveyance legal.

"I can see no other way for me to raise sufficient to settle with you and the other creditors, but for them to take property; and should you think best to do this, please forward the notes to some one here, and I shall settle it as soon as the sale can be made; or should you not prefer my offer for the estate as above, you will please take the property for your equal share among the creditors, according to the laws of this State. Signed A. A. Goodman."

In this letter, there is a clear and an unequivocal acknowledgment of the indebtment, claimed by the plaintiff. The writer speaks first of a payment of $300, which he had made and for which he requested a receipt, or the surrender of one of the notes.

He then states that the "old demand of the plaintiff," against the estate of his father was a subject of no little anxiety, and he proposes a mode of payment, of property and money, amounting to the sum of $2,638, which was about the balance due on the four notes. As he was jointly and severally bound with his father in all the notes, an acknowledgment of the indebtment would operate against him. But this acknowledgment was coupled with a special mode of payment, in property and money, favorable to the defendant and the estate he represented. And the question arises here, whether this mode of payment must be considered as a condition annexed to the acknowledgment of the debt.

If the acknowledgment can be considered separate and distinct from the mode of payment proposed, there can be no doubt of the plaintiff's right to a judgment. The rule established by the Court is, that an unqualified admission of the indebtment authorises an implied promise to pay, on which an action may be sustained. The original debt is referred to as the foundation of the promise, but the action rests exclusively on the acknowledgment and the implied promise, and not upon the original contract. That is barred by the statute, and cannot be asserted as a ground of recovery. It is not the renewal of the former ground of action, but a new action founded upon the acknowledgment of the original debt and the implied promise.

This, it must be admitted, is a technical device of the Courts, under the Statute, which does not seem necessarily to belong to the subject. The Statute of limitations is founded upon public policy, to protect individuals against stale claims. It is founded at least in part, upon the presumption that where a debt, without an acknowledgment, or payment of interest, is permitted to run beyond the Statute, it has been paid. Now it would seem, that a distinct and an unequivocal acknowledgment of the indebtment, after the Statute had run, should remove the bar and give legal force to the demand. But the current of decisions in our courts is that the acknowledgment does not revive the original cause of action, but is the foundation of a promise on which an action may be sustained.

In the case of *Bell* v. *Morrison*, 1 Peters, 855, this subject was considered at great length, and the Court say: "There is some confusion in the language of the books, resulting from a want of strict attention to the distinctions here indicated. It is often said that an acknowledgment revives the promise, when it is meant, that it revives the debt or cause of action. The revival of a debt supposes that it has been once extinct and gone; that there has been a period in which it had lost its legal use and vitality. The act which revives it, is what essentially constitutes its new being, and is inseparable from it. It stands not by its original force, but by the new promise, which imparts validity to it. Proof of the latter is indispensable to raise the assumpsit on which the action can be maintained. It was this view of the matter which first created the doubt, whether it was not necessary

13a

that a new consideration should be proved to support the promise, since the old consideration was gone. The doubt has been overcome; and it is now held, that the original consideration is sufficient, if recognized, to uphold the new promise, although the Statute cuts it off, as a support for the old. What indeed would seem to be decisive on this subject, is, that if the new promise is qualified or conditional, it restrains the rights of the party to its own terms; and if he cannot recover by those terms, he cannot recover at all."

Here a principle is laid down, and it is this: the action must be brought and sustained on the new promise, with no other reference to the old promise, which is barred, than as the consideration of the new one. If the acknowledgment of the indebtment be clear and unequivocal, and without condition, the law implies a promise to pay; but if terms of payment are connected with the acknowledgment of the debt, the new remedy is on the terms proposed.

Almost numberless citations of decisions might be made, on this question, but they would rather confuse than make clearer the above statement. It embodies the principle upon which the modern decisions under the Statute rest.

It only remains to apply the above principle to the case before us.

In his letter the defendant says, "I think (I) could raise some cash to pay on a month's notice, provided you would take the Willoughby house and lot in Ohio, to settle up the whole demand. The house and lot were appraised at $1333, and $300 I have paid you, and I can get from our Cleveland debt $500, and I can borrow $500 more in cash. That will make $2638," (which sum is about the balance due on the notes.) And if Kempshall the plaintiff, declines this proposition, he proposes to give to him an equal share of the property among the creditors.

Here are two modes of payment proposed. First to pay $2633, about the balance due on the notes, in property and money, some time being given; and if this should be declined, that Kempshall should take his proportionate share of the property with the other creditors. This is the new obligation' assumed on the consideration of the old indebtment; and under the above rule, the remedy must be on the new obligation. Whether it has been so acted on by the plaintiff, as to make it obligatory, is not now a subject of inquiry.

It is true that the defendant was a joint and several promissor with his father, since deceased; and the propositions of payment seemed to refer to the property of the deceased, on which he had administered; but the terms of the new promise must be taken as they were made, seeing the old promise was barred by the Statute.

It appears to me that it would better have promoted the ends of justice, to consider the admission of the subsisting indebtment, as removing the obstruction of the Statute, instead of affording ground for a new action. But the decisions of the Courts have been otherwise, and we are bound by them and especially, by the decision in the case of *Bell* and *Morrison.*

From this view of the case, the verdict which has been found by the jury, must be set aside, and a non-suit entered.

IN ADMIRALTY.

BRIG FASHION *v.* WARD & WARD.

1. A decree in Admiralty is the Judgment of the Court, on the subject in controversy submitted by the pleadings, and must correspond with and apply to that issue.

2. The opinion of the Judge on collateral matters not involved in the Record, is not to be incorporated in the judgment of the Court.

8. When a recovery in damages is sought in case of collision between two vessels, and the proof exhibits fault in both, or no fault in either, and the libel is therefore dismissed, the decree need not set forth the ground assumed by the Court, unless the pleadings presented such issue.

4. Especially will such course be avoided in framing the decree, if the Court is apprised that the same matter is litigated between the parties in another district.

. *H. H. Emmons,* for Libellant.
Frazer, & Gray, for Respondents.

OPINION OF THE COURT BY JUDGE WILKINS.

In this case a motion was made, in open Court, by the Proctors of the Brig Fashion, that a decree be entered dismissing the Libel with costs, according to the judgment of this Court previously pronounced in the case.

After the Court had pronounced its opinion, directing the libel to be dismissed with costs, and one of the Proctors had notified the court of the intention of the libellants to appeal, the Court was requested by the Senior Proctor for the libellants, to direct the Clerk to suspend entering a decree, as the form of the same would be amicably agreed upon by the Solicitors on both sides.

To this, Mr. Gray, the Proctor of the respondents assented.

The Court are now apprised that such agreement cannot be had, and are asked by the motion to direct the decree to be entered as specified in the motion under consideration. This is resisted by the libellants, on the ground, that inasmuch as the Court, in the opinion pronounced, declared, that from the evidence, no fault could be found in the management of the steamer Pacific, and that therefore the collision was the result of inevitable accident, that such conclusion should be incorporated in the decree to be entered of record.

Before proceeding to the trial, the Court was informed that a suit had been instituted in the District of Ohio by the respondents, who had there libelled the steamer Pacific, which suit was still pending and undetermined. The form of the decree is deemed of importance, as the libellants here, desire as defendants there, to arrest further proceedings on the ground that all the matters in controversy have been adjudicated upon by this Court, and determined here.

Such would be their right if such had been the case, in the litigation in this Court, and the form of the decree would be of little consequence, if the pleadings exhibited the same. If to a libel the plea of jurisdiction is alone set up in the answer, and on hearing the libel be dismissed, the decree need not state, as the cause of the dismissal, the want of jurisdiction, for that sufficiently appears by the record of the case, the decree having reference to the issue. What is the decree but the judgment of the Court, on the subject matter submitted,—the judicial determination of the issue? It must correspond with, and apply to that issue.

So far as the opinion of the Judge embraces collateral, or matters not involved in the issue, so far the opinion is but judicial reasoning, and illustration, and cannot and should not be made the basis of, or be incorporated in, the judgment. In the present cause the libel exhibited a case of collision between the Brig Fashion and the Steamer Pacific, and specified certain allegations upon which a recovery in damages was sought. They were these:

1st. The unskilful navigation of the Brig Fashion, in starboarding her helm, when she should have ported; by reason whereof the collision occurred.

2d. The unseamanlike conduct of the officers and crew of the Fashion, in not pursuing her course up the river close to the Canada shore, but suddenly changing that course and crossing the track of the Pacific when it was too late for the latter to avoid a collision.

Thus was gross negligence and fault charged by the libel on the vessel of the respondents.

The answer denied both these averments, and alleged that the course of the Fashion was on the American side of the channel, and that she was not starboarded, and did not cross the track of the steamer.

The evidence was not strictly confined to this issue; other matters were embraced in the examination, and in the argument of the counsel. It was strenuously and ably urged upon the Court, that if the evidence did not make out fault upon the part of the Fashion, yet there was no fault proved upon the part of the Pacific, and that consequently the damages should be apportioned between the colliding vessels. The Court took the whole matter into consideration, and having determined that the preponderance of the testimony was with the respondents, so declared its conviction, and that on the issue presented, the libel must be dismissed, not being sustained. Here the opinion would have rested, and such was the intention of the Court, and is so declared. But the question of the apportionment of damages resting on the circumstances of the collision's being an inevitable accident, the Court went further than the pleadings warranted, and having fully considered and analyzed the testimony in regard to that proposition, could not, from the testimony, come to any more satisfactory conclusion, than that stated at the close of the written opinion. The examination and consideration of the question were due to the able counsel who presented the argument, but were not incorporated in the written opinion as forming the basis of the judgment of the Court.

The language is emphatic, viz: "the libellants having failed to establish fault in the Fashion, the libel must of course be dismissed."

Although still of the opinion that the preponderance of the testimony as to the speed of the Pacific, the only point determined by the court, was no more than the necessary steerage power under the circumstances, yet I cannot conscientiously so direct the form of the decree, as to preclude the respondents from recovering in their suit, by a prejudgment in this Court, when the defense of 'casualty is not set up in their answer, and the point was not directly specified in the issue.

I more readily adopt this course, as the libellants have notified the Court of their intention to appeal, which is attended without cost, where the testimony can be more minutely examined with reference to this point, and where my error of judgment, can and will be corrected by the Circuit Judge, and consequently where no damages but the delay of a few months can accrue to the libellants.

H. H. Emmons & Newberry, for Libellants.
Frazer, Vandyke & Gray, for Respondents.

DISTRICT COURT OF THE UNITED STATES.

ILLINOIS.—OCTOBER TERM, 1854.

~~~~~~~~~~~~

MARGARET B. LANE *v.* CHARLES DOLICK ET AL.

1. By the laws of Illinois, when a married woman, who is a resident of the State, conveys her real property by deed, it is the acknowledgment that gives effect to the deed, and that must be made substantially in conformity with the law; and if not so made, the deed is invalid.

2. The form of acknowledgment, when a *femme covert* pleads her right of dower, is different from that by which she transfers her estate of inheritance.

3. Where a *femme covert* was the owner of real estate in fee, and executed a deed with her husband, purporting to convey the estate, and the acknowledgment to the deed was in substance a mere relinquishment of dower, *held* that the deed did not convey the estate of the wife.

Messrs. *N. W. & B. S. Edwards*, for plaintiff.

Mr. *Logan*, for defendants.

OPINION OF JUDGE DRUMMOND.

This is an action of ejectment brought by Mrs. Lane against the defendants, for the west half of lot 43 and the west half of lot 15, in Belleville, Madison County. It is admitted by both parties, that on the 6th of July, 1834, the title to the property was in the plaintiff as her estate of inheritance, she, at that time, being a *femme covert*. On that day, Mrs. Lane and her husband, both being residents of Illinois, executed a deed, through which the defendants claim. The deed was acknowledged on the 8th of July, 1834. Mrs.

Lane's husband died in 1847, and since his death she has brought this action. A jury has been waived, and both law and fact submitted to the Court. The case depends upon the effect to be given to the deed already mentioned. In the deed both Mrs. Lane and her husband are named as grantors, and the body of the deed is in the usual form. The certificate to this deed is as follows: The officer certified that there appeared before him, "James S. Lane and Margaret B., his wife, known to me to be the persons whose names are subscribed to the written instrument of writing, and acknowledged the same to be their free and voluntary act and deed, for the purposes therein mentioned; and the wife of the said James S. Lane being by me examined separate and apart from her said husband, and the contents of the within instrument of writing fully made known to her, she declared that she signed, sealed, and delivered the same, of her own free will and accord, and that she relinquished her dower in the premises therein mentioned, voluntarily and freely, without coercion or compulsion of her said husband."

The Statute under which this deed was acknowledged, declares that the officer " shall make her acquainted with, and explain to her the contents of such deed or conveyance, and examine her separate and apart from her husband, whether she executed the same voluntarily and freely, and without compulsion of her said husband; and if such woman shall, upon such examination, acknowledge such deed or conveyance to be *her act and deed*, that she executed the same voluntarily and freely, and without compulsion of her husband, and does not wish to retract," the officer shall make a certificate, "*setting forth* that the contents were made known and explained to her, and *the examination and acknowledgment aforesaid*," and " *such deed*" shall be as effectual to pass the title as if she were sole and unmarried.

Our law is different from the law of many of the states, in

requiring the certificate to set forth the particular facts which must concur to render the deed valid.

The certificate in this case states that the wife was examined separate and apart from her husband, and the contents of the deed were fully made known to her. The law required that it should appear that the officer made her acquainted with, *and explained* to her, the contents of the deed. In *Hughes* v. *Lane*, 11 Illinois Reports, 123, the Supreme Court of this state held, that the words "was made acquainted with the contents of the written deed," were equivalent to the words; "that the contents were made known and explained to her;" and if this is correct, then it follows that the words in this case, "and the contents of the within instrument of writing [being] fully made known to her," are also equivalent to the words of the Statute. That was the case of a conveyance by a *femme covert*, of two lots of land, to one of which she had the right of dower, and to the other the fee; and, it is to be observed, the certificate contained some of the words necessary when a married woman relinquishes her dower alone, and the Court seemed to have overlooked the difference between the law for the relinquishment of dower and that for the conveyance of the wife's fee, or they laid no stress on that difference. Now it was all one law, January 31, 1827, with different provisions; and when the wife was to relinquish her dower, she did it by joining her husband in the deed, and the officer acquainted her with the contents, and then, on an examination separate and apart from her husband, he has to ascertain whether she relinquished her dower. The object of this part of the law is to declare how the wife's dower may be released. Then, in the next section of the same law, it is declared how a married woman shall convey her own real estate, which is, by executing with her husband a deed for the conveyance of her land; and after its execution, the officer shall make her acquainted with, *and explain* to her, the contents of such deed. Now, it would seem as though this alteration of the phraseology, this addition to the sentence, was not without a purpose. In the case of dower, the wife grants nothing. She joins in the deed, and makes the proper acknowledgment to relinquish her dower. The officer acquaints her with the contents of the deed, and asks her whether she executed it and relinquished her dower freely, etc. In the case of a conveyance by a *femme covert* of her estate, she executes the deed to grant the inheritance, and as has often been decided, the deed must contain words of grant by her. *Agricultural Bank* v. *Rice*, 4 Howard's Reports, 241. And to give effect to the deed as a grant from her, she must not only be made acquainted with the contents of the deed, but they must be explained to her, the Legislature appearing to think that it was quite possible, as all experience proves, that a woman might be made acquainted with the contents of the deed and yet not understand it; that is, she might read it, or hear it read, and yet not comprehend its effect. In Kentucky, the law required the deed to be shown and explained to the *femme covert,* and the Court, in *Nantz* v. *Bailey*, 8 Dana, 114, say, it is necessary that the nature and effect of the deed should have been first explained to her. "It was the duty of the clerk, when ·he made the privy examination, to show and explain the deed, so as to have enabled the wife, in the absence of her husband, to understand truly the legal effect of the act she was about to acknowledge, and if he omitted to make the required explanation, the acknowledgment was void. The only explanation the clerk could or should make was, that by the deed, if she should acknowledge it voluntarily and understandingly, she would forever relinquish her fee simple right." It shows clearly that the Court did not understand that a mere reading of the deed would in all cases be sufficient, *Miller* v. *Shackleford*, 3 Dana, 291. Our Statute is even stronger than that of Kentucky, but, as already stated, the Supreme Court have decided that if she were made ac-

quainted with the contents of the deed, they were explained
to her, that is, it is one and the same thing. The object of
these remarks will become apparent hereafter.

The certificate in this case does not contain the words "and
does not wish to retract," and, in this respect, is like the
certificate in *Hughes* v. *Lane,* in which case the Court held
it was not necessary the certificate should contain those
words, saying, they were inserted in the statute to afford a
married woman an opportunity to avoid a deed, by informing
the officer that she wished to retract, notwithstanding she
had voluntarily executed it. The Court admit there may be
a question whether this is the proper construction of the law,
and say, they think it capable of that construction, and that
it was the duty of the Court, if possible, to adopt such a
construction as would uphold rather than destroy titles. I
agree that we should give a fair, and, it may be, a liberal
construction to these laws for the purpose mentioned; but still
we must look to the law as our guide, and not destroy and
impair its provisions piece-meal, and while we insist the law
must be observed, by our decisions contradict our professions.
The law makes the acknowledgment a solemn act, and gives
it all the sanctity of a record, and will not suffer it to be
changed by parol. It is that which gives validity to the
deed, and without it the wife's interest in her estate will
not pass. *Mariner* v. *Saunders,* 5 Gilman's Reports, 125;
Elliott v. *Peirsol,* 1 Peters' Reports, 828; *Hepburn* v. *Dubois,*
12 Peters' Reports, 374.

In the case referred to, of *Hughes* v. *Lane,* the Court expressly waive giving any opinion as to whether the certificate
of acknowledgment, showing that the *femme* had released her
dower only, would be sufficient. That is the question to be
decided in this case.

What is the acknowledgment here? The officer certifies
that he examined the wife separate and apart from her
husband, and the contents of the deed were fully made known

Margaret B. Lane v. Charles Dolick et al.

to her, and this examination having taken place, she declared that she signed, sealed, and delivered the deed of her own free will and accord, and that she relinquished her dower in the premises therein mentioned, voluntarily and freely, without coercion or compulsion of her husband. If it was an acknowledgment certified under this part of the law for the relinquishment of dower, it would be she acknowledged that she executed the deed and relinquished her dower in the premises therein mentioned, voluntarily and freely, and without compulsion of her husband. "Of her own free will and accord," is nothing more than voluntarily and freely in the release of dower. I can only look on it, therefore, as in substance an acknowledgment of the relinquishment of dower. It raises, then, the question whether the certificate of the relinquishment of dower is sufficient.

The true rule is this : If it clearly appear from the certificate, that the law has been substantially complied with, that the wife understood the nature and character of the transaction, that is sufficient. Does that appear in this case? Let us assume the necessary hypothesis. She had executed a deed with her husband, conveying her estate. This she knew; she appeared before the officer for the purpose of acknowledging the fact. Does she declare that the conveyance is her act and deed; that she executed the same voluntarily and freely, and without compulsion of her husband, and does not wish to retract, on the private examination? No. She declares she executed it of her own free will and accord, and relinquished her dower in the premises, or this the officer states in his certificate. If she did, and we must take this as true, is it not manifest she did not know what her estate was, or that she supposed she was granting something different from what she in fact had the right to grant? Does it affirmatively appear there was that intelligent understanding of the transaction on her part, which is necessary to give validity to such a contract? It seems to me this declaration made by her, shows that she did not fully understand what she was doing; and I think it most probable, nay, certain, that the officer who took the acknowledgment and wrote it, did not himself understand that the wife was conveying her own estate, but supposed she was merely releasing her dower to her husband's land. I do not go the extent of saying that whenever an acknowledgment contains a relinquishment of dower, it follows as a necessary consequence, in all cases, that the wife's estate will not pass; but I hold that when there is such acknowledgment, it raises a strong presumption in itself, that the wife did not fully understand her position and her rights, and there should be sufficient in the acknowledgment to rebut that presumption, to show clearly she knew she was passing an estate of inheritance. If it be said very few married women know what dower means, or the difference between that and an estate in fee, it is only an additional reason why the law and the courts should give every possible opportunity for her to become acquainted with her rights before she divests herself of her estate. It seems to me, if the guards which have so long been thrown around the estates of married women as a shield against the improvidence, folly, or imprudence of the husband, are to be removed, it must be by the Legislature, and not by the courts.

It has been held in many cases, that if the acknowledgment only contains a relinquishment of dower, it is not sufficient to pass an estate in fee, and in Missouri under a Statute precisely like ours, it was held insufficient, though the acknowledgment would have been ample without the relinquishment of dower. *McDaniel* v. *Priest*, 12 Missouri, 545; *Gregory* v. *Ford*, 5 B. Monroe's Reports, 482; *Lewis* v. *Richardson*, 7 Monroe's Reports, 66; *Barnett* v. *Shackleford*, 6 J. J. Marshall's Reports, 532; *Powell* v. *Mason*, etc., 3 Mason's Reports, 347; *Raymond* v. *Holden*, 2 Cushing's Reports, 264; *Bruce* v. *Wood*, 1 Metcalf's Reports, 542.

If we adopt the construction contended for by the defendants' counsel, then we strike out all of the words after "free will and accord," as surplusage; and in that event we leave out the words "without the compulsion of her husband," because as it reads in the certificate, these words apply not to the execution of the deed, but to the relinquishment of dower. It is said the words "of her own free will and accord," are the same thing in substance as the words of the Statute. I am not quite prepared to concede this. The Statute uses the words "voluntarily and freely,', and if these words were employed, it might with the same propriety be insisted that was enough; but the law has superadded other words. However, I do not put the decision so much on this ground, as on the one already stated. It has sometimes been said that unless the certificate showed that the wife did understand what she did, if she has the legal means of understanding, it is sufficient. Some such language is used in the case reported in 3 *Dana,* already mentioned and cited by the Court, in *Hughes* v. *Lane;* but that was a case where the wife said she relinquished her inheritance in the land, and nothing is said about dower; and the law of Kentucky, while like ours it requires several facts to concur to render the wife's deed to her property valid, did not like ours, require that all these material facts should be set forth by the officer, and the courts of Kentucky have uniformly held, if the necessary facts were not set forth, they will presume the other facts, *Gregory* v. *Ford,* 5 B. Monroe 482. But as already stated, they have also held that an acknowledgment like this, which showed only a release of dower, was insufficient to free the life estate.

We may now apply some remarks that were heretofore made. If the words in this acknowledgment, "the contents of the deed were fully made known to her," are to be presumed to mean that she was acquainted with the contents, and they were explained to her, what are we to infer when the certificate shows that if any explanation was made, it was an erro-

neous one? or that the officer did not know what interest the
wife was passing, and therefore could not explain? If
this acknowledgment be sufficient, then all that courts have
to do, is, not to look to the certificate to ascertain what estate
is transferred, but to the kind of estate the wife had, and if
she makes the acknowledgment necessary to convey the fee,
and has it not, her dower passes, or if she makes the acknowledgment necessary to release dower, and has it not,
then the fee passes; that is, we are to adapt the words to the
estate, and give an effect to the deed contrary to its plain import, and contrary to the provisions of the Statute. Are
we prepared to go this length? And it seems as though we
must, for I see no distinction in principle between the two
cases. I will go far to sustain titles, but in *Hughes* v. *Lane*
there is obviously a strong effort on the part of the majority
of the Court to support a deed that was supposed to be all
fair and just, but it seemes to me they have, to say the least,
gone quite far enough, and I do not feel inclined to go beyond even that case, as I would be obliged to do, if I held this
acknowledgment good. It has also been said here, that it
was the clear intention to transfer the fee. It may be so.
But where can the Court look for that intention except to the
certificate, and to the law applicable to it? It is clear that
is the only safe guide. Some complaint has been made of
the hardship of this case upon the defendants, but we must
put these cases upon some principle that we can stand on,
and not shift our ground with every new deed that comes up.
Parties when they are purchasing estates must exercise some
degree of vigilance as to their titles, and if they are wanting
in this respect, they alone are in fault.

I have gone into a more minute and critical examination of
the phraseology of the Statute than I otherwise should, on
account of the stress that was laid on the case of *Hughes* v.
Lane in the argument. If that case governed this I should
feel obliged to follow it as a rule of property binding upon

Courts of the United States; but as I understand that case, the question involved in this is left open, and consequently I am at liberty to decide it according to my own views of the law.

The issue and judgment will therefore be for the plaintiff.

COLUMBUS INSURANCE CO. v. CURTENIUS ET AL.

1. The whole legislation from the ordinance of 1787 to the present time, clearly indicates that Congress has intended that the Mississippi and its navigable tributaries should remain free from all material obstruction to their navigation.

2. A State cannot authorize any material obstruction to be placed in the channel of a navigable tributary of the Mississippi.

3. The declaration alleged that the defendants had placed piers in the principal channel of the river Illinois, so as essentially to obstruct its navigation, and that in consequence of such obstruction a loss was sustained. The defendants pleaded that in placing the piers there they had complied with an Act of the Legislature of Illinois, authorizing a bridge to be constructed. *Held* that the plea was not a good defense to the action, but that it must go further, and deny that the bridge was a material obstruction to the navigation of the river.

Messrs. *Lincoln & Chumasero*, for the plaintiffs.
Messrs. *Logan & Powell*, for the defendants.

OPINION OF JUDGE DRUMMOND.

This is an action brought by the plaintiffs as insurers of a canal-boat and cargo of wheat, which were lost by the canal-boat's striking the piers of the bridge built by the defendants, near Peoria, while on the passage from Peru to St. Louis, and which loss the plaintiffs have been obliged to pay. The canal-boat was towed by the steamer Falcon at the time of the loss, 19th March, 1849.

The declaration alleges that the defendants *placed piers in the principal channel of the Illinois river, a navigable river*

14a

free to all the citizens of the United States, so as essentially to obstruct the navigation of the same, and that *in consequence of such obstruction* the loss above mentioned occurred. There are different counts, varying the form of the statement, but this is the substance in each.

There are several pleas put in by the defendants which rely upon the following defense. That by an Act of the Legislature of Illinois, of 26th January, 1847, they were authorized to erect the bridge, and place as many piers in the bed of the river as might be necessary for the support and construction of the bridge, *provided a space of at least seventy-five feet from pier to pier, and embracing the principal channel of the river be left and always kept open for the passage of all craft navigating the river,* and they aver that the demands of the law have been complied with, and particularly that they have in the precise language of the above proviso, left and kept open the proper space, embracing the principal channel, for the passage of all craft navigating the river.

A demurrer has been interposed to these pleas, and the question for the Court to determine is, whether the matters stated in the pleas constitute a defense to the action. In other words, had the State of Illinois the power to authorize the construction of such a bridge? This is the only question which has been argued.

The allegation by the plaintiffs is, that the piers which have been placed in the principal channel of the river by the defendants, essentially obstruct its navigation. The only way in which this is met by the defendants, is by the statement that they have kept open a space of seventy-five feet, embracing the principal channel, for the passage of all craft navigating the river. If, therefore, under the law as it stands and the pleadings in this case, the defendants should establish that they had left a space of seventy-five feet, embracing the principal channel, for the passage of river craft, that would be a complete defense to the action, though it might be true that the piers were so placed as to constitute an essential obstruction to the navigation of the river, and by reason thereof the plaintiffs suffered the damage complained of. And as a necessary deduction from this we must admit that if the Legislature should declare that a certain space left in a navigable river was sufficient for the free navigation of the same, that declaration would be binding and conclusive on all the world. And, in fact, that is the ground assumed on the argument by the defendants' counsel, and they have even gone further, if this indeed is going further, and insisted that the State had the right totally to obstruct the navigation of the river. It will be seen, therefore, that the question, as it is now presented, is not whether Illinois had the power to authorize the construction of a bridge across a navigable stream, provided it did not essentially impede the navigation of the river ; neither is it, whether this particular bridge, built by the defendants, is an essential obstruction, because that is a question of fact to be determined by evidence ; but whether the Court will presume that it is not an obstruction, because the defendants have left open a passage of seventy-five feet, in opposition to the assertion placed upon the record that it is.

The first point to be determined is, whether the river Illinois, over which this bridge has been erected, is in law a navigable river free to all citizens. The tide does not ebb and flow there, and technically, according to the common law, it is not navigable, though it is so in fact. But, even if it is considered navigable, and if in this respect it stands upon the same footing as rivers where the tide ebbs and flows, it does not follow that the power of the State is not plenary over it, because, as we shall see hereafter, the States have in some instances totally obstructed navigable streams. The question is, is it navigable *and* is it free?

By the ordinance for the government of the Territory north-west of the river Ohio, of 1787, it was provided (Art.

4) that the navigable waters leading into the Mississippi and St. Lawrence should be common high-ways, and forever free to all the citizens of the United States.

It is said that this provision of the ordinance is not in force. This seems to be the doctrine now established by the Supreme Court of the United States, contrary to what has been the general understanding for many years, in the States carved out of that Territory. *Permoli* v. *The First Municipality*, 8 *Howard*, 589; *Pollard* v. *Hagan*, 3 *Howard*, 212; *Strader* v. *Graham*, 10 *Howard*, 82.

It was never doubted but that any provisions of the ordinance which were contrary to the Constitution of the United States, and the laws passed in pursuance thereof, or to the Constitutions of the States formed out of that Territory were abrogated, because the " common consent " mentioned in the ordinance was then presumed. But it seems certain that Congress did not exactly regard the ordinance as at an end, by the adoption of the Constitution of the United States, as is plain from the very first law on the subject *adapting* it to the Constitution, 1 *Stat. at Large*, 50. And in allowing the various States which were formed out of that Territory to adopt State governments, provision was made that they should not do anything repugnant to the ordinance, with certain specified exceptions. As to Ohio, Act of April 30th, 1802, Sec. 5, 2 *Stat. at Large*, 173. As to Indiana, Act of April 19th, 1816, Sec. 4, 3 *Stat. at Large*, 289. As to Illinois, Act of April 18th, 1818, Sec. 4, 3 *Stat. at Large*, 428. And the same is true of the States since admitted, Michigan and Wisconsin. And Congress extended the provisions of this ordinance, except the introductory clause, over some of the south-western States. But without dwelling upon this part of the subject, which is only mentioned for the purpose of showing how fully this ordinance was followed up by Congress, let us see how the question stands upon Acts of Congress passed from time to time since the organization of the Gov-

ernment. The Government started with the declaration that
the navigable waters leading into the Mississippi should be
common high-ways and forever free.   It is said by the Court
in the case of *Strader* v. *Graham*, already referred to, that
the new Government (Constitution and Laws of the United
States) secured to the people of the north-western States *all
the public rights of navigation and commerce* which the ordinance did or could provide for.   It would be a curious commentary upon this language to say that the Western States
can materially obstruct or dam up the great navigable rivers
within their borders.   But the legislation of Congress seems
to warrant the opinion expressed by the Court.   Besides the
Acts already referred to, many others may be mentioned as
indicating the views of Congress as to Western rivers.   In
the Act providing for the sale of lands north-west of the
Ohio and above the mouth of the Kentucky, of May 18th,
1796, 1 *Stat. at Large*, 464, the ninth section declares that all
navigable rivers within the Territory to be disposed of by that
Act, shall be deemed to be and *remain* public high-ways.
And so in relation to the rivers within certain boundaries, by
the 6th sec. of the Act of June 1st, 1796, 1 *Stat. at Large*, 491.
The same provision was'applied to all the rivers of the Indiana
Territory, North of the Ohio and East of the Mississippi, of
which Illinois then formed a part, by the sixth section of the
Act of March 26th, 1804, 2 *Stat. at L.*, 277; the 17th section
of the Act of March 3rd, 1803, 2 *Stat. at L.*, 235, made the
same rule applicable to all navigable rivers within the Territory of the United States South of the State of Tennessee.
And so, as to the navigable waters in Louisiana, Act of Feb.
20th, 1811, sec. 3.   And it was an express condition of her
admission into the Union, that the Mississippi and the navigable waters leading into the same should be forever free, Act
of April 8th, 1812, 2 *Stat. at L.*, 642, 703.   The same rule
was applied to the rivers of Alabama, Act of March 2d, 1819.
And to Mississippi, Act of March 1st, 1817, 8 *Stat. at L.*,

492, 849. And to Missouri, Act of June 4th, 1812, sec. 15, 2 *Stat at L.*, 747. Indeed, without proceeding further, it may be safely affirmed that in no instance has Congress permitted an occasion to pass without declaring that the Mississippi and its navigable tributaries shall remain public high-ways and forever free. These various enactments clearly prove the extraordinary solicitude with which Congress has from the very foundation of the Government watched over this subject. It would seem impossible to misapprehend the motive of such legislation.

But it is said, that the new States having come into the Union upon an equal footing with the original States, these various laws in relation to the navigable rivers are not binding on the new States, unless as regulations of commerce, and that, being contained in land laws, most of them are mere Territorial regulations, and temporary in their character. Now, it is immaterial whether Congress has legislated under the impression that a part of the ordinance of 1787 was still in force, although it is not; provided it is apparent from its whole tenor of legislation that it has re-enacted such part and given it continued operation. And that does seem to be the fact in this instance. If we find a law of Congress, and more especially if we find a series of laws all tending to the same result, the main question is not, whether Congress was looking to this or that part of the Constitution for the power to enact, but is the power in the instrument? If it is, it is a binding, valid law, no matter what part of the Constitution Congress was thinking of at the time of its passage. It has sometimes happened that Congress has passed laws as they supposed under one part of the Constitution, and the Supreme Court has given them effect under another. I think, therefore, that Congress has intended, and carried that intent into effect, to make the Mississippi, and the navigable waters leading into it from this State, common public high-ways and free to all the citizens of the United States. To hold otherwise would be in effect to decide that Illinois and Missouri, or Illinois and Iowa would have the right to shut up the Mississippi river anywhere above a port of entry, if indeed it may be considered thus qualified. For though it has been thought that there is some magic power about a port of entry, it will be found, on examination, that the distinction which is sometimes taken between navigable waters above and below a port of entry, is rather fanciful than real.

If, then, Congress has legislated rightfully on this subject, the next thing to be considered is, how far that legislation has restricted the power of the States. Do the navigable rivers declared free by Congress stand upon the same footing, and not otherwise, as rivers where the tide ebbs and flows? If there is no difference, then the subject is by no means free from difficulty, because the States have in some instances partially, and in others, totally obstructed rivers navigable at common law. In Massachusetts, the doctrine seems to be maintained that the State has the power materially to obstruct the navigation of a river. In the *Commonwealth* v. *Breed*, 4 *Pick.*, 460, it was proved that a bridge built over a navigable stream prevented the passage of vessels that were accustomed to pass there before. And the Court say that it was a power that had been exercised from the commencement of that Government without objection. And they say further that, though great vigilance has been exercised in requiring bridges to be provided with suitable draws for the passage of vessels, yet in some instances the passage of vessels of a description which before had been accustomed to pass had been entirely prevented. And they say it rests with the Legislature to determine when the public convenience requires these partial obstructions. There seems to have been no question made as to what would have been the effect of the exercise of the power of Congress to regulate commerce.

The Supreme Court of the United States have gone even further than the Court of Massachusetts. The State of Delaware had authorized the erection of a dam across a navigable stream, and it was erected accordingly. Some persons navigating the creek with a vessel licensed and enrolled, took away the dam as an unlawful obstruction to the navigation. Suit was brought, and the question was raised as to the power of the State to erect the obstruction. And the Supreme Court, in conceding the power to the State, do it upon the express ground that Congress had not legislated on the subject, admitting that it would be different if Congress had ever exercised the power with which it was vested. *Wilson* v. *The Black Bird Creek Marsh Co.*, 2 *Peters*, 245.

In New York, the right of a State has been placed on somewhat narrower ground. The Legislature of New York had authorized the construction of a bridge across the Hudson river, at Troy, where the tide ebbed and flowed, and it was navigable; but it was required to be done so that the stream should be restored to its former state, or in such manner as not to impair its usefulness. An information was filed on the part of the State, alleging that the place where the bridge was built was an arm of the sea, in which the tide ebbed and flowed, and navigable for vessels trading in pursuance of the Acts of Congress. The defendants relied upon the Act of the Legislature, and averred that they had left over the main or principal part of the channel an opening for a convenient and suitable draw to enable vessels navigating the river to pass and repass, and so as to restore the river to its former state, or in a sufficient manner not to have impaired its usefulness as a public navigable river. The point was thus made as to the power of the State to give the authority. It will be observed that there was no averment on the part of the people that the bridge, as constructed, essentially obstructed the navigation of the river. *The People* v. *Saratoga and Rensselaer Railroad Co.*, 15 *Wend.*, 113. The Court decided that it was the exercise of a valid power, but say, that the place where the bridge was built is one which coasting vessels have a right to pass, and where any obstruction *entirely preventing or essentially impeding* the navigation would be unlawful. They admit that a power exists in the States to erect bridges over navigable waters, if the wants of society require them, provided such bridges do not essentially injure the navigation of the waters which they cross. But they say that the power must be considered as surrendered by the States, so far as may be necessary for a free navigation.

As has been already mentioned, the ordinance of 1787, with the exception of the anti-slavery article, was extended over some of the south-western States, for instance, over Alabama. By that ordinance the new States were to be admitted into the Union upon an equal footing with the original States in all respects whatever. This applied to Illinois and to Alabama. It was a trust which the general Government was obliged to fulfill. But when Alabama was admitted into the Union, there was a compact made by which all navigable waters within the State were to remain public high-ways, and free to all citizens of the United States. And the Supreme Court say, in *Pollard's Lessee* v. *Hagan*, already cited, that this compact would be void, if inconsistent with the Constitution of the United States. Alabama being equal with the other States, no restriction could be imposed on that State which Congress had not the right to impose upon others. If in the exercise of the power, Congress could impose th same restrictions upon the other States as were imposed by that compact on Alabama, then it was a mere regulation of commerce among the several States, and therefore as binding on the other States as on Alabama; that is, as binding, if the power was exercised by Congress: for obviously they do not mean to be understood as asserting that Congress could not exercise this power as to some of the navigable rivers of the United States, leaving it dormant as to others. And they conclude, as by the compact Congress had no more power over Alabama than over the original States, it was nothing more than a regulation of commerce to that extent among the several States.

It will be remembered that it had been decided in the leading case of *Gibbons* v. *Ogden*, 9 Wheaton, 1, that the power to regulate commerce included the power to regulate navigation. If this be nearer to the circumstances under which Illinois was admitted into the Union, it will be difficult to distinguish between the two States in this respect. The ordinance of 1787 was extended to Alabama; but that ordinance only referred to the rivers leading into the Mississippi and St. Lawrence. Many of the rivers of Alabama flowed into the Gulf of Mexico, and therefore, when in 1819, it was proposed that State should be admitted into the Union, it was one of the conditions, and, Alabama acceding to it, it became a compact of admission, that *all* the navigable rivers within the State should be forever free. This being so, the only question was whether there was anything for the compact to rest upon in the Constitution of the United States. And the Supreme Court, as already mentioned in the case cited, decided that there was. Now it is not unimportant to observe, that in the resolution of Congress admitting Alabama into the Union, it speaks of the ordinance of 1787, as articles of compact between the original States and the people and States in the Territory North West of the Ohio, and the same language is used in many of the acts of Congress when referring to this ordinance. And in the act of Congress authorising the people of the Illinois Territory to form a State government, it is required that their Constitution shall not be repugnant to the ordinance of 1787, between the original States and the people and states of the Terrritory north west of the river Ohio. And the very preamble of the Constitution of Illinois sets forth, that " the people of the Illinois Territory, having the right of admission into the general Government, as a member of the Union, consistent with the Constitution of the United States, the ordinance of Congress of 1787," &c.,

And when Illinois was admitted into the Union, on the 3d of
December, 1817, the resolution referred to the ordinance as
articles of compact between the original States and the people and States in the Territory north west of the river Ohio.
There is great reason for saying, therefore, independently of
the various statutes which have been referred to, that if the
ordinance of 1787 is not in force in Illinois *propria vigore*
this part of it which we are now speaking of, is in force by
virtue of the compact which may be said to have been made
since the adoption of the Constitution, between the United
States and the States formed out of the north west Territory,
and that the compact is binding on the States of the north
west Territory, for the same reason that it is binding on Alabama, Mississippi or Louisiana.   However this may be, that
Congress has always understood that the navigable rivers of
the north west leading into the Mississippi were free public
highways, and so treated them, is most manifest.   It may
without exaggeration be said, that it has exercised in this respect, from the very foundation of the government, a vigilance
that has never slept.   Judge Woodbury, in giving a very elaborate opinion in the case of the *United States* vs. *The New
Bedford Bridge*, 1 Wood. & Minot, 401, says, that he has no
doubt that the power to regulate commerce, vested in Congress, authorizes it to keep open and free all navigable streams
from the ocean to the highest ports of delivery or entry, if
no higher, and to protect the intercourse between two or more
States in all our tide waters.   In *Washington Bridge* v.
The State, 18 Connec. R., 53, there had been a bridge erected
across the Housatonic, below a port of delivery.   This was
one of the objections taken, but the Court refused to express
an opinion on that point, deciding the case upon other grounds.

There is a case not yet finally decided, but which is reported
on an interlocutory order in 9 Howard, 647, *Pennsylvania* v. *the
Wheeling and Belmont Bridge Co.*, which it may not be improper
to refer to.*   In that case no particular stress seems to have

* Since finally decided, 13 Howard, 519.

been laid on the fact that Pittsburgh was a port of entry, and it was not noticed in the pleadings that were originally filed in the Supreme Court. The State of Pennsylvania made application for the removal of the bridge at Wheeling, on the ground that it was an obstruction to the navigation of the Ohio, a navigable river, free to all the citizens of the United States. The defendants justified under charters from Virginia and Ohio, that they had complied with the provisions of the charters. There was a section in the charter from Virginia, which provided that if the defendants built a bridge which should be an obstruction to the river as usually navigated, it should be abated as a nuisance. The defendants admitted that the Ohio river was a free navigable river, but insisted that it did not essentially obstruct the navigation of the same, and introduced and relied upon an act of the Legislature of Virginia, of January 11, 1850; which declared that the bridge built was in conformity with law. This of course was equivalent to saying that the bridge, as erected, was not an obstruction to the navigation of the river. And yet it is clear that the Supreme Court did not consider this act of the Legislature of Virginia as conclusive upon all the world, because the main question referred to the commissioner, by the interlocutory order of the Court, was to take proof whether or not the bridge was an obstruction to the free navigation of the Ohio river. And it is upon this report of the commission, that the cause is now being argued on the final hearing.

In this case, to adopt the reasoning of the defendants would be in effect to admit that the act of the Legislature could not be examined; in other words, that no citizen who was injured by an illegal act of the Legislature could go behind it to show its illegality. It seems to me, therefore, that the pleas ought to go further than they have done, and they must deny that the bridge is a material obstruction, so that the plaintiffs may show, if they can do so, that it is, and that in consequence thereof, they have sustained the damage mentioned in the declaration.

GEORGE FOSTER *v.* THE SCHOONER MIRANDA.

1. The 5th section of the act of Congress of 3d March, 1849, required a vessel navigating the lakes in the night, while on the starboard tack, to show a red light, and a vessel having the wind free, a white light. It also required sailing *vessels* to have reflectors to their lights, and that they should be such as to insure a good and sufficient light, as well as *propellers* and *steamers.*

2. In a collision, in the night, between a brig and a schooner, at the foot of Lake Michigan, the weight of the evidence is that the brig, close hauled on the wind on the starboard tack, had a white light. This was in violation of the act of Congress and was such a fault as to preclude the brig from recovering full indemnity for the damage done by the collision, which occurred while the brig carried such a light.

3. The act of 1849 did not intend to abrogate the rules which have been generally observed for the management of vessels: it only added a new one. But it once being established that the brig had the wrong light, the burden of proving that the loss was not the consequence of it, is thrown upon the b ig. The proof clearly shows that, at the time of the collision, the schooner had not a competent look-out. The schooner also should have kept away and not held on her course. It cannot be said, therefore, within the meaning of the act of 1849 that the loss *resulted* entirely from the neglect of the brig to carry the proper light.

4. Both vessels were in fault, and the loss was divided equally between them.

Mr. Hurd, for libellant.
Mr. Goodrich, for claimant.

OPINION OF JUDGE DRUMMOND.

This is a libel filed by the owner of the brig S. F. Gale, against the schooner Miranda, for damages sustained by the brig, from a collision with the schooner in the fall of 1849.

The brig S. F. Gale from Chicago with a load of wheat, was proceeding down the lake on her way to Buffalo. When near the foot of Lake Michigan, off Point Wabbeshanks, not far from the light-ship stationed near that Point, about three o'clock in the morning of the 11th of October, the collision took place. The wind was south-south-east. The brig was close hauled upon the wind with her starboard tacks above, steering nearly east. It was a clear star-light night, and a vessel could be discerned and a brig distinguished from a schooner a mile or more distant. Some time before the collision occurred, the light carried by the Miranda, was seen from the S. F. Gale, two points on her bow. The man at the helm was ordered to keep the brig clear to the wind, because the light of the Miranda indicated a vessel approaching from an easterly direction. The brig was accordingly kept as clear to the wind as possible. The Miranda was bound up the lake, on a voyage from Cleveland to Chicago, and was standing about west by north, and consequently had the wind free. Some time before the collision those on board of the Miranda had seen the light of the brig, and, believing it a white light, supposed it was a vessel on the same course with themselves, and immediately preceding the collision, the watch on the deck of the Miranda had gone aft to lower the peak, with a view to haul round the light-ship—a usual and proper precaution—the captain being at the helm. As the two vessels approached, the mate of the brig shouted to those on the schooner, not to run into them. When this was done the helm of the schooner was put hard-a-port, and that of the brig put down; but the vessels ran so near that at that moment, when apparently for the first time those on each vessel entertained apprehension of a collision, it was impossible to prevent them from meeting, and the Miranda struck the S. F. Gale on the larboard bow near the forerigging. Both vessels were injured, but the brig suffered the most.

By the 5th section of the act of Congress, of 3d of March, 1849, making appropriations for light-houses, &c., and for other purposes, 9 *Statutes at L.*, 382, vessels, steamboats and propellers navigating the northern and western lakes, are required to comply with certain regulations "for the security of life and property," among which are the following:—Dur-

Foster *v* The Miranda.

ing the night, vessels on the starboard tack shall show a red light, and vessels going off large or before the wind, a white light; and it is provided, "if loss or damage shall occur, the owner or owners of the vessel, steamboat or propeller neglecting to comply with these regulations, shall be liable to the injured party for all loss or damage *resulting from such neglect.*"

This law is undoubtedly binding upon all the classes of vessels mentioned. It follows that it was the duty of the S. F. Gale to carry a red light, and of the Miranda to carry a white light at the time of, and previous to the collision. There was no point made as to the light of the Miranda. Those on board of the brig admit that the schooner showed a white light. The evidence, however, proves that it was an ordinary globe lantern without reflectors; and if so, it could hardly be said to come up to the standard required by the law; because I think the words in the act, "*said light* shall be furnished with reflectors, &c., complete, and of a size to insure a good and sufficient light," apply as well to the lights carried by vessels as to those carried by steamboats and propellers.

The libel alleges that the S. F. Gale carried at the time a red light. The answer of the claimant denies it, and asserts it was a white light. Of course, the dispute is to be determined by the proof. And here is to be found the conflict of evidence which so often occurs, in these cases between the persons on board of the different vessels. A brief examination will show where the weight of the testimony is upon this point.

Langley, the captain of the brig, merely says they had a red light. Scott, a seaman, states they had a red light on the pall bitts, but he did not notice the Gale's light when he went on deck. It being his watch below at the time, he did not go on deck till the collision occurred. Hitchcock, also a seaman of the brig, who was at the helm, says that at the time the Miranda's light was first discovered, and for more than an hour previous, and up to the time of the collision, the brig showed a red light suspended from the pall post.

This is the whole testimony on the part of the libellant. The witnesses simply declare the fact to be so, without adverting to any circumstances which show that their attention was particularly called to it, or that they had any special reasons for recollecting it.

On the other hand Durand, the captain of the Miranda, says that he saw the light of the Gale about fifteen minutes before the collision, a mile or more distant: that it was a white light. He is positive it was a white light, because the second mate and himself had previously talked of it, and there was no other light in sight except that of the light-ship, and he is certain also, because the Gale carried the same light (white) when she shot across the bows of the schooner. Wilgus, the first mate of the Miranda, declares he *noticed the signal light* of the Gale. It was a white light, but burned low, giving a dull light. He still saw the same light hanging after the two vessels parted. Isaac Brown, the second mate, was one of the watch on deck at the time. He and the captain spoke together of the *white light* carried by a vessel then ahead of them as they supposed. They stood some time on the forecastle deck and saw a white light and that only. If the Gale had carried a red light, he says, they would not have gone aft to lower the peak of the mainsail. Joseph Brown, a seaman of the Miranda, states the brig had a white light, which burnt dim at the time. The light was so near he could not but observe it; and he says it was remarked by others at the time that the Gale carried a white light. Turner, also a seaman of the Miranda, says that the Gale carried a dim, white light; and is positive it was a white light, because he had heard the captain and second mate previously talking of the light in sight as a white light, and because, when he found the brig was close hauled on the wind, with her starboard tacks aboard, he noticed that she showed the wrong light.

It is apparent from the foregoing statement of the evidence upon this point, it predominates strongly in favor of the conclusion that the S. F. Gale showed a white light. The witnesses who testify on that side, had their attention particularly drawn to the fact: it was the subject of remark at the time. They saw the light before the collision, and after; their opportunity for observation was favorable, and it seems clear that those on board of the brig who speak to this point were mistaken; or, at all events, the S. F. Gale did not show that kind of light which the law required. There can be no doubt the act demands the exhibition of such a red light (when the vessel during the night is on the starboard tack), as under ordinary circumstances, and more especially in so clear a night as that when this collision occurred, can be distinguished from a green or white light. It is possible the explanation may be found, as has been suggested, in the fact that the S. F. Gale, just before the light-ship was passed, had been sailing with the wind free, and her officers had neglected to change their white light when they changed their course. However this may be, I am forced to the conclusion that the brig was not at the time showing the proper light, consequently those who had charge of her were themselves in fault in that respect. There is some doubt, also, whether there was a good look-out kept on board of the brig. The captain of the Miranda says, if a good look-out had been kept on the brig, the collision might have easily been avoided. This might have been so, but those on board of the S. F. Gale had a right to suppose, as they were close on a wind, the usual rule would be observed by the Miranda—to keep away; whereas, as we shall presently see, the course of the schooner was unchanged until the collision was unavoidable.

The S. F. Gale not being free from blame, it follows the owner cannot, under the maritime law, sustain a claim for full indemnity for the damage done.

The next question is, whether within the meaning of the

15a

act of Congress the loss or damage resulted from the neglect of the brig to comply with the requirement of the law, because if that is the case, so far from the Miranda being liable to the S. F. Gale, the latter would be liable to the owner of the Schooner for the injury done to the Miranda. And perhaps we cannot bette rillustrate the principle than by supposing this were a libel filed by the owner of the Miranda against a brig for injury done to the former. Could it be sustained under the circumstances of this case? *Conkling's Admiralty*, 302.

We have to set out with the admitted fact, that the S. F. Gale violated an express law of Congress. In the case of the collision of the De Soto and Luda, *Waring* v. *Clark*, 5 Howard's R., 441, the Supreme Court went out of its way to decide, that if a collision occurs between steamers at night, and one of them has not signal lights, it will be held responsible for all losses until it is proved that the collision was not the consequence of the absence of signal lights. The Court say they do not put the decision of the case on that ground, and they do not determine whether there was an absence of signal lights or not. The real ground of the decision on the merits was, that the Luda was run downwhilest in the accustomed channel of upward navigation, by the De Soto, which was out of that for which it should have been steered to make the port to which it was bound. The opinion of the Court in *Waring* v. *Clark*, was given under the act of 7 July, 1838, which made it the duty of the master and owner of every steamboat running between sunset and sunrise, to carry one or more signal lights. It is said this principle applies also to the act of 1849 which we are now considering, and that the Miranda cannot be accountable for any loss to the S. F. Gale, until it is shown it was not occasioned by the brig carrying a white light.

Did the collision happen in consequence of the neglect of those who had charge of the brig? It may be admitted that the fact of the brig not having the proper light throws upon

the libellants the *onus* of proving the damage was the result of some fault on the part of the Miranda. I have come
to the conclusion, after an attentive examination of the evidence, that while it may be said the collision might not have
happened if the brig had shown the right light, it may also be
said it would not have occurred if there had not been fault on
the part of the Miranda. It is insisted, if it be proved that
the brig violated the law, it follows as a necessary consequence that the Miranda must stand excused. I do not so
understand the law. There are certain rules which are settled in the maritime law, respecting the conduct of vessels at
sea, but the neglect of these by one party will not excuse the
other for the want of ordinary care and diligence. In a recent case, it seems to be implied that every proper precautionary measure must be taken on the part of the collided
vessel to pass the other in safety; and then if a loss happen
in consequence of the fault of the other, the damage is attributable to the neglect of this last. *Newton* v. *Stebbins*, 10
Howard, 605; and see *St. John* v. *Paine*, 10 *How.*, 55, and
The Cynosure, 7 *Law Reporter*.

If the S. F. Gale showed the wrong light, it was not the
less the duty of those on the Miranda to observe the usual
nautical rules in the management of their schooner. It was
not the intention of the act of Congress to abrogate those
regulations which have always been observed in the management of vessels. Notwithstanding the brig carried a white
light, it was the duty of the Miranda, having the wind free, to
keep away, and not to hold on her course. It was a clear star-
light night, those on the Miranda had a right at first to presume
that the brig was on the same course with themselves. But
if it be true as stated, that the Captain and mate of the Miranda looked at the light of the S. F. Gale for some time,
they must have seen that they were overhauling the vessel
ahead at a very rapid rate. It is to be borne in mind that
the evidence shows the two vessels were approaching each

other at the combined speed of from eight to ten miles an hour. It should have been enough to have excited to watchfulness. The law of Congress is obligatory, but so are all the laws of the sea. There have been many rules and regulations established by the wisdom and experience of nautical men and sanctioned by the courts, for the conduct of vessels, but there is none of more imperative obligation, than the one which declares that when a vessel is approaching another in the night a competent and vigilant lookout should be kept on board of each. It is a rule prescribed alike by the law, and by common sense and common prudence. Did the Miranda keep such a look-out? It seems to me not. According to the evidence the officers knew they were approaching a vessel. What if it was a vessel on the same course with themselves? They were not the less bound to be vigilant in looking out for her and watching her movements. I concur entirely in the opinion of one of the nautical witnesses examined in court, Capt. Napier, that even if they had supposed the vessel ahead was on the same course with themselves, still it was their duty to keep a good look-out, and to call all the watch on deck to lower the peak, at a time when they were so near another vessel. It is impossible to escape the conclusion that if this had been done, in so clear a night as that was, it would soon have appeared that the brig ahead was in fact approaching them from an opposite course close hauled on the wind, notwithstanding the white light, and thus the collision might have been avoided. It was also the duty of the schooner, having the wind abaft the beam, to keep away. It seems clear that if the Miranda had had a competent watch at the time, and kept away as she ought to have done, no collision would have taken place. The loss that was sustained was not the result altogether of the neglect of the brig to show the right light, and was not the consequence alone of that neglect, but to say the least it was occasioned in a measure by the neglect of those in the Miranda. I find, therefore, that the two vessels were each in fault.

But it is urged, conceding there was a fault on the part of the Miranda, yet it was not such an omission as that of the brig. The latter had violated an express law, by neglecting to do that the omission of which no circumstances could excuse, and it is not like other rules, which vary according to contingencies. I cannot yield my assent to this doctrine. The law of Congress under particular circumstances requires a particular light. The maritime law requires a vessel under certain circumstances, to be managed in a certain way. Both are equally binding upon those who have the charge of vessels. And I think that is a sound rule, which, if sustained and enforced by the courts, conduces, to the greatest extent, to unremitting vigilance on the part of seamen. The doctrine laid down by Dr. Lushington in the case of the *Hope*, 1 W. Robinson's R., 1540, seems to be founded in good sense, and may be applied to this case: that if the brig carried the wrong light, and the master of the Miranda should say, " we will keep our course nevertheless," he would be to blame. It would be a dangerous doctrine, to authorize the master of the Miranda to say under the circumstances of this case: "That vessel has the wron light; I will not trouble myself to avoid hert: he consequences be upon herself."

Both vessels then being in fault, the next inquiry is how is the loss to be apportioned?

The rule laid down by Lord Stowell in the case of the Woodrop Sims, under his second possibility by which a collision may occur, when both parties were to blame, or where there is a want of due diligence on both sides, is, that the loss must be apportioned equally between them as being occasioned by the fault of both. This seems to be the well settled doctrine in the English Admiralty, and is the general rule of the maritime law. *Story on Bailment*, §608, *and Abbott on Shipping*, 230-3, *part 3, Chap. 1, Shee's Edition. Conkling's Admiralty*, 300. It has, however, been said in the argument, that the rule has never been adopted in this country. No case was cited in which the doctrine has been applied by a court of Admiralty in this country, and it is certainly singular, in the many cases which have arisen, there are so few in which the fault has been found to be common to both parties, so as to determine what the rule is in such cases. But the doctrine to divide the loss appears to have been approved, and whenever it is referred to, it seems to be considered as a part of the maritime law to be administered by our Admiralty courts. *Story on Bailment, ubi supra;* 8 *Kent Com.*, 231, 232. It is treated as settled law by Judge Hopkinson in *Reeves* v. *the Constitution, Gilpin's R.*, 584, by Judge McKinley in *Strout* v. *Foster*, 1 *Howard's R.*, 92, and by Judge Woodbury in his separate opinion in *Clark* v. *Waring*, 5 *Howard*, 503. And it was expressly decided and applied by the District Court of Massachusetts in 1846, and treated as the settled doctrine in Admiralty, *Rogers* v. *the Brig Rival*, 5 *Law Reporter* 28, and authorities there cited. And see the case of the *De Kock* v. ——, *Law Reporter*, 611.

It is admitted that the rule in the common law courts is different, but all the text writers and judges who have mentioned the subject, seem to regard it as a fixed rule in Admiralty. And on the whole, though it has sometimes been considered objectionable by able judges and writers, yet after some reflection I am satisfied the strength of the argument, reasoning upon general principles, is in favor of the rule, and sustains the authorities, in spite of a sneer that has occasionally been thrown out of its being *rusticum judicium.* It is safer to adopt this rule in cases of collision, than it is to measure out to each party in a particular case, the precise quantum of damage that he may have sustained.*

As the parties wish me to decide the question of damages on the proof now in, without referring it to a commissioner, I will state my views on the subject.

* The rule has since been sanctioned by the Supreme Court. *The Schooner Catharine* v. *Dickinson*, 17 *Howard's R.*, 170.

The evidence is that the S. F. Gale was injured to the amount of $336, for which repairs were actually made and about that amount paid. The other damage is stated by the captain at $300. One of the witnesses puts it from $300 to $500. They do not give all the particulars of the injury, from which the court might ascertain with accuracy the amount. It is stated that the new fore-sail was worth $40 more than the old. On the whole I have thought that $600 would, under the proof, be a fair amount to fix upon as the damage sustained by the S. F. Gale. The witnesses say that the damage done to the Miranda was $300. The whole damage done by the collision was then $900, one half of which would be $450. The S. F. Gale being injured $300 more than the Miranda, I shall order a decree to be entered against the claimant and his sureties for $150, and that divides the loss equally between the parties.

I shall allow costs to neither party; each one must therefore pay his own.

SAMUEL WARD, EBEN B. WARD AND THOMAS G. BUTLIN, v. THE SCHOONER M. DOUSMAN.

In a collision which took place between a steamer and a schooner as they were entering the harbor of Chicago, the evidence shows that the schooner was ahead, and was sailing the channel usually taken by vessels when the wind was as at that time, and that the steamer attempted to pass, in a narrow space, between the schooner and the pier, without any considerable abatement of speed. This was a fault, and under the circumstances the steamer cannot maintain a libel for the injury done by the collision. The steamer should have allowed the schooner to continue her course without interruption, and if necessary should have stopped.

When it appears in a case of collision, one party is in fault, before a Court of Admiralty will allow any compensation by apportionment or otherwise to such party, the evidence must clearly show there was a fault on the other side. If it is conflicting so as to leave it doubtful, or if it should appear that there might be some slight mistake or error which was occasioned by the original flagrant fault of the first named, no apportionment will be made.

Ward v. The M. Dousman.

Whenever a sail vessel is entering upon difficult navigation, as approaching a harbor, &c., a steamer following should take extreme precaution to keep out of the way. A steamer is considered under command, and should avoid sail vessels; and this rule is to be enforced with peculiar strictness under the circumstances of this case.

Messrs. H. G. & E. S. Shumway, for libellant.
Mr. Goodrich, for claimant.

OPINION OF JUDGE DRUMMOND.

This is a libel filed by the owners of the steamer Arctic. It alleges that the steamer, being about to enter the harbor of Chicago, on the 13th day of August, 1851, turned to pass around the north pier; that after the steamer commenced turning, the schooner M. Dousman, which was entering the harbor at the same time, with *the wind free,* and being on the easterly side of the steamer, negligently and improperly changed her course, struck the steamer on the larboard side and damaged her to a considerable amount. It states that there was sufficient room and depth of water for the schooner to enter the harbor without changing her course northerly, and that with proper care on the part of the schooner the collision might have been avoided; that the steamer was so situated at the time the schooner approached, it was impossible for the Arctic to get out of the way: the steamer being between the schooner and the north pier. The owners of the Arctic claim compensation for the damage done by this collision.

The answer states that the schooner, loaded and drawing eight feet of water, with the wind north, was entering the harbor in the channel usually taken by vessels with such a wind; that at the mouth of the harbor, and south of the channel the vessel was sailing, there is shoal water—usually called the middle ground—on which the schooner would have been in danger of grounding and of being lost or injured, if she had kept too far south. That the Arctic, just after the M. Dousman had doubled the north pier, undertook to pass between the schooner and the pier; that in so doing she came in contact with the schooner and did some damage to the latter. The owner denies that the schooner changed her course more than was prudent to keep her off the middle ground, and that there was not sufficient room for the Arctic to pass between the schooner and the pier; and avers that the steamer ought to have been stopped or backed so as to allow the schooner to pass into the harbor.

There is the usual conflict of testimony in this case. In a collision between two vessels, there is generally an effort by those on board of one to cast the blame on the other. There are, however, some main facts in this case which cannot be controverted. The M. Dousman was a schooner under sail, with the wind about north, trying to make the harbor of Chicago by the north channel. The entrance to the harbor is quite narrow. At the time the schooner changed her course to run into the harbor, the Arctic was several hundred yards astern of the schooner. As the wind was then, vessels coming in by the north channel keep as near the north pier as they can with safety, on account of the current which sweeps around the pier. The Arctic, astern of the schooner, and herself about to make the harbor under a full head of steam, undertook to go to wind ward of the schooner, and between her and the north pier. Those who had the management of the steamer knew, or were bound to know, the risk they run in attempting so very difficult and delicate a maneuver.

When we come to the details of the collision, we find great discrepancy in the evidence. According to those on the Arctic, no collision would have taken place if the schooner had not suddenly changed her course and luffed up across the line of the steamer, while according to those on the schooner the collision could not have been avoided, and whatever change of course there was, was caused by a fear of striking the middle ground, a bad shoal lying near the mouth of the harbor.

It seems that the helmsman of the schooner, when he saw the approach of the Arctic and the danger of a collision, kept the schooner away without any direction to that effect, whereupon the captain ordered him to keep the vessel straight and not mind the steamer. The people of the M. Dousman concur in saying that the vessel luffed to avoid grounding. Those on the Arctic, on the contrary, affirm there was plenty of room with good water to the southward of the course of the vessel.

It is true that the schooner cannot escape the consequences of its own fault by showing that the steamer was also in fault, but I do not think it necessary to weigh and examine the testimony very minutely to determine whether there might not have been some trifling fault on the part of the schooner, because the faults of the steamer were so many and flagrant, that whatever error, if any, of the schooner there was, (and I am not prepared in this conflict of testimony to say there was any,) it might well be considered, under the circumstances, as trivial.

I think the weight of the evidence is, that the collision occurred as the Arctic was in the act of swinging as she changed her course to enter the harbor. All the witnesses on the schooner do not agree as to this; but the master of the brig Mary, which was a short distance behind, and about to enter the port, speaks particularly on this point, and his position gave him the best opportunity of judging. Besides, this conclusion is strengthened by the manner of the contact, and by the nature of the injury that was done to the steamer and to the schooner. The luffing up of the schooner may have contributed slightly to it, but it is not certain that the collision would not have taken place in any event. It would not be surprising if the helmsman of the schooner was a little alarmed when he saw the imminence of the danger, and should try to avoid it; nor that the captain, through an apprehension of running aground, should give an order to luff. These are niceties which need not be severely criticised. We must recollect that the captain of the schooner had a right to presume that the steamer would keep out of his way; and though we should hold him to the exercise of all reasonable skill and prudence, still we must judge of these by the light of the circumstances which surrounded him.

The first and second mate of the Arctic unite in giving it as their opinion that the checking bell was not rung, and that her speed, which had been from eight to twelve miles an hour, had not been slackened. It is true one of the men says that the checking bell was rung fifteen minutes before the collision; and yet this same witness declares, in another part of his testimony, that at that time they were only seventy or eighty feet from the pier. No reliance whatever can be placed on the evidence of this witness. He was examined before me; and his whole manner indicated a total recklessness as to the facts, and his eagerness to screen the Arctic involved him in endless contradictions. It is manifest that the Arctic, whether her speed had been lessened or not, was going at too rapid a rate. It would be attended with very ruinous consequences to sanction such speed under such circumstances. Coming into a harbor with a narrow passage, right in the wake of another vessel, at a speed of ten miles an hour! Steamers cannot be too stringently held to caution and circumspection in this particular. They are constantly violating all the rules we adopt, and I do not feel disposed to relax those wholesome restraints which the Courts have thrown around their management.

The schooner was ahead, and had the right to choose her course; in this instance, with the wind north, it was her only course. It was the duty of the steamer to keep out of the way of the schooner; and there can be no doubt it was a gross fault for the steamer to attempt, under the circumstances, to pass between the schooner and the north pier. This is the opinion of the nautical witness who has been examined on that point, and I concur fully in its correctness. It was attended with great risk and peril in every aspect, as well to the steamer as to the schooner.

I think it may be laid down as the rule, without exception, that whenever a sail vessel is entering a harbor so difficult of access as that of Chicago, a steamer following should take extreme precaution to keep out of the way of such vessel, and, if need be, stop entirely. It is the only safe rule. The general rule applicable to steamers is, that they are always considered under command, and should keep out of the way of sailing vessels; and it seems to me this rule should be enforced with peculiar strictness upon a steamer situated as the Arctic was in this case.

If this were a libel promoted by the owners of the M. Dousman, I should have no hesitation in awarding to them compensation for the damage their vessel sustained, as it is, I dismiss the libel with costs.

CIRCUIT COURT OF THE UNITED STATES.

INDIANA.—NOVEMBER TERM, 1858.

WILLIAM JOLLY ET AL. *v.* THE TERRE HAUTE DRAW-BRIDGE COMPANY.

[This term was held by Judge Leavitt, of the Ohio District, by the appointment of Judge McLean, pursuant to the Act of Congress of the 29th July, 1850, in the place of Judge Huntington, of the Indiana District, who was unable to attend, owing to sickness in his family.]

Under the grant of power to Congress, to regulate commerce among the several States, as given by the Constitution of the United States, the general government has jurisdiction over navigable streams, so far as may be necessary for commercial purposes.

A steamboat, enrolled and licensed pursuant to the Act of Congress, is entitled to the protection of the general government, while engaged in carrying on commerce between different States; and her owners have a right to use the navigable streams of the country, free from all material obstructions to navigation.

In relation to the States carved out of the N. W. Territory, the guaranty in the ordinance of '87, as to navigable streams, is still in force.

The Courts of the Union, having jurisdiction of the parties in a civil suit, are competent to administer the common law remedy for an injury sustained by reason of an unlawful obstruction in a navigable stream, without any express legislation by Congress, giving the remedy, and prescribing the mode of its enforcement.

The national jurisdiction over navigable streams does not deprive the States of the exercise of such rights over them, as they may deem expedient, subordinate to the power granted by the Constitution of the United States.

A bridge of sufficient elevation, or with a proper draw, is not necessarily an impediment to navigation; neither is any structure or fixture such an impediment, which facilitates commerce, instead of being a hindrance.

The inquiry in this case is, whether the bridge with the draw erected by the defendant at Terre Haute, is a material obstruction to the navigation of the Wabash river.

If it occasions merely slight stoppages and loss of time, unattended with danger to life or property, it is not such an obstruction.

The Terre Haute bridge was built under a charter from the State of Indiana, which required a "convenient draw" in the bridge. This imports a draw which can be passed without vexatious delay, or risk; and, if not such a one, the charter is violated; but if it meets the requirement of the act of incorporation, and is yet a material obstruction, the Act is a nullity, for the want of power in the Legislature to pass it.

If the jury find the bridge is a material obstruction, but that the injury sustained by the plaintiffs' boat was the result of recklessness, or want of skill in those having charge of her, the Bridge Company are not liable; and evidence of the good professional reputation of the pilot will avail nothing, if, in this particular case, he was reckless and unskilful.

If the jury find for the plaintiffs, they may include in the damages given, the probable earnings of their boat, for the time she was delayed in repairing the injury sustained.

Messrs. *O. H. Smith & S. Yandis*, for plaintiffs.
Messrs. *R. W. Thompson & J. P. Usher*, for defendant.

OPINION OF THE COURT BY JUDGE LEAVITT.

This suit is brought by the plaintiffs, as owners of the steamer American Star, to recover damages sustained by that boat in passing through the draw of the bridge across the Wabash river, at Terre Haute.

The material facts presented to the jury by the evidence are, that the Star, a stern-wheel boat, duly enrolled and licensed at the port of Cincinnati for the coasting trade, with the usual complement of officers and men, under the command of William Jolly as master, also a part owner, was engaged in the navigation of the Wabash river, making regular trips for the conveyance of passengers and freight, from Cincinnati to the highest point of navigation on said river; that in March, 1852, the water being at a high stage, as she was descending the river, in passing through the draw of the Terre Haute bridge, bow foremost, and partially laden, she struck with considerable violence against one of the piers of the bridge, her guards on one side being thereby broken, the top of the pilot-house carried away, and one of her chimneys thrown down, with some other minor injuries; that as the result of the collision, the boat was detained nearly two days at Terre Haute, in making the necessary temporary repairs, to enable her to prosecute her trip, and one week at Cincinnati, in making permanent repairs; the actual cost of which is proved to have been $371; that owing to her crippled condition after the injury, she was unable to receive freight offered below Terre Haute, to the amount of some $150 or $200; and that one entire trip was lost, the usual and estimated profit of which is stated at $1,000.

The bridge was a wooden structure, with a draw having a space between the piers of about sixty feet, and at the top of the draw, when raised, of thirty or forty feet. It was erected by the defendant, under an act of incorporation granted by the Legislature of the State of Indiana, containing a provision requiring the corporators to construct "a convenient draw" in the bridge.

This brief outline of the case will suffice as preliminary to the consideration of the questions of law, which have been presented and argued with great ability by counsel, and upon which the instructions of the Court have been requested.

It is not controverted by the counsel for the Bridge Company, that the Wabash is a navigable stream; nor is it denied that the plaintiffs' boat, at the time the alleged injury was sustained, was employed in carrying on commerce between ports and places lying in different States. But, it is insisted, that as this bridge was erected under the authority of the State of Indiana, and in conformity with the charter granted by the State, it cannot be deemed an obstruction to navigation, in the sense of entitling the plaintiffs to compensation for the injury complained of.

The Constitution of the United States contains an explicit grant of power to Congress, to regulate commerce among the several States. Under this grant, there can be no question of the competency of Congress to exercise jurisdiction over all the navigable streams, to the extent that may be necessary for the encouragement and protection of commerce between two or more States. This doctrine is so well settled by the uniform legislation of Congress, and the frequent adjudications of the Supreme Court of the United States, as to render its discussion here wholly unnecessary. It is regarded as equally clear that the boat, the owners of which in this case are seeking compensation for an injury sustained, having been duly enrolled and licensed by the proper officer, in pursuance of an Act of Congress, was rightfully employed in the navigation of the Wabash river, and that her owners, while she was so employed, had a right to the free use of that river, and were entitled to protection against all unlawful obstructions to its navigation. It follows, that for any injury attributable to such obstructions, the law will give the needful redress. Nor is it necessary for this purpose, that there should be any express legislation of Congress giving the remedy, and regulating the manner of its enforcement. The Courts of the Union, if the plaintiff is a citizen of a State other than that in which he brings his suit, have jurisdiction, and are competent to administer civil remedies for such injuries, upon the principles of the common law, without any statutory enactment for that purpose. This doctrine is clearly established by the decisions of the Supreme Court of the United States, in the *Wheeling Bridge Case; 13 Howard's S. C. Rep.*, 518.

There is another ground on which the right of every citizen of the United States to the free and unobstructed navigation of the Wabash river, may be confidently asserted. The State of Indiana is one of the States carved out of the North Western Territory, and therefore subject to the operation of that article of the compact contained in the ordinance of 1787, which declares that "the navigable waters leading to the Mississippi and the St. Lawrence, and the carrying-places between the same, shall be common high-ways," &c.   While it is admitted that some of the articles of compact in that ordinance have been superseded by the admission of the States within the North Western Territory into the Federal Union, it has been held by repeated judicial decisions, that the solemn guaranty referred to is still in full force, and is a perpetual inhibition to such States from authorizing any impediments or obstructions to the free navigation of the water-courses within its scope.   *Spooner* v. *McConnel et al.*, 1 *McLean*, 337; *Palmer* v. *Commissioners of Cuyahoga County*, 3 *Mc Lean*, 226 ; *Hogg* v. *Zanesville Man. Co.*, 5 *Ohio R.*, 416.

But, in maintaining the paramount jurisdiction of the national government over navigable streams, and the operative force of the guaranty in the ordinance of '87 in regard to them, it does not follow that the States are deprived of all power of legislation.   Judge McLean, in the case above cited from the third volume of his Reports, says: "A State, by virtue of its sovereignty, may exercise certain rights over its navigable waters, subject, however, to the paramount power of Congress to regulate commerce among the States."   This principle is distinctly recognized in all the cases referred to, whether arising under the commercial power of the general government, or the ordinance of '87·   It has never been claimed that the States do not rightfully possess jurisdiction upon and over the navigable water-courses within their limits. Such a claim is clearly in derogation of the sovereignty of the States, and therefore, wholly inadmissible.   But, while the right of the States is thus conceded, it is well settled that, in the exercise of their jurisdiction, they shall not infringe on that granted to the national government by the Constitution of the United States; and that in reference to the States

16s

formed from the North Western Territory, they cannot disregard the provision of the ordinance referred to.

This limitation of the power of the States is not inconsistent with their claim of sovereignty; nor does it involve necessarily any conflict of jurisdiction between them and the government of the Union. The States have all the power over their water-courses, which is necessary for local or State purposes. The right of a State to punish crimes committed on its streams, and to authorize and enforce such police regulations as may be necessary for the protection of its citizens, has never been questioned. It is equally clear that a State may adopt such measures, in reference to its water-courses, as are required by its citizens in facilitating trade and commercial intercourse. Hence, they properly exercise the right of establishing and licensing ferries, and authorizing the construction of wharves. They may also sanction an apparent obstruction of a navigable stream, by authorizing the erection of dams and locks; for the obvious reason that these are not hindrances to navigation, but are promotive of its benefits. Nor can there be a doubt that it is competent for a State to authorize the erection of a bridge across a navigable stream within its limits. But in all the cases referred to, the power must be exercised subject to the restriction, that the right of free navigation is not essentially impaired. If a bridge is erected, it must be sufficiently elevated to admit of the safe and convenient passage of such boats or vessels as are most advantageously used for the conveyance of travelers or freight upon the river or water-course spanned by the bridge; or, if not thus constructed, there must be a draw of such size and structure as not materially to infringe the right of free and unobstructed navigation.

It is, however, a question not clear of doubt, whether it is practicable to place a draw-bridge across a stream, subject to high floods, and with a rapid current, as is the fact in reference to the Wabash, without materially impairing its safe navigation. This description of bridge is obviously better suited to tide-water streams, or such as have little or no current, in reference to which they may be used with little hindrance to navigation.

The jury, however, in this case, may properly limit their inquiry to the question, whether the Terre Haute Bridge, with its draw of the size and structure proved, at the time and under the circumstances in which the injury to the plaintiffs' boat was sustained, was an essential impediment to the navigation of the Wabash; and this leads necessarily to the further inquiry, what constitutes such an impediment?

Without going at length into the consideration of this question, it may be stated that slight difficulties occasioning short stoppages, and some loss of time, such as proceed from ferries, locks, dams, and even bridges, as already intimated, are not to be viewed as material obstructions. But, if these involve much loss of time in passing them, or danger of accident or injury to life or property, or the use of extraordinary caution, they do essentially impair the right of free navigation, and subject those placing such obstructions in a navigable stream, to damages for the injuries which they occasion.

In reference to the Terre Haute Bridge, it will be proper for the jury to give due weight to the evidence of the witnesses, who have had much experience in steamboat navigation on the Wabash, and who say that in their judgment this bridge, especially in descending the river, is a serious obstruction to navigation. There is also a clear preponderance of proof to the effect that it is the more usual practice in descending the river, to round to, some distance above the bridge, and thus by means of a rope made fast at the shore, to let the boat descend, stern foremost, slowly through the draw. This process, as stated by some of the witnesses, occupies from ten to thirty minutes; and by some, it is stated the detention is an hour, and sometimes an hour and a half. The Court has no hesitation is saying, if the difficulties presented by this bridge are of a character requiring this precaution and this loss of time, it is a material obstruction to navigation.

In the Wheeling Bridge case, before referred to, it appeared that of the great number of steamers upon the Ohio river, there were but seven which could not safely pass under the bridge at ordinary stages of water, without lowering their chimneys. These seven boats could let down their chimneys, but the operation was attended with delay and some danger; or they could navigate the river, though with less speed, with chimneys considerably reduced in height; and yet the Supreme Court of the United States held, that the bridge was an essential impediment to navigation—in fact, a public nuisance; and decreed that unless so altered as not to impede the passage of any of the boats used on the Ohio, it must be abated. This decision, emanating from the highest Court of the Union, is obligatory on this Court, and must be received as the law, so far as applicable to the present case.

Having reference to the principles here stated, it will be the duty of the jury to pass upon the question, whether, from the evidence, the Terre Haute Bridge is an impediment to the navigation of the Wabash river. It is insisted by the counsel for the Bridge Company, that the structure has been erected in compliance with the charter granted by the State of Indiana, and therefore, that the company are not liable for the injury complained of. The charter, as before stated, authorizes the erection of the bridge, with "a convenient draw." This clearly implies that it shall be such a draw as may be used without vexatious delay or loss of time; and also with safety to persons and property. Nothing less than this will meet the requirement of the act of incorporation. And if the jury find the charter has not been complied with, it cannot shield the defendant from liability for the injury sustained by the plaintiff in passing the bridge. Or, if the jury come to the conclusion from the evidence, that the bridge and draw are in accordance with the charter, and yet a material obstruction to navigation, the company are liable, if ordinary skill and care were used in navigating the plaintiffs' boat through the draw. For reasons already stated, it was not competent for the Legislature of Indiana to authorize a structure across the Wabash, which would be an essential hindrance to its navigation; and any law conferring such authority, is a nullity.

It will therefore be a proper inquiry for the jury, whether the plaintiffs' boat, in passing the bridge, was managed with ordinary skill and caution. For, conceding the bridge to be an unlawful obstruction, yet if the plaintiffs' injury is clearly referable to the reckless and unskilful management of the plaintiffs' boat, the company are not responsible for such injury. On this point, as on all others involving the weight and credibility due to the witnesses, the jury are the exclusive judges. If the evidence of the pilot who was at the wheel, and of others connected with the boat, is entitled to credit, the proof is satisfactory that the boat was managed with skill and caution. She was not let down stern foremost by a rope, as was the more usual way of passing the draw; nor is it regarded as essential to the plaintiffs' right to recover for an injury sustained in passing the draw, that such a precaution should have been used. Some of the witnesses express the opinion that this is the safer course, while others, having skill and experience in the navigation of the Wabash, say that neither prudence nor safety requires it. The pilot of the boat has testified very intelligently, and with apparent candor, and says he did not consider it necessary to pass the draw stern foremost. He also says that great care and caution were observed in passing through the draw, and that the injury to the boat was not the result of either carelessness or want of skill. He thinks the boat would have passed safely through the draw, but for a strong wind which suddenly struck her, and caused her to veer from the course he was

steering. In this statement the pilot is corroborated by several of the plaintiffs' witnesses, while most of the witnesses
for the defendant say they have no recollection that there
was any wind, exceeding a moderate breeze. This is not
viewed as a material point in this case, as the liability of the
Bridge Company is in no way affected by the state of the
wind, or its influence in causing the collision. If the bridge
is an unlawful obstruction, and the plaintiffs used ordinary
care and skill in passing it, the company are responsible for
the injury, irrespective of the agency of the wind. And this
for the obvious reason that, wind or no wind, the injury could
not have been sustained, but for the fact that the bridge was
there.

It is proper here to remark, in reference to the pilot of the
plaintiffs' boat, that the evidence is satisfactory as to his professional character. He had served in that capacity for some
years, on the Wabash, and it is in proof that he is esteemed
a safe, prudent and skilful pilot. But notwithstanding this
evidence of general good professional reputation, if in this
particular case he evinced recklessness and want of skill, and
the injury to the plaintiffs' boat is attributable to that cause,
they must bear the consequences of his misconduct.

In this case, a large proportion of the evidence for the
plaintiffs is in the form of depositions of persons who were on
the boat at the time of the accident, and of others experienced in the navigation of the Wabash, who have been examined as experts. These depositions were taken at Cincinnati, without previous notice to the opposite party, and
without the attendance of his counsel. This mode of taking
testimony is expressly authorized by an Act of Congress. It
is liable to the objection that the opposite party is preclu-
ded from the opportunity of cross-examining the witnesses,
and thus testing the truthfulness of their statements. It is,
however, the right of the party against whom depositions
thus taken are to be used, to re-call and re-examine the same

witnesses, if he deems it necessary. The defendants in this case have not availed themselves of this right; and the plaintiffs' depositions are therefore committed to the jury, as taken by the other party, without any cross-examination by the defendant. Under these circumstances, it is insisted by the defendant's counsel that these depositions should be viewed with suspicion, and that they are entitled to very little weight by the jury. On this point, it is only necessary to remark, that these depositions are by law admissible to the jury as evidence; and, although they would be entitled to greater weight, if taken upon notice to the other party, and with an opportunity for cross-examination, they are nevertheless entitled to credit, unless otherwise impeached.

It has been before noticed that a part of the evidence for the plaintiffs in this case, consists in the opinions of experts —those experienced in and familiar with the navigation of the Wabash—as to the practical effect of the Terre Haute Bridge upon the navigableness of that river, and the correctness of the professional conduct of those entrusted with the management of the plaintiffs' boat in passing the bridge. In reference to this description of evidence, it is only necessary to remark that, for obvious reasons, that those best acquainted with any particular art, profession or business, in all matters directly concerning them, are accounted more satisfactory and reliable witnesses, than those who have no such skill or experience. Hence it is well settled, that the testimony of intelligent and credible experts is entitled to the most respectful consideration. The principle here stated applies as well to navigation as to any other art or occupation.

It only remains for the Court to say, that if the jury find the plaintiffs are entitled to their verdict, the amount of damages to be awarded is wholly with them. The actual expenses of repairing the injury sustained by the plaintiffs' boat forms, of course, an element in estimating the amount. But it is moreover proper to bring to the notice of the jury, a late decision of the Supreme Court of the United States,* having a direct bearing on the question of damages in this case. That Court has held, that in an action for an injury by collision with another boat, the boat of the plaintiff not being in fault, he was entitled to compensation, in damages, for the profits his boat would have made during the the time necessarily lost in repairing the injury sustained. No reason is perceived why the same principle does not apply to the present case. If, therefore, the jury find for the plaintiffs, they should include in their verdict, the amount of the probable earnings of the plaintiffs' boat during the time she was delayed in making the repairs necessary to refit her for service. This amount will be settled by the evidence before the jury, on that point.

The jury returned a verdict for the plaintiffs, assessing their damages at $1,000. A motion for a new trial by the defendants was overruled.

SAMUEL CULBERTSON *v.* ABNER T. ELLIS ET AL.

Where, in a contract for the construction of a public work, the contractor undertakes to complete it by a specified time, and it contains a clause authorizing the engineer, if at any time he has reason to believe the work will not be so completed, to declare a forfeiture of the contract; and the engineer in good faith annuls it, and such annulment is confirmed by the directors of the company, no liability to the contractor is thereby incurred on the part of the engineer or the directors, though it should subsequently appear that the contractor was not in default, and that the forfeiture was declared under a mistaken view of the facts.

But the declaration of forfeiture, in such case, will not prevent the contractor from recovering the amount due him on the contract at the time of forfeiture.

If the declaration avers, as the foundation of the claim for damages, that the forfeiture was wrongfully and maliciously declared by the engineer, and affirmed from like motives by the defendants, then being directors of

----

* The case referred to is that of *Williamson and others* v. *Barrett and others*, 13 *How. S. C. Rep*,. 101. The same principle was decided in that case by the Circuit Court of Ohio, 4 *McLean*, 589.

Samuel Culbertson *v.* Abner T. Ellis et. al.

the company, the plaintiff must prove facts from which the inference of bad motives may be drawn.

Proof that some of the defendants had expressed the opinion, prior to the forfeiture, that it would result in a large saving to the company, is not a sufficient ground for inferring corrupt motives, in the absence of other facts showing that such motives were the influential cause of their acts.

If, from the evidence, there are reasonable grounds for the inference that the plaintiff, by retaining the contract, would have been a loser by it, or would have made no profit, the forfeiture, though declared or assented to from wrong motives, will not entitle him to damages.

If the evidence justifies the conclusion that the plaintiff would not have finished the work within the contract time, had no forfeiture been declared, as the contract would then have been terminated, and the plaintiff, by its terms, would have been liable to a deduction of one-sixth upon the whole of the work performed, he cannot recover for any alleged injury from the forfeiture.

The allegation of a malicious arrest of the plaintiff's person, on a warrant of the peace sued out by one of the defendants, not being set forth as a distinct cause of action, is not a proper basis for a verdict against the defendants; but, if the averment of malicious motives in the forfeiture, and the assent given to it, is sufficiently proved, the malicious arrest may be considered in aggravation of damages.

If the jury are satisfied that, in the prior suit brought by the plaintiff against the Wabash Navigation Company, the jury took into consideration and included in their verdict, the loss which they supposed the plaintiff had suffered by the forfeiture, he cannot recover any thing in this action for such loss, even if the jury should conclude from the testimony that there was an actual loss to him.

Mr. Kilgore and Mr. Smith, for plaintiff.

Mr. Judah, Mr. Crawford and Mr. Crittenden for defts.

OPINION OF THE COURT, BY JUDGE LEAVITT.

This is a special action on the case, brought for the recovery of damages, on grounds set forth in the plaintiff's declaration, and which will be indicated with sufficient clearness by the following brief statement. A company had been incorporated by the Legislatures of the States of Indiana and Illinois, by the name of the Wabash Navigation Company, for the improvement of the navigation of the Wabash River at the Grand Rapids, by means of a crib lock and dam.

On the 21st of August, 1847, the President and Directors of said Company entered into a written contract with the plaintiff, and one Isaac Culbertson, since deceased, by which the Culbertsons agreed to construct the lock and dam, in the manner and upon the conditions specifically stated in said contract. One of the conditions was, that the work should be completed by the first of November, 1848, with a clause to the effect that if the work was not prosecuted with the force and diligence necessary to ensure its completion by the time stated in the contract, it should be competent for the engineer of the Company to declare it forfeited, and take possession of the work in behalf of the Company. ' It was also agreed, in case the Culbertsons failed to complete the lock and dam within the contract time, they were to be subject to a deduction of one-sixth of the amount of the work done by them. Soon after the execution of the contract, the Culbertsons procured tools, implements and other property, and commenced the execution of the work, and continued their operations during the autumn of 1847, and the summer of 1848; and, on the 2d of September, in the last named year the engineer declared the contract to be forfeited, and the Company took possession of the work and carried it on to its completion.

The averments in the declaration are, in the substance, that the plaintiff had faithfully performed his part of the contract, up to the time of the forfeiture, having made all the progress therein that was practicable, and was then engaged on the work in the vigorous prosecution of the same; that the engineer, at the instance of the defendants, wrongfully and without any sufficient reasons, declared the contract to be forfeited; and that the defendants, being at the time Directors in said Company, corruptly conspiring together to injure the plaintiff, wrongfully and maliciously urged the engineer to declare the forfeiture, and with the same purpose and motive affirmed the act of the engineer, and wrongfully took possession of the tools, implements and other property of the plaintiff; and as a means to accomplish their unlawful purpose, maliciously filed a false affidavit that they were in fear of personal injury and violence by the plaintiff, and on the 7th of September, 1848, sued out a warrant of the peace against him, and procured him to be arrested and held in custody thereon.

The plaintiff claims damages for the loss, which he alleges he sustained by reason of the forfeiture of the contract, and the illegal proceedings of the defendants in getting possession of his property and arresting and imprisoning his person.

The defendants plead, first, not guilty, thereby putting in issue all the allegations in the plaintiff's declaration; and secondly, that the plaintiff, in a prior suit against the Wabash Navigation Company, tried in this Court, obtained a verdict and recovered judgment for nearly ten thousand dollars, in which was included his claim for the injury sustained by him arising from the annulment of the contract.

It is not deemed necessary, in committing this case to the jury, to re-state, or minutely analyze, the great mass of evidence which has been introduced on this protracted trial. It will be my purpose to bring to the notice of the jury, with as much brevity as possible, the legal principles involved, and leave them in the discharge of their rightful duties—to apply these principles to the facts before them.

Upon the first issue made by the parties, two principal enquiries arise: first, whether, in the forfeiture of the contract by the engineer, the affirmation of that forfeiture by the defendants, and the acts consequent thereon, the defendants were influenced by the malicious or improper motives imputed to them by the plaintiff; and, secondly, whether the forfeiture resulted to the injury of the plaintiff, by depriving him of profit which otherwise would have enured to him from the fulfilment of the contract.

In relation to the first of these enquiries, it will be noticed by the jury, as a fact not controverted in the case, that the

contract between these parties contains an explicit provision
to the effect, that in case the Culbertsons shall not prosecute the work in such a way as to ensure its completion within the time stated, the engineer may declare it forfeited, and
take possession of the unfinished work in behalf of the company. It is not pretended that any fraud or undue means
were used, to induce the plaintiff to become a party to this contract. It was voluntary on his part. The clause of forfeiture
is one usually inserted in contracts for the construction of
important public works, and is obligatory on the parties to it,
not being against law, or condemned by any principle of public policy. For the purpose indicated by this clause in the
contract between the parties, they constitute the engineer
their mutual agent, and are bound by his decision, if made in
good faith. It has been held by the Supreme Court of the
United States, in reference to a clause of forfeiture in a contract similar to this, that if the engineer declares a forfeiture
under the belief that the contractor was not prosecuting his
work with proper diligence and energy, and an apprehension
that the work would not be completed within the contract
time, damages are not recoverable for the forfeiture, though
it should appear that the contractor was not in default, and
that the engineer acted under a mistaken view of his conduct.
13 *Howard's Reports*, 307. This principle is, however, stated
by the Court, with the limitation, that the forfeiture shall not
deprive the contractor of what was previously earned by or
due to him under the contract.

As the result of this doctrine, thus settled by the Supreme
Court, it will be observed, the plaintiff in this action has no
egal claim for damages arising from the act of forfeiture,
unless the engineer, with the knowledge and approbation of
the defendants, and from corrupt and malicious motives, annulled the contract, and the act of annulment, from like
motives, was sustained and affirmed by the defendants. The
motives of the engineer and defendants, in this transaction,
are proper for the consideration of the jury; and these can

only be inferred from their acts, as adduced in evidence. If there was reasonable or probable cause for the declaration of forfeiture, it affords at least a *prima facie* presumption that it was done in good faith, and without any improper motive. In the consideration of this subject, it will be the duty of the jury to scrutinize the evidence, and decide according to the light which it affords. The work which the plaintiff contracted to perform, was one of very considerable magnitude; and it was obviously important to the company of which the defendants were the representatives, as well as to the public, that it should be completed within the time stated in the contract. The work, while in progress and in an unfinished state, would be a hindrance to the navigation of the Wabash river, in those stages of water when it could be used for that purpose; and if unnecessarily protracted, would subject the company to damages for its obstruction. Hence the propriety and necessity of the clause of forfeiture in the contract, to secure the prompt and timely completion of the work. The contract, as already stated, was dated in August, 1847, and the locks and dams were to be completed by the first of November, in the following year. The declaration of forfeiture was made the second of September; leaving but two months from that date, for the completion of the work. The testimony of a number of witnesses is before the jury, touching the manner in which the work had been prosecuted, prior to the forfeiture, and the amount of work then to be done. It also appears, that the season of 1848 was not favorable to the prosecution of the work, owing to the occurrence of frequent floods in the river, and to the sickness of both the Culbertsons, resulting in the death of one of them. I do not propose to advert specially to the testimony on these points. The engineer who superintended the work from its commencement, and by whom the forfeiture was declared, has been very closely examined on all the points involved in this controversy. He is wholly unimpeached as a witness, and appears to be a gentleman of great intelligence and candor. It will be for the jury to decide what weight shall be given to his testimony. He has stated very clearly the progress of the work, up to the time of the forfeiture, and what then remained to be done. With a full knowledge of all the facts, he gives it as his opinion, there was not even a remote probability, that the work would be completed by the first of November; and that under this conviction, and wholly uninfluenced by the defendants or others, and solely on his own responsibility, he declared the annulment of the contract. It moreover appears from his testimony, that so far from any act being done to obstruct the progress of the work, he and the defendants evinced the greatest anxiety for its rapid advancement, and its completion by the plaintiff within the contract time. And to this end, it appears the Board of Directors, during the summer of 1848, passed several resolutions of a conciliatory character, enjoining upon the plaintiff to apply more force to the work, and prosecute it with greater energy.

Some testimony has been introduced by the plaintiff, proving that some of the defendants, on different occasions, and to different persons, expressed the opinion that by annulling the contract, a considerable saving would result to the company; and it is insisted in behalf of the plaintiff, that this was the motive in declaring the forfeiture. If such an inference is fairly sustainable, the jury will be fully justified in finding the allegation of evil motive, as alleged in the declaration, to be true, and returning a verdict accordingly. If a wrong has been committed in this transaction, with the low and mercenary design of benefiting the company, it affords a fair implication that the annulment was wrongful and malicious, and the plaintiff is well entitled to recover the full amount of any injury which he has thereby sustained. The jury, however, must be satisfied beyond a fair doubt, that the defendants were actuated by a motive so dishonorable and fraudulent. And they will not be justified in such a presumption, by the fact, that some of the defendants expressed an opinion that the forfeiture would result in a saving to the company.   Such an opinion may have been entertained, without presuming that it necessarily induced the act of forfeiture.   Indeed, such an inference is in direct contradiction to the testimony of the engineer, who, as before stated, testifies that he declared the forfeiture from a conviction of duty, and on his sole responsibility.   He also swears, that in his judgment, no saving would accrue to the company by the annulment of the contract.

In no aspect of this case, can the plaintiff's alleged loss from the forfeiture of the contract, be taken into consideration by the jury, in estimating damages, if they are satisfied' that by retaining the work he would have realized no profit, or that there would have been an actual loss.   Some of the witnesses for the plaintiff express the opinion, that the plaintiff would have made some profit on his contract, if he had been permitted to complete it.   Others, among whom is the engineer, having an accurate knowledge of all the facts necessary to a correct judgment on this point, say the plaintiff would have lost money by holding on to the contract, and completing the work.   It will be for the jury to decide, as to the preponderance of the testimony relating to this point of the case.   Whether, on the supposition of a loss to the plaintiff from the forfeiture, he is not barred from recovering it in this action, by his recovery in the prior suit, will be a proper subject of inquiry, in considering the second plea of the defendants.

With reference to the question of loss or profit by the plaintiff, if the contract had not been annulled, there is evidence which is entitled to the consideration of the jury, proving that the plaintiff had no hope or expectation of completing the work, within the contract time.   By the terms of the contract, in the event of a failure to finish the work according to its requirements, he was subject to a deduction of one sixth upon the entire value of work done; and his profit, if any, would be reduced by this amount. And moreover, without question, failing to complete the work by the first of November 1848, the contract would then be at an end, and the work pass into the company's hands. These suggestions are submitted to the jury, to aid them in coming to a just conclusion in reference to the probabilities of profit to the plaintiff, if the contract had not been annulled.

With reference to the issue on which the jury are to pass in this case, it is perhaps not necessary to decide, whether the sickness of the plaintiff and his brother, during the summer of 1848, and the prevalence of high water in the Wabash, during that season, which may have retarded the progress of the work, would have afforded a legal excuse for not completing it, within the contract time, if there had been no annulment of the contract. These contingencies were not provided for, in the clause of forfeiture, and did not affect the right of the engineer to annul the contract, if, without reference to these, the facts justified the act. In the posture in which this case is before the Court and jury, the question is not, whether the plaintiff is excusable for not prosecuting the work with more diligence and energy, but whether the plaintiff's allegations of malicious motives in the forfeiture, are sustained by the evidence.

As to the arrest and imprisonment of the plaintiff, on a warrant of the peace, issued at the instance of one of the defendants, with the alleged malicious purpose of compelling a transfer or sale of the plaintiff's tools, implements, etc., to the company, which, it is insisted by counsel, is of itself a sufficient ground to justify a verdict of damages in this action : it will be noticed, that it is not set forth in the declaration as a distinct and substantive cause of action. It is stated, as one of a series of acts showing the malicious purpose of the defendants in the entire transaction. Isolated from the other facts of the case, it can not consitute a legal basis for a general verdict against the defendants; but, if the jury believe the main fact charged, namely, that the defendants maliciously procured the declaration of forfeiture and subsequently affirmed the act, and that the arrest and imprisonment of the plaintiff were without probable cause, and with a bad purpose, the latter facts may properly be taken into consideration in aggravation of damages.

The views of the Court on the plea of a former recovery, interposed by the defendants, will now be briefly stated. As before noticed, it is insisted by counsel that the jury may include in their verdict the prospective profit of the plaintiff, on his contract with the company, if there had been no annulment, even if the jury in the former suit estimated such profit in their verdict. The Court, on this point, has no hesitancy in saying, if the jury are satisfied the supposed profit on the contract was taken into consideration by the former jury, and was included in their verdict, it can not be embraced in the verdict to be returned in this case. It is a plain principle of law, and an obvious dictate of justice, that a party shall not have two recoveries for the same cause of action. The former action, as appears from the record, was in debt, against the Wabash Navigation Company, and the amount recovered was nearly ten thousand dollars. Three of the jurors in that case testify that their recollection is distinct,—that the prospective profit of the plaintiff on his contract with the company was included in their verdict. In addition to this, it is proved by two gentlemen who were of counsel in that case, on opposite sides, that this claim was insisted on in argument to the jury; and they have no doubt, from the amount of the verdict, that it was considered and allowed by them. This evidence would seem to be satisfactory on this point. But the present action against the defendants as individuals, is not barred by the recovery in the former action. If the jury find that the acts charged in the

17a

declaration are proved, and were done with the malicious motives imputed.to them, it will be competent for them to return a verdict for such damages as they may deem just, excluding from their computation the amount of any supposed loss to the plaintiff, from the forfeiture of the contract.

DISTRICT COURT OF THE UNITED STATES.

LEWIS F. WEIMER *v.* RUSH R. SLOANE.

To sustain the allegations of the declaration in this suit, which is for aiding or abetting in the escape of slaves, under the Fugitive Slave Act of 1850, it must appear that the alleged fugitives were slaves who had escaped from service, and had been arrested by the owner or his agent; and that the defendant, with knowledge of these facts, aided and abetted their escape.

The Statute authorizes an arrest, either by the owner or his agent, with or without warrant; but, when made by an agent, he must be authorized by a written power of attorney, executed and authenticated as required by the Statute.

To make the defendant liable, it must appear that he had notice or knowledge that the slaves were fugitives, and were, at the time of the alleged unlawful interference, in custody under an arrest; but this notice or knowledge may be inferred from circumstances.

The test of the legality of an arrest is the law, and not the opinion of the defendant.

Any words or actions tending to effect an escape, and which lead to that result, are sufficient to implicate the defendant in the charge of aiding or abetting the escape.

An intention to effect an escape must appear, but such intention may be inferred from the facts. Every one is presumed to have intended the result necessarily and legitimately flowing from his acts.

A party acting as counsel for a fugitive slave, is protected from the consequences of his acts, so far only as they are within the proper limits of his professional duty.

Messrs. *Coffin & Stanbery*, for the plaintiff.
Messrs. *Vinton & Hunter*, for the defendant.

Lewis F. Weimer *v.* Rush R. Sloane.

OPINION OF THE COURT BY JUDGE LEAVITT.

GENTLEMEN OF THE JURY: This action is founded on the seventh section of the Act of Congress, of the 18th of September, 1850, known as the Fugitive Slave Act, and is brought to recover the value of three persons named in the declaration, who, it is alleged, were the slaves of the plaintiff, owing him labor or service as such, in the State of Kentucky, and who escaped from him into the State of Ohio. There are several counts in the declaration, but as a verdict is insisted on, upon the third count only, charging the defendant with having aided, assisted, or abetted, in the escape of the alleged fugitives, the inquiries of the jury will be limited to that charge.

To sustain this charge, it must appear to the satisfaction of the jury, that the persons named in the declaration, at the time of the alleged illegal interference by the defendant, were the slaves of the plaintiff, owing him labor or service in the State of Kentucky; that they escaped into the State of Ohio, and had been arrested either by the owner, or his agent or attorney; and that the defendant, with knowledge that they were slaves, and had been arrested as fugitives, unlawfully aided, abetted, or assisted them to escape.

As it is not controverted, that the alleged fugitives were the slaves of the plaintiff in Kentucky, and that they escaped into Ohio, it is not necessary to advert specially to the evidence proving these facts. I will briefly notice the testimony touching the nature and extent of the defendant's interference with the rights of the plaintiff, before I advert to the legal principles involved in the case.

The first witness introduced by the plaintiff is James P. Patton, who says, that being at Sandusky city, in pursuit of some slaves who had escaped from his service, he received at that place a power of attorney from the plaintiff, authorizing him to arrest the slaves named in the declaration; that on the 20th of October, 1852, the slaves arrived in the cars, and were seen by the witness at the depot of the Mansfield rail road. They were conducted by a colored man, from the depot to the steamboat Arrow, then lying at the wharf of the city, and were put on board. Witness called on Rice, a police officer of the city, and one Hedges and another person to assist in the arrest of the negroes. They went on board the steamboat, and the witness Patton saw and recognized them. He enquired of them, if they did not wish to return to Kentucky. George, one of the negroes, replied, that he did not care about going back. They were then arrested, it being about half after seven in the evening of the 20th of October, and, followed by a large crowd, proceeded to the Mayor's office. The negroes were taken into the office, and took their seats on a settee on the south side of the room. The Mayor, Mr. Follett, was in the office; the room was crowded, and there was a good deal of excitement. Witness stated to the people present that the negroes were slaves, and informed the Mayor that he wanted a trial, to prove property. The power of attorney under which he made the arrest, with some others in his possession, had been laid upon the table at which the Mayor was writing, by Rice. After some time, the Mayor said he doubted whether he had any authority to try the case, and refused to do so, at the same time referring witness to a magistrate. Witness said he was determined to hold the negroes. The defendant stepped out of the crowd, and said, Who is it that detains these colored people? Witness replied that he did. Defendant then enquired if Marshall Rice was in the room, and Rice replied that he was. Defendant asked Rice if he had a warrant to arrest the negroes, who said he had no warrant. Defendant then asked witness if he had a warrant, and was informed that he had none, and that he had arrested the negroes without any warrant, and brought them before proper authority, etc. Defendant said to witness, you should have had a warrant, and could not arrest without a warrant. Witness replied that he could arrest without a warrant, and intended to hold the negroes, and would hold every one responsible, if they were taken from him. Defendant smiled at this. Some conversation then followed about the value of the slaves, and witness said to defendant, he would hold him individually responsible, if he interfered with them, and that he might expect to pay $1000 for each of the negroes, if he caused them to be taken out of his custody. Some conversation then took place, as to the ability of the defendant to pay for the slaves. Witness said he would have to pay for them if he interfered in their rescue, as he would certainly be sued. Defendant then took off his hat, and waved it over his head and said, Colored friends, arise, and take those colored friends of yours out of the room, with a row, or a rush. Witness is not quite certain which of these words were used. The crowd, of whom some twenty were colored men, some of them armed with clubs, rushed towards the slaves, and forced them out of the room, with a rush. Witness has never seen them since, and they have never been retaken. On his cross-examination, the witness stated that the power of attorney from the plaintiff was delivered to him at Sandusky, about a week before the arrest, and that before going to the Mayor's office, he had handed that, with others, to Rice. At the office, the Mayor requested witness to select the power identifying the negroes; he selected it, with another, and handed them to the Mayor. Witness was armed with a revolver. Says he did not know till next morning, that the defendant was a lawyer.

W. W. Hedges says, he was at Sandusky city in pursuit of some negroes who had escaped from him in Kentucky. First saw the plaintiff's negroes on the steamboat Arrow, on the night they were arrested. Was informed they were there, and assisted Patton, Rice, and another person, to take them. Patton had requested him to assist. The negroes were arrested at the cook-room of the boat. Witness went with the crowd to the Mayor's office, after the arrest. Rice was in company, and on going into the office, he laid some papers on the Mayor's desk. Some conversation took place between Patton, Rice, and the Mayor, which witness did not hear. Heard some one ask, who brought the negroes there. Did not know defendant then. Now thinks it was the defendant who made the enquiry. Defendant then enquired for Rice, and asked him if he had a warrant to arrest the blacks. Then asked Patton if he had a warrant. Patton said he had none, but was authorized to arrest them. Defendant then took off his hat and waved it, saying: Colored people, remove your friends with a rush or row. On his cross-examination, the witness says he thinks defendant had a white hat. Says that two of the negroes, a man and a woman, recognized Patton on the boat, before the arrest. Says, also, that he heard defendant distinctly at the Mayor's office, and that he spoke loud.

Oliver Rice testifies, that in October, 1852, he was acting as a constable and marshal of Sandusky city. Was at the steamboat Arrow. Patton and one Shrove had some negroes in charge. Patton said he had arrested them as slaves, and handed his papers to witness. Went to Mayor's office; there was quite a crowd, and a good deal of excitement. Witness laid the papers on the Mayor's desk. Did not hear much of the conversation between Patton and the Mayor. After some time, defendant came into the room. Some conversation between defendant, Patton, and the Mayor. Defendant had taken his seat near the Mayor. Heard him ask if Rice, the marshal, was present. Witness replied that he was. And defendant then enquired of him if he had a warrant to arrest the negroes. Witness replied that he had no warrant. Defendant then raised his hat, and said: Friends of these colored people, remove them with a rush; and they all went out. There were a good many colored persons present, armed with clubs. Witness heard one of them say, they should

never take the negroes away alive. · On cross-examination,
says, he thinks Patton was at the railroad depot. Patton
had informed witness before what his business was, and that
he wished witness to assist him. Witness's object in going
to the steamboat was to suppress any riot, etc. Says defendant spoke in a loud voice at the Mayor's office, and that
he wore a white hat.

On the part of the defendant, a good deal of testimony
has been introduced to prove the occurrences at the Mayor's
office, and to discredit the statements of the plaintiff's witnesses.

John B. Lott says, he was on the steamboat at the time
the negroes were arrested, and went with the crowd to the
Mayor's office; called on the defendant at his office, to procure his services for the negroes as counsel. Defendant proceeded to the Mayor's office, enquired for Rice, asked him if
the negroes were in his custody, and wished to see the authority by which they were held. Said he saw nothing to authorize their detention. Witness heard some one then say, hussle
them out, and they all left the room.

Marshal Burton says, defendant is an attorney at Sandusky city. Witness was at the Mayor's office, evening
of October 20, 1852. It was much crowded. Heard defendant enquire by what authority the negroes were detained.
Defendant was near the center of the room. Witness heard
no answer to defendant's inquiry. Thinks defendant asked a
second time for the authority by which the negroes were held.
No reply to this. Defendant said, he saw no reason why
they should be detained. Some one said, hussle them out.
Witness saw defendant in the room. Thinks he had no hat
on. Saw no movement of his hat. Heard nothing said by
defendant about moving the colored people with a rush.
Thinks he would have heard it, if it had been said. Did not
hear defendant enquire for Rice. Thinks he would have heard
it, if such enquiry had been made.

H. M. Cheeseborough : Was present at the Mayor's office. Was there ten or fifteen minutes before anything was done in the way of business. Did not notice defendant, till he heard him enquire by what authority the negroes were held. Did not seem to address this enquiry to any one in particular. Witness heard some one ask for Rice. Some person said, the papers were with the Mayor. Defendant repeated his enquiry as to authority. He paused, turned partly round, and said, there appeared to be nothing against these persons to detain them. Some one said, hussle them out, and the room was soon clear. When defendant spoke of there being no authority to detain the negroes, he turned toward the place where they were sitting. Did not see his hat, or any motion with a hat. Did not see Rice in the room at all. Heard nothing from defendant about colored persons removing their colored friends with a rush. Thinks he would have heard it, etc.

Mr. Jennings says, he was at the Mayor's office. Saw defendant come in. Was accompanied by a colored man. Thinks he had a book in his hand. Heard defendant enquire, by what authority the negroes were detained. Thinks he heard the Mayor say, he had no jurisdiction of the matter. Heard defendant ask for Rice. Rice came forward, as witness thinks. Defendant enquired if the negroes were in his custody. Rice said they were not detained by a warrant in his hands. Defendant then said, if there is no authority for holding them, they can go. All went out in a hurry. Thinks defendant had no hat on. Not positive as to this. Did not hear him say colored friends, etc. Thinks he would have heard the words, if they had been used. When defendant said, if there is no authority to hold the negroes, they can go, he turned round to the crowd.

Mr. Clark : Was at the Mayor's office. Heard defendant enquire twice, by what authority the negroes were detained. Heard no reply. Defendant then said, he saw no reason why they should be detained. A colored man by the name of Locke, then said, rush them out, and they all left. Defendant had no hat on, and did not appear to be excited.

Joseph Jibbeau testifies as to what happened at the Mayor's office: Defendant enquired for authority, etc. Asked for Rice, who came forward, and defendant asked him if he had a warrant. Rice said he had no warrant, etc. Defendant then asked, if there were any papers or authority by which the negroes were detained. Asked two or three times. No reply to this. After a short pause, defendant said, Colored friends, I don't see any thing to detain your friends. Locke then said, hussle them out, and they went out in quick time. Defendant spoke in a medium tonè of voice. Thinks he had no hat on. Did not wave his hat. Did not use the words attributed to him by plaintiff's witnesses. Thinks he heard some one say, in reply to defendant's enquiry for authority, that the Mayor had the papers.

Mr. Follett: Was Mayor of Sandusky city, October 20, 1852. Heard a noise in the street. The crowd came into the office. Witness was writing at the time. Knew there were slaves there. Negroes were seated in the room. Witness paid no attention, but kept on writing, with his back to the negroes. After some time, Rice came in and laid the papers on witness's desk. Did not look at the papers. Mr. Bill asked, what he was going to do. Witness replied, he had no jurisdiction. Thinks he never spoke to Patton, or Patton to him. After some time, Rice came to his desk, and witness handed the papers to him. Rice asked witness if he had examined them, and witness replied that he had not. Witness went towards the door. Defendant came in, turned round and said, By what authority are these persons held in custody? Are there any papers to show why they are held here? Thinks Patton said, Rice has the papers. Defendant then said, Colored citizens, I see no authority for detaining your colored friends. The negroes and the crowd then went out. Patton then came up to defendant, and said, Here's the papers; those slaves are mine, and I will hold you responsible. Witness supposed that claimant had not before made known his claim. There was not much noise or excitement. Recollects distinctly that defendant had no hat on, or with him. Thinks it was after the crowd had left, and before Patton said, Rice has the papers, that defendant made the remark, that he saw no authority for detaining the negroes, etc. Defendant may have used these words before. Witness says defendant did not use the words testified to by Patton, Hedges, and Rice. That Patton did not come to his desk, and ask him what he was going to do, and select the papers, etc.

Having given this condensed statement of the material facts in evidence, I do not propose to analyze, or make any comments upon them, with a view of aiding you in coming to a conclusion, as to what is or is not proved. That duty belongs exclusively to the jury, and I leave it to their deliberate and unbiassed action. I shall merely state the legal principles involved in the case, and leave it to the jury to make the application of them to the facts.

As before stated, there is no dispute in this case, that the three persons named in the declaration as the slaves of the plaintiff, were in fact such in Kentucky, and that they escaped thence into the State of Ohio. But it must moreover appear, that they were in legal custody, by an arrest, either with or without warrant, by the owner or some person legally authorized by him to recapture them. The 6th sec. of the Act of Congress before referred to, provides, "that where a person held to service or labor in any State or Territory in the United States, has heretofore, or shall hereafter escape into another State or Territory of the United States, the person or persons to whom such service or labor may be due, or his, her, or their agent or attorney, duly authorized by power of attorney in writing, acknowledged and certified under the seal of some legal officer or Court, of the State or Territory in which the same may be executed, may pursue and reclaim such fugitive person, either by procuring a warrant from some one of the Courts, judges or commissioners aforesaid, of the proper circuit, district or county, for the apprehension of such fugitive; or by seizing and arresting such fugitive, where the same can be done without process; and by taking or causing such person to be taken before such Court, judge, or commissioner," etc.

It will be seen from the foregoing provision of the Statute, that the authority is expressly given to the owner of the fugitive, or his agent or attorney, to arrest without warrant. The arrest in this case was made by Patton, as the agent of the plaintiff, without any warrant for this purpose. It appears also, that the power of attorney under which he acted as agent, was executed and authenticated according to the requirement of the Act of Congress. The arrest of these fugitives was therefore clearly authorized by law, and they were legally in the custody of the plaintiff's agent, at the time of the alleged interference by the defendant.

But to sustain the present action, it must appear to the satisfaction of the jury, that the defendant had notice or knowledge that these persons were fugitives, and were legally in custody, when he aided in their escape. It is one of the material allegations in the plaintiff's declaration, that defendant knowingly, willingly, and illegally aided or abetted the escape of the fugitives. This must therefore be proved, as essential to the plaintiff's right of recovery. But the knowledge of the defendant, both as to the persons' being fugitives and being in legal custody, either may be established, by positive proof, or may be inferred from circumstances. In the case of *Giltner* v. *Gorham et al.*, 4 *McLean*, 420, it was held, that " to bring an individual within the Statute, he must have knowledge that the colored persons are fugitives from labor, or he must act under such circumstances as show that he might have had such knowledge, by exercising ordinary prudence."

It is in evidence in this case, that the defendant was employed as counsel for the fugitives, and it is not perhaps an unreasonable presumption, that he was apprised of all the facts which rendered it necessary that his professional aid should be invoked in their behalf.

As already intimated the jury must be satisfied that the defendant had knowledge that the fugitives had been arrested, and were in custody at the time of his alleged interference. If the plaintiff's agent held them without authority, they were illegally detained, and no one could have incurred liability by aiding them in their escape. It will be for the jury to determine, in reference to all the circumstances, whether the defendant may not be presumed to have known that the fugitives had been arrested. It is in evidence, both by the plaintiff's and defendant's witnesses, that on entering the Mayor's Office, he enquired by what authority the colored persons were held. If the witnesses for the plaintiff are entitled to credit, he was informed distinctly that the negroes were claimed by Patton as agent of plaintiff, and that he had arrested them, as he was authorised to do, without warrant. From the occurrences which followed the announcement of the fact, that the arrest had been made without warrant, it seems most probable the defendant supposed the negroes could only be taken and held in custody, by an arrest under a warrant. The power of attorney, proving the agency of Patton, was laid on the Mayor's desk, and could have been seen by the defendant, if he had wished or requested to see it. If, under the erroneous belief that a warrant was necessary to justify the arrest of the fugitives, he did not ask for its production, or use reasonable diligence to ascertain the existence of the instrument, he is not protected from the consequences of his acts. As before stated, no liability was incurred by the defendant, without a legal arrest and detention of the fugitives; but the test of the legality of the arrest is to be determined by the Statute, and not by the opinion of the defendant. On

receiving information that there was no warrant, it would have
been altogether proper for the defendant to have required the
production of the written power under which the plaintiff's
agent acted ; and if this request had been evaded or refused,
there would have been reason for the conclusion, that the
fugitives were in custody without any authority to detain
them.

If the jury are satisfied that these persons were fugitive
slaves and were legally in the custody of the plaintiff's agent,
at the time of their escape, and that these facts were known
to the defendant, or that, from the circumstances, he is fairly
chargeable with such knowledge, the further enquiry remains,
whether he aided, abetted, or assisted in their escape, in the
sense of being liable to the penalty fixed by the Statute. On
this subject, I have only to remark, that any words or actions
tending to produce an escape, if the result follows, will subject a party to the penalty of the law. It is not necessary
that there should be any physical force used, to effect the
escape. It is true, the party implicated must have intended
such a result, but this intention may be inferred from the
facts. Every one is presumed to have intended whatever is
the necessary and legitimate result of his acts. If therefore
an escape follows, as the result of certain words or acts, the
law raises the presumption, that it was intended, and holds
the party responsible.

In the case of *Vaughan* v. *Williams*, 3 *McLean*, 530,
which was an action for damages for rescuing certain slaves
from the possession of the plaintiff, the learned Judge said,
in reference to what constituted an interference, subjecting
the defendant to the penalty of the Statute, that "if he (the
defendant) countenanced and encouraged, from time to time,
the movements of the crowd which resulted in the rescue,
or being present, sanctioned it in any form, he is liable to
the penalty. A man cannot incite others to the commission
of an illegal act, and escape the consequences by the plea,

that he did not put forth his hand in the consummation of the act."

As to the occurrence at the Mayor's office, there are some discrepancies between the witnesses for the plaintiff and those for the defendant. It is the exclusive province of the jury to decide upon the credit due to the testimony of witnesses. It will be their duty, if practicable, to harmonize their conflicting statements, and thus avoid the conclusion that any have wilfully falsified the truth. But if this cannot be done, they must receive or reject the testimony, as their best judgment shall dictate. If the witnesses for the the plaintiff are accredited, there is no room for a doubt, that the defendant unlawfully interfered for the rescue of the slaves. The words attributed to him by these witnesses, could have no other effect, under the circumstances of the case, than to induce the crowd to interfere for the rescue of the slaves. Rice, one of the plaintiff's witnesses, is impeached by proof of bad character for truth; and unless his testimony is corroborated by other witnesses entitled to credit it will be the duty of the jury to reject it.

The points of difference in the narratives of the witnesses, as to what took place at the Mayor's office, are doubtless obvious to the jury, and need not be specially noticed. If, however, the jury shall reject the statements of all the plaintiff's witnesses, as unworthy of credit, it will be proper for them to enquire whether, upon the defendant's evidence, a verdict ought to pass for the plaintiff. What is sufficient to constitute an illegal aiding, abetting or assisting, the escape of a fugitive slave under the Statute, has been stated by the Court. It will be for the jury to make the application of the principles laid down, to the facts before them. It will be for them to enquire and decide, whether the evidence warrants the conclusion that the acts and words of the defendant were the direct cause of the escape of the negroes. If, without implicating the defendant, they can find a satisfactory reason for the sudden and hurried movements in the Mayor's office, resulting in the escape of the slaves, it will be their duty to do so. The Statute under which this suit is instituted, is highly penal in its provisions, and the party seeking a recovery upon an alleged violation of it, should be held to strict proof.

There is one point which has been strenuously urged by counsel, to which it is the duty of the Court to call the attention of the jury. It is insisted, that the defendant acting as counsel for the fugitives, did no more than he was warranted in doing from his professional relation to them. In the case of *Norris* v. *Newton et al.*, 5 *McLean*, 102, one of the defendants acting as counsel for the slaves it was contended that in that character he was protected from liability. The Court stated the law to the jury in these words: "So far as his acts were limited to the duties of counsel he is not responsible. But, if he exceeded the proper limits of a counsellor at law, he is responsible for his acts, the same as any other individual." This is doubtless the true principle, as applicable to this point. Persons arrested and in custody upon the charge of being fugitive slaves, have an undoubted right to all the benefits of counsel. And it is in no sense improper, that counsel should advise and assist persons in that situation. In their professional character, they may enquire into the authority by which the fugitives are held, or insist on a legal investigation of the question whether they are slaves; and on the hearing before competent authority, may urge their discharge from custody. If satisfied they are illegally restrained of their liberty, the great remedy by writ of *habeas corpus* may be rightfully resorted to. In short, any proceeding which is in accordance with the law of the land, may be instituted to test the question of the legality of their detention. But it would be extending the principle of professional privilege too far, to say that a lawyer is justified, even in behalf of a fugitive slave, in aiding and assisting his escape, in any mode which the law does not sanction.   There is perhaps good reason to infer, from the evidence in this case, that the defendant supposed the slaves could not be held in legal custody, without an arrest by warrant.   As already stated, the law does not require this process to authorize an arrest.   And if the defendant under a misapprehension of the Statute has brought himself within its penalties, he is not protected from responsibility by his professional character.

But it is quite unnecessary to detain the jury with further remarks, in committing this case to them.   The trial has been conducted throughout, by the counsel, not only with great ability, but with great fairness.   No efforts have been made to introduce any false issues, or in any way to divert the minds of the jury from the merits of the case.   This is creditable to the gentlemen concerned, and worthy of their distinguished professional standing.   It remains for the jury, excluding every extrinsic consideration from their view, to decide this case in accordance with the duty their oath imposes. If, in their judgment, the plaintiff has sustained an injury for which the law, applied to the facts, entitles him to redress, I have the fullest confidence they will award it to him by their verdict.   If, on the other hand, they should come to the conclusion that the defendant is not implicated as charged, the jury will cheerfully acquit him of all censure, by a verdict in his favor.   And I need not say that in the decision of this case, the individual views of the jurors, as to the justice and expediency of the law upon which the action is founded, should have no weight.

[The jury returned a verdict for the plaintiff, which, on a motion for a new trial, the Court refused to set aside.]

CHARLES M. GIBBONS *v.* RUSH R. SLOANE.

[This suit was brought to recover the value of a slave owned by the plaintiff, who escaped and was rescued at the same time and under the same

United States *v.* Linus Hand, Francis G. Stratton et al.

circumstances, as in the preceding case of *Weimer* v. *Sloane.* The evidence was the same in both cases, except as to the manner of the execution of the power of attorney to Patton, who made the arrest as the agent of Gibbons; and by the consent of the counsel, both cases were submitted to the jury at the same time. In this case, it appeared that Gibbons had executed a power of attorney in the State of Kentucky, as required by the act of Congress, in which either no name was inserted as the agent of the plaintiff, or, if any, that of some person other than Patton; and that afterwards and before the arrest of the fugitive by Patton, his name was inserted by the plaintiff or some other person, at Sandusky City, in the State of Ohio, without any acknowledgment of the instrument in that State. The Court instructed the jury, that under the act of 1850, this was not a valid power to Patton, and did not authorize him to make the arrest. The jury returned a verdict for the defendant.]

UNITED STATES *v.* LINUS HAND, FRANCIS G. STRATTON ET AL.

A recognizance taken by a Commissioner of the Circuit Court, conditioned for the appearance of the principal "to answer the charge of a wilful and corrupt conspiracy to burn the steamboat Martha Washington on the Mississippi river," is void, as not describing an offense made punishable by any Act of Congress, and cognizable by the Circuit Court.

By the 23rd Sec. of the Act of Congress of March 3rd, 1825, defining and punishing the crime of conspiring to cast away, burn, or destroy a vessel, the *intention* thereby to injure underwriters is an essential ingredient of the crime; and without the averment of such intention, no offense is described in violation of any Act of Congress.

The authority of a Commissioner in arresting, holding to bail, or committing to jail, is expressly limited to complaints or charges importing an offense against the laws of the United States.

The recognizance in this case, was void *ab initio*, and created no obligation on the principal to appear.

The bail was not therefore bound by this recognizance for the appearance of the principal, as it is of the essence of every undertaking by the bail or surety of another, that there should have been a valid obligation of the principal.

Mr. *Morton*, District Attorney, for the United States.
Messrs. *Ward & Swayne*, for the defendants.

OPINION BY JUDGE LEAVITT.

This is a suit by *scire facias* on a recognizance taken by a Commissioner of this Court, by which Nicholson as principal, and Hand and Stratton as bail, acknowledge themselves, jointly and severally, to owe the United States the sum of five thousand dollars, upon the condition that said Nicholson shall appear before this Court, at the term then next following, "to answer a charge of wilful and corrupt conspiracy for burning the steamboat Martha Washington, on the Mississippi river." The *scire facias* avers that the recognizance was duly returned to said Court, and that, Nicholson failing to appear, a default against all the parties was entered.

The *scire facias* has been returned served on the defendants Hand and Stratton, and not found, as to Nicholson. The defendants on whom service has been made, have appeared, and filed a general demurrer to the *scire facias*.

The main point urged in support of the demurrer, is, that the act charged in the recognizance, to answer which the defendants undertook for the appearance of Nicholson, is not an offense by Act of Congress, and therefore not cognizable by this Court; and that the recognizance is a nullity, creating no obligation on the principal or his bail.

This objection is fatal to this action. There is no Statute of the United States, which punishes a conspiracy to burn a steamboat on the Mississippi river. This recognizance was probably intended to provide for the appearance of the principal, Nicholson, to answer to charge of conspiracy to burn the steamboat named, with intent to injure certain underwriters. This is a crime, defined and punished by the 23rd Section of the Act of Congress of the 3rd of March, 1825—4 *vol. Laws U. S.*, 122; but by its terms, the *intent* with which the alleged conspiracy is entered into, is an essential ingredient of the crime. By an inadvertence, this intent, as descriptive of the crime, is omitted in the recognizance ;.

and the act set forth is not in violation of any Act of Congress, and therefore not within the cognizance of this Court. Under the clause contained in the Constitution of the United States, vesting in Congress the power to regulate commerce among the States, it was no doubt competent for that body to punish the offense defined in the section above referred to; and this Court, by its decision, has sustained an indictment framed under it. But, in that case, the *intent* of the alleged conspiracy was set forth in the language of the Statute; and it is clear, without such averment, the indictment could not have been sustained.

It results from this view, that the Commissioner had no authority to take the recognizance of these parties, for the offense which it describes. The power conferred by the 33rd Sec. of the Judiciary Act of Sept. 24th, 1789, upon a judge or justice of the United States, or of a State, to issue warrants in criminal cases, and commit or hold to bail, is expressly limited to violations of the laws of the United States. And the same limitation is contained in the Act of 23rd of August, 1842, by which Commissioners of the Circuit Court are authorized to exercise the same powers as are vested in a judge or justice, under the said 33 Sec. of the Act of 1789.

This recognizance, being void *ab initio*, imposed no legal obligation on the principal to appear and answer to the charge which it set forth. And it is clear, if there was no legal obligation on the part of the principal, there was none on his bail. It is of the essence of all contracts or undertakings by a surety or bail, that there should have been a valid obligation of the principal. It is well said by a writer on this subject, that " the nullity of the principal obligation, necessarily induces the nullity of the accessory."

The demurrer to the *scire facias* is therefore sustained.

United States *v.* James Bougher.

The 41st Section of the Steamboat Act of 1852, declaring that "all penalties imposed by this Act, may be recovered in an action of debt, by any person who will sue therefor," does not preclude the United States from suing for a penalty in an action of debt.

The right to sue under this provision as an informer being limited to a *person*, the United States cannot sue in that character.

But when an Act is declared to be unlawful by Statute, and a penalty is prescribed, a person who violates the law may be proceeded against by indictment, or by an action of debt, if no mode of suing for the penalty is specially provided by the Statute.

At common law, debt is a proper action to recover a pecuniary penalty imposed by Statute.

By the 9th Section of the Judiciary Act of 1789, the District Courts have cognizance of all suits at common law, where the United States sue, and the matter in dispute amounts to one hundred dollars, exclusive of costs.

Mr. *Morton*, District Attorney, for the United States.

Mr. *A. E. Gwynne*, for the defendant.

OPINION OF THE COURT BY JUDGE LEAVITT.

This is an action of debt prosecuted in the name of the United States. The declaration avers, in substance, that the defendant, being the master of a steamboat used for the transportation of passengers on the Ohio and Mississippi rivers, employed a pilot to serve on his boat, without being licensed for that purpose, as required by law; and that thereby he has incurred a penalty of one hundred dollars.

A demurrer has been filed to the declaration; and it is insisted in argument, that the United States cannot maintain an action of debt for the penalty, and that it can only be recovered in a suit brought by an informer.

The 10th sub-division of the 9th Section of the Act of the 13th of August, 1852, to amend the Act " to provide for the better security of the lives of passengers on board of vessels propelled in whole or in part by steam," (*Pamphlet Laws*,

U. S., 1 *Session*, 32 *Congress, p.* 61,) declares that "it shall be unlawful for any person to employ, or any person to serve as, an Engineer or Pilot on any steamboat" used for the conveyance of passengers, who has not procured a license from the proper Inspectors for that purpose; and it provides that any one violating this provision, shall forfeit one hundred dollars for each offense. The 41st Section of the Act just referred to, provides that "all penalties imposed by this Act may be recovered in an action of debt, by any person who will sue therefor, in any Court of the United States." This is the only provision of the Statute, relating to the manner of enforcing the penalty for employing an unlicensed pilot, or serving as an unlicensed engineer. It is true the 1st section of the Act, provides that the owner of a steamboat, for the offense of permitting a boat to be navigated with passengers on board, without complying with the terms of the Act, shall be subject to the penalties contained in the 2nd Section of the Act of July, A. D. 1838. But it is very clear this provision cannot, on any just principle of interpretation, include or apply to the case set out in the declaration in this action. And it is equally clear, that this action is not sustainable upon the 11th Section of the Act of 1838, which enacts that penalties imposed by that Act, may be sued for and recovered, in the name of the United States, in the District or Circuit Court of the proper District. That provision is restricted in its terms to offenses created by the Act of 1838, and cannot be held to extend to those created by the subsequent Act, although in its title, the latter Statute purports to be an amendment of the former. It was doubtless competent for Congress, in the Act of 1852, to have declared that all penalties incurred under it should be prosecuted in accordance with the 11th Section of the Act of 1838. But having failed to do so, it would violate all settled rules for the construction of penal Statutes, to hold that the provisions of that section can be transferred to, and made a part of, the Act of 1852. The 1st Section of the latter Act, adopting the provisions of the Act of 1838, and prescribing the manner of prosecuting for violations of the Act, must be restricted to the cases specified in that section. These, as before noticed, include only offenses by the *owner* of a steamboat, in fitting out and navigating the same, without complying with the requirements of the Statute. Violations of the Statute in the service or the employment of unlicensed pilots or engineers, are not specified in the 1st Section of the Act of 1852. In reference to the manner of enforcing the penalty against the defendant for the offense set out in the declaration, the Act of 1838 must be wholly excluded from the consideration of the Court.

Having thus referred to the statutory enactments relating to this subject, the question raised on this demurrer is, whether the United States can sue in debt, for the penalty which it is alleged the defendant has incurred, under the 41st Section of the Act of 1852, before cited. The right to sue under this provision is limited to a person; and it is clear that the government, in its sovereign capacity, is not a *person* to whom this right attaches.

It was strenuously insisted in the argument, that under the provisions of the Statute referred to, if the United States could not maintain this action, as an informer, it could not be sustained on any other basis. In other words, that as the 41st Section of the Act of 1852 provided that all penalties imposed by the Act, may be recovered in an action of debt by any person who will sue therefor, in any Court of the United States, every other mode of enforcing a penalty under the Act is prohibited. On the other hand, it was contended by the counsel for the government, that this is merely a cumulative provision, not intended to abridge or deny the right of the government to proceed in any other mode known to the law, and usually resorted to in practice, but to sanction a remedy deemed necessary to the efficient enforcement of the law, and one which could exist only by express legislative enactment. The latter view is the one adopted by this Court, as best suited to carry into effect the intention of the law, and not in conflict with either the provisions of the statute, or any just principles of construction. It is most obvious that the requirements of the Statute in relation to steamboats, would have been wholly inefficient, if the enforcement of its penal provisions had been referred solely to the action or interposition of common informers. Such, clearly, was not the intention of Congress in the provision referred to, giving an informer the right in all cases arising under the Statute to prosecute for the penalties.

The words of the Statute are merely permissive to an informer to sue, and do not import that that is the sole remedy for its violation. This is also inferrible by a reference to the 1st Section of the Act of 1852, from which it will be seen, as to one class of offenses, the penalties provided and the mode of proceeding authorized in the 11th Section of the Act of 1838, are expressly adopted.

The right of the United States to prosecute for violations of the Act of 1852 is, therefore, in no way affected by the provision securing to an informer a right to sue for the penalties incurred under it. It is most obvious, that it was not designed to restrict the manner of prosecuting for a penalty to one particular form of proceeding, but as authorizing a supplemental or additional remedy.

In this view, the only remaining inquiry is, whether the United States can maintain the action of debt, for the penalty for the alleged offense, without an express statutory provision authorizing such mode of procedure. On this point no authorities were adduced in the argument, nor have I been able to recur to any bearing directly upon it. I suppose, however, that it is hardly a controvertible proposition, that upon the facts alleged in the declaration, the defendant could have been prosecuted by indictment, although the Statute does not authorize it in terms. The Statute makes it an offense for any one to employ an engineer or pilot on a steam-boat, or for any person to serve in such capacity, without a license, and subjects the party offending to a penalty of one hundred dollars. It is silent as to the manner of prosecuting for penalties, except that the 41st Section confers upon an informer a right to sue in debt, in any case arising under the Statute in which a penalty has been incurred. But if no one chooses to avail himself of this right by instituting a suit, the guilty person may be proceeded against by indictment. In all cases when an act is declared to be unlawful, and a punishment or penalty is annexed to the doing of the act, it pertains to the sovereignty of the State, through the agency of the judicial department, to punish it by indictment; and it does not require any express statutory authority as the warrant for such a proceeding. Is it not equally clear, upon the same principle, that if the government chooses to waive the right of proceeding in this way, and to adopt the milder form of an action of debt for the penalty, it is competent to do so? It is a long settled principle of the common law, that the action of debt is maintainable to recover a pecuniary penalty imposed by a Statute, and when such a penalty is incurred by a violation of a Statute of the United States, it accrues to the government, and may be sued for in its name ; and it certainly can constitute no just ground of complaint on the part of the person implicated, that he is called upon to answer for the violation of a law, in a civil suit, instead of being arraigned for it, upon the finding of a Grand Jury.

In addition to these views, it may be stated, that the right of the United States to sue in this Court, for the penalty alleged to have been incurred by the defendant, and the competency of the Court to entertain the jurisdiction of the case, may be deduced from the clause in the 9th Section of the Judiciary Act of 1789, relating to the jurisdiction of the District Court; which declares that said Conrt shall have cogni-

zance of all suits at common law, where the United States
sue, and the matter in dispute amounts, exclusive of costs, to
the sum of One Hundred Dollars. 1 *vol. L. U. S.*, page 77.
This case certainly meets all the conditions of this clause. It
is a suit at *Common Law*, brought by the *United States*, and
the matter in dispute amounts to *One Hundred Dollars*.
Demurrer overruled.

M. E. LUCAS ET AL. v. THE STEAMBOAT THOMAS SWANN, T. SWEENY ET AL. OWNERS.

A libellant claiming damages on the ground of a collision with another
boat, must make it appear that there was no want of ordinary care and
skill, in the management of his boat, and that the injury for which he
claims compensation, resulted from the sole fault of the other boat. But
the faulty management of one boat, will not excuse the want of proper care
and skill in the other.

A case of damage resulting from inevitable accident, is defined to be,
"that which a party charged with the offense could not possibly prevent,
by the exercise of ordinary care, caution and skill."

There is no ground for the conclusion in this case, that the injury was
unavoidable; but on the contrary, it is a case of mixed or mutual fault.

But to constitute a proper basis for a decree apportioning the damages
equally to each boat, as in a case of mixed or mutual fault, the evidence
must enable the Court to find the specific faults of each, from which the
injury resulted.

If the Court is satisfied that both boats were in fault, and yet, from the
conflict in the evidence, cannot find, with reasonable certainty, the specific
faults of each, it constitutes a case of inscrutable fault; and, in such case,
in accordance with the law as settled in the United States, a decree for
the equal apportionment of the damages resulting from the injury may
be entered.

The present is adjudged to be such a case, and a decree is entered in
accordance with the principle stated.

Messrs. Walker, Kebler and Force, for libellants.
Mr. T. D. Lincoln, for respondents.

OPINION OF THE COURT BY JUDGE LEAVITT.

This is a case in Admiralty, brought by the libellants, as
owners of the steamboat "Fanny Fern," to obtain compen-

sation for an injury to that boat, by a collision with the
steamboat "Thomas Swann," of which the respondents are
the owners.

This collision occurred a little after 4 o'clock in the morning of 28th February, 1854, on the Ohio river, some ten or
twelve miles below Wheeling, in the channel between Little
Grave Creek Bar and the Ohio shore, near the head of the
bar, and at the distance of something upwards of one hundred
yards from that shore. The Fern was a stern-wheel boat of
about 450 tons burthen; the Swann is a side-wheel boat, of
the largest class of Ohio packet boats, and was, at the time
of the collision, one of the boats of the Union Line, from
Louisville to Wheeling.

The libellants allege, that as the result of the collision,
their boat immediately sunk in fourteen feet of water; and
they claim damages for the full value of the boat, as being a
total loss. They also allege, that the injury to the Fern was
caused solely by the fault and misconduct of those having
charge of the respondents' boat; and set forth as the foundation of their claim for indemnity, that the Fern was descending the river, in the proper and usual place of a descending
boat, a short distance above the head of the Grave Creek Bar,
and that her pilot, noticing the lights of a boat coming up near
the Ohio shore, and having no signal from her, when the boats
were within from a quarter to less than a half a mile of each
other, he gave two taps of the large bell of the Fern, thereby
indicating his wish to take the left-hand side of the channel.
The ascending boat proved to be the Swann; and the libellants
aver, that she made no response to the Fern's bell, and that
the Fern continued her course down, in her proper place,
when her pilot, seeing the Swann veering across the channel,
towards the Virginia side, promptly gave the order for stopping
and backing; that the boat was stopped and backed, and
every precaution used to prevent a collision; but that the
Swann, wrongfully pursuing her course across the channel,

struck the Fern nearly at right angles, on the starboard side, near the foot of the stairs, about fifteen feet from the bow of the boat, cutting her about two-thirds through, and causing her to go down in less than one minute.

The respondents, on the other hand, deny that there was any fault or misconduct on the part of those having charge of their boat; and insist that the Fern, before entering the channel between the bar and the shore, was not in the proper place of a descending boat, being not more than thirty yards from the Ohio shore, and so near thereto, that in the line of vision from the pilot-house of the Swann, the lights of the Fern were so blended with the lights on shore at that point, that they could not be distinguished; and that from this cause the pilot of the Swann did not know, and had no reason to suppose, that a boat was coming down, till the bell of the Fern was heard, at which time the boats were not more than 200 or 250 yards apart; and that instantly, on being apprised that a boat was coming down, the pilot of the Swann gave one tap of the large bell, to indicate that he could not take the Ohio side of the channel, and almost simultaneously rang the bells for stopping and backing. The respondents also insist that, when the Fern's bell was heard, the Swann was in the proper place of an ascending boat of her size, at that stage of water, following the channel, and slightly quartering towards the Virginia shore; and that the Fern, being close to the Ohio shore, and with every facility for passing the Swann on that side, had no right to signal for the Virginia side; and that the Fern improperly attempted to cross the channel, and was nearly at right angles with it, when the boats came together. And they insist also, that having made the attempt to cross, she was wrong in stopping and backing; and that the collision was the result of this improper navigation, and not of any faulty conduct on the part of the Swann.

It may be noticed here, as one of the facts about which there is no contradiction in the evidence, that the Swann

struck the Fern at an angle of about 72° with her stern; and
that she sunk near the head of the bar, about one hundred
yards from the Ohio shore: her stern being in deep water,
and very near the line of navigation usually followed by
both ascending and descending boats at that point.

This brief outline presents the nature of the controversy
between these parties. Their theories and assumptions, both
in the pleadings and by the evidence, are in direct conflict;
and it may be added, both cannot be sustained. The libellants claim that their boat was without fault, and therefore
that the respondents are answerable for the whole damage
she has suffered from the collision; while the respondents
claim that the injury to the Fern was not occasioned by any
fault on their part, but is chargeable solely to her mismanagement.

The evidence affords no ground for any unfavorable presumption against either of the parties, for any failure to
comply with the requirements of the Act of Congress of
1852. Whatever of contradiction there may be in the proofs
in other respects, it satisfactorily appears that each of the
boats was provided with the requisite signal lights, and that
they were in good order at the time of the collision; and
also that each was manned with the usual and necessary
number of men and officers. And it is specially worthy of
notice here, that the proof is ample, on both sides, to show
that the pilot of each boat on duty at the time of the collision
was, in all respects, trustworthy, and well qualified for the
duties of his station.

With a view to some proper basis for a decree in this case,
I have carefully read and reflected on the great mass of evidence presented on the hearing, partly oral, but mostly in the
form of depositions. In this effort, I have encountered great
difficulties, arising from the discrepant and contradictory
character of the evidence, for and against the opposite claims
of the parties. It is impossible, by any mental process, or

upon any known principle of estimating the preponderance of evidence, to decide with even reasonable certainty, in what direction the scale should incline. With equally favorable opportunities of witnessing the occurrences to which they testify, and with the presumption that the witnesses on either side are equally intelligent, truthful and credible, it would seem to be an arbitrary exercise of the discretion of a judge, to reject the testimony given by one party and accredit that given by the other.

To show the difficulty, if not the utter impossibility, of sustaining the hypothesis of either of these parties, it is only necessary to state some of the essential features or aspects of the case, in regard to which the evidence is in direct and irreconcilable conflict. And first, it is a conceded fact in the case, that the signal bell of the Fern, the descending boat, was first sounded; but as to the relative position of the boats, when the bell was tapped, and when the pilot of the Swann was apprised that a boat was approaching, the testimony of the parties is essentially variant. The witnesses for the libellants testify that the Fern, at that point, was in the proper place of a down-going boat, some one hundred and thirty yards out from the Ohio shore, and nearly on a line with the inner side of the bar. On the other hand, the respondents' witnesses testify, that when the bell of the Fern was first tapped, she was so near to the Ohio shore, that her lights were blended with, and could not be distinguished from, lights along the shore; thus rendering it impossible for the pilot of the Swann to know that a boat was coming down, until her bell was heard; and also, excluding the descending boat from the right of choosing the outer or Virginia side of the channel, and making it altogether wrong in her to cross the channel, for the purpose of getting on that side. And the evidence is not less conflicting, in reference to the position of the Swann, the ascending boat, at the point where she was first seen by the pilot of the Fern. On one side, the proof is, the Swann was coming up the Ohio shore; on the other, that she was out in the channel, quartering to the Virginia side. And as to the distance between the boats when the Fern was first seen by the pilot of the other boat, a point of vital importance in the decision of the case, the evidence is very discrepant. The pilot of the Fern swears the distance was near a half a mile, and other witnesses for the libellants state it as upwards of a quarter of a mile; while for the respondents it is proved it did not exceed two hundred and fifty yards, and in the opinion of one witness, was not more than one hundred and fifty yards. There is also a direct contradiction between the testimony of the parties as to the course of the two boats, and their position at the time they came together. The libellants' witnesses swear the Fern was running straight down the river, up to the time when the pilot tapped her bell, and was then turned slightly across towards the Virginia side; whereas the respondents' witnesses say she was running nearly square across the river, and was struck by the Swann almost at right angles. And there is the same conflict in reference to the position of the latter boat. The witnesses for the libellants prove that the Swann turned out from the Ohio shore and was pointed across the channel ,towards the Virginia shore, when the collision took place. The witnesses on the other side say her course was not changed from the time the Fern was seen, and was but slightly inclined towards the Virginia shore. And again, while the witnesses on one side state positively that the Swann ran into the Fern, those on the other are equally clear that it was the Fern that struck the Swann.

These are some of the points in reference to which the evidence is conflicting, to an extent that makes it difficult to come to a conclusion for or against either of the parties. The libellants, as the result of this unfortunate collision, are the sole sufferers, no injury having been sustained by the other boat; and, as already stated, they claim indemnity for the

whole amount of the injury they have sustained. They are
entitled to a decree for this, only on making proof that the
injury resulted from the fault of those having charge of the
respondents' boat, and that there was no want of ordinary care
or skill on the part of the libellants, to prevent the collision.
On the other hand, it is a well settled principle of maritime
law, that the fault of one boat or vessel will not excuse any
want of care, diligence or skill in another. Now, if the
Court was at liberty to regard the evidence for the libellants,
to the exclusion of that offered by the other party, there
could be no hesitation in decreeing indemnity for the full
amount of the injury. That evidence proves the respondents' boats to have been in fault, without any blame imputable to the libellants. But, if the evidence of the respondents is
received and accredited without regard to that adduced by the
libellants, the fault would rest upon the boat of the latter; and,
the result would be, a decree dismissing the libel, at the costs
of the libellants. But for the reasons stated, I am unable
satisfactorily to come to either of these conclusions, or enter
a decree upon either of the grounds indicated.

Without thinking it necessary, in the view I take of this
case, to enter minutely into the examination of the evidence
presented on both sides, I am prepared to state, as the conclusion of my mind, that the collision in controversy was not
the result of inevitable or unavoidable accident. This is defined to be, " that which a party charged with an offense
could not possibly prevent, by the exercise of ordinary care,
caution and maritime skill." 2 *Dods.*, 83; 2 *Wm. Rob.*,
205; *Flanders on Mar. Law*, 298. It is not a reasonable
supposition, that the injury sustained by the libellants' boat
could have been inflicted, without some fault, and as the mere
result of unavoidable necessity. There was, at the time of
this occurrence, not less than twelve feet water in the channel of the river, and it was then rising. At the place where
the Fern sunk, near the outer edge of the upper part of Grave

Creek Bar, there was a depth of fourteen feet. There was deep water the whole width of the channel between the edge of the bar and the Ohio shore, which, at that stage of water, was from one hundred to one hundred and twenty yards wide; and even upon the bar itself there was six feet water. There was then ample verge for these boats to have passed, without coming in contact. And moreover, there is no disagreement in the statements of the witnesses, that the night was calm, and, although somewhat cloudy, not so dark as to render navigation difficult or dangerous. With these facts in view, there would seem to be no difficulty in reaching the conclusion, that there was a censurable want of care, caution, or skill, in the management of these boats; and that the injury cannot be fairly placed to the account of inevitable accident.

It follows from this conclusion, that if this is a case warranting a decree of indemnity, it must be regarded either as one of mixed or mutual fault, or of inscrutable fault. If it be a case belonging to the first of these classes, by the well settled principles of the maritime law—differing in this respect from the common law—the decree must be for an equal apportionment of the injury sustained, between the two boats, with such order in respect to costs, as the Court may deem equitable. While I do not affirm that such a decree might not be justified in this case, there would seem to be an objection to such a disposition of it. As I understand the maritime law, the Court not only must find, as a basis of such decree, that the blame is imputable to both parties, but must find specifically the faulty acts of each, to which the injury is to be charged. As already intimated, it may be well doubted, whether the most searching analysis of the evidence would result in a satisfactory conclusion as to the precise acts which were the direct cause of the collision. The contradictory character of the evidence involves the facts of this case in great doubt, and renders it extremely difficult to attain such a result with reasonable certainty. Nearly every fact stated by the witnesses,

19a

importing censure in the management of either of the boats, is so far impugned by opposing evidence, as to create doubt and uncertainty. In this state of the case, the Court would scarcely be justified in assuming a theory, which could only be maintained by arbitrarily repudiating the evidence on one side, and accrediting that offered by the other. For the reasons which will be stated hereafter, there is no necessity for a resort to this desperate expedient, to attain the ends of justice in this case.

It is true, there is one exception to the remark just made, that nearly every material fact implicating either boat is contradicted by opposing testimony. It has not escaped the attention of the Court, that the evidence shows conclusively, that the Swann, as the ascending boat, failed to give the first tap of the bell, as required under certain circumstances, by the rules of the Board of Supervising Inspectors, adopted pursuant to the Steamboat Law of 1852. This act of Congress confers on this Board ample authority to adopt such rules; and they are obligatory in cases to which they fairly apply. And a violation of any of these rules, resulting in disaster, raises a presumption of culpability, which can only be removed by proof that the collision is attributable to some other cause. The rule referred to requires the pilot of an ascending boat, "so soon as the other boat shall be in sight and hearing, to sound his bell," etc. But if, with ordinary diligence, the descending boat is not seen or heard in time to enable the pilot to comply with the rule, no censure can attach for not doing so. It would seem from the evidence of the respondents, that the Fern, from the fact that she was too near the Ohio shore, and from the impossibility of distinguishing her lights from those on the shore, was not seen and known to be a steamboat, until her bell was heard by the pilot of the Swann. This fact would excuse the pilot for not complying with the rule referred to. In reference to some other requirements contained in these rules, which have been noticed in the argument, I have only to say, that I doubt their application to the then state of the river, and the circumstances in which these boats were placed, immediately preceding the collision. There was not only a wide channel between the Ohio shore and the bar, but, in point of fact, there was water enough on the bar itself, for either of the boats to have passed over it. Without further remarks on this point, I have only to say, in reference to the rules referred to, that they must be construed in subordination to the paramount rule of navigation, that a collision must always be avoided if possible; and an injury inflicted will not be justified, unless inevitable, on the ground that the injured boat had violated a prescribed rule.

But I do not propose to enter into an elaborate inquiry, whether this is a case of mixed or mutual fault, justifying a decree on that basis. In my judgment, there are, as before intimated, obstacles in the way of entering such a decree in this case. And as it may be disposed of on another principle, according, as I think, with strict justice and the doctrines of the maritime law, I prefer to place it on that ground. In its results, so far as the interests of these parties are concerned, the decree which I propose to enter, for an equal apportionment of the loss sustained by the collision, is the same as if based on the finding of mixed fault.

As already intimated, I cannot upon the evidence before me, with any reliable certainty, adopt the conclusion, that the injury suffered by the libellants arose from the sole fault of those in charge of the respondents' boat; nor can I find the reverse of this proposition to be satisfactorily established, and thus hold, that the respondents are absolved from all liability for the injury sustained. It is equally clear, for reasons before adverted to, that this injury cannot be fairly charged to inevitable accident. It is a fair deduction from the facts before the Court, that the cause of this collision is to be found in the faulty management of one or both of these boats. And I have no hesitation in concluding, that in the excitement produced by the occasion, the pilots of both were in fault. This is a reasonable implication from all the circumstances involved in the transaction. And yet, from the conflict in the evidence, as before remarked, it is difficult, if not impossible, to determine to what direct and specific acts the collision is to be attributed. And this, as I understand the maritime law, makes it a case of damage or loss, arising from a cause that is inscrutable. It is not, of course, to be inferred from this, that any doubt exists that the immediate cause of the injury to the Fern, was the collision between the boats; but it implies that the causes which led to this result are involved in 'obscurity and doubt.

In this view it only remains to inquire what decree shall be made in this case. This is the only occasion on which this point has been before this Court, and I confess, that from my limited experience in the administration of maritime law, I enter upon its consideration with some hesitancy, and with great reason to distrust the conclusions to which I might be led, unaided by the light which others have thrown upon the subject.

It is insisted by the counsel for the respondents, that the maritime law gives no redress for an injury resulting from the collision of boats or vessels, unless the Court can find from the evidence that it was the result of the *sole* fault of one; or that it was *mixed* or mutual fault. This ground supposes that there can be no decree for an apportionment of the loss, if, for any reason, the cause of the injury is inscrutable, or left in such doubt that there can be no satisfactory finding of specific facts.

The English admiralty decisions referred to by counsel would seem to sustain this position. They certainly show, that where the cause of the injury is inscrutable, and the proof does not implicate either of the parties as in fault, there can be no decree for an apportionment of the loss. I do not think they establish it as the law in England, that where there is reason to conclude one or both parties were in fault, but the evidence leaves it uncertain which, that no decree can be rendered for a contribution by moieties. I do not, however, propose a critical examination of these cases, as I consider the question referred to as satisfactorily settled in this country.

In his commentaries on Bailments, Secs. 609, 610, Judge Story discusses this question, and maintains the right and expediency of dividing the loss, as between colliding vessels, where the fault is inscrutable. His language is: "Another case has been put by a learned commentator on commercial law. It is, where there has been some fault or neglect, but on which side the blame lies is inscrutable, or is left by the evidence in a state of uncertainty. In such a case, many of the maritime states of continental Europe have adopted the rule to apportion the loss between the vessels." The writer referred to by Judge Story is Mr. Bell, whose commentaries on the laws of Scotland have given him a distinguished reputation as a jurist. And in reference to the doctrine asserted by this author, Judge Story remarks, that "if the question be still open for controversy, there is great cogency in the reasoning of Mr. Bell, in favor of adopting the rule of apportioning the loss between the parties. Many learned jurists have supported the justice and equity of such a rule; and it especially has the strong aid of Pothier, and Valin, and Emerigon." In a note appended to the section before cited, Judge Story has inserted the argument of Mr. Bell in the maintenance of his views, the force and clearness of which certainly entitle it to the highest consideration.

I am not informed whether the doctrine, thus approvingly referred to by Judge Story, has been distinctly asserted by him in any case calling for its judicial recognition. But another learned American judge, eminent for his profound research in the doctrines of the maritime law, and his able and judicious administration of that law, holds the rule for the apportionment of damages, in cases of an injury by collision, where the fault is uncertain or inscrutable, as indisputable, in the United States. In the case of the *Scioto*, reported in *Davies' Reports*, 359, Judge Ware, the learned Judge of the United States for the District of Maine, says: "This rule in admiralty—a contribution by moieties—seems to prevail in three cases: *first*, where there has been no fault on either side; *second, where there may have been fault but it is uncertain on which side it lies;* and *third*, where there has been fault on both sides." In the syllabus of this case, the point is stated thus:—"But if it—the collision—happens without fault in either party, or if there was fault, and it cannot be ascertained which vessel was in fault, or if both were in fault, then the damage and loss are divided between them, in equal shares."

I may be permitted to remark, though I have not seen the reported cases, that I am informed that since the decision in the case of the *Scioto*, before referred to, Judge Ware has asserted the same principle in other cases. To what extent other American judges have affirmed it, I have not the means of information. But having the high sanction of Story and Ware—both known as able exponents of the maritime law— and sustained, too, by the most distinguished jurists of continental Europe, I have no hesitancy in applying it to the case before the Court.

A late elementary writer on maritime law in this country, of high reputation for accuracy and learning, affirms, that "without question, the doctrine above stated is the *American* law on this subject." This writer says: "Where the collision is evidently the result of error, neglect, or want of precaution, which error, neglect, of want of precaution is not directly traceable to either party, but is inscrutable, or left by the evidence in a state of uncertainty, there the rule of the maritime law is, that the loss must be apportioned between the parties, in equal moieties." *Flanders on Mar. Law*, 296. This writer admits that a different rule prevails in England, but very justly remarks "that the rule adopted in England does not necessarily determine the law for us, in the United States. And accordingly, we find that the Courts of Admiralty in this country adhere to the rule of the ancient maritime law." *Ibid*, 298.

Adopting this view of the law, and satisfied that the application of the principle adverted to meets the real equity of the case, I shall decree an equal apportionment of the loss between the parties. As already stated, the contradictory and irreconcilable character of the evidence leaves the mind in doubt and uncertainty, as to some of the important facts in the case; but there is a satisfactory ground for the conclusion that both the colliding boats were in fault, and therefore that each shall contribute to the loss. And I may remark here, that in my judgment, the enforcement of the principle here sanctioned, is not only vindicated as in itself just and equitable, but in its application to the navigation of the western waters, as altogether expedient. Heretofore, in cases of collision, the great object of each party has been to prove his adversary exclusively in the wrong, and thereby avoid all pecuniary liability. And it is almost proverbially true, that in collision cases, each party has but little difficulty in sustaining, by the proofs, any state of facts which may be insisted on. In most cases, the witnesses on either side, from a misapprehension of the facts, or a dishonest purpose of representing them falsely, involve the transaction in such doubt and uncertainty as to render it impossible to reach a satisfactory conclusion. If, under such circumstances, a reasonable ground is furnished for the conclusion that there is fault on both sides, and that each party should share in the loss sustained, there would be greater caution and vigilance in navigation, and less effort and less temptation, by corrupt or unfair means, to misrepresent or distort facts.

It appears satisfactorily, that the injury resulting from the collision fell almost exclusively on the Fern. The injury to the Swann is so slight that the respondents have set up no claim to remuneration. The result, therefore, of the decree will be, that one-half of the actual loss or injury sustained by the Fern, must be paid by the respondents. The value of the Fern is variously estimated by the witnesses who have testified on that subject, at sums ranging from $12,000 to $20,000. For the purposes of this decree, the Court fix her value at $15,500. There is proof in the case that the Fern has been raised, but no evidence was offered of her value, including her engine and machinery, after the collision. This value, whatever it may be, will be deducted from the sum of $15,500, and the respondents are decreed to pay the libellants one-half of the balance. It will be necessary to appoint a Commissioner to inquire into and report the value of the Fern after the injury. This will be provided for in the decree to be entered. In refernce to the costs, under the circumstances of the case, no discrimination will be made between the parties, and they will therefore be paid equally.

JAMES M. BROADWELL v. J. C. BUTLER & Co.
JAMES M. BROADWELL v. KEYS, MALTBY & Co.

It is a part of the obligation of a common carrier, to deliver the property placed in his charge within a reasonable time; but what is a reasonable time depends on the circumstances of the case.

The words, *privilege of reshipping*, in a bill of lading, are intended for the benefit of the carrier, but do not limit his responsibility.

If he undertakes to deliver goods within a specified time, he is liable for any delay beyond that time, unless the cause of the delay is within the exceptions in the bill of lading, or occasioned by the act of God, or the public enemy.

The subsidence of the water in the Ohio river, preventing a boat from passing up the falls with its cargo, is not strictly within any of the reasons which excuse a carrier for the failure to deliver goods within a reasonable time.

But proof of a usage long established, uniform and well known, to the effect, that under a bill of lading in the usual form, with the words *privilege of reshipping* inserted, a boat from below bound to any place above the falls, may wait there for a rise of water for a month or more, without incurring liability for not delivering the cargo, in a reasonable time, is admissible.

The proof in this case is conclusive of the existence of such usage; and therefore, the detention of the boat with its cargo, for thirty days or upwards, does not deprive the owner of a right to recover full freight to the place of consignment, if the property was delivered with promptness, after the first rise in the river.

Messrs. *Lincoln, Warnock & Smith*, for Libellant.
Messrs. *Coffin & Groesbeck*, for Respondents.

OPINION OF THE COURT BY JUDGE LEAVITT.

As the questions in these cases arise on nearly the same facts, and depend on the same principles, they will be considered together. They are suits in admiralty, brought by the libellant as master, for the owners of the steamboat Princess No. 3, to recover freight alleged to be due for the transportation, in the first named case, of a large quantity of molasses, and in the other, of sugar, from New Orleans to Cincinnati.

The facts necessary to be noticed, in the decision of the points presented, are, that on the 19th of February, 1853, the agents of the said Butler & Co. shipped, on the Princess No. 3, at New Orleans, four hundred barrels of molasses, and the agents of Keys, Maltby & Co., at the same time and place, shipped on said boat, one hundred and eighty-nine hogsheads of sugar, consigned to those houses respectively, at Cincinnati. Bills of lading were signed by the libellant, in both cases, as master, in the usual form, undertaking for the delivery of said property to the consignees, at Cincinnati; the dangers of the navigation and of fire only excepted, at a rate of compensation stated in the bills. To both the bills of lading were attached, the words, *"privilege of reshipping."*

Within a day or two after the date of the bills of lading, the boat proceeded up the river, and arrived at the foot of the falls of the Ohio river, without accident or detention, on the 5th of March. It is admitted by the answers of the respondents, that their agents, at the time of the shipments, were apprised of the fact that, from the size of the steamboat, it could not pass through the locks of the canal around the falls, and consequently, that the cargo could not reach its destination, on that boat, in any other way than by passing over the falls. It is also an admitted fact, that on the arrival of the boat at the falls, the river had fallen so low, that there was not depth of water sufficient to permit its passage over them, and that it continued in that stage for about one month. At the expiration of that time, there was a swell in the river, which enabled the boat to proceed up ; and, on the 10th of April, it arrived at Cincinnati, and the cargo was delivered to the consignees.

It is satisfactorily proved, that the time usually occupied in making the trip from New Orleans to Cincinnati, in favorable weather, and no accident occurring, is from ten to twelve days. There was therefore a detention of the boat, at the falls, of upwards of thirty days. It is clearly established by the evidence in these cases, that during the period of the detention of the boat, there was a decline in the price of molasses, at Cincinnati, of from two to five cents the gallon, and in sugar, from one-eighth to three-eighths of a cent in the pound. The respondents respectively allege, that they are entitled to a set-off against the claim for freight, equal to the decline in the market value of the articles shipped, occurring while the boat was delayed at the falls. And this is the principal question arising in these cases.

The respondents insist, that the libellant failed to deliver the property shipped, according to the obligation of the bills of lading, and that the owners of the boat are therefore liable for any loss sustained by reason of such failure. They insist, that by the terms of the bills of lading, the carrier was bound to deliver the cargo, with all practicable diligence, and that if, by reason of low water at the falls, the boat could not pass up, he was bound to reship, or by some other means ensure the prompt delivery of the property to the consignees.

On the other hand, the libellant contends, that the molasses and sugar were shipped by the agents of the respondents, with a knowledge that the falls of the Ohio might present an obstruction to the upward passage of the boat, and that his contract, by a fair construction of the bills of lading, was to deliver the cargo, with reasonable diligence, in contemplation of such obstruction; and that proceeding to Cincinnati with promptness and diligence, as soon as the state of the river would permit, and safely delivering the cargo there, was a full discharge of his contract as contained in the bills of lading. The libellant also insists, that the words, " privilege of reshipping," inserted in the bills of lading, instead of creating an obligation to reship at the falls, in case of low water, are to be construed as a privilege, enuring to his benefit, and designed to secure the right, should the interests of the owners of the boat require it, to reship the cargo at the falls, or at any other point.

I am not aware of any judicial decision, settling the legal import and construction of these words, with reference to a state of facts similar to those presented in these cases. The phrase "privilege of reshipping" is one in common use, in carrying on the commerce of the western waters; and questions have been of frequent occurrence, in suits against carriers to recover for the loss of, or injury to property, where there has been a reshipment under the right secured by these words in the bill of landing. But I know of none—nor have any been referred to—determining their effect, in a case asserting a loss, from a failure to deliver within a reasonable time. In the cases referred to, involving liability for loss or damage, it is well settled, that the privilege of re-shipping in a bill of lading, is intended for the benefit of the carrier, but does not limit his responsibility. He is bound for the safe delivery of the property committed to him, precisely as if such words were not used in the bill of lading. The stringency with which the law holds him to this liability is well known, and need not be here stated.

That it is a part of the obligation assumed by a carrier of goods for hire, to deliver them within a reasonable time, is not controvertible. But what shall constitute a reasonable time, depends on the peculiar circumstances of the case. *Parsons on Con.*, 657; *Flanders on Shipping*, 312. And this is the principle which must govern, in giving a construction to these bills of lading. No time is stated in them, within which the carrier obligated himself to deliver the goods. If such a stipulation had been a part of the contract, there would have been a liability for any delay beyond that time, unless it was occasioned by the act of God, or the public enemy; or was owing to the usual perils of navigation or fire, which are expressly excepted in the bills of lading. In strictness, the subsidence of the water in the Ohio river, which prevented the boat from passing over the falls, was not a cause of delay, which within any of these principles would excuse the carrier from the obligation imposed by law, to deliver the property within a reasonable time. It was practicable to have delivered the cargo at Cincinnati, by draying the molasses and sugar around the falls, and reshipping on other boats. But this would have been attended with very considerable expense to the carrier, and some loss and injury to the cargo. Was the carrier bound to incur this expense, and was he justified in detaining the property at the falls, awaiting a rise in the river?

Apart from all extrinsic facts, there would seem to have been an obligation on the carrier to avail himself of all the means within his power, to forward the sugar and molasses to the consignees, in the fulfilment of his undertaking, according to the legal import of the bills of lading, to deliver them within a reasonable time. But it is insisted, that the uniform usage among those connected with the commerce of the Ohio and Mississippi rivers, either as shippers or carriers, sanctions a different construction; and that, in conformity with that usage, the libellant in these cases was justified in waiting at the falls, till there should be a stage of water that would enable the boat to pass up.

That evidence of such usage is admissible, seems clear upon the authorities applicable to the subject. It is well settled, that a written contract cannot be varied, controlled, or contradicted by parol proof. But in the case of *The Reeside*, 8 *Sumner*, 567, Judge Story said, " the true and appropriate office of a usage or custom is to interpret the otherwise indeterminate intentions of parties, and to ascertain the nature and extent of their contracts, arising not from express stipulations, but from mere implications or presumptions, and acts of a doubtful or equivocal character. It may also be admitted to ascertain the true meaning of a particular word, or of particular words in a given instrument, when the word or words have various senses," etc.

In the case of *Wayne* v. *Steamboat Pike*, 16 *Ohio R.* 421, it was held, that where terms used in a bill of lading, have by usage acquired a particular signification, the parties will be presumed to have used them in that sense; but usage will not be permitted to control the terms used, unless it is established by clear and satisfactory proof; other decisions to the same effect have been made, to which it is not deemed necessary specially to refer. At this day, there can be no doubt, that proof of usage is admissible in explanation of the intention of the parties, if that intention is doubtful or equivocal. And when clearly proved, it will be regarded as in the contemplation of the parties, at the time the instrument was executed, and as virtually embodied in it. In the 1st *Vol. of Parsons on Contracts, p.* 661, it is said, that "usage so long established, so uniform, and so well known, that it may be supposed the parties to the contract knew it, and referred to it, becomes, as it were, a part of the contract, and may modify in an important manner the rights and duties of the parties."

The evidence of a usage fixing the meaning and construction of the words, *privilege of reshipping,* fully meets the requirement of these authorities. A number of witnesses, of high standing and intelligence, and great experience, in the commerce and business of the West, embracing both shippers and carriers, say, that this phrase has been known to them for many years; and that when used in shipments from below, to any point above the falls of the Ohio, it is intended for the benefit of the carrier; leaving it to his choice to reship or not, as he may deem most for his interest; but it is never understood as creating an obligation to reship. These witnesses say, in reference to the obstruction at the falls of the Ohio, the words not only do not import the duty of reshipping, but that in case of inability to pass the falls from low water, the carrier incurs no liability for the detention, though it should be for an entire season. And several of the witnesses testify, that in all cases where it is intended to impose the obligation to reship, the words, "to be reshipped," are uniformly used.

The proof therefore of a well known and established usage, in the particular referred to, is full and satisfactory. It results, that the libellant has not violated his contract by detaining his cargo at the falls for the period of something more than thirty days, and is therefore entitled to a decree for full freight to Cincinnati, according to the rates specified in the bills of lading, with interest thereon from the time it accrued.

John Allen *v.* William M. Hunter.

A patent is *prima facie* evidence of the right of the patentee.

The thing invented or discovered must be so clearly described, as to enable a person well skilled in the subject matter of the invention to construct or make it.

In a matter of science, no individual can be a fit expert, who does not understand the science involved.

And a jury in such a matter will give weight to the witnesses as they may be competent to speak on the subject.

A specification in regard to a chemical compound, is not addressed to persons who are ignorant of chemistry.

A specification must be construed according to the true import of the words used, rather than by their grammatical arrangement.

In a case of a prior invention, a patent is not to be superseded unless the thing patented was invented before the invention patented.

Nothing more than experiments being made before the emanation of the patent, although such experiments resulted in the invention or discovery subsequently patented, the first patent must stand.

A caveat is intended to give notice of an invention or discovery, and prevent a patent from being granted to another for the same thing.

Messrs. *Stanbery, Coffin & Newton,* for plaintiff.
Mr. *Matthews,* for defendant.

INSTRUCTION OF THE COURT.

This, gentlemen of the jury, is an action for the infringement of a patent. The plaintiff, who is the patentee, "claims to have invented a new and useful mode of setting mineral teeth on metallic plates," and he describes as follows the composition and mode of application.

"The cement may be formed of any of the known fluxes, combined with silex, wedgewood and asbestos intermixed with gold and platinum scraps, which form a metallic union with the plate upon which the teeth are set. The compound which I prefer is composed of silex 2 oz., white or fluid glass 2 oz., borax 1 oz., wedgewood 1½ oz., asbestos 2 drms., feldspar 2 drms., haolin 1 drm. This compound should be intermixed or underlaid upon the plate, with gold or platinum scraps. The gum color consists of feldspar ½ oz., white glass 1 oz., oxyd of gold 1¼ grs.: moisten and apply with a brush."

After describing how the application is to be made, the patentee says, "I claim as my invention, and desire to secure by letters patent, a new mode of setting mineral teeth on metallic plates by means of a fusible silicious cement, which forms an artificial gum, and which also unites single teeth to each other, and to the plates on which they are set."

"I also claim to be the inventor of said cement or compound, a full and exact description of which is herein given."

"I also claim the combination of asbestos with plaster of paris, for covering the teeth and plates for the purpose of sustaining them in their proper position, while the cement is being fused."

A caveat was entered by the plaintiff, in the office of the commissioner of patents, the 29th of April, 1851. This notice to the office that the plaintiff was the first inventor, for which he claimed a patent, was to answer a double purpose. First, to give notice of his claim as inventor, and second, to prevent a patent from issuing to another for the same thing.

The patent issued to the plaintiff bears date the 23d of December, 1851. Under the law, before this patent could be issued, a thorough examination of the claim was made by examiners of the patent office, who were appointed, it is to be presumed, on account of their knowledge and experience in matters of science, mechanism, chemistry and natural philosophy, which enables them to judge of the feasibility and utility of inventions and discoveries made, and for which the inventors or discoverers apply for a patent. A claim which has thus been examined and sanctioned by the granting of a patent, gives to the patentee a *prima facie* right to the invention or discovery claimed. And the individual who disputes the right, must produce evidence to counterbalance the legal presumption of right in the plaintiff from his patent.

On the subject of patents, we are governed by the law, and not by our own notions of policy. Some individuals who prefer their own theories to the practical results of society, which have been established and sanctioned by the wisdom of ages, hold that there can be no property in a discovery or an invention. And these notions may have an influence on their judgment, when they are called to act on the subject of patents. Such an influence should be regarded as unjust and against law. You are sworn, gentlemen, to act on the subject before you according to the law and the evidence.

The defenses made to the right claimed by the plaintiff are:

1. That the patent is void upon its face, for want of certainty in its specifications.

The law requires "every inventor to swear that he does verily believe that he is the true inventor, or discoverer of the art, machine, or improvement for which he solicits a patent; and he shall deliver a written description of his invention, and of the manner of using or process of compounding the same, in such full, clear and exact terms as to distinguish the same from all other things before known, and to enable any person skilled in the art or science of which it is a branch, or with which it is most nearly connected, to make, compound and use the same."

In requiring this particularity, the law has two objects in view. 1. That the invention or discovery claimed may be clearly distinguished from all other inventions or discoveries. 2. That when the patent shall expire and the invention or discovery shall become public property, any one skilled in the art or science may construct or compound it.

Patentees are not monopolists.

This objection is often made, and it has its effect on society. The imputation is unjust and impolitic. A monopolist is one

20a

who, by the exercise of the sovereign power, takes from the public that which belongs to it, and gives to the grantee and his assigns an exclusive use. On this ground monopolies are justly odious. It enables a favored individual to tax the community for his exclusive benefit, for the use of that to which every other person in the community, abstractly, has an equal right with himself.

Under the patent law this can never be done. No exclusive right can be granted for any thing which the patentee has not invented or discovered. If he claim any thing which was before known, his patent is void. So that the law repudiates a monopoly. The right of the patentee entirely rests on his invention or discovery of that which is useful, and which was not known before. And the law gives him the exclusive use of the thing invented or discovered, for a few years, as a compensation for "his ingenuity, labor and expense in producing it." This, then, in no sense, partakes of the character of monopoly.

Inventors are often great benefactors. And how ill are they generally rewarded! If the invention or discovery be of great value, a system of piracy is commenced, not so much to injure the patentee, as to benefit the actors. And it cannot be denied that this course of action is made popular in the community, by the charge of monopoly against the patentee, and his realization of large profits. His expenses are not considered, the benefit he has conferred on society, nor the shortness of seven or fourteen years, to which his exclusive right is limited. For the maintenance of his right, he is subjected to legal controversies, which, not unfrequently, involve him in an expenditure beyond the amount of his profits. Inventors and discoverers are proverbially poor. It is said that the man, by the operations of whose genius the streets of the City of London were first lighted, was a wanderer and a beggar in those streets. The gas company who were made rich by his invention, eventually made some provision for him.

What have inventors done for our country? The application of steam to the propulsion of vessels upon the water, and carriages upon the land, have advanced our country a century in commercial intercourse, in civilization and in every thing which constitutes a great nation. And look at the numberless labor-saving machines, the cotton gin, the planing machine, the reaping machine, and many other machines and inventions, which by the force of machinery accomplish wonderful results.

It then appears that patentees, so far from being monopolists hanging as dead weights upon the community, are the benefactors of their country.

By the law an extension of a patent can be given, only where it is made clearly to appear, that by the profits from the term of the grant the patentee has not been remunerated for his ingenuity, labor and expense, in bringing his invention into operation.

In this case the patentee says, that the cement may be formed of any of the known fluxes; and it is argued, that as this includes all fluxes, "if there be any which cannot be so used, the patent is void."

The words of the specifications are to be taken together, and they are to be so construed as to give effect to the meaning and intention of the person using them. Words are not to be distorted from their meaning so as to effect what may be supposed to have been the intention of the person using them. But they are to have a reasonable construction, as connected with the sentence in which they are used.

The words, known fluxes, belong to chemistry, and none but those who understand the science of chemistry should have weight as experts on this subject. A dentist who extracts and fills teeth, or who sets teeth, may be expert in what he professes, and yet be ignorant of chemistry. This has been verified in the present case. As the invention is claimed to be a new and useful mode of setting teeth, &c., it seems to be supposed that dentists are proper experts to define the meaning of chemical terms. But if they have not a scientific knowledge of chemistry, they are not experts in the application of chemical terms.

The law says the description shall be such as to enable any person skilled in the art or science, of which it is a branch, or with which it is most nearly connected, to make, compose, and use the same. If the person called be not skilled in chemistry, he cannot be considered as an expert in regard to chemical affinities. A mechanic may as well be called as an expert on this subject, as a practical dentist, who has no knowledge of chemistry. The same may be said in regard to the term borax. The making up of the compound or the manufacture of teeth is not necessarily connected with dentistry.

The specifications must be so full and clear as to enable a competent person to make the compound without experiment. And the enquiry for the jury is, has this been done in the plaintiff's patent. In passing upon this point, the jury will be governed in matters of science by the opinion of experts.

Doctor Clark, of New Orleans, has practiced dentistry fourteen years, and now has the largest practice in that city. He has received his composition for setting teeth from Doctor Allen. He says he could make the compound from the patent. Doctor Samuel Hazlett, of New York, says he could make the compound and the teeth from the patent. Doctor Stockton says, a dentist properly informed would be at no loss to make the compound from the formula of Doctor Allen. Doctor Barlow says, that Doctor Allen's plan requires mechanical skill. He has made the compound and set the teeth under Doctor Allen's direction. Doctor Chapman says, from Doctor Allen's formula he constructed the work. And Doctor Kingsly, who is a dentist, says, a manufacturer of teeth would know borax cannot be used in a crude state, but must be fritted before used under Doctor Allen's plan. Doctor Wardle manufactures teeth, and he put up the work by Doctor Allen's plan; and he thinks that a man of ordinary skill could make the gum from the directions given. Professor Silliman says, borax is usually prepared, which is done easily.

Several witnesses in behalf of the defendant were examined.

Doctor White, a manufacturer of teeth, says, without the knowledge he now has, he would have been at a loss how borax was to be used according to Doctor Allen's formula. Doctor Semple, dentist, purchased a right of Doctor Allen, with special instructions how to use the compound. Doctor Rochart made an experiment on Doctor Allen's formula, put the teeth in eleven times in all. Doctor Babcock made the experiment on Doctor Allen's formula, but could not make the compound, and he considers the recepe of no practical utility. Doctor Porter says, the formula of Doctor Allen is not practicable. Doctor Smith tried the formula of Doctor Allen, and found it impracticable.

Doctor How purchased a right of Doctor Allen, but could not set the teeth, to do well, without back plates. Doctor Doughty tried Doctor Allen's formula without success, on a gold plate or silver. Doctor Talbert tried Doctor Allen's formula without success. Doctor Maine says, from Doctor Allen's specification he would have used, in making the gum, the borax of commerce. And Doctor Hays says, that from the specifications to Doctor Allen's patent he could not make the compound of Doctor Allen.

This is substantially the evidence in regard to the specifications of the plaintiff. Whether they are sufficient is a mixed question of law and fact. The opinions of the experts who have been examined, are in conflict; and so far as my personal knowledge goes, this has been uniformly the case where experts have been examined. This may show, however honestly witnesses called by the respective parties may swear, that slight circumstances, imperceptibly or otherwise, influence the opinions of men, even in matters of science. The fact to be established by the plaintiff was, whether his compound and the setting of teeth were so described, as to enable a person of competent knowledge, to make the compound and set the teeth.

In regard to the compound, no one can be competent to testify as to it, who is not acquainted with chemistry. He must know something of the affinities of the constituent parts of the compound, and of its strength and durability. A mere mechanical dentist is no more competent to judge of this matter than the ordinary mechanic whose skill consists in applying the materials made ready to his hands, for the structure of a machine, without knowing by what process these materials were formed.

It is, therefore, gentlemen, your duty, in considering the testimony, to give weight to it in proportion to the competency of the witnesses to judge of the matters sworn to. In this view, no one may be supposed to have misrepresented the facts, speaking from the lights of his own knowledge; and yet, the statement of one witness who has a thorough knowledge of chemistry, and speaking on that subject, should be relied on more than the statement of any number of witnesses, who speak without the requisite knowledge.

Some of the witnesses say, that in making the compound by the formula of Doctor Allen, they would use borax in its crude state, or what is called the borax of commerce. The most, if not all of these witnesses do not profess to have a knowledge of chemistry; while other witnesses say, who are acquainted with the science, they would know that borax was not referred to by Dotor Allen in its crude state. And these are the men who can be confided in as experts, and to whom, under the patent law, the specifications are addressed. The description must be such, the law says, as "to enable any person skilled in the art or science of which it is a branch, or with which it is most nearly connected, to make, compound, and use the same."

The objection that, as all the fluxes are claimed in making the compound, if any one can be found which cannot be used for that purpose, the patent is void, cannot be sustained.

The word flux is derived from the latin word *flus*, to flow, and is applied in chemistry to substances which are in themselves very fusible, or which promote the fusion of other bodies. Any substance or mixture used to promote the fusion of metals or minerals, as alkalies, borax, tartar, or other saline matter, are called fluxes. Now, in the first place, it is not shown that there is any one flux which may not be used to make the compound; and if this were made to appear, it could not affect the validity of the patent, as the reference to fluxes was general, and should be held to include those which are in general use, and which will overcome, by their chemical attractions, the opposing powers of the other ingredients of the compound. This, all chemists would understand, and to such persons is the description addressed.

Formerly, a strict construction was given in this country and in England to the claims of a patentee, but a more liberal and favorable view is now taken of his claim. He must describe it within the law; but Courts do not go beyond the law for technical objections to defeat it.

The next question for your consideration, gentlemen of the jury, is whether defendant has infringed the plaintiff's patent.

An infringement consists in constructing a machine, or making a compound, substantially in the same mode as that for which a patent has been obtained.

Certain publications which have been made in the "Dental Recorder," in New York, and the "Dental Register," in this city, which show the formulas, the plaintiff alleges, are claimed by the defendant, and which are similar to those claimed in the patent.

Doctor Slack, one of the oldest and most experienced chemists in this country says, that the formula of defendant is in substance the same as that claimed by the plaintiff. And he strongly illustrates his opinion by saying "they are as much so as two and two make four, or that three and one make four."

Doctor Locke, Jr., who is a professed chemist, and who analyzed the formulas of Doctors Allen and Hunter, says there is no substantial difference. Other witnesses called by the plaintiff, corroborate the statement, that the two formulas are substantially the same.

But on the part of the defendant several witnesses have been examined, who give their opinion that the formulas are different. This with most of them is supposed to consist in the mode of combining the ingredients, that the finer particles of the pulverized ingredients were separated by a sieve, by the defendant, which left the larger particles granulated, which on being fused make a stronger gum.

It will be for you, gentlemen, to determine the fact of infringement, from this conflict of testimony. I have only to refer you to the rule before stated, of giving weight to such witnesses as were best qualified to judge of the matter about which they have testified. A further remark on this point is not only justified, but called for by the justice of the case. That one of the two chemists who have sworn that the formulas were in substance the same, has analyzed the ingredients of both, and he finds them substantially the same. His testimony then is given, not as matter of opinion, but as a fact clearly demonstrated. This is the only mode by which the human judgment can rest upon absolute certainty. There are but few questions which may be decided by the power of analysis, chemically or mathematically. But where this is done satisfactorily, truth is attained.

An unsubstantial or colorable alteration in a machine or a compound, does not protect an individual from the character and consequence of an infringer.   Where the machine is constructed, or the compound formed, on the same principle, however varied in form, there is an infringement.   In a machine where the same powers are employed, with only formal alterations as to the size or position of the machinery, to produce a certain result, the principle of the machine remains the same.   And so of a compound, where the ingredients are the same, and the change is merely in the mode of combining them.   Or where there is a substitute of one ingredient, having the same qualities and producing the same result, being within the scope of the claim.

The next point for your consideration will be, whether the discovery was useful.

Of this there can be no doubt, if the claim of the plaintiff shall be sustained.

Doctor Jobson, of London, England, considers the improvement the greatest in dentistry of the present age.   He is corroborated by many other witnesses who speak from experience.   It is unnecessary to advert to the testimony on this point, as there is no conflict in it.   Every invention or discovery must be useful, to entitle the party to a patent.

Whether the plaintiff was the first and original inventor of what he claims, is the subject of your next enquiry.

To sustain his patent, the plaintiff must show that he was the first and original inventor or discoverer.   That he was neither, is strongly urged in the defense.

It is contended that a work published by Doctor Fitch, of New York, on dental surgery, which was a translation from a French work by Delabarre, was substantially the same as the plaintiff's.   If this be so, it bars the plaintiff's right.   So cautiously does the law guard the public rights, that if the thing invented or discovered has been described in any foreign publication, it is declared to be fatal to the patentee. This provision goes upon the presumption, if such foreign publication has been made, the patentee may have acquired a knowledge of it. And this presumption is not rebutted by proving, as far as a negative can be proved, that the inventor had no knowledge of it. The publication may be proved, as to its contents, and the fact of publication by the production of the book, or by parol testimony.

Doctor Clark, of New Orleans, says that Delabarre's formula was somewhat like that of the plaintiff's, but that it was different, and was impracticable, and has been long since abandoned. Doctor Fitch, the translator, says Delabarre's system was never brought into practical use.

Doctor Jobson, evidently eminent in his profession, was personally and intimately acquainted with Delabarre, in Paris. And while in France, the Doctor became acquainted with the most eminent dentists in Paris, and he says that they all considered the plan of Delabarre as a failure, and that it had been abandoned by him; but although abandoned, yet if he published substantially the formula of the plaintiff, it is fatal to his right.

Several other witnesses speak of Delabarre's formula, as having been abandoned in this country.

On the part of the defendant, a set of teeth was given in evidence to the jury said to have been made on Delabarre's plan, and which were worn by the famous Aaron Burr. The teeth in this specimen were very irregular, some inclining one way and some another, so as to form no continuous and even circle. Doctor Jobson, on examining it, said, the teeth may have been set on Delabarre's plan, as their irregularity was the defect in his system.

Several of the witnesses called by the defendant, considered the plan of Delabarre as similar, or very much like the plaintiff's.

To defeat the plaintiff's patent on this ground, Delabarre's plan must be shown to be substantially the same as Doctor Allen's.

It is further alleged that Steamer communicated to the plaintiff his alleged discovery. If this be true, the plaintiff's right cannot be supported, as he could not, if the supposition be true, be the original inventor or discoverer.

Steamer states that he was employed by the plaintiff, and sold to him, in 1851, a formula for an enamel; and also, that he prepared in Allen's laboratory the gum used by him, for which he agreed to pay thirty dollars. This witness seems to have been a worker in metals. It is proved, however, that he took back the facts stated, in a publication under his signature. The equivocations and inconsistencies of the witness, do not recommend his statements to the confidence of the jury.

Mr. Thonin, who is a manufacturer of porcelain teeth, says, that Doctor Allen proposed to pay witness what Steamer owed him, if he would procure Steamer's signature to a certain paper. At the same time Doctor Allen observed that he had paid Steamer a hundred dollars for his services. It does not appear, however, what the paper was, which Doctor Allen was anxious Steamer should sign.

Doctor Darling is a dentist, and he says that Doctor Allen called on him, and advised him not to purchase a formula for setting teeth from Steamer, as the Doctor alleged Steamer procured it from his laboratory, and he threatened to sue Steamer.

Elias Wildman, who has been a dentist since 1836, he considers the formula of Delabarre sufficient, and that it is substantially the same as Doctor Allen's.

Doctor Lane says, that in 1845 he became acquainted with a continuous gum for setting teeth, as practiced by Doctor Dodge of New York, who not long afterwards died, and no further account of his plan has been given.

These facts, disconnected and certainly not very satisfactory from their nature or the manner of relating them by the witnesses, are left with the jury, with the remark that the plaintiff's patent ought not to be avoided in this particular, except on clear and undoubted evidence.

But the defendant claims to have discovered the same thing as contained in the formula of the plaintiff, before he made the discovery. If this be so, the plaintiff cannot recover.

Mr. Aldrich states that Doctor Allen, in the fall of 1847, made an upper set of teeth with the gum, for his wife. Witness is the brother-in-law of Doctor Allen, who, to the knowledge of the witness, has been engaged, for several years in making experiments on the subject of setting teeth.

Mrs. Aldrich says she wore the set of teeth first made by Doctor Allen, four or five years. Then a full set were made, which she now wears alternately with another set.

Doctor Wickersham knows, that in April, 1847, Doctor Allen was experimenting to find how to set teeth by a continuous gum on a platina plate.

Doctor Curtis states, that Doctor Allen made for him a full set of teeth in 1849, having the continuous gum. These lasted until 1853, when a new set was made, which the witness now wears. He thinks, in 1843 Doctor Allen informed him that he was experimenting to fasten teeth on a plate. The last set of teeth made for the witness had a back plate. This was done at his own request.

Doctor Ward. Ten years ago Doctor Allen was working night and day, to make an improvement in setting teeth.

Doctor Bacharjin, is a manufacturer of teeth, and he says that Doctor Allen was experimenting to set teeth by a continuous gum on a plate, in 1843. The witness saw a specimen similar to what is called for in his patent.

Doctor Taylor, was at the convention in Louisville in September, 1851. Several specimens of Doctor Allen's work were presented to the convention.

In April, 1851, a paper was published in Cincinnati, in which the editor speaks of the improvement of Doctor Allen, which will supersede block work. In July, 1851, Doctor Allen showed witness a specimen somewhat improved from the one he had before seen, and of which he spoke in terms of high approbation in the dental paper of which the witness was editor. He says that Doctor Allen, some two years before his patent, exhibited to him a specimen of work similar to the one described in his patent. He saw Doctor Hunter's improvement, which he supposed was block work, in April, 1852. The work of Hunter is like that of Allen's in many respects. He says Hunter's work was block work, up to 1851, and he supposed Hunter's work was intended to be an improvement on block work. He thinks, in principle the improvement of Hunter, as claimed, and Allen's, are the same; Hunter's mode of fastening is different from Allen's.

The report of the Convention of Physicians at Louisville, in the fall of 1851, spoke in high terms of the improvement of Doctor Allen, and the convention voted him a gold medal.

Hugh McCullum says, two or three years after 1841, Doctor Allen said he was making improvements to fasten teeth on a plate with a continuous gum, but that he had not yet perfected his improvement.

Professor Wood states that in the College Session of 1851-2, Doctor Allen made a specimen in which the teeth were fastened to the plate by a continuous gum. Several unavailing efforts were made to break the teeth from the gum; at length one of the teeth was broken.

Mr. Colburn, dentist, says, that Doctor Allen's method of setting teeth is the best, and that the old plan has been abandoned. The platina plate is used.

Peter Van Emmon, dentist, was eleven years in company with Doctor Allen, and he says the improvement of Allen has superseded the other modes of setting teeth. Between five and six years ago, he saw the first specimen. A dentist accustomed to block work could make the work of Doctor Allen, and would know how to use borax.

Doctor Putnam is a dentist, has manufactured teeth, made fluxes, &c., and practiced under Doctor Allen.

Doctor Robinson, of London, England, has been a dentist

twenty-three years, and he considers Doctor Allen's plan as new and useful. Doctors Stockton, Chapman, Barlow, Kingby, Harlet, Wilson, Halman, Shope and Smith, all speak of Doctor Allen's plan as the best, &c.

Mrs. Bartlett, lives in Covington. In 1846 or 7, Doctor Allen made for her a temporary set of teeth, then a set with springs, at her request, with a gum like the set she now wears, which was within five months of the time her teeth were taken out.

C. E. Allen, is not the inventor; he heardSteamer say that he regretted injustice had been done to Doctor Allen through his instrumentality.

C. Buchart regrets that Doctor Allen was unjustly dealt with.

Mr. Monter, dentist, was employed by Doctor Allen in 1852. Was acquainted with Steamer, who had no knowledge of dentistry.

Doctor Darling says, Steamer's enamel was of no value for dental purposes. Has been working on Doctor Allen's plan three years and finds it good.

Dr. Irwin. Allen's plan is new and very useful.

Doctor Miller, has treated between two and three hundred cases on Doctor Allen's plan, which is best; thinks Hunter's plan would be better for block work.

Doctor Wardle, says he is a manufacturer of mineral teeth. He makes the compound from Doctor Allen's formula; thinks a man of ordinary skill could make the gum by the formula.

Defendant's evidence as to his priority of invention or discovery.

Mrs. Guilford. In January, 1851, Doctor Hunter made her a set of teeth which she has worn ever since, and on which the continuous gum was used. In 1848 he made a set for her, somewhat different. Her present teeth are better than the natural teeth.

Doctor King, in November, 1850, saw a specimen of upper

teeth which Doctor Hunter said he had prepared for the World's Fair.

Mr. Toland, Doctor Hunter frequently purchased teeth of him. In the fall of 1850, he showed the witness specimens which he intended to send to the World's Fair. This was three months before the fair. The witness saw the teeth after they were returned from the fair.

Mr. Jones, says, prior to 1848, in 1846 or 7, Hunter stated to him his object was to set teeth on a plate by a continuous gum. In the fall of 1850 he saw the experiments, now exhibited, three or four months before the World's Fair.

Doctor Crane, has known Doctor Hunter for twelve years, and knows that he was experimenting on continuous gum work. In 1847 Doctor Hunter said he had succeeded so far as to convince himself that he would succeed in setting a full set of teeth in a continuous gum. In the fall of 1850 he saw the specimens now exhibited.

Mr. McKinney, saw at the Crystal Palace in London the specimens before the jury, connected together.

Doctor Lesley. In 1846 he knew that Doctor Hunter was making experiments to overcome shrinkage. He stated his object was to unite the teeth single on a plate by a gum. At the Louisville convention, being one of the committee to whom the paper presented by Doctor Allen was referred, in regard to his invention, he differed from the other members of the committee, and made a counter report to that which was made by the other members of the committee.

Doctor Locke, sen., says, in 1844 or 6, he knew that Doctor Hunter was experimenting, and about a year before October, 1851, Doctor Hunter said to him that he had succeeded in making a gum in which to set teeth.

Doctor Taliaferro, has known Doctor Hunter ten years, and knows that he experimented to improve teeth. In 1848, he made a set of teeth for witness, perhaps block work. The teeth were soldered to a back plate.

Mr. Wayne says, in 1847 Doctor Hunter was experimenting,—object was to make a compound to fasten teeth.

Doctor Maise says, in 1846 a lady got him to insert a tooth in an artificial set, and the teeth appeared to have been set in a gum body. The witness saw the work of Doctor Dodge in New York, could see no other fastening than the gum. This was prior to July, 1850.

Doctor Brown says, in the fall of 1850, Doctor Allen enquired of the witness what kind of work Hunter was getting up. Witness replied he was getting up a gum work.

Doctor Hamlin says, the teeth in Hatch's mouth looked like Levatt's enamel; but Allen showed a plan with a gum that adhered to it.

Doctor Crane says, five or six years ago, Levatt's enamel was the same as Doctor Allen's work in Hatch's mouth. That a gum body cannot be made out of it.

In Doctor Hunter's specifications, he says, " the teeth are first arranged on the plates according to the knowledge of the manipulator and state of the patient, after which the gum is applied, which does not shrink in the fire, and the whole brought up to the proper degree of heat in a muffle, and suffered to cool, when they will be ready for soldering to the plates, without having changed by working or otherwise in the fire, thereby enabling any dentist who cement single teeth well, to make block work with a greater degree of certainty, and much more accuracy than by carving, and without that act."   :

In the Dental Register of the West, published in this city, October, 1852, there was published a "new method of supplying artificial teeth and gums, by Doctor Hunter, parts of which were read as rebutting evidence by the counsel. He says, 15th page, " Where is the new principle in the patent claim now made ? A flux is combined with what is technically termed a body or base, and the application is in every respect similar."

"I stand upon the ground that I have perfected a body, (as applied to certain bodies and enamels made into artificial teeth, by Jones, White and McCurdy,) which does not materially contacrt in the fire, and possesses more strength than any other body known to me, and which, with skillful handling, requires but one heat, independent of the soldering of the teeth to the plate, to make perfect work."

"It is applicable, he says, to the ordinary gold plate as used by dentists, generally, in the form of block work, and is made by me in continuous arches where a full denture is required, and it is equally applicable to cases where a few teeth are required, and can be fastened to the plate by soldering, riveting, or any other known method now in use."

In regard to the first inventor, gentlemen, it is not sufficient to defeat a patent, that another person has conceived the possibility of effecting what the patentee has accomplished.

To constitute a prior invention, the party alleged to have made it must have proceeded so far as to have entitled himself to a patent, in case he had made an application. And you will apply this test to the work of the defendant.

The caveat of the plaintiff was filed in the patent office the 29th of April, 1851, and bears date at Cincinnati, 7th of April, 1851. In this paper the plaintiff says, "What I claim as my invention is a fusible cement of which an artificial gum is formed, applicable to artificial teeth, by means of which mineral teeth are firmly united to each other, and also to the metallic plate upon which they are set."

And he says, "The mode of applying the cement is as follows: When the teeth and plate are properly arranged upon a cast of plaster of paris, and the teeth covered with the plaster, I use the cement under, between, and around the teeth. This cement is composed of silex, oxide of tin, oxide of lead, manganese, potash and wedgewood. The teeth, being thus arranged, are put into a furnace, and other cement is used; the cast is then removed, and when cooled, the out-

21a

side plaster is taken off. I then use a preparation of the oxide of gold, so combined with the cement and so applied, as to produce, when finished, a true gum color. Again the cast is put into the furnace until the latter preparation flows; it, is then removed, cooled slowly, and is ready for the mouth."

The caveat, which is in evidence, shows beyond controversy how far the plaintiff had progressed with his invention on the 29th of April, 1851, when the caveat was filed in the patent office; and as it bears date, at Cincinnati, on the 7th of that month, it may be presumed that it was prepared at that time to be forwarded to Washington.

' This peculiarity of the plaintiff's invention and discovery, supposed to exist in the mode of fastening his teeth on the plate, with or without back straps, and without rivets, by the consistence and strength of the paste he uses, which keeps the teeth firmly in their places, and lessens the weight and size of the work in the mouth.

The patent of the plaintiff bears date the 24th of December, 1851. From that time his specifications became public, and every one had a right to inspect them, and for proper purposes to obtain a copy of them.

The question arises under the caveat and the patent of the plaintiff, whether he is protected from the experiments and invention of the defendant. He is protected by the law, unless the defendant's invention entitled him to a patent, before the plaintiff applied for his patent.

If both the plaintiff and defendant are inventors of the thing claimed by them respectively, the one who perfected his invention first is protected by the law. A general remark that he had accomplished his object, without particularizing what he had invented or discovered is not satisfactory. But a statement of the thing invented or discovered should be considered as evidence, so far as it agrees with the patent subsequently obtained, or with the work claimed to have been perfected.

One of the specimens exhibited by the defendant in the fall of 1851, and which he expressed an intention of sending to the great Fair, was block work ; the other is alleged to be a continuous setting of the teeth, to fit the mouth, and not consisting of parts put together, as block work. These specimens, or at least one of them, some of the witnesses saw at the World's Fair, in 1852.

The defendant has made no application for a patent; and it would seem, from his publication in the "Dental Register" above referred to, he contests the fact of any discovery having been made by the plaintiff. In page 14, he says, "to Delabarre must be given the credit of having first conceived and executed the union of artificial teeth already baked, with an artificial gum and plate." "To Adibran," he says, 15th page, "must we give the credit of having first made the claim, so far as I am informed, of having overcome the shrinkage of material, which claim was made in his published work, and was contested twenty years after Lefoulon, but which principle is claimed by no other author."

"Desirabode and Lefoulon both gave Delabarre credit for having done this kind of work, and published his formula, the principle of which consisted in uniting a flux with the material used as an ordinary base or body, that it might fuse at a less heat than the teeth then in use."

And the defendant then asks, "Where is the new principle in the patent claim now made?" This publication, as before stated, was made in October, 1852.

Several witnesses have been examined by both parties, to show that each, for a number of years, has been experimenting to obtain, what both of them, as they allege, have accomplished. The caveat and the patent show what the plaintiff has attained, and the defendant's work is shown by the evidence. The evidence of the plaintiff has shown the work done by him on his principle before his patent was obtained.

The acrimony excited in the course of this controversy, as shown by the testimony, is much to be regretted. The subjects involved are interesting to the cause of science and the arts, to the public at large, and especially to the parties in this suit. The plaintiff claims no more than nominal damages, as he is desirous only of sustaining his claim under his patent.

Neither the Court nor the jury can enter into the feelings of the parties in any cause. It is their duty to consider and decide every case on its merits, as the law requires. There should be no other solicitude felt than to attain this result. And having attained this, in the careful exercise of their best judgments, they have nothing to apprehend.

After being out a short time, the jury returned with a verdict for the defendant.

A motion for a new trial was made, which remains undecided.

FREDERICK ROTH v. THE CITY INSURANCE CO.

Where an agent of an Insurance Company makes the survey and the representation of the property to be insured, being as well acquainted with the situation of the property as the assured, any misrepresentation does not avoid the policy.

When the survey and representation of the premises are filled up on the representation of the assured, the agent having no knowledge of the premises, the policy is void, if any fact upon the risk be omitted or misrepresented.

Like all other contracts, the contract of Insurance must be made in good faith.

Where the form of the instructions required the assured to apply to an agent of the company, if there be an agent in his district; and if the assured shall undertake to make the survey and representation himself, he shall be held strictly to conform to the requirements to make a valid policy, would seem to imply that if the agent be called to make the survey and representation and acts, the assured is not bound for the accuracy of the representations.

There are many facts on which a jury should pass, in regard to the risk, &c.

Mr. *Walker*, appeared for the plaintiff.

Mr. *Swayne*, for the defendant.

OPINION OF THE COURT.

This is an action on a policy of Insurance, which bears date the 5th of May, 1852, of two thousand dollars, for one year, on a brick dwelling house in Nashville, in the State of Tennessee. The damages claimed fall short of the amount insured.

The declaration was in the usual form, in answer to which the defendant filed the general issue and several special pleas. To some of the pleas demurrers were filed, and to others issue was joined. But the parties waived the questions raised by 'the pleadings, except in regard to concealment and misrepresentation of the premises, on the application for insurance, and submitted the case on the questions of law.

The policy contained the following clause: "This policy is made and accepted in reference to the proposals and conditions hereunto annexed, which are to be used and resorted to, in order to explain the rights and obligations of the parties hereto, in all cases not herein otherwise specially provided for."

The conditions referred to are, "All applications for insurance must be made to the Secretary, and the subject offered for insurance accurately described."

"If the property offered for insurance is within the district of a surveyor of this company, he will examine and report thereon, unless the party applying shall elect to make his own survey, in which case such survey shall be made according to the printed form of instructions issued from the office of this company, and the party furnishing such survey shal be responsible for the accuracy thereof; but if the property offered for insurance is not within the district of a surveyor, then the applicant must himself furnish an accurate and just description thereof, viz., the dimensions of each building; of what materials constructed; the internal division and arrangement thereof; how warmed, (and where stoves are used, how in particular the pipes are conducted,) how occupied, whether as private dwellings, or how otherwise; the name of the present occupant or occupants; how situated in respect to contiguous buildings; the occupation of such contiguous buildings, and the materials with which they are constructed," &c.

"If any person insuring any building or goods in this office shall make any misrepresentation or concealment; or if after the expiration of a policy of insurance, and before renewal thereof, the risk of the building shall be increased by any means whatsoever; or if, after insurance effected, either by the original policy or by renewal thereof, the risk shall be increased by any means whatever, within the control of the assured; or if such buildings or premises shall be occupied in any way so as to render the risk more hazardous than at the time of insuring or renewal, such insurance shall be void and of no effect."

The application for insurance represented the building to be insured, as brick, situated on the North side of Lower Water Street, in the city of Nashville, Tennessee, occupied as a dwelling house by the assured, worth from two thousand eight hundred to three thousand dollars, " and that buildings were on each side of the dwelling house assured, from sixty to seventy feet."

The parties agree that the steam saw-mill is between fifty four and fifty-five feet from the dwelling-house insured, by actual measurement; and it appears that the house took fire by the sparks from the saw-mill, which was burnt down.

Mr. Warne, who is agent for the company, and took the insurance, being sworn, states that Roth, having an insurance

on his house in one of the Nashville offices, which was about
to expire, said to witness, that as some of his friends had
insured in the Cincinnati Insurance Office, he was desirous of
having his house insured by it; and the deponent states that
he was well acquainted with Roth's property, being his family
physician; the blank survey was filled out by the witness,
and after being read to the plaintiff was signed by him, and
witness forwarded it to the Cincinnati office and received the
policy.   The witness was well acquainted with the locality of
the buildings.   When the question was asked of Mr. Roth,
how far his dwelling was from the saw-mill, his answer was,
I suppose some forty or fifty feet.   The distance was not
measured by the witness, but was put down in the survey
"about fifty feet."   He says Mr. Roth is a German, and
speaks the English language so as scarcely to be understood.
Witness believed himself the distance to be about fifty feet.
As witness was so well acquainted with the property, Roth
could not have misrepresented its situation.   The injury to
the insured was fully two thousand dollars.

On the 10th of September, 1852, the Secretary of the
Insurance Company wrote to the agent, "We are in receipt
of Mr. Roth's proof of loss, and we regret to say it corroborates the report that came to us, that the steam saw-mill was
nearer the dwelling than is set forth in Mr. Roth's survey, on
which the policy was issued.   Besides the erroneous statement of the distance, we find that the survey is silent as to
the nature of the occupancy of the contiguous buildings.   By
his silence we were led to suppose such buildings were not of
an extra hazardous occupation; had the survey been explicit
on that point, we should, without hesitation, have declined
the risk; and we have thus been led into the issuing of the
policy, under an erroneous representation of the hazard."

There being no controversy about the facts, the cause is
submitted to the Court on the above statement.

In the argument the plaintiff denies the concealment and misrepresentation which are set up in the defense, and insists that the survey having been made by the agent of the company, who was well acquainted with the locality of the premises, being the family physician of the plaintiff, the plaintiff is not chargeable in law with any misrepresentations or concealments in the description of the premises. That the distance was not measured between the house insured and the nearest houses on both sides, but it was assumed in the survey as about fifty feet. These are the words of the agent in his deposition; but in the survey the distance is stated to be "sixty to seventy feet." The memory of the witness is inaccurate in this respect. And as the parties agree that the measured distance is a little short of fifty-five feet between the saw-mill and the dwelling-house, there was a misrepresentation in this respect of five feet. This is the misrepresentation on which the defendant relies.

The concealment charged consists in not responding to two enquiries in the printed form of the survey, whether the nearest buildings are frame or brick, and how they are occupied. A note, in the form of the survey furnished, states, if the nearest building is wood, no answers need be given to the interrogatories respecting the walls, sub-divisions, roof and gutters, and that the description may be given in writing, or by a diagram.

And the question is, whether the inaccuracy of distance, and the omission to describe the steam saw-mill, which was the nearest building, are fatal to the rights of the plaintiff. A steam saw-mill is alleged to be more combustible than an ordinary wooden building, and that, consequently, the risk was increased, and therefore it was the more important that it should be accurately described.

The main enquiry, as to the liability of the company is, whether the survey, having been made out by its agent, relieves the plaintiff from the objections made.

There could not in fact have been any inaccuracy as to distance, in the statement of the plaintiff, for the agent of the company says in his deposition, in answer to his enquiry as to the distance the plaintiff replied, forty or fifty feet. Nor can he in fact be said to have concealed anything, as, being an ignorant man, and slightly acquainted with the English language, he relied upon the agent to make out the description. But notwithstanding this, if Warne was legally the agent of Roth in making out the description, and not the agent of the company, the plaintiff must be held responsible for the inaccuracy and concealment charged.

The plaintiff contends, if there had been no agent present and consenting to the whole negotiation, that the facts concealed or misrepresented, were not such as to avoid the policy. That to work this result, it must be a fact which the company, not having the means of knowing, cannot be presumed to know; or a fact material to the risk, and which, if known, would have prevented the officer from taking the risk, or at least from taking it at the premium charged. The difference of ten or five feet in the distance, the counsel argues, can be of no importance. This may be so, but can it be disregarded when the policy has made the statement of the distance a condition?

The policy uses the word contiguous in reference to the distances to be described. The word imports contact, or adjoining; but this cannot be the sense in which it was used in the policy. Whether the saw-mill increased the risk, would seem to be a matter of fact for a jury, and with propriety the effect of the inaccuracy of distance might also properly be enquired into by a jury.

On reference to the authorities there will be found much conflict on the questions raised. The general principles in regard to misrepresentation and concealment, are found in the elementary works. 1 *Phillips*, 80; *Duer*, from 281 to 400, and in *Carter* v. *Rocker*, 3 *Burrows*, 1909. These go upon the ground that the contract is made on the good faith of the representation by the insured, to whom all the facts are known, and which he is bound to state. Any concealment of the facts important to the risk, or misrepresentation of them, so as to mislead the underwriters, is fatal to the policy. For any failure in this respect, neither the ignorance nor inadvertence of the party can afford an excuse.

In *Curry* v. *Con. Ins. Co.*, 10 *Pickering*, 535, the assured had been threatened by a person who had been arrested by the plaintiff, that he would burn his house when released, which was concealed by the plaintiff, perhaps, because he considered it an idle threat; yet the Court instructed the jury, if they considered the threat material to the risk, and would have influenced the underwriters, it was a matter for the jury. In *Fowler* v. *Ætna Ins. Co.*, 6 *Cowen*, 673, where the plaintiff represented his two story frame house was filled in with brick, which was not true, it was held to be fatal to a recovery.

When a description is false and not included in the policy, it must be material to the risk, or it will not vitiate the policy. *Delonguemore* v. *Tradesman's Ins. Co.*; 2 *Hall*, 509. It is a general rule, to make a representation a warranty, it must be a part of the policy.

Where the written application was a part of the policy, and the conditions required a description of buildings within ten rods of the house insured, any misdescription should avoid the policy. The building insured was a grist-mill, having space on all sides, no mention being made of a barn within six rods, nor of the fact that there was a turning lathe and carpenter's bench and tools kept and used in the building; although these facts were spoken of at the time of insurance; held that these omissions were fatal to the policy. *Jennings* v. *The Chenango Mut. Ins. Co.*, 2 *Denio*, 75.

Lord Mansfield held that there is a material distinction between a representation and a warranty. A representation may be equitably and substantially answered; but a warranty must be strictly complied with. In *De Hahn* v. *Hartley*, 1

Term Rep., 343, it is said in 1 *W. Blackston*, 427, and in 3 *Burr*, 1419, that a false warranty will vitiate the policy, though the loss happens in a mode not affected by the falsity.

In *Masters* v. *The Madison County Mut.Ins. Co.*, 11 *Barbour*, 624, it was held that the surveyor and agent of an Insurance Company, on being applied to for an insurance upon the plaintiff's mill, went to see the property, and made survey thereof, the plaintiff not accompanying him, but leaving him to transact the business and to do whatever was necessary. The agent then made out the application for the plaintiff to sign, using the printed blank furnished to agents for that purpose. He was informed at the time by the plaintiff's son that there was a mortgage on the premises, which was a lien thereon. But the application made no mention of any incumbrance. Held that the notice given to the agent, of the prior incumbrance, was sufficient notice to the company; and that the omission to set forth the mortgage in the application, was not a breach of warranty, or a concealment of importance affecting the risk; notwithstanding the application, by a memorandum in the margin, required the applicant to state whether the property was incumbered, by what and to what amount, and if not, to say so, and although the by-laws of the company made the person taking the survey the agent of the applicant.

Held also, "that under these circumstances, the plaintiff could not be prevented from recovering against the company, upon the policy, by the omission to mention in the application, the fact that there were other buildings standing within ten rods of the property insured, in answer to an interrogatory upon the margin of the application." *Ibid.*

"The fact that an applicant for an insurance merely mentions the nearest buildings, without professing to do more, or to make any further statement, does not amount to a warranty that there are no other buildings within the given distance of ten rods." *Ibid.*

"If there are other buildings, it amounts to the withholding of information called for by the interrogatory; and then the question arises, whether it is material to the risk. If the risk is not increased by the other buildings, then the withholding of the information is immaterial. This is a question of fact, proper to be submitted to the jury." *Ibid.* "Although the by-laws of an Insurance Company make the person taking a survey in its behalf, the agent of the applicant, still he is the agent of the company also, and it is bound by his acts." *Ibid.*

On the part of the defendant it is contended that the plaintiff having signed the survey, he is bound by the conditions of the policy. That the agent who filled up the blank survey acted in doing so, as the agent of the plaintiff and not as the agent of the company. That the policy was declared to be made on conditions annexed to it; and this would be the effect of the policy if the survey had not been made.

The condititions in this policy, it is argued, are a warranty. They stipulate

1. That what is stated by the plaintiff is true.

2. That any misrepresentation and concealment shall avoid the policy.

These, it is alleged, are the conditions of the policy, and if not fulfilled, no liability on the part of the company attaches.

In *Saxton and Others* v. *The Montgomery County Mutual Ins. Co.*, 9 *Barbour*, 191, it was held, "Where, by the conditions annexed to a policy it is provided that, 'in all cases the insured will be bound by the application, for the purpose of taking which the surveyor will be deemed the agent of the applicant as well as of the company,' the surveyor is the agent of the applicant, and the applicant will be affected by any omission of such agent in describing the property insured." "Where, in the application to an Insurance Company for insurance on personal property, which application was annexed to the policy issued and was referred to therein, and made a part therof, opposite to the usual printed inquires, 'where situated, of what materials and size of building, &c., and relative situation as to other buildings, distance from each if less than ten rods,' &c., was written a description of several buildings standing within ten rods of the one in which the goods insured were; but several other buildings within that distance were not mentioned. Held that had this been an insurance upon buildings, the statement in the application as to the distance from other buildings, would have been a warranty." *Ibid.*

" Where it is one of the conditions of a policy of insurance that, in case of any misrepresentation or concealment on the part of the assured, the insurance shall be void; in an action upon such policy, the defendant's concealment of a material fact, the question of concealment and its materiality should be submitted to the jury." *Ibid.*

In *Kenedy and Others* v. *The St. Lawrence County Mutual Ins. Co.*, 10 *Barbour*, 285, where a policy of insurance against fire, referred to the application of the insured thus, "reference being had to the application, &c., for a more particular description, as forming a part of this policy." Held that the application formed a part of the contract, and was a warranty.

Where the insured was required to state in his application the number of buildings within ten rods of that in which the goods insured were deposited, and he omitted to state all the buildings within that distance. Held that the warranty was broken, and that the insured could not recover. *Ibid.* This rule applies as well to a policy of insurance on goods deposited in a store, as to a policy on the building itself. *Ibid.*

" If there be in the policy a warranty with respect to the number of buildings within ten rods, and the warranty be broken, the fact that the agents of the insurers drew the application, and knew of the existence of the buildings omitted, is immaterial." *Ibid.*

Jennings v. *Chenango Mutual Ins. Co.*, 2 *Denio*, 75. Conditions of insurance annexed to a fire policy, and the written application of the assured, when referred to in the policy, as forming part of it, are parcel of the contract, and have the same effect as if written in the body of it.

Statements, in the application, when it made a part of the policy, of the purpose for which the insured building is to be occupied, and of its situation as to other buildings, are warranties, and if untrue, the policy is void, though the variance be not material to the risk. *Ibid.*

And parol evidence that the assured truly informed the agent of the insurer, who prepared the application, as to these particulars, is not admissible. *Ibid.*

Where the conditions which were made a part of the policy declared that all applications for insurance must be made in writing, and must state the relative situation of the property as to other buildings, and the distance from each, if less than ten rods, and the printed application was so filled up as not to show the distance of other buildings from the insured property, though there was one within ten rods. Held that the insured cannot recover. So where the conditions required the application to state for what purpose the insured property was occupied, and in the application it was only called a grist-mill, and it was proved that carpenter's work was accustomed to be done in it, with instruments and fixtures which were kept there. Held that the policy was void. *Ibid.*

In *Wall* v. *Howard Ins.Co.*, 14 *Barbour*, 883. A representation to be a warranty must be contained in the policy, or by reference in the policy must be made a part of it. A warranty must be strictly complied with, even where it does not seem to affect the risk. *Ibid.* But a misrepresentation in a matter that does not affect the risk or the amount of the premium, will not avoid the policy unless made with a fraudulent design. *Ibid.*

A misrepresentation whereby a less premium is paid than would be payable if a true statement had been made, even without a fraudulent intent, would, upon common principles of insurance, be sufficient to render the policy void. *Fitzherbert* v. *Mather*, 1 *Term Rep.*, 12.

These cases are cited as they seem to have a direct bearing on the case before the Court. But it must be observed that they are not altogether consistent with each other. In some of them it is held that where the representation is made a warranty by being inserted in the policy, or by reference made a part of the contract, any misrepresentation, though not affecting the risk, avoids the policy, whilst in others the policy is held to be avoided, if the misrepresentation has a bearing on the risk.

Now, I cannot see why the misrepresentation of a fact, which was in no way material to the risk, and, consequently, could have had no effect to increase the premium, if known, can be held to make the policy void. The contract of insurance, like all other contracts, requires good faith in the parties; and it is said that in these cases, the assurer generally relies on the assured, who has full knowledge of the locality of the property, and the company is not presumed to have such knowledge, every fact bearing upon the risk should be truly stated. And if this be not done, whether the omission be chargeable to fraud, negligence or inadvertence, is immaterial, as the effect on the insurers is the same; the policy is avoided.

But it may be said, can there be no distinction between that which is included in the contract, and that which is outside of it. Such an enquiry may lead technical minds to make a distinction, where none in fact exists. That which the contract includes is held to be a warranty, and that which is outside of the contract is considered to be a mere representation. Now, if there is a misdescription in the latter, which misleads the assurer, the policy is void; and from this it seems to have been inferred that where there is a warranty, the misrepresentation of any fact which does not and cannot mislead the assurer, because it has no relation to the risk, yet it shall vitiate the policy. And this we are told is the distinction between a simple representation, and one which is made a part of the policy. The former is said to be a proposition for a contract, the latter a part of it. The former, if fraudulent, avoids the contract; the latter, if untrue, is a breach of the contract.

It is admitted that a warranty, as stated by *Ellis on Insurance*, may be considered a condition precedent to the contract, and consequently requires a strict construction and performance, before the assurer can be held responsible. But it is said by the Supreme Court in a late case, "there is no more reason for claiming a strict literal compliance with the terms of a policy than in ordinary contracts. Full legal effect should always be given to it, for the purpose of guarding the company against fraud or imposition; beyond this we would be sacrificing substance to form, following words rather than ideas."

Lord Eldon, in the House of Lords, in *McMorran* v. *New Castle Fire Insurance Co.*, 3 Daw. R., 255, took a sensible view in saying, "the insurance was made with the New Castle Fire Insurance Company, and the mill was burnt; and in an action against the insurers the question was, whether the mill, which was warranted as in the first class of risks, was not truly of the second class. It turned out to be in the second class, and it was held that an action on such a policy could not be sustained, Lord Eldon observing, whether the misrepresentation was in a material point or not, or whether the risk was equally great in the one class as in the other, were questions which had nothing to do with the case; the only question being, Is this *de facto* the building which I have insured?" But in this case it was held or considered, that in a case of warranty, it would be a good answer that the mistake or misrepresentation was to be attributed solely to the insurers or their agent."

The materiality of a representation or an omission is a matter for the jury. *Grant* v. *Howard Fire Insurance Co.*, 5 *Hill* (*N. Y.*) *Rep.*, 10 ; *McLarahan* v. *Universal Insurance Co.*, 1 *Peters* 188. Lord Mansfield says, " Good faith forbids either party, by concealing what he privately knows, to draw the other into a bargain, from his ignorance of that fact, and his believing the contrary. But either party may be innocently silent as to grounds open to both, to exercise their judgments upon." And again, "there are many matters as to which the insured may be innocently silent; he need not mention what the underwriter knows." And again, " the reason of the rule against concealments, is to prevent fraud and encourage good faith."

In *Satterthwaite* v. *Mutual Beneficial Institution*, 2 *Harris* 393, the Supreme Court of Pennsylvania says " where the constitution and by-laws of a Mutual Fire Insurance Company, do not require from an applicant for insurance, a statement as to the condition of the property designed to be insured; but where the by-laws provide for a survey at the instance of the company, the policy is not void by reason of omission on the part of the assured to state a fact material to the risk, where no enquiry is made on the subject."

There is another point to be considered, and that is, what effect is to be given to the fact, that the survey was made by the agent of the company, who, from the evidence, was as well acquainted with the building insured and the adjacent buildings as was the insured. He filled up the blanks in the form furnished by the defendant, which was signed by the plaintiff. If this be considered as the representation of the plaintiff, unaffected by the agent of defendants, there is an end of this controversy. And I admit that the greater number of decisions on this point are against the plaintiff. They treat Mr. Warne, in making the survey, as the agent of the

22a

plaintiff. And although this point was pressed in the argument with great cogency, I was not convinced that it was reasonable or just. It is, undoubtedly, the rule of decision in New York, and also in Massachusetts. And he who takes a ground, on a question of insurance, in opposition to a rule well established in these two great commercial States, may be considered as hazarding something, if he has anything to hazard. But if I am wrong, the parties will not be injured, and I myself may be put right by my brethren at Washington.

I do not take ground that, in all cases, where the survey is made out by the agent of the assurer, the assured is not answerable for the representation. But if such agent actually makes the survey, being as well acquainted with the locality of the premises as the assured is, and when he takes the whole authority of making the representation on a view of the premises, I must think, until overruled, that the assured is not responsible either for concealment or misrepresentation. But where the representation is made out under the direction of the insured, or without a view of the premises by the agent, it would be just to hold the insured responsible. The employment of the agent, and the circumstances under which the survey was made, are matters for the jury, as well as some other matters before noticed.

In the case cited from 11 *Barbour*, where the agent made the survey, the direction of the insurer was not complied with, by stating there was a mortgage on the premises, yet as the son of the insured stated the fact to the agent, it was held sufficient. This was under the general rule that a notice to the agent was notice to the principal. Under the by-law of the company, it was declared that their agent, in making the survey, acted as the agent of the insured. In the above case the Supreme Court of New York say, the agent is in the employment of the company, soliciting risks and making contracts for the company with every body who might wish to insure; and he also makes out the application, and prepares the necessary papers to effect insurances, and hence the Court were of opinion that it would be little better than legalized robbery to allow those insurance companies to escape from liability upon the merest technicality possible, and that too when created by its own by-laws.

But whether such agent is declared to be the agent of the assured when he makes the survey, cannot be material. He is known to be the agent of the company, and it is expected of him that he will assist the uninstructed in making their applications, for which purpose he is furnished by the company with the necessary blanks to be filled up under his direction. His connection with the company, and the interest he is expected to excite in its behalf, recommend him to those who desire to be insured, and they rely upon his fairness and intelligence. And if, under such circumstances, he should intentionally or unintentionally make any concealment or misrepresentation in the application, acting upon his own survey, and having an intimate knowledge of the premises insured, the company should not be permitted to defeat a recovery on such ground. No hardship is imposed on the company, if it be presumed to have the notice of the agent who made the survey. Ordinary prudence would suggest the propriety of giving such instructions on this point, as should secure full information, at least in all cases where the survey is made by the agent.

From the language of the conditions made a part of this policy, an inference may be drawn that, where an agent of the company is called on to make the application, the insured incurs no responsibility. The words are, "If the property offered for insurance is within the district of a surveyor of the company, he will examine and report thereon, unless the party applying shall elect to make his own survey, in which case such survey shall be made according to the printed form of instructions issued from the office of the company, and the party furnishing such survey, shall be responsible for the accuracy thereof." Now if the party shall elect to make his own survey, he may make it, though the property to be insured is within the district of a surveyor of the company, yet in such case of election, he makes the survey under the responsibility stated. But if the agent of the company examine and report thereon, he is authorized to do so, which, it would seem, relieves the party from the responsibility of making his own report, and for the accuracy of which he is held responsible.

In the case of *Bruner* v. *Howard Fire Ins. Co.*, 2 *Law Register*, 510, held by the Supreme Court of Pennsylvania it was competent to show that the description of property insured, annexed to a policy, though signed by the insured, was drawn up by the agents of the insurer, and that they knew all about the property from the verbal description by the insured and from actual survey, and therefore that the omissions and misrepresentations were chargeable to the agents of the assured.

In the case of the *Protection Ins. Co.* v. *Harmer*, 22 *Ohio*, 452, an interesting and well considered case, sustains, as I think, sound doctrines on the law of insurance.

A jury may be called at the convenience of the counsel, and exceptions can be taken, so as to present to the Supreme Court the points ruled.

LESSEE OF WILKINS *v.* WRIGHT ET AL.

The distinction between a deed of trust and a mortgage, is somewhat technical.

Before a default in payment, the property mortgaged may be sold on execution as the property of the mortgagor.

This cannot be done under a deed of trust.

To perfect a title under a mortgage, a judicial sale must be had.

Under a deed of trust, a sale is not required.

So nearly are these instruments assimilated, that different minds may come to different conclusions in regard to the character of the same instrument.

Messrs. Andrews for the plaintiff.
Mr. Parker for the defendant.

OPINION OF THE COURT.

The lessee of plaintiff are heirs at law of Diana Rapelye, deceased, and claim under a deed to their ancestor from Joseph Evans, dated 19th June, 1817.

Defendant's title is under a later deed from Evans. The case turns on the character of the deed to Rapelye. On its face this deed is absolute. But the following indorsement is made upon it: " It is perfectly understood between Diana Rapelye and Joseph Evans, that the said Diana is to hold the within mentioned tracts of land, as a deed of trust, for the said Joseph Evans, and as security for her, until he pays the five hundred and the one thousand dollars with interest, which he has given his notes for," &c. If the notes were not paid at the time specified, "the said Diana will have full power to sell or to act as she thinks proper; but the said Evans is to have the privilege of selling the lands, at any time within the period specified in the notes, but the notes to be taken up before the deed is returned; the interest on the notes are included, but if taken up before due, then the interest to be deducted from the date." Notes were drawn payable in two and four months. If the notes should be paid, then "the deed for the land to be again made to Evans, free from all incumbrances whatsoever."

The question arises whether the above deed, with the indorsement, is a deed of trust or a mortgage.

If it be a mortgage, before forfeiture it may be sold on execution against the mortgagor, subject to the mortgage. But if it be a deed of trust, nothing remains in the grantor which can be reached by execution. If it be a mortgage, on the payment of the money the title reverts to the mortgagor. But if it be a deed of trust, a reconveyance of the land is necessary. In either case, the land is a security for the money.

But under the mortgage a sale would be necessary to perfect the title in the mortgagee or in any other person. But if the instrument be a deed of trust, the fee stands vested in the grantee, and no sale is necessary.

The distinction between a deed of trust and a mortgage, is somewhat technical, and in many cases different minds might incline to the one character or the other of the same instrument. The parties in this case call the instrument a deed of trust, and provide that on the payment of the money, the title should be reconveyed to the grantor, free from all incumbrances. This is not the language of a mortgage, which provides that, on the payment of the money the conveyance should be of none effect. From expressed language of the parties, they would seem to have considered the instrument as a deed of trust. And as this kind of instrument best secures the right of the grantee, we may presume the form was adopted with that view.

Upon the whole, we think the instrument may be considered as a deed of trust, but we decide nothing more. Any equitable rights which the defendants may have, are neither shown nor considered in the case.

UNITED STATES v. JAMES WHITAKER.

Where a post-master is charged with abstracting a letter from the mail, containing money, to fix the charge it is usually necessary to examine the post-masters and assistant post-masters, between the office where the letter was deposited to be mailed, and the office to which it was directed.

And at such office the clerks or persons who received and opened the mail should be examined. This testimony is especially necessary on the part of the prosecution, where the accused proved an exemplary character during his whole life.

Mr. *Morton*, District Attorney, for plaintiff.
Mr. *Joliffe* for defendant.

OPINION OF THE COURT.

This is an indictment against the defendant, who acted as assistant post-master at   post-office, for stealing a letter from the mail containing ninety-three dollars.

The letter was proved to have been mailed at Withamsville, the money being counted and handed to the defendant to be enclosed in a letter and directed to Stephen Clark, Cincinnati, but was never received, as proved by Mr. Clark, nor did it appear to have been received by the account of mails received at the Cincinnati office.

The defendant, sometime after the deposite of the money, called one or more witnesses to notice the fact that he enclosed the money in the letter, sealed it, but no one swears to the fact that it was mailed, but such were their impressions, as at the time of enclosing the money he was putting up the mail.

A proposition was made to the defendant, if he would pay, or secure the payment of the money to Mr. Clark, the matter would not be prosecuted, which the defendant refused.

The persons who usually opened the mail in the Cincinnati office were examined, but all the persons through whose hands the letters passed were not examined.

In the defense it was shown that letters directed to Cincinnati, on the same route, west of the defendant's office had miscarried, and also, that letters directed to the Cincinnati office on other routes had never been received.

It was proposed to prove that the assistant post-master at Mount Washington, the next office to the Witham office, on the route to Cincinnati, was suspected, and that at one time he had been charged with passing counterfeit money. But the Court overruled the testimony, on the ground that the person had not been examined as a witness, and that his general character could not be assailed.

Some ten or twelve witnesses were then called, who proved the good character of the defendant. In the cross examination of one or two of the witnesses to the good character of the defendant, they were asked whether the defendant had not, at one time, been charged with passing counterfeit money. This was not objected to by the defendant, and was explained by showing of whom he had received the bank note, as good, on which the charge was founded. This circumstance, it was proved, had not in the least affected the fair character of the defendant in his neighborhood.

The Court remarked to the jury that the exemplary character of the defendant, as proved, should have weight in their deliberations. That before the letter reached Cincinnati it passed through the office at Mount Washington, and one or two other offices before it reached Cincinnati, and at that office it passed through the hands of clerks, and there were others who had access to it. The defendant admitted the letter and the money were deposited in the office, to be forwarded in the mail. Upon the whole, the Court remarked, unless you come to the conclusion that the defendant is guilty, beyond reasonable doubt, you will acquit him.

The jury found the defendant not guilty.

●   ————

Joseph W. Wayne v. T. Winter et al.

Parol evidence is not admissible to show at what time a patent was applied for.

The Patent-Office contains written evidence of the fact, and it must be proved by such evidence.

Mr. *Miner*, for plaintiff.

Messrs. *Stanberry and McCormick*, for defendant.

OPINION OF THE COURT.

The plaintiff introduced the patent under which he claimed a right to a washing machine, which the defendants were charged with infringing, dated 30th October, 1849. An assignment to the plaintiff by the patentee, on the 15th January, 1851, was shown, and which was recorded in the Patent-Office in 1853. The face of the wash board was covered with zinc, with numerous elevations, so as to make a rough surface on which the clothes, on being washed, are rubbed. The invention consists in extending the zinc plate with sharpened edges beyond the board on which it was laid, so that the zinc plate extended into the side pieces fastened to the board and made it firm.

From the evidence it appears that this wash board had been in use more that two years before the date of the patent, which, it was contended, was a dedication of the improvement to the public. The counsel for the plaintiff offered parol evidence to show when the patent was applied for, but the Court overruled the testimony. A non suit was suffered, which was set aside on motion and payment of costs.

ROCHUS HEINRICH v. JOHN LUTHER.

A patent is prima facie evidence of the right of the patentee.

Where the patentee claims three distinct improvements, he must show himself entitled to each, to sustain an action.

Since shears were invented, some contrivance has been used to stop the handles, so as not to strain the joints of the cutting knives.

This has been done by the enlargement of the handles so as to come in contact at the proper point.

Several witnesses proved that a screw was used for this purpose, others have known wires to be used.

The invention consists, not in avoiding the pressure of the joint of the shears, but in accomplishing that result by a new means.

The beak which performs this office in the plaintiff's shears, was cast in the handles of the shears, and is as permanent as any other part of the handle.

There is no special claim in writing that the beak should be so made, but the drawing shows how it was a part of the upper handle, and the drawing is a part of the specifications.

Messrs. *Stanberry and Parker*, for plaintiff.

Messrs. *Andrews and Swayne*, for defendant.

OPINION OF THE COURT.

This action is brought against the defendant, gentlemen of the jury, for infringing the plaintiff's patent. It was issued to secure to the plaintiff an improvement in tailors' shears. The patent bears date the 27th of February, 1839.

The invention claimed, is, 1. The projection at the point of beak *e*, on the upper bow, as described. 2. The addition of the convex protuberance of, or swelling of *f* and *g*, on the right side of the upper and lower bows, so as to fill the palm of the hand in using the shears.

The third is the concave lip *h*, on the left side of the upper bow, for the thumb to rest upon as described.

To entitle the plaintiff to recover, these three inventions as claimed, must be found to have been invented by him as claimed.

Before the patent is granted, the invention claimed is examined by one or more examiners skilled in the arts, and compared with the patents which have been issued in this and other countries; and if the invention is found to be new and useful, and the applicant swears that he is the first and original inventor, the patent is granted. And this gives to the patentee a prima facie right.

In this case the patent has been issued for the improvements above specified, so that if the plaintiff shall fail to establish his right to either of the things specified, he will not be entitled to your verdict.

That the improvement in the shears is useful, is abundantly shown. One evidence of this, as stated by several of the witnesses, is, that wherever the improved shears have been known, they have been generally used.

It is proved that the defendant, before the commencement of this action, manufactured and sold shears similar to those described in the plaintiff's patent. On a comparison, several witnesses say the shears made by the defendant are the same in principle as the plaintiff's.

The improvements, it is alleged, as specified, enable a person to hold the shears with a firmer grasp, by bringing the entire muscles of the hand and thumb in contact with the handles, and to use them with more power and greater ease than the ordinary shears. And that the beak *e*, which projects from the lower part of the upper handle, checks the action of the handles at the proper point, so as to avoid a strain at the joint of the shears.

An objection is made that the plaintiff abandoned his right to the public, by permitting his invention to go into public use. But unless this use exceeded two years, before he applied for his patent, there is no abandonment. A former patent, it seems, had been obtained by the plaintiff, embracing some of the improvements made to the handles of the shears, but these are not claimed in the present patent.

The principal controversy arises on the novelty of beak *e*, as appears on the drawing.

From the first formation of shears, there has been some contrivance to prevent the strain on the joint of the cutting knives. This was generally effected by enlarging the upper and lower handles, so as to come together at the proper point. But this required an additional weight in large shears used by tailors, by an increase in the size of the iron handles, so as to make the use of them unwieldy and tiresome to the hand.

Several of the witnesses speak of shears, some one or more

years before the date of the plaintiff's patent, on which a screw was used to keep the handles apart, answering the same purpose as the beak. Other witnesses say they have known wires to be used for the same thing. But the plaintiff contends the proof shows that the screw and wires were abandonded as useless, before the plaintiff's beak was invented.

Now the invention does not consist in a resting point for handles, so as to avoid a strain upon the joint of the shears, for that was always guarded against by the enlargement or shape of the handle, or by some other mode. Neither the screw nor the beak, in this respect, produces a new result. But the invention consists in the beak, by which an old result is produced by new means.

A knob of porcelain on a door is common. As porcelain was well known before it was so applied, and as knobs were common of other materials, the use of porcelain for this purpose gave no right to a patent. But if a new and useful mode of fastening the knob on the spindle was invented, that is a sufficient invention for a patent. And so in regard to the beak claimed by the plaintiff. If it be more substantial than the screw, being cheaper and fastened to the handle of the shears in a new mode, different from the screw or the wire formerly used, it is an invention for which a patent may issue.

The beak, you will observe gentlemen, is cast with the handle of the shears, so that it is a part of the handle, and as durable as any other part of it. It is true that in the written specifications the beak is not claimed to be cast with the handle, but there is a reference to the drawing which shows how the beak is made, and the drawings are a part of the specifications.

It is replied that the drawings would be the same if the beak were soldered on the handle. The model which the plaintiff was required to file in the Patent Office, when he applied for his patent, showed, as the shears used in evidence show, that the beak was cast. And it is considered that the drawing shows, with reasonable certainty, that the beak was a part of the handles of the shears, as permanently fixed as the thumb piece or the handles.

As an evidence that neither the screw nor the wire was of any value is shown, it is contended, by the abandonment of both. What, then, was there in the screw which the plaintiff copied? There is nothing new in preventing the strain of the joint, and if the old mode of producing this result by a wire or a screw should be used, it would be no infringement of the plaintiff's patent; nor would there be an infringement if the handles were so enlarged, as formerly, to produce this result. The invention consists in the beak, which is made a part of the handle of the shears. In this the principle of the invention consists, and in nothing else.

The parties have agreed that if the patent of the plaintiff should be sustained, the jury should find in damages a verdict for five hundred dollars.

The jury returned a verdict for that sum.

UNITED STATES v. FOULKE.

The jury are to weigh the evidence in every case, and where there is a conflict in a criminal case which creates reasonable doubt, they will acquit the accused.

These doubts should not arise from our sympathies or hopes, but from a deliberate consideration of the evidence.

Mr. *Morton*, District Attorney, for plaintiff.

Mr. *Upton*, for defendant.

OPINION OF THE COURT.

The defendant stands charged, gentlemen of the jury, with stealing a letter out of the mail containing money, he being a post-master.

Mr. Chapman, who acts as special agent for the Post-Office Department, states that the defendant was post-master at Moultrie, situated on the railroad to Cleveland. The witness mailed a letter at New Franklin post-office, Stark County, addressed to the post-master at Osnaburg, with a request that it should be returned to Cleveland. There was but one office, Paris, between New Franklin and Osnaburg. The letter contained a ten dollar bank note.

This letter was received by the post-master at Osnaburg, which is thirteen miles west of Moultrie. Mr. Koons, the post-master at Osnaburg, states that he received the letter from Chapman and forwarded it the next day, the 21st July, to Cleveland. It had to pass through Paris and New Franklin before it reached Moultrie post-office, on the railroad. The letter was directed to one Milton, Cleveland, requesting him to make and forward to the writer a plow. A fictitious name was signed to the letter.

Mr. Chapman states that on the evening of the 21st of July, he received from Cleveland, by the conductor of the train, the same ten dollar note he enclosed in the above letter.

The post-master of Paris, which was the first office after it left Osnaburg, states that he took, on the 21st, no letter out of the mail which was not directed to his office. The post-master at New Franklin also stated that he took no letter out of the mail which was not directed to his office. The next was the Moultrie office.

: Mr. Cleland, the conductor of the train, states that, on the 21st of July, the defendant was post-master at Moultrie, and kept a tavern. He generally received the mail from the cars and changed it. On the above day, the defendant asked him to change a ten dollar bill, as he wanted small bills, and the witness gave him smaller notes for the bill which he identified, and that was the bill which he on the same day handed to Chapman, the agent of the Post-Office Department.

Mr. Grey, assistant post-master at Cleveland, was requested by Chapman to look for the letter he had caused to be forwarded, which he did on the evening of the 21st of July, and for several evenings afterwards, but no such letter has been received at the Cleveland post-office.

Mr. Meeker was present when Cleland, the conductor, changed the bill at the request of the defendant. Cleland at first objected to the bill as not good, but Foulke assured him it was good and that he would be responsible for it.

Mr. Arnold saw Cleland and Foulke talking together on the above day, but did not hear the conversation.

DEFENDANTS' WITNESSES.

Mr. Randolph, being called by the defendant, states that he saw defendant on the 21st of July, 1853, in Chambersburg. He was arrested about the 9th of August. On the 21st he saw A. Koons, the post-master at Osnaburg, at Root's, in Chambersburg. Mr. Root came across the street and spoke to defendant, taking him out of the crowd. Witness saw they had money passing between them, and the witness says the defendant got a $10 bill of Root, in the presence of three or four persons who witnessed the exchange. The bill received by Foulke was doubted at first. The witness had the $10 bill in his hand. The bill had two crosses near the letter B. The bill being presented to the witness, he believes it to be the same.

Samuel Loder was at Chambersburg on the eve of the 21st or 22d of July, 1853, and heard Randolph, Foulke and Harris talking together, witness being present. They talked about the ten dollar bill. Witness on looking at it thought it was not good. He saw Root in close proximity with Foulke. Witness thought the bill was not good. Witness has known Root five years. Witness stood near Randolph.

Mr. Harris, was at Chambersburg on the 22d or 23d of July. He thinks Loder took up some work. Witness lived with Loder. Witness saw Mr. Root come down, call Foulke out and change some money with him; handed the bill to Randolph; Foulke had the note, but does know the size of it; and witness saw Foulke give change for the note; heard Mr. Randolph say it was a base counterfeit.

Mr. Thomas, lives in Chambersburg. On the 22d of July 1853, had some hands at work who came to his house on the same evening, and he made an entry of the date as above. Witness saw a bill in the hands of the defendant, who said it did not look like a good bill. Root said if it were not good he would make it good. Witness did not examine the bill, and did not know the amount of it. On the same evening a wagon and sulkey were taken away by Mr. Randolph.

Joseph Estel was the mail carrier about five months, and was the carrier at the above time, three times a week each way Tuesdays, Thursdays and Saturdays.

Mr. Lever, Mr. Wallace, John McClury, Wm. H. Gill. Wm. W. Hamilton, Charles M. Austin, Judge Riddle, Joseph H. Quinn and Mr. Aster were sworn, all of whom testified to the good character of the defendant. They represented him as having filled various responsible trusts, and exercising great influence with the people of his county.

The plaintiffs called some rebutting witnesses.

Mr. Root says he is the brother-in-law of Koons; that he had some dealings with the defendant the latter part of May or the beginning of June; bought a horse from defendant; paid thirty dollars, and gave a note for the balance; that he sold goods, and had more accounts against the defendant. Chambersburg was only a few miles from Moultrie.

Mr. Koons says he was not at Chambersburg on the 21st of July; that he was there on the 20th, and a short time afterwards; that he never promised Root to change a bill for him with the defendant.

The defendant then called Mr. Eustine, who says, he heard

Root say he had changed with Foulke a ten dollar bill, which was suspected; and that he promised to make it good if it were not so.

This is the substance of the testimony, gentlemen; and it is your duty to consider it well, and to come to a decision as to the guilt or innocence of the defendant.

If the postmasters of Osnaburg and New Franklin have sworn truly, the letter was mailed at Osnaburg, and, passing through the New Franklin office, in all probability was received at the Moultrie office: and, if the conductor of the train, Mr. Cleland, and the Postoffice agent, Chapman, remember correctly, the note which the latter endorsed to test, as he says, the Moultrie office, was received by the conductor from the defendant on the 21st of July, and handed by him to Chapman, the agent, on the same day. And, as the conductor was apprised by the agent of the experiment, both he and the agent would necessarily charge their memories with the facts and the date. These witnesses are not impeached.

The defense rests mainly on the fact alleged, that the identical note was received by the defendant from Roth on the 21st of July, the same day the conductor received the note from the defendant. The witnesses vary somewhat as to the time the note was received by the defendant from Roth. It was sometime in the afternoon. Now, if this note was not received until after the cars had passed the Moultrie office, the defense must fail. Chambersburg is but a short distance from Moultrie. Supposing the note received from Roth was the identical note passed to the conductor by the defendant, there is no question that he must have received it from Roth, and returned to his office before the cars arrived. It is said that the daughter of the defendant, in the absence of her father, generally opened the mail.

The attempt is openly avowed to implicate Mr. Koons, the Postmaster at Osnaburg, in this transaction. The letter in question was enclosed to Mr. Koons by Chapman, open, and

23a

he stated the object. It is then suggested that Koons had the power to abstract the letter, hand it to his brother-in-law, Roths, who passed it off to Foulke with the view of entrapping him. Mr. Koons was not suspected by the agent of the Postoffice Department, nor is there any evidence, beyond what you have heard, to cause suspicion against him.

Koons swears he was not at Chambersburg on the 21st of July, and the same is corroborated by the oath of Roth, his brother-in-law; and one or two of the other witnesses state, that it was on the twenty-second or third that the ten dollar note was passed to Foulke by Roth. But, several of the witnesses say that the note was passed to the defendant on the 21st; and they identify the note now presented to them by a mark which was observed at the time; and here, too, the witnesses state facts which would be likely to remain impressed upon their memory. The note was minutely examined by Mr. Randolph and others, as it was suspected to be a counterfeit; and several of them, on looking at the note now, are able to identify it by certain marks which were observed when they saw it at Chambersburg.

If this evidence be false, it has been most ingeniously contrived. But, such a supposition most seriously implicates the defendant's witnesses, who have not been impeached, and who appear to be respectable. It will be your duty, gentlemen, to reconcile the testimony if you can; but, if this can not be done, it will become your painful duty to weigh the facts, and decide where the truth lies.

By a large number of respectable witnesses the defendant has shown a good character. This the law permits, from the infirmity of human testimony, and for the safety of the accused. Where an individual has so acted as to secure the confidence and good feeling of his neighbors, and of those with whom he has had intercourse or business, he will not be supposed, except upon the clearest evidence, at once to abandon so desirable an inheritance. There may be such instances, but they form exceptions to the general rule.

You, gentlemen, are to judge of the weight of evidence, and the credibilty of witnesses. There is no tribunal but that before which we must all appear, which can rightly judge of the motives of human action. We have no such standard; and, at best, we can only determine matters of controversy, civil and criminal, on the highest probability of facts, from the evidence. But, in every criminal case, where a conviction is utterly ruinous to the accused, a jury will acquit, if they have reasonable doubts of his guilt; but, these doubts must not arise from our sympathies, but from a deliberate consideration of the evidence.

The jury found the defendant not guilty.

EX PARTE H. H. ROBINSON, MARSHAL OF THE UNITED STATES.

A writ of *habeas corpus* may issue to relieve an officer of the Federal government who has been imprisoned under State authority for the performance of his duty.

Where concurrent jurisdiction may be exercised by the Federal and State authorities, the court which first takes jurisdiction can be interfered with by no other court, State or Federal. It is a subversion of the judicial power to take a case from a court having jurisdiction, before its final decision is given.

It may be considered an open question, whether one decision on a *habeas corpus* is final.

It should be considered whether all the evidence was heard, and a full trial was had by a Judge or court having jurisdiction.

The federal authorities follow the established construction of a State law by the Supreme Court of the State.

And the rule should be reciprocal—by the State courts in regard to the federal laws.

The powers of the Federal courts, in regard to the exercise of its powers under the constitution and laws of the Union, are as distinct as the courts of distinct governments.

Mr. Pugh for the Marshal.

Messrs. Chase & Joliffe against the discharge.

BEFORE JUDGE McLEAN AT CHAMBERS.

A petition and affidavit of Hiram H. Robinson, Marshal of the United States for the above district, stating that he was imprisoned under the order of the Hon. Judge Parker, one of the Judges of the Court of Common Pleas for the county of Hamilton, for the performance of his duty as Marshal, under process issued by a Commissioner of the United States, and praying for a writ of *habeas corpus*, was presented; which, being granted, the Sheriff, in obedience to the command of the writ, brought the petitioner into court, with the following return:

"April 8, 1855, for return and answer to the *habeas corpus*, the Sheriff of Hamilton county says, that, by virtue of an order of the Court of Common Pleas, and in pursuance of the command of said order, he arrested the within named H. H. Robinson, and committed him to jail as commanded; and that he now holds him in custody by virtue of said order."

It appears from the facts of the case, that, on the 30th of March last, an affidavit of Lewis Van Slyke was made to Judge Parker, representing himself to be the guardian of Rosetta Armstead, and that said Rosetta was then held in illegal imprisonment by Hiram H. Robinson, United States Marshal, under a certain pretended warrant issued by John S. Pendery, claiming to sit as a Commissioner of the Circuit Court of the United States for the Southern District of Ohio, from which said imprisonment said Rosetta was discharged by order of the honorable court on Thursday, the 29th day of March current, in violation of which said order of this court, and immediately after the said minor was placed in the custody of the affiant, the said Hiram H. Robinson again seized the said minor under the same pretended warrant of said Pendery, and now holds her in illegal imprisonment, &c. Upon which affidavit a writ of *habeas corpus* was issued. To this writ the Marshal made the following return:

"The answer of Hiram H. Robinson, Marshal of the Southern District of Ohio, says that, on the 20th day of March, 1855, he was and ever since has been Marshal as aforesaid, duly appointed and qualified; that on said day a warrant was delivered to him by John L. Pendery, Commissioner of the United States, appointed by the Circuit Court of the United States, which commanded him to arrest Rosetta, a fugitive from labor, &c.; and that, on the 24th of the same month, he produced the said Rosetta before the Commisioncr, as commanded; and thereupon the hearing of the claim, made by —— Dennison, specified in said warrant, was regularly commenced.

"That the hearing of the claim has been adjourned from day to day and from time before the said Commissioner, and that the determination thereof yet remains to be made.

"That on the 30th of March aforesaid, and before the delivery to the respondent of this writ, the Commissioner adjourned the trial and determination of the claim until Tuesday morning, the 3d day of April, at ten o'clock; and that the Commissioner did then direct the respondent, as Marshal, to produce the body of the said Rosetta before him, on the day and at the hour stated, to abide his determination as Commissioner in the premises.

"This respondent, therefore, respectfully denies the right and jurisdiction of the Court of Common Pleas of Hamilton county to compel him to produce the body of the said Rosetta before it, under the circumstances stated."

It is admitted that before the warrant of the Commissioner was issued, the colored girl Rosetta was taken by a *habeas corpus* at Columbus, in Ohio, while passing through the State with the agent of her master, before a Judge of Probate, who decided that she was free, and at the same time appointed Van Slyke her guardian.

The seventh section of the act of Congress of the 2d of March, 1833, provides "that either of the Justices of the Supreme Court, or a Judge of any District Court of the United

States, in addition to the authority already conferred by law, shall have power to grant writs of *habeas corpus* in all cases of a prisoner or prisoners, in jail or confinement, where he or they shall be committed or confined on or by any authority or law, for any act done or omitted to be done in pursuance of a law of the United States, or any order, process, or decree of any judge or court thereof; any thing in any act of Congress to the contrary notwithstanding. And if any person to whom such writ of *habeas corpus* may be directed shall refuse to obey the same, or shall neglect or refuse to make return, or shall make a false return thereto, in addition to the remedies already given by law, he or they shall be deemed and taken to be guilty of a misdemeanor, and shall, on conviction before any court of competent jurisdiction, be punished by fine not exceeding one thousand dollars, and by imprisonment not exceeding six months, or by either, according to the nature and aggravation of the case."

This section, which regulates the writ of *habeas corpus*, was enacted to meet the nullification doctrines proclaimed by South Carolina, but which, in this respect, it is believed, were never acted upon by that State. Little was it supposed that the principle could ever have a necessary application to the Northern or Western States, whose members of Congress advocated and voted for the law.

The right to issue the writ can only arise by a total nullification of the Federal authority, and the imprisonment of one of its officers, not for a crime, but for the performance of duties enjoined on him by law, and which he has sworn to perform.

It is contended that the case under consideration is not within this statute. The Marshal omitted to do the act ordered to be done by the honorable Judge Parker, because it would be in express violation of his duty under an act of Congress. This is literally within the act. But it is alleged the Commissioner has no authority to act judicially, as he was not appointed as judges are required to be appointed by the Constitution.

The second section of the second article of the Constitution provides "that Congress may by law vest the appointment of such inferior officers as they think proper in the President alone, in the Courts of law, or in the heads of Departments."

By the fugitive act of 1850, the Commissioners appointed by the Circuit Courts of the United States have concurrent jurisdiction with the Judges of the Circuit and District Courts of the United States, &c.

These Commisioners were appointed under the act of 1842; and under that act they had power to issue warrants, to arrest persons who had committed offences under the law of the United States, and on hearing, commit them, hold them in bail to answer, or to discharge them, as in their judgment the law required.

The nature of the duties of the Commissioners under the act of 1850 is not, in principle, different from those which they previously discharged. The inquiry of a Commissioner or a Judge under the fugitive act is not strictly whether the person is free, but whether he owes service to the claimant. In its results the inquiry may involve the liberty of the fugitive; but the principle applies to an apprentice as well as to a slave.

It must be admitted that this inquiry is somewhat in the nature of judicial power; but the same remark applies to all the officers of the accounting departments of Government. They investigate claims, and decide on the evidence. The examiners in the Patent Office determine on the merits and novelty of inventions. This becomes a judicial duty in every suit between conflicting patents. It is impracticable, in carrying on the machinery of government, to prescribe precise limits to the exercise of executive and judicial power in deciding upon claims. The Supreme Court has had the acts of these Commissioners before it, and has always treated them as having authority under the law.

Two grounds are urged by counsel as sustaining the jurisdiction of the State Judge:

1. That before the fugitive was arrested by the Marshal, she was declared to be free by the Probate Court.

2. That the warrant was defective in not stating that the girl escaped from the State in which she was held as a slave.

It must be admitted that the authorities are not uniform on the point, whether the decision on a *habeas corpus* is final. This may be said of the authorities in this country and in England. I have been myself inclined to think such a decision should be considered final, where there was clearly jurisdiction and a full and fair hearing; but that it might not be so considered when any of these requisites were wanting, or when new and important evidence could be obtained. Some years since I was consulted by a Commissioner on the propriety, after a hearing, of giving time to obtain new evidence. Several unimpeached witnesses swore positively to the identity of the fugitive. I advised that time should be given, and eventually it was satisfactorily shown that the first witnesses were mistaken, and that the fugitive was living in Canada. This discharged him from custody.

It would be difficult to find any provision in the act of 1850 under which a State Judge can exercise jurisdiction. The act is special and stringent. Officers are named in the statute whose duty it is to act when cases are brought before them. There is no reference to State authorities, I believe, either directly or indirectly. There is no law in Ohio which authorizes State Judges to act. It is true that the act of 1793 did authorize State Magistrates to exercise jurisdiction under it, and that act has only been repealed so far as repugnant provisions are contained in the act of 1850.

But it is not necessary to the decision of the case in hand

to hold that the decision of the Probate Judge was not final; nor is it necessary to show that the warrant had no defects. It may be admitted that the first decision on the *habeas corpus* was a bar to the inquiry before the Commissioner, and that the warrant was defective; but can a State Judge take jurisdiction on these grounds? It is the exercise of an appellate power, which is not given by the laws of the United States or the laws of the State. Suppose these objections had been made before the Commissioner, he could have considered them. In regard to the warrant, he could have amended it if necessary. But it would not have been necessary. The fugitive being in the custody of the Marshal, with the consent and at the request of the master, she was lawfully held for the purpose of the inquiry. And as to the decision of the Probate Court, whether it constituted a bar to the proceedings, it was a matter for the decision of the Commissioner.

I think these grounds are unprecedented in judicial proceedings, except, perhaps, in the decision of the Supreme Court in Wisconsin. That court sat as a Court of errors on the proceedings of the District Court of the United States. That case, I observed, received high commendation in the argument before the State Judge; but, as it may come before the Supreme Court for revision, it is not fit that I should speak of it in regard to the federal powers. I will, however, refer to the Revised Statutes of Wisconsin, page 730, sec. 22, which authorizes the prisons of the State to be used by the United States, and the Sheriff and his deputies are required to keep the prisoners safely "until they be discharged by due course of the laws of the United States."

It must be recollected that when the *habeas corpus* was served upon the Marshal, the case before the Commissioner was in progress, and near its termination. Is there any precedent for such a procedure? If the State Court had a concurrent power, the proceeding would have been irregular and void. Under the same government I could not have interposed. But that a court of a different government could interpose in this form, is sanctioned by no law or precedent. Before the Supreme Court of Wisconsin reversed, as a court of error, the decision of the District Court, it had the grace to wait until that Court had finally decided.

It is not usual in legal proceedings to plead a former recovery or a former acquittal. Can any court interfere in such cases and take the case from the court in which the jurisdiction is vested? If the Commissioner did wrong, does that authorize the State Judge to interpose by writ of *habeas corpus*, and withdraw the case from the Federal jurisdiction?

It is a general principle of law, to which I know of no exception, that the laws of every Government shall be construed by itself; and such construction is acted upon by the judiciary of all other countries.

By the Federal Constitution "the judicial power of the United States is declared to be vested in one Supreme Court, and in such inferior courts as the Congress may from time to time ordain and establish." Under this provision the judiciary of the Union gives a construction to the laws, which is obligatory on the State tribunals. The Constitution again declares that "the Constitution and laws of the United States which shall be made in pursuance thereof, and all treaties made or which shall be made under the authority of the United States, shall be the supreme law of the land; and the judges in every State shall be bound thereby, any thing in the Constitution or laws of any State to the contrary notwithstanding."

The construction of the statutes of the different States, except where the Supreme Court of the Union exercises an appellate power, has uniformly been followed by the Courts of the United States. This has been carried so far by the Supreme Court as to reverse its own decisions to conform to a change in the decisions of the State Court, and this was on the ground of policy, to avoid two rules of property in the same State. It has been considered as no degredation by the Supreme

Court to follow the established construction of the local laws by the Courts of the States. There is no instance, it is believed, where a Federal Court has disregarded the decisions of a State Court, where it possessed no appellate power.

Some years ago an individual was indicted for a capital offence in the Circuit Court of the United States, in which that most learned and able man, Judge Story presided. The same individual was in prison under State process for debt, or some petty offence. The District Attorney of the United States moved the Court to issue a *habeas corpus* to bring the defendant before the court; but that learned Judge held he had no power to issue the writ for that purpose.

A year or two ago a case similar in principle occurred in the Circuit Court of the United States for Ohio, and that court held it had no power to take the defendant from the State jurisdiction. In such cases in this State, an arrangement has been made with the State authority to order the accused to be delivered to the Marshal, with a pledge that he should be returned to the State jurisdiction; and where a concurrent jurisdiction exists in the Federal and State Courts, the Federal Courts have uniformly held the suit in these courts to be abated where the same cause of action has been sued in the State Court.

I cannot withhold the expression of my surprise at the earnest, if not indignant manner in which the counsel spoke of the conduct of the Commissioner in issuing his warrrant after the decision of the Probate Court on the *habeas corpus;* and an intimation was thrown out that, if the peace of the country is to be preserved, more respect must be shown by the Federal authority to the decisions of the State Court.

There is not the least foundation for this feeling and expression. It arises from an entire misconception of the case under consideration. The Commissioner of the United States issued his warrant to arrest the supposed fugitive from labor on the application of the master. There is no evidence that he had any knowledge of the previous decision of the Probate Judge. No one, I suppose, will allege that he had legal evidence of the fact. But suppose the record had been presented to him, did he show any want of respect to the State Court by issuing the warrant and inquiring into the complaint? This by no means prejudiced the right of the fugitive, as the previous decision could be set up in bar of the procedure, if such decision were final.

But I have an authority on this point. Some years ago a *habeas corpus* was issued by the Circuit Court of the United States for the Eastern District of New York, to bring before it an individual who had been arrested as a fugitive from justice under our late treaty with England. The Circuit Court was held by Judge Betts, the District Judge, who, on a full examination, remanded the prisoner to be given up under the treaty. Judge Nelson, out of court, issued another *habeas corpus*, and the prisoner being brought before him, he adjourned the case to the Supreme Court. When the matter was in discussion before the Court, I urged that the second *habeas corpus* was irregular. The case was dismissed for want of jurisdiction, but a majority of the Judges intimated the opinion that the first decision by the Circuit Court was no bar to the second writ. I differed with my brethren on the question; but as the court did not take jurisdiction, no decision was given in the case. The writ of *habeas corpus* being returned to Judge Nelson, he discharged the prisoner.

Every one who examines the authority in this country and in England, will find that there have been diversity of judgments on the point whether the decision on a *habeas corpus* is final; and, after the case above cited, the sympathies of the counsel for the indignity done to the Judge of Probate may well be spared, as also all apprehensions of the public peace being disturbed for any want of respect by the Federal authorities to the State Courts. State rights are invoked by the counsel. If these rights are construed to mean a subversion of the Federal authorities, they may be somewhat in danger.

That the Commissioner had jurisdiction in the case is clear. While duly engaged in the investigation of the matter, the honorable Judge of the Common Pleas, whose motives I by no means question, by a *habeas corpus*, took from the custody of the Marshal the body of the fugitive, which left the Commissioner without a case. It wrested from him, without any authority of law, the subject of his jurisdiction. This, so far as I know, is without precedent. Had any Commissioner or Federal Judge interposed, and by the same means disregarded and disturbed the jurisdiction of a State Court, I should have felt not less concern than the eloquent counsel.

A sense of duty compels me to say that the proceedings of the honorable Judge were not only without the authority of law, but against law, and that the proceedings are void, and I am bound to treat them as a nullity. The Marshal is discharged from custody.

JOSEPH LAMB'S HEIRS v. JAMES H. GILLETT.

A claim of title under a tax sale, can only be sustained by showing a substantial compliance with the Statute.

Under the tax law of Ohio, of the 14th of March, 1831, which declares that the deed of a County Auditor for land sold for taxes shall vest a good and valid title in the grantee, both in law and equity, and shall be received in all courts as prima facie of a good and valid title, the deed is admissible in evidence, without proof of the preliminary proceedings.

The deed being received in evidence, the *onus* of impugning its validity, by showing that the prior proceedings were irregular or illegal, rests on the other party.

The recitals in the County Auditor's deed, being made under the sanction of his official oath, are presumed to be true till the contrary is proved.

In proof of the proceedings, preliminary to the sale, it is only necessary

Joseph Lamb's Heirs v. James H. Gillett.

to show by the County Auditor's record, such facts as the Statute expressly requires to be of record; and parol proof is admissible of any facts, not required to be recorded.

The doctrine of presumption in favor of the acts of sworn public officers, applies in cases involving the validity of tax proceedings.

Messrs. Swayne and Baker, for plaintiff.
Messrs. Mason and White, for defendant.

OPINION OF THE COURT, BY JUDGE LEAVITT.

This is an action of ejectment for a tract of land in Clark County. By agreement of counsel the case was submitted and argued at the last term, without the intervention of a jury, and with the understanding that the evidence offered was to be received, subject to all legal exceptions to its competency.

The lessors of the plaintiffs, as proof of title, have introduced a patent from the United States, dated the 17th of June, 1817, granting the tract in controversy to Joseph Lamb's heirs; and, in connection with this, they have proved that they are the legal heirs of the said Lamb.

The defendant sets up a title under a sale of the land for taxes. He has offered in evidence, 1st. A deed from J. S. Halsey, County Auditor of Clark County, dated 28th of March, 1835, to Landaff W. Andrews, which, after reciting fully the prior proceedings, shows a sale of the tract on the last Monday of December, 1832, to James L. Torbert, for the taxes of 1831 and 1832, and an assignment of the certificate of purchase by Torbert to said Andrews. 2d. A deed from Andrews and wife to Joseph Wheldon, dated the 17th of March, 1837. 3d. A deed from Wheldon and wife to the defendant, dated the 16th of May, 1839.

The defendant also offered in evidence, an abstract from the books of the County Auditor's office, from which it appears that the land was entered upon the duplicates in the name of Joseph Lamb's heirs, for the years 1831 and 1832; and having been returned delinquent for those years was offered for sale, and sold by the County Treasurer to the said

James L. Torbert.   In connection with these abstracts, the duplicates from the offices of the County Treasurer, the County Auditor, and the Auditor of the State for the years above named, as also an authenticated copy of the delinquent lists from the office of the State Auditor, were exhibited. The defendant also introduced James S. Halsey, the County Auditor of Clark County during the progress of these proceedings, as a witness, who testified that the duplicates exhibited as those delivered by him to the County Treasurer for the years 1831 and 1832, were the same that were made out and delivered by the witness to the Treasurer, with the proper year marked on the back of each.

The lessor of the plaintiffs also offered certain abstracts from the books of the County Auditor's office, with copies of the certificates appearing on the duplicates in that office for the years 1831 and 1832, to prove, from the dates of those certificates, that the duplicates had not been made out and delivered to the Treasurer within the time prescribed by the Statute, and that in other respects the law had not been complied with.

In explanation of the dates of the certificates referred to, the defendant examined Mr. Halsey, who stated that the dates affixed to them had no reference to the time when the duplicates for the use of the County Treasurer were made out, or the date of their delivery to him by the witness as County Auditor.   And the witness also stated that he had no reason to doubt, and did believe, that the duplicates referred to were made out and placed in the hands of the Treasurer in proper time.

This statement, it is believed, presents substantially, the evidence offered in this case, though probably not in the precise order of its introduction by the parties.   It shows, however, with sufficient distinctness the matters in controversy requiring the consideration of the Court.

There is no disagreement between the counsel as to the

correctness of the principle that, to sustain a tax title, the party claiming under it must show a substantial compliance with the requirements of the Statute under which the proceedings have taken place. This has been too well settled; as applicable to the acts of all public officers deriving their authority from the statutory enactments, to be now questioned. In general, the Courts of Ohio have applied it with great stringency to proceedings constituting the basis of tax titles. In some of the more recent cases, however, which will be particularly noticed hereafter, the Supreme Court of Ohio have relaxed from the strictness and severity of their earlier decisions. But the right of a party resisting the validity of a tax title, to impugn it by showing defects and irregularities in the preliminary proceedings, has been uniformly recognized by that Court. And in this Court also, in the few cases which have been before it, involving tax titles, the same principle has been sanctioned. Yet it must be admitted that in this class of cases, questions of no small difficulty sometimes arise as to what constitutes a substantial compliance with the law, and under what circumstances parol proof is admissible to show what has been done, and to what extent the doctrine of presumption in favor of the acts of public officers, may be properly applied to sustain those acts.

Before we consider the question whether the defendant has proved that in the proceedings under which he claims title, there has been a substantial compliance with the Statute, it may be proper to ascertain under what circumstances the deed of the County Auditor is to be received and treated by the Court as prima facie evidence of title in the grantee. This point has been discussed by counsel, and several authorities have been cited applicable to it. On the one hand, it is insisted that the deed, including all its recitals, is to be received and accredited as prima facie evidence of title, without other proof; and that, being so received, the onus of showing defects and irregularities in the prior proceedings, affecting its validity, falls on the party who resists the title set up under it: or, if the deed is not thus received, and this effect given to it without extrinsic proof, it is necessary only to show preliminarily, that the land sold for taxes and conveyed by the deed, had been duly entered on the duplicate for taxation, and had been returned delinquent and sold for the taxes. On the other hand, it is urged that the Auditor's deed is not *per se*, to be received as *prima facie* evidence, and only when it is sustained by proof of a strict compliance with all the provisions of the Statute.

This point, in the precise form in which it has been discussed by counsel, does not necessarily arise in this case. The defendant, without pressing the question of the admissibility of the deed, unsustained by other proof, has introduced the record of the proceedings on which it is based; and that record constitutes an item of evidence in the case. In this view, the Court might properly restrict their enquiry to the question of the sufficiency of the Auditor's deed, sustained as it is by the extrinsic proof offered by the defendant. We will, however, briefly consider the provision of the Statute under which this deed was made, and the authorities referred to by counsel bearing on the question of its construction. And here it may be remarked, that on this question, in accordance with a principle long sanctioned by the Supreme Court of the United States, we shall be guided in our conclusions by the construction given to the Statute by the Supreme Court of Ohio, so far as it is fixed and ascertainable.

The Statute under which the land in dispute was sold for taxes, was the act prescribing the duties of County Auditors, passed March 14, 1831. 3 *Chase*, 1807. This Statute, among other things, requires that if land returned delinquent for the non-payment of taxes and sold, is not redeemed by the owner within two years from the date of the sale, the County Auditor, after the expiration of that time, shall make out and

24a

deliver a deed therefor to the purchaser or his assignee. And the 39th sec. declares the effect of the deed in these words:— "The deed so made by the Auditor, shall vest in the grantee, his or her heirs or assigns, a good and valid title, both in law and equity, and shall be received in all Courts as prima facie evidence of a good and valid title in such grantee, his or her heirs or assigns."

Some cases from the Ohio Reports have been cited by counsel, on the point under consideration, which originated under Statutes differing in their general provisions, and especially in the language used declaring the effect of a deed executed for land sold for taxes, from that under which the proceedings in this case were had. It will not be necessary to notice these with much particularity. In the case of *Holt's Heirs* v. *Hemphill's Heirs*, 3 *Ohio R.*, 232, it is not stated in the report under what Statute the tax proceedings took place, nor what was the peculiar language of the law in regard to the effect of the deed for land sold for taxes. The Court held that the deed was no evidence of title, unless accompanied with proof that the proceedings prior to the sale had been conducted according to the requirement of the Statute. And, in the case of *Carlisle* v. *Longworth*, 5 *Ohio R.*, 368, which involved the validity of a tax deed under the act of February 1, 1825, the same principle was settled. The 9th section of the act provided, that "the deed made by the County Auditor, as *herein before specified*, shall be received as *prima facie* evidence of title, and shall convey to the purchaser or purchasers, a good title in law and equity," &c. The Court say : "Before the deed made by the County Auditor can be received as evidence, it must be shown that he had authority to make it. This is done by showing that the land had been advertised and sold for taxes." And again : "In connection with this preliminary evidence, the deed will be received, and the Legislature has declared its effect." In the case of the *Heirs of Thompson* v. *Gotham*, 9 *Ohio R.*, 171, the Court say: "In order to sustain a title under a sale for taxes, it is not sufficient to produce the Collector's deed. There must be evidence to show that the tax has been levied, that the steps, required by law to authorize the sale, have been taken, and that the person making the deed had authority to make it." The tax in the case here cited, was not assessed under a general tax law, but by a corporation, having power under its charter to levy taxes for certain purposes.

· The next case presenting the question whether the Auditor's deed, under a tax sale, could be received in evidence without extrinsic proof to support it, was that of *Turney* v. *Yeoman*, 14 *Ohio R.*, 20. In this case there had been a forfeiture of the land to the State, for the nonpayment of taxes; and the land was sold under the act of the 14th March, 1831, providing for the sale of lands forfeited. 8 *Chase*, 1817. By the 6th section of the act, the County Auditor was required to execute a deed to the purchaser, "which deed," it is declared, "shall be *prima facie* evidence of title in the purchaser or purchasers." The deed of the County Auditor was objected to, as inadmissible without proof of the preliminary proceedings. In the commencement of their opinion, the Court say: "The objection to the introduction of this deed, presents a new and interesting question," from which it is to be inferred that there had been no previous decision of the Court on that point, that was regarded as authoritative. After a critical examination of the Statute, the conclusion to which the Court arrives, is, that effect must be given to the clear and explicit provision of the Statute declaring that the Auditor's deed shall be *prima facie* evidence of title in the grantee. The Court say, "it makes the deed, while unimpeached, evidence in and of itself, without any other proof." And adverting to the decision in the case of *Carlisle* v. *Longworth*, the Court arrived at the conclusion that it rested on the peculiar phraseology of the 9th section of the act of 1825, which declared the Auditor's deed evidence, only after proof that the preliminary requisites of the Statute had been complied with.

This case would seem to be decisive on the question now under consideration. It is true the tax title set up in that case was based on a sale of land forfeited to the State for non-payment of taxes, pursuant to the act of the 14th of March, 1831, to provide for the sale of lands thus forfeited. But in principle, no distinction is perceived between a sale under that Statute and the Statute authorizing the sale of lands delinquent for the nonpayment of taxes. In either, there must be a substantial compliance with the requirements of the Statute. It is noticeable, however, that there is some difference in the phraseology of these Statutes, in reference to the effect of the County Auditor's deed. In the law respecting sales for delinquent taxes, the Legislature have declared that the deed made by the Auditor shall "vest a good and valid title" in the grantee, both "in law and equity," and shall be received in all courts as *prima facie* evidence of a good and valid title," whereas, in the act relating to forfeited lands, it is simply declared that the Auditor's deed "shall be *prima facie* evidence of title in the purchaser or purchasers." It seems clear, that if under the latter Statute the deed is admissible in evidence, unsustained by proof of the preliminary proceedings, much more is it so under the act relating to sales of delinquent lands, in which the Legislature, *ex industria*, have declared that the deed shall vest in the purchaser a good title, both in law and equity, and in mandatory terms have required all Courts to receive such deed as *prima facie* evidence of title.

The ruling of the Supreme Court of Ohio, in the case of *Turney* v. *Yoemans*, just referred to, has not been changed in any case which has since been before that Court, but has, as we think, been affirmed in two cases which will now be noticed. In *Douglas* v. *Dangerfield*, 14 *Ohio R.*, 522, a tax title was in question, originating under the statute of 1831, the same under which the proceedings in the case before the Court took place; but the question whether the Auditor's deed could be received, *per se*, as *prima facie* evidence of title, was not distinctly presented, for the reason that the party claiming under the deed had introduced evidence of the prior proceedings, in support of the deed. But in their opinion, the Court make the pregnant remark, that "it would not, perhaps, be going too far to say that the production of the Auditor's deed alone was sufficient to put the defendants on their defence." It is obvious, we think, that if there had been no extrinsic evidence offered, the deed would have been received, in accordance with the decision in the case of *Turney* v. *Yeomans*. In a subsequent case between the same parties, 16 *Ohio R.*, 24, the Judge who gave the opinion of the Court, refers to the former case, and speaks of the point decided as "the late decision of this Court, which gives effect to tax deeds without other proof to support them."

In view of these cases, we think there can be no doubt that the Supreme Court of Ohio intended to give a construction to the provision of the Statute declaratory of the effect of an Auditor's deed, by which such deed is receivable in evidence, without extrinsic proof, as *prima facie* evidence of title; and that its reception throws upon the party resisting the tax title the burden of impeaching it by proof that the prior proceedings were not in accordance with the Statute. And we accord fully with that Court in this conclusion as we do not see, from the plain and explicit language of the Statute, that any other is admissible.

In accordance with this view, the proper order of proof would be, that the evidence impugning the proceedings on which the Auditor's deed was based, should follow the introduction of the deed. But, as before stated, as we understand the course pursued by counsel in the trial, the defendant, in connection with the deed, offered transcripts from the books of the Auditor, with other proof to sustain it. In this posture of the case, it will perhaps be more convenient and appropriate to advert to this evidence before considering that offered by the plaintiffs in support of their exceptions to the proceedings prior to the tax sale.

As before noticed, the defendant has offered transcripts from the Auditor's books showing the preliminary proceedings, accompanied with the duplicates for the years 1831 and 1832, and an authenticated copy of the list of lands returned as delinquent for the nonpayment of the taxes for those years. From an inspection of these papers, it satisfactorily appears that the land in controversy was duly entered on the duplicate of 1831, for Clark County, as subject to taxation, in the name of Joseph Lamb's Heirs, and was returned by the County Treasurer as delinquent for that year. It was again entered in the name of the same persons on the duplicate of 1832, charged with the tax of that and the preceding year, with the interest and penalty added, and again returned as delinquent. It also appears from the record of sales of lands sold for taxes in Clark County, that a list of lands delinquent for the years named, embracing the tract in question, in the name of Lamb's Heirs, was published for four weeks successively after the 1st of October, and prior to the 1st of December, 1832, in the *Western Pioneer*, a newspaper printed at Springfield, with a notice that the several tracts named in said list would be offered at public sale at the Court House, on the last Monday of December, in said year; and that the tracts, pursuant to the notice, were offered for sale by the Treasurer: and that the tract in the name of Lamb's Heirs was returned as sold to the said Torbert.

If we are right in the conclusion before stated, that by the express provision of the Statute, the Auditor's deed is to be received as *prima facie* evidence of title, it was not incumbent on the defendant to offer any proof to sustain it, until impeached by the other party. We suppose, as a necessary result, all the recitals of the deed are to be received as true till the contrary appears. Such was clearly the intention of the Statute, in the provision declaring the effect of the Auditor's deed. The deed is made by that officer under all the sanctions of his official character, and, upon the soundest principles of law, is to be viewed with every presumption in its favor, until it is invalidated by proof. In its recital of the preliminary proceedings, it is to be regarded as a solemn certificate by the officer that they transpired precisely as they are set forth. Having carefully-examined the recitals of this deed, and compared the facts stated with the requirements of the Statute, we find that all these requirements have been fully and accurately complied with. Everything necessary to be done, is certified to have been done in the precise manner pointed out by law.

Viewing the Auditor's deed in this light, the enquiry is presented, whether it is efficiently impeached by the proofs offered by the plaintiffs. Before noticing the exceptions insisted upon as invalidating the deed, it may be proper to remark, that they can only be sustained by positive proof that the facts relied on as the basis of the tax title, and which, by the Statute, give it legal vitality, do not exist. It is the undoubted right of the party impugning such title, to show that it has no foundation in fact or law on which to rest. As to him, the County Auditor cannot be regarded as his agent, and he is not concluded by his acts, and may even contradict facts appearing of record on the Auditor's books. He may defeat the tax title by showing that the land taxed was by law exempt from taxation, or that it was not entered on the duplicate, or that the taxes had been actually paid, or that the land was never returned delinquent, and was not in fact sold for taxes. All this he may show by substantive proof; but he cannot rest on mere presumptions to rebut and negative the recitals of the Auditor's deed, or the facts exhibited by the records and transcripts from his office.

The exceptions to these proceedings, as stated and insisted

on by the plaintiffs' counsel, refer, 1st. To alleged defects and irregularities connected with the duplicates; as that it does not appear on the duplicates exhibited, for what years they were made, or that they were the duplicates for Clark County, or were even in the County Auditor's office, or that they were made out by the 15th of August, and delivered in due time to the County Treasurer. 2d. To alleged defects and irregularities connected with the delinquent list, and the sale of the land; as that it does not appear that the Treasurer made oath to the delinquent list for 1831, or that he gave public notice of the sale immediately after the 15th of August. This statement embodies, it is believed, the exceptions relied on by the plaintiffs' counsel, in resisting the title asserted under the tax deed.

These exceptions, it will be noticed, are founded upon, and suppose facts, which are in opposition to the recitals of the Auditor's deed. As before stated, that deed recites, with great specialty and minuteness, all the proceedings preliminary to the sale, as having been conducted in exact accordance with the requirements of the Statute. The objections urged, are rot based on any positive proof of any act of official neglect or misconduct on the part of those charged with the enforcement of the law, but on inferences of such neglect or misconduct, deduced from certain documents offered in evidence by the plaintiffs. In accordance with the views before expressed, as to the legal effect and operation intended to be given to the Auditor's deed under the Statute, we think that nothing has been shown to impeach its validity, and that it vests in the grantee a good title.

But, if this conclusion is erroneous, and it should be conceded that the plaintiff has so far impeached the proceedings on which the tax title rests, as to make it incumbent on the defendant to sustain the recitals of the Auditor's deed, no reason is perceived why that is not satisfactorily done by the evidence before the court, which has been before noticed. This evidence consists in abstracts and transcripts from the books of the County Auditor's office, explained as to some facts, by the parol testimony of the person who held the office of County Auditor, while these proceedings were in progress. This evidence corroborates and sustains the recitals in the deed. It is indeed insisted, that parol evidence is inadmissible to establish any fact, connected with these tax proceedings; but, upon the authority of cases, to which we shall hereafter refer, we think, this objection is not sustainable. We suppose the principle applicable to this point is, that those acts which the statute expressly requires to be of record, or in writing, must be so proved; but as to matters where this is not required, parol or secondary proof is competent. The application of this principle, in connection with the verbal testimony of Mr. Halsey given on the trial, disposes of several of the exceptions to these proceedings, if otherwise well taken. He testifies that the duplicates for Clark County for the years 1831 and 1832, made out for the various purposes designated by the statute, and offered in evidence, were made by himself, and identifies those exhibited to him as the duplicates for those years. He also proves that the copy required by the 23rd section of the Statute, to be made out and delivered to the County Treasurer, was made out and delivered by him. with the proper year inscribed, and as the witness believes "on or before the 15th day of August" as directed by the Statute. As the law does not require the Auditor to make any record, or memorandum in writing of the making and delivery of this duplicate, there can be no doubt, that it is competent to prove it by parol.

The counsel for the plaintiffs has referred to the case of *Kellogg* vs. *McLaughlin*, 8 *Ohio R.* 114, as an authority against the admissibility of parol evidence, in support of a tax proceeding. That case involved the validity of a tax sale, under the act of March, 1831. It seems that written evidence of the publication of the notice of sale, taken from the books of the County Auditor, had been offered in evidence, and rejected in the Court below, on the ground that it did not appear that the publication had been made as required by the Statute. The 80th section provides, that prior to the sale, the delinquent list and notice of sale, shall be published for four successive weeks "between the *first day* of October and the *first day* of December." The record showed that the publication was for four successive weeks between the *first Monday* of October and the *first Monday* of December. The Supreme Court held that the evidence was properly rejected, as the record did not show that the last of the publications was before the *first day* of December. This case settles the principle, that as the Statute made it the express duty of the Auditor to record the delinquent list with the notice of sale annexed, it must be proved by the record that the Statute had been complied with, and that parol evidence was not admissible to show the publication was in fact made as prescribed by the Statute. Such proof would have contradicted the record, and was therefore clearly incompetent. But, in that case, it is not held or intimated that parol proof may not be received to establish any fact, which the law does not require to be recorded or in writing.

In the case of *Thevinin* vs. *Slocum*, 16 *Ohio R.* 519, the distinction adverted to, is distinctly recognized. It was a tax title case, under the act of 1822. Parol proof, in connection with documentary evidence was offered, and held to be admissible, in regard to any fact, which the Statute did not require to be in writing. One of the questions was, whether the delivery of a written order for the sale of the land, required under the Statute referred to, could be proved by parol. The Judge delivering the opinion of the Court said, " I find nothing in the law of 1822, which made it necessary that the fact of delivery should be recorded by the Auditor of the County." " It might then be proved as any other matter in *pais* by parol, and the man who received the list was as competent to prove its delivery as any other person." And in another part of the opinion, on another point in the case, the same doctrine is distinctly laid down.

It is to be noticed in this connection, · that the tax law of 1831 requires in express terms, that certain matters shall be placed on record by the County Auditor. By the 26th Sec., the County Auditor and the County Treasurer are required to make a settlement on the first Monday of January, when a delinquent list is to be made out, and sworn to by the Treasurer; which list properly certified by the Auditor, he is required to record in his office. And by the 31st Section, the Auditor is required to record the delinquent list, with a copy of the notice of sale, from the newspaper, in which it is published. And by the 34th Sec., it is made the duty of the Auditor to attend all sales of delinquent lands, and to make a record thereof.

As the Statute requires nothing to be of record, but the matters specified in the sections referred to, the implication is strong, that the Legislature did not intend that any other part of the proceedings should be recorded. And hence, the reason and propriety of the distinction adverted to, between the mode of making proof of acts of record and those not of record.

Without deeming it necessary minutely to analyze the several exceptions urged to these proceedings, it only remains to say, they are fully met and answered by the well established legal doctrine of presumption in favor of the acts of sworn public officers. This doctrine is too well known and sanctioned, to require the citation of authorities to sustain it. It has also been applied by the Supreme Court of Ohio, in cases involving the validity of tax titles, as will appear from the cases, to which some reference will now be made.

In the case of *Winder* vs. *Sterling*, 7 *Ohio R.* 190, one of the questions before the Court was, whether the record showed a compliance with one of the provisions of the tax law of Feb. 1, 1825, which required the delinquent list to be verified by the oath of the Collector, administered by the County Auditor. The Collector had signed a certificate, in the form prescribed by the Statute, which was set out in the record, but there was no evidence that he had been sworn to it. Yet the Court held, that the absence of any proof that an oath had been administered, as required by the Statute did not vitiate the proceeding. In thus deciding, the Court must have presumed, that the statutory requirement had been complied with; there being no evidence justifying the contrary presumption. In the same case, a similar doctrine was recognized and applied. It appeared from the transcript from the Auditor's office, that the delinquent list and notice of sale was published in a paper printed in an adjoining county, but did not show, as the reason for such publication, that no paper was printed in the county, in which the land was situated; or, that the paper containing the notice was in general circulation in such county. The Court overruled this objection remarking, that "in this matter, the law is directory to the officer, and when he has exercised his discretion, we are disposed to believe in the absence of all proof to the contrary, that he has done his duty."

In the case of *Sheldon* vs. *Coates*, 10 *Ohio R.* 278, the tax deed was objected to, on the ground that it appeared from its recitals, that the certificate of sale, on which the deed was based, was signed by the officer executing it, by the official designation of Collector, instead of Sheriff. Though such signing was deemed to be erroneous, the Court held the objection not sufficient to set aside the deed, stating in their opinion among other things, that "it is a general rule in sales by public officers, that where there is a sufficient power to warrant a sale, a slight variance or omission will not be held material." In the same case, a further exception to the proceedings was insisted on that the Sheriff, who, under the Statute then in force was *ex-officio* Collector of taxes, and as Collector, was required to give bond, had not done so, within the time directed by the Statute. The law required this bond to be

given before the first Monday of August, and that the duplicate should be withheld till bond was given. The bond was
not given till the 10th of September, and the duplicate was
not put into the hands of the Collector till the 20th of that
month. But this objection was overruled, as was also another,
based on an irregularity in the notice of sale.

In the case of *Gwynne* vs. *Neiswanger*, 18 *Ohio R.* 400, it
was objected that the transcript from the County Auditor's
books did not show that the list of taxes in arrears, required
by the Statute to be made out and forwarded to the Auditor of
State, on or before the 1st of August, was made out and forwarded by that day. In disposing of this objection, the late
Judge Hitchcock, who delivered the opinion of the Court said:
"The time in which it was sent, does not appear, but I suppose, under this law, we may venture to presume that it was
sent in time, and that the officer performed his duty." And,
to another objection that it was not stated in the notice of sale,
at what hour the sale was to commence, and that it did not
appear from the return of the officer that the sale was at public auction, as directed by the Statute, the Court replied, that
"the first is not necessary and the last will be presumed."

In the recent case of *Ward* vs. *Barrows*, 2 *Ohio State Reports* 241, the doctrine of presumptions in support of the acts
of public officers in tax proceedings, is fully considered, and
conclusively settled. The objection to the tax title was the
same as in the case of *Winder* vs. *Sterling* before referred to,
that it did not appear that the return of the list of delinquent
taxes, required by law to be made by the Collector, was sworn
to by him before the County Auditor as expressly directed by
the Statute. He was required by the law to sign the delinquent list, "and testify to the correctness of the same under
oath or affirmation." As in the case of *Winder* vs. *Sterling*,
the Collector had affixed his name to a certificate purporting
to be an oath, in verification of the list, according to the form
given by the Statute, but it did not appear that an oath or af-

firmation had, in fact, been administered to him. In their opinion, the Court refer with approbation to the decision in the case just named, and properly infer that the objection to the tax proceeding could only have been overruled by the application of the doctrine of presumption in support of the fact, that the delinquent list had been duly authenticated by the oath of the Collector. They say, the conclusion of the Court was correct that there was "presumptive proof that the oath had been administered." And in reference to the omission in the case before them, the Court say, "under such circumstances, unless the Statute makes written evidence indispensable, the officer will be presumed to have done his duty, until the contrary appears." And again—"Facts presumed are as effectually established, as facts proved where no presumption is allowed."

These authorities seem to be decisive of the question under consideration, and justify the conclusion that the exceptions urged to this tax title cannot be sustained. Adverting to those exceptions, not one of them implies a more material omission, or irregularity than that which was held unavailable in the cases of *Winder* vs. *Sterling* and *Ward* vs. *Barrow*. In those cases there was no evidence of a fact which might well be deemed essential to the validity of the proceedings, but which the Court held was presumptively established. This principle is certainly broad enough to cover the exceptions in this case. They do not embrace any act, required by the Statute to be of record, or in writing, and under the decisions referred to, constitute no objection to the title asserted by the defendant. Judgement for the defendant.

F. A. ROSS ET AL. v. THOMAS D. CARPENTER ET AL.

By the 29th Rule of the rules regulating the Chancery practice of this Court, a Bill is not amendable after replication filed, unless the plaintiff

F. A. Ross et al. *v.* Thomas D. Carpenter et al.

shows, that "the matter of the proposed amendment is material, and could not with reasonable diligence, have been sooner introduced."

If the amendment asked for, is the introduction of a new party to the bill, whose interest was known to the original plaintiffs or their agent, when the bill was filed, the amendment will not be allowed.

As the 29th Rule makes no provision for an amendment of the bill, after the cause is at issue, and depositions have been taken and filed, it may fairly be construed as prohibiting it. If granted, it must be under very special circumstances.

In a case which has been pending and at issue for a long time, especially if the answer denies the equity of the bill, and sets up lapse of time in bar of the plaintiff's claim, no reason is afforded for the relaxation of established rules of practice.

Mr. *H. Stanberry*, for plaintiffs.

Mr. *H. H. Hunter*, and Messrs. *Swan and Andrews*, for defendants.

OPINION OF THE COURT, BY JUDGE LEAVITT.

In this case, a motion has been filed for leave to amend the bill, by adding the name of Bezer Latham, as one of the plaintiffs. This motion is resisted by the defendants, on the ground, that when a bill has been long pending, and answers and replication have been filed, and depositions taken by the parties, an amendment of the bill cannot be allowed.

The bill sets up an equitable interest in the tract of land, described in it. It was filed in this Court, on the 25th of June, 1847. In 1849, the answers of the defendants were put on file, denying the plaintiffs' equity, and calling for strict proof of the allegations of the bill. The case was put at issue, by a replication, filed in July, 1851; after which depositions were taken by the parties, from time to time, and placed on file.

In September, 1853, the deposition of Allen Latham was taken, who disclosed the fact, that prior to the commencement of this suit, he had conveyed an interest in the tract in question, to the said Bezer Latham, whose name it is now sought to introduce as a party to the bill, which interest still remains in the said Bezer Latham. It also appears from this deposition, that Allen Latham was cognizant of, and had a direct agency in the institution of this suit. He states that he procured the assent of the persons, in whose names the bill was filed, that the suit should be so brought; and that in concert with one Bela Latham, since deceased, who was the agent of said Bezer Latham, a resident of the State of New Hampshire, he retained counsel, and authorized the suit to be brought in this court.

On these facts, it is insisted, leave to amend the bill ought not to be granted; and it does not seem to be allowable from the language of the 29th Rule of the rules adopted by the Supreme Court, for the equity practice in the Circuit Courts of the United States. In relation to the amendment of bills, that rule provides, that " after replication filed, the plaintiff shall not be permitted to withdraw it, and to amend his bill, except upon a special order of a Judge of the Court, upon motion or petition, after due notice to the other party, and upon proof by affidavit, that the same is not made for the purpose of vexation or delay, and that the matter of the proposed amendment is material, *and could not with reasonable diligence, have been sooner introduced into the bill,*" etc.

It is very clear, the last requirement of this rule, has not been complied with. No showing of " reasonable diligence" in procuring this amendment appears; nor is any reason given for the great delay which has occurred, in asking for it. Indeed, from the facts before the Court, it would seem to be impossible that this provision of the rule can be complied with. As before noticed, this suit was brought not only with the knowledge, but by the immediate agency of Allen Latham, who was apprised of the interest of Bezer Latham in the land in controversy, and of the necessity of his being a party to the bill. And no reason or excuse is given, why he was not made a party.

The rule cited prescribes only the conditions, on which the

bill may be amended, after replication filed, but is silent, as to amendments, when the further progress of taking depositions in the case has been made. This marks another stage in a chancery cause. And as the rule does not contemplate the right of amendment, after depositions have been taken, it may perhaps be fairly inferred, that it is prohibited.

By the practice of the English Courts of equity, it seems, that unless under very special circumstances, a bill cannot be amended, after the case is at issue. It will not be allowed, in any case, unless the plaintiff shows not only that the proposed amendment is material, but that the party was not in a condition to have made it, at an earlier stage in the cause. *Story's Com. on Eq., Sec.* 332—and the authorities there cited.

But, if it be conceded, that even after the parties have taken their depositions, circumstances may exist, which may make it proper to grant leave to amend the bill, it is a conclusive answer to the present motion, that the facts of this case do not bring it within such an exception. As before intimated, from the agency of Allen Latham, in the institution of this suit, and the relation, in which he stood to the plaintiffs, they are chargeable with knowledge of Bezer Latham's interest in the land. And after the case has been pending for seven years, and has been at issue three years, and the parties have taken their testimony, it is clearly too late to allow an amendment of the bill. It would be unreasonable, after the defendants have been so long in court, and have made all their preparations for a hearing, on the pleadings and evidence as filed, that they should be put to answer a new case, by allowing an amendment of the bill. There is a reason too, why this motion should be regarded with little favor, in the fact, that the defendants not only deny in their answers, the equity of the plaintiff's claim, but set up the lapse of time as a bar to their right to a decree. It is, certainly, in no aspect, a case calling for, or justifying, a relaxation of the settled rules of equity practice. The motion for leave to amend is therefore over-ruled.   25a

INDIANA.—MAY TERM, 1855.

JAMES THOMPSON *v.* JAMES N. HOLTON, TREASURER OF BENTON COUNTY.

Under a compact with the United States, a law of Indiana was passed declaring that lands sold by the United States, within the State, should not be taxed until after the expiration of five years from the time of sale.

In 1847, an act of Congress was passed declaring that in all the States which came into the Union previous to the year 1820, the restriction of taxation in such States should be annulled.

The act of Indiana, however, remained unrepealed until 1852.

Prior to the repeal certain lands were sold, and after the repeal, but before the five years had expired from the time of the sale, and the purchaser asked relief—the Court held that the repeal of the act after the purchase, and before the termination of five years from the purchase of the land, impaired the contract made with such purchasers, and was consequently void.

Messrs. *Morrison, Ray and Morrison,* for plaintiff.
'Messrs. *Gregory and Jones,* for defendant.

OPINION OF THE COURT.

This is a bill to enjoin the defendant from collecting taxes alleged to have been illegally assessed, on the lands of the complainant, in Benton county, Indiana, for the year 1853.

It is averred that the lands were not and are not yet taxable; because at the time of the purchase, which was in March 1852, the laws of the State then in force exempted from tax-tion, "all lands sold by the United States until the term of five years from the day of sale shall have expired;" *Revised Statutes of* 1843—208.

This exemption was no doubt induced by the act of the 19th April, 1816, " to enable the people, of Indiana Territory to form a constitution," &c., and the irrevocable ordinance of the people of the Territory accepting the propositions contained in the act, one of which was, " that all lands sold by the United States after the 1st of December, 1816, should be and remain exempt from any tax until the expiration of five years from the time of sale."

Congress by its act of the 26th January 1847, assented that the several States admitted into the Union prior to the 4th of April, 1820, may impose a tax upon all lands that might be sold by the United States, in said States, from and after the day of sale. But the law of Indiana exempting such land from taxation remained in force until the 17th of June, 1852. The complainant purchased his lands in Benton county, in March, 1851, more than a year before the exemption was repealed.

At the time the complainant purchased his land, a law of the State exempted it from taxation for five years from the time of purchase, and this it is contended, is not a contract between a State and the complainant. What is a contract? By the Supreme Court, and by every body, it is defined to be an agreement to do or not to do a certain thing. As in the case before us, by this law the State agreed not to tax lands purchased of Congress within the State, for five years after the purchase. Here is a stipulation, as express as words could make it, to all purchasers ; and every purchaser accepts the proposition by making the purchase. Here is a contract as express as words can make it. For aught that appears, the exemption was the motive to the purchase. And no one can say that the policy of the State in this respect is an unwise one. It is an object with every new State to increase its population, and this is done by exempting lands purchased from taxation for a greater or less period of time. In the case under consideration, it exonerated the plaintiff from the annual payment of near $1000 in taxes. This is a considerable sum to the purchaser, and it may enable him to improve his farm in a few years.

It is argued that if the land in question be exempted from taxation on the same principle, the land purchased by revolutionary soldiers in the State would forever be exempted from taxes. The law, at present, exempts the lands of revolutionary soldiers from taxation, consequently a purchase by such soldiers of land in Indiana, would make the exemption perpetual. Now this case has no analogy whatever to the one under consideration. The exemption in the one case is for the term of five years, in the other it is for the present, not for any specific time or for all time to come, but merely from present taxation. In the one case, it is a matter for the exercise of the discretion of the Legislature, in the other no such discretion can be exercised, as the exemption is for five years. In the one case there is a specific contract, in the other there is no contract; and no obligation to extend the exemption beyond the present time; the next year the law may be repealed, and there is no ground of complaint; but in the other a repeal of the exemption before the termination of five years, would impair the obligation of the contract.

The Legislature of Arkansas chartered a bank on the funds of the State, and provided in the act that the notes of the bank should be receivable in payment of public dues to the State. By an improper management of the bank its specie became exhausted so that it could no longer pay specie for its notes; the notes consequently were discredited, and the State refused to receive them in payment of taxes, and the Legislature repealed the section declaring the notes should be received in payment of public dues. A tender being made of

James Thompson v. James N. Holten.

the notes to the Treasurer, or by the Treasurer in paying an amount due the State, the notes were refused, and suit was brought by the State against the debtor. In the Supreme Court of the State a judgment was entered in behalf of the State against the defendant, the Court holding that after the repeal of the above section, the notes could not be paid into the State Treasury.

A writ of error was presented to the Supreme Court of the United States, which decided that every individual who held a note of the bank, at the time of the repeal, had a right under the charter to pay it into the State Treasury for public dues, and that, as against such holders of the notes of the bank, the act of the Legislature of Arkansas impaired the obligation of the contract between the State and the holder, and was, consequently, void. But that notes received subsequent to the repeal were not so payable. The State being the owner of the bank had a right to repeal the charter, but that, by such repeal, it could not impair the right of the holder of the paper received before the repeal, and under the guaranty that the notes should be receivable in payment of debts to the State.

The case before us is a much stronger one than that referred to, from Arkansas. In *Hanna and Others*, v. *the Board of Commissioners of Allen County*, 8 *Black*. 352, the Court say "the purchasers could not complain, because the first act contained no exemption, express or implied, and by the second the right to repeal the act exempting the lands from taxation was expressly reserved in the act itself." The Court, however, say, "if no reservation had been made of the right to repeal the act of 1834, we should certainly have been obliged to conclude that the State was deprived of the power of taxing the lands therein referred to," &c. This point, it was true, was not involved technically in the case, but in effect it was, when the court was obliged to put the power to repeal on the reservation in the act; consequently, if there had been no reservation, there could have been no power to repeal.

The injunction heretofore allowed in this case is made perpetual, at the costs of defendant.

JOHN M. HARPER v. EDWIN W. NEFF AND JAMES BLAKE.

A mortgage having been given on certain articles of property to secure the payment of $1,500, a subsequent agreement was entered into between the parties to deliver over to the mortgagor the articles of property, on his giving security to sell the same at reasonable prices, and account to the mortgagee every fifteen days for the proceeds, and pay the same over to him, &c.

The security was given, and an action being brought on the new agreement, the security pleaded that the original mortgage on the articles had been assigned to him.

To this plea the defendants demurred.

The Court held that this plea was no answer to the declaration; that the new agreement was substituted for the mortgage, the plaintiff relying on the personal security given instead of the lien on the articles of property.

Henderson and Mackenzie for the plaintiff.
------ ------ for the defendants.

OPINION OF THE COURT.

The plaintiff states in his declaration, that on the 21st of January, 1858, by their deed of that date, the defendants bound themselves to the plaintiff. to pay him the sum of $1,500, which deed was and is subject to a certain condition thereunder written, which condition—after reciting that said Neff was then indebted to the plaintiff by a judgment in the Marion Circuit Court in about the sum of sixteen hundred dollars, and that the plaintiff then had a bill of sale on cer-

tain articles of jewelry, tools, &c., such as were usually kept
in jewelry and watch stores, to secure the payment of said
sum of about sixteen hundred dollars, and that said articles
of jewelry were then deposited by the plaintiff in the safe at
S. A. Fletcher's Banking House, and were then of the cost
price of fourteen hundred and twenty-nine dollars, and that
said plaintiff was then about to re-deliver to the said Neff
said articles of jewelry, &c., to be by him sold to the said
Neff, retruning the proceeds to the plaintiff or his attornies—
was and is, that if the said Neff should use due and proper diligence to make sale of the said articles at reasonable prices,
and would, every fifteen days after the same should be delivered to him as aforesaid, render an account and pay over the
proceeds of such sales to Henderson & Mackenzie, or the
other authorized agents of the plaintiff, until, of such proceeds,
the plaintiff should receive the sum of fourteen hundred and
twenty-nine dollars, with accruing interest thereon, the obligation should be void.

To which condition there was and is also thereunder written
this proviso, that if said Neff should prefer to re-deliver to
the plaintiff said jewelry or any part thereof, the same should
be received by the plaintiff at its cost price on said obligation,
and should operate as a payment of fourteen hundred and
twenty-nine dollars.   The plaintiff avers the delivery to Neff
of the jewelry, &c., and that he neither re-delivered the jewelry nor paid the proceeds, or any part thereof, of the sales
made, &c.

The plea alleges "that at and before the time of executing
by said Blake & Neff of the writing obligatory in said declaration mentioned, the said plaintiff held a mortgage or bill of
sale executed by said Neff, which is the same bill of sale
named in said declaration, by which said Neff mortgaged and
sold to said Harper all the jewelry, goods, tools, &c., named
in said writing obligatory, and a large amount not mentioned
in said writing obligatory, amounting in all to the sum of two

thousand, forty-three dollars, and thirty-one cents; which mortgage was conditioned that said Neff should pay to the said Harper the sum above stated, with all interest due and to become due thereon, for which said Neff had executed his certain promissory notes, amounting in the aggregate to the sum aforesaid, which mortgage was in full force and unsatisfied at the time of the execution of said writing obligatory in said declaration mentioned, and said Harper was then holding said goods, jewelry, tools, &c., in said writing obligatory named, by virtue of said mortgage; and the said defendants say that after said writing obligatory had been executed and delivered to plaintiff, the said plaintiff for value received did, after said jewelry, tools, &c., had been, under the terms thereof, delivered to said Neff for the purposes therein stated, assign said mortgage to James Blake, by means whereof the said Blake became and was the owner of said goods, jewelry, &c., in said declaration mentioned, and the said writing obligatory became and was void and of no effect," &c.

To this plea the plaintiff filed a general demurrer.

The plea is no answer to the declaration. The agreement on which the action is founded recites a previous mortgage given on the jewelry, tools, &c., to secure the payment of a sum amounting to sixteen hundred dollars. This mortgage in the agreement is called a bill of sale, but that does not alter the legal effect of the instrument. The jewelry, &c., at this time, was in possession of the plaintiff, and the agreement states, that he was about to re-deliver the jewelry, &c., to Neff, the mortgagee, who bound himself to sell it at a reasonable price, and pay to the plaintiff or his attorneys, every fifteen days, the amount received on such sales, until the sum of $1,429 should be paid; and Neff had the option to return the articles to the plaintiff, at their cost, in payment of the sum last mentioned, and Blake was security for Neff that he would faithfully perform the agreement. In his declaration, the plaintiff sets forth, as a breach of the undertaking, that Neff had neither paid over any part of the proceeds of the sales, nor returned to the plaintiff the articles, &c.

The defendants plead that the original mortgage, which was superseded by the new agreement, was assigned over by plaintiff to Blake, one of the defendants. The plaintiff had relinquished the mortgage by the new agreement, in which Blake was security. The assignment of the mortgage, therefore, could have no effect on the new agreement. The plaintiff, in delivering the jewelry, tools, &c., to Neff, abandoned the mortgage, and relied on the personal security of Blake; and, if the mortgage could have any effect whatever in the hands of Blake, it could have no other than to operate as an indemnity to him for the liability he had incurred by signing the new agreement.

The demurrer is overruled, and judgment must be entered on the new agreement.

ÆTNA INSURANCE CO. v. ELIJAH SABINE.

An action being brought against the defendant, charging him with an abuse of his powers, as agent of the plaintiff, it is essential that he should be alleged to have acted as agent of the company.

Unless he was authorized to act as agent of the company, he could not bind it; and any ratification of the contract would relieve the defendant from an alleged abuse of his powers.

If the plaintiff ratified what the defendant had done, and which did not bind the company, except by such ratification, the defendant is not chargable with any remissness of duty.

Mr. *Henderson* appeared for the plaintiff.
Mr. *Crawford* for the defendant.

OPINION OF THE COURT.

This action was brought on a policy of insurance against defendant for having exceeded his powers, &c., by which plaintiff was injured. The declaration contained four counts. The defendant filed a general demurrer to the declaration.

To the first count it was objected, on demurrer, that plaintiff alleges no authority to the agent to make the insurance; and on this it is argued that the plaintiff could not be liable on the policy until a ratification of it was proved; and, if there were a ratification, the plaintiff would be estopped to charge the defendant, as the validity of the policy depended not on the original contract, but on the subsequent ratification of it by the plaintiff.

The declaration, it is said, does not state the case of an agent who has a general authority, but acts in violation of his private instructions in not taking good security for the payment of the premium, and in the insurance of Kentucky flatboats.

If, while the agent is exercising general powers, he has private instructions, the agent could bind the company, but would be liable to it for any abuse of his power; but, in the first count it is alleged he had no power at all. By reason of this defect, the ground for a recovery is not laid, and consequently the demurrer is sustained as to this count.

The second count is also subject to exception, as the allegation of the defendant's agency is not made, which was essential to establish his liability. If he be not authorized to act, the policy is not binding on the plaintiff, and a ratification of the policy by the company would relieve the defendant from responsibility, and remove from the plaintiff all ground of complaint.

The same objection applies to the third count as is above stated to the first.

MAY TERM, 1855. **395**

Paine et al. *v.* Wright and the Indianapolis and Bellefontaine R. R. Co.

In regard to the fourth count, it appears there is a sufficient allegation of the agency, as it is stated that defendant, while acting as agent for the company, received large sums for insuring, which he has failed to account for or pay over to the plaintiff. If, under such circumstances, he has received money on account of the plaintiff, he is bound in good conscience to pay it over. This count, the court think, is sustainable, and as to it the demurrer is overruled; but it is sustained as to the first, second, and third counts. The court will give leave to amend the declaration generally.

PAINE ET AL. *v.* WRIGHT AND THE INDIANAPOLIS AND BELLEFONTAINE RAILROAD COMPANY.

Where a portion of the stockholders are citizens of other States, they may seek relief in the Circuit Court against an illegal taxation of their property by a State, although there be no allegation that the tax is in violation of the constitution or laws of the United States.

And in such case, the corporation doing its business in the State, in order to obtain relief, may be made defendants.

The Circuit Court will give relief under the laws of the State, the same as the State Court.

And if the construction of the tax law has been fixed by the Supreme Court of the State, such decision will constitute a rule of decision for the Circuit Court.

A tax can be just and equal on Railroad Corporations only by taxing the profits.

The investments in such an enterprise are materially different from investments in real estate.

Messrs. *Barbour, Porter & Yandis* for complainant.
Messrs. *Walpole, McDonald & Henderson* for defendant.

OPINION OF THE COURT.

This bill is filed by a great number of persons represented to be citizens of other States than Indiana, and stockholders in the Indianapolis and Bellefontaine Railroad Company, to an amount exceeding sixteen thousand dollars, against the President and Directors of said Company, whose place of business is in the State of Indiana, and William Wright, Treasurer of Marion county, in Indiana.

The controversy arises on the amount of taxes assessed on the stock or property of the Railroad Company. The Secretary of the company returned, under oath the stock of the company, amounting, to $335,367 90 in value, on which the legal tax was assessed by the Auditor, and a duplicate made out for the taxes of 1853, which was handed to the Treasurer of the proper county, and which tax the complainants allege was fully paid to the Collector.

The county Auditor was directed, subsequently, by the Auditor of State, to institute an inquiry whether a full return of stock, under the tax law of the State, had been made; and, on inquiry, the county Auditor reported that instead of the value of the stock returned by the Secretary of the company, which omitted the land owned by the company by a misapprehension of the law, he should have returned $799,000 in stock, &c., for taxation; and that the Auditor decided there should be added to the sum returned $383,733, and that an additional tax on the sum omitted should be assessed, which added to the tax at first assessed, the sum of $2,533 19.

The bill prayed that the Treasurer might be enjoined from the collection of the above sum of $2,533 19, as an illegal assessment.

An objection to the jurisdiction of the court is made in the answer.

The complainants are citizens of different States, none of them being citizens of Indiana, so that on that ground there would seem to be no just exception to the jurisdiction. The complainants sue as stockholders of the Railroad; and they make the Treasurer of Marion county, who collects the tax, defendant, and also the President and Directors of the Railroad Company. No substantial objection is perceived to this form of suit. The stockholders own a large amount of stock, and they allege that an illegal tax has been imposed on the stock of the company, injurious to the stockholders, and on this ground they ask relief against the Collector of the tax, and that he may be enjoined from collecting the same.

It is true the railroad could not, in its corporate name, bring a suit in this Court against the Collector, because the business of the company is transacted in the State of which the defendant is a citizen. But the complainants, being citizens of other states, may claim the protection of their stock against an illegal taxation, and make the corporation a defendant, and enjoin it from paying over the tax; and the corporation being made a defendant, being a party on the record, the same relief may be given to it as if it had been made a complainant.

This principle is exemplified in a case where a plaintiff, being a citizen of another State, sues in the Federal Court, making the person against whom the relief is prayed, and others, citizens of the same State, who are jointly interested in the relief prayed. The rule is, that the court having jurisdiction, relief may be given to the parties on the record, whether plaintiffs or defendants, as the principles of equity shall require. The corporation, however, should have answered, admitting the facts stated in the bill, and praying that equity may be done. This, however, under the view taken by the court, is not material.

This case is brought under the original jurisdiction of this court, on the ground that the controversy arises between citizens of different States. It does not come before us in the exercise of an appellate power, but as a Court having concurrent jurisdiction with the State Court, in giving effect to the laws of the State. And the question is, whether the tax law for 1853 requires the tax to be assessed upon the entire property of the Railroad Company, or upon what, in common language, constitutes the stock upon which dividends are paid.

The 32d section of the tax law, 1 *Revised Statutes*, 113, makes it " the duty of the President, Secretary, Agent, or other proper accounting officer of every railroad, to furnish to the Auditor of the county, where their principal office is situated, a list of all the stock in said company, and its value, attested by the oath of the officer making the same; and shall furnish a statement dividing the aggregate amount of all the stock of such company amongst the several counties in proportion to the value of the superstructure, buildings, and real estate of such company in each county; and if any such company shall not have in this State its principal office for the transaction of its financial business, it shall be the duty of the President, Cashier, Secretary, Treasurer, Engineer, or constructing agent of such company to furnish the Auditor of the county, where the work first enters the State, a statement, under the oath or affirmation of the officer making it, specifying the amount and value of all real estate owned by such company within this State, the amount expended in the construction of said work within the lines of the State, and the amount invested in machinery and rolling stock of every kind; which said machinery and rolling stock shall be assessed for taxation in the same proportion to its total amount, that the length of line of the work in this State completed, bears to the entire length of the line of said work completed."

From the language of this section, there would seem to be no doubt that the Legislature intended to tax the entire property of the Railroad Company; and that a list, to be furnished to the Auditor of the county, "of all the stock in said

company, and its value, attested by the oath of   a-
making the same," was intended to include the whole p   of
of the company.   And this is the construction given to
section by the Supreme Court of Indiana, in *Dunn* v. *Ham
ton, Auditor of Marion county in* 1854.

That decision of the Supreme Court of the State constitutes a rule of decision for this Court.   It has long been so
settled in the Federal Courts.

By the 37th section of the Tax Act, if the company shall
fail to make a return of its property for taxation as required,
"the proper county Auditor shall proceed to make out such
list from the best information he can obtain," &c.   Now, if
an imperfect list shall be made, the power here given will
enable the Auditor to act, by making out a new return, or
correcting the errors of the one returned.   This is within the
purview of the above section.

Railroads have contributed more to the facilities of intercourse, the interest of agriculture, to build up towns and extend our internal commerce, than all other improvements.
But, in the construction of these works, heavy expenditures
have been incurred, and large debts contracted by way of
loans of money and otherwise, so that the companies are ill
able to bear the pressure of a heavy taxation.   The expense
of running the cars, making repairs, and meeting contingencies is very great ; and when to this shall be added the interest on debts incurred, little or no profit can be realized to
the stockholders for some years after the road is in operation.
Lands, of necessity, are often received in payment of stock.
These lands are taxed, the same as lands held by an individual,
on the plausible ground that the lands of a corporation should
be taxed the same as the lands of an individual.   But these
lands are never held by the corporation for the purposes of
culture, but to be converted into money, or for the occupancy
of the road.   They do not, in the general, as the lands of an
agriculturalist, afford a profit by an increase of value.   But

zens of di~
exercisg
curr~ ~his

~nds, and also for the strao-
· This, in effect, is a tax—
an addition to the interest.
onnected with the public in-
&c., which require a large in-
mode of taxation so equal or
Such investments are subject
to not affect real estate. No
liture required on a railroad,
nor the losses of a bank. As common carriers, the railroad
is responsible for injuries done to persons and property,
through the neglect or want of skill in its agents; and experience has shown that juries are inclined most liberally to
compensate all who suffer, by finding liberal, if not extravagant damages. Banks are liable to imposition and losses
through the failures of borrowers, counterfeit notes and
drafts, which no one can foretell. These casualties place at
greater hazard the monies invested in railroads and banks
than in real estate; and, although these establishments may
be owned by individuals, yet they are so intimately connected
with the public interest and welfare, that stockholders are dis-
tinguishable from the owners of other property.

Taxation should be so laid on each classification of property,
as to operate equally. Now, nothing can be more unequal
than the above taxation of railroads. The cost of the work
affords no criterion in regard to the profits. This depends
upon location and other circumstances, which have no connection with the cost of construction; and yet all of them afford more or less public accommodation.

These great improvements are made, generally, with the
means afforded by capitalists of other States or countries, and
we are enriched by the expenditure. These roads will not
be kept in good repair, and be safe for passengers, unless the
stockholders shall receive a reasonable interest for their advances. And this, and an entire equality of taxation, can

only be attained by a charge on the profits. From indications not to be mistaken, these great lines are in danger of being embarrassed, if not destroyed, by taxation.

Believing that the tax in this case is not unconstitutional under the Federal or State constitutions, and seeing that the tax law has been construed by the Supreme Court of Indiana against the right set up by the complainants, the bill is dismissed at the complainant's cost, and the injunction is dissolved.

E. M. CURTIS v. THE CENTRAL RAILWAY.

A special plea which amounts to the general issue is demurrable.

A plea which states facts in bar to the plaintiff's demand, is not good, if the facts so stated do not constitute a bar.

The law and practice of the State having been adopted in regard to the taking of depositions, a subsequent modification of the law, which was followed for a long time, will be considered as adopted by usage.

But the law of the State can make no change in the act of Congress, as to the circumstances under which depositions may be taken. The person whose deposition is taken, under the act of Congress, must reside more than a hundred miles from the place of holding the court.

A conductor of a train of cars is engaged in an important business, and is bound to use reasonable care for the safety of passengers. And at cross roads, or where the tracks lie very near each other, a more than ordinary degree of care is requisite.

Any carelessness in loading a freight train of cars, or in not attending to the adjustment of the load of lumber, by which an injury is done to a passenger in another train, will make the owners of the freight train responsible.

Messrs. *Morrison, Ray & Morrison*, for plaintiff.

Messrs. *Newman & Test*, for defendants.

INSTRUCTION OF THE COURT TO THE JURY.

This case is brought to recover damages against the defendant, for an injury done to the plaintiff, through the

26a

carelessness of the agents of the defendant, by which the plaintiff was injured while traveling in the cars of another line of railroad. The declaration alleges that the plaintiff was a passenger on the train of cars running eastward, towards the state line of Indiana and Ohio, and the defendants' train running westward, on a track parallel to that on which the plaintiff was a passenger, and within five feet six inches of the track on which the eastern cars were running; the western cars being freighted with cross ties and other materials of lumber, which were so negligently loaded by the servants of the defendant, that in passing the eastern train, the projecting end of a cross tie or piece of timber, being loaded as aforesaid, struck the left arm of the plaintiff below the elbow, as the arm rested on the sill of the window of the car in which the plaintiff was a passenger, and with great violence and force thereby cut, lacerated, bruised and wounded the said left arm, &c.

The defendant pleaded in bar to the action, that the injury was received through the carelessness of the plaintiff, by resting her elbow and arm on the sill of the car window, by which she exposed her arm to danger and injury, &c.

Several other special pleas were filed, to which the plaintiff demurred.

These pleas were disposed of on the ground that they amounted to the general issue, or did not state a complete answer to the declaration, admitting the facts stated to be true. In some of the pleas there was an averment of carelessness by the plaintiff, but no denial of the careless loading of the lumber so as to project over the side of the car, as alleged in the declaration, by reason of which the injury was done.

The demurrer filed authorized the defendant to test the sufficiency of the declaration, and it was alleged to be defective in not showing any connection between the cars on which the plaintiff was a passenger and those which were owned by the defendant; but this objection was overruled by the court.

The fact of the tracks of those two roads being near each other, imposed the greater diligence on the agents of both companies.

Exceptions were taken to several depositions, as not having been duly taken. By a rule of court, depositions were admitted to be taken under the State law, and in pursuance of the State practice.

The first exception alleged, that notice of taking depositions was served on the Treasurer of the railroad company, and not on the President. It was proved that this notice was served on the Treasurer in the absence of the President. This is a sufficient service of the notice under the revised acts of 1852. 2 *Vol.*, *p.* 85.

The State law has been somewhat changed in regard to taking depositions, since the above rule of court was adopted, but it seems that the State law as altered was followed by the uniform practice in this Court, and this was held by the Court as a usage in practice which would be sustained.

It was objected to depositions taken before the Mayor of Columbus, Ohio, who did not certify that the parties were or were not present. The Mayor certified that the defendant was not present, and this, we think, is sufficient.

To the deposition of Churchman and wife, it was objected that they reside in Indiana, and it nowhere appears that they live more than one hundred miles from the place of holding the Court. This is a fatal objection. In adopting the State practice the Court did not dispense with the requirement of the act of Congress, which authorizes depositions to be taken where the witness lives more than one hundred miles from the place where the case is to be tried. The adoption of the State law only referred to the form and mode of taking depositions.

The injury was proved, substantially as alleged in the declaration. A short distance after leaving Richmond, the two tracks were laid five feet six inches only apart, and this was continued for a considerable distance. When the passenger cars came to this part of the road, the freight cars had stopped on the eastern part of it, and moved slowly forwards as they were approached by the passenger cars. A stick of timber, called a tie, for the road, was proved to have projected some six inches or more over the other loading of the freight cars, and this timber struck the passenger cars two or three times, broke off a part of the moulding of the car window where the plaintiff was sitting, and severely injured her left arm.

Under the injury, she at first fainted, but when she came to, she thought herself fortunate in not being more injured. Every possible attention was paid to her by the conductor and others. There were differences among the witnesses as to the position of the arm of the plaintiff. Some of them stated that her arm protruded two and a half inches over the side of the car; others who were near to her said her arm did not extend beyond the side of the car.

The Court called the attention of the jury to the facts proved, and instructed them, if the injury was caused by the negligence of the defendant's agents, the plaintiff was entitled to recover. It was not enough that the freight cars should be shown to have been carefully loaded, but as the ties were thrown crosswise the open cars, it was the duty of the conductor of the freight cars to see that the timbers had not slipped from their places, so as to endanger the lives and limbs of the passengers on the train which they were to meet. That if they believe the arm of the plaintiff rested on the window sill where she sat, yet if her arm was not so extended as to endanger it in passing the tracks near to each other, under ordinary circumstances, the alleged carelessness is no excuse for the defendant.

The conductor of a car performs a most responsible duty. The propelling force which he controls, with the train moved by it, increases in a wonderful degree the facilities of commercial intercourse and exchanges; but by its mighty power it crushes to death all living beings which it encounters. Hence the care, the vigilance, and the skill of the conductor must be in continual exercise to avoid collisions. In passing over a cross road, or over tracks near each other, his vigilance should be in proportion to the danger he encounters.

That the tie which scraped the passenger car, and tore off some of its moulding at the window must have projected several feet beyond the side of the freight cars, is clear, from the fact that it struck the car in which the plaintiff was sitting. In almost every car passengers are warned not to stand on the platforms between the cars, and this is done for the benefit of the passengers. Still the conductor of the cars is bound to exercise reasonable diligence. He is bound not to endanger his own passengers, or the passengers in other cars, by any carelessness or want of diligence on his part.

In the case before the jury, carelessness is shown, by the fact that the timber carried by the freight train struck, with force, the passenger car. This degree of carelessness is sufficient to charge the defendant. Had the freight train been properly laden, no one will pretend that the position of the plaintiff would have subjected her to injury. The circumstances of her admitting that she was in fault, after being told that her arm was on the window, will have but little weight with the jury. She was not in a position to judge of the facts, and therefore her admissions should be cautiously received.

If the jury find from the evidence that the plaintiff was injured through the carelessness of the defendant's agents, either in loading the cars or in not keeping the load properly adjusted, she is entitled to recover what may be considered a reasonable compensation for the suffering she endured, the expenses for medical treatment, and otherwise, while she remained disabled. These are called compensatory damages. There is nothing in the case which would seem to authorize vindictive damages. No proof is given from which an intention to injure any one by the defendant's agents, can be presumed.

The jury found a verdict for $1500.

THE UNITED STATES *v.* JOHN M. EMERSON.

On a charge for stealing letters out of the mail by a post master or other person, it is important to have as witnesses the post masters through whose offices the letters passed or were distributed.

When such witnesses are not called, although there may be proof of the mailing of the letters, and that they were never received, it is not sufficient for the conviction of any post master on the route.

If a witness swear positively as to the commission of the offence under improbable circumstances, whose character is bad, it will have little weight with the jury.

And this is especially so where the accused shows a good character. Under doubtful circumstances of guilt, good character will lead to an acquittal of the defendant.

District Attorney of the U. S., for plaintiff.
Mr. *Morrison* and Mr. *Walpole,* for defendant.

OPINION OF THE COURT.

This is an indictment which charges the defendant with embezzling various letters, which contained articles of value, while acting as post master at Hamilton, in Steuben County, Indiana.

E. B. Mott, a witness, states, that on or about the 1st of January, 1853, he mailed a letter at the office of defendant, directed to James Akright, New London, Huron County, O., which contained two certificates of deposit, dated the 3d of December, 1852, given by the Tompkins County Bank, New York, in favor of James A. Gibbons, assigned to Akright. The package was directed to the distributing office at Toledo.

S. W. Spratt stated that three letters or packets were

mailed about the same time, one of which contained two certificates of deposit, each for fifty dollars; the other two packets contained a deed and other papers, all of which by their direction were to pass through the Toledo post office. The first letter was mailed the same evening, &c.

Mr. Brown, the post office agent, in a short time after the loss of the letters was suspected, examined the distributing post office at Toledo, and found that no such letters as described had passed through that office, at or near the time that they should have been distributed at that office.

Dugan, a witness, was called by the prosecution, who swore that on the 1st of January, 1853, he called at the post office in Hamilton, about ten o'clock at night, knocked at the door, and no one answering, he went across the street on some business. In a short time he returned, and seeing a light in the window of the post office, he crossed over the fence and approached the window, where he saw the post master sitting near the window engaged in opening letters; and he saw him take money and other articles out of the letters thus opened, which he put in his pockets, and one or two of the letters, after the contents had been taken out, he laid upon the window, so that the witness could see the directions on the letters, and he says the directions were to the same persons as sworn to have been mailed on the 1st of January. One he specially observed was directed to James Akright. He observed that one of the letters opened contained a deed, or what appeared to be a deed, or a patent for land. After the defendant had completed his work, he stepped into an adjoining room, opened the door of a stove and threw the letters into it.

Dugan, by a large number of respectable witnesses, was proved to have a bad character, and every one stated that he was not worthy of credit under oath.

The defendant's character, was proved to be good. He was a physician of respectable standing in society, and he was evidently a man of intelligence. It was also proved that Dugan was once arrested for perjury, at the instance of the defendant, on which account he was hostile to the defendant, although that difficulty had been settled between them.

The Court charged the jury that the evidence, without the statements of Dugan, did not authorize a conviction. That the letters were mailed at the office of the defendant at the time stated, there could be no reasonable doubt. The witnesses were highly respectable, and nothing has been stated to their discredit.

But from the office of the defendant to the distributing office at Toledo, a distance of more than fifty miles, there are several post offices where the mail was opened, but none of the post masters have been called as witnesses.

The examination of the Toledo office where the mail is distributed, is satisfactory to show that no such mail as should have been forwarded from the Hamilton office was distributed at Toledo. But if the letters were abstracted at Toledo, where they passed through the hands of the post master or his clerks, if they were carried in the mail to that point, and they have not been called as witnesses. Nor is there any evidence to show that the letters deposited in the Hamilton office have not been received.

These defects in the evidence are fatal to the success of the prosecution, unless the jury shall believe the evidence of Dugan. The credibility of witnesses must be considered and judged of by the jury.

In the first place, this witness is discredited by his neighbors. Many of them have been examined, and they agree in saying Dugan's character is bad, and that they would not believe him under oath. There is no better test of the character of a witness than the opinion of his neighbors. Every man has a character where he is best known,—where his daily walk and conversation are observed and spoken of. Local prejudices or excitements may sometimes do injustice to an individual. But this is generally temporary. So that upon the whole, there is no criterion so safe, in determining as to the truth of a witness, as the opinion of his neighbors.

The relation of the witness in regard to the acts of the defendant, which he observed through a window at a late hour of the night, cannot be said to have been impossible; but they were very extraordinary. They were of a character to create strong doubts of their truth, unless they proceeded from a credible person.

It appears that the witness and the defendant had been at enmity. This not unfrequently affords a motive for revenge, where injuries supposed or real had been inflicted on the witness. Of these matters, gentlemen, you are to judge and determine.

The defendant has proved a good character. He is a professional man, and stood well with his neighbors. He has left the neighborhood, but he seems to have left few enemies behind him. Indeed, from the evidence, no witness speaks to his prejudice, except the witness, Dugan.

Character, gentlemen, under all circumstances, is the best earthly inheritance. It is a shield to the innocent when unjustly accused. And in this case you will give weight to it, in connection with the other facts of the case.

Verdict not guilty.

UNITED STATES v. SOLOMON STANLEY.

A false reserving to obtain a pre-emption right, is made perjury by statute.

The person commencing an improvement has a right to continue, and any one who intervenes may be considered a trespasser.

But if a first occupant give way to a second, and the right of pre-emption is granted to the second, it is good against all the world except the first occupant.

And if he abandon his right, the right cannot be questioned.

Where perjury is charged on a written affidavit, and it appears clearly from several witnesses that the affiant stated the facts truly, and was advised that they were substantially the same as stated in the writing, by a lawyer in whom the affiant confided, and he yielded to such an influence in taking the oath, it is not perjury, the guilty motive being wanting.

District Attorney of the United States, for plaintiff.
Messrs. *Walpole*, for defendant.

CHARGE TO THE JURY.

This is an indictment for perjury, under the 13th section of the act of Congress of the 4th September, 1841, for swearing falsely to establish a pre-emption right, which, by that act, is made perjury. The act of the 3d of August, 1846, provides "that every actual settler, being the head of a family, or widow, or single man over the age of twenty-one years, who is now in possession, by actual residence as a house-keeper, of any tract of public land within the limits of the several cessions by the Miami Indians, in Indiana, which have not yet been proclaimed for sale by the President, or any such person who shall hereafter erect a dwelling house and become a house-keeper upon any such tract of land, shall be entitled to the same benefits and privileges with respect to said land, as were granted to settlers on other lands by the act approved 22d June, 1838, entitled an act to grant pre-emption rights, and the several amendatory provisions of said act," &c.

And in the 2d section of said act, it was provided "that in every case, the affidavit of the claimant under that act should be like unto that prescribed by the act of the 22d June, 1838, and the same shall be filed, and proof and payment made for the land claimed, at any time before the day fixed by the President's proclamation for the public sale of said land."

The written affidavit was read on which the perjury was assigned, and which was made and filed by the defendant, at the time of application to the Register of the Land Office for the pre-emption. A pre-emptive right to a quarter section was claimed on the ground that John Stanley had built a dwelling house on the same, which he with his family occupied, within the above cession of the Miami Indians. This affidavit was made the 23d March, 1854.

It appears from the testimony that a man by the name of Majors, and hands employed by him, entered upon the land in controversy, on the 18th March, 1854, cut logs for a cabin, and the next day it was built up to the roof. Finding the building in this condition, John Stanley, the brother of defendant, came to the cabin with his loaded wagon and entered into it, by cutting a door, and had it covered with materials which had been prepared by Majors.

When Majors returned to finish the house, he found the defendant in possession of it, who said that his brother had gone to the Land Office to enter the land, and he remained to protect the possession. Majors entered into the house and his trunk was handed in. His entry was resisted by defendant, and finding that he could not stay there, Majors took possession of another quarter section.

The affidavit of defendant stated that "he knows from personal observation, that the said John Stanley did, on the 14th day of March, 1854, enter into a dwelling house with his family, consisting of himself and wife and two children, which the said John Stanley previously caused to be erected on the above described quarter section of land, and that he, the said Stanley, continues to make said house his only home."

After the affidavit was drawn up, the defendant stated that he did not feel free to swear to it. And he then observed that when he first saw the house, it was a pen, there being no roof on it; that his brother cut out the door and covered the house on the 14th, but he did not say who built the pen. After the statement of the above facts, the defendant was induced to make the affidavit on the advice of a connection of his who was present, and who was a lawyer, believing that it contained the facts substantially as stated by him.

Some nine or ten persons proved the good character of the

defendant, and that his standing was as fair and unexceptionable, as any other person of his age in that part of the county where he lived.

The Court, in their charge to the jury, said there could be no doubt that John Stanley was guilty of a trespass in entering into the partly built cabin, and that he could not have procured the pre-emptive right to the quarter section, had Majors claimed it, and had all the facts been represented to the Register and Receiver of the Land Office. Majors was entitled to the possession of the improvement, so far as it was made by him. But he relinquished his right, as appears from the testimony, and settled upon another quarter in the neighborhood. This abandonment left John Stanley in possession of the improvement, and he made the house habitable by cutting out the door and putting a roof on it.

But the inquiry for the jury is not as to this particular matter, but whether the defendant was guilty of wilful and corrupt perjury. It does not appear that he had any knowledge who had constructed the pen of the cabin, but he knew that his brother had cut out the door and put on the roof. And he objected to swearing to the written affidavit, it appears, until his friends, and especially the lawyer, who was a connexion of his, advised him to swear to it, as it embraced only the facts substantially as stated by him. If you believe, gentlemen, that he yielded to this influence in swearing to the paper, and that in his repeated relations he gave a true statement of the facts as they transpired, according to his knowledge of them, he is not guilty of perjury. To constitute perjury there must be a wilful and corrupt statement of a falsehood, material to the matter in hand. You are to determine the facts in the case, and judge of the guilt of the defendant. He has shown an excellent character, and this, under the circumstances, and indeed under all circumstances where the evidence of guilt is not clear, will receive due consideration by a jury.

Verdict of not guilty.

CIRCUIT COURT OF THE UNITED STATES.

MICHIGAN—JUNE TERM, 1855.

JAMES NALL, JR. ET. AL. *v.* THE STEAMER ILLINOIS ET AL.

On an appeal in Admiralty, from the District to the Circuit Court, reasonable diligence should be used in prosecuting the appeal.

If the party delay perfecting the appeal for six months, and until a day or two before the term of the Circuit Court, the appellee may, under the rule, notice the cause for a hearing, and the Court will require him to take his depositions during the session of the Court, so as to come to a hearing. At the home port of a vessel, the local law must regulate the lien. A purely maritime lien may arise in every other port, under the maritime jurisdiction, unless it be in the home port. This must be regulated by the local law.

The lien cannot arise under the local law and also under the maritime.

Mr. *Howard* for libellants.
M. *Newberry* for respondents.

OPINION OF THE COURT.

This is an appeal in Admiralty from the District Court.

The libel is for articles furnished the steamer Illinois, an account of which is stated and satisfactorily proved by the libellants.

In their answer, the respondents allege that articles were furnished, but they deny that the claim in said libel mentioned is a lien upon the steam boat, her tackle, apparel, and furniture, &c.

In the libel there are some defects, which, if they had been taken advantage of in time, would have required amendment.

The proceeding, though in the Admiralty, is under the act of Michigan, which gives a lien on the vessel. In such a case the law should be specially referred to and substantially stated. So the tonnage of the vessel should be stated to show, that it comes under the Admiralty jurisdiction and has a license.

The libel asserts a lien on the vessel, by the maritime law, and the law of Michigan. This is inconsistent, as a lien must arise at the home port of the vessels under the local law. No lien attaches upon a domestic vessel, for work and labor done and performed on her, except by statute. *Read v. The hull of a new Brig*, 1 *Story's*, 6, 6. *Rep.* 244. By the common law, material men have no lien for articles furnished a vessel, whether she be foreign or domestic, and such is the law of the English Admiralty. But by the civil law, they have such a lien. In the United States they have it only in the cases of foreign ships, or ships of one of the states of the United States, furnished in another state. *Lane v. The Brig President*, 4 *Wash.* 6, 6, *Rep.* 458. It is of no importance how a lien arises under the local law, whether by statute, or common, or municipal law; whenever its existence is established, the jurisdiction of the Admiralty attaches to it. The *Schooner Marian*, 1 *Story's Cir.* 6, *Rep.* 68. A common law lien is always connected with the possession of the thing, and is simply a right to retain. But a maritime lien does not depend upon possession, but is an interest in the thing, and may be enforced, wherever the Admiralty jurisdiction is exercised.

The libel alleges, that, "the articles were delivered to the said steamer at Detroit aforesaid, to be used in furnishing and completing her; and it alleges some of them were put in

and upon, and worked into said steamer by the work and labor of the libellant," &c.   Now if the articles were not all so
used, it would be difficult to say, what part of them were so
used, and the libel could not be sustained.   The averments
should be positive, in order that the extent of the lien may
be seen.

Although the forms of procedure are less technical in Admiralty, than at common law, yet there should be certainty
in the material matters to give jurisdiction.

As an Admiralty Court, the District Court has a general
jurisdiction, yet it can enforce no liens against a vessel which
is not of a size and character to engage in maritime navigation.

It has been strongly suggested by some writers, that the
lien under the statute is the same as the common law lien
for mechanics, which depends for its validity on possession.
But this point has not been raised in the pleadings, and it
need not be examined.

The maritime lien arose out of the conveniences, if not necessities, of commerce.   The floating vessel is constantly
changing its locality, and the master is often under the necessity of contracting debts for the repairs of his vessel, &c;
the work and labor done, or articles furnished for the ship, is
presumed to be done or furnished on the credit of the vessel.
A personal liability of the master only, would not be sufficient
to meet the exigency.   The vessel is, therefore, bound in such
cases.

The motion which was made in this case for a continuance
was overruled, on the ground that as the decree in the District Court had been made six months before this Court commenced, the appeal being filed a day or two before its commencement, showed such a want of diligence in the appellants in the prosecution of their appeal, as not to entitle
them to further delay.   A continuance would necessarily give
a delay of eighteen months, from the decree in the District

Court. The Court considered the circumstances as coming within the rule which authorized the appellants to notice the cause for trial; and that it would impose no unjust hardship on the defendants, to take their depositions during the present term. When this decision was announced, the Court stated, all the time would be given, to take the depositions during the term, which could be given.

A statement has been made of what the defendants' counsel expected to prove, and which, if admitted, could not affect the justice of the case.

The correctness of the charges are admitted by Mr. Newberry, who built the vessel, and also by Mr. McKnight, who purchased her. In addition to these admissions, the items are proved by the clerk who sold the articles. As these articles were used in building and furnishing the boat, under the Michigan law, they constitute a lien on the boat, whether it be in the hands of Newberry the builder, or McKnight the purchaser, both of whom are defendants.

Upon the whole, the decree of the District Court is affirmed with costs.

WM. H. MATCALM v. OSMOND SMITH.

All persons interested, should be made parties to a bill to foreclose a mortgage.

This is indispensable where a party may be chargeable with any balance, which the sale of the mortgaged premises may not satisfy.

Mr. *Howard*, for plaintiff.
Mr. *Clark*, for defendant.

OPINION OF THE COURT.

This is a bill in chancery to foreclose a mortgage. Charles D. Parkhurst executed three several promissory notes to plaintiff, each for five hundred and forty-four dollars, and to receive the payment of these notes, Smith and wife executed a mortgage for sixteen hundred and thirty-three dollars on the premises stated in the mortgage, dated 7th December, 1851, given by the said Parkhurst as collateral security. But if the money should not be paid, the party of the second part to sell the mortgaged premises. There was a failure to pay the sum due, $1280 70, on 1st July, 1853, and this bill is brought to have the mortgaged premises sold.

And the bill states that Eben Sherwood, who is also made a defendant, claims to have some interest or estate in the mortgaged premises, mortgaged to him by Parkhurst, dated 8d June, 1850, which required Parkhurst to pay to Sherwood $687,41, in three equal annual payments to be paid in sawing, and the said Sherwood to deliver the logs at the mill ponds.

And the bill requires Sherwood to answer whether he has not received from Parkhurst the notes, &c., and whether the mortgage has not been fully paid; and whether the said mortgage ought not to be discharged of record. What amount, if any is due, on the mortgage. Whether he has delivered the logs, &c., at the mill pond. How many feet of lumber had been sawed by Parkhurst. Whether the said Parkhurst did not make the notes, and the said Smith and wife did not execute the mortgage; and whether the amount stated to be due on said notes is not due.

To the bill the defendants demur, and for cause of demurrer state, that Charles D. Parkhurst, alleged to be a citizen of Michigan, is not made a party, when the object of the bill is to foreclose a mortgage to pay his debt.

It is clear that Parkhurst should be made a party. The mortgage was executed by Smith and wife to pay his debt The debt was incurred by Parkhurst for the purchase of the premises mortgaged. He sold to Smith, and Smith and wife agreed to pay to the mortgagee the original consideration, for

27a

which the premises were sold, and himself and wife executed a mortgage to secure such payment.

It seems Parkhurst had mortgaged the premises, while he owned them to Sherwood, for six hundred and eighty-seven dollars and forty-one cents, to be paid in three equal annual payments in sawing lumber, &c., Sherwood to deliver logs to be sawed at the mill pond.

Parkhurst is a necessary party to show in his answer how much of the original consideration was paid, and especially is it necessary that he should answer how much he paid, on Sherwood's mortgage, if the whole of it were not discharged. Sherwood is called on to answer as to what payments were made, but Parkhurst has a direct interest in showing the payments to Sherwood, as he would be answerable to him for any remaining balance, or to the plaintiff, should Sherwood's mortgage be first satisfied, it being prior in date. The demurrer to the bill is sustained.

Leave given to amend the bill.

OGDEN *v.* HARRINGTON.

In a sale of land for taxes, any material act which the law requires, or which may prejudice the rights of the owner, will be fatal to the title of the purchaser.

But mere technicalities which do not come within this rule, and cannot prejudice the interest of the land holder, do not vitiate the sale.

A payment of the money received on the sale into the County Treasury, instead of the State, or the treasury of the county, instead of the treasury of the township, cannot affect the title.

The officer who pays or receives the money wrongfully, is liable to pay it over to the proper treasury.

Mr. *Walker* appeared for the plaintiff.

Mr. *Lathrop* for defendant.

OPINION OF THE COURT.

This is an action of ejectment to recover the possession of the north-east and north-west quarters of section 30 T. B. N., Range 16 east, three hundred and twenty acres. The patent was issued to J. W. Edmonds, 15th August, 1837, which covers the land. In 1842 the patentee conveyed the land to plaintiff.

The defendant claims under a tax title, and the points raised in the case are in regard to the validity of the procedure in the sale for taxes.

It is objected that the warrant of the Supervisors to the township, however, is defective. It is directed merely to the Treasurer, &c., whereas, it should have been issued in the name of the people of the State of Michigan. A reference is made to the 6th article of the Constitution of Michigan, which relates to the judicial department, and which declares in the 7th section, that "The style of all process shall be 'in the name of the people of the State of Michigan.'" And in the act regulating the commencement of suits, (Revised Laws, 132), it is provided that the style of all process from courts of record in this State, shall be "in the name of the people, &c."

These regulations, it would seem, were intended to apply only to judicial process; and if the same form had been used, to some extent, in directing certain things to be done, from a superior officer of the State to one who is inferior, it is mere matter of form, and need not be followed. It appears, indeed, where the form of the warrant, as it is called, which authorizes the Treasurer to call the tax, is given by the proper authority, the form of judicial process is not followed. In such a case, where the form is not imperative, it can be of no importance. It is only necessary to direct or require the Treasurer to collect the tax as stated on the duplicate.

It has again been objected that the land has not been legally assessed.

The 2d section of the revised law provides, that "undi-

vided shares or interests in lands shall be assessed to the
owners thereof, if such ownership is known to the assessors,
and no tract in the same section, originally entered as one
parcel, shall be subdivided in assessing, unless the fact of a
subdivision having been made by the owner or owners shall
be known to the assessors.

The entry of the land is proved by the Register. The
mode of assessing lands owned by more than one person depends upon the personal knowledge of the assessors. Where
there is no evidence as to the extent of ownership, to the
assessors, the Court will presume that the assessment has been
correctly made; this presumption always arises in favor of
the acts of an officer. It appears in this case there was no
possession of the premises at the time it was assessed, so that
it does not appear the assessors had any means of ascertaining
the interest of such proprietor. The objection, therefore, that
the assessment was erroneously made is not sustainable.

An accurate description of the land is required, but to the
description given by the assessors there is no objection except the one above stated.

It is again objected that the tax is not charged in dollars
and cents.

The signs of dollars and cents do not appear at the heads
of the columns, but the valuation is stated, and the tax or the
amount is so plainly stated as not to be mistaken, and in the
last column the total amount of the tax is stated. The purposes of the tax are stated in each column, as for township,
school, library and other purposes, so that there seems to be
no force in this objection. In Sibley v. Smith, 2 Michigan
report 499, Chief Justice Shaw says: "Our rule is very plain
and well settled, that all those measures which are intended
for the security of the citizen for ensuring an equality of
taxation, and to enable every one to know, with reasonable
certainty, for what polls, and for what real and personal estate he is taxed, and for what all who are liable with him for
taxes are, essential."

The County Treasurer, who is collector, is directed to retain in his hands the sum of one hundred and fifty dollars for township purposes, and the further sum of one hundred and nine dollars and fifty cents, for school and library tax, and hold it, subject to the draft of the officers authorized by law to receive the same. And he is authorized, in addition to the aforesaid sums, to retain four per cent. for collection; and he is required, also, to pay over to the Treasurer of the county of St. Clair the sum of five hundred and forty-seven dollars and fifty cents, for county purposes; and the further sum of forty dollars and eleven cents, for and on account of State assets; and the further sum of fifty-one dollars and fifty cents, for and on account of the militia; and four hundred and five dollars and forty-four cents, on account of delinquencies in the tax for highways.

It is objected, that the militia tax should have been directed to be paid to the Township Treasurer, instead of the County Treasurer; but this cannot be material. A wrong application of the money cannot vitiate the sale for taxes. But in this case, if the payment be made into the county treasury, instead of the township, the error can be easily corrected by the payment of the sum to the township by the County Treasurer.

The tax assessed on the roll was, for State, county, township, school and militia purposes.

There is a further objection to pay to State assets. In answer to this, it is only necessary to repeat, that a wrong payment of the tax by the officer who collected it by a sale of property, cannot affect the sale. The officers through whose hands the money passes, and to whom it is paid wrongfully, are liable to pay the sum to the proper treasury.

Upon the whole, we do not see any such error in the proceedings under the tax sales, as affects the validity of the sale.

The jury were instructed accordingly, and they rendered a verdict for the defendant.

LYELL *v.* MILLER, *et. al.*

There can be no taxation of costs, except under the act of 1853.
That law abolishes all previous laws on the subject, without any reservation.

OPINION OF THE COURT.

This is a motion in regard to the taxation of costs. The above cause was submitted to a jury, and before a verdict was rendered the plaintiff submitted to a non-suit. A motion was made to set aside the non-suit, which was overruled by the Court.

The taxation is made in part under the present fee bill, and in part under the late one. The act of 26th February, 1853, which is now in force, declares, "That in lieu of the compensation now allowed by law to attorneys, solicitors and proctors in the United States Courts, to United States District Attorneys, clerks of the District Courts, marshals, witnesses, jurors, commissioners and printers, in the several States, the following, and no other compensation, shall be taxed and allowed."

The above law applies to all taxations of costs, after it took effect, and it abolished all prior laws on the subject. As there is no provision in the present act that, for services previously rendered, cost should be taxed under the former law, there can be no taxation under it.

PHILLIS JOHNSTON *v.* JAMES A. VANDYKE.

1. The Common Law of England, except so far as modified by Statute, was the law of property in the late Territory of Michigan.

2. At Common Law the widow was entitled to dower in all lands of which her husband was seized at any time during coverture.

3. A and B were married in the territory of Michigan in 1810. A was seized of certain real estate in 1816, which he sold and moved out of the territory, and continued a non-resident until his death in 1850. In 1846 the State of Michigan restricted, by statute, the right of dower to lands of which the husband, *died*, seized; but providing expressly, *that no right which had already attached* or vested, should be affected thereby. Held, that the right of dower was an inchoate right during coverture, only made consummate by the death of the husband, and was embraced within the saving clause of the restrictive statute.

4. The dower to be set off, must include all casual and natural enhancement from circumstances, and excluding all improvement actually made by the tenant.

5. The mode indicated by the statute of the State as a judicial process for setting off dower, will be pursued in the U. S. Court.

Messrs. *Campbell & O'Flynn* for plaintiff.

Frazer & Emmons for defendant.

BY JUDGE WILKINS.

A special verdict was rendered in this case, finding that *the* George Johnston, mentioned in the declaration, was married to the plaintiff in the year 1810: that about that time they resided on the premises in question; that the husband was seized of the same on the 24*th of Sept.*, 1816, and from that time continued so seized until the 28*th of Oct.*, 1816, when he sold, and conveyed the same to one Stephen Mack, and that the defendant now owns and holds the same by mesne conveyances from said Mack.

The verdict furthermore finds that the said Johnston and his wife removed and settled in the Territory, and now State of, Wisconsin, in the year 1820, where they continued to reside until the year 1850, at which time the said George Johnston, the husband, died, and that the plaintiff removed to this State in the fall of 1853, subsequent to the institution of this suit. The verdict further finds that the premises described were in *October*, 1816—the time of alienation—worth the sum of 1800 dollars, *and embracing the improvements since made*, are *now* worth the sum of $40,000; that the improvements made are worth $8000; that dower was demanded on the 31st of March, 1851, and in May, 1852, according to the allegations in the declaration.

Upon this verdict, the plaintiff now moves that judgment be entered in her favor, assigning her dower in the premises demanded, and declaring the defendant guilty of withholding the same : and that the court appoint three disinterested and respectable freeholders commissioners for the purpose of making the admeasurement of the dower of the plaintiff, out of the lands described in the Record, according to the provisions of the 55th section, of Part 8d, Title 111 and Chap. 2 of the Revised Statutes of the State of Michigan of 1838, page 479; and that, in making such admeasurement, the said commissioners be directed to admeasure the same to the plaintiff, irrespective of any improvements made by the defendant, and allowing to the widow all advances in the value of the said premises arising from extreme circumstances since the alienation.

In resisting this motion, two objections are urged :

1st. That the plaintiff, when this action was brought, was a non-resident widow; and, therefore, not entitled to recover dower, her husband *not being seized of the same at the time of his death.*

2d. That, conceding the existence of her right, yet her dower is to be set off according to the value of the premises when they "were aliened" by her husband, according to the provisions of the Revised Statutes of Michigan of 1846.

1. The Revised Statutes of Michigan of 1846, Title XIV, Chap. 66, page 267 and 270, in relation to Estates in Dower and Estates by the Courtesy, provides :

SEC. 1. That the widow of every deceased person, *shall* be entitled to dower, or the use during her natural life, of one-third part of all the lands whereof her husband was seized of an estate of inheritance *at any time* during the marriage, unless she is *lawfully* barred thereof "—and by

Sɛc. 21st. That, a woman being an alien, *shall* not on *that account* be barred of her dower; and *any* woman *residing out of the State*, shall be entitled to dower of the lands of her deceased husband, *lying in this State, of which her husband died seized*, and the same *may be assigned* to her or recovered by her, in like manner, as if she and her deceased husband had been residents within the State at the time of his death."

These provisions are not in conflict. They are parts of the same Statute; and, while the first section is general, re-cognizing the right of "the widow of *every* deceased person," whether resident or non-resident, to dower of *all* lands where-of her husband was seized *during marriage*; the 21st section cannot be fairly construed as restrictive of or limiting such right to any particular class of widows, or to a certain classi-fication of lands. For this section (the 21st) must be con-sidered in connection with the eight preceding sections, and as especially descriptive of those who *shall not be barred* of dower. The Statute declares elsewhere that dower may be barred by voluntary conveyance or jointure, and then, in *this* section further enacts, that an alien, "on *that* account *shall not* be barred;" and, that a non-resident widow *shall* have dower assigned her, of the lands of which her husband died seized, *in like manner*, as if she had been a resident within the State at the time of her husband's decease. But the Statute no where creates, *as to the right of the widow*, a distinction between lands aliened during the life-time of the husband, and lands of which he died seized: her right of dower, as to both the one and the other being clearly em-braced within the general provisions of the Statute.

The 21st section certainly does not confine the alien widow to such limitation; and it is not to be reasonably inferred as the intention of the Legislature, by the terms employed, to favor in this respect, the resident alien, more than the non-resident citizen. Wherefore should the Legislature establish a distinction between the resident and the non-resident, which in the same section is repudiated as between the alien and the resident ?　But, as provision is made in the 8th section, that, "When a widow is entitled to dower in lands, of which her husband died seized, and when her right of dower is not disputed, that she may have it assigned to her, in whatever counties the lands may lie by Judge of Probate of the county in which the estate is settled :" it would seem that this 21st section was alone intended to extend to the non-resident and alien widows, the same privilege with the resident, of having dower assigned and recovered, and not to deprive her of a right conferred by the contract of marriage, and not subsequently barred by any act on her part.　It is true, that the Statute speaks of "a married woman, residing *within the State* barring her dower by deed of conveyance" according to a specified form; and " *a woman*" *without* defining her residence, accepting a jointure before marriage in lieu of dower; and "a woman residing out of the State, having dower assigned," and also of " lands of which the husband *died seized,*" and lands held "during marriage ;" but, it is not perceived how this difference of phraseology, in the connection in which the same is employed, marks any distinction with reference to *whom* the right of dower pertains, or, as to the estate to which it shall apply.　The Legislature never intended that a non-resident widow, whose husband, during coverture, was seized of lands, and who sold the same without her consent, as required by the 13th section, should be barred of her right of dower, merely by the fact of her non-residence at the time of her husband's decease.　If such was the intention, it would make the existence of the right of every married woman to dower in her husband's lands, contingent upon his *continued residence* within the territorial limits of the State, defeat the beneficent policy of the law, by enabling him at all times capriciously to bar the wife's dower by a removal, and consequently make this sacred right of the widow dependent upon his will.　This would be inconsistent with the other provisions of the Statute, which most carefully protect the interest of the wife, whether resident or non-resident, and requires that where she joins in any conveyance of lands by her husband, the acknowldgement of the act shall be before some public functionary—under certain prescribed solemnities, and with the evidence of the act being voluntary and without the coersion of the husband.

This Statute, then, in providing that *"any woman residing out of the State shall be entitled to dower in the lands of which her husband died seized, and that the same may be assigned her as if she had been resident within the State,"* is not considered as restrictive of the right of a *non-resident* widow in the recovery of dower, or, as inhibiting the same as to lands sold during coverture.

But, giving the construction contended for by the defendant's counsel, and holding that a non-resident, under the Statute, is only entitled to dower in land of which her husband died seized—the facts presented by the verdict, are such as render this Statute inapplicable. The marriage occurred in 1810, seizen and alienation in 1816; the death of the husband in 1850. By the Common Law of England, the widow was entitled to be endowed of *all* lands and tenements, of which her husband was seized in fee simple or fee-tail at *any time* during coverture, and if the seizin was in the husband but for a single moment, the right of dower attached. *Cro. Eliz.* 503; *Coke, Litt.* 81.

No statutory provision of the late Territory of Michigan contravened this rule of property, and the Revised Statutes of the State of 1838 and 1846, expressly declare that every woman shall be entitled to her dower, as at common law. The ordinance of 1787 saves in *all* cases to the widow of an intestate the 3d part of the real estate for life, and declares "that the law relative to dower shall remain in full force, until altered by the Legislature."

As the law treats marriage in no other light than as a civil contract, between parties able and willing to contract, and although the husband and the wife are as *one* person as to many legal consequences of *their* union, yet, the latter is at *the time of the contract*, vested with a personal individual interest in her husband's real estate, which the law shields and protects for her exclusive benefit. This right is always implied, and in many ecclesiastical nuptial celebrations, it is expressed "*in totis verbis;*" "of all my worldly estate, I thee endow," cannot be considered as mere words of ceremony without substantial meaning. It is a right inchoate then at the time of marriage, suspended during coverture, yet untransferrable without her consent, attaching to the reality as a valid title of an estate for life, on the death of the husband, and can only be barred by her own act, and not by subsequent Legislative provisions.

But, the act of 1846, was not designed to operate retrospectively. Such a construction is apparent from its terms. The future tense is used throughout, wherever the right in the process to secure it, is indicated. The phrases "*shall* be entitled,"—"*shall* purchase lands during coverture,"—"*shall* be entitled to an election," &c., and phraseology of like *prospective* import, are the terms employed. And where there is no positive enactment, or, a clear, unavoidable inference of a retrospective intention, as in this statute of 1846; the rule of interpretation is adverse to a retroactive operation, especially where civil rights will be thereby affected. Such the doctrine of *Dark* v. *Vanklent,* 7 *John,* 477; *Given* v. *Marr,* 27 *Mann,* 112; *White* v. *White,* 5 *Barr,* 474; *Munday* v. *Munroe, Manning R.* 1, 369; *Sayre* v. *Wisener,* 8 *Wendell* 661. Not a word in this Statute applies to the past or affects in any way the right of dower, previously vested; and the repealing clause, at the close of the volume, expressly protects every right which had accrued antecedent to the adoption of this revised code of 1846.

But had such been the obvious intention, the law would

have been invalid; for this right of dower vests in the woman, whenever *marriage* and *seizure* combine. On this principle, and to avoid dower, must the woman join in the conveyance by her husband, and her joint execution of the deed as a voluntary act be made manifest on the instrument itself. If such a right was not a vested right, wherefore the necessity of the provisions in regard to barring dower? The wife's execution of the deed, separate and apart from her husband is for *some* purpose; it does, or does not transfer *a right*. If the latter, the act is an useless form; if the former, then the right was *vested* in her during coverture. 1 *Greenleaf's Cruise,* 198; *Kelly* v. *Harrison, 2 Johns, Cases;* 8 *Wend.* 661.

In *Kelly* v. *Harrison,* the Court in New York held, "that the right of dower was an inchoate right, and deemed so sacred, that no revolution or change of government could affect it."

From 1810, the period of her marriage, to 1816, when the estate was sold by her husband, the plaintiff was vested with this inchoate right of dower, and the property being transferred without her consent, this right remained suspended until the death of her husband in 1850. The law of 1846 could not, and did not design to interfere with a private right so vested. It is saved by the ordinance of 1787, and it is protected by the provisions of the existing Statute.

2. But, it is contended, that by the 7th section of the act of 1846, the plaintiff is only entitled to *dower,* to be assigned her according to the value of the lands in 1816, when they were aliened by her husband.

This section declares that, "When a widow shall be entitled to dower out of the lands, which shall have been aliened by the husband in his life time, and such lands shall have been enhanced in value after the alienation, *such lands shall be estimated* in setting out the widow's dower, *according* to their value *at the time when they were so aliened.*"

Now, whatever right was acquired by the marriage and

seisin, was certainly a right vested in the widow antecedent
to the statute of 1846, and could not, therefore, be affected by
any of its provisions. The Legislature could change the process by which the right was ascertained, such as directing the
mode of setting off dower, but could not curtail or diminish the
right itself. The title is to a life estate in one-third of the lands
of which the husband was seized. Such was the common law
title. And such was the title vested in the plaintiff in 1816. It
was not a right to one-third of an estimated value in dollars
and cents at any period, but an absolute right to the enjoy-
ment and possession of so much of the real estate, according
to quality, as should be set off by metes and bounds.

At common law, where improvements have been made by the
heir, or where the estate has been impaired in value by the heir
or tenant, the widow is endowed according to the value at the
time of the assignment of dower; because in the one case the
heir improves with a knowledge of the widow's right, and in
the other, the assignment being by metes and bounds, she
must resort, for the damages sustained, to another form of
action. *Coke, Litt.* 82 *a.* But should a feofee improve the
land, the widow shall only be endowed according to the value at
the *time of the feoffment,* and not according to the value when
dower is assigned; because the increased value is the consequence of the labor and expenditure of the feofee.

Whatever right existed in the widow, it was incohate, dormant and contingent during coverture, becoming only consummate on the death of the husband. It was a right that
could not be realized in any form, or be applied or attached
to the land, as long as the husband lived; and in case of her
prior death the right ceased, and could never attach. It had
then no *specific* appropriation when the property was aliened
in 1816, and none at any subsequent period up to 1850,
when the husband died; and she was then entitled to have
dower set off in the premises, and not before.

The jury find that in 1816 the farm was worth but $1,800;

that it has been improved by its various proprietors to the amount of $8,000, and is now worth $10,000, *inclusive* of these improvements.

Had the husband died before the statute of 1846, and the property had been so far enhanced in value from like improvements and the corresponding advance of the country around, the widow's dower *then* attaching, would, under the existing law, have been one-third set off by metes and bounds, exclusive of the improvements made by the vendees. She claims no more in this action. And if the law *then* allowed her this, as her right of dower, it may well be asked *can* the law of 1846, or rather *does* it impair or diminish it? But she does claim that the assignment of her dower, shall be with reference to the enhanced value of the land, arising from the circumstances of the gradual advance of the country in population and prosperity. To this she is entitled. Her right pertained and was incidental to the tenure of the land. She never parted with her right. It was connected and concurrent with the estate,—was even manifest in the chain of title, and as circumstances, independent of and uncontrolled by the present proprietor or his vendors, increased the value of the premises, there is no reason why she alone of those having a legal interest in the same, should not reap her share in the common blessing. To assign her dower according to the value of the lands when aliened, would be depriving her of the benefits in which all the inhabitants of the country, and especially landholders, have participated; and to allow her the advantage of the improvements made by the various vendees, would be giving her a share in the labors of others, made, to be sure, with a presumed knowledge that *their* chain of title was incomplete, (and allowed at common law,) but inconsistent with the settlement and advance of a new country, and consequently not recognized in the United States.

At common law the widow was not excluded from improvements of any kind, whether made by the heir or the vendee.

This has been authoritatively settled by Lord Dennean, in *Ridder* v. *Guinnel*, 41 *Eng. Com. Law*, 728.

In the United States a distinction is held in several of the States between improvements made by purchasers, and the natural rise in value of the property from other causes.

In Mass. the widow is not excluded from this casual advance.

In Powell *v.* Monson & Brimfield, Manufacturing Company, 3d Mason, (C. R. 347,) Mr. Justice Story, after a full review of the English and American cases, declares that the Common Law never excluded the widow from *any* improvements, and that, in the United States, she is only excluded from improvements actually made by the tenant or purchaser.

This learned Jurist was not aware, at the time he gave this able review of the English and American law, of the case, in 41st English Common Law just cited. He says, that "the doctrine that the widow was thus entitled to the value, at *the time her dower shall be assigned her*, stands upon solid principles and the general analogies of the law. If the land has, in the intermediate period between alienation and assignment, risen in value, the widow must receive the benefit; for, if it had depreciated, she must sustain the loss. *Her title* is consummate by her husband's death, and that title is, in the language of Lord Coke, '*to the quantity of the land*, viz: one-third part.'"

This case may well be considered the leading American case. In it, the Judge fully reviews *all* the preceding cases, and especially considers the cases of Humphrey & Finney, and Hale & James, in 2d and 6th Johnston, holding the contrary doctrine of "the value of the land at the time of the alienation."

In the first case, the Court based its opinion upon the statute of New York, (which, by express provision, restrained dower to the time of alienation), intimating at the same time, that such was the rule of the Common Law, and re-asserting the same views in the last case.

It is only necessary to observe, in support of the opinion of Mr. Justice Story, that since Chancellor Kent decided Hale *v.* James, in 6th Johns. Chan. cases, the Court of Queen's Bench, in Great Britain, has settled the controversy as to what was the Common Law of England, in Riddle *v.* Gwinnel, and the fact that there is no legal process known to the Common or to the Statute Law by which the value of improvements made is to be ascertained, strongly strengthens the view of the Common Law rule as given in third Mason.

Judge Story strongly approbates, as "high authority," the learned judgment of the Supreme Court of Pennsylvania, in Thompson *v.* Morrow, 5th Sarg't & Rowle, 290, and states that, had that case earlier fallen under his observation, he would have been spared the laborious research he had given to the question.

Most carefully was the point examined and considered by Judge Tilhman in Thompson & Morrow; tracing the Common Law to its source, searching through the year books from 1st Edward to the 8th Henry, and the ancient elementary works of Littleton and his massive Commentator, and leaving no preceding American case without a full examination. All the New York cases already alluded to were revised, and the rule adjudged to be "that the widow must be endowed, according to the value of the lands, at the time her dower shall be assigned her, exclusive of the improvements made by the purchaser."

The reasoning of the Judge applies to the facts in this case. I repeat his language; he says:

"Dower is a *right* favored both by Court of Law and Equity. A right founded on marriage, and marriage is so highly regarded as to constitute a valuable consideration for the settlement by jointure of property on the wife.

"Without jointure, the law gives to the wife, in case she survives her husband, one-third of his real estate seized during coverture for her life. It is inchoate at the marriage, and

28a

not consummate until the death of the husband. No act of
the husband can lessen or defeat this right; neither can she
be deprived of it, but by her own voluntary act, for which
the law makes many salutary provisions to prevent fraud and
coercion. Her dower is in *the land* as found when her title
is complete *at the death of her husband.* Where the husband
has aliened during coverture, and the aliene has improved,
in *this* country, she takes her third without estimating the
improvements, and this, for two reasons: 1st, because, had the
husband never aliened, the improvements might not have been
made, and, 2d, because a contrary admeasurement would
affect the prosperity of the country, and discourage improvements in building and agriculture."

Such is the clear language of the Court in this case, and
adopted by Judge Story. The subsequent Pennsylvania case
in 3d *Penson and Watt,* does not conflict, but is deemed in
direct affirmance of *Morrow* v. *Thompson.*

With the exception of New York and Virginia, wherever
the point has been raised, the same rule has been established
in the other States. Ohio, Maine, Kentucky, Delaware, Mississippi and Indiana, have maintained the doctrine as deduced
by Justices Story and Tilhman, so that it may be said, "that
the preponderance of authority is with the rule," that the
widow has her dower, according to the value of the lands,
when it is assigned. 6. *Ohio R.* 76, 2 *Harrington,* 336;
1. *Dana.* 348, 8 *Shipley,* 371; 28 *Maine,* 509, 3 *How. Miss.
R.* 860 ; 5 *Black,* 406.

The cases in New York, have already been considered in
connection with the Pennsylvania and Massachusetts cases,
and the case in Virginia. 4 *Leigh,* 509, from its being the
opinion of a divided Court, and mainly founded upon a Statute, and the prior decisions in New York, is not of sufficient
authority to shake the well considered adjudications of *Powel*
v. *Monson and Brimfield,* manufacturing company, and
Thompson v. *Morrow.*

As this case is an ejectment for dower, and the judgment of the Court is moved upon the special verdict, that judgment must not only embrace the declaration of the rule, but the process by which the rule is to be enforced. The motion calls for judgment of dower in the premises demanded, and for the appointment by the Court of Commissioners to admeasure the same.

This appointment of commissioners is but a mode prescribed by the law of the State, of assigning the dower as declared by the judgment of the Court. It is properly the process of execution. And as a question of practice, must be settled by the existing rules of the Court.

By the 70th rule, the practice of this Court is governed by the revised Statutes of 1848, in all cases where no special provision is made; and these Statutes direct, Section 55, page 479, that, § "If an action be brought to recover the dower of any widow, which shall not have been admeasured to her, before the commencement of such action, instead of a writ of possession being issued, the Court upon the record of judgment, and upon the motion of the plaintiff, shall appoint three disinterested freeholders, as Commissioners to make the admeasurement of dower to plaintiff, out of the lands described in the record. And the said Commissioners shall proceed in like manner and with like obligations, as Commissioners appointed by a Judge of Probate, to set off dower and report their action to the Court for confirmation, &c., suppose such confirmation, a writ of possession, issues, &c."

These Commissioners inspect the premises, determine their value, and set off one-third of the same to the widow. So much, then, of the special verdict, as finds the value of the land in 1816, and in 1850, is immaterial as unnecessary. The issue, for the jury, was, whether or not the plaintiff was entitled to dower, and their finding the marriage, and seizure and death of husband, and demand of dower, comprehended their entire duty. It is for the Commissioners to admeasure the value of the premises.

Such was the judgment in 3d *Mason*, the N. S. Court, carrying into execution the process appointed by the Statute of the State. In that case it was decreed,

1st. That the widow should have her dower, exclusive of the increased value of the lands, arising from the improvements made by the alienee.

2d. Reasonable damages for the detention of dower, which (in the State ——) is a proceeding indicated by Statute. *Statute* 1838, 471, *and* 477.

3d. That the plaintiff recover legal costs, &c., and,

4th. That Commissioners be appointed to admeasure and report as soon as practicable, setting off the widow's dower by metes and bounds according to present value.

JUDGE M'CLEAN'S OPINION.

As I do not entirely agree to some of the views presented by my brother Judge in this case, I have thought proper to state, succinctly, my opinion.

This action is brought to recover dower in a tract of two hundred and seventeen acres of land near the city of Detroit.

A patent from the government to Antoine Shapeto, as appears by the county records of deeds, was offered in evidence. This was objected to as not the best evidence. The Court said, the original patent or a certified copy from the land office at Washington, was the best evidence, and that as the patent was not required to be recorded in the county where the land lies, a certified copy of it could not be received in evidence. But a confirmation of the title by Congress, on the report of Commissioners, as appears from the 1st vol. of American State papers, published under an act of Congress, was received as showing title in Shapeto.

A conveyance to Santabart from Shapeto, indorsed on the copy of the patent, was then offered in evidence. To this, objection was made for want of certainty as to the tract conveyed, but the Court held, that although the indorsement on

Phillis Johnston *v.* James A. Vandyke.

its face was defective in not describing the land, yet, by reference to the description of the land in the copy on which the indorsement was made, there was the requisite certainty, and the deed was admitted in evidence. A deed from Santabart to Jōhnston, the husband of the plaintiff, was then given in evidence.

The facts being submitted to the jury, it found the following verdict :

"That the said George Johnston was married to the plaintiff in the year 1810; that they lived on the farm in question for one or two years, about the year 1810; that said George Johnston was seized of the property in question on the 24th of September, 1816, until the 28th of October, 1816 : that he then sold and conveyed the same to Stephen Mack, and that the defendant now owns the same by mesne conveyances from said Mack ; that said Johnston and wife, about the year 1820, removed and settled at Green Bay, then in the Territory of Michigan, but now in the State of Wisconsin, where they remained until 1850, when said Johnston died; that the plaintiff removed to this State in the fall of 1853; that the said farm at the time of alienation was worth the sum of eighteen hundred dollars, and is now worth, embracing the improvements made since said alienation, the sum of forty thousand dollars, and that said improvements, so made after alienation, as aforesaid, were worth eight thousand dollars; that said dower was demanded of defendant on the 1st of May, 1851, and also the 31st of March, 1851, according to the allegations in said declaration ; and under the facts aforesaid, so found, the jury submits to the Court, what judgment should be rendered on the verdict."

Should the plaintiff be entitled to dower, it becomes important to inquire to what extent she may claim. Does her right extend to the improvements made on the land by the purchaser, or is she limited to the value of the premises at the time her husband aliened; or is she entitled to the increased value of the land, excluding all improvements, at the time dower was demanded?

The decision of the Courts in the different States have not been uniform on this subject. In some instances the statutes adopted may have influenced the decisions referred to, but in others the differences seem to arise from views of the common law, and the notions of policy which were entertained.

In New York, in the case of Dorchester *v.* Coventry, 11 John., Rep. 510, the Court laid down the rule without qualification, that the dower of the widow was limited to the value of the land at the time of the alienation, though it had risen greatly in value afterwards, exclusive of buildings erected thereon by the alienee. The same doctrine was sanctioned afterwards in Shaw *v.* White, 13 John., Rep. 179; Walker *v.* Schuyler, 10 Ware, 480.

In Tod *v.* Baylor, 4 Leigh's Rep, 498, the Court of Appeals of Virginia held, that in equity as well as at law, the widow was to take for dower the lands according to the value at the time of alienation, and not at the time of the assignment of dower; and that she was not entitled to any advantage from enhancement of the value by improvements made by the alienee, or from general rise in value, or from any cause whatever.

Where the husband died, seized of the land, and the claim of the dower is made from the heirs, it would seem to be reasonable and just that the widow should have the proceeds or possession of one-third of the premises as improved. But where the estate by the deed of the husband passed into the hands of a purchaser, the dower cannot, in justice, extend to improvements made by him; but the claim should embrace the enhanced value of the land, exclusive of improvements made by the occupant. This increase of value arises from the general progress and improvement of the country, and applies to land unimproved. This is conformably to the principles of the common law, and is the rule adopted by the

Courts of most of the States. It appears to be the settled
rule in England, Massachusetts, Pennsylvania, Ohio, and
many other States. In the Queen's Bench, Doe. ex. dem. Riddle *v.* Gwinnell, 41 Com. Law. Rep. 728; Powell *v.* Monson &
Brimfield, Manufacturing Company, 8 Mason's C. C., Rep.
347; Thompson *v.* Morrow, 5 Sarg't. & Rowle's Rep. 289.
This is in accordance with the views of Chancellor Kent and
Professor Greenleaf; 4 Kent Com. 68, and notes 1 Greenleaf's cruise 193. The decisions in Ohio, Indiana, and other
States of the same import might be cited; but it is not
deemed necessary.

It is made a question in the case, whether the claim of
dower is governed by the revised acts of 1838 or 1846. If
the rule of decision be found in the former act, which gives
dower to the widow as at Common Law, in the lands of her
husband, and places upon the same footing persons who live
out of the State as those who live within it, there must be an
amount of dower under the rule above stated, and this is
claimed by the plaintiff.

The 21st section of the act of 1846 declares, "That a woman being an alien, shall not, on that account, be barred of
her dower, and any woman residing out of the State shall be
entitled to dower of the lands of her dec'sd. husband, lying in this
State, of which her husband died seized." The 24th and
25th sections of the same act define, to some extent, the
dower rights; but if the 21st section governs the case, there
can be no dower, as the husband lived in the State of Wisconsin at the time of his death, and was not seized of the
premises in controversy.

From the finding of the jury, it appears that George Johnston, the husband of the plaintiff, was seized of the premises
from the 24th of September, 1816, to the 28th of October
following, making one month and four days; that Johnston
sold the land to Mack, and about the year 1820, he removed
to Green Bay, with his family, then in the Territory of Michi-

gan, but which was afterwards included in the State of Wisconsin, where the husband died in 1850.

Two grounds are urged by the plaintiff's counsel, as showing the inapplicability of the act of 1846:

1st. It is said that law has not been adopted by any act of Congress, or by any rule of this Court.

2d. That the act of 1846, from its language, was not intended to operate retrospectively, and that if such were the intentions of the Legislature, this Court would not give effect to it.

The first objection is answered by saying, that the 21st section of the act of 1846 is not a rule of practice, but of property, and as such is obligatory on this Court, without adoption. The 34th section of the judiciary act of 1789 provides, "That the laws of the several States, except where the constitution, treaties or statutes of the United States shall otherwise provide, shall be regarded as rules of decisions in trials at Common Law in the Courts of the United States, in cases where they apply."

The second objection urged, if the right arises under the 21st section, is not without difficulty.

Dower existed under the Common Law, and to establish the right, it was necessary to show seizen of the husband, his marriage with the claimant, and his death. But almost all the States of the Union have regulated dower by statute.

It is not easy to define the right of dower before the death of the husband. In his commentaries, 4 vol., 50, Chancellor Kent says: "Dower is a title inchoate, and not consummate till the death of the husband; but it is an interest which attaches on the land as soon as there is the concurrence of marriage or seizen." Marriage without seizen would not create this right, nor would seizen without marriage create it. Both these must concur, to give the incipient right to dower. But still it is not only an inchoate right, but contingent. It depends upon the death of the husband. If he survive his wife, she has no right transmissible to her heirs, nor during

Phillis Johnston *v.* James A. Vandyke.

the life of her husband can she give it any form of property, to her advantage; nor even after the death of the husband, can she convey her dower, until it shall be assigned to her.

It is true the statute gives the wife an interest in the land of her husband, on the contingency that she shall survive him, and of which no act of the husband can divest her. But still it is not, in a proper sense, a vested right. So long as the husband shall live, it is only a right in legal contemplation, depending upon the good conduct of the wife and the death of the husband. Until the death of the husband, the right, if it may be called a right, is shadowy and fictitious, and, like all rights which are contingent, may never become vested. The marriage, seizen, and the death of the husband, must concur to create a right in the wife, which can be reached by any legal principle, for her protection.

And the question is argued, whether this right be of a character to place it beyond the reach of legitimate action.

If Johnston and wife had remained residents of Michigan until the death of the husband, the wife, it is admitted, would have had a right of dower in the land; but thirty years before the death of the husband, they removed to a remote part of the Territory, and which is beyond the State of Michigan, and for many years has been within the Territory or State of Wisconsin.

The 21st section of the act of 1846 so far modified the right of dower as to limit it to lands of those who live out of the State of Michigan, and who own lands within it, so as to require seizen in the husband at the time of his death. No objection is made to this law in regard to subsequent rights of dower, but it is earnestly contended it cannot operate in any case where marriage and seizen concurred before the law was passed.

There is nothing in the constitution of the United States which prohibits a State from passing a retrospective law. In Saterlee *v.* Matheson, 2 Peters, 380, it was held, that no part

of the constitution of the United States applies to a State
law, which divested rights vested by law. That was a case
in which, on an action of ejectment, the Supreme Court of
Pennsylvania held that the relation of landlord and tenant
could not exist between persons holding under a connectical
title in that State. The Legislature of Pennsylvania declared by an act, that such relation should be held to exist,
and the Supreme Court of Pennsylvania reversed their former decision, and held that the relation of landlord and tenant
did exist under the law. This case was taken to the Supreme
Court of the Union, which affirmed the judgment of the State
Court. Similar doctrines have often been advanced in the
Supreme Court.

The mode of relinquishing dower is provided for by Statute,
and varies in the different States. A statute of Pennsylvania declares valid all deeds made prior to September 1st,
1836, though the certificate of acknowledgment be defective.
A similar statute was passed in South Carolina, Purd Dix.,
205, both of which have been held valid by their respective
Courts. Retrospective laws have been passed in many of the
States, and in all cases, it is believed, effect has generally
been given to them where they did not impair the obligation
of contracts, and in some cases, as in the instance above
cited, these laws have modified vested rights.

I am aware of the impolicy and, indeed, danger of such
legislation, and I have been opposed to it, except where the acts
were more clearly just and related to the remedy. Where an
objection to such laws is made, it is necessary to consider
what effect must be given to them, as on that their validity
may depend.

But the decision of this point is unnecessary, as the repealing clause in the laws of 1846 provides that the acts repealed
by it "shall not affect any act done, or right accrued or established, or any proceeding, suit or prosecution had or commenced in any civil case previous to the time when such re-

peal shall take effect; but every such act, right and proceeding, shall remain as valid and effectual as if the provision so repealed had remained in force."

The concurrence of marriage and seizen, having taken place long prior to the law of 1846, those acts are within the reasoning, and of course, the right growing out of them are not affected by the repealing act.

The dower in this case will be in one-third of the land, exclusive of the improvements, whether it be assigned in the land or by an estimate of its annual rents.

Judgment for dower as estimated, and the appointment of Commissioners, &c.

THE UNITED STATES *v.* H. F. BACKUS.

A State regulation that the estates of deceased persons shall be settled in the Probate Court, which shall appoint commissioners to adjust the claims against the estate, and prescribe the time within which such claims must be presented, and if not presented, shall be barred, is not obligatory on the federal government, in the collection of its debts.

The amount claimed has been adjusted by the accounting department of the Government, and must be collected under its own laws.

It has a priority of claim, and cannot, therefore, do any injustice to general creditors by enforcing its claim. A law of a state, which gives eighteen months before suit can be brought against executors, does not apply to a demand by the Federal Government.

If the act could be so construed, it would be in conflict with acts of Congress, and would consequently be in operative.

Mr. *Hand, District Attorney* for plaintiffs.
Mr. *Backus*, for defendant.

OPINION OF THE COURT.

This action was brought against H. F. Bachus, James D. Doty, and Lindsey Ward, executors of Michael Drousman, deceased, to recover a balance due, from the estate of the deceased, as late Post Master at Mackinaw. These persons were appointed executors in the will of the deceased, and on the 11th of October, 1854, proof of the will was made in the Probate Court, and letters testamentary were granted.

By the act of Michigan, Revised laws of 1846, in relation to the payment of debts and legacies of deceased persons, page 290, it is provided that when letters testamentary are granted the Probate Court is required to appoint "two or more suitable persons to be commissioners, to receive and examine and adjust all claims and demands of persons against the deceased, except in cases where no debts exist, or the value of the estate, exclusive of the furniture, shall not exceed one hundred and fifty dollars." This amount is assigned to the widow, and in law is a final administration, and bars all claims against the estate. At the time of granting letters, the Probate Court is required to "allow such time as the circumstances of the case shall require for the creditors to present their claims to the commissioners for examination and allowance, which time shall not exceed eighteen months; and all creditors are required to present their claims for the action of the Commissioners within a limited time, or they shall be barred." The Commissioners allow or disallow the claims thus presented.

All cases pending against the deceased at the time of his death, the Statute requires to be presented against the executor for judgment, which when entered, shall be transmitted to the Probate Court, and the amount thereof shall be paid in the same manner as other claims duly allowed against the estate. Eighteen months were allowed by the Probate Court, for creditors to present their claims.

The writ was returned served on Backus, and non est as to the others; and the declaration was filed against Backus, the other defendants not being served.

The defendants pleaded the above Statute, and alleged that the defendants not served were citizens of Wisconsin, and it was also alleged that this writ was brought, before the time expired allowed by the Probate Court, to the Commissioners, for the adjustment of the claims against the estate, and that said Court, under the Statute, has exclusive jurisdiction over the estates of deceased persons, and that suit cannot be brought against the estate, until after the expiration of the time allowed, and in such form as the Statute authorized, &c.

To this plea the plaintiff's demurred.

The objection that two of the executors are citizens of Wisconsin, and consequently this action against the defendant is not sustainable, we think, is obviated by the provision of the act of February, 25th, 1839, which declares, "that the non joinder of parties, who are not found within the district, shall constitute no matter of abatement, or other objection to the suit." By the Statute, the judgment against the party served with process, shall not prejudice other parties. And we suppose that this provision applies as well to persons jointly liable as executors, as to any other joint liability. It is a well settled principle, that an executor is not liable to be sued, in any other jurisdiction than that under which the letters testamentary were granted. And if the suit must abate on the ground stated, the effect would be to defeat the demand of the Government.

The exclusive jurisdiction given to the Probate Court, in the settlement of decedents' estates, cannot affect the claims of the Government, however it may bear on private claims. The mode of proceeding in the Probate Court, and the time given for the settlement of accounts, cannot regulate the claims of the government, nor affect the remedies given to it under its own laws. The demand in this case has been adjusted by the accounting department, under the laws of Congress, and there can be no obligation to present the account for adjustment, to the Probate Court of Michigan. Such a rule of procedure, would subject the action of the Federal Government, to the regulation of a state Government.

The Federal Government being entitled to a priority over

James Lyell, a citizen of G. B. *v.* The Supervisors of Lapeer Co. Michigan.

other creditors, by the enforcement of its demand, no injustice is done to the general creditors. It could not have been contemplated by the Legislature of Michigan, that the law should apply to the General Government as a creditor. Such a construction of the act is not required from its language. It is true, there is no exception in it, but the exception necessarily arises from the nature of the case.

Executors are responsible under the laws of the State, but their liability attaches on the acceptance of the trust. The eighteen months given for the adjustment of accounts against the estate of the deceased, relates to the remedy, and cannot apply to a demand of the Federal Government. If the Statute could be so construed, it would be in conflict with the laws of Congress, and would be, consequently, inoperative.

The demurrer to the plea is sustained.

JAMES LYELL, A CITIZEN OF GREAT BRITAIN *v.* THE SUPERVISORS OF LAPEER COUNTY, MICHIGAN.

MOTION FOR A NEW TRIAL.

1. Counties are established by Law, and need not be proved.
2. The Revised Statutes of Michigan of 1846, page 70 and Section 40, providing, *"that the County Treasurer shall pay money on the order of the Board of Supervisors, countersigned by the Chairman and signed by the Clerk,"* an order in that form will be presumed to be correct, and the official act of the Board of Supervisors.
3. Such an order is a County liability, drawn by one County officer upon another, for payment out of County funds, and no presentment and demand and notice of dishonor necessary.
4. The Statute expressly authorizes such orders for County indebtment, to be drawn by the Board of County Supervisors, and does not provide that they may not be negotiable.
5. An action lies against the County upon such County orders in the U. S. Court, when the sum in controversy and the character of the parties confer jurisdiction.

Gray, Campbell and *Toms,* for plaintiff.
Hand and *Goodwin,* for defendant.

By Judge Wilkins.

This action was brought by the plaintiff, a subject of the Queen of Great Britain and Ireland, against "The Board of Supervisors of the County of Lapeer, on a County order described in the declaration as follows:

"$500 —— —— receivable for Taxes,——, No. 1089, Treasurer of Lapeer County, pay to G. Williams or bearer, $500. By order of the Board of Supervisors, with interest.

G. A. GRIFFIN, Chairman.

WM. BEECH, Clerk.

LAPEER, June 22, 1848."

During the trial a number of exceptions were taken to the rulings of the Court, and the questions raised form (with the principal objection as to the power of these County functionaries to grant such orders to County creditors,) the basis of the present motion.

The order having been produced and identified by the plaintiff, it was further proved that it was *in the form usually observed* by the various Boards of Supervisors of the organized Counties of the State, in the liquidation of County indebtment; and that the parties by whom it was executed, held, at the time, to the organized County of Lapeer, the official relation of chairman and clerk of the Board of Supervisors, which the paper represented, and that a demand was made by the bearer upon the Treasurer of the County for payment.

1. It was contended by the defendant's counsel that "the Board of Supervisors of Lapeer County" was not a corporation, and there was no evidence of such fact given to the jury.

The County of Lapeer was organized by a public law of the State, and therefore need not be proved. And by the Revised Statutes of 1846, each organized County is declared to be a body politic and corporate, with authority to contract debt for County purposes, and with liability to be sued on its

James Lyell. a citizen of G. B. *v.* The Supervisors of Lapeer Co., Michigan.

contracts. *Rev. Stat.* 62, *Sec.* 3. By a subsequent section, it is provided that "whenever any controversy or cause of action shall exist between any County and an individual, such proceedings shall be had in law or equity, as in other suits between individuals, and in all such suits, the name in which the County shall sue or be sued, shall be "The Board of Supervisors" of such "County."

These legislative provisions are not superceded by the 1st section of article 10 of the Constitution of 1850, which declares "that all suits and proceedings, by or against a County, shall be in the name *thereof*." It is certainly not to be reasonably supposed that the new Constitution, by this clause, restricts suits for or against Counties, to the political or geographical designation by which one County is territorially known from another. The law of 1846, in existence when this contract was made, employs the same language as designative of geographical bounds; and to carry into effect its provisions in relation to suits, directs *by name* the functionaries upon whom process is to be served.

A County is an empty name, for judicial purposes. It would serve no object to sue in that name, without further provision as to the functionary which should legally represent the County in Court. The legal name of the County is given by law, and that name or title is the Supervisors of said County. The Constitution leaves the old law in force. But if the objection was valid, it should have been pleaded in abatement, and the right name given. Great injustice would now be done by countenancing such an objection, after the case has progressed to an issue.

2. It is further urged that this Court has no jurisdiction in the cause, the defendant being a political body of the State, and not amenable to legal process in the United States Court.

By the *Revised Statutes* of 1846, *p.* 66, *Sec.* 2 and 7, it is provided that "the Board of Supervisors of each County shall have power to examine, settle and allow all accounts against

James Lyell, a citizen of G. B. *v.* The Supervisors of Lapeer Co., Michigan.

the County, and that all such accounts *shall* be presented to and be adjusted by the Board of Supervisors, who shall have power to direct the raising of such moneys by taxation, as shall be necessary to defray the County charges and expenses."

This provision, it is contended, gives to the Board of Supervisors the exclusive jurisdiction of all claims against the County, and even limits their subject matter to accounts and County charges for incidental expenses.

The County warrant upon which the suit is instituted, purports on its face, to be " by order of the Supervisors," and for an account settled and adjusted by them ; and consequently within the power conferred upon the Board " to examine, to settle and to allow:" It is drawn upon the Treasurer of the County, as the officer intrusted with the County funds. It is made payable *with interest,* forasmuch as the Board, knowing the pecuniary concerns of the County, and that its Treasury was *then* unable to meet the demand, thus "settled" the same, anticipating the exercise of the other power conferred—"the raising of the money by taxation."

The note described in the declaration, and introduced as part of the plaintiff's testimony, is properly termed *the evidence of the claim,* and of its allowance by the legal authority of the County. It is the custom of such organizations, when claims are allowed, to issue their orders on the treasury for *their* payment. The debt exists, independent of the order or warrant, and the form in which such instruments may be framed, does not affect the question of power.

The case of *Brady v. The Mayor & Aldermen of New York,* in 2 *Sanford,* so much relied upon, does not cover the facts of the case under consideration.

The Statutes of New York required that every claim should *first* be presented to the Board of Supervisors for audit, and consequently the Court held that as such had not been the

29a

fact, that the action did not accrue until after such presentation. Such was the principle of the decision. But here the
order for payment is evidence that the claim has been duly
presented, as required by the Statute, and properly allowed by
the competent authority. The Board has already acted on
the subject matter, and adjudicated the claim. Wherefore
the necessity of a re-presentment of this order to every new
Board as a County charge? The Treasurer must have funds
wherewith to pay, and if the Treasury be empty, it would be
but a repetition, *ad infinitum*, of the same matter for allowance and settlement. Such is not the requirement of the
Statute. Unquestionably, the matter of claim must first be
presented to the County Board for allowance and by it be settled; but when allowed and settled, and the claim assumes,
by the action of the County Board, the shape of a County warrant or order, it may, if unpaid from any cause, be the subject of a suit against the County.

The Statute having declared the organized Counties of the
State corporations for the purposes of suit, and conferred
upon them the power to contract debt, it follows that such
contracts may be enforced by suit. The rights of the contracting parties are reciprocal. If the County can sue, it can
be sued. And whatever remedies the State may bestow upon
its Counties to enforce their just claims, and whatever tribunals may be organized by State legislation for the determination of controversy between its own citizens and bodies
politic, yet such legislation cannot affect remedies conferred
upon others by the laws of the United States. It cannot
compel foreign suitors to select the tribunals of the State in
which alone to seek the recovery of their just demands; it
cannot deprive a party of a right of action secured to him by
the Constitution and laws of the United States.

The plaintiff, a foreigner, brings his action of assumpsit,
and specially declares upon the County order exhibited in
evidence, and it has been settled in the case of the *Bank of*

Columbia v. *Patterson Administrators*, 2 *Peters' Condensed*, 501, that assumpsit is the proper form of action. The claim having been allowed, the County *assumed* its payment, and gave to its creditor this evidence of their assumption.

It is unnecessary to consider the argument of the counsel in relation to the power of the United States Court to issue a *mandamus* to State officers, as the question does not necessarily arise. This Court is now asked for judgment upon the verdict. The proper enforcement of that judgment by the appropriate process, is another matter.

But the form deemed necessary by the supervisors, in framing their warrant upon the County Treasurer, has occupied other objections to this verdict upon the part of the defendant.

The order is numbered 1089, as a measure of precaution, by the clerk, and as a check upon the Treasurer. A declaration is prefixed, forming no part of the substance of the order itself, that it will be "*Receivable for Taxes.*" And the Treasurer is directed to pay the sum specified to a person named, "or to bearer."

Now it is contended that the case made by the plaintiff on such paper does not entitle him to recover, because the instrument on its face is *negotiable*, and the Statute conferring no such authority upon the Supervisors of the County; that it is a bill drawn by one set of County officers upon another County officer, and by the bearer ordered to be paid to the present holder; and that, being negotiable, there was no proof of acceptance or notice for non acceptance. The Statute meets all these objections. By its clearly expressed provisions, the Board of Supervisors are directed to meet annually in their respective Counties, to organize by the selection of one of their number as chairman. The County clerk is directed to serve as clerk of the Board, and to keep a record of its proceedings, to preserve and file all accounts audited and allowed, and to attest by his signature all orders of the Board on the Treasurer for the payment of money.

This Board, thus organized, are also expressly authorised "to *examine, settle* and *allow*" *all* accounts presented against the County, to direct the payment of the same by the necessary orders, and (in the language of the Statute law) "as it incidental may deem expedient."

This Board is also authorized to borrow money, not exceeding $15,000, for the erection of County buildings and bridges, and to provide for the payment of the same *with interest thereon.* It is also fully authorized to make provision for all the expenses of the County.

The Statute also provides that a County Treasurer shall be biennially elected, who shall have the custody of the moneys belonging to the County, from whatever source derived, and who is restricted in disbursing the same to the written or printed orders or drafts of the Board of Supervisors, signed by its clerk, and countersigned by its chairman.

No particular form of words in which these orders shall be framed, is anywhere prescribed in the Statute. Nor is the Board of Supervisors confined, in the negotiation of a loan of money for the purposes specified, to any particular record or evidence of the transaction. The clerk must make a record of it, and the Board can direct such further evidence of the same, as they may deem expedient, to be given to the capitalist loaning the County his money; and the same, when received, is directed to be placed in the County Treasury, subject to the drafts or orders of the Board of Supervisors, signed and countersigned by the clerk and chairman.

And when such orders are so granted, they import ability and fidelity in the auditing tribunal, which allowed the accounts on which they are based. It is not for the Court to go back of the order, in a case like the present, and inquire whether or not the Supervisors were deceived or misled,— whether or not they exceeded their power in borrowing more money than the law allowed. The order speaks for itself; and being under the sum of $2,000, the limit fixed by section

10th, over which a loan cannot be negotiated without special notice, it will be presumed that it was fair in its inception, and in its transfer to other parties, and was for a legitimate consideration. Fraud cannot be inferred from the face of the paper; and it is not consistent with the policy of the Statute, nor would it subserve any public purpose to sanction, without evidence of fraud, the repudiation by one County Board of the solemn acts of its predecessors.

The Board, having power to contract for certain purposes, "as may be deemed expedient, and having power to borrow money, it is within the spirit and scope of their authority, to issue—either in payment of adjusted accounts, or, as certificates or evidences of money loaned, such orders on the County Treasury, as that described in the declaration. And more especially where an account has been examined and allowed, is it competent for the Board to direct it to be paid by the Treasurer in such way as shall work no injustice to the County creditor, by affording him the power, in the form of the draft, to raise money upon it, should the County Treasury not be in sufficient funds at the time to liquidate the amount."

And, although the instrument is in mercantile form—" payable to order "—it is not mercantile currency, and subject to the mercantile law as to presentment and notice of dishonor. It is no more than a County order, made payable to bearer for the convenience of the County creditor, and correspondent with the existing exigency of the County Treasury. It is the evidence of a County liability, assumed by the appropriate functionaries; drawn by one County officer upon another, and calling for payment out of the County funds. On its face it is official, on its face it is notice to the County, and being outstanding, the evidence of its non-payment is of County Record. It is in effect, a bill, drawn by the County on itself, of which there need be no notice of dishonor. Notice is only required where knowledge is necessary to enable the drawer or indorser to take means for self-protection.

The principle does not apply where the drawer and drawee are identical.

In carrying out the provisions of the Statute, in relation to public buildings, or other necessary County improvements, (a Statute designed to meet the wants of a new County) it was necessary to clothe the Counties with authority to contract debt, and to anticipate the resources of future taxation. To induce emigration, roads must be made, bridges built, Court Houses and Jails erected, &c. The spirit of the Statute embraces the negotiation of loans upon the prospective value of the taxable property of the County.

Each organized County is required by law, at its own expense, to provide suitable Court Houses and Jails, and fireproof offices for public and private Records : and for these purposes money can be legally borrowed by the Supervisors. The history of the County shows, that newly organized Counties could not, without great oppression, respond to the demand of the Statute, and borrow money, for any purpose, without making provision for interest, and the immediate negotiability of their corporate evidences of indebtment.

The objection to this verdict on the ground that the Board of Supervisors could not lawfully make a negotiable order on the County Treasury, payable on demand to bearer, and with interest, is not considered sufficient.

The other reasons for a new trial are embraced within the view taken by the Court as to the extent of the official authority of the County Board. It does sufficiently appear, that the order or draft, upon which the action was instituted, was made by the statutory authority of the County legally expressed. The Statute provides, that the Treasurer shall pay such drafts, when signed and countersigned by chairman and clerk as required—there was evidence that G. Griffin was the reported Chairman, and William Beech was the reported Clerk, in the year 1848, of the Board of Supervisors of Lapeer County. If such was not the fact, the testimony could have been easily rebutted or overcome by higher proof within the power of the defendant, viz: the public Records of the County in *possession* of *defendant*.

JUDGE MCLEAN'S OPINION.

This case was taken under advisement at the last term, it having been tried by a jury at a previous term, before the District Judge, at which time certain questions of law were raised, with the view of having them adjudged by a full bench.

This action was brought on the following instrument;

$500, receivable for taxes, No. 1089. Treasurer of Lapeer County, pay to G. Williams or bearer, five hundred dollars, by order of the Board of Supervisors with interest. Lapeer, June 22d, 1848. Signed, Wm. Beech, Clerk, and G. A. Griffin, Chairman.

The declaration set forth this instrument specially, to which the general issue was pleaded, without affidavit. Afterwards an affidavit was filed, without application to the Court or notice to the plaintiff. Under the rules of Court, a copy of the declaration was served on the defendants, which was notice to them, and they have appeared. At the trial parol evidence was given of the signatures of the parties to the instrument, and that they acted in the capacities assumed.

It was objected that the defendants are not a corporation, and that on the trial there was no proof of that fact.

The Counties of a state are organized under a general law, of which the Court will take notice. There was, therefore, no proof on this point required.

It is also objected, that the action is misconceived, as the first section of the tenth article of the Constitution of 1850 declares, "that all suits or proceedings by or against a County, shall be in the name thereof." This, it is supposed, supercedes the 27th section of the revised law of 1846, page 65, which authorizes suits to be brought against a County, in

the name of the "Board of Supervisors." This would be
the case had a proper plea been filed, and had not the new
Constitution in the same section provided, that the existing
law should remain in force until changed.

It is also urged, to show a want of jurisdiction in this case,
"that the Board of Supervisors has exclusive jurisdiction of
the subject matter of this suit; and that the Statute requires
all demands against a County to be presented to and settled
by such Board. And the case of *Brady* v. *Supervisors of
New York*, 2 *Sand. Rep.* 460, is referred to as sustaining
the objection. That the Statutes of New York and Michigan are the same, that "all accounts against any County
shall be presented to and settled by the Board of Supervisors."

The decision referred to in Sandford was right, as it involved an open account, which had never been adjusted. But
that has no application to the case before us. The note, or
whatever it may be denominated, is an order by the Board of
Supervisors, on the Treasurer of the County for the payment
of five hundred dollars, with interest. This is, therefore, a
promise of payment of a debt acknowledged to be due.

The 82d section of the act which regulates proceedings
against Counties, declares, revised Statutes 1846, that when a
judgment shall be recovered against the Board of Supervisors,
&c., no execution shall be awarded or issued upon such judgment; but the same, unless reversed, shall be levied and collected as other County charges, &c.; and it is argued the
only mode by which this duty of the County officers can be
enforced is, by mandamus; and that as this Court cannot issue such a writ to a State officer, it can exercise no jurisdiction in the case. And the cases of *Kendall* v. *U. States*,
12 *Peters Rep.* 524 *and* 615; *McIntire* v. *Wood.* 2 *Cond.
Rep.* 588. Where it was held, that the power of the Circuit Courts of the United States'to issue the writ of mandamus is confined exclusively to those cases in which it may be
necessary to the exercise of their jurisdiction." And it was

held in the case of Kendall, that the jurisdiction of the Circuit Court of the United States for the District of Columbia, in this respect, under the law of Congress, was greater than the other Circuit Courts of the United States.

On the obtainment of a judgment, it is the duty of the Supervisors to levy a tax on the County and pay it. Now, the objection which is urged against the jurisdiction of this Court is, that the County officers in the present case may fail to do their duty, and this Court cannot coerce them by mandamus.   This is a presumption which cannot be entertained, as now urged, and consequently, the point need not be decided.

This Court, sitting within the State of Michigan, administers its laws, following in most instances, the remedies provided by the local laws.   Those remedies are adopted by acts of Congress, or by rule of Court, and they become, in effect, the laws of the United States.   And these laws are acted on by the Courts of the United States, under the construction given to them by the State Courts.

Under the Statute of the State, the Courts of the Union sustain a creditor's bill, and give effect to a new remedy created by Statute, where such remedy is appropriate to the exercise of a common law or chancery jurisdiction.   But the question as to the power of this Court to issue a mandamus in the present case, is not now before us, and need not be decided.

It may be that the remedy in the State Court may be more simple and more effectual than in this Court, but this is not a matter for our consideration.   The plaintiff having a right to sue in this Court, has sought his remedy here, and we can exercise no discretion in the case, which does not rest upon legal principles.   A verdict has been obtained by the plaintiff, and the question is now made, whether he shall realize the fruits of the verdict, or be thrown out of Court, and pay the costs which have accrued.

The objections to the form of the order, on which the action is brought, are not sustainable. It is evidence of indebtment by the County, and a peremptory order to the Treasurer to pay the amount. A Bank might as well say, when one of its notes is presented for payment, that it is no evidence of an obligation to pay, as for the Treasurer in this case to object. As the Supervisors have power to borrow money, a presumption may be raised that the order in question was given for money loaned, or in payment for labor, or some article of value received. It is evidence of indebtment which can only be set aside by showing fraud in the County officers, in which the plaintiff participated.

The want of power in the Supervisors to give such an instrument is alleged. The law gives them power to loan money, and have they no power to acknowledge the indebtment? Under such a restriction, they could hardly be expected to be successful borrowers. The powers of the Supervisors are ample under the Statute, and there is nothing in the case which shows that their powers were not strictly and legally exercised.

A demand on the Treasurer was proved on the trial. If the Treasurer had set up in his defense, that he had the means of payment in his hands, and was always ready to pay the order, it might show that the suit had been prematurely commenced. But as the order bears date seven years ago, it is not probable that the Treasurer has had the means of payment.

A County cannot claim the immunity of not being sued under the eleventh amendment of the Constitution. If every County could throw itself on its sovereignty, and hold at defiance the judicial power of the Union, we should have in the country more sovereignty than law.

It is again objected that the Supervisors have no power to contract to pay interest. They have the power to loan money, but no power, it is contended, to agree to pay interest.

This argument would have been stronger, had it rested on a usage not to pay interest, instead of a want of power to agree to pay it.

Upon the whole, I see nothing in this case, which authorizes us to set aside the verdict. A judgment is, therefore, rendered.

SUYDAM AND OTHERS *v.* TRUESDALE & KIBBE.

1. Leave to file a supplemental answer to a bill of foreclosure, based upon a fact which *was known to the party* at the time of the original answer, and which was not omitted through mistake, refused.

2. A supplemental answer must embrace new matter discovered after the putting in of the answer on file.

3. It is an application to the discretion of the Court, and will of course be denied, if it is apparent from the Record, that it was known to the party before his first answer.

4. The rule as to parties to proceedings in equity is not inflexible, and will not be enforced so as to work injustice.

Davidson & Holbrook for the motion,
Toms & Campbell for the complainants.

OPINION OF JUDGE WILKINS.

The motion which has been argued in this case, and been held under consideration by the Court, is made on the part of defendant Kibbe, and is for leave to file a supplement to his answer, and based upon his affidavit, setting forth that, at the time he filed his answer, "he had no notice or knowledge" of the matter now proposed to be introduced by way of amendment; or in addition to what he has already placed upon record as matter of defense.

A full understanding of the merits of the application requires a brief statement of the proceedings in the order of their occurrence.

The complainants filed their bill on the 18*th of April*, 1850, against Westley Truesdale and wife, to foreclose a mortgage, alleging therein that Augustus S. Porter was, by deed of assignment, a subsequent incumbrancer of the mortaged premises, with a prayer that he might be made a party.

On the *25th day of November*, 1850, the complainants filed their supplemental bill, exhibiting Terry & Kibbe as purchasers of the premises at an assignee's sale, on the 24th of July, 1850, for a mere nominal consideration, and making them parties. The bill was taken as confessed against Terry, and on the 8TH OF FEBRUARY, 1851, Kibbe filed his answer, and *four days after* filed a cross bill against the complainants and David M. Price and John Stephens, the statements of which, as appears by the bill itself, were sworn to by the said Kibbe as true on the 1st *day of February*, 1851, *eleven days* before the same was filed of record. In this bill, "he shows to the Court and charges the fact to be," that some time in the year 1850, the complainant in the original bill, viz: Suydam, Reed & Co., executed and delivered to John Stephens and David M. Price, a deed for the said mortgaged premises, and that they, the said Stephens & Price, were *then* in possession of the same.

EIGHT DAYS then, before he filed his answer, *Kibbe knew* that the mortgaged premises had been sold, and a deed executed and delivered therefor to Stephens and Price by the complainants, Suydam, Reed & Co. On the 20th day of October, 1851, more than eight months afer his answer had been filed, he makes his affidavit, on which he asks the Court for leave to file a supplemental answer, swearing as follows:

"That previous to the time said complainants filed their said supplemental bill, they sold all their right and title in the premises described in the bill of complainant to Price and Stephens, and that, *at the time*, the said deponent Kibbe filed his answer to said supplemental bill, he had *no notice or knowledge* of said Price and Stephens' title, and that *this* GROUND of defense, viz: the sale and conveyance to Stephens and Price, he, the said Kibbe, had no knowledge of till *some time after* his said answer had been filed."

Now, it is apparent, that the *sworn statement* in the cross bill,—*sworn to before the answer was filed*, showing that Price and Stephens were then in possession, and that the complainants, Suydam and Reed, had delivered them a deed therefor, *is a fact* directly antagonistic to the fact alleged in the affidavit of the 20th of October, "that *this* ground of defense, viz: the sale and conveyance to Stephens and Price," was not known to affiant until some time after his said answer had been filed, which said answer was filed on the 8th of February, 1851.

This self-contradiction in regard to the principal fact, on which the granting of the present motion must depend, leaves the Court in great uncertainty which statement to believe.

If we credit the oath of the 1st of Feb. 1851, then the matter of defense is *not new*, and was known before, and should have been incorporated in his answer, filed on the 8th, and if we grant his request upon what is sworn to *now*, it must be upon the ground that his former oath was a careless, if not a perilous one. For we are estopped from concluding that it was a *mistake*—the *very statement of the fact* shows his knowledge at the *time* of its existence. Leave to file.

A supplemental answer, as observed in Talmage *v.* Pell, is the proper course where a new matter of defense is discovered *after the putting* in of the answer, but which existed before; 9, Paige 413. But as the application is to the discretion of the Court, it is essential that the new matter of defense should have been recently discovered. If known before the answer was filed, the application will of course be refused, especially if the introduction of the new matter is calculated to embarass the further proceedings in the case, and is not essential as substantial matter of defense.

It is true that where the party has assigned, pendente lite, the whole of his interest in the subject matter of the suit, the adverse party can object that the suit has abated as to such assignor, and bar the proceedings, until the assignee is made a party, who has a right to be heard for the protection of his

interest. But such *adverse* party may, after he becomes acquainted with the fact of such assignment, *waive his privilege*
of objecting that the suit has abated in consequence of a
transfer of interest. Such was the conduct of the defendant
Kibbe, who makes this application; for, knowing as he did,
on the 1st of February, 1851, *this* matter of defense, he should
have inserted and relied upon it in his answer of the 8th, and
not doing so, he waived all objection to the suit proceeding.

Although Courts of Equity require all parties in interest to
be brought before them, in order that the controversy may
be finally settled, yet, the Court will not extend a ready ear
to such applications, when by doing so justice must be defeated, and by refusing the application, no injury can be done
to the defendants. In this case, the complainants, who are
citizens of New York, were, when their bill was fixed, the
sole parties in interest. The affidavit alleges the transfer
of that interest to individuals—who appear by the papers on
file, to be citizens of this State. The amendment proposed
then, is the introduction of matter, which would cause the
dismissal of the Bill, for want of jurisdiction. What just
end, then, is to be attained by making Stephens & Price parties complainant? If any interest is shewn in them, by the
affidavit, it is the same which is sought to be secured by the
decree now prayed for by the complainants, which must inure
to their benefit.

And how is the defendant profited? Does it enable him
to establish his defense—of fraud in Truesdale?

But, again, conceding the new matter as true, the mortgages sold pendente lite, and the interest of their vendees, is
comprehended within the interest represented by the complainants; and being one and identical, the decree of foreclosure, (if any is eventually rendered,) *is* a decree for *their*
benefit, and if the Bill be dismissed, for any or all the causes
shown in the answer of Kibbe—they, the assignees, having
no other title than that conferred by the complainants,

the controversy, as to the subject matter, is finally ended: which object is the spirit of the rule of the Supreme Court, as declared in Ellmendorf vs. Taylor, 10th Wheaton 152. A final decree can be made without affecting their rights. They are not active, but passive parties—they hold under complainants—who prosecute for their benefit. This rule as to parties in Equity is not inflexible, and will never be so rigorously enforced as to defeat its purpose and work iniquity. It is a discretionary rule, and the Court will consider its application to the circumstances of the case, and require or deny its enforcement according to its discretion.

But, again, the proposed amendment is chiefly technical in its character; it introduces no substantial matter of defense. The omission of other parties in supposed interest, whose rights may be affected by the decree, does not in this case impair the rights of those of Record; neither, under the showing of the affidavit, can it affect the interest of those who are not of Record; The policy of the rule, as given in Mandeville vs. Riggs, 2 *Pet.* 282, is, to prevent future litigation. The alleged transfer, then, to Stephens & Price, is not such substantial matter, without the consideration of which justice cannot be done to the parties litigant. If the proposed new matter was as to fraud, or, that the assignment was anterior to the mortgage, and that the latter was fraudulently obtained, or antedated, or that there never had been a mortgage *bona fide,* or, that it had in fact been paid: I should be disposed to grant the application; but, as it is, going not to the merits, but, to dismiss on purely technical considerations, I cannot, with satisfaction to my own conscience, grant the motion. Motion refused.

DWIGHT SCOTT vs. PROPELLER PLYMOUTH.

1. A steam Propeller, built by ship-builders at Cleveland, Ohio, under a contract with parties resident in Buffalo, New York: the former place is *her home* port until after her delivery and her first voyage.

2. Painting a vessel before her completion, and while still in the custody of the ship-builder, is work done at the home port, and creates no lien in favor of the painter on the vessel.

8. When the interest of a witness is balanced, his testimony is competent.

Libel filed for the recovery of a bill for painting the Propeller while lying in the port of Cleveland, Ohio. It appeared in the proofs that the Propeller was built by the firm of Lafronier & Stevenson, boat builders, Cleveland, under contract with George H. Bryant & Co., merchants, Buffalo, N. Y. That a considerable sum had been advanced, and the balance due satisfactorily adjusted before the delivery of the vessel, which formally took place in May, 1854, when she sailed on her first voyage to Buffalo, the libellant interposing no claim, and making no objection, although aware of the delivery of the vessel to Bryant & Co.

The libellant was a ship-painter, and was engaged, when he performed the work for the Plymouth, in painting other vessels in the ship-yard of Lafronier & Stevenson, with whom he kept a general account of work and cash payments.

The painting of the Plymouth was at the request of Lafronier & Stevenson, and amounted in all to about thirteen hundred dollars, upon which five hundred had been paid, and credited to Lafronier & Stevenson when the propeller was delivered to Bryant & Co. Subsequently, Lafronier & Stevenson failed in business, and the libelant institutes this action against the vessel for the balance due.

Miller & Campbell for Libellant.

Contended—1st. That there was a maritime lien, inasmuch as the owners resided in Buffalo, and the work was on *their vessel. There was no owner until the vessel was finished; and when finished, by the contract she was owned in a foreign port.* In support of this proposition, the Counsel cited: 3d *Kent Com.* 132 and 143; *Conklin Admiralty* 56; *Davies Reps.* 202; *9th Wheaton* 65.

2d. If the libellant had not a maritime lien for the painting, he acquired such lien under the local law of Ohio, which will be enforced in the United States Court. *Swan's Statutes of Ohio*, 185, 551; *Conklin's Admiralty*, 57; *2 Gallison*, 474; *1 Story*, 244; *1 Sumner*, 78; *Gilpin's Rep.*, 473.

3d. The allegations of the answer unsupported, because the testimony of Lafronier & Stevenson is incompetent, and should not be received.

Contra, Messrs. *Lathrop & Duffield*, who replied:

1st. That the ownership of the Plymouth, when the debt was contracted, was in Lafronier & Stevenson: Bryant & Co., having no interest until she was finished and delivered.

1. *Taunton*, 318, *Muchlow* v. *Munger*; 9 B. & C. 72, *Oldfield* v. *Low*; 5 B. & C. 857, *Simmons* v. *Swift*; 9 B. & C. 277, *Atkinson* v. *Bell*; 4 Ad. & E. *Clark* v. *Spence*; 2 *Mees & Welch*, 602, *Laidlow & Bell*, and *American Laws*; 4 *Rawle* 260; 7 *Johnst.* 473, 11 *Wendell*, 135; 6 *Pick.* 209; 9 *Pick.* 500.

2d. No lien given by the law of Ohio. *Jones* v. *The Commerce* 14*th Ohio*, 408.

3d. The interest of Lafronier & Stevenson balanced and therefore competent.

OPINION OF THE COURT.

1. Under the proofs submitted, the libellant acquired no maritime lien. His contract was with Lafronier & Stevenson, to whom alone he gave credit. Bryant & Co., had no property in the vessel until delivered; and the work, for which the suit is instituted, was performed by the libellant before the vessel was delivered. Cleveland was her home port, when in process of construction, and the fact that the libellant kept a general account with Lafronier & Stevenson for painting the various vessels built by them, and that he was engaged in painting other vessels at the same time with the Plymouth, shows, that he looked to them for his payments, and not to the future vessel.

Until completed, there was no vessel in existence on which a maritime lien could attach. The material man and his employer resided at Cleveland, and not until after her first voyage was her home port at Buffalo. So far, therefore, the libel sets forth a claim for work and materials, furnished at

30a

a home port, and, consequently, created no lien. *Abbot on Ship.* 143, Note.

2. No lien was given by the Statutes of Ohio. The Mechanics' Lien Law of that State, *Swan's Edition of Statutes*, Chap. 69, passed March 11, 1843, creating a lien in favor of mechanics, does not apply to this case, as the pre-requisite acts to perfect the lien, prescribed in the substitute for section 7th, have not been complied with. And the Statute of 1840, commonly called the Boat and Vessel Law, according to the construction of the Supreme Court of Ohio, gives no such lien. *Jones* v. *The Commerce*, 14 *Ohio*, 408.

3. Lafronier & Stevenson, under the circumstances, are considered by the Court as competent witnesses. Their interest, in this controversy, is balanced. They are answerable to the libellant for the amount claimed, should he fail in this suit; and should he recover—Bryant & Co., having paid for the Propeller according to contract, they would be obligated to refund them the amount recovered here. Libel dismissed.

UNITED STATES *v.* CHARLES PATTERSON.

1. In an indictment for embezzlement, under the post office law, it is sufficiently certain to charge "that defendant was a person employed in one of the departments of the Post Office Establishment of the United States."

2. When the embezzlement is of a letter containing a bank note, it is not necessary to describe the note.

3. In larceny such description is necessary.

4. The verdict being general, if one count is good, judgment will not be arrested.

George E. Hand, District Attorney.
Betham Duffield, Esq., for defendant.

BY JUDGE WILKINS.

The motion made to arrest the judgment in this case is founded principally on two reasons:—

1st. That the offense is not described in the indictment with sufficient cetainty and precision.

2d. That no offense is charged against the defendant in the last four counts.

1. The offense in the fifth count is described thus:—"That Charles Patterson, a person employed in one of the departments of the Post Office Establishment of the United States, a certain letter which came to the possession of him, the said Patterson, and which was intended to be˙ conveyed by post, and containing a bank note of great value, viz: of the value of $50, did then and there, with force and arms, feloniously embezzle," &c.

Stripped of the verbiage descriptive of time, place, and circumstance, and what is the charge here specified? Is it not "that Charles Patterson, employed as stated, embezzled a certain letter which came to his possession as deputy post master?"

The language employed is the language of the Statute creating and defining the offense, which is sufficient.

The time has gone by when the technical objections so ably urged in the argument, and for which there is so much authority in England and in our State tribunals, can be of any force in the courts of the United States.

The cases of the *United States* v. *Lancaster*, 2 *McLean*, 432, and the *United States* v. *Marlin*, 2 *McLean*, 254, cover the whole ground as to this objection; and certainly settles the law in the VII. Circuit until reversed by the Supreme Court.

And the cases of the *United States* v. *Mills*, 7 *Peters*, 142, and the *United States* v. *Gooding*, 12 *Wheaton*, 460, declare the law of the United States to be "that it is sufficient to charge the offense in the words of the Statute;" Mr. Justice Story intimating in the last case that any other description would be fatal.

If the offense was the simple larceny of a letter and bank note, indictable at common law, a description of the letter and of the note would have been necessary. But the offense is embezzlement, a criminal breach of trust, and that the thing embezzled was a bank note of a certain value, is but an aggravating circumstance, and the description of the same not held essential. And the form in *Arch.* 156, which was for the embezzlement, as clerk, of a bill of exchange, a particular description of the bill, other than its amount, is omitted. This objection is not sustained,

2dly, It is urged that it is not succinctly or grammatically charged that the defendant committed the offense.

Separating the 1st clause of the charging matter from the concluding part, and making two sentences instead of one, there is doubt and obscurity as to the offender; but, considering the whole as one continuous sentence, there can be no misunderstanding as to the party accused. The Court can reject the unnecessary word "*that*" as surplusage; as, in the case of *Rex* v. *Cooke*, 4th *Hargrave's State Trials*, the omission of the words "*et ipse idem Petrus Cooke*," which was not fatal. Consider the "Charles Patterson" in the first clause as the nominative case, and that he did embezzle the letter and money mentioned.

Charles Patterson is charged with being employed in the Post Office Department, and with embezzling a certain letter and bank note, which then and there came into his possession. The repetition of the nominative case, namely, "that he, the said Charles," did embezzle, might have saved the Court and the counsel an argument and research; but its omission does not make the charge so equivocal as to warrant the arrest of the judgment, and the consequent discharge of the accused.

It is clear, some intelligent being did the act, and equally clear that no other being is connected with the description of the offence than Charles Patterson, whose name is repeated twice in the sentence: once as being the person entrusted with the letter in question, and once as being employed in the Post Office at the time. To hold, judicially, that the indictment leaves it in doubt who is meant, would be grammatically straining words beyond their usual import. Some one mentioned *did* embezzle; who was it? Not White, for Patterson is described as his deputy, and "the deputy," or " the said Patterson," must be the nominative preceding, and giving signification to the verb.

But could I have sustained this objection, it would have been of little avail to the defendant. Here, as in the 1st objection, English and State authorities may be considered as fully sustaining the position of defendant's counsel, but the United States cases are the other way.

The verdict is general on an indictment containing seven counts, two of which are unquestionably good; but it is authoritatively ruled by Mr. Justice McLean in 3d McLean, 411, and by the Supreme Court of the United States, in 5th Wheaton, 184, (the case of Furlong and others), " that each count in an indictment is a distinct substantive charge, and that on a general verdict, if one be deemed bad, the judgment of the Court may be pronounced upon that count considered sufficient."

Here, the Court hold *all* the counts as sufficient, and only allude to those U. S. authorities in order to remark that where such exist, and are applicable, this Court will not regard as of any weight whatever, either the English or State decisions, and this intimation will supercede hereafter a laborious research, so commendable in counsel, but which must prove, eventually, labor lost.

Motion refused.

THOMAS BUTLER *v.* STEAMER ARROW.

1. When a receipt is introduced as evidence of the contract of affreightment, the whole document is in proof, and one part cannot be separated from the other in its judicial interpretation.

2. After the voyage had been completed, the Clerk of a Steamer sailing between Sandusky, Ohio, and Chatham, Canada, touching at Detroit and other intermediate ports, gives the following receipt to the owner of a horse lost between Detroit and Chatham.

" Received of T. B., three dollars for transporting horse from Sandusky to Chatham. One dollar for the steamer Ploughboy, and two dollars for the steamer Arrow. The horse (by consent,) transferred to the Ploughboy, October 30, 1852." Part evidence admitted to explain the receipt.

Clark, for libellants.

Campbell, for respondents.

JUDGE WILKINS.

The libellant alleges, that on the 30th of October, 1852, he shipped by the Arrow from Sandusky, Ohio, his horse, for the village of Chatham, in the Province of Canada West, for the sum of $3,00 then paid. That the steamer, then lying at Sandusky, through her Captain, then and there contracted with libellant to deliver the said horse to one John Davis at said village of Chatham, and that the said horse was never so conveyed or delivered.

The answer of the owner, fully denies this allegation, and the contract as exhibited and further shows, " That the steamboat was employed at the time alleged in running between Sandusky and Detroit, and no other route and no further than Detroit, and that the same was then *well known to libellant.* That the libellant at the time alleged, applied to the clerk of the steamer to receive on board a horse to be carried to Detroit, and there to be delivered to steamboat Ploughboy, (a boat running from Detroit to Chatham), to be conveyed to Chatham. That the clerk of the Arrow agreed to receive said horse, convey him to Detroit, and there deliver him to said steamer Ploughboy, to be conveyed to Chatham. That the said libellant paid to the clerk, the sum of two dollars, for the transportation of the horse to Detroit, and also the further sum of one dollar to be paid to the Ploughboy, for conveying the horse from Detroit to Chatham. That the said horse was conveyed to Detroit on the Steamer Arrow, and by the mate thereof, placed on the Ploughboy shortly after her arrival at the wharf, and the one dollar paid for the transportation to Chatham as directed."

The libellant claims the value of the horse which was lost from the Ploughboy. The only proof brought to support the exhibits of the libel, is a receipt by the clerk of the Arrow, given to the libellant, *after* the voyage had been completed by the Arrow, and she had returned to Sandusky. That receipt reads as follows. "Received of Thomas Butler, $3,00, for transporting horse from Sandusky to Chatham, $1,00, for the Ploughboy, and $2,00 for the Arrow ; the horse by consent was put aboard the Ploughboy, October 30th, 1852."

This proof by no means establishes the contract of affreightment as exhibited in the libel. The contract set forth, was that the Arrow was to deliver the horse to one John Davis at Chatham. But here, part of the consideration is specified as being paid to *another* boat, and a statement that the horse was delivered to such other boat. The whole document and not a part, is in proof, and the one part cannot be separated from the other, in its judicial interpretation.

Without explanation it is ambiguous, the three dollars for the transportation to Chatham is subsequently divided between two vessels, and without proof that they ran in connection, this receipt would not be satisfactory to charge the Arrow, especially from the answer of the owner, which corresponds with the document, and with its closing declaration that "the horse was put on board the Ploughboy."

Without impinging upon the rule, then, that a written instrument cannot be modified by parol proof, we are necessarily compelled here to resort to the proof furnished by the claimant of the Arrow, and this completely sustains the defense.

1st. That the agreement was to deliver the horse at Detroit, and to the steamer Ploughboy, for conveyance to Chatham; and that such agreement was fully performed.

2d. That the route of the Arrow at the time of the alleged contract, *terminated* at Detroit, and that this was known to libellant.

3d. That the clerk of the Arrow, did not receive the whole consideration for the whole route as compensation to the Arrow, but only two dollars for the Arrow, and agreed to act as the agent of the libellant in paying the other dollar to the Ploughboy.

4th. That the Arrow under the circumstances is not answerable for the loss of the horse, sustained in consequence of the neglect of the Ploughboy. Libel Dismissed.

MOORE & FOOTE *v.* HENRY L. NEWBURY.

A receipt of payment by a note is not conclusive, but only a *prima facie* evidence of payment.

A clerk invested with general authority to collect debts, presented a bill for supplies which were furnished on the credit of the vessel, and the debtor, not denying the claim, said that he was not then able to pay. On a subsequent application, the clerk expressed his willingness to take a negotiable note, if a certain third person would join in the note, and said he would then give the debtor the time desired, but if this were rejected, he should be compelled to attach the vessel. The note was given, and a receipt given of "payment by note." The note was endorsed by libellants, cashed the same day, and not being paid at maturity, returned to them, and was now produced in Court and offered to be cancelled.

Held, that the original debt was not extinguished, and that the lien on the vessel was not waived or abandoned.

Alfred Russell, for libellants.
John S. Newberry, for respondent.

BY JUDGE WILKINS.

The clerk of the libellants, invested with a general authority to collect debts, presented a bill for the amount claimed, to the respondent, on the 22d of May last, 1854, and demanded payment. The respondent, not denying the accuracy of the account, stated that he was not able at the time to make payment. At a subsequent interview, the clerk renewed his application, expressed his willingness to take a negotiable note for the amount, if a certain individual, whom he named, would join in the same, and that *then* he would extend to the respondent the time desired, but that if this proposition was rejected, he would be compelled to attach the vessel.

The note indicated was procured by the respondent, received by the clerk, and the account adjusted by a receipt, given in this language:

"Received payment by note.
"MOORE & FOOTE,
"By G. F. BAGLEY, *Clerk.*"

This note, being endorsed by the libellants, was, on the same day, cashed at a broker's office, and not being paid at maturity, was returned to them; it is now exhibited in court, and offered to be cancelled.

This libel is exhibited on the original account. The answer alleges payment, and denies the existence of the maritime lien. Such being the facts, two questions are presented:

1st. Was the original debt extinguished by the note?

If not, 2dly. Does the transaction show an abandonment or waiver of the lien?

The Circuit Court for the United States, for this district, in *Allen* v. *King*, 4 *McLean*, 128, and in *Weed* v. *Snow*, 3 *McLean*, 265, has settled the law for this Court, namely, that a receipt of payment by note is not conclusive, but only *prima facie* evidence of the payment of the debt, and that such evidence may always be explained by other extraneous circumstances, showing the intention of the parties when the receipt was given, and that there was in fact no actual payment of the debt. This renders unnecessary the consideration of the conflicting decisions in other States. This Court will follow the rulings of the Circuit, as long as they are unreversed by the Supreme Court of the United States. Most of the cases cited were considered in *Allen* v. *King*, and there is nothing in this receipt which takes it out of the ruling in that case.

Here there is no proof of an agreement that the note should discharge the pre-existing debt, and no proof that it should not so operate. Our judgment must rest on the intention, as manifested by the conversation and conduct of the parties at the time. The receipt, unexplained, as in *DeGraff* v. *Moffat*, cited by the respondent's proctor, would have been conclusive.

The proofs exhibit these facts: The master was not able or not willing to pay when the account was first presented. He did not contest the sum due. But he wanted time as a convenience to himself. The agent or clerk was willing to give time on certain conditions. With this spirit of accommodation the note in question was procured and received. The statement of the clerk, that unless the proposed arrangement was acceded to, the vessel should at once be attached, can, by no fair principle of construction, be held to signify his design to receive the note as absolute payment, and an extinguishment of the debt. Moreover, it appears that the agent was only authorized to collect debts. He had no power to exchange securities, especially a higher for one of less grade,—a security *in rem* for one merely *in personam*. Such power is not necessarily implied in a simple agency to collect. And certainly the cashing of the note by the broker was solely on the strength of the contract of endorsement. Had the intrinsic credit of the drawers been sufficient, the face of the obligation would have been otherwise.

Holding, therefore, that the note, independently, was not a satisfation of the debt, the only question remaining is,— Was the lien abandoned by the libellants' receiving the note, and thus recognizing the act of the clerk?

It is to be observed that, as the transaction took place in Chicago, the libellants did not, in fact, receive the note, but only the money raised by its discount, when it was too late for them to disavow or repudiate the transaction.

Where materials are furnished a vessel, the credit is given either to the owner, the captain, or to the ship, and the law creates the lien on the latter. Such lien, however, may be waived, either at the time the materials are furnished, or be abandoned by a subsequent agreement, expressed or implied, on the part of the creditor. He may, at his option, look to other security, and if so, no lien attaches to the ship.

In the case of *De Graff* v. *Moffatt*, so confidently relied upon, the contract, at the time it was entered into by the parties, *embraced a credit by the notes of the respondent.* After the libellant had closed his proofs, the respondent introduced in evidence a settlement between the parties—an account current in the handwriting of the libellant—in which sundry promissory notes were credited and admitted as cash. This account was balanced, and for the sum remaining due, a receipt in full was given, being expressed at the foot of the account as a payment by note, which was not produced or offered for cancellation. No evidence was introduced showing any understanding modifying or contradicting this receipt, and it was, of course, held, as in *Allen* v. *King*, *prima facie* evidence of payment. Besides, the original agreement, as shown by the account, certainly waived all lien upon the vessel.

Although a note under certain circumstances will not operate as an extinguishment of the debt, yet, when the creditor accompanies the act of receiving it in payment with the manifest *intention* to take it as his sole security, and not to look to the ship, such intention clearly expressed or certainly implied, operates as the abandonment of the lien which the law gave him. Such an intention was not manifested in this case. There was no understanding to release the vessel. It is true that she was not yet attached by process; and it is true that the clerk threatened it; but it is alike true that, at that interview between the clerk and the respondent, *all the latter wanted was further time to pay the debt.* The former wanted the money due; and under these circumstances the note was given and taken.

But if the note was not taken with the understanding that it was absolute payment, can it be inferred that it was received as additional security? If it was, it would not help the respondent's defense. He pleads payment, and relies upon a change of securities. The note was not a higher security than the ship. Why, then, collateral, or why a change? There can be but one answer. The note was received to raise the money at the time for the mutual accommodation of the clerk and the respondent, by placing the former in possession of funds which he *then* needed, and extended to the latter further time to meet an acknowledged obligation then due. This intention of the parties is too obvious to be disregarded or overlooked. The one did not receive the note in discharge of the lien; the other did not give it with such an understanding. The intention must govern. The note was to be payment, if paid at maturity; if unpaid, all the relations of the parties as to the vessel and the debt, remained unchanged. The circumstance, so ingeniously pressed, that the note was cashed, and the libellants thereby received the amount of the lien, (which then ceased and could not be revived,) does not materially vary the transaction, or exhibit a different intention. The note gave thirty days' time to the respondent. Until that time elapsed, the vessel could not be attached. Why? Certainly not because the debt was paid, or the lien waived, but because the note and its discount evidenced an understanding to await its maturity, and the default of the makers to meet it.

It was in proof that the note was discounted on the endorsement of the libellants. That it was never paid by the respondents, but by the former, fully appears by their present possession. The witness stated that the note was returned by the endorsees, who had cashed it in May last, and that the libellants were charged with the amount in their account current with the broker. In other words, the note, when due, was lifted by the libellants.

In cases of this description, the material man is not to be deprived of any of his remedies, except upon the most conclusive proof that exclusive credit has been given to other security than the owner, the master, or the ship. Looking to either of the former, to the exclusion of the latter, releases the lien, but must be clearly established. In no case will either be released, unless such was the manifest intention of the party. The maritime law guards, with most scrupulous care, its various subjects. The material man, the furnisher of supplies, and the mariner are equally protected.

That credit was originally extended to the vessel in this case, is not questioned. The schedule appended to the answer, reads:

"Steam Boat Fashion,
              "To MOORE & FOOTE, Dr.
"To merchandise rendered on account."

To this the receipt is attached upon which the defense is based. So that the lien was in existence and recognized the day the note was given. There is no proof that it was ever waived—no proof of an intention to waive it.

The Court was forcibly impressed during the hearing with the fact that the instrument was negotiable, and had been discounted, and that, therefore, as the libellants had received the money, their relation to the vessel had ceased. But the subsequent production of the note, and its tender for cancellation, removed all difficulty as to sustaining the lien. This note is not now outstanding. No innocent endorsee can be affected by the decree, nor can it be discovered how sustaining the libel on the principle stated will peril vessels hereafter by secret liens. The purchaser of a ship or any vessel afloat, purchases with a presumed knowledge of the existing legal responsibilities. The note and the lien cannot both be sustained. While the one is still current as cash, or outstanding, the other is without force or vitality; but if the former is itself dead and as waste paper, the legal existence of the latter is not impaired. Here the ship contracted the debt. That debt never has been paid. The note was but a promise to pay—a broken promise. It was made and accepted with the sole view to an extension of time. Certainly in this tribunal, as a Court of equity, the respondent cannot complain of being dealt with inequitably by a decree enforcing payment of the debt of the boat from the boat; a debt not denied either in its character or amount.

Decree for the entire claim and costs, and the cancellation of the note on payment of the decree.

FULLER ET. AL. vs. S. H. IVES ET. AL.

An individual may, *bona fide*, convey his property in trust for the benefit of his creditors.

But if previous to his assignment he has appropriated his funds, in the name of another, to delay and defraud his creditors, the Court will set aside the assignment, and his previous conveyances or fraudulent investments, and make them answerable to his creditors.

When an individual, having given acceptances to another with a view to his own indemnity, receives a large amount of property, which he applies to his own purposes, and leaves his acceptances unpaid, his acts are fraudulent.

Messrs. *Howard, Lockwood and Clark,* for plaintiffs.
Mr. *Walker* for defendants.

OPINION OF THE COURT.

This is a creditor's bill, which was filed the 3d of July, 1854, and which represented, that plaintiffs had obtained a judgment against defendants on which execution was issued and returned no property found. That Ives had fraudulently conveyed his property, so as to place it beyond the reach of his creditors. The assignment was made in the following terms—"Whereas, I, Stephen H. Ives, of Detroit, in the State of Michigan, being unable to pay my debts and liabilities, and being desirous of having all my property finally distributed among my creditors—Now, therefore, in consideration of one dollar to me in hand paid by Jno. S. Wright, of said Detroit, I do hereby transfer, assign and set over to said John S. Wright with all my property of every name and nature, real, personal and mixed, including bonds, notes and shares in actions of every kind, excepting only such property assigned as is by law expressly exempt from sale by execution, which property so assigned I shall hereafter more particularly describe in a schedule to be attached hereto, for the following purposes, viz: First, to pay all debts or demands due from me for personal and family expenses; all debts incurred by me since the 20th of February, 1854, including all fees and charges for services, retainers and expenses due or to become due to my counsel, and all expenses connected with my litigation with George W. Markham, and all debts due Cyrus W. Jackson, J. S. and N. H. Wright or either of them.

Second, to pay all my other creditors share and share alike.

Third, to pay over to me or my assigns any surplus; and the said John S. Wright is fully authorized to turn all of said property, as soon as it can reasonably be done; and is clothed with all necessary powers to effectuate and promptly to carry this trust into effect, and for this purpose to use my name or otherwise as may be most desirable."

It appears from the statement of Ives under oath, on his examination by the Master in Chancery, the 30th of August, 1854, that on the 1st July, 1854, he executed an assignment in the evening at Mr. Walker's office, in the presence only of Mr. Walker, his counsel, and he left the assignment with him and has not since seen it. That during the year previous to the assignment up to the 14th of February, 1854, he had been engaged in the banking and broker's business, under the firm of S. H. Ives & Co., and on that day the firm was dissolved.

He received from that firm for his good will, five thousand dollars. On the 20th of February he received a sum in a check on the bank for five thousand three hundred and five dollars, and near the same time a check for three hundred dollars. These sums balanced his account with the bank. He received on the 20th February, not included in the above, the sum of four thousand seven hundred dollars. C. & N. Ives gave defendant a draft or certificate for three thousand five hundred dollars; and a certificate of Indiana bank stock for fifteen hundred dollars. On the 1st of August, 1853, he received for his quarter profit in banking, nineteen hundred and sixty-three dollars—for the ensuing quarter six thousand two hundred and fifty-six dollars, and for the two succeeding quarters ten thousand seven hundred and eighty-seven dollars. And the defendant received from G. W. Markham some twenty-nine or thirty thousand dollars in merchandise. His acceptances for Markham amounted to about forty thousand dollars. These acceptances the defendant alleges were the cause of his failure, and compelled him to assign his property.

From the above exhibit of moneys and property received by the defendant, the necessity for his failure is not perceived. On account of Markham he could not have lost more than fifteen thousand dollars, in converting the merchandise he received from him into money and paying the full amount of his acceptances. This would allow five thousand dollars loss on the merchandise, which was estimated at the wholesale prices. And the moneys he received from other sources very much exceeded the sum of fifteen thousand dollars. But we do not rely on this estimate only, to show the fact and motive of his failure.

It does not appear that any part of the acceptances of Markham have been paid. Ives has received about thirty thousand dollars of merchandise and in addition a considerable amount of debts, for his indemnity, but he seems to have made some other appropriation of the means thus received, than the payment of the debts for which he was security. He being a banker in good standing, it is not to be doubted that it was in his power to have paid his acceptances, on a reasonable indulgence being given. But it does not appear that he proposed any adjustment to his creditors, or asked for any indulgence. But it does appear that he purchased a valuable real estate in Detroit in the name of a near connexion—the deed being made to this person. A valuable block of expensive buildings was constructed, which required a very large expenditure. His father-in-law, who received the deed, was shown to have been in limited circumstances, and wholly unable to buy the ground or build the block of buildings. The evidence is clear to show that the means were furnished by Ives in purchasing the ground and making the improvements.

The facts in the case, without going further into a detail of them, show satisfactorily to the Court, that the assignment of Ives was made to hinder and delay his creditors, and we feel bound to declare it to have been fraudulent under the Statute. The Court will direct a decree to this effect to be entered, and will refer the matter to a Master, &c.

31a

LYALL VS. MILLER & LITTLE, ADMINISTRATORS OF LITTLE.

A deed of trust, having been, *bona fide*, given to pay a debt of twenty
thousand dollars—surplus on sale by the trustee to be paid over—divests
the grantor of the title, so that his assignee in bankruptcy cannot maintain
an ejectment, nor can the purchasers under him bring an ejectment.

The claim of the bankrupt was limited to the surplus, if any, and this is
all that the purchaser under the bankrupt's assignee can claim.

Mr. *Holbrook* for plaintiff.
Mr. *Jay* for defendant.

OPINION OF THE COURT.

This is an action of ejectment. On the trial of the case a
verdict was found for the defendant, and a motion for a new
trial was made, on the ground that the District Judge charged
the Jury that the following instrument conveyed the estate
of Mackie to Eleanor Wood.

Mackie took the benefit of the bankrupt law in New York,
and the land in question was sold and conveyed by his assignee in bankruptcy. Under this deed the action of ejectment was brought.

"This indenture, this 10th of April, 1841, between John
F. Mackie of the first part, and Eleanor Wood of the second
part, witnesseth—Whereas, the said party of the first part is
indebted unto the said party of the second part in the sum of
twenty thousand dollars, which bond conditioned to pay the
same. Now, therefore, this indenture witnesseth that in order to pay the said sum of twenty thousand dollars, and in
consideration of one dollar to the said party of the first part
in hand paid by the party of the second part, at and before
&c, the said party of the first part, hath granted, bargained,
sold and assigned and made over, and by these presents doth
grant, bargain, sell, assign, transfer, and make over unto the
said party of the second part, her heirs and assigns forever,
all and singular, the lands, hereditaments and real estate of

him, the said party of the first part, in which he is interested
either in law or in equity, situate and being at Saginaw or
elsewhere, in the State of Michigan, and all the right, title
and interest of said party of the first part.

In trust, nevertheless, that the said party of the second part
shall proceed and sell and dispose of the herein granted and
assigned premises, at such time or times, in such manner and
on such terms, and for such prices, as in her discretion shall
be most advantageous for the parties interested therein, and out
of the proceeds pay and discharge the expenses of this trust
and the aforesaid indebtment of twenty thousand dollars, or
such and so much thereof as shall then remain due, and refund the balance or surplus of such proceeds to the said party
of the first part, his heirs or assigns.

And the said party of the first part hereby constitutes
and appoints the said party of the second part his true and
lawful attorney irrevocably in the premises, and authorizes
and empowers her to sell and dispose of at public or private
sale the above granted premises, and every part and parcel
thereof and to execute and deliver good and sufficient and valid
deeds and conveyances to the purchaser or purchasers," &c.

The District Judge, on the trial, held that the above instrument was a deed of trust, the fee being vested in the
trustee for the purposes specified, and, consequently, that the
plaintiff claiming under the sale of the assignee in bankruptcy,
was not vested with the legal title.

And we think the instruction to the Jury was correct. The
assignee, on the supposition that there was no fraud in the
deed of trust, could take under the assignment only the interest of the bankrupt, which was any surplus which might
remain, after the above debt was paid. If the deed of trust
were a mortgage, the suit of plaintiff could not be sustained,
as on failure to pay by the mortgagee he could not recover the
possession against the mortgager. But the deed is not

strictly a mortgage, but a deed of trust with power to sell, which is not affected by the bankruptcy of the grantor.

The motion for a new trial was properly refused. Judgment, &c.

JOHN JACKSON *v.* THE JULIA SMITH.

IN ADMIRALTY.

1. Where the possession of a vessel is not tortious, but, under color of right,—a contract of affreightment made with the Master, will bind the vessel.

2. Where the contract is violated the proper measure of damages is the value of the property at the place of shipment, with interest from that time, unless there be other damages connected with and proximate to the contract.

Mr. *Gray* for libellant.
Mr. *Lathrop* for claimant.

BY JUDGE WILKINS.

The libel and evidence in this case, exhibit a contract of affreightment, entered into at Chatham, Canada West, between the Libellant and the Vessel, on the *8th of June,* 1854, for the transportation and delivery of a quantity of tobacco, at Garden Island, near the Port of Kingston.

It is further shown, that the tobacco was duly shipped and that the vessel departed on her voyage,—but that it was not transported and delivered according to contract, having been intercepted at Detroit in consequence of the cargo having been landed at that place in supposed violation of the Revenue Laws of the United States.

Damages are claimed for the breach of contract in not delivering the cargo at Garden Island.

It is in proof, as matter of defense, that on the *9th of September*, 1853, one George S. Lester was the owner of the vessel; and that under contract of sale with one James Reeve of Canada, he then gave him the *exclusive possession* of the same, and that this exclusive possession continued in the said James Reeve until the 11*th of June*, 1854, three days subsequent to the contract of affreightment made with the libellant.

It is also in proof, that while the possession continued, the vessel was employed in the coasting trade between different ports in the Province of Canada, and that at the time the contract of affreightment was entered into, she was under the command and control of James Bruce, as Master, holding his appointment from the said Reeve. That when the tobacco was shipped at the Port of Chatham, Bruce, the Master, contracted, for a stipulated compensation, to deliver the same in good order to her consignees at her port of destination.

It is conceded that the contract of sale between Lester and Reeve was broken by the latter,—that the vessel was not paid for,—that in order to avoid being seized by Lester under process she kept in foreign waters, and that on the 11th of June, 1854, while lying at anchor in the British Channel of the Detroit River, she was forcibly brought into the jurisdiction of the State of Michigan, and Lester having sued out from the appropriate Court a writ of Replevin, she, *with her cargo*, was taken possession of by the Sheriff of Wayne County, and against the will of her Master was brought into the Port of Detroit and sold and delivered to the Respondent.

Her cargo was discharged at the wharf, and being seized by the Revenue officers of the United States, was sold and bought in by Lester, who alleges that he now holds the same subject to the order of the owners.

Under the circumstances disclosed, the possession of Reeve was not tortious. His neglect or refusal to carry out his contract with Lester, did not affect the character of his possession, especially as to third parties not privy thereto. He had possession with Lester's consent, and was therefore clothed with power to use her in trade as long as that possession continued. Bruce was her lawful master, and at the time of the contract of affreightment, rightfully represented and could bind the vessel.

It is not, as was contended, the case of a vessel stolen, or where the possession had been fraudulently obtained. She was delivered to Reeve at the time of the contract of sale, and his failure to fulfil his engagement did not make his possession unlawful *ab initio*, or vitiate the contracts of the vessel while the possession continued. Such a rule would be destructive of all maritime confidence, and place the shipper in a foreign port on inquiry as to title, which is not necessary, and would, in most cases, be impracticable. Ostensible ownership, with present undisputed possession, confers authority and is sufficient to bind the vessel. The rights of seamen and shippers cannot be affected by the unknown private contracts of other parties claiming interest in, or controverting her title. As long as she navigates and sails from port to port in the business of commerce, her captain speaks her voice and binds her by his contracts.

The cargo never having been delivered, the next question is,—What shall be the measure of damages?

Where goods regularly shipped are not delivered according to contract, the carrier is bound to make good to the shipper the actual loss which he has sustained; or, in other words, to place him in as good a position as he was, as to his property, when the contract was made. In this admeasurement of damages, the Court has nothing to do with the antecedent or subsequent relation which Lester bore to the vessel. The contract of affreightment was with the Julia Smith. Whether or not Lester had a right to retake the vessel, and whether the damages accrued in the exercise of a legal right, are not now subjects of consideration. The vessel is deemed responsible, and must make good to the libellant his loss consequent on the failure to perform the contract.

Making good the loss clearly embraces the value of the property shipped at the port of Chatham, at the time of the contract—there being no proof of loss consequent upon the non-delivery to the consignees at Castle Island.

The Court cannot go beyond this principle. The expense incurred by the libellant in visiting Detroit, in search of his property, and in the legal steps taken by him to recover the same, are not considered as proximate to the non-delivery at the port of destination. The landing of the goods without manifest was not the act of the vessel, and should not enhance the damages in this suit. Either the present owner or Reeve may be responsible for this expenditure in another form of action, but as it was not necessary for the libellant, who held the security of the vessel, to prosecute or defend, the damages in this procedure cannot include his expenses in endeavoring to recover the cargo.

It is decreed that the clerk take proofs as to the value of the cargo at Chatham on the 8th of June, 1854, which sum, with interest from that time is to be recovered from the vessel libelled.

FREDERICK W. BACKUS v. THE SCHOONER MARENGO.

A bill of lading is conclusive to establish the articles shipped, unless fraud or mistake be shown.

Such an instrument has some of the characteristics of a bill of exchange

Good faith in the agents of commerce is requisite.

Messrs. *Howard & Gray*, for plaintiffs.
Mr. *Holbrook* for respondents.

This is an appeal in Admiralty, from the District Court. A libel was filed by the plaintiff on a contract of affreightment of five thousand, seven hundred and ninety and forty-six hundreths bushels of wheat from the ports of Amherstburg and Colchester, in Canada, to Buffalo, for the consideration of two hundred and forty dollars.

The bill of lading, signed by the captain of the vessel, specified the above number of bushels, and which being received in good order was safely to be delivered at Buffalo.

The wheat received fell short of the quantity specified, at the port of delivery, seven hundred and sixty bushels.

The defence relied on is, that all the wheat received was delivered except about ten bushels, which, being wet, the consignee refused to receive.

The libellant on the bill of lading paid for the quantity specified.

The two witnesses who kept tally of the wheat received at Malden were sworn, and they agree in the quantity. And the amount of wheat received at Colchester was also sworn to, by the person who kept the tally at that place, and from these two ports the entire cargo was received.

In support of the defense the deposition of the Mate of the vessel was read, who stated that twelve hundred bushels of wheat were received at Malden, which he tallied; and that no account was taken of the quantity of wheat received at Colchester. He says that he nailed down the hatches and consequently, that no wheat could have been taken from the vessel until it arrived at Buffalo. The hatches, he says, were not raised until the vessel went under the elevators at Buffalo, to discharge her cargo. And he swears that all the wheat received was delivered at Buffalo; and he states the vessel could not carry more than five thousand one hundred bushels.

H. Rowell, a hand on board, confirms the statements of the mate, except that on another occasion, the vessel being filled to her utmost capacity, carried five thousand three hundred bushels.

Several witnesses on board the vessel corroborate, generally the statements of the above witnesses. The person who built the vessel stated that she was overhauled some years since and her capacity considerably enlarged.

It is clearly proved that the wheat delivered at Buffalo was carefully weighed and tallied. As the accounts agreed, kept by the witnesses, who were highly respectable men, there could have been no mistake. The Captain swore to the manifest, which contained a statement of the amount received at the two ports. And it is proved that he declared at Malden that he had engaged to transport six thousand bushels of wheat, and he should charge for the transportation of that amount.

It is clearly and satisfactorily proved that thirteen hundred and fifty-two bushels were delivered at Malden, instead of twelve hundred, as sworn to by the mate; and it is proved that the vessel instead of being two or three miles from the shore when loaded at the port of Colchester, as sworn to by the mate, was only about one-quarter of a mile from the land.

H. Reynolds, a colored man, who was cook, says, that he was on board the vessel the above trip, and that after she was unloaded at Buffalo she was taken into a canal or slip where witness saw that water, to the depth of about eighteen inches, had been in the hold of the vessel. There was a considerable amount of wheat in the vessel, but it being wet the consignees refused to receive it. This wheat covered the floor of the vessel, about eighteen inches deep.

There was some wheat sold after the schooner left the elevator. He heard the mate ask the captain what should be done with the wet wheat. At first he answered that he did not know; but afterwards he told the hands to throw it overboard. The next morning the crew threw a considerable part of the wet wheat overboard. They were engaged, the witness says, two or three hours in throwing the wheat overboard. A Dutchman came on board and offered to buy it, and he paid three dollars for the wet wheat that remained. This sale was sanctioned by the captain and mate. The captain was told that about eighty bushels were sold to the man. The hands were engaged in removing the wheat from seven in the morning to near twelve. The seams of the vessel were open and she leaked badly.

The bill of lading is an instrument of commerce. It possesses some of the qualities of a bill of exchange. It is considered as conclusive evidence of the cargo shipped, and cannot be contradicted unless fraud or mistake be shown. The purchase money was paid on the faith of this instrument, and no fraud or mistake is shown. The witnesses for the defence are so contradicted, in regard to the amount of the wheat shipped and delivered, as to render their testimony unworthy of credit. It is extraordinary that the mate and the hands on board should swear that all the wheat received into the vessel was delivered at Buffalo, when they were engaged for several hours in throwing the wet wheat overboard, and in selling some eighty bushels that remained. These facts were within the knowledge of the defendant's witnesses, while they swore that all the wheat received, was delivered.

The quantity of wheat shipped at Malden and also at Colchester is so clearly proved as to remove all doubt on the subject. And the deficiency is accounted for by the leakage of the vessel, the refusal of the consignees to receive the wet wheat, and the subsequent dispositon of it.

In all commercial transactions the strictest morality and truth should be observed. If these shall be disregarded, commerce will become a curse instead of a blessing. The richness of its products will be more than counterbalanced by the evils it will disseminate. Especially, when the sacredness of oaths shall be violated by the agents of commerce, it will destroy the confidence of high and honorable men, which is essential to commercial prosperity.

The decree of the District Court is affirmed with costs.

LEVI BUZZARD *v.* THE SCOW PETREL.

All vessels are required to use reasonable diligence to avoid collisions.

A vessel anchored in a river having a rapid current should keep a watch.

A sail vessel, in descending the river when there is no breeze, will be carried by the current, and will not obey the helm. In such case the vessel anchored in the current, by porting her helm, may avoid the floating vessel.

If no watch be kept, under such circumstances, by the anchored vessel, and a vessel descending the river floats against her, not being under the command of her helm, and her captain and crew by outcry endeavored to give notice to the crew of the anchored vessel, no damages for an injury done can be recovered.

Under such circumstances, the omission to station a watch on the anchored vessel, amounts to negligence.

Mr. *Miller*, for appellant.

Messrs. *Walker & Russel*, for the defendant.

OPINION OF THE COURT.

This is an appeal from the decree of the District Court in Admiralty.

The scow Petrel and her boats, tackle, apparel and furniture were attached on a libel filled by the plaintiff, as owner of the schooner Avenger, which is a vessel of more than twenty tons burthen, viz., seventy tons; that said schooner, being on a voyage from port St. Clair to the port of Detroit, had come to anchor on the St. Clair river below Newport, was carelessly and negligently run into and damaged by the scow Petrel, &c.

The collision is not controverted, though in the answer the manner of describing it in the libel is denied. It appears that the Avenger got under way from St. Clair, about dark, in December, 1852, being loaded with lumber, and drifted down the river to opposite the mouth of Belle river, where she came to an anchor, as the witnesses of the plaintiff say,

nearer to the American than the Canada shore; other witnesses considered her in the channel, very near the middle of
the river. It was a bright moonlight night. At about
twelve or one o'clock at night, the scow Petrel, in descending the river, struck the Avenger on the starboard bow, at
the cat head, her jib-boom entering between the foremast and
fore rigging of the schooner. The two vessels then dragged
down. The Avenger lost an eye bolt and a flying jib-boom,
guys, and one of her martingale back ropes; also, two
stanches, a chalk plate and a piece of her sail.

The captain of the scow came on board and wanted, as
some of the witnesses say, while others state differently, to cut
the rigging of the schooner, which the captain of the schooner
would not permit; but an anchor was thrown out astern.
The object was to bring the schooner's head round, but there
being no windlass, there was nothing to which the chain or
rope of the anchor could be fastened, which could resist the
force of the current, and the anchor, hawser and line were
lost. But the vessels were shortly afterward separated and
the scow sheared off.

The captain of the scow states that he was descending the
St. Clair river on the night of the collision, that he remained
on deck until between twelve and one o'clock, and seeing the
watch on deck, went below, where he had not been more than half
an hour when he heard one of the deck hands say that there was
a vessel down the river to leeward. The captain then came on
deck, and seeing that there was no wind, the man forward was
ordered to let go the anchor. When he left the deck, there
was a breeze sufficient to give steerage way, but when he returned to it, there was no wind. The anchor being let go,
they payed out twenty to twenty-five fathoms of chain. At
this time the Avenger was off from a quarter to a half mile.
Perceiving that the chain would not bring the Petrel up, the
captain got up on his vessel—loaded with lumber—so that he
could see the Avenger. He hallooed as loud as he could to

the men on board of the sloop to shift their helm. The scow was then drifting down the middle of the river.

Other men who were also forward continued to halloo to the men on the schooner to shift their helm. After the chain was all payed out, it was found the anchor would not hold the Petrel, it then being about a quarter of a mile from the Avenger. The hallooing was continued on board the Petrel until it was within a very few yards of the Avenger, and in the act of running into her. The mate of the Petrel was at this time on the deck and at the helm. The helm, in going down the river, was hard to port, to try and get the vessel to the American side, but there was not wind enough to allow her to mind the helm. When the jib-boom was nearly or quite over the Avenger, the captain saw a man jump out of the cabin of the Avenger and cry out there was a vessel running into them. Previous to this he had neither heard nor seen any one on the Avenger. At this time some four or five persons came out of the cabin. The scow struck the schooner on the starboard bow.

The supposition that there could have been a watch on the Avenger, is inconsistent with the facts as proved by several witnesses. If a watch had been asleep on the deck, he must have been wakened by the outcries of the persons on board the scow, as they approached the Avenger. No person was seen on deck until the moment of contact, which was too late to avoid the mischief. Had the helm of the schooner been shifted, it is urged, the scow would not have struck it.

The stress of the argument in behalf of the libellant is, that there was on board the scow a larger anchor, which, if it had been thrown, would have arrested the drifting of the vessel. Such an anchor was on board the scow, but the smaller one, it seems, was generally used, which was thrown. Whether this was negligence on the part of the commander of the Petrel, depends upon the circumstances under which he acted, and the degree of vigilance required by the colliding vessel.

Before this point is considered, it may be well to inquire what duties, if any, were imposed by usage or otherwise, on the anchored vessel. That the Avenger was in the channel of the river, is proved by the floating of the scow. For want of wind the scow refused to obey her helm; she therefore followed the course of the current and ran into the Avenger. The excuse of the captain of the schooner for not approaching nearer the American shore, was that the wind had lulled and the vessel could not be so directed. It was, therefore, anchored in the channel, and consequently subjected to greater danger from descending vessels, carried by the current. At the place of anchorage, the current ran at from six to seven miles an hour.

It is proved by experienced commanders and seamen well acquainted with the navigation of the St. Clair river, that what is called an anchor watch, is necessary when the vessel is anchored in the current. That when there is no current, such watch is not usual 'or necessary. And this usage is shown by a majority of the witnesses, and by those who are most experienced in the navigation of the river. The propriety of this usage appears from the occurrence under consideration. Had the Avenger been anchored out of the current, the collision could not have happened. The master of the schooner Fortune, in his deposition, says that a watch on board a vessel anchored in the current, is necessary for the "safety of the crew and of others navigating the river."

It seems that in descending the river, the captain of the Petrel was on deck, with others, until between twelve and one o'clock; that he then left the deck and went below, where he had not remained more than thirty minutes before he returned to the deck, having heard some one say there was a vessel ahead. He saw the vessel ahead to the leeward, at a distance of from a quarter to a half mile. He directed the bow anchor to be thrown, with the view to stop or retard the movement of his vessel. But the anchor dragged by the force of the current. Seeing this, the captain ascended to the highest part of his vessel, and by an outcry endeavored to arrest the attention of the persons on board the schooner. And as they approached the schooner, to the outcry of the captain, several of the crew joined in the request to shift the helm of the schooner. But there was no response made by those on board the schooner, nor were they apprised of the approach of the Petrel until she was in contact, when nothing to prevent the collision could be done.

From the known usage to keep an anchor watch, when a vessel is moored in the current of a river, the captain of the Petrel had a right to expect the usual watch was kept, and that the helm could be so shifted as to avoid the collision. With this presumed knowledge, the conduct of the Petrel must be examined. On approaching the Avenger, the captain, and mate, and some others, were on deck. The anchor which had been thrown must have retarded the vessel, but it was not under the command of the helm, and they expected by their outcries to arouse the crew of the Avenger, until they had approached too near to arrest the floating of the Petrel by casting the large anchor.

The rule is a reasonable one that the moving vessel is to avoid a collision. But this is founded on the supposition that the vessel is under the command of her helm. Where this is not the case, the reason of the rule fails, and the obligation imposed by it.

The officers and crew of the Avenger were all below, without a watch, and some of them, as stated, were about to retire. This showed great remissness in those who had charge of the schooner, especially as she was at anchor in the current of the river.

Reasonable care was required from the captain and crew of the Petrel to avoid the collision, and this they seemed to have exercised. An extraordinary effort, under ordinary circumstances, is not required. During the twenty minutes that the captain remained below, after midnight, the breeze subsided, which was felt when he left the deck, so that when he returned, on hearing there was a vessel ahead, the Petrel was floating on the current, and her direction could not be changed by her helm. On perceiving this the working anchor was cast and the chain paid out, and the outcry was made. This was at least reasonable diligence, and all that could be necessary for the safety of the schooner was, that her officers should also have used ordinary vigilance. Having failed to do this, her owner can have no claim against the Petrel for damages.

The judgment of the District Court is affirmed.

Dennison *v.* Larned.

A note with a blank indorsement authorizes the holder to receive the amount as the *prima facie* owner, and to sue the indorser by filling up the indorsement.

When the action is brought against the indorser by the indorsee, the action is maintainable in this Court, though the assignment was made by a citizen of Michigan to a citizen of New York.

Mr. Hand for the plaintiff.
Mr. Clark for defendant.

OPINION OF THE COURT.

This suit is brought on a note given by Roloefson to defendant, for the payment of fifteen hundred dollars at Lyell's bank, in Detroit. The note was not paid at maturity, and it was protested. It seems that the note was given for the accommodation of the defendant.

The note was the property of Stephens & Fields, who left it at Lyell's bank for collection; after protest it was returned to the holders. The note was then sold to plaintiff, with whom the firm'of Fields & Stephens do a large business in New York.

The defense is, that Fields & Stephens are still the owners of the note, and that it was handed over to the plaintiff to bring suit in this Court.

It was proved by Stephens, that this firm, having large dealings with the plaintiff, in New York, the note was assigned to him, and charged to his account.

This action being brought by the indorsee against the indorser, there can be no objection to the jurisdiction of this Court. The indorsement by Fields & Stephens was made by the defendant in blank when the note was handed to the bank for collection, as an authority to the bank to receive the proceeds. The note having been returned to the owners, they filled up the blank indorsement, to the plaintiff. This they had a right to do; or if the note was sold to the plaintiff with a blank indorsement, the plaintiff, being the holder of the note, had a right to fill the blank indorsement at any time during the trial or before it.

It is proved that the defendant applied to Stephens to intercede with the plaintiff for indulgence in the payment.

The jury found for the plaintiff. Judgment.

BARNARD & LOCKWOOD v. CONGER.

Where a person has agreed to deliver a quantity of lumber at specified prices, and he fails to comply with his contract, the plaintiff is entitled recover in damages the difference in price between the lumber contracted for, and the market price at the place of delivery.

If the market price at the place of delivery was as low, or lower, than the price agreed to be paid in the contract, the plaintiff will be entitled to no damages.

The rule is, that no damages can be recovered where none have been sustained.

Mr. *Clark* appeared for the plaintiffs.

Messrs. *Emmons & Jones* for defendant.

OPINION OF THE COURT.

This action is founded upon a contract for the delivery of five hundred thousand feet of lumber, at Albany, in New York, at certain prices stipulated, dated 19th of April, 1854; to be delivered the same year before the close of navigation. Of the first and second quality, the defendant was permitted to deliver, at the prices stated, as he might choose. Thirty-two dollars for the clear, per thousand feet, and twenty-four dollars for the second quality. Two hundred thousand feet of said lumber, which may be delivered, shall be counted at two dollars per thousand feet less than the prices above named, in consideration that the said Barnard & Son advanced to said Conger on the contract the sum of three thousand dollars, they charging interest on said advance from the payment, until the money shall be repaid by the delivery of that amount of lumber. The delivery to be made at the plaintiff's wharf in Albany.

It was proved that in the summer and fall of 1854, the market price of clear lumber was thirty-five dollars per thousand feet; twenty-seven dollars per thousand for the second quality. Other witnesses stated that in September and October, 1854, lumber sold, first quality for thirty-four dollars per thousand, and second quality for twenty-four dollars. Boat loads sold, at first quality, thirty-two dollars, second quality, from twenty-two to twenty-three dollars per thousand.

The Court instructed the Jury, that if lumber embraced by the contract was worth more in the market in Albany than the prices stipulated in the contract to be paid to the defendant at the period within which the lumber was to be delivered, the plaintiff was entitled to recover, by way of damages, the difference. But if the price of lumber in the Albany market was

F. W. Backus v. Schooner Marengo.

as low or lower than the prices agreed to be paid by the plaintiff, he suffered no damage by the failure of the defendant. If the plaintiff with the money in hand, could, in the market at Albany, purchase lumber at the same price that he had agreed to pay the defendant, he was entitled to no compensation, as he sustained no loss.

A sale of lumber in small quantities or by retail, will not fix the prices in the present case; nor would prices paid for a much larger amount than is named in the contract, fix the price. This would bring down the price too low, while the retail price would place it too high. The true rule will be found in such quantities as provided for in the contract, and if you shall find that a purchase could have been made by the plaintiff, at the time the defendant should have delivered the lumber, at the contract or a less price than that agreed to be paid, at the place of delivery, the plaintiff is entitled to no damages.

The three thousand dollars advanced, with the interest, it is understood will be satisfactorily arranged. The jury found a verdict for the defendant.

———

FREDERICK W. BACKUS v. SCHOONER MARENGO.

If the Appellant delay to perfect his appeal, so that the record is filed a very short time before the term of this Court, the Appellee may notice the cause for hearing or continue it, at his option.

No one should take advantage of his own remissness, to the prejudice of the other party.

Mr. *Holbrook* for appellants.

Mr. *Howard* for respondents.

OPINION OF THE COURT.

On the 6th of June last, the notice of appeal in this case

was entered in the District Court. The record was filed a day or two since, and a motion is now made by the Appellant to continue the cause.

The rule on this subject declares, " that eight days' notice of hearing on appeal shall in all cases be given, by the service thereof on the adverse party, or on his proctor.

" When an appeal from a decree in the District Court is interposed less than twenty days before the next stated session of this Court, the Appellee may, at his option, notice the cause for hearing at such session, on the first or either day thereof, or have the same continued to the next stated session.

" When an appeal from the decree of the District Court is interposed, twenty days before the next stated session of this Court, it may be noticed for hearing at such session by either party."

As this case was appealed within less than twenty days before this term, the appellee has a right to notice the cause for hearing on the first day of Court, or to continue it as he may prefer. This avoids delay and is just. If the appellant do not file the record in time, the other party may continue the cause. The motion for a continuance is overruled.

CHAPIN & BUTTS v. NORTON ET AL.

Under a contract made by the complainants with the defendants, the complainants agreed to purchase all the lumber sawed by the defendants on Grand river, on the terms specified, taking it at the mill and transporting it to Chicago, &c. Among other conditions, the complainants agreed to furnish supplies for the hands of the defendants, &c.; which, after about a year, they refused to do; on which the defendants abandoned the contract.

Where one party refuses to do a certain thing, under the contract, which was necessary to enable the other party to perform his part of the contract, he may abandon the contract.

And in such case the party first refusing, is liable to the other for damages.

But such damages must be limited to the immediate consequences resulting from the refusal to perform the contract, and cannot extend to probable profits which might have been realised if the contract had been carried out.

The party who abandoned the contract on the failure of the other party to perform in a material part, is not liable for damages.

A large quantity of the lumber being in possession of the defaulting party, it would seem that he, having repudiated the contract, cannot afterwards claim the benefit of the contract, in disposing of the lumber on hand. Under any circumstances he would be entitled to a reasonable compensation for selling the lumber.

In the process of a continuing contract, if accounts are received and adjusted without objection, it is too late to make an objection at the trial.

And where an inconvenience is suffered by the delay of the other party, notice should be given.

Messrs. *Willing & Gray* for complainants.

Mr. *Lathrop* for defendants.

OPINION OF THE COURT.

This is a bill in Chancery, in which the complainants ask the foreclosure of a mortgage.

On the 20th of February, 1850, the parties entered into an agreement substantially as follows :—The complainants are lumber merchants and reside in Chicago, and they entered into an agreement with the defendants, who owned a steam saw mill on Grand river, in the State of Michigan, and were engaged in sawing lumber, to purchase all the lumber that they should manufacture at their mill, for five years, on the following terms :

1. Five dollars per thousand feet was to be paid for merchantable ; two dollars fifty cents for culls, and one dollar per thousand for pine laths.

2. The complainants were to receive the lumber at the mill and sell it in Chicago, and in addition to the above prices, were to pay the defendants one-half the net profits.

3. They were to procure vessels to take the lumber from

the mill to Chicago, the amount to be ascertained by tally on delivery at Chicago.

4. The complainants were to furnish to the defendants all the supplies needed to carry on their mill.

5. The lumber to be paid for on the receipt of the price of sale.

6. For all moneys advanced by complainants, they were to receive interest at ten per cent.

7. The expense of the transportation and all other expenses of sale, &c., were to be deducted out of the proceeds, before the division of the profits.

8. At the close of each month an account of sales was to be rendered to the defendants, and at the close of the year a settlement was to be had.

At the date of the agreement, the complainants loaned to the defendants two thousand dollars and took from them a mortgage for the payment, with interest at ten per cent., in one and two years; and also conditioned for the repayment of all advances made under the contract, and also for the performance of the contract.

In November, 1851, the defendants refused to deliver any more lumber under the contract, alleging that the complainants had broken it by a refusal to furnish supplies.

In February, 1852, the defendants commenced an action at law against the complainants, in Ottaway county, to recover damages for the alleged breach of the contract. That suit, under the act of Congress, was removed to this Court, and is still pending.

In the fall of 1852 this bill was filed, to foreclose the mortgage.

The answer admits the execution of the mortgage, but alleges that complainants first violated the contract, which released the defendants from all obligation under it. And they claim damages from the complainants.

In order that the decision of this case may finally settle the controversy, it was agreed by both parties that the matter between them, arising under the contract, shall be finally settled in this suit, and a decree entered against either party as the Court shall decide.

The complainants claim the mortgage and interest, amounting to the sum of two thousand eight hundred and sixty-six dollars and sixty-six cents; and also a balance on the account current, including interest, amounting to the sum of one hundred and seventy-nine dollars and forty-seven cents. These items make the sum of three thousand forty-six dollars and thirteen cents. And a large amount is claimed as damages for the failure of the defendants to perform the contract.

The defendants claim damages from the complainants for breaking the contract, by refusing to furnish the necessary supplies, which compelled them to sell their lumber at a lower price than was stipulated in the contract, in order to continue their manufacture. And they allege that at the close of the fourth quarter, as appears by their own account, the complainants had on hand 578,122 feet of lumber, for which they have never accounted. And they say the interest and discounts have been regularly charged by them.

The expenses charged are, they aver, unreasonable, and ought not to be allowed. And in the answer damages are claimed for stopping their mill by an injunction, obtained by complainants. Breaches of contract are also set up, as a ground for damages, in not sending for the lumber in proper time, by which means large amounts of it were piled upon the wharf at the mill, which caused great inconvenience and damage to the defendants. The accuracy of the accounts rendered by the complainants are questioned, and damage was suffered by the defendants, it is averred, by the complainant's selling at a longer time than was agreed on.

Before the question of damages is considered, it is important to ascertain whether the complainants or defendants are responsible for breaking up the contract. On this point the evidence is clear. Every one acquainted with the business in which the defendants are engaged, must be aware that it requires a large expenditure. A large number of hands must be constantly employed in procuring the logs and bringing them to the mill, and in sawing the lumber. Teams and vehicles must be used in the business. All these must be supported and wages paid to the hands. It appears thirty-five hands were employed in the above business, and sometimes, it is supposed, a greater number. Supplies, it appears, could not be purchased at Grand River, nor its vicinity, and the nearest market where the necessary articles could be purchased was Chicago. These supplies consisted of provisions for the hands, food for the cattle, and several expensive articles used in running the mill. And in the agreement the complainants undertook to furnish these supplies. We see from the account rendered that in the course of a year they required a large expenditure.

From the nature of these supplies, the manufacture of lumber must stop if they were withheld. And, as appears from the evidence, they were withheld by the complainants. The pretence assigned was, that they had already made large advances under this head and could make no more. At this time, it appears, they had in their possession lumber that would more than cover the amount of the advances. And it also appears that large quantities of lumber were piled up at the mill, which it was their duty to remove. They must have known that withholding supplies at the beginning of winter, without notice, must stop the mill and greatly embarrass, if not ruin, the defendants.

From the evidence it appears, that the complainants were desirous, not only to get rid of the contract, but to possess themselves of the defendants' property. This motive was so often expressed to various persons at Chicago, and elsewhere, and so carried out by their acts that, reluctantly, we are brought to the conclusion that such was their intentention. And to bring out this result, the defendants were to be led on unsuspectingly by certain devices, so that the refusal to furnish supplies would be most injurious to the defendants and beneficial to the complainants. The facts proved, necessarily lead to this conclusion.

It is unnecessary to say, that in all contracts where certain things are to be done by the parties, a failure by one party will justify the other in abandoning the contract. But in a matter where the performance of the one party was necessary to enable the other party to perform, as in this case, the contract may be considered as abrogated.

This view settles the question against the complainants' claim for damages, by reason of the acts of the defendants. They must stand upon their mortgage and matters of account.

The complainants claim mortgage money and interest together, with a balance on account current of one hundred and forty-seven dollars and interest—the latter item may be affected by some other items in the account current, which are disputed. The other claims, except the one for interest, are cut off by the breach of the contract on their part.

In their answers the defendants claim damages on account of the injunction in this case, which necessarily suspended the operation of their mill, and the cutting or removing of timber from their lands. This was no doubt very injurious to their interests, but it was an injury for which no redress can be given. The suspension resulted from the allowance of the injunction; and although the complainants were active in procuring the writ, yet they are protected by the act of the Court. The counsel for the defense yields this point. Nor are the defendants entitled to damages for the reduction of the lumber received at Chicago, by the tally at that place. This claim is also very properly yielded by the defendants' counsel. The contract stipulates that the Chicago tally shall fix the amount of lumber received, and this amount must stand, unless a mistake or fraud shall be made to appear in taking it.

It seems to be usual at Chicago to make a deduction in the lumber for shrinkage, and several witnesses think the amount deducted on this account not greater than usual.

It does not appear that the charges of expense of the transportation of the lumber to Chicago, or in the tally and sale of it at that city, was objected to by defendants, when the monthly or quarterly accounts were rendered; and it is too late to raise the objection at the hearing, unless fraud or mistake can be shown.

On the 1st of December, 1851, it appears the complainants had on hand 738,508 feet of lumber, and 98,450 pieces of lath; and the defendants insist that as complainants refused to go on with the contract, by a failure to furnish supplies, they are not entitled to the advantage arising, under the contract, for the sale of this lumber. There is much force in this suggestion. But the complainants could not be required to sell the lumber, without a reasonable compensation. It would seem proper that, as the complainants refused to perform their part of the contract, so as to authorize an abandonment of it by the defendants, in regard to the lumber on hand, they could not go on under the contract. This point is not now finally decided, but reserved.

There can be but little doubt that the defendants are entitled to damages for the refusal of the complainants to furnish supplies. But these damages must be limited to the act of refusal, and the immediate consequences resulting therefrom. The injury cannot be extended to the profits arising from the contract, if it had been performed by the complainants. Such damages are remote and contingent. But the contract was abandoned by defendants, which, under the circumstances, would limit their claim, as stated.

The damages claimed on account of the large amount of

lumber which accumulated at the mill, covering the wharf to the great inconvenience and damage of the defendants, by reason of the complainants' neglect to remove it, might have constituted a ground for allowance had the complainants been notified of the fact and requested to remove it. But, without such notice, there seems to be no ground for an allowance. The loss by fire of sixty thousand feet of lumber, at the mill, cannot be charged to the complainants, or any part of it.

Interest is charged, in the current account, for payments made under the contract. If these payments were made in advance, the charge is a proper one; but if they were made on a sale of the lumber, as the contract required, no interest should be charged. The account current is not before me, but a succinct statement of items taken from the account. Without that account, a final decision is impracticable. Nothing more can be done than to require a report from a master on the items allowed to the defendants.

It appears from the briefs, that from the 20th of February to the 1st of May, 1852, no account of sales was rendered, but only a statement of the profits. This would be unsatisfactory, if the complainants shall be required to account for the sale of this lumber under the contract.

It is therefore ordered that the account current and all the evidence in this case, be referred to a master in chancery, who shall report at the ensuing term, on the claims for damages as above stated. And the master will specially report:

First. What would be the proceeds of the lumber on hand on the 1st December, 1851, at the current prices in Chicago, after allowing the usual per cent. for selling, the cost of transportation, and the money paid by the complainants under the contract.

Second. What amount of damages was sustained by the defendants, under the restrictions stated, for refusing to furnish supplies.

Third. What, if any, deductions should be made from the items of interest charged in the account current.

Fourth. Any items incorrectly charged in the account current, through mistake or otherwise.

YATES & WOODRUFF v. W. L. P. LITTLE AND WIFE.

Three persons having an interest in fifty lots in Saginaw city, they selected certain persons to appraise lots, and on this appraisement they made partition and executed quit claims. To the complainants were assigned lots one and two, with the warehouses and wharf, valued at seven thousand dollars. To the defendants was assigned lot three, with the wharf, at two hundred dollars.

The warehouse, after the papers were all executed, was found to extend twenty feet on lot three, which adjoined lot numbered two.

The warehouse was worth six thousand and five or six hundred dollars, it being divided into stores of thirty-three feet.

The defendants claim twenty feet of the warehouse on the lot three, from which the plaintiffs gave a quit claim, not supposing that any part of the warehouse was on it.

A bill was filed to correct the mistake, to which the defendants demurred.

The Court overruled the demurrer, holding that, under the circumstances stated in the bill, the mistake was a matter for equitable jurisdiction and relief.

Mr. *Holbrook*, for complainants.
Mr. *Campbell*, for defendants.

OPINION OF THE COURT.

This is a bill in chancery, which represents that the complainants owned three equal undivided fourth parts, and the defendant, William L. P. Little, was seized and possessed of one undivided fourth part of all the real estate in the city of Saginaw, known and commonly called the improved fifty lots. That the complainant Yates was entitled to two-fourths, and the complainant Woodruff to 'one-fourth; and to make an equitable partition of the lots in value, it was agreed between them that they should be appraised by Eleazer Jewett, Gardner D. Williams, and Charles L. Richmond, in regard to the above lots and other property, which embraced the interest of other parties. And on the 14th of September, 1848, the appraisers met at Saginaw city, and after viewing the premises and duly deliberating thereon, did determine on their report, in regard to the fifty lots as follows:—Lots one and two in block thirty, with the warehouse and wharf were worth seven thousand dollars; that lot number three, in the same block, with the wharf, was worth two hundred dollars; that lot number one in block thirty-five, vacant, was worth seventy-five dollars; that lot eleven, in block thirty-four, with dwelling house, was worth three hundred and fifty dollars; that lot seven, in block twenty-eight, and Richmond's store, were worth five hundred dollars; that lot eight, vacant, was worth sixty dollars; that lot nine, same block, with Cushway's house, was worth five hundred and sixty dollars; that lot ten, vacant, was worth sixty dollars; that lot six, in block eighteen, with the shoe shop on it, was worth one hundred and sixty dollars; that lots one, two, seven and eight, in block twenty-seven, with Webster's house and barn, were worth four thousand dollars; that lots three, four, five and six, vacant, were worth forty dollars each, one hundred and sixty dollars; that lots nine, ten and eleven, were worth two hundred and twenty-five dollars; that lot twelve, in the same block, with joiner's shop, was worth three hundred dollars; that lot seven, block thirty-two, with Little's office was worth one hundred and ninety dollars; that lots eight and nine, with Little's house, were worth thirteen hundred and eighty dollars; that lots one, two and three, in block one hundred and twenty-one, vacant, were worth seventy-five dollars; that twelve lots in block one hundred and sixty-six, were worth five hundred and thirty dollars; that south of Cape street, lots one, two, three and four, vacant, in block ten, were worth one hundred and ten dollars; that lots five, six, seven and eight, same block, were worth one hundred and sixty dollars; that lots three and four, in block seventeen, were worth sixty dollars.

After the partition, it was agreed that the fifty lots, so called, owned by the parties, have been partitioned, and it was further agreed that Messrs. Yates and Woodruff shall take, as their portion of the property, block numbered twenty-seven, entire, with all the buildings, improvements and appurtenances; also lots numbered one and two, in block numbered thirty, and lots numbered seven and eight, in block numbered twenty-eight, with the buildings and improvements thereon.

And W. L. P. Little agreed to quit claim unto the said Yates and Woodruff, all his right and interest above allotted to them as above. And the bill states that the above agreement was consummated, with a slight exception of a modification agreed to, as to the property which was to be released to the complainants, but not as to the appraisal, which remained the basis of the partition. On the 1st of May, 1849, the defendant executed a quit claim deed from the above property to the complainants; and they executed a like deed to the defendant for lot three, on block thirty, north of Cape street, together with other lots.

The complainants allege that the appraisement of lots one and two was made and accepted, under the belief that the warehouse stood wholly on those lots, and that lot numbered three was a vacant lot, with a wharf in front thereof, which was released by the complainant to the defendant at the valuation thereof; and the bill charges that such was the belief of the defendant. But the complainants allege they have since discovered that lots one and two extended only one hundred feet in front on the Saginaw river, and that the warehouse, which is a very commodious one, fronts on the river one hundred and twenty feet, being twenty feet on lot number three.

And the complainants say that until after the agreements

were all executed, the above discovery was not made; and since it has been made the complainants have tendered to the defendant the full value of the ground occupied by the warehouse on number three. That the warehouse, being divided into stores of thirty feet front, will be irreparably injured by cutting off twenty feet. That lot three was valued and conveyed to the defendant as a vacant lot, with a wharf in front. And the complainants pray, that relief may be given, and the mistake corrected, &c.

To the bill the defendant files a demurrer. And for cause of demurrer states, that complainants have made no case for relief; that they have not set out the deeds and writings, that the charges are not made specifically, and that the complainants have not offered to do equity, &c.

The case made in the bill is one of flagrant injustice, though it occurred, not by the contrivance of the defendant, but through the mistake of the appraisers and of the parties. Lots one and two, with warehouse and wharf, were valued at seven thousand dollars. Can any one suppose that one hundred feet only, of the warehouse was valued? Can any one doubt, that the entire warehouse and the ground on which it stood, with the wharf, were included in the valuation? The facts are so clear, looking at the face of the bill, in this respect, that no proof could be more satisfactory. By this mistake the defendant has got more than he was justly entitled to, and the question is whether he can conscientiously retain this advantage. Twenty feet of the warehouse, at the rate at which it was valued, not including the ground, could not be less than ten or eleven hundred dollars. And although the defendant has been applied to, he has refused to correct the mistake. His lot adjoining, with the wharf, was appraised at two hundred dollars, and the defendant received it at that price. And he has refused three hundred and fifty dollars for the twenty feet of lot, which would be within twenty-five dollars of the sum charged him for the entire lot.

This does not present a very favorable aspect of the defendant's case ; and yet he refuses to do justice, or, in other words, is determined to hold twenty feet of the warehouse, which is on his lot. And the question is, can he do so conscientiously.

The counsel for the defendant insist that he can, and that the complainants, by reason of their negligence are not entitled to relief.

It is insisted that the relief prayed cannot be given, as the appraisers were appointed by the parties, being judges of their own choosing, and that their decision cannot be set aside. The bill does not specially pray to have the award set aside, but for general relief, from the mistake in the partition, by the parties themselves, and the consequent injustice to the complainants.

A mistake of the arbitrators is a ground to set aside an award, and no mistake could be more palpable than the one committed in this case. Lots one and two, including the warehouse and wharf, were valued at seven thousand dollars, which, in the partition, were assigned to the plaintiff. Now these lots were not specifically valued, but as connected with the warehouse; and in this view, the appraisers estimated the value of twenty feet more ground than the lots one and two contained. And when to this ground is added, the twenty feet of the warehouse, both of which the defendant claims, instead of the vacant lot, as described and valued, it makes a clear case of injustice, that any Court, having the power, would, in some mode correct. To refuse this, on the ground that the plaintiffs had been negligent of their rights, under the circumstances, would be a mockery of justice. The injustice is so clear that it is matter of surprise, how the defendant should consent to take advantage of the mistake. And it is hoped for his own sake, that the allegations of the bill are not accurate.

If the conveyance had been executed for the ground in

front occupied by the warehouse, which would have taken twenty feet from lot numbered three; it would have given no more, in all probability, than was in the mind of the appraisers. And yet, under such circumstances, Chancery would have corrected the error, by making the proper deduction from lot number three.

The parties were misled and very naturally, by the report of the appraisers. In making partition and executing conveyances, they were governed by that report. They failed to do what the plaintiffs and defendant intended to do, and it is most unjust and inequitable for the defendant to claim the advantage, in the partition, which the mistake has given him. The mistake has chiefly arisen from the parties themselves, and although the mistake of the appraisers led to the thing that was done, the case is not more the error of the arbitrators, than the error of the parties. Suppose a party had agreed to purchase a certain tract of land, and through mistake a different tract was conveyed to him, would not this be corrected? Such a mistake often occurs in the conveyance of town lots. No honest man would hesitate to correct such an error, and a refusal to do so, would authorize a Court of Chancery to correct it.

Where an individual has been grossly negligent of his own rights, in some peculiar cases, Chancery will not relieve him; as where an individual fails to procure evidence in a trial at law which he might have procured, equity will not relieve him. But the case before us is not one of mere negligence within the meaning of the books. The plaintiffs were non-residents, as appears from the declaration, and this may account for the mistake in the partition, unless the contrary be shown.

Acts done through mistake, by principal or agent, are not binding. *Lessee of Hormer's Heirs* v. *Moore and Gwynne*, 1 *McLean's Reports*, 49. Mistakes and fraud are equally relievable in equity. *Dunlap* v. *Stetson*, 4 *Mason*, 249. A

33a

mistake of facts, going to the essence of the contract, avoids it. *Hammond* v. *Allen*, 2 *Sumner's Reports*, 887. A bargain, founded upon material misrepresentations of matters of fact, even though they were inadvertly made through the mutual mistake of the parties, or by mistake of the grantors alone, will be annulled in equity. *Daniell* v. *Mitchell*, 1 *Story*, 172. A mistake in the description of lands intended to be mortgaged, may be corrected in equity. *Bank of United States* v. *Piatt*, 5 *Ohio Reports*, 540; 1 *Ohio, Hunt* v. *Freeman*, 490.

In Story's Commentary on Equity, 1 vol. sec. 150, it is said: "In like manner, where the fact is equally unknown to both parties, or where each has equal or adequate means of information, or where the fact is doubtful from its own nature, in every such case, if the parties have acted with entire good faith, a court of equity will not interpose; for, in such cases, the equity is deemed equal between the parties; and when it is so, a court of equity is generally passive, and rarely exerts a jurisdiction. Thus, where there was a contract by A to sell to B for twenty pounds, such an allotment, as the commissioners under an inclosure act should make for him; and neither party, at the time, knew what the allotment would be, and were equally in the dark as to the value; the contract was held obligatory, although it turned out, upon the allotment, to be worth two hundred pounds." This turned upon the uncertainty of what the value of the allotment would be, and whether it was more or less, the contract was valid.

In section 151, it is said: "The general ground, upon which these distinctions proceed, is, that mistake or ignorance of facts in parties is a proper subject of relief, only when it constitutes a material ingredient in the contract of the parties, and disappoints their intentions by a mutual error; or where it is inconsistent with good faith, and proceeds from a violation of the obligations, which are imposed by law upon the conscience of either party."

And again, in section 152, the author says :-"One of the most common classes of cases, in which relief is sought in equity, on account of a mistake of facts, is that of written agreements, either executory or executed. Sometimes, by mistake, the written agreement contains less than the parties intended; sometimes it contains more; and sometimes it simply varies from their intent, by expressing something different in substance from the truth of that intent. In all such cases, if the mistake is clearly made out by proofs entirely satisfactory, equity will reform the contract, so as to make it conformable to the precise intent of the parties." *Durant* v. *Durant.*

In *Calverley* v. *Williams*, 1 *Verper*, 210, Lord Thurlow said: "No doubt, if one party thought he had purchased, *bona fide*, and the other party thought he had not sold, that is a ground to set aside the contract, that neither party may be damaged; as it is impossible to say, one shall be forced to give that price for part only, which he intended to give for the whole; or that the other shall be obliged to sell the whole for what he intended to be the price of part only. Upon the other hand, if both understood the whole was to be conveyed, it must be conveyed. But again, if neither understood so, if the buyer did not imagine he was buying any more than the seller imagined he was selling this part, then this pretence to have the whole conveyed, is as contrary to good faith upon his side, as the refusal to sell would be in the other case. The question is, does it appear to have been the common purpose of both to have conveyed this part."

The argument is, that relief cannot be given, as the Court cannot say what the appraisement would have been without the twenty feet. The answer to this is, that the partition was intended to be made on the estimated value of the parcels of property made by the appraisers, so that this objection is not insuperable. Lapse of time, and change of value in the property, is alleged in the argument; but this does not arise on the demurrer.

If it be admitted that no decree can be made against the wife of the defendant, on the final hearing, or before it, the Court can protect her interests.

Upon the above view of the case, the demurrer must be overruled.

CIRCUIT COURT OF THE UNITED STATES.

NORTHERN ILLINOIS—JULY TERM, 1855.

THE UNITED STATES v. THE RAILROAD BRIDGE COMPANY.

This case was argued before Judge McLean, at Chambers, at Washington City, in the spring of 1855; and the opinion was delivered at the Circuit Court of Northern Illinois, at the above term.

A military reserve may be abandoned by the Government, when it becomes useless for public purposes, and by giving notice through the Secretary of the Treasury, now the Secretary of the Interior, it may be considered as a part of the public lands, from which it was temporarily reserved.

Such lands having been surveyed and offered at public auction, may be open to entry as other lands.

The reserve on Rock Island, though surveyed, never having been offered for sale at public auction, does not come technically within the act of 1852, authorizing Railroad Companies to locate their roads through the lands of the United States. The act of 1819, authorizing the sale of military reserves, &c., which had become useless, embraced only those lands which had been reserved and become useless, at the time the above act was passed. The power given to the defendant to construct the road and build a bridge across the Mississippi, is not controverted.

In all the Western States, within which there have been public lands, it has been the uniform practice to make public roads through the lands of the United States.

This every State may do, under its power of eminent domain.

And this power is exercised by a State, subject to no power vested in the Federal Government. The proprietary right of the United States can in no respect restrict or modify this exercise of the sovereign power by a State

It is essential to the welfare of the citizens of the States, that this power should be exercised.

So far as easements by establishing public roads, are concerned, within a State, by its legislature, the jurisdiction is exclusive.

The power to regulate commerce among the States is vested in Congress, but the judicial power cannot act until Congress shall prescribe the rule in regard to commerce.

Where there is an obstruction to commerce which operates to the irreparable injury of an individual, the Court may act to prevent the injury.

This was the ground on which the jurisdiction was sustained against the Wheeling Bridge, at the instance of the State of Pennsylvania.

And in a similar case, relief could be given to the United States.

But the facts in regard to the injury done to the land on Rock Island, do not authorise such an interference.

If the amount of injury were to be considered, to the land on Rock Island as alleged, the benefits conferred would be as five to one.

The Bridges to be constructed over both branches of the Mississippi, at Rock Island, with the draws proposed, at the place selected, will not cause any appreciable obstruction to commerce.

The Bridge is thrown over a sluggish current more than half a mile below the rapids, which are only half the width of each of the two draws.

This is an application by the United States for an injunction against the Railroad and Bridge Company, to prevent them from constructing their railroad across Rock Island and bridges connected therewith, over both channels of the Mississippi river.

The case was ably argued by the Attorney General of the United States, and Mr. Hoyne, District Attorney for the Northern District of Illinois, for the complainants; and by Mr. Reverdy Johnson and Mr. Sargeant and Mr. Judd, on the part of the defendants.

The bill states that as early as 1812, the western extremity of Rock Island was occupied as a military post, called Fort Armstrong; that various buildings and fortifications were erected thereon by the United States, which were occupied for military purposes from 1816 to 1886, at which date it was evacuated by the troops of the United States, and ceased to be a military garrison.

In April, 1825, the island was reserved for military purposes by the Secretary of War, of which the Commissioner of the General Land Office was informed, and by him due notice was given to the register and receiver of the land office in which the reservation was situated.

By the order of the Secretary at War in 1835, the whole of Rock Island was reserved for military purposes, and the register and receiver of the land office at Galena, a new land district, which included the island, were duly notified by the commissioner of the general land office.

Since the troops were withdrawn from the island, it has been occupied, as the bill states, by the Indian Department, by the ordnance department, as a depot for arms, &c., and by agents of the quarter-master's department, for the protection of the property of the United States, up to the time of filing the bill. And the complainants allege, that the defendants have located their railroad over the island and by their agents have made large and deep excavations of earth and embankments, on the line of the road over the island, removing rocks and cutting timber, greatly to their injury and the injury of the soil, for which injuries no adequate remedy can be had by an action at law.

And the complainants also allege, that preparation has been made by the company for the construction of a bridge over the western channel of the river, which will materially obstruct the navigation of steamboats, many of which ply upon the river, several hundred miles above Rock Island; that steamboats, in carrying on a commerce on the river, frequently take boats or barges in tow on each side of them, which would require a much wider draw to pass down the river than the one proposed to be made in the bridge, and that it would at all times be difficult and dangerous, from the rapidity of the current, for a steamboat to pass through the draw. On these grounds substantially, and on the ground that the power to regulate commerce among the several States is vested in Congress, &c., an injunction is asked.

The defendants rely on two acts of the legislature of the State of Illinois, one dated in 1847, and the other in 1851, incorporating and authorizing them to locate a railroad, with one or two tracks, by the way of La Salle, from Chicago to the town of Rock Island, on the Mississippi river; and they allege that on the 17th day of January, 1853, the legislature of Illinois created the defendants a body corporate with power to build a railroad bridge across the Mississippi at or near Rock Island, or so much thereof as is within the State of Illinois, and to connect by railroad or otherwise, with any railroads in the States of Illinois or Iowa, in such manner as shall not materially interfere with or obstruct the navigation of the river, &c.

And the defendants set up the following report of the Secretary of War, dated the 30th of December, 1847:

Sir,—In compliance with a resolution of the Senate of the 22d instant, requiring the Secretary of War "to inform the Senate, if Fort Armstrong, on Rock Island, in the State of Illinois, is now occupied as a fort; and if not, how long the same has been abandoned, in whose charge the same is, and on what terms; and also that he communicate his opinion, if the interest of the government requires that said site should be reserved from sale for military purposes," I have the honor to transmit, herewith, reports from the adjutant general, the acting chief of ordnance, and the quarter-master general, containing the information desired; and to state that in my opinion, the interest of the government does not require that said site be longer reserved from sale for military purposes.

(Signed,)

WM. L. MARCY.

The adjutant general reported that Fort Armstrong, on Rock Island, was evacuated May 4th, 1836, in pursuance of general orders, No. 9, dated January 25th of the same year.

He says it was subsequently used by the ordnance department as a depot on a small scale for arms and munitions; but it is understood the stores were all removed some years since. Rock Island, he states, is not believed to be of any value for military purposes, and is considered as finally abandoned.

The quarter-master general reported "that Fort Armstrong is now in charge of his department; and that Thomas Drane is employed at a compensation of sixteen dollars per month to take care of it." It is of no further use to the public as a military site, and he recommended that it be transferred to the land department. The chief of ordnance reported that as far as regards the ordnance department, he considered the reserve no longer necessary for military purposes.

On the 11th of February, 1848, the Secretary of War enclosed the above report to the Secretary of the Treasury, and says, "that the site of Fort Armstrong is no longer required for military purposes, and it is therefore hereby relinquished and placed at the disposal of the department which has charge of the public lands."

(Signed,)

WM. L. MARCY.

A return of the survey of the land on Rock Island, as public lands are surveyed by the surveyor general, is in evidence.

Under the act of June the 14th, 1809, which authorized the President of the United States to erect such fortifications as may be necessary in his opinion for the protection of the northwestern frontier, Fort Armstrong was built. But the reserve was not made in form until 1825, as above stated.

By the Act 3d March, 1819, the Secretary of War was authorized, under the direction of the President, to cause to be sold such military sites belonging to the United States, as may have been found, or become, useless for military purposes. And the Secretary of War is thereby authorized, on the payment of the consideration agreed for, into the

Treasury of the United States, to make, execute and deliver all needful instruments for transferring the same in fee, and the jurisdiction over the reserve ceded by a State shall cease.

In 1850, the Secretary of War instructed the adjutant general to write to Col. Mason, directing the sale of the reservation on Rock Island, on terms most favorable to the United States. In three or four months afterwards a telegraphic despatch postponed the sale "until further orders."

By the Act of the 4th of August, 1852, the right of way was given to all rail and plank roads or macadamized turnpike companies, that were or might be chartered over and through any of the public lands of the United States, &c., with the following proviso: "That none of the foregoing provisions of this Act shall apply to, or authorize any rights in any lands of the United States, other than such as are held for private entry or sale, and such as are unsurveyed and not held for public use, by erection or improvement thereon."

The case involves several very important questions, some of which have not been heretofore raised for judicial consideration.

The suit is brought by the general government, not in its sovereign capacity, but for the protection of certain public public trusts committed to it, which require, as is supposed, the exercise of the judicial power. This is more in accordance with the principles of our government, than a resort to military force. The President, under exisiting laws may remove trespassers from the public lands, by a military order, or by a civil action, or an indictment.

Where a suit is brought by a State, or by the general government, it is subject to the forms of pleading and the rules of procedure applicable to suits between individuals; and wherever an injury is inflicted on the public rights protected by law, a remedy, civil or criminal, is given.

Congress has the exclusive power, under the constitution,

to regulate commerce between two or more States, and it is contended that, in virtue of this power, the complainants have a right to maintain this suit, on the ground that the bridge proposed to be constructed will be an obstruction to commerce, and this presents a new question.

The commercial power of the constitution is that which the federal government exercises in its sovereign and legislative capacity. It has regulated commerce on the Mississippi river and the other navigable rivers of the United States, so far as navigation by steamboats is concerned; and ports of delivery have been established. This regulation has extended on the Mississippi a great distance above Rock Island.

But this commercial power can only be exercised and carried out by legislation; and when this shall be done, any violation of the laws will subject the offenders to the penalties provided. The instrumentality of the judiciary can be invoked only by the government to give effect to its laws, civil or criminal, but the judicial power cannot precede that of legislation. The rule of action on all questions of policy, within the federal powers, must be prescribed by Congress.

There is no federal common law which pervades the Union, and constitutes a rule of judicial action. But in all the States the common law is in force, in a greater or less degree. Its existence and extent are shown by the Statutes of the States respectively, and the usages of the Courts. But there is no common law in regard to regulations of navigation. These must be adapted to the peculiar circumstances of a country, and the facilities which exist for traffic. In this respect, the legislation of Congress is the only remedy known to the constitution.

If it be admitted that the bridge would be an obstruction to the commerce of the Mississippi river, is there any power in the judiciary to remedy the evil? The commercial power is in Congress, but until it shall prescribe the rule, the power is dormant. Congress has power to punish the counterfeiting of the current coin of the Union, the violation of the mail, and many other acts, but, until the law shall fix the punishment, the Courts of the United States cannot punish.

Neither can a proceeding by indictment or information be instituted in the judicial courts of the Union, without statutory authority. The law of redress must be enacted before redress can be given. In this respect, as a suitor, the government occupies the same position as an individual or a corporation.

If there be an obstruction in or over a navigable water which injures private right, redress may be found by an action. On this ground the Supreme Court sustained the complaint of the State of Pennsylvania against the obstruction of the Wheeling bridge, because it was an injury to the line of transportation over its roads and canals, which it had constructed, and from which a revenue was derived. The State sued as an individual might have sued, on the ground of an injury, which, at common law, was irreparable. For such an injury the general government may obtain an injunction.

But no such special injury to the property of the government is alleged in this case, except as to the reserved land on Rock Island, which allegations will be hereafter examined. The power to regulate commerce is not property, nor is it in this view a subject of judicial action where it has not been exerted.

Under the commercial power, Congress may declare what shall constitute an obstruction or nuisance, by a general regulation, and provide for its abatement by indictment or information through the Attorney-General; but neither under this power, nor under the power to establish post roads, can Congress construct a bridge over a navigable water. This belongs to the local or State authority, within which the work is to be done. But this authority must be so exercised as not, materially, to conflict with the paramount power to regulate commerce.

If Congress can construct a bridge over a navigable water, under the power to regulate commerce or to establish post roads, on the same principle it may make turnpike or railroads throughout the entire country. The latter power has generally been considered as exhausted in the designation of roads on which the mails are to be transported; and the former by the regulation of commerce upon the high seas and upon our rivers and lakes. If these limitations are to be departed from, there can be no others, except the discretion of Congress. It is admitted, that in the regulation of commerce as a question of policy, the only limitation imposed by the constitution is, that no prefence can be given to a port in one State over those of another.

Was Rock Island a military reserve at the time the alleged trespass was committed? That it was reserved for military purposes in 1825 is clear. The Secretary of War, acting under the President, and by his authority, reserved it, and it was so entered on the books of the land offices at Edwardsville and Galena. And it was occupied as such until the year 1836, when it was abandonded as a military post; the troops were withdrawn, and sometime afterward the buildings were sold.

The abandonment of Rock Island as a military post, and for all public purposes, was as complete as its reservation had been, by all the public authorities by whom it was selected or used.

The suspension of the sale under the act of 1819 was ordered by Mr. Poinsett, Secretary of War, not because it was wanted for public purposes, but on the ground that the act did not authorize its sale. On the 8th of November, 1838, he wrote to the general land office that "the reservation would not be sold under the above act, and that it was left to the general land office to take such measures for the sale of the reservation as it may deem proper under exisiting laws."

In this view Mr. Poinsett was correct. The act referred to provided "That the Secretary be, and he is hereby autho. rised, under the direction of the President of the United States, to cause to be sold such military sites, belonging to then Uited States, as may have been found or become useless for military purposes." "And the Secretary of War," the act provides, "is hereby authorized, on the payment of the compensation agreed for, into the treasury of the United States," to execute a deed, &c.

This law, from its language, was not intended to be a general regulation; but authorised the sale of military reserves, which, at that time, had become useless. It changed the settled mode of selling public lands, as it authorized the Secretary to sell for a price agreed on, which precludes, or at least renders unnecessary a sale by public auction, as the general law for the sale of the public lands required. This consideration, as well as the purport of the section, showed that it was not a general regulation, but was intended to operate upon military reservations which then existed and which were unnecessary.

The Attorney-General contends that "the frequent interposition of Congress, especially authorising the sale of military reservations, negatives the idea that they could be sold without Statute authority."

When land has been purchased by the United States for military or other purposes, it is admitted the land cannot be sold without the special authority of Congress. In such cases the purchase is made for a specific object, and being purchased with the consent of the State, under the Federal Constitution, there is a cession of jurisdiction as well as of property. Now, to transfer property so acquired and relinquish the jurisdiction, the authority of Congress is indispensable. And this shows the reason why the act of the 28th of April, 1825, was passed. It provides in the first section, "that in all cases where lands have been, or shall hereafter be conveyed to or for the United States, for forts, arsenals, dock yards, light houses, or any like purpose, etc., which shall not be used as necessary for the purpose, for which they were purchased or other authorized purposes, it shall be lawful for the President of the United States, to cause the same to be sold for the best price to be obtained, and to convey the same by grant or otherwise."

Now, from this Act it does not follow, that where the government reserves its own land from sale, for any public purpose, that a special Act of Congress after its abandonment is necessary for the sale of it. The President, under a general power given him by the Act of 1809, selected a part of the land on Rock Island for a military site, on which Fort Armstrong was built. And when he finds the place no longer useful as a military post, or for any other public purpose, he has a right to abandon it, and notify the land offices where the reservation was entered. The entry on the books of the land offices within which the reserved site is situated, and the occupancy of the place by the government, are the only evidence of the reservation. And when this evidence is withdrawn, and the site is abandoned, the reserve falls back into the mass of the public lands subject to be sold under the general law. But before such land can be sold at private sale under the general system, it must, by proclamation, be offered at public auction. The proclamation should give notice of the sale of the reserved tract as other lands. In this mode, I think, the sale would be a valid one.

The right claimed in the case of *Wilcox* v. *Jackson*, 13 *Peters*, 509, was a pre-emption under the Act of 1834, which declared that no entry or sale of any land shall be made under the provisions of the act, which shall have been reserved for the use of the United States, or which is reserved for sale by Act of Congress or order of the President, or which may be appropriated for any purpose whatever." Before the entry was made as a pre-emptive right by

Beaubin, a light house upon the reserve was built by the government, and the possession of it for public purposes had never been abandoned.

Under the circumstances stated, Rock Island cannot be considered as a military reserve. The possession of it was abandoned, and the right of government released through the same authority, by which it was appropriated. And no act has been done by the government, by which a new appropriation of the ground for military or any other public purpose is shown or can be presumed. The buildings had been sold by the government. The sale of the reserve was suspended, it is presumed, because there was no power to sell by the war department under the Act of 1819. That the suspension of the sale was in no respect influenced by a desire to retain Rock Island for any public purpose, appears by the subsequent action of the war department.

The next inquiry is, whether the land in question is within the provision of the Act of Congress of August the 4th, 1852, which grants the right of way through the public lands to all roads, etc.

The first section of that Act grants to "all railroads and McAdamized turnpike companies, that may be chartered within ten years, over and through any of the public lands of the United States, may be authorized by an Act of the Legislature of the respective states in which public lands may be situated," etc. To the 3d section of that Act there are several provisos, the last of which is: "That none of the foregoing provisions of this Act shall apply to or authorize any rights in any lands of the United States, other than such as are held for private entry and sale, and such as are unsurveyed and not held for public use by erections or improvements thereon."

This act required the proper officers of such road to transmit to the Commissioner of the General Land Office, "a correct plan of the survey of the road, together with the survey of sites for depots, which were granted on the line of such selection, which shall become operative." This survey of the road and of sites for depots on it, were transmitted to the Commissioner of the General Land Office, as the act required.

In a report of the Commissioner of the General Land Office to the Secretary of the Interior, dated 19th of January, 1854, the Commissioner says, by way of note: "As regards the right of way for the road, (now under consideration,) it is already granted by the general act entitled, 'An Act to grant the right of way to all railroads,' &c." In the same report the Commissioner states, "that several bills have been reported to Congress of late years, materially changing the mode of disposing of such reservations, which are now on special file."

The opinion of the Commissioner, as to the right of way or the necessity of legislation, before reserves can be sold, whether right or wrong, can have no influence in the decision of this case. A part of the land on Rock Island has been granted, and it is proposed to make, in addition, one or more private grants. This shows, at least, that the reserve does not, in the opinion of Congress, remain to the extent of the island.

Although this land cannot be now considered a military reserve, yet it is not "held," in the language of the law, "for private entry and sale." Under the general law, no public land can be so considered, which has not been offered at public auction, under the proclamation of the President. In giving a construction to this act, the Court is not at liberty to change the meaning by changing the copulative conjunction into a disjunctive. If effect could be given to the argument, in this respect, it would pervert the meaning of the act. But this reading, if it were admissible, would not change the effect of the act. Land is not held for private entry, which has not been offered at public sale; nor is land

34a

held for sale in the meaning of the law, which has not been so offered. It is true the land was directed to be sold under the act of 1819; but as that act did not authorise such a sale, the land cannot be considered to have been held for private sale.

The other member of the sentence describing lands within the act is: " And such (lands) as are unsurveyed and not held for public use by erection and improvements thereon." ، Now this provision applies to the period of time, when the right is claimed by the railroad. The ground in question was appropriated for military purposes, but when the entry on the land complained of was made, it was not a military reservation; and any improvements thereon had been, not only abandoned and sold, but the former reservation was relinquished and annulled. To hold then, under the circumstances, that the land was still a military reservation for any public use, would disregard the facts in the case. Whether the government might not have again reserved the land for some public purpose is a question not involved in the decision. It would be in it, if there were any evidence that such reservation had been made. To presume such a reservation would be against the evidence.

The improvements under the above Statute having been abandoned and sold, may be considered as not having been made, and so as to the reservation. But still the provision is not technically within the Statute. It refers to lands " unsurveyed," and the lands on Rock Island have been surveyed. This is a technical objection, and to such objections some minds on the bench and at the bar are strongly inclined. My taste does not lie in this line, as it often defeats the great ends of justice, and preserves nothing of any value.

The charter granted by the State of Illinois, to the defendants, authorises them to locate and construct their road, to purchase the right of way, to condemn the land where necessary, and have the damages assessed as provided for in the charter. And in regard to the construction of a railroad across the Mississippi river, the company is vested with power to build, maintain, and use a railroad bridge over the river, or that portion of it which is within the jurisdiction of the State of Illinois, at or near Rock Island, in such manner as shall not materially obstruct or interfere with the free navigation of the river; and to connect by said road or otherwise, such bridge with any railroad, either in the State of Illinois or Iowa, terminating at or near said point; to unite or consolidate its franchises and property with any or all bridges or railroad companies in either of said States."

That the State of Illinois had power to grant the charters for the road and bridge, has not been questioned. A doubt might once have been entertained, whether a State could, under the power of eminent domain, confer the power of appropriation to private companies; but this power has been so long exercised and acquiesced in, that it is now, probably, too late to question it.

Whether a State has power by an act of incorporation or otherwise, to authorize a rail or turnpike road through the lands of the United States, has not, it is believed, been raised or judicially decided. The first impression would be, probably, that a State cannot exercise such a power. But first impressions are rarely to be followed on constitutional questions. They should be deliberately and deeply considered, in relation to their bearing on the Federal and State powers. That the Federal Government is one of enumerated powers is not controverted; nor that the States reserved to themselves all powers not conferred on the General Government, absolutely or by necessary implication.

In the admission of new States into the Union, compacts were entered into with the Federal Government, that they would not tax the lands of the United States. This implies that the States had power to tax such land, if unrestrained by compact.

The Constitution provides, "that Congress shall have power to dispose of and make all needful rules and regulations respecting the territory or other property belonging to the United States." Under this provision Congress organized Territorial Governments. Having power to sell the public lands, beyond the limits of any State, a territorial government was the only mode by which the purchasers and occupants of those lands could be protected in their rights of persons and property. Hence the implied power to establish such a government.

The constitution was adopted a short time after the ordinance of 1787 was passed; and as that ordinance provided for the government of all the territory owned by the United States, no express provision for a territorial government was deemed necessary. In that ordinance it was declared that the States to be formed out of the territory "should never interfere with the primary disposal of the soil by the United States, in Congress, nor with any regulation Congress may find necessary for securing the title in such soil to *bona fide* purchasers."

Within the limits of a State, Congress can, in regard to the disposition of the public lands and their protection, make all needful rules and regulations. But beyond this it can exercise no other acts of sovereignty which it may not exercise in common over the lands of individuals. A mode is provided for the cession of jurisdiction when the federal government purchase a site for a military post, a custom-house, and other public buildings; and if this mode be not pursued, the jurisdiction of the State over the ground purchased remains the same as before the purchase. This, I admit, is not a decided point, but I think the conclusion is maintainable, by the deductions of constitutional law.

Under acts of Congress, trespasses on the public lands are

liable to a civil or criminal prosecution. And yet the Statutes of Congress are numerous, giving the settlers upon those lands without authority, (which makes them trespassers,) pre-emption rights. And this latter policy has become so popular as to induce settlers to take possession of the best portion of the public lands, before they are surveyed or offered for sale. This policy of punishing acts in some, which are rewarded in others, seems to be inconsistent. The only excuse for the provision is, that he who takes the timber from the ground, renders it less valuable and enriches himself; while the other settles on the land with the view of purchasing it. But he is not obliged to make the purchase, and while in possession he may take from it the most valuable timber.

It is a fair implication, that if the State were not restrained by compact, it could tax such lands. In many instances the States have taxed the lands on which our custom houses and other public buildings have been constructed, and such taxes have been paid by the federal government. This applies only to the lands owned by the government as a proprietor, the jurisdiction never having been ceded by the State.

The proprietorship of land in a State by the general government, cannot, it would seem, enlarge its sovereignty or restrict the sovereignty of the State. This sovereignty extends to the State limits over the territory of the State, subject only to the proprietary right of the lands owned by the federal government, and the right to dispose of such lands and protect them, under such regulations as it may deem proper.

The State organizes its territory into counties and townships, and regulates its process throughout its limits. And in the discharge of the ordinary functions of sovereignty, a State has a right to provide for intercourse between the citizens, commercial and otherwise, in every part of the State, by the establishment of easements, whether they may be common roads, turnpike, plank or railroads. The kind of easement must depend upon the discretion of the legislature. And this power extends as well over the lands owned by the United States, as to those owned by individuals.

This power, it is believed, has been exercised by all the States in which the public lands have been situated. It is a power which belongs to the State, and the exercise of which is essential to the prosperity and advancement of the country. State and county roads have been established and constructed over the public lands in a State under the laws of the State, without any doubt of its power, and with the acquiesence of the federal government. In this respect the lands of the public have been treated and appropriated by the State as the lands of individuals. These easements have so manifestly conduced to the public interest, that no objection, from any quarter, has hitherto been made. And it is believed that this power belongs to the States.

It is difficult to perceive on what principle the mere ownership of land by the general government within a State, should prohibit the exercise of the sovereign power of the State in so important a matter as the easements named. In no point of view are these improvements prejudicial to the general interest; on the contrary, they greatly promote it. They encourage population, and increase the value of land. In no respect is the exercise of this power by the State inconsistent with a fair construction of the constitutional power of Congress over the public lands. It does not interfere with the disposition of the lands, and instead of lessening enhances their value.

Where lands are reserved or held by the general government for specified and national purposes, it may be admitted that a State cannot construct an easement which shall, in any degree, affect such purposes injuriously. No one can question the right of the federal government to select the sites for its forts, arsenals and other public buildings. The right claimed for the State has no reference to lands specially appropriated, but to those held as general proprietor by the government, whether surveyed or not.

The right of eminent domain appertains to a State sovereignty, and it is exercised free from the restraints of the federal constitution. The property of individuals is subject to this right, and no reason is perceived why the aggregate property, in a State, of the individuals of the Union, should not also be subject to it. The principle is the same, and the beneficial result to the proprietors is the same, in proportion to their interests. These easements have their source in State power, and do not belong to federal action. They are necessary for the public at large, and essential to the interests of the people of the State.

The powers of a State to construct a road, necessarily implies the right, not only to appropriate the line of the road, but the materials necessary for its construction and use.

Whether we look to principle, or the structure of the Federal and State governments, or the uniform practice of the new States, there would seem to be no doubt that a State has the power to construct a public road through the public lands.

A grant to this effect is sometimes made by Congress, as in the act of 1852; but this does not show the necessity of such a grant. Generally, Congress appropriates to the road a large amount of lands. The positions are believed to be irrefragable—first, that the right of eminent domain is in the State; and secondly, that the exercise of this right by a State is no where inhibited, expressly or impliedly, in the federal constitution, or in the powers over the public lands by that instrument, in Congress.

If this view be correct, the question is narrowed to the simple inquiry, whether the construction of the road, through Rock Island, connected at both ends by bridges over both channels of the river, which include the island, will do an irreparable injury to the public land on the island. Several witnesses have been examined on this point, and, as usual, there are among them differences of opinion. But the weight of the evidence does not show an irreparable injury. On the contrary, it appears that the works complained of will add greatly to the value of the island. From the nature of the improvement, this is so palapable as to require no illustration. By the flow of the river, on either side of the island, its inhabitants are cut off from all intercourse with the shores, except by a ferry. But the bridges proposed, and the railway, will connect the island with both shores, and bring over it a line of travel for passengers, and for the transportation of merchandise, which must add several hundred per cent. to the value of the island and its products.

The testimony in regard to the obstructions to commerce by the proposed bridge, is contradictory. Many witnesses have been examined on both sides, and while those called by the plaintiffs say the bridge will, in a great degree, destroy the commerce of the river, those called by the defendants think it will be no material obstruction. This discrepancy manifestly arises from a mistake in the locality of the bridge. The defendant's witnesses live in the neighborhood of the structure, and speak of it as located, whilst the witnesses of the plaintiffs fix the bridge much higher up the river, and where, from the rapid current occasioned by the falls and the ledges of rock which confine the water to a width of sixty feet, at the foot of the rapids, there is a short turn to the left in the channel, very near the supposed bridge, which would render the passage through the draw, if not impracticable, extremely dangerous. But the experienced engineer, Mr. Brayton, who superintends the building of the bridge, has taken the soundings of the river, and surveyed and measured the distance on it from the side of the bridge to the falls, and above them. This work is laid down on a map which he refers to.

He says, "from the bridge up and on the sides of the river

there are two chains of rock which at the bridge are widest apart, and gradually converging as you ascend, until at the distance of about two-thirds of a mile above the bridge, the channel becomes quite narrow, not exceeding in width sixty feet; that this narrow opening is in nearly a right line with the channel, as it runs through said point to the proposed draw in the bridge." And it appears from the soundings that the bridge is thrown over the deepest water in that part of the river. The engineer says "the plan upon which the bridge is being constructed is a wooden superstructure, built upon Howe's patent, supported by two stone abutments and six piers, laid in water cement. The span between the piers is two hundred and fifty feet in the clear, except the draw. The draw is to be a turn-table draw, two hundred and eighty-four feet in length, supported in the center by a circular stone pier of solid masonry, leaving an opening on each side of such turn-table pier, one hundred and twenty feet in the clear. That such draw is over the main channel and deepest water of the river on the line where the bridge crosses;" and that it is the line of navigation uniformly taken by the boats running up and down.

Except the earth used for the embankment across the Island for the road, but few of the materials for the work have been taken from the Island. The rock on the Island was unfit for masonry, and some of it has been used to fill up the unexposed part of the abutments of the bridge and a small amount of rif-raf work. The embankment is shown to be half a mile from the principal building at Fort Armstrong. Convenient passage ways have been made under the railroad, so that there is no obstruction to the passage from one end of the Island to the other. It seems that about one hundred and fifty thousand dollars have been expended by the company on the road over the Island, and on the bridges. Thirteen acres and a half of the land on the Island appears to be occupied by the road. Several of the witnesses estimate the value of the land without the bridge and the road, at one hundred and fifty dollars per acre ; the road being made, and the bridges, they suppose it will be worth one thousand dollars per acre.

One of the witnesses for the defendant states, that he has long acted as a pilot for steamboats and rafts over the rapids, and is well acquainted with the river ; that for more than half a mile above the bridge, the channel from the draw up is straight, running to the opening in the rocks, known as " Shoemaker's Chain," and that the velocity of the current from the chain to the bridge, is little more than two and a half miles per hour.

The piers, except where the draws are placed, are two hundred and fifty feet apart, which affords ample space for rafts, the bridge being elevated above low water some thirty-three feet, and twenty feet above high water.

The falls, it would seem, must, from the rapidity, sinuosity, and narrowness of the channel, present the principal obstructions to the navigation of this part of the river. Rafts or barges attached to steamboats are loosened, before descending the falls, and they are floated down under the direction of a pilot. This, it is said, is never done in the night, unless the river is high. Whatever improvements may be made in widening this channel, it is hardly probable that it will be extended to double its present width, which would make it equal only to either of the draws below. And if this were done, the passage of the draws over a deep, straight and sluggish current, would be much safer than the rapids. Indeed, from the concurrent views of the witnesses who speak of the bridge where it is being constructed, there will be but little or no delay or hazard in passing the draws. If any injury should result to boats from any want of attention by the bridge company, or the structure of the draw, they being managed with reasonable care, an action at law may be resorted to, as in other cases of wrong.

Having considered this great case, in regard to the legal principles involved under the Federal and State Governments, the magnitude of the enterprise, the interest of the public in the road and in the commerce of the Mississippi river, I am brought to the conclusion that the complainants are not entitled to the relief asked; and, therefore, the motion for an injunction is overruled.

CYRUS H. MCCORMICK v. JOHN H. MANNY AND OTHERS.

1. The plaintiff's first patent for a reaping machine being dated in 1834 has expired, and whatever invention it contained now belongs to the public.

2. Improvements were made by McCormick, for which, in 1845, he obtained a patent, and in 1847 a patent for a further improvement, which last patent was surrendered and re-issued in 1853.

3. A machine may consist of distinct parts, and some or all these parts may be claimed as combinations. In such an invention, no part of it is infringed, unless the entire combination or the part claimed shall have been pirated.

4. In his patent of 1845, for improvements in the reaping machine, the plaintiff claimed the combination of the bow L, and dividing iron M, for separating the wheat to be cut from that which is left standing, and to press the grain on the cutting sickles and the reel. The defendant's wooden divider does not infringe that claim of complainant's patent which embraces the combination of the bow and the dividing iron, as he does not use the iron divider which the plaintiff combined with the wooden.

5. Where the plaintiff's patent calls for a reel post, set nine inches behind the cutters, which is extended forward, and connected with the tongue of the machine to which the horses are geared, it is not infringed by a reel bearer extending from the hind part of the machine and sustained by one or more braces. The only thing common to both devices is supporting the end of the reel nearest to the standing grain. In their combinations and connections, and in everything else the devices are different.

6. Where reaping machines, prior to the plaintiff's invention, had a grain divider or reel post similar to the plaintiff's, the defendants may use the same without infringing the plaintiff's patent.

7. The invention embraced in plaintiff's patents of 1847 and 1853, was not a raker's seat, but it was the improvement of his machine, by which it was

balanced, and the shortening of the reel so that room was made for the raker's seat on the extended finger-bar. This being his invention and claim, to this his exclusive right is limited. Had he claimed generally a seat for the raker, the claim would have been invalid, by reason of the prior knowledge and use of rakers' seats in reaping machines. McCormick's rakers' seat was new in its connection with his machine; but his invention did not extend to a raker's seat differently arranged.

8. A mechanical equivalent is limited to the principle called for in the patent, including colorable alterations, or such as are merely changes as to form.

9. Manny's reaping machine does not infringe either of McCormick's patents. The divider and reel bearer used in Manny's machine being different in form and principle, do not infringe McCormick's patent of 1845.

10. The stand or position for the forker, invented and patented by John H. Manny, is a new and useful improvement, and different in form and principle from McCormick's patents of 1847 and 1853.

This was a bill in Chancery filed in the Circuit Court of the United States for the Northern District of Illinois, by Cyrus H. McCormick against John H. Manny and others, charging them with infringement of his patents for improvements in the reaping machine, dated January 31st, 1845, October 23d, 1848, re-issued May 24, 1853. The defendants filed their answer, setting up various grounds of defence, but relying chiefly on the defence that the reaping machines manufactured and sold by them at Rockford, Illinois, under the name of Manny's Reaper, differ in form and principle from the improvements patented by McCormick, and that the raker's stand or position was an improvement invented and patented by John H. Manny. Issue being joined, a large volume of testimony was taken, showing the state of the art of making reaping machines before and after the date of McCormick's patents. The cause standing for hearing on the bill, answer, exhibits and testimony, it was by agreement of counsel heard at Cincinnati, in September 1855, before the Honorable John McLean, Circuit Judge, and the Honorable Thomas Drummond, District Judge of the United States for the Northern

District of Illinois, and was argued for the complainant by Reverdy Johnson and E. N. Dickerson, Esq'rs., and for the defendants by Edwin M. Stanton and George Harding, Esq'rs.

On behalf of the complainant it was submitted that letters patent had been granted to the complainant January 31st, 1845, for improvements in reaping machines. In this patent, among other things, there was described and claimed a device for dividing and separating the grain to be cut, from that which was to be left standing, as the machine passed around the grain field. And also a device to support the end of the reel on the side nearest to the standing grain, so that the cut grain could be brought freely on the platform of the machine. Another patent was granted to the complainant, October 23d, 1847, and re-issued to him, on an amended specification, May 24th, 1853. This patent specified and claimed an improvement for supporting the raker's body on the machine, while he raked off the cut grain and deposited it in gavels on the ground at the side of the machine. It was contended that the defendants had made and sold for the harvest of 1854, eleven hundred reaping machines, and for the harvest of 1855, three thousand reaping machines, in all of which there were devices for dividing and separating the grain, for bearing up the reel and devices for supporting the raker, substantially the same as were specified and claimed by the complainant. A decree of a perpetual injunction and an account of profits were asked for.

On behalf of the defendants it was submitted, that prior to the date of complainant's inventions and patents, various devices for dividing and separating grain had been described, patented, or used, and on this point especial reference was made to the machines of Dubbs, Cummings, Bell, Phillips, Duncan, Randall, Schnebly, Hussey, Ambler, and others. That anterior to the same date, reaping machines, containing devices for bearing up the reel out of the way of the cut grain, had been described, patented or used, by Cummings, Bell, Ten Eyck, Phillipps, Duncan, Schnebly and Randall.

And that prior to McCormick's invention, devices for supporting the raker's body had been used in the machines of Hussey, Randall, Schnebly, Woodward, Nicholson and Hite. Defendants' counsel contended that McCormick's patents of 1845, 1847, and 1853, on their face, purport to be for special improvements in the machine patented by him in 1834, and not for the discovery of any new principle, method, or combination for reaping, in general. His exclusive right is, therefore, limited to the specific improvements he invented, described, and claimed in his patent.

The patents for these improvements are to be construed in reference to the general state of the art, to McCormick's prior inventions, and to the particular description of his improvements, and the specification of his claim.

And so that, while securing him the exclusive right contemplated by law, at the same time to guard against his withdrawing from the public anything before discovered, known, or used by others, or that was contained in his original patent. For a patentee has no right to extend the term of his monopoly over anything embraced in his original invention, under color of some improvement on it.

The claims for the seat, the reel post, and the divider, are efforts to acquire a monopoly of the reaping machine, by enlarging, modifying and changing the description and specification of particular improvements, and expanding them so as to cover principles, methods and results, in violation of the principles and avowed policy of the patent laws. And the result aimed at by the complainant would withdraw from the public the contribution of many minds, and subject an instrument of great public utility to a private monopoly, without even a decent color of right.

The merit claimed for McCormick, of being the first man who brought the reaping machine into successful use, was wholly aside from the present question. For, even if that merit justly belonged to McCormick, it is not the ground on which the patent law confers an exclusive right to the machine. And, besides, it could only extend to his own improvements; whereas, to the principal parts constituting the machine, he has not the shadow of any claim, as inventor.

The opinion of the Court was delivered at Washington, on the 16th of January, by Mr. Justice McLean, as follows:

JUDGE M'LEAN'S OPINION.

This is a bill to restrain an alleged infringement of the plaintiff's patent, by the defendants, and for an account.

By consent of the parties, the case was adjourned from Chicago to Cincinnati, at which place it was argued on both sides with surpassing ability and clearness of demonstration. The art involved in the inquiry was traced in a lucid manner, and shown by models and drawings, from its origin to its present state of perfection. And if, in the examination of the cause, the entire scope of the argument shall not be embraced, no inference should be drawn that the Court was not deeply impressed with the artistical researches and ingenuity of the counsel.

It is proper that I should say here, that after the close of the argument at Cincinnati, no time was afforded for consultation with my brother judge. At my request he has lately transmitted to me his opinion on the points ruled, without any interchange of views between us, and there is an entire concurrence on every point.

Cyrus H. McCormick, a citizen of Virginia, represented to the Patent Office, that he had "invented a new and useful improvement in the machine for reaping all kinds of small grain," which improvement was not known or used before his application, on which he obtained a patent, dated 21st of June, 1834. As that patent has expired, and whatever of invention it contained now belongs to the public, no further notice of it in this place is necessary. The same individual, in representing to the Patent Office, that he had invented certain new and useful improvements on the above machine, obtained a patent for those improvements, dated the 31st of January, 1845.

After describing certain improvements in the cutting apparatus, the divider, and the reel post, he makes the following claim:

1. The carved (or angled downward, for the purpose described,) bearer for supporting the blade in the manner described.

2. The reversed angle of the teeth of the blade, in the manner described.

3. The arrangement and construction of the fingers (or teeth for supporting the grain) so as to form the angular spaces in front of the blade, for the purpose designed.

4. I claim the combination of the bow L and dividing iron M, for separating the wheat in the way described.

5. Setting the lower end of the reel post (R) behind the blade, curving it at R^2, and leaning it forward at the top, thereby favoring the cutting, and enabling him to brace it at the top by the front brace (S,) as described, which he claims in combination with the post. And afterwards, McCormick applied for another patent, for improvements made on his reaping machine patented in 1845, and it was issued to him the 23d of October, 1847.

This patent was inoperative, as the patentee afterwards alleged, by reason of a defective specification; and he surrendered it, and obtained a corrected patent the 24th of May, 1853. In his specifications of this patent, he says, " the reaping machines heretofore made may be divided into two classes. The first class having a seat for a raker, who, with a hand rake equal in length to the width of the swath cut, performs the double office of gathering the grain to the cutting apparatus and on to the platform, and then of discharging it from the platform on the ground behind the machine."

The defects of the first class were remedied, he says, by the second class, in which a reel was employed to gather the grain to the cutting apparatus, and deposit it on a platform, from whence it is raked off by an attendant, who deposits the grain on the ground by the side of the machine, where it can lay as long as desired; the whole width of the swath being left unencumbered for the passage of the horses on the return of the machine to cut another swath.

And he states that the length of the reel leaves no seat for the raker, who has to walk on the ground at the side of the machine and rake the grain from the platform, and, he says, the weight of the machine is too great, back of the driving wheel. For these defects he has provided a remedy by his improvements, which places the driving wheel back of the gearing that gives motion to the sickle, which is placed in a line behind the axis of the driving wheel and the cog-gearing, which moves the crank forward of the driving wheel, so as to balance the frame of the machine with the raker on it. And also in combining with the reel, which deposits the grain on the platform, a seat, or position for the raker to sit or stand, so that he may rake off the grain, thrown upon the platform by the reel, on the side of the machine farthest from the standing grain.

And in conclusion he says, " what I claim as my invention, and desire to secure by letters patent, as improvements on the reaping machines secured to me by letters patent dated the 24th of June, 1834, and the 31st of January, 1845, is placing the gearing and crank forward of the driving wheel for protection from dirt, &c., and thus carrying the driving wheel further back than heretofore, and sufficiently so to balance the rear part of the frame, with the raker thereon ; and this position of the parts is combined with the sickle back of

35a

the axis of motion of the driving wheel, by means of the vibrating lever, substantially, as herein described."

And he claims " the combination of the reel for gathering the grain to the cutting apparatus, and depositing it on the platform, with the seat or position for the raker, arranged and located as described, or the equivalent thereof, to enable the raker to rake the grain from the platform, and lay it on the ground, at the side of the machine."

The defendants in their answers, deny the validity of the plaintiff's patent for want of novelty, and on other grounds; but in their argument they disclaim any such purpose; and place their defence on a denial of the infringement charged. The infringement of the plaintiff's patent is alleged to consist in his divided reel-post, and its connections, and the raker's seat.

The fourth claim in the plaintiff's patent of 1845, is " the combination of the bow L and dividing iron M, for separating the wheat in the way described." He describes the divider " as the extension of the frame on the left side of the platform, three feet before the blade, for the purpose of separating the wheat to be cut, from that to be left standing, and that whether tangled or not." This divider gradually rises from the forward point, with an outward curve or bow, so as to throw off the grain to the left, and thus separate it from the grain to be cut. And this is combined with a dividing iron rod or bar, made fast by a bolt to the timber extended, as a divider, which bolt also fastens the bow.

From this bolt the iron rises towards the reel at an angle of thirty degrees, until it approaches near to it, when it is curved to suit the circle of the reel. This iron is adjustable to suit the lowering or elevation of the reel, by a bolt and slot in the lower end. By its gradual rise, this iron divider elevates the tangled grain, and presses it against the cutting sickles of the machine.

There can be no doubt that this combination of the bow and

iron divider, as claimed, is new, it not having constituted a part of any reaping machine prior to the complainant's.

In the specifications of the defendant's patent, he says, "the divider F. projects on the left side of the machine in advance of the guard fingers, and divides the grain to be cut from that which is to be left standing, &c., and the machine constructed under his patent has a wooden projection, somewhat in the form of a wedge, extended beyond the cutting sickles some three feet; and which, from the point in front, rises as it approaches the cutting apparatus, with a small curve, so as to raise the leaning grain and bring it within the reel on the inner side of the divider, and on the outer side by the projection, to disentangle the heads and stalks, so as to leave them with the standing grain."

This is not dissimilar in principle from the wooden divider of the plaintiff's machine; the curve outward may be less, and the elevation from the point which enters the grain may also be less than McCormick's, but it performs the same office, and in principle they may be considered the same, and the question necessarily arises, whether in this respect, this divider is not an infringement of the plaintiff's patent.

A satisfactory answer to this inquiry, is not difficult.

The plaintiff claims that his wooden divider is in combination with the iron rod on the inner side, which rises from its fastening at an angle of thirty degrees. The adjustability of this iron, by giving it a lower or higher elevation, is also important, and would of itself be a sufficient ground for a patent. But in this inquiry, the adjustability of the iron divider is not important, as it may be considered stationary.

A patent, which claims mechanical powers or things in combination, is not infringed by using a part of the combination.

To this rule there is no exception. If, therefore, the wooden divider of the defendant's machine, be similar to that of the plaintiff's, there is no infringement; as the combination is not violated in whole but in part. But there is another, and an equally conclusive answer, to the objection.

The plaintiff's wooden divider was not new, and therefore, could be claimed only in combination. The English patent of Dobbs in 1814, had dividers of wood or metal. The outer diverging rod of Dobbs' divider rises as it extends back, and at the same time, diverging laterally from the point of the divider, acts the same as the McCormick divider of 1845, to raise stalks of grain inclining inwards, and to turn them off from other parts of the machine.

The English patent of Charles Phillips, in 1841, had a dividing apparatus, consisting of a pointed wedge-formed instrument, which extended some distance in advance of the cutting apparatus and reel; its diverging inner side, like the corresponding side of McCormick's divider of 1845, bears inward upright grain within the range of the reel and cutting knives; while at the same time, its outer diverging edge, like the outer edge of McCormick's divider, bears off standing grain without the range of the reel. And there is an inclined bar, which, being attached by its front to the lower piece, extends backwards and upwards, until it meets the frame of the machine, at a point above and behind the cutting apparatus.

Ambler's machine had also a divider, not dissimilar to the defendant's.

Bell's machine, made in 1825, had dividers on it to press the grain away from the machine on the outer side, and on the inner side to press it to the cutters.

Hussey's machine, too, had a point which projected into the grain, and divided it before the cutting knives; the inside to be cut, the outside to remain with the standing grain.

In Schnebly's machine, the grain to be cut was separated from that which was left standing, by a divider projecting on the side of the machine.

In the plaintiff's patent of 1834, he says, on the left end

of the platform is a wheel of about fifteen inches diameter, set obliquely, bending under the platform to avoid breaking down the stalks, on an angle that may be raised or lowered by two moveable bolts, as the cutting may require, corresponding with the opposite sides. The projection of the frame at this end is made sufficient to bear off the grain from the wheel, and he claims " the method of dividing and keeping separate the grain to be cut from that to be left standing."

This patent having expired, whatever of invention it contained, now belongs to the public, and may be used by any one. The inner line of the projecting divider of the defendant's machine, it is contended, has a gradual rise from the point; which answers the purpose of the iron divider of Mr. McCormick's to crowd the grain on the reel and cutters; but, in this respect, the wooden divider of the defendant's is not materially different from those above referred to, and others in use, before the plaintiff's patent of 1845.

In regard to the divider in the defendant's machine, it is clear, that it cannot be considered as an infringement of the plaintiff's patent.

The reel-post, as claimed, with its connections, by the plaintiff, seems not to have been infringed by the defendant.

In defendant's machine the end of the reel, next the standing grain, is supported by an adjustable arm, which is nearly level, slightly inclined upwards, and supported by a standard towards the rear of the machine. In McCormick's patent of 1845, the reel-post is set back of the cutter, some nine inches at its foot, rising upwards and projecting forwards, and supported at its top by a brace running to and connected with a standard on the tongue of the machine. The reel-post of the defendant is substantially like the one in Bell's reaping machine, and also the patent granted to James Ten Eyck, in 1825. The reel-support or beam of the latter has not the features of vertical and horizontal adjustability contained in the reel-beam of the defendant's; but it is attached to the machine behind the platform on which the cut grain is received, and it extends forward to hold the reel, and to leave the space beneath it unobstructed.

In his patent of 1834, McCormick placed his reel-post before the cutting apparatus, standing perpendicularly, and being braced as described. But in the patent of 1845, that post was set nine inches *behind* the sickles, leaning forward so as to bring the part of it which supported the reel to its former perpendicular, the post still extending forward so as to admit of being braced directly to the tongue of the machine to which the horses are harnessed.

This was rendered necessary, as the first post being in advance of the cutter, encountered the fallen grain, which adhered to it, and clogged the machine.

The reel-post, so called, in both these machines, were alike, only as bearers of the end of the reel next to the standing grain; but their structures in every other respect are different. McCormick's reel-post served as a brace to the machine, its foot being morticed into the left sill of the machine, nine inches behind the cutting sickles; its top, leaning forward, was braced to the tongue of the machine. The defendant's reel-post, like that of Bell's, was connected with the hindmost post of the machine, and was sustained by braces, as the reel bearer.

In giving strength to the machine it was unlike the plaintiff's, and if this were not so, the defendant's is sustained by similar reel-posts in other machines, prior to McCormick's.

But in addition to these considerations, the plaintiff claims his reel-post in combination with the tongue of the machine, as described. There is no pretence that this combination has been infringed.

From the structure of McCormick's reaper, it was impossible to find a seat for the raker, without an adjustment of the machine which should balance it with the weight of the raker behind the driving wheel. For this purpose the gearing and crank were placed further forward, the finger piece was extended, and the reel shortened, so as to make room for the raker, and enable him to discharge the grain at the side of the machine, opposite to the standing grain. This improvement was claimed as a combination of the reel with the seat of the raker.

In his specifications to the patent of 1853, McCormick describes two classes of machines, the first class having a seat for a raker, who, with a hand-rake, having a head equal in length to the width of the swath cut, performs the double purpose of gathering the grain to the cutting apparatus and on to the platform, and then of discharging it from the platform behind the machine. This was defective, principally, he says, because the grain was discharged behind, in the wake of the machine, rendering it necessary to remove the grain before the return of the machine, and he alleges these defects are obviated by his improvement. In the specifications to John H. Manny's patent, of the 6th of March, 1855, he says, after referring to McCormick's, Schnebly's, Woodward's and Hite's machines, in regard to the seats of the rakers, "the improvement of mine consists, in combining with the reel, which gathers the grain to the cutting apparatus, and deposits it on the platform, a seat or position arranged between the inner end of the platform and the end of the machine next the standing grain, for an attendant to sit or stand on, and which gives due support to him while operating a fork to push the cut grain towards the outer end of the platform, where the grain is first compressed against the wing or guard provided for the purpose, and then by a lateral movement of the fork discharged properly on the ground behind the platform, in gavels, ready to be bound into sheaves."

And in the summing up, the defendant, Manny, says, "what I claim is the combination of the reel for gathering the grain to the cutting apparatus and depositing it on the platform, with the stand or position of the forker, arranged

and located as described, or the equivalent thereof, to enable
the forker to fork the grain from the platform, and deliver
and lay it on the ground at the rear of the machine, as described."

With a few verbal alterations, this claim is the same as
made by the plaintiff, with the exception of the seat of the
raker, and the place of deposit for the grain.

It must be admitted that the combination of the raker's
seat with the reel, as claimed by the plaintiff, was new. And
a very important question arises, how far this claim extends.
Is it limited to the mode of organization specified, or may it
be considered as covering the entire platform of the machine,
and all combinations of the seat and reel ?

The reel was not new, nor was a seat on the platform, or
connected with the platform, for the raker, new; but the position for the raker, *as described* by McCormick, was new. Mr.
Justice Nelson, in the case of *McCormick* v. *Seymour & Morgan*, in his charge to the jury said, " the seat was the object
and result he was seeking to attain, by the improvement
which he supposed he had brought out. What he invented
was the arrangement and combination of machinery which he
has described, by which he obtained his seat. That, and not
the seat itself, constituted the essence and merit, if any, of
the invention."

The reel was advanced in front of the cutters, and shortened, and the driving wheel was put back and the gearing
forward, so as to balance the machine with the weight of the
raker on the extended finger piece. In this peculiar organization, the improvement of McCormick consisted. It was
adapted to no other part of the machine.

To place the raker on any other part of the platform or
machine of McCormick, than on the extended finger board,
would derange its balance, which was so well adjusted by the
improvements described. No such change can be made
without experiment and invention; consequently, the im-

provement of the plaintiff, in this respect, is limited to his specification.

In 1844, Hite made a new and useful improvement on McCormick's reaping machine, patented in 1834, by attaching thereto a seat mounted on wheels, for a raker to occupy when raking the grain from the platform, on which it is deposited by the reel. And a patent was issued in 1855, for this improvement, although from the evidence, the presumption was, that the improvement had gone into public use more than ten years before.

William Schnebly, at Hagerstown, from 1825 to 1837, constructed reaping machines. At first a revolving apron was used, but this was discontinued, and after the grain had been thrown on the platform by the reel and the proper motion of the machine, he says he sat upon the machine in rear of the platform, sometimes upon the guard board, and sometimes astride a cap or cross beam, suitable for that purpose, and raked off the grain with a three or four pronged fork, from the platform, and deposited it on the ground at the side of the machine.

In the specifications of Woodward's machine, patented in 1845, he says, the raker stands upon the platform L, and as the grain is cut and falls upon the platform, he with a fork or rake conveys it to the hinged box, and when a quantity is accumulated therein sufficient, the rear end of the box falls and deposits the wheat on the ground in the form of a gavel. This box was often dispensed with. The raker rode on the machine.

In 1844, Nicholson represented that he had made an improvement on a machine for cutting grain, &c., and he says, "the machine is provided with a pair of shafts, L, for the animal to draw by, and a place, A, for the driver to sit on, and a suitable stand for a raker's seat. And as a part of his improvement he claims a mode of depositing the grain in a line out of the track of the horse, as described. In 1855 a and that is, that Hussey, in the construction of his machine in Ohio, at a very early day used a reel in connection with his cutter and raker. It is insisted that this use of the reel in connection with a raker, in Hussey's machine, before the discovery of the plaintiff, destroys his claim to originality. In answer to this, it is claimed, on the part of the counsel for this plaintiff, that the contrivance of Hussey into which the reel was introduced, was substantially different from the plaintiff's contrivance. It appears that Hussey's reel, like the reel of the plaintiff, when his first seat was put on in 1845, interfered with the raker, so as to prevent his raking the grain the whole length of the platform. Hence Hussey had an endless apron, by which the grain, when cut, was deposited at the feet of the raker, so that he could shove it off with his rake."

I have cited largely from the learned judge, not only because the opinion was greatly relied on by the plaintiff's counsel in the argument of this case, but for the reason that the opinion is sound. The reel, it seems, interfered with Hussey's plan, which was obviated by an endless apron. McCormick dispensed with the apron by putting back the driving wheel and placing forward the gearing, &c., so as to balance the machine, which, with the shortening of the reel, completed his improvement.

Now, if a raker be seated on a different part of the machine, and where he can rake without balancing the machine, and without interruption from the reel, it is a contrivance and an invention substantially different from McCormick's. To seat the raker on Manny's machines does not require the same elements of combination that were essential in McCormick's invention. His invention in procuring a seat for the raker, being new and useful, was unaffected by those which preceded it. But Manny's contrivance required no such modification and combination of the machinery for a raker's seat, as McCormick's; it is substantially different from his. The seat

was not the thing invented, but the change of the machinery,
to make a place for it.   And where the seat may be placed
on the platform, or on any part of the machine, which does
not require substantially the same invention and improvement as McCormick's, there can be no infringement of his
right.

In McCormick's claim for the improvements which gave
him a seat for the raker, arranged and located as described,
he adds, "or the equivalent therefor."

The words of this claim, "or the equivalent therefor," can
not maintain the claim to any other invention, equivalent or
equal to the one described.   This would be to include all improvements or modifications of the machine, which would make
it equal to, McCormick's.   This part of the claim can not be
construed to extend to any improvements which are not substantially the same as those described, and which do not
involve the same principle.   It embraces all alterations
which are merely colorable.   Such alterations in a machine
afford no ground for a patent.

As stated by Mr. Justice Nelson, the improvement of
McCormick consisted, not in the seat for the raker, but in
the modification and new combination of parts of his machine, so as to secure a place for a seat.   Had a construction
of the seat merely, been the invention, that learned judge
admitted the prior seat for the raker on Hussey's machine
would have nullified the claim.

Having arrived at the result, that there is no infringement
of the plaintiff's patent by the defendant, as charged in the
bill, it is announced with greater satisfaction, as it in no respect impairs the right of the plaintiff.   He is left in full
possession of his invention, which has so justly secured to him,
at home and in foreign countries, a renown honorable to him
and to his country—a renown which can never fade from the
memory, so long as the harvest home shall be gathered.

The bill is dismissed at the costs of the complainant.

PITTS & PITTS v. WEMPLE ET AL.

A patent for a combination of machinery is not infringed if less than the entire combination is used.

A combination is usually formed by using known processes or mechanical powers, in which case the invention consists in the union of those powers.

The constituent parts remain with the public, as before the combination.

But the combination cannot be used though something be added to it.

An improvement on a combined machine, for which a patent may be obtained, gives no right to use the combined machine.

Nor, under such circumstances, has the inventor of a combined machine the right to use the improvement.

The inventions of the original and improved machine, are separate and distinct.

Messrs. *Chickering & James*, for plaintiff.

Messrs. *Larned & Goodrich*, for defendant.

OPINION OF JUDGE M'LEAN.

This action is brought to recover damages from the defendant, for an infringement of the plaintiffs' patent for a new and useful improvement in machines for threshing, separating and cleaning grain. The patent was dated the 27th of December, 1837.

In their specifications they say, "We claim as our invention, the combination and use of an endless apron divided into troughs and cells in a machine for cleaning grain, operating substantially in the way described."

This is not a claim to the invention of an endless apron only, but for an apron divided into troughs and cells in the machine, operating substantially as stated.

"We claim, also, the revolving rake, for shaking out the straw, and the roller for throwing it off the machine, in combination with a revolving apron. We claim the guard slats in combination with a belt, constructed as above described, to receive the grain, straw and chaff from the thresher." And they also claim the combination of the additional seive and shoe with the elevator for carrying up the light grain, in the manner and for the purpose herein set forth.

Here are four distinct claims, each of which is a combination, and the whole of which constitute the machine claimed to have been invented by the plaintiffs, and which they denominate "a new and an improved combination of machinery for separating grain from the straw and chaff, as it proceeds from the threshing cylinder."

The defendant, Wemple, in his patent, claims as his invention, and desires to secure by letters patent, "The employment of a cylinder (H,) having tangential or other suitably projecting plates across or along its periphery, for the purposes of separating the grain and breaking the impinging effect produced by the threshing cylinder on an endless apron; the said cylinder being so situated and operating in the rear of the threshing cylinder, as gently to feed over the straw and headings as they are delivered from the threshing cylinder."

A patent was also issued to Samuel Lane, on the 6th of April, 1831, on his claim of having invented "a new and useful improvement in the machine for threshing and cleaning wheat and other grain."

The three patentees claim an improvement in the machine for threshing and cleaning grain. The endless apron is claimed as a part of the combination of each. The apron performs important functions in each. It is used in each to carry the threshed grain and straw thrown upon it by the trasher to the upper cylinder, where the grain is separated from the straw and chaff. In Lane's machine the straw and grain, after the threshing is completed, are received by the apron, and passing on rollers are carried up to the endless seive and rake.

In Wemple's machine, the grain, straw and chaff, are thrown by the thresher upon a cylinder, which feeds over the straw and headings, and breaks their force on the endless apron.

This is called a separator of the grain from the straw, both of which are carried on the apron to the machinery for separating the grain from the straw and chaff.

The function performed by the endless apron in each of these two machines, is substantially the same. In Wemple's machine there is a cylinder which breaks the force of the threshing operation; and there are slats on the apron at certain distances, but these make no substantial difference in the effect produced.

The Wemple machine, by reason of its additional cylinder and slats, may separate a small portion of the wheat from the chaff, but in regard to the endless apron they operate substantially on the same principle. But the endless apron of the plaintiff's machine produces a different effect and operates on different principles. The apron in Lane's and Wemple's machine merely carries the wheat in the chaff. In the plaintiff's machine it operates not only as a carrier, but as a separator of the wheat from the straw. And this is clearly indicated by the plaintiffs, in calling their machine, " a new and improved combination of machinery for separating grain from the straw and chaff, as it proceeds from the threshing machine."

To save the apron from the force of the contents of the thresher, guard slats are used. The endless apron in plaintiff's machine is divided into cells, so that in passing over the rollers the grain is shaken from the straw and falls into the cells, which are deep and narrow, while the straw passes over them. This mechanical contrivance should have been called a separator, or an endless apron separator.

This shows that in the use of the apron by the plaintiffs, there was no infringement of Lane's patent, nor of the plaintiff's patent by the use of the apron in Wemple's machine. The endless apron separator is materially different in its form and principle, and the effect produced by it, from the aprons used by the two other machines. The slats can in no correct sense be considered as mechanical equivalents, for the cells in the plaintiff's apron.

The cylinder F, near the thresher, is substituted in Wemple's machine for the guards used by the plaintiff. And these are different in their mode of operation, although the effect may be somewhat similar. The rule is, that where the invention consists of a combination of known mechanical powers, the use of less than the whole will be no infringement. If the whole of the combination be taken, though something be added, still it is an infringement. An improvement on a combined machine may be patentable; but in such a case, the patentee cannot use the combined machine without a license; nor can the owner of such machine use the improvement, without a license.

As the endless apron used by Wemple is materially different from the one used by the plaintiffs, and as that constitutes only a material part of his entire combination, it follows that it cannot be considered as an infringement of his patent.

As Wemple's endless apron is substantially on the same principles as Lane's, if Wemple's be considered as an infringement, in this respect, of the plaintiff's patent, the same rule of construction would invalidate the plaintiff's patent, as being the same as Lane's, of prior date.

But it will be perceived that in the four specific claims of invention by the plaintiffs, each one consists of combinations of mechanical powers which produce a given result, and these minor combinations are claimed as new, and if they are new, they are entitled to protection.

The first claim under this view is, for the endless apron connected with the other machinery. The second claim, of the revolving rake, is connected with the apron, so as not to be separated from it. The third claim of the guard to break the force of the contents of the thresher, thrown upon the

36a

apron as already stated, has not been infringed by defendants.

The fourth claim of the plaintiffs seems to present the only difficulty. That is the claim of the additional sieve and shoe, with the elevator for carrying up the light grain to the sieve, for a more effectual cleaning. This appears to be new and distinct.

Where the parts of a combination have been invented, whether such invention be of a new machine, or a combination of mechanical powers, it is protected in its distinctive character. The defendants' model has the elevators which return the grain for a more perfect winnowing. The only difference I perceive between the two modes is, that Wemple's elevators convey to the thresher the imperfectly cleaned wheat, whilst the plaintiff's return it to the sieves. The only difference is, that the heads of the wheat, by passing through the thresher, may produce a somewhat better effect than where they are thrown upon the sieves. I find no specific claim for the elevators in Wemple's patent, but they are represented in his model, and if used, they are an infringement of the plaintiff's patent.

On this opinion being given, the counsel of the defendants stated, that they did not use the elevators, and had not for sometime, and that they did not consider them as an improvement of their machine.

FORSYTHE v. BALLANCE.

A grant made by Congress to certain settlers in the village of Peoria, whose buildings had been destroyed by a company of militia, in the service of the United States, cannot be considered as a gratuity.

The grant, when made, referred back to the consideration and fully recognized it.

· The individual who made the settlement, and whose property was destroyed, died before the grant was made. The property descended to his heirs, and when the patent was issued, it was properly made to the legal representatives of the deceased.

Under the laws of Illinois, where the administrator finds it necessary to sell the real estate of a deceased person for the payment of his debts, he may make the heirs, if not residents of the State, or of the United States, parties to the proceeding by publication under the order of the Court.

When this proceeding is offered collaterally, it cannot be objected to, the jurisdiction being undisputed.

The heirs being content, a stranger cannot object to the irregularity of the proceeding.

Mr. *Williams*, for plaintiff.

Mr. *Browning*, for defendant.

OPINION OF JUDGE M'LEAN.

This is an ejectment to recover the possession of a certain lot of land in the town of Peoria, of which the defendant is in possession, under a title adverse to that under which the plaintiff claims. The plaintiff claims under Lecroix, who was an early settler in Peoria, and who claimed under the acts of Congress of 1820 and 1823.

The first was entitled an Act for the relief of the inhabitants of the village of Peoria, passed the 15th day of May, 1820. The 1st section provides, "that every person, or the legal representatives of every person, who claims a lot or lots in the village of Peoria, shall, before the first day of October, deliver to the Register of the Land Office at Edwardsville, a notice in writing of his or her claim, and the Register is to make report to the Secretary of the Treasury of the evidence in support of the claim, and his opinion whether it ought to be confirmed."

The Register reported, among others, that Michael Lecroix claims a lot in the village of Peoria, eighty feet by three hundred in depth. And it appears from the facts in the report, that Lecroix purchased it and three other lots in 1808 or 9, very soon after which he built on the above lot a large two story dwelling house, a large store house, and other out buildings, &c., and that he continued to occupy the same until the year 1812, when the village of Peoria was destroyed by Capt. Craig, who commanded a company of Illinois militia, in the service of the United States, because his company was fired upon at night, whilst at anchor in their boats in the lake opposite the town, by Indians, who were supposed to be friendly with the inhabitants.

On the 8rd of March, 1828, Congress passed "an act to confirm certain claims to lots in the village of Peoria, in the State of Illinois. The first section declared, "That there is hereby granted to each of the French and Canadian inhabitants, and other settlers in the village of Peoria, in the State of Illinois, whose claims are contained in a report made by the Register of the Land Office at Edwardsville, in pursuance of the act of 1820, and who had settled a lot in the village aforesaid, prior to the 1st of January, 1818, and who had not heretofore received a confirmation of a claim or donation of any tract of land or village lot so settled upon and improved, not exceeding two acres, shall be confirmed."

A survey of the lot in question was made by the United States in 1840, and a patent was issued to the legal representatives of Lecroix. The patent recited the report of the Register, that "Michael Lecroix is the inhabitant or settler within the purview of the confirmatory act of Congress, 3d March, 1828, &c., and that it has appeared to the satisfaction of said Register and Receiver, that the said inhabitant or settler, did not, prior to the said act, receive in confirmation of claims or donations of any tract of land or village lot from the United States, and that the legal representatives of the said Lecroix, in virtue of the confirmation act aforesaid," are entitled, &c.

In March, 1848, the administrator of Lecroix filed his petition to have the lot sold for the payment of debts. Lecroix, having made a will, distributed his property between his wife and children, illegitimate, but recognized by him. He died in 1821. The Court of Probate, to whom the petition was presented, ordered publication, as required by the Statute, as notice to the absent heirs who lived beyond the State of Illinois, some or all of them living in Canada. These heirs were made defendants in the petition, as well as the legatees of the deceased.

After the requisite notice was given and the necessary proceedings had, the Court directed a sale of the premises in pursuance of the Statute, and a purchase was made by the administrator or executor of Lecroix, who afterwards sold to the plaintiff.

The right asserted by the defendant, originated before the patent, under which the plaintiff claims, was issued; and it is insisted that the title was a gratuity, and that until the patent was issued, no right vested in the representatives of Lecroix. That in this view the title of the defendant is paramount to that of the plaintiff.

In no correct sense, can this lot be considered as a gratuity to Lecroix. It is true that the early settlers at Peoria had no right to the lots they occupied. They were the pioneers in that part of the country, and encountered privations and dangers incident to such a settlement. The country became involved in a war with England, and a consequent war with the Indians on our frontier. During this contest a Captain Craig, who commanded a company of militia, in the service of the United States, being fired on by some Indians from or near the village of Peoria, on the supposition that the people of the village were friendly to those Indians, in revenge destroyed the village. This was a great outrage, and was so considered by the Government, and it was bound to remunerate the sufferers. It was done, to a limited extent, by giving to them the lots which they had occupied.

The act of 1820 was passed for the relief of the inhabitants of Peoria. This was a recognition of the obligation by the

Government, but of a more limited extent than the merits of the inhabitants required, or was suited to the dignity or justice of the Government. The report was made under the act of 1820, designating the extent of the claim of Lecroix. It seems he had constructed a large dwelling house, a large store house, and other buildings, on the lots awarded to him, and this was confirmed by the act of 1823, which granted the lots stated in the report to the former proprietors. This grant recognised the consideration of the former settlements and improvements, which had been burnt by the troops under the United States. The title related back, and took effect from the settlements made.

To call this a gratuity would be to apply the term unjustly, as it supposes the thing to have been done without consideration, and would exclude the remuneration which was declared and intended by the Government. Lecroix died before the act of 1823, but the proof of his loss was made, and the proceedings for his remuneration were not only commenced, but nearly completed. His claim was recognised by the Government, and its final confirmation can not be separated from the basis on which it rests. It was property, property which, on the death of Lecroix, descended to his heirs. This was fully recognised by the Government, by the issue of the patent to his legal representatives.

This was not only a pre-emptive right, which is the right of purchase, but it was an absolute right to the property,—a right sanctioned by legislative grant, which is the highest evidence of title.

This lot was sold as the property of the heirs of Lecroix, for the payment of his debts. The heirs, under the Statute, were made parties to the suit. The proceedings are not alleged to be void for want of jurisdiction, or any other ground. No fraud is charged. No person but the heirs can now object to the sale, and there is nothing in this case which shows that they are not content. The purchase was made under a judicial sale, and there is no presumption that it was not fairly made.

Can a stranger to this title object to the regularity of the sale. I think not. Under the laws of the State, the title of the heirs was transferred by the sale and the deed made under it. That sale was sanctioned, and the deed made, under the direction and special sanction of a Court having jurisdiction of the case. The Courts of the United States follow the decisions of the State Courts in construing its Statutes.

The defendant, a stranger to this title, which is paramount to the one under which he claims, objects to the judicial proceedings under which the plaintiff claims, when they are offered in evidence collaterally. This cannot be done where the jurisdiction of the Court is unquestionable.

In *Grignon* v. *Astor*, 2 *Howard*, 319, in a case where there was a sale of property by an administrator for the payment of the debts of a deceased person, the Court say, "The power to hear and determine the case is jurisdiction; it is *coram judice*, whenever a case is presented which brings the power into action. If the petitioner presents such a case, as, on demurrer, the Court would render a judgment in his favor, it is an undoubted case of jurisdiction." And, "If the law confers the power to render a judgment or decree, the Court has jurisdiction; what shall be adjudged or decreed between the parties, and with which is the right of the case, is judicial action by hearing and determining it."

A case so adjudged, however erroneously, when the judgment is given in evidence, must be considered as conclusive of the matters determined.

I think the legal title is in the plaintiff.

Judge Drummond considered the grant to the legal representatives of Lecroix as a gratuity, which could not be reached by the creditors of the deceased.

BANK OF CIRCLEVILLE v. NICHOLAS P. IGLEHART.

On the failure of a bank to pay specie, it may be forced into liquidation under the laws of Ohio, and Receivers are appointed to collect the debts and pay the liabilities of the bank.

If there be a deficiency of assets and the stockholders are required to contribute *pro rata*, on the amounts of stock they owe, and to pay the whole amount, if necessary, on such a decree an action of debt cannot be sustained.

To maintain an action of debt, the sum decreed, must be certain so as to require no further action of the Court.

In such a case, a mandate from the Supreme Court of Ohio, to the Common Pleas, requiring it to carry out the decree, and to issue an execution, if necessary, for the whole amount of the stock debt against the stockholders respectively. An order for such an execution being made, the execution being issued and no property found, does not change the nature or effect of the original decree.

An action being brought on the decree as originally given, is subject to the condition expressed, and the facts must be shown to authorize an execution for the whole amount.

The original decree was not joint, but several, that contribution be made *pro rata*. In such a case, an action may be sustained against one of the stockholders, on the original decree, who is a citizen of Illinois.

A suit in equity may be brought to give effect to a decree, where the conditions of the original decree are not appropriate to the powers of a Court of Law.

Mr. *Hunter* for complainant.
Messrs. *Arnold, Larned & Lay* for defendant.

OPINION OF THE COURT.

This is a bill in Chancery to enforce a decree entered against the defendant, in the State of Ohio.

The defendant, with others, became a large stockholder in the Bank of Circleville, established at Circleville, in the State of Ohio, which Bank, being in embarrassed circumstances, was forced into liquidation under the laws of Ohio, and William B. Thrall and two other persons were appointed receivers, to wind up the bank by collecting its debts, &c. Finding that the assets of the bank were wholly insufficient to pay its debts, a bill was filed against its stockholders to compel them to pay the amount, in full, of their subscriptions of stock. The defendant owed on his stock the sum of twenty-nine thousand seven hundred and fifty dollars. Other stockholders owed large sums on their stock, and the cause being certified to the Supreme Court in which a decree was entered against the stockholders, requiring them to pay to the receivers the full amount of their subscriptions of stock, with interest thereon from the date of the decree, "if in the process of closing up the affairs of said bank, by the receivers, it should be found necessary to require the full payment thereof." But if the whole amount should not be required, then the said defendants should pay to the receivers, such parts of the amounts due from them collectively, as with the other assets of the bank will be sufficient to pay its debts; the stockholders to pay a just proportion according to their respective balances due. But the decree was not to bind the stockholders to pay any demand against the bank which had not been previously presented, or reduced to judgment, or exhibited within one year after 1848. And the bill states that the demands against the bank amount to twenty-five thousand dollars, and may greatly exceed that sum.

And the bill alleges that all the stockholders except the defendant, Baker, Crane, and Renich, are insolvent, and that it is necessary that these persons should pay the full amount of their installment, or at least so much thereof as shall be necessary to enable the receivers of the bank to liquidate its liabilities. The bill states the other stockholders are citizens of Ohio.

The first receivers having resigned, others were appointed, who are now prosecuting this suit. The defendant is called to answer, as to the extent of the liabilities of the bank, and how much remains unpaid, and whether any assets belong to the bank except as aforesaid; and the complainants pray that an account may be taken of the amount due and owing by the defendant, and that he be required to pay to the receivers of the bank or their successors, the amount found to be due by said defendant, or such part thereof as may be necessary, with the other available assets of the bank, to enable the receivers to pay the liabilities of the bank, including costs and expenses.

The defendant demurs to the bill, and for cause of demurrer says, that the complainants have not in their bill stated such a case as entitles them to any such discovery or relief as is prayed.

It is first objected that there is an adequate remedy at law.

That an action of debt may be sustained on a decree for money, is admitted. And it appears from the decree, to enforce which, this bill is filed, that the defendant was found to owe to the bank, on account of his stock, twenty-nine thousand, seven hundred and fifty dollars; and to this amount he was held liable to the receivers of the bank. But the decree was not absolutely for this amount. It was that he was liable on his subscription of stock to the above amount, and that he should pay, by way of contribution, with other stockholders, similarly liable, such amount, not exceeding the said sum, as with the other funds, will pay the debts of the bank.

It is clear that on such a decree an action at law cannot be sustained. The sum is not certain, nor has a Court of law the means of making it certain. The debts of the bank must be ascertained, the amount of the assets and what per cent. on the stock debts will make up the deficiency. And by looking into the bills it appears that these facts are called for in the answer of the defendant, and they must be ascertained, before the relief prayed for can be given. " A bill in equity will lie to carry a former decree into execution, when from neglect of the parties or other cause, subsequent events have intervened, making the further aid of the Court necessary, *Leniton* v. *Detts*, 5 *Black's Rep.* 896.

It appears that the Court of Common Pleas, of Pickaway

county, Ohio, after the cause was remanded to it, by the Supreme Court, ordered the Sheriff to collect the full amount decreed against the stockholders. The complainant claims nothing under that order, but relies upon the equity of the original decree. And we must take the case as made in the bill, and which is presented by the demurrer.

The decree was remanded to the Court of Common Pleas to be carried out, and if found necessary to pay the debts of the bank, it had power to award execution for the full amount of the stock indebtment. The Court directed the execution for the full amount, under the authority of the mandate, but this was merely in the execution of the decree. The execution was returned without realizing any fruits of the decree. And the decree is now brought before this Court, for execution, the same as it was before the Common Pleas of Pickaway county.

By the bill the decree is brought before this Court for execution, and it becomes necessary that we should give effect to it, according to its terms, and we are not bound by an executing order of the Common Pleas of Pickaway county. It is no part of the decree, but a mode of giving effect to it, under which no amount was collected.

It is urged, that from the bill, the liabilities of the bank do not appear to have been presented within the time limited in the decree.

The decree embraced all demands presented before it was entered, and all judgments against the bank and all demands which might be presented within one year from the first day of January, 1848. From the notice of this decree it is seen, that it could not have been entered for a specific sum to be paid absolutely.

The complainants allege that the costs chargeable to the bank will not be less than three thousand dollars, and that the liabilities of the bank, exclusive of interest, amount to the sum of $22,640, and that adding thereto the costs and expenses of winding up the affairs of the bank, the liabilities will be above the sum of fifty thousand dollars.

Until a full exhibit of the debts of the bank shall be made, it will not be possible to designate, with precision, their amount. The decree entered by the Court was the only one which could be given, before the exhibit of the debts were made. It graduated the charge on the stockholders so as to make their contributions equal, *pro rata* on the amount of the stock debts. We think this part of the bill is sufficient.

The Courts in Ohio which entered and sanctioned the decree, are Courts of general jurisdiction, and this will be recognised by this Court, without any allegation to that effect in the bill.

It is also urged that the bill is defective, for want of proper parties. That the other stockholders who were parties to the decree are necessary parties. These individuals in the bill are alleged to be citizens of Ohio, and cannot be made parties. No decree is asked against them, and they can, in no respect be prejudiced by any decision which shall be made in this case. And in addition to this consideration, the liability of the defendants under the decree is distinct and separate; each one being required to contribute *pro rata* on his debt for stock, so as to pay the liabilities of the bank. Each is liable on his own subscription for stock, and the only inquiry in this case will be how much of the stock must be paid to carry out the decree. If the whole amount shall be required, the other parties to the original decree cannot be injured, nor will they be injured if the Court should find that the payment of less than the whole will be sufficient. No decree that this Court shall make in this case, can affect injuriously the interests of other parties to the decree. The *pro rata* contribution by the decree is the rule of action of this Court, in giving effect to it, the same as in the Court of Ohio.

This view is not in conflict with the case of *Bargh & Arcularius* v. *Page Ingersoll et al.* 4 *McLean* 11. In that case the suit was brought on a joint liability, one of the parties being a citizen of the same State with the plaintiff. But in this case the defendant is a citizen of Illinois, and his brother and partner died some years ago, insolvent; so that the present defendant stands on his individual responsibility, in no respect so connected with others, as to affect the jurisdiction of this Court. As regards the question of distribution, the principle being fixed by the Ohio decree, it may as well be made, so far as the defendant is concerned, by this as the Ohio Court. The report of a Master can lay the facts before us.

The act of 1839 authorizes this Court to take jurisdiction on a joint demand, under the statutory provision, that a judgment against a joint obligor shall not prejudice his co-obligor.

Upon the whole, the demurrer is overruled and a rule for answer is entered.

DIKE ET AL. v. PROPELLER ST. JOSEPH.

Where a part of the cargo is thrown overboard for the safety of the vessel, and the lives of the passengers, a contribution may be required from the owner of the vessel, and the cargo saved.

This is given in the exercise of a maritime jurisdiction and on the principle of a general average.

Though there may be a remedy at law, on bonds given, yet that does not take away the jurisdiction in admiralty.

Where a lien in Admiralty attaches, it follows the proceeds into the hands of assignees.

Mr. *Wate* for libellants.
Mr. *Hayne* for the respondent.

OPINION OF THE COURT.

This is an appeal in Admiralty. On a voyage from Buffalo to Chicago, in the fall of 1851, the propeller St. Joseph being laden with a cargo of merchandise, by stress of weather was driven on the Michigan shore of Lake Huron, at half past seven o'clock in the evening. It was found impossible to back or heave the vessel off. All hands were immediately employed to construct a temporary dock on which to convey the cargo to the shore. The next morning, the hands commenced carrying the goods on shore, and continued the same during the day; but in the evening the wind hauled to east south east, blowing a gale, and causing the boat to strike heavily and leak badly. The temporary dock, was broken up by the heavy sea.

The danger of the loss of the vessel and cargo became imminent, unless she was speedily lightened and got off. And to accomplish this, large quantities of merchandize were thrown overboard, by means whereof, the remainder of the cargo, and the vessel, were saved.

A libel was filed claiming contribution from the vessel on a general average.

The answer admits the allegations of the libel, but the lien on the vessel is denied; and it is alleged, that when the goods were delivered to the consignee, an average bond was entered into, in which the owners agreed to pay the balance of the average, and that thereby the lien on the vessel and cargo saved, were waived.

The District Court entered a decree against the defendant.

In returning the answer the counsel rely on the case of *Cutler* v. *Rae*, 7 *Howard*.

That was a case where a vessel on a voyage from New Orleans to Boston, was run ashore in a storm in Massachusetts Bay, by which the vessel was lost, but the cargo and the lives of the passengers were saved, the amount of the cargo being of the value of five thousand four hundred dollars, which was delivered to the consignee at Boston.

The Court in that case held, that the goods having been delivered to the consignee, the lien under the general average was terminated.

Average contribution is the creation of the maritime law, and is founded in the great principles of equity. This principle is fully recognized in the Rhodian laws, and is sanctioned by all civilians, who have either spoken or written on the subject. It is nothing more nor less than the sacrifice of the cargo or a part of it, to preserve the lives of the passengers under the greatest emergencies. Or to strand the vessel to save the lives of the passengers and the cargo. In such cases those who have suffered loss to save the cargo or vessel, shall have a general average of the property saved, whether vessel or cargo, or a part of the cargo, in proportin to the loss sustained. No subject can be more purely maritime than this. And it is said the contribution may be recovered in equity and in law. If the demand be a lien upon any property within the reach of the Court, the proceedings may be *in rem.* And if any individual within the process of the Court is liable, the proceedings may be against him *in personam.* The lien still continues on the property in the hands of assignees. This doctrine is laid down in *Sheppard* v. *Taylor,* 6 *Peters,* 675. And it has been the rule of decisions in the Courts of the United States.

A maritime lien adheres to the proceeds of the thing into whose hands soever it may go; and the owner becomes personally liable, and may be proceeded against *in personam* This lien upon proceeds often extends to judicial sales.

It is argued that there is no jurisdiction in this case, as appears from the decision of *Cutler* v. *Rae,* above cited; from the remarks of the Court in that case, it does seem to have turned upon a question of jurisdiction. The Court say, " We think the case is not within the Admiralty jurisdiction." On this ground the judgment was reversed and the cause was remanded to the Circuit Court, with orders to dismiss the libel.

In the case of *Cutler,* the libel was filed *in personam,* by the owner of the vessel, against the consignee, claiming contribution from the part of the cargo saved, for his lost vessel. The Court say, in general average, "the party entitled to contribution has no absolute and unconditional lien upon the goods liable to contribute. The Captain has a right to retain them until the general average with which they are charged has been paid or secured. This right of retainer is a qualified lien, to which the party is entitled by the maritime law. But it depends upon the possession of the goods by the master or ship owner, and ceases where they are delivered to the owner or consignee. It does not follow them into their hands, nor adhere to the proceeds."

This would not seem to be a decision of want of jurisdiction, but on the merits. It might be a matter of doubt whether the defendant being consignee and not owner, having received the property as damaged and saved property, not having undertaken by bond or otherwise to pay an average contribution, was personally liable to pay it.

But the libel in the present case was a proceeding *in rem* against the vessel, on a general average; so that there is an important difference between the case in 7 *Howard*, and the one before the Court. The decision, however, in the case of *Cutler*, was by a divided Court, and it has not been satisfactory to the profession, nor was it a decision in accordance with the prior decisions of the Supreme Court. I should conform to it in a case that could not be distinguished from its principles.

It seems to be a settled principle, that where the maritime jurisdiction attaches, the demand may be recovered *in rem* or *in personam*. It does not follow that where an action may be maintained on the contract, as in this case, the maritime jurisdiction may not be exercised.

The jurisdiction of our Court of Admiralty, is not limited by that of the English Admiralty.

The decree of the District Court in this case is affirmed.

JAMES B. RUSSELL *v.* JOHN BARNEY.

The 8th section of the revised Statute of the 3d of March, 1845, requires three things to protect the tenant in possession. 1. He must have entered upon the land in good faith, under color of title. 2. He must have been in possession for seven years, before suit was brought. 3. He must have paid all taxes assessed on the land during that period.

To protect the possession under the ninth section, two things only are required. 1. Color of title made in good faith. 2. He must have paid all taxes assessed on the land seven years before suit was brought. The above sections impose a limitation on titles.

On the grounds stated, they declare the land shall be held and adjudged to belong to the occupant or the person who has, for seven years, paid the taxes.

The act does not operate directly on the title, but conditionally. It is a Statute of limitations, and therefore, does not impair the obligation of the contract.

An individual must claim under one section, and cannot claim under both. Having been in possession less than seven years, he cannot claim under the 8th section, nor can he claim under the 9th section where the land is not vacant and unoccupied for seven years.

Under this section, the tenant must bring himself strictly within the Statute.

Mr. *Weed*, for plaintiff.

Mr. *Peters*, for defendant.

OPINION OF JUDGE M'LEAN.

This is an ejectment brought to recover a tract of land in the possession of the defendant, and which he claims under a tax title, having paid the taxes thereon for seven years before the institution of this suit. It is admitted the defendant, resting only on his deed from the auditor on the tax sale, could not maintain his right, as there are in the proceedings prior to the sale, certain defects, which would be fatal to his title. But he does not rest his defence on his tax deed, although upon its face it is prima facie a good title; but he relies on the act of 1839, republished in the revised Statutes of 1845, the 8th section of which provides, that "every person in the actual possession of lands or tenements, under claim or color of title, made in good faith, and who shall for seven successive years, continue in such possession,

37a

and shall also, during said time, pay all taxes that are legally assessed on such lands and tenements, shall be held and adjudged to be the legal owner of said lands or tenements, to the extent and according to the purport of his or her paper title. All persons holding under such possession by purchase, devise, or descent, before said seven years shall have expired, and who shall continue such possession, and continue to pay the taxes as aforesaid, so as to complete the possession and payment of taxes for the term aforesaid, shall be entitled to the benefit of this section."

There are three essential requisites, under the above section to constitute a valid defense in this case. First, the defendant, in the purchase at the tax sale and obtaining the deed, must have acted in good faith. He must have made the purchase with the belief that he was acquiring a good title under such sale; and the deed upon its face must purport to convey a good title. And this is wholly inconsistent with any fraudulent contrivance or unfairness in the purchase, or any knowledge, at the time, that the sale was void.

In the second place, he must have entered into the possession with an honest intention to occupy it, believing it to be his, and that possession must be continued by him or his assignee for the term of seven years, before an action for the title shall be brought.

In the third place, he or his assignee must not only have remained in possession for seven years, but he must have paid all taxes legally assessed thereon.

These three requisites having been complied with, the Statute declares, "he shall be held and adjudged to be the legal owner of the land."

What is the character of this act. It varies somewhat in form from an ordinary Statute of limitations. But in considering an act we must regard its effect rather than its phraseology. A Statute of limitations in regard to real estate generally provides that " every real possessory action shall be brought within —— years next after the right or title accrues, and not after." Now the right of action accrues so soon as an adversary possession is taken, and the effect is, if the action be not brought before the expiration of the time specified, that the right of entry is gone. In other words, his right is declared to be unavailable.

The above, does not in terms render the title of the original owner inoperative and void, but it takes from him the means of recovery. The right of entry is gone, and without this his interest in the land, in effect, is extinguished. And this consequence results from the adversary possession of the defendant. The eighth section above cited provides, that the person whose possession and payment of taxes bring him within its provisions, shall " be held and adjudged the legal owner."

In both cases the claim of the occupant is protected, and the effect to both parties is the same. The former owner has lost his right of entry on the premises, and is barred; and in the other case the owner is barred, by the right given to the occupant under the Statute. In both cases the title of the former owner is barred. Barred from bringing his action, in the one case, and in the other, by the paramount right of the occupant.

Statutes of limitations are founded upon public policy. They have been adopted in all civilized countries, whether under the civil or the common law. They have had a salutary effect in giving quiet and greater certainty to titles of real estate.

The objection that this section acts upon the title and not upon the remedy of the owner, is more specious than sound. Whether the Statute operate upon the right of remedy or the right of property, in a case stated, it produces the same result to the original owner. In either case his title is without effect.

The objection that the Statute cannot operate except on titles acquired subsequent to its date, is not sustainable. Statutes of limitations affect all titles to real estate without having regard to their dates, as they have upon personal obligations. The question is, has the Statute run the time limited, against the title claimed, or the chose in action declared on.

Whether the Statute provide any savings for disabilities,

is a matter of policy, addressed to the discretion of the legislature, but does in no respect affect its power.

The 8th section is not indefinite as to time. It provides that
if any person shall remain in possession of lands or tenements
seven successive years, under a color of title made in good
faith, and shall pay the taxes during that period, he shall be
held and adjudged to be the legal owner. If he remain in possession a less number of consecutive years, or shall fail to pay
the taxes for the same time, he has no claim under the section.

But in this case, although the defendant may have paid
the taxes for seven successive years, it is admitted that he
has occupied the premises in controversy only a part of that
time. He, therefore, cannot defend his possession under the
8th section of the act. The claim he asserts, must rest upon
the 9th section, or, partly, on both.

The 9th section provides that, " whenever a person having
color of title, made in good faith, to vacant and unoccupied land,
shall pay all taxes legally assessed for seven successive years he
or she shall be deemed and adjudged to be the legal owner of
said vacant and unoccupied land, to the extent and according
to the purport of his or her paper title." And the benefits
of the Statute are extended to purchasers under the tax payer.

This section dispenses altogether, with an adversary possession, by which notice to the original owner is presumed.
This is a new and an extraordinary provision in a Statute of
limitations. It requires only a color of title for the land
made in good faith, and the payment of the taxes assessed
upon it, for seven successive years, to protect the possession
of the occupant. The title must be of the same character,
as the title under the 8th section, as above described. And
this title, under the 9th section is avoided, if it shall appear
that the owner has paid the tax in any one or more years,
within the successive seven years, for which the taxes are
alleged to have been paid, by the claimant.

Under the provisions of the Statute, this title may be acquired, without notice to the owner, either express or implied. No act is required to be done, from which any presumption of notice can arise. The payment of the taxes cannot be construed into notice to the owner, as is often done by different claimants of the same land without notice to either. The only negligence chargeable to the owner is, that for seven successive years he has failed to pay the tax. No sale of the land for taxes is necessary. The payment of the tax prevents the State officers from taking any steps against the land, for the collection of the tax, which would require public notice to be given. The acts of the party who seeks to appropriate the land, are necessarily known only to himself and the person to whom he pays the tax. And indeed the person receiving the tax, may suppose it to have been paid for the owner.

Under neither of the above sections need the color of title emanate from the State. It must be made in good faith, by a person who believes himself to have a title; and the deed, upon its face, must purport to convey a good title. If it be defective upon its face, in this respect, it does not convey a title within the Statute. But it is not necessary that the fee should actually pass by the deed, for in such a case the Statute would be unnecessary. It was intended to protect the right of the occupant who cannot trace his title to a legitimate source, or which may be defective in the deraignment of title behind the instrument under which he claims.

Do either of the above sections impair the obligations of the contract within the 10th section of the first article of the Federal Constitution, which declares "no State shall pass any law impairing the obligation of contracts"?

If these sections operate as limitations, they cannot be held to impair the obligations of the owner's title. He is bound under the 8th section, by a failure to pay his taxes for seven years in succession, and his presumed acquiescence in the adversary occupation by the claimant. Under the 9th section, the bar is made complete by the defalcation of the owner to pay the tax in any one year for seven successive years; and in the payment of those taxes for that term by the claimant.

The law is founded upon a public policy, and does not act directly upon the title in either of these cases, but conditionally. There must be great negligence, on the part of the owner, in a public duty, and there must be positive action by the claimant. On the concurrence of these two conditions, under the 9th section, the possession is protected; and under the 8th section or third requisite, possession is required.

The case of *Fletcher* v. *Peck*, 6 *Cranch*, 87, does not apply to the facts in this case. The Legislature of Georgia declared the grant to Peck, made by a prior Legislature, void. And the Supreme Court held, " a grant made in pursuance of a contract, is an executed contract, and its obligations may be impaired by a law of a State."

It is argued that the above act is in violation of Article 5 of the amendments to the Constitution, which declares, "Nor shall any person be deprived of life, liberty, or property, without due process of law." This provision is intended to restrain the action of the Federal Government, and like the 7th Article, secure, in cases, at common law, a trial by jury, where the controversy shall exceed twenty dollars, is not obligatory on the States.

But if the above restriction did apply, it would not nullify the law, as it contemplates an inquiry and the establishment of the facts required to protect the right of the occupant.

There is no power in the Federal Constitution, or the laws of Congress made under it, to set aside the provisions of either of the above sections, and their construction must rest with the Supreme Court of the State. I regret that this question has not been decided by the judiciary of Illinois, as I should follow such decision as a part of the Statute of the State. This is uniformly done in the construction of Statutes which do not conflict with the Constitution or laws of the Union.

The right of the claimant under the 9th section is technical, and without any other merit than that of contributing in a very small degree to the revenue of the State. And this act, though legal, is stript of all merit when the motive which prompted it is considered. It is a mode of acquiring real estate, not dishonest, because legal. This being the aspect in which I feel bound to consider the claim, the most rigid technical rules of construction shall be applied to it. As the acts to sustain the claim are without merit, the right must be maintained by a strict compliance with every tittle of the Statute. No implication can arise in favor of the right set up; no waiver of the letter of the act for a substantial compliance with it. The claimant rests upon the letter, and by the letter his right should be adjudged.

The right of the defendant cannot stand this test. His claim under the 8th section cannot be sustained, as his possession of the premises was only a part of the seven years required. He cannot sustain it under the 9th section, as a part of the seven years the land claimed was not "vacant and unoccupied." He must claim under one of the sections, as he cannot claim under both. It was competent for the legislature to provide for the operation of the right under the 9th section although the claimant occupied the premises a part, of the time. But as the Statute now stands, the land was not "vacant and unoccupied," if occupied by the claimant or any other person. It may be said that the occupancy of the land by the claimant is more favorable to the owner, as it may be notice to him; but the answer is, in the words of the Statute, the land must be "vacant and unoccupied." The facts bring the case within the reason of the 9th section, but not within its words. In such cases the Supreme Court of Illinois has held that the Statute does not constitute a bar, but they may be considered omitted cases, which the legislature has not deemed proper to limit. *Bedell* v. *Janney*, 4 *Gilman*, 194. A special power granted by Statute, affecting the rights of individuals, and which directs the title of real estate, ought to be strictly pursued, and should so appear on the face of the proceedings. *Smith et al.* v. *Hilemon*, 1. *Scammon*, 323.

Upon the whole, my opinion is, that a judgment should be entered for the plaintiff.

CIRCUIT COURT OF THE UNITED STATES.

THE UNITED STATES *v.* JAMES H. FORSYTHE.

To sustain an indictment under the 16th section of the subtreasury law, the proof must be clear that the defendant has violated some specific provision of the act.

A duly certified transcript from the treasury is made evidence and declared to be, *prima facie* evidence of embezzlement; but where the items of such evidence have been estimated and made up from hearsay, they are not admissible.

Where the expenditures of the Collector's Office are greater than its receipts, to convict, the evidence must show beyond a reasonable doubt, that he has used the money, or refused to pay it over, in violation of the law.

An offer to make a deposit of fourteen thousand dollars, to secure the government, for any balance that might be found against him, is nothing more than a proposed compromise, to avoid the prosecution, and cannot be received as evidence of indebtment to any specific amount.

Mr. *Morton*, District Attorney, for plaintiffs.
Messrs. *Spaulding & Backus*, for defendant.

OPINION OF THE COURT.

The defendant having been appointed Collector of the Customs for Port Miami, in the State of Ohio, gave bond and security, as the law requires, for the performance of his duty, dated 30th of September, 1848. He remained in office until the 11th of November, 1850, when he was removed, and his successor, Mr. Riley, was appointed. From the 31st of March, 1849, to the time of his removal, one year and seven months, he made no returns, and on this ground he was removed from office, and indicted under the 16th section of the Sub-Treasury law. That section provides that if any one charged with the safe keeping of the public money and the disbursement thereof, shall convert to his own use, in any way whatever, or shall use, by way of investment in any kind of property or merchandise, or shall loan or exchange it for other funds, or deposit it in bank, or any failure to pay over or to produce the public moneys intrusted to such person, shall be held to be *prima facie* evidence of embezzlement, and he shall be sentenced to imprisonment, for a term not less than six months nor more than ten years, and to a fine equal to the amount of the money embezzled.

And it is declared that a transcript from the books and proceedings of the Treasury, shall be *prima facie* evidence of the balance in his hands. And it is further provided, that a refusal to pay any draft, order or warrant, whether in or out of office, of the Treasurer, for any public money in his hands, shall be deemed as *prima facie* evidence of embezzlement.

A jury being sworn, it was proved that after his removal, being at Washington, the defendant proposed to deposit fourteen thousand dollars in the Treasury to secure the payment of any amount of moneys which should be found in his hands. But the government officers refused to receive the money for the purpose proposed. From the returns entered upon the transcript, the government would appear to owe the defendant above twelve hundred dollars.

A number of witnesses were examined who paid duties to the defendant, on imported merchandise from Canada. The transcript being offered in evidence was objected to, on the ground that the items were not set down from the returns of the defendant, but were returned by his successor, from talking with the persons who had paid duties into the office.

The Treasury transcript is made evidence when duly certified. There is no objection to the authentication of this document, but the items of which a considerable part of it is composed, though put into the transcript, are not evidence. They were not ascertained and established by the ordinary official action of the department, and consequently they are not evidence. Many of the items were put down by an estimate, and others had no better proof of their verity than hearsay, which is not admissible.

The evidence of the payment of duties was not satisfactory, as it led to no certain result. The expenditure of the office was greater than its receipts, so that it does not appear that the money he had in his hands was greater than the sum he paid out. And the Court instructed the jury, that as this was a criminal procedure, the proof must clearly show that he was guilty of appropriating money to his own use, or that he loaned it, or failed to pay it over when demanded. The transcript is no evidence for the reasons stated, nor does the parol evidence show, beyond reasonable doubt, that he has violated any specific provision of the act.

The proposal by the defendant to deposit fourteen thousand dollars to secure the government in any amount that might be found due to it, was not an admission of any amount being due, but a proposal of compromise to avoid a criminal prosecution.

The Prosecuting Attorney has read the first section of the act of March 3d, 1849; which declares that from and after the thirtieth day of June, 1849, the gross amount of all duties received from customs, from the sales of public lands, and from all miscellaneous sources, for the use of the United

States, shall be paid by the officer or agent receiving the same, into the Treasury of the United States at as early a day as practicable, without any abatement or deduction on account of salary, fees, costs, charges, expenses, or claim of any description whatever.

This act was intended to take away all excuse from Collectors to withhold payments into the Treasury, under the pretence that they were responsible, as Collectors, on various grounds, to individuals for services rendered, &c. This was the evil which the law was intended to remedy. And it was a regulation in civil cases and can have no direct application to the case before us. The law did not take effect, until three months after the default of the defendant is alleged to have commenced. Under the circumstances, it is not perceived how this act can have a serious or direct bearing in the case. It is not a paying office, and there is no evidence, that the defendant received any instructions upon the subject.

The jury found the defendant not guilty.

DISTRICT COURT IN ADMIRALTY.

LEMUEL WICK *v.* THE SCHOONER SAMUEL STRONG.

Motion to dismiss the libel for want of jurisdiction.

Otis & Sears, for the motion.
Keith & Coon, against the motion.

STATEMENT OF THE CASE.

The schooner Samuel Strong was built at the mouth of Black River, Lorain County, in this State, in the summer of 1847, by citizens of that County. In the course of her construction she contracted a large debt to the libellant, then and still a resident of Cleveland. She was originally registered at the port of Cleveland, and was run by the parties who built her until in or about the month of July, 1848, when her then owners sold one-half of her to parties in Wisconsin, and her registry was changed from the port of Cleveland to the port of Chicago. On the 18th of June, 1855, the schooner, then lying in the port of Cleveland, was attached by the libellant. The present claimants, who allege themselves to be *bona fide* purchasers and sole owners of the schooner, filed their claim and also their answer, which, among other grounds of defence, excepted to the jurisdiction of the Court over the schooner, upon the ground that the Statute of this State known as the "Common Carrier" act, *Swan*, 185, did not create a lien but conferred a remedy merely. In order to save costs, it was agreed by the counsel that the motion to dismiss the libel should be heard before any steps were taken to substantiate the libellant's claim, or the other grounds of defence.

OPINION OF THE COURT BY JUDGE WILLSON.

The libel in this case was filed on the 18th of June, 1855. It seeks to enforce a lien for materials furnished by the libellant, from May to October inclusive, in the year 1847, in the building of said schooner at Black River, in the District of Ohio. The libellant is now, and was in the year 1847, a resident of the city of Cleveland; and in the third article of his libel, he avers among other things, that by the maritime law, and the law of Ohio, a lien is given him in the premises, which he can enforce and by which he can obtain redress in Admiralty.

To the libel a defence is interposed by Walker, Bean & Alvord, claimants, and residents of the State of Wisconsin, who have duly filed their claim, answer and exceptions. The defence made by the pleadings consists of,

1st. The Statute of limitation, in bar of recovery after the lapse of six years from October, 1847.

2d. A judicial sale of the schooner Samuel Strong, by virtue of a decree in Admiralty, rendered by the United States District Court for Wisconsin, on the 19th of May, 1851, in a cause civil and maritime.

3. That this Court has not jurisdiction of the subject matter of this suit.

I have not thought it necessary to examine all the questions which arise out of this record, because from the view I have taken of it, the decision of the cause must turn upon the single question of the jurisdiction of the Court, and as the question of jurisdiction is in its nature a preliminary inquiry, it is certainly proper, in whatever form it may be presented, that it should be brought to the consideration of the Court at the earliest opportunity, and be decided before incurring expenses which would be rendered fruitless by the dismission of the cause for want of jurisdiction.

It is claimed by the counsel for the libellant in this case, *that a maritime lien and a proceeding in rem are correlative,* and that wherever a proceeding *in rem* is competent, a lien exists, and *vice versa.*

This is true beyond a question, when a preceeding *in rem* in the Admiralty Court for wages, salvage, collision or bottomry, goes against the ship in the first instance. But this rule does not obtain in the case of a domestic vessel for materials furnished, and when the question of lien depends upon the local Statute. This is evident from the language of the 12th rule in Admiralty prescribed by the Supreme Court of the United States. This rule provides that "in all suits by material men for supplies or repairs, or other necessaries, for a foreign ship or for a ship in a foreign port, the libellant may proceed against the ship and freight *in rem*, or against the master or the owner alone *in personam*, And the like proceedings *in rem* shall apply to cases of domestic ships, when, *by the local law, a lien is given to material men for sup-plies, repairs or other necessaries.*"

It may, therefore, be laid down as a well established prin-ciple of maritime law, fully recognized by the Federal judici-ary, that the District Courts have a general Admiralty jurisdiction *in rem*, in suit, by material men, in cases of foreign ships, or ships of another State; and that in cases of domestic ships no lien is implied, unless the local law gives lien; in which event it may be enforced in the District Court. In the case of the *General Smith*, 4 *Wheaton*, the Court de-cided with great clearness that, " when the proceeding is *in rem* to enforce a specific lien, it is incumbent upon those who seek the aid of the Court, to establish the existence of such lien in the particular case. When repairs have been made or necessaries have been furnished to a foreign ship, or to a ship in a port of a State to which she does not belong, the general maritime law, following the civil law, gives the party a lien on the ship itself for security, and he may well maintain a suit *in rem* in Admiralty to enforce his right. But in respect to repairs or necessaries in the port or State to which the ship belongs, the case is governed altogether by the municipal law of that State, and no lien is implied unless it is recognized by that law."

The case before us is one where the materials were fur-nished to a home vessel in her home port, and the question for the Court to determine is, whether the law of Ohio gives a lien, for materials furnished in the building of a ship or vessel in this State, which can be enforced in Admiralty.

It is claimed by libellant's counsel that such a lien is given by an act of the Legislature of Ohio, entitled, "An act pro-viding for the collection of claims against steamboats and other water crafts, and authorizing proceedings against the same by name," passed February 26th, 1840, and the act explanatory thereof, passed 24th February, 1848.

The first section of the act of 1840 provides "that steamboats and other water crafts navigating the waters within and bordering on this State, shall be liable for debts contracted on account thereof, by the master, owner, steward, consignee, or other agent, for materials, supplies, or labor, in the building, repairing, furnishing or equipping the same, or due for wharfage," &c.

In the second section it is provided that "any person having such demand, may proceed against the owner or owners, or master of such craft, or against the *craft itself.*" The next section merely gives directions how to proceed to obtain a warrant of seizure when the craft itself is sued; and the fourth section enjoins upon the Clerk to issue a warrant returnable as other writs, directing the seizure of such craft by name or description, as provided in the third section of the act, or such part of her apparel or furniture as may be necessary to satisfy the demand, and to detain the same until discharged by due course of law.

These are the main provisions of the Statute, at least so far as the Statute itself concerns our present inquiry. Does this Statute give a lien in the technical legal sense of the term? or in other words, does the lien attach to the watercraft, except on seizure, by virtue of the warrant issued, and in the mode and under the regulations prescribed in the Statute?

It was clearly the object of the Legislature in passing this act, to subject water craft, of the description named, to be sued, whose owners resided out of the State, or if residents, whose names were unknown to the creditors. The evil formerly existing, and intended to be remedied by the law, was, that creditors could not always discover the names of the owners; and without having their names they could not bring suit against the person, or by attachment against the property. I regard this law as affording a remedy only. There are no words in the act expressly giving a lien, and in the language of the Court in the case of *The Canal Boat*

Huron v. *Simmons*, 11 *Ohio Reports*, "The boats responsibility is not in the nature of a lien." I apprehend that it is the seizure which creates the lien, and that until the water craft is actually taken by warrant, and in the mode prescribed by the law, no lien attaches to the property.

This Statute is said to be a transcript of the New York Statute, under which liens have been enforced by adjudications of the Federal Courts in Admiralty proceedings.

The Statute of New York provides for proceedings *in rem*, in almost the precise language of the Ohio Statute, except in one important particular. It declares "that ships or vessels of all descriptions, &c., shall be liable for all debts contracted by the master, commander, owner or consignee thereof, on account of any work done, or any supplies or materials furnished by any mechanic or tradesman, or others on account, or towards the building, repairing, fitting, furnishing or equipping such ships or vessels, and *that such debt shall be a lien upon such ship or vessel, her tackle, apparel and furniture*, and shall be preferred to all other liens thereon, except for seaman's wages."

These Statutes are in derogation of the common law, and by a well established rule should be construed strictly. But I can conceive no rule of construction by which a creditor, with a claim fairly established against a vessel under the New York Statute, could be divested of his lien, or be deprived the right of enforcing it in the Admiralty. His lien, by law, attaches the moment the debt is contracted. By the Ohio Statute, it is provided simply, that the vessel *shall be liable*, and, as in a case of an execution, a lien is established when seizure is made of the property.

The Ohio water craft Statute of 1840 was not intended by its authors to become a lien law in the legal sense of the term; had it been so, the Legislature would have so declared it, and it is legitimate to look to the subsequent legislation of the General Assembly to ascertain the intention of the law making power.

The Legislature of Ohio, on the 11th of March, 1843, passed "an act to create a lien in favor of mechanics and others in certain cases." In the first section it is provided, that any person who shall perform labor, or furnish materials or machinery, for constructing, altering, repairing any boat, vessel or other water craft, or for erecting or repairing any house, &c., shall *have a lien* to secure the payment of the same, upon such boat, vessel, or other water craft, and upon such house, &c." This section gives the creditor a specific lien, which, by the act, continues two years from the commencement of the work. It is known, denominated and recognized, as a lien law. If the law of 1840 gave a lien which attached before seizure, what reason or necessity for the act of 1843?

But whatever may be my own views as to the intent and construction of this water craft law, I am bound to follow and adopt the construction given to it by the Supreme Court of Ohio. In cases depending on the Statutes of a State, the Federal Courts adopt the construction of the State, when that construction is settled or can be ascertained. Chief Justice Marshal, in delivering the opinion of the Court in the case of *Elmendorf* v. *Taylor*, 10 *Wheaton*, remarked that, "This Court has uniformly professed its disposition in cases depending on the laws of a particular State, to adopt the construction which the Courts of the States have given to those laws." This course is founded on the principle supposed to be uni versally recognized, that the judicial department of every goverennmt, where such department exists, is the appropriate organ for construing the legislative acts of government. On this principle the construction given by the Courts of the several States to the legislative acts of those States is received as true, unless they come in conflict with the Constitution, Laws and Treaties of the United States. What, then,

38a

have been the adjudications upon this question by the Supreme Court of Ohio?

In the early cases in which that Court were called upon to give a construction to this act, we find but little to aid in determining the question before us. The first case, 10 *Ohio R.* 384, merely decides that a suit cannot be sustained for debts incurred prior to the passage of the act. The case in 11 *Ohio R.* 438, decides, that suits may be brought under the act for provisions and other necessary supplies. These are the points decided. Yet we find the *obiter dicta* of the judges delivering the opinion, in the two cases, in direct conflict. In the first case Judge Hitchcock says—"This law gives a lien upon such crafts for certain claims against them." In the second case, Judge Reed says—"The boat's responsibility is not in the nature of a lien." And up to the time of the decision of the case of the *Steamboat Waverly* v. *Clements,* this question was regarded as open and unsettled by the Supreme Court; for the judge, in delivering the opinion of the Court in that case, used the following language:—"It seems to us entirely unnecessary to decide whether the liability of the boat for the debts contracted on her account, is strictly to be regarded as a lien or not. When it becomes necessary to decide that point, our opinions will be expressed; but sufficient unto the day is the evil thereof." Whatever *dicta* may be found, therefore, in the reported cases previous to this, should not be regarded as binding authority. In the case of *Jones & Watkins* v. *Steamboat Commerce,* 14 *Ohio R.* 410, the question was fairly and legitimately raised, and decided with great clearness and ability by the Court. I shall make no apology for quoting somewhat at length from the opinion of the Court, delivered in that case, by Judge Birchard. After stating the case he proceeds to comment on the language of the act, and says, " The craft *shall be liable.*" These words have sometimes been spoken of as creating a lien for the demand. But these words are not those usually employed in

Statutes when the Legislature intend to create a lien, strictly speaking. The first section of the act regulating judgments and executions, (*Swan, Stat.* 467,) provides that "lands, tenements, goods and chattels shall be subject to the payment of debts, and *shall be liable to be taken* on execution and be sold." Here the words are the same, and yet this part of the act has never been construed to create a lien. The owner, notwithstanding this clause, can transfer any of the property named, and clothe the bona fide vendor with a good title, no matter how much he may be indebted. The 2d section creates a lien: The lands, &c., "shall be bound" from the date of the judgment: The goods and chattels "shall be bound" from the time they are seized in execution. Now if the intention had been to create a lien, that is, to *bind the boat*, instead of creating a liability to *mesne process* and be substituted as defendant in place of the owners, the fair presumption is, that the words and phrases commonly used to convey that intention, and not those used to convey a different meaning, would have been employed. *We therefore declare that the first section of the act does not create a lien.* It merely declares a liability, leaving the mode of enforcing it to the subsequent provisions in the act." I have quoted the language used by the Court in deciding the case referred to, lest its force might be lost. Aside from its binding authority, I regard the decision as founded on reason and sound principles of law. Neither do I consider its authority invalidated by the case of *Webster* v. *The Brig Andes*, 18 *Ohio R.* The language of the Court in that case took a wide range, but the question we are now considering was not legitimately involved in its decision.

It is to be regretted that the Legislature, in conferring quasi Admiralty powers and jurisdictions upon the State Courts, should have so framed that act as to deprive a class of creditors (whose interests it evidently sought to advance and protect) from availing themselves of a Court of Admiralty to enforce their claim: and I have no doubt that the same reasons which induced the passage of the act of 1840, will prompt future legislation to enable the Federal as well as the State Courts, to carry out the just intentions of the authors of the act referred to.

As the law now is, I am constrained to dismiss this libel for want of jurisdiction.

UNITED STATES *v.* TIMOTHY O'CALLAHAN.

Offences of the same class may be included in the same indictment.

Though offences of different classes, may not be joined. This is the English rule.

Offences of the same class, under a Statute and at common law in England, may be united in the same indictment.

But a late act of Congress, requires offences which may be joined, to be included in the same indictment.

Offences committed by substantially the same act, it would seem, ought not be punished as acts committed at different times and under circumstances wholly disconnected.

Mr. *Morton*, District Attorney, for plaintiff.
Mr. *Backus*, for the defendant.

OPINION OF THE COURT.

The defendant's counsel move to quash this indictment, on the ground that it contains several charges of distinct offences.

In point of law there is no objection to the insertion of several distinct felonies of the same degree, though committed at different times, in the same indictment against the same offender, and it is no ground either of demurrer or arrest of judgment. Upon this ground it has been holden, than an indictment on 37, George 3, c. 70, may, without any repugnancy, charge the double act, that the defendant endeavored to incite a soldier to commit mutiny, and also to incite him in

United States *v.* Timothy O'Callahan.

traitorous practices. Thus, too, in arson, counts at common law, and on the Statute may be joined, without danger ; a count for a robbery may be joined with another for stealing privately from the person ; and burglary and theft, forcible entry and detainer, have been frequently united in the same proceeding. A count for embezzlement on the 39 *George*, 8 c. 35, may be joined with a count for a larceny on 2 *George*, 2 c. 25, because these offences are felonies ; and a count for embezzling bank notes upon the 39 *George*, 2 c. 85, may be joined with a count for larceny at common law. 2 *Hale* 178; 2 *Leach* 1108; 12 *Ward* 425 ; 8 *East* 41; 3 *Term* 2; 106 ; *Cro.* 6 c. 41; 8 *Ward* 211 ; 1 *B. & P.* 180 ; 2 *Leach* 799 . 1 *Leach* 478; 2 *East P. C.* 935-6 ; 2 *Leach* 1108; 3 *M. & S.* 589.

In *Archbold's Criminal Pleadings, page* 55-6, he says, if a defendant be charged with two or more offences in the same count of an indictment, the count will be bad for duplicity, except in one or two excepted cases. But he remarks, " as to charging a defendant with different offences in different counts, it admits of a different consideration." A defendant, he says, ought not to be charged with different felonies in different counts of an indictment ; as for instance, a murder in one count, and a burglary in another.

But a late act of Congress has a bearing upon this question and settles it. In the 1st section of the act " to regulate the fees and costs to be allowed clerks, marshals and attorneys of the Circuit and District Courts of the United States," &c., it is declared, " That whenever there are or shall be several charges against any person or persons for the same act, or transactions connected together, or for two or more acts or transactions of the same class of crimes or offences which may be properly joined, instead of having several indictments, the whole may be joined in one indictment, in separate counts; and if two or more indictments shall be found in such cases the Court may order them consolidated."

The distinct offences, charged in the indictment before us, belong to the same class; it being a charge for passing counterfeit coin, purporting to be gold and silver pieces, at different times, and on different occasions. This may, perhaps, have been done to meet the proofs.

But, however this may be, the act of Congress referred to, with the view of saving costs, authorizes the charges as they are made; and if distinct indictments had been found, on the separate charges, the act of Congress would authorize the Court to consolidate them.

I should be extremely reluctant, where an offence was committed, under a law, in several distinct ways, by the same transactions, to hold the defendant punishable under each. This would be contrary, it seems to me, to the genius of our laws, and to the humanity which characterizes them. Still it must be admitted, where offences of the same class may be charged in the same indictment, committed at different times and under different circumstances, that the punishment, appropriate to each, must be inflicted.

The motion to quash is overruled.

The United States *v.* John N. Sander.

A count in an indictment, which alleged that the defendant, did secrete and embezzle a certain letter, is not defective.

When a Statute makes one or more distinct acts connected with the same transaction, indictable, they may be charged as one act.

Where a letter is delivered to an authorized agent, the letter cannot be charged with having been embezzled. Whether the alleged agency existed, the jury must determine from the evidence.

Mr. *Morton*, District Attorney for plaintiff.

Messrs. *Adams & Bliss*, for defendant.

OPINION OF JUDGE WILLSON.

This is an issue, upon a plea of not guilty, to an indictment founded upon the last clause of the 22d section of the act entitled "an act to reduce into one the several acts establishing and regulating the Post Office Department," of the 3d March, 1825. By this clause of the Statute it is provided, "that if any person shall take any letter or packet not containing any article of value or evidence thereof, out of a post office, or shall open any letter or packet which shall have been in a post office, or in custody of a mail carrier, before it shall be delivered to the person to whom it is directed, with design to obstruct the correspondence, to pry into another's business or secrets:—or shall secrete, embezzle or destroy any such mail letter, or packet, such offender, upon conviction," &c.

The indictment contains two counts. The first charges that the defendant on the 5th day of May, 1855, at Vermillion, &c., did open a letter which had been put into the mail at Coldwater, in the State of Michigan, to be conveyed by post, and directed to Phœbe Sturdevant, Vermilion, Ohio, with a design to obstruct the correspondence, and to pry into another's secrets.

The second count charges that the "defendant at Vermilion, in the district aforesaid, on the 5th day of May, 1855, did secrete and embezzle a certain letter which had before been in the post office at Vermilion, in said district, before it had been delivered to the person to whom it was addressed and directed, and which letter was then and there directed to Phœbe Sturdevant, at said Vermilion, and which said letter had, before that time, been put into the mail of the United States at Coldwater, in the State of Michigan, and was intended to be conveyed by post to Vermilion aforesaid, and which said letter had before that been conveyed by mail, and and was deposited in said post office, at Vermilion, and had not, before the same was so secreted and embezzled by said defendant, been delivered to said Phœbe Sturdevant."

At the commencement of the trial of the cause, the defendant's counsel made a motion to quash the second count of the indictment, for duplicity. The court overruled the motion, with an intimation to counsel, however, that if the court, on reflection, should deem the ruling wrong, they would direct the jury to exclude the testimony, as impertinent to the second count of the indictment.

We are satisfied that the second count is not defective for duplicity. When a Statute makes two or more distinct acts, connected with the same transaction, indictable, each one of which may be considered as representing a stage in the same offence, it has been repeatedly held that they may be coupled in one count. Thus, setting up a gaming table, and inducing others to bet upon it, may constitute distinct offences: for either, unconnected with the other, an indictment will lie. Yet, when both are perpetrated by the same person, at the same time, they constitute but one offence, for which one count is sufficient, and for which but one penalty can be inflicted.

In describing an offence under this Statute, no technical words are necessary. In the case of the United States vs. Mills, 7 Peters' Rep. 142, the court say—"the general rule is, that in indictments for misdemeanors created by Statute, it is sufficient to charge the offence in the words of the Statute. There is not that technical nicety required as to *form*, which seems to have been adopted and sanctioned by long practice in cases of felony." In the case of Mills the indictment was substantially, in form, like the second count of this; both charge the secreting and embezzling in one count, and both are founded on the same section of the post office law. The same ruling has been adopted by this Court in the case of the United States vs. Lancaster, 2d McLean's Rep. 431.

But a more serious and grave question is raised by defendant's counsel in requesting the Court to charge the jury, "that if they should find the letter in question had been delivered by the post master at Vermilion to the defendant, who was at the time a fully authorized agent of Phœbe Sturdevant, to receive it, that any embezzlement by him thereafter, and before delivery to her, does not constitute an offence under the Statute. It is claimed by counsel that a delivery to an authorized agent is a delivery to the principal, and that when this is done the functions of the Post Office Department, and the powers of the Federal Government, are at an end in the premises.

We believe this position of counsel to be well taken.

It is a familiar principle of law, that an act done by an authorized agent, within the scope of his authority, is an act of the principal: "*Qui facit per alium facit per se.*" Hence it is that the delivery of goods by a third person to an agent, and his acceptance of them for his principal, is, in contemplation of law, a delivery to, and acceptance, by the principal. So, payments made by a third person to the agent in the course of his employment, is payment to the principal, and whether actually paid to the principal or not, by the agent, it is conclusive on him.

A letter, packet, or other thing valuable, having been committed to the Post Office Department for carriage and delivery, if once parted with by the post master to a person authorized to receive it, from that moment ceases alike to be under the control of the Department and the power and authority of the General Government. The sanction, by the Federal Courts, of the contrary doctrine, would be dangerous in its tendency and subversive of reserved State authority. No power is given to Congress to legislate upon the subject, except what is incident to, and necessary to carry out, the grant contained in the 8th section of the first article of the Constitution. The grant is simply, "*that Congress shall have*

power to establish post offices and post roads," and while we
would not adopt the limited and narrow construction given
to this grant by President Monroe, in his special message to
Congress of 4th May, 1822, yet we would not extend implied
powers further than what is necessary to carry out, with
safety to the public, the legitimate operations of the post office
establishment.   When the functions of the Department are
exhausted by the proper delivery of mail matter (once placed
in its charge) such mail matter is then beyond the reach and
authority of any legislation of Congress.

It is for the jury to determine from the testimony, whether
the defendant was the authorized agent of Phœbe Sturdevant
to take this letter from the post office at Vermilion. If he
so received it, without any criminal purpose at the time, you
will have done with the case by returning a verdict of not
guilty.   But on the contrary, if you are satisfied from the
testimony, beyond a reasonable doubt, that the defendant at
the time he obtained the letter from the post office, did it with
the criminal intent of opening it for the purpose of prying
into another's business or secrets, then, although he may have
had the previous consent of Phœbe Sturdevant to bring her
letters from the post office, you will be required, nevertheless, to examine the evidence as to the offence charged in the
first count of the indictment; for in that case the offence had
its inception at the time of his taking the letter from the
office, as that act was, in itself, a larceny.

We do not intend to recapitulate the testimony or comment
upon it. We will say, however, that there is in this country
a growing unwillingness to rest convictions on confessions
alone. Yet it is hardly to be supposed that a man who is
innocent, will make statements to different persons, and perform acts at different times, which, taken together, go directly
to prove an alleged commission of a crime. When it is a
question of intention of the accused, for an alleged violation
of law, the jury in no case can have furnished them, by the

prosecution, positive proof; when the intent is material, however, it must be shown by the Government; and this is to be done by proving overt acts of the defendant from which the intention can be implied, as every man is supposed to intend the necessary consequences of his own acts.

Take the case, gentlemen, and under the rules of law, as given to you by the court, return a verdict according to the evidence.

The jury retired, and after several hour's deliberation came into court and asked to be discharged as there was no possibility of their agreeing upon a verdict. They were accordingly discharged by the Court and the case continued.

Thomas D. Simpson *v.* The Mad River Railroad Co.

A person who approves of an improvement of a patented right, but refuses to pay the price charged for it, is inexcusable for using it.

The fact of use is evidence of its utility, and should subject the defendant to damages.

Messrs. *Curtis & Scribner*, for the plaintiffs.

OPINION OF THE COURT.

This is an action for the violation of a patent right. On the 30th of September, 1845, the plaintiff obtained a patent for "an improvement in the mode of removing truck wheels, of locomotive and other engines."

The agent of plaintiff was called on by the agent of defendant, who on examination was pleased with the improvement; and when the price of two hundred and fifty dollars was stated to him he refused to pay it. He had had the improvement in operation two weeks, as witness understood, and he said to the witness, he might bring suit.

United States *v.* Joseph S. Wilson.

There is no defence set up by the defendants, and the Court instructed the jury that they could assess the damages, to which the plaintiff is entitled, for the violation of the patent. From the statement of the witness, it appears to be a very useful improvement in removing truck wheels of engines or cars, when they become defective and need repair. It saves much labor and expense, and also time. It is natural to conclude that from the time the improvement was first used by the defendants, nothing to the contrary appearing, it was continued in use, up to the time this suit was commenced. The case proved is evidence of the utility of the improvement.

The jury found a verdict of five hundred dollars, in damages. Judgment.

UNITED STATES *v.* JOSEPH S. WILSON.

The Court this morning (Nov. 28d) decided the motion to quash the indictment found in this case at the July Term.

Two objections were taken to the indictment:

1st. That the Grand Jury were illegally selected.

2d. That during the whole time in which the Grand Jury were deliberating and considering upon the bill of indictment, one of the Grand Jurors was absent, and did not consider upon, consent to, or have knowledge of, the action of the Grand Jury—that the indictment was found and returned into Court by *fourteen* Grand Jurors.

The Court, in an "elaborate" and able opinion, delivered by Judge Wilson, overruled the motion and sustained the indictment.

The District Attorney, Hon. D. O. Morton, in argument, contended that the indictment was well and properly found and returned, and cited the Court to various authorities, and among others, to the case of *Joseph Tuck,* 7 *Ohio Rep.,* 241.

The defendant, by his counsel, Mr. Upham, contended that the indictment was null and void—that the Grand Jury which found and returned it were illegally selected, and were no more the Grand Jury contemplated in the Constitution, and provided for by the act of Congress, than any other unauthorized association of men; that the number of "good and lawful men" who composed it was "too short;" that "no principle was ever established by the case of *Joseph Tuck* 7 *Ohio*, 241," or in any other case in Ohio, which made fourteen men a Grand Jury; and if there was any such case, that subsequent rulings of the Courts of Ohio have settled the question, having a slight regard to the Statutes of the State, that the Federal Courts in the selection of Juries, were bound by the State laws, for the reason that the act of Congress so provides; that although the law only requires the agreement of twelve of "the good and lawful men who compose the Grand Jury" to find and return the indictment, yet it gives to the person charged with crime the privilege of having the advantage or accident of the deliberations of fifteen; that it is not in accordance with the reason, spirit, or letter of the law, that a Grand Jury which the law requires to be composed of fifteen "good and lawful men" should organize, and then one, two or three of their number leave and abandon the Jury. Numerous authorities were cited by the Counsel.

Messrs. *Upham, Carter, Adams, and Brooks* for the defence.

OPINION OF THE COURT.

This is a motion to quash the indictment, and three causes are assigned—

The 1st is, that the Grand Jury who found and returned the bill, was not drawn, selected and designated, according to law.

The 2d is, that the bill was found by fourteen Grand Jurors only; or, in other words, that one of the fifteen Grand Jurors was absent when said bill of indictment was found.

The 3d is, that said bill of indictment was returned into Court by fourteen Grand Jurors only.

From the view I have taken of the causes urged for granting this motion, it is perhaps unnecessary to consider the point in controversy between counsel as to the right or propriety of allowing the defendant to change his plea. I supposed, when that application was made and leave granted, that it was fully understood, and agreed to, by opposite counsel. This motion will therefore, be disposed of without any intention on the part of the Court to furnish the precedent, of allowing a plea in bar to be withdrawn, in order to file a plea in abatement, or of a motion of the character of a dilatory plea.

To the first question, then, raised by this motion—"Was the grand jury of the last July Term of this Court a legally constituted Grand Jury?"

By the act of Congress of the 20th of July, 1840, it is provided "that jurors to serve in the Courts of the United States, in each State respectively, shall have the like qualifications and be entitled to the like exemptions, as jurors of the highest *Courts of Law* of such State *now* have and are entitled to, and shall hereafter, from time to time have, and be entitled to, and shall be designated by ballot, lot, or otherwise, according to the mode of forming such juries *now* practiced, and hereafter to be practiced *therein*, in so far as such mode may be practicable by the Courts of the United States, or the officers thereof; and for this purpose, the said Courts shall have power to make all necessary rules and regulations for conforming the designations and empannelling of juries, in substance, to the laws and usages *now in force* in such States; and further, *shall have power*, by rule or order, from time to time, to conform the same, to any change in these *respects* which may be hereafter adopted by the legislature of the respective States for the State Courts."

By the first clause of this Statute the enactment is positive in its requirements, that so far as the *qualifications* and *exemptions* of jurors in the Federal Courts are concerned, they should be the same as those of the highest Courts of law of the State, and that the mode of forming such juries, should, so far as *practicable*, conform to the mode of the State for the highest Courts of law in such State. So far as relates to the qualifications and exemptions of federal juries, the Courts have no discretion. The law is positive that they shall have the like qualifications, and be entitled to the like exemptions as jurors of the highest Courts of law of such State had at the time of passing the law, or should thereafter have in such State. By the latter clause of the Statute the language used is—" The said Courts *shall have power* to make all necessary rules and regulations for conforming the *designation* and *empannelling* of juries, in substance, to the laws and usages *now in force* in such State; and further, *shall have power* by rule or order, from time to time, to conform the same to any change in these respects which may hereafter be adopted by the Legislature of the respective States for the State Courts."

It was clearly the intention of the framers of this law, to confer upon the Federal Courts a *discretionary power*, to be exercised as they should deem proper, in forming rules and regulations for the designation and empannelling of jurors.

The Courts, from necessity, were to exercise a discretion as to the *practicability* of designating and empannelling juries according to the mode prescribed for selecting juries of the highest Courts of law in the State. They have the power and the discretion to change the mode from time to time. The Court may exercise the power or refrain to exercise it, as it may now deem *practicable.*

But what was the mode of seleciing Grand Juries, at the time this act of the 20th July, 1840, was passed, in the highest Court of law in the State of Ohio?

The highest Court of law in the State, at that time, was the Supreme Court of Ohio, and the jury law then in force was the act of the 9th of February, 1831.

The only provision for selecting juries for the Supreme Court is found in the fifth section of the act. This section provides, "that the Clerk, at least thirty days previous to the sitting of the Supreme Court, in the presence of the Sheriff, shall draw out of the box in which is contained the names selected as aforesaid, *twelve persons,* and shall forthwith deposit in the office of the Clerk of the Supreme Court of said county, a list of the names so drawn, and the Clerk

of the Supreme Court shall immediately issue a venire."
It would hardly be claimed by a lawyer of discrimination and
candor, that a Court should receive commendation for selecting and empannelling a *Grand Jury* according to any mode
which existed in the highest Court of law in Ohio on the 20th
of July, 1840. Neither will it be found that any material
change has taken place, by legislative enactment, in the selection of juries in Ohio, since the adoption of the new Constitution. This Court, therefore, from the necessity of the
case, was obliged to exercise that discretionary power, conferred on it by the act of Congress, determining the mode of
designation and empannelling Grand Juries.

By the 4th rule the mode is assimilated to that practiced in
the *inferior Courts of the State*, and the Court has seen to it,
that in practice, that mode has been substantially carried out.
As a matter of fact, the first fifteen names drawn from the
box, constitute the grand jury, and for those the venire
issues. The rule contemplates, that in case any of the fifteen
should fail to attend, the Marshal should fill the panel from
the remaining nine names drawn. It was hoped by this careful mode of selection, the grand inquest of the District would
be composed of men whose character and standing would
command the respect and confidence of all; and however sin-
cere counsel may be in imputing to the Court a disregard of
law, and an indifference in the formation and adoption of the
rule, we are nevertheless satisfied, that it secures for this
Court, what all must desire, viz: jurymen of integrity,
intelligence and impartiality.

In relation to the second cause urged in support of this
motion, I must confess that its consideration has been attended by no small degree of embarrassment. At the last term, in
the absence of the presiding Judge of this circuit, some days
elapsed, in which the Grand Jury, fourteen in number, were
desirous to come into Court and report several bills, and this,
probably among the number. I then had doubts as to the

power of fourteen Grand Jurors to report a bill, and my
doubts were increased by reading the sententious language of
the learned Judge who delivered the opinion of the Court
in the case of *Doyle* v. *the State,* 17 *Ohio Reports.* On the arrival of the presiding Judge, the Grand Jury reversed their
application. The experienced Judge presiding took the
ground at once, that the Court should not look beyond the
endorsement upon the indictment of a *true bill,* signed by the
foreman; especially when a greater number than twelve appeared in Court to make the presentment. This was upon
the hypothesis, that fifteen qualified Grand Jurors had been
empannelled, sworn and sent out, as the grand inquest of the
District.

To this ruling of my learned brother I assented, though
reluctantly at the tim e, and the fourteen Grand Jurors came
into Court and reported several bills.

There is doubtless a broad and substantial distinction to be
observed between the *action* of an illegally constituted Grand
Jury, and that of a jury all of whom are legally qualified
members.

In the limited time which I have had to examine the question, I find no case where the indictment has been declared
vitiated by the irregularity of one member of a properly constituted Grand Jury, while on the contrary, numerous adjudged
cases are to be found, where the action of the whole panel
has been pronounced void, in consequence of containing one
or more unqualified members.

In England, it would seem that formerly, twelve Grand
Jurors could return a bill. Lord Mansfield, in 1760, when
application was made to have the panel exceed twenty-three
names, refused the application, and held that for the purpose
of finding or reporting a bill, twelve men of the panel agreeing would be regarded as the Grand Jury; 2 *Burrows,* 1088.

The act of 11 *Henry 4th* provided, that the Grand Jurors
should be of the King's liege people, returned by sheriffs or

89a

baliffs of franchise, and of whom none should be outlawed, or fled to sanctuary for treason or felony, otherwise the indictment should be void. And by the same act it was provided that if any one of the Grand Jurors should be an outlaw, the indictment should be void. The case of *Hovey* v. *Hobson, Taunton,* is a leading authority for construing the act, and declares that the mischief was, that persons were put on the jury who were not qualified to serve, that they had no right on the jury, and that their presence vitiated the whole panel, and rendered their action void; and for the plain reason, that the bill must be found by at least twelve, and that the disqualified juror might be one of the twelve.

The American cases have nearly all proceeded on this same principle. It is recognized in the case *Commonwealth* v. *Parker,* 2 *Pickering,* 549 referred to by counsel, and very earnestly contended for by the Court in the case of *Doyle,* 17 *Ohio.* The principle established is, that if a person is on the panel not having the qualification of a juror as required by law, the action of the whole jury is vitiated and an indictment found by them would be void.

The Statute of Ohio has always required that regular juries should be composed of persons having the qualifications of electors, and the Supreme Court of the State, in its intepretation and construction of the Statute has gone to the full extent of strictness adopted by the English Courts in their decisions upon the Statute of 11 *Henry 4th.*

But a very different question is presented by this motion. It is not claimed that any of the jury were disqualified to serve by reason of not being qualified electors in the District. Taking for granted that the whole panel was composed of good and lawful men, the counsel claim that the absence of one of the fifteen vitiates the action of the whole, and that this irregularity of the jury can be inquired into by motion to quash the indictment.

On this question the case of *Joseph Tuck,* 7 *Ohio Reports*

241, is to the point, and decisive of this motion. The Court here held, that if twelve jurors agree in finding an indictment, it cannot be invalidated by showing misconduct of one of the fifteen jurors, nor can inquiry be made upon what grounds any one of the twelve jurors concurred in the finding. In that case the exception was taken by plea; in which plea it was averred, "that Geo. Parsons, one of the grand jurors, was not present at the finding of the indictment, did not hear any witness, nor examine, nor inquire touching any allegation of the indictment, and that as to him there was no inquest whatever."

The Court there overruled the plea, and its decision enunciated the principles of law, familiar to all, that the *record cannot be contradicted;* that a record is proved by itself, and is of such validity that no fact can be averred against it.

In the motion now before the Court, how stands the case? The record shows the Grand Jury found the bill of indictment on their oaths. The intendment and legal effect and presumption is, that it was found on proper evidence, with due deliberation, and by the concurrence of twelve of their number.

The case of *Doyle*, 17*th Ohio*, does not invalidate the authority of the case in 7*th Ohio*. In *Doyle's* case one of the Grand Jurors was not an elector, and had not the Statute qualification of a juror, and the simple and legitimate question for the Court to decide there was, whether an illegally constituted Grand Jury, (by the disqualification of one of its members), rendered the indictment void, and the Court very properly held it did. The question now before this Court was not embraced in that case.

The 3d point urged in support of this motion, is substantially embraced in the 2d, and would stand or fall with it.

Upon consideration, therefore, of all the points, the Court overrules this motion.

CIRCUIT COURT OF THE UNITED STATES.

OHIO—OCTOBER TERM, 1855.

COOK & COOK v. THE COMMISSIONERS OF HAMILTON COUNTY.

Where the Commissioners of Hamilton county were authorized by an act of the legislature, to construct the necessary county buildings on the old court house lot, and such lot was large enough for a court house only; the Commissioners made a contract to build the court house on such lot, and the jail on some other lot, with the sanction of the legislature.

These contracts were valid, as to the court house and also as to the jail, on the happening of the condition expressed.

By constructing the court house on the old court house lot, they acted wisely, as accommodation was thereby afforded to more of the officers of the county, than any other plan could have given.

The Commissioners dismissed the contractors in about four months, after they commenced the work, without cause.

This subjected the Commissioners to an action for damages, for the work done and the materials furnished, also for the profits of the work had it been completed under the contract.

In such case, the cost of materials and of labor will be estimated as of the time the contract was broken up. The wrong doers cannot complain of this rule, as they put an end to the contract wrongfully and voluntarily.

The act of 1851 authorised the Commissioners to make the contract which was made.

The expense of the buildings was left to the discretion of the Commissioners, as they were to construct all the necessary county buildings, on such plans and of such materials as they might determine.

As the buildings were necessarily to be large and substantial, it may be presumed that they should be also ornamental. A fair contract being made, the decision of the people by a popular vote, affords no justification for an abrogation of the contract by the Commissioners.

The result shows, that under the pretence of reform, the people are subjected to imposition and increased expense.

Messrs. *Fox, Stanbery, and Pugh,* for plaintiffs.
Messrs. *Caldwell, Groesbeck, and Tilden,* for defendants.

OPINION OF THE COURT.

This action is brought on a contract between the parties, for the building of a court house and jail by the plaintiffs, for Hamilton county.

The contract was dated the 15th of July, 1851, by which the plaintiffs agreed to build the court house and jail on the old court house lot, in Cincinnati. The jail to be built on another lot, should the consent of the legislature be obtained.

The building was to be constructed according to the requisitions of plans and sections thereon, drawn by J. Rogers, architect, which plans, sections and specifications, are referred to and made a part of the contract. These plans were numbered from one to seventeen. The work to be done under the direction and superintendence of the architect. For the construction of the court house, the defendants agreed to pay the sum of four hundred sixty-eight thousand, seven hundred thirty-two dollars and fifty-five cents. And for the building of the jail, the sum of two hundred twenty-six thousand, five hundred twenty dollars and seventy-four cents.

It was stipulated that the buildings should be commenced immediately, and prosecuted with all reasonable speed, and that they should be completed and ready for use, by the 1st of May, 1855.

On the 4th of November, 1851, less than four months after the work was commenced, the contractors were dismissed by the defendants, no special cause for the dismissal being assigned, and this action is brought to recover damages against the defendants for breaking up the contract.

The defendants pleaded several special pleas, to which the plaintiffs demurred, and which demurrers were sustained by the Court, 6 *McLean*, 112. It was, however, agreed by the parties, that the case should be tried on its merits, on the general issue, each party having the right to give in evidence any matter which might be pleaded.

On the evidence being offered to the jury, a question was raised at what time the price of the materials should be proved, necessary to complete the work, and also the price of labor.

The Court held that the proof must be limited to the time the plaintiffs were discharged from the work. Whether the materials and labor were higher or lower after this period could not be shown, as affecting the merits of the case. The rights of the parties became fixed, on the wrongful dismissal of the plaintiffs, by the defendants. No other rule is practicable or certain; and the defendants cannot be heard to complain of hardship, as their own voluntary action fixed the rule of their liability.

By the contract, the architect, Rogers, not only superintended the work, but he had power to dismiss the contractors. So far from being dissatisfied with the progress of the work, he states that there was no ground of complaint against them. In laying the foundation, for some defect in a part of the work, he directed it to be taken up and the defects remedied. He says, the work, so far as the plaintiffs were permitted to progress with it, was well and substantially done, and that they would have completed it, as he thinks, within the contract.

Whatever pretences were set up by the defendants, in regard to the progress of the work, there was no ground connected with its progress, or the manner in which it was executed, which authorized the defendants to dismiss the contractors. Nor was there any reason for such a step, connected with the interest of the public. It is argued that the people decided against the contract, as extravagant and injurious to the public. That contracts should be submitted to a popular vote, after they have been solemnly entered into, or notice given, as the law required, is a new principle of constitutional law. It certainly affords no justification for breaking up the contract.

The people, when left to their own unbiased judgment, will generally, if not always, decide matters submitted to them judiciously, but, under an excited canvass, the result depends upon the means used. A fit illustration of this is found in the case before us. The contract, it is said, was annulled, in obedience to the decision of the people of Hamilton county; and the consequence is, that the extravagant compensation complained of, will, probably, be increased about one hundred per cent., and the buildings, when completed, will be inferior, in every respect, to the first plan.

When the sacredness of contracts, fairly entered into, shall be disregarded, under any pretence, there will be an end of all confidence and protection of persons or property. And where a contract is broken up without cause, it places the injured party on the same ground, in regard to an action for damages, as if he had performed the contract. The responsibility is thrown upon the wrong doer, and if he be a public agent, the public must suffer. Our government is founded upon the theory, that the people will protect their own interests, by electing to places of trusts, honest and capable men.

The plaintiffs are entitled to compensation for the work done and the materials procured, at the time they were discharged from the contract. And they are entitled to damages, which shall cover the profits on the work, had it been completed. These are ascertained by estimating the cost of the materials under the contract, and the expense of construction. It appears the plaintiffs purchased a steam engine and derrick, which were necessary in placing the heavy materials in the building; but as these were retained by the plaintiffs, they cannot be charged against the defendants.

For the work done by the plaintiffs and the materials procured, the amount can be ascertained from the evidence.

In regard to the materials to complete the building, a question is made and argued, whether they shall be estimated, as the best that can be procured. The court house is designed to be a structure of large dimensions, and it was intended to be substantial and ornamental. The plans of the architect were to govern the contractors, and the jury, in assessing damages, will also be governed by them. And the materials to be used should be estimated as the best for the purpose intended.

The price of the work will not be estimated by the old plan, of carrying the brick and mortar in the hod, but by the use of machinery to elevate, not only the brick and mortar, but the heavy materials required, by the contract, to be put into the building. By this mode the labor of many hands, formerly required, is dispensed with, which lessens the cost of construction.

The contract is alleged to be void, because it is impossible to perform it. The impossibility is supposed to arise from the requirement that the court house and jail shall be constructed on the same ground. The contract in regard to the jail is as follows: "It is further agreed that said court house and jail are to be erected on the old court house lot, corner of Main and Court streets, now in use, as at present understood; but should the Commissioners of Hamilton county, at the next session of the legislature, obtain permission to build the said jail in the rear or adjoining the said court house lot, or on any other lot in Cincinnati, east of Main street and west of Broadway, and south of Fourteenth street, then and in that case the said party of the second part agrees to erect and build said jail in the rear of or adjoining to said court house, or on any other lot in the above limits, without any additional charge."

An act was passed the 20th April, 1852, which declared, "that the county Commissioners of Hamilton county are hereby authorised and empowered, in the erection of public buildings, as heretofore by any law provided for, to proceed with the erection of the same, either by contract or otherwise, as in their opinion the public interest may require." This does not meet the above condition, nor was it intended for that purpose. It is supposed to have been intended to carry out the reform required by the vote of the people, by enabling the agents of their choice to construct the buildings under their own superintendence, without inviting bids, by public notice, for the performance of the work.

Another act was passed the 14th of March, 1853, which is entitled an act to provide for the purchase of property and the erection of a work house in Hamilton county. And the act carries out the intention expressed in the title. Not a word is said in it about the building of a jail. Neither this act nor the one above cited, authorized the construction of a jail, within the contract, on which this action is founded. The action is not brought to recover damages, on the special ground, that the Commissioners made no effort to procure the passage of a law authorizing the jail to be constructed on any other lot within the limits specified.

The contract was not for the construction of a court house and jail on the same ground. Seeing that the court house covered the entire lot, provision was made to build the jail on some other lot, should the Legislature authorize the same. This is not a contract against law, as upon its face it is to be binding only, on the condition that the law making power shall sanction it. Such a contract is legal and binding on the parties, on the condition stated. Without the legislative sanction, the contract, in regard to the jail is not binding, and as no action of the legislature has been had as contemplated by the contract, the plaintiffs cannot recover damages, under the contract to build the jail.

But it is insisted that the Commissioners had no authority to make the contract. The principle is admitted, that the powers of the Commissioners are limited by the laws. The act of 1851 is entitled, "An act to authorize the Commissioners of Hamilton county, to erect public buildings."

The 4th section provides, "That Richard K. Cox, John Patten, and David A. Black, Commissioners of Hamilton county, and their successors in office, be and they are hereby authorized and empowered, to erect all such suitable and necessary buildings for the said county, upon the same place or lot of ground which is now known as the old court house property, in the city of Cincinnati, upon such plan and of such materials as to them shall be deemed proper." This power is ample. The plan and materials are to be determined by the Commissioners.

The 4th section declares, "That the Commissioners and their successors shall have power to appoint a Superintendant of such buildings, &c, and shall make such necessary arrangements and contracts for the work and materials to be furnished for said public buildings, and require the faithful performance of all contracts in relation to the same." Proposals for the work were required to be invited and notice given. The powers conferred on the Commissioners were full and complete, and required no prior law to be consulted. The 9th section declared, "if there be any thing, in any prior act, inconsistent with these provisions, it is repealed."

A subsequent section authorizes the Commissioners to borrow two hundred thousand dollars, and to provide the means of paying it, by a tax on property within the county. This power to tax is in addition to the power of taxation in any general act.

The second section in the act of 1848, declares the Commissioners shall not incur any expenditure exceeding fifty dollars, without public notice, &c. And the third section provides, " That the Commissioners shall not enter into any contract to build any poor house, or any other public building, which requires an expenditure of more than five thousand dollars, without first submitting, as to the policy of such outlay, to the qualified voters of the county at the annual spring or fall election, by giving public notice, &c. And all contracts in violation of this section shall be void, as against the county."

The 4th section authorizes the Commissioners to lay a tax on the county levies, sufficient to pay the outstanding debts of the county, existing at the time such tax is laid.

And the 5th section authorizes the Commissioners to lay a tax &c., and in the close of this section the following provision is made : "And said Commissioners are by law authorized to levy taxes to pay all and every item within each current year, for which said Commissioners are by law authorized to levy taxes, provided that such law is not to apply to loans made."

It is argued that the above contract is void, because it is contrary to public policy.

It is not contrary to, but promotive of, the provisions of the act of 1851, except as to the place where the jail is to be built ; and before the contract was to take effect a modification of the law, in this respect, was to be procured.

The contract rests upon the act of 1851, and upon no prior Statute. For the ordinary business of the county the general Statutes, regulating the powers and duties of the Commissioners, were sufficient. But county buildings being contemplated, new powers were necessarily conferred on the Commissioners, not only to make contracts and borrow money, but also to impose a tax annually which should meet current expenditures. This was done by the above act.

The act did not specify a court house and jail, but authorized the Commissioners to erect " all such suitable and necessary buildings for the said county, upon the old court house lot, &c. Finding that the lot afforded space enough for a court house only, the Commissioners wisely determined to build the court house on the lot specified; and to ask the authority of the legislatuse to construct the jail on another lot. By doing this they made a larger and better provision for the county officers, and the courts, than any other plan could have given. Almost all the county offices, numerous as they are, will be accommodated in this building, to the great convenience of the officers and of those who have business with them.

· The contract is alleged to be void because the expenditure incurred by it, greatly exceeded the sum which the Commissioners were authorized to borrow.

The Commissioners must have known, and every intelligent man in the county, that the county buildings for this great city and densely populated county, could not be built for two hundred thousand dollars. And looking at the act, it is clear that a large expenditure was anticipated, as new powers were given to the Commissioners to tax so as to meet the annual expenditures. Where a public contract is of such magnitude as to require five years for its completion, no wise government will appropriate at once an amount of money, which shall meet the entire expenditure.

Having noticed the principle objections made to the validity of the contract, I will make a few remarks on the testimony.

A great number of witnesses, gentlemen of the jury, have been sworn, as measurers of the work and as experts; and as usual in such cases, many of them differ widely in their estimates.

It is proper that I should say, that the engineer, Mr. Rogers, was employed by the Commissioners to make an estimate of the work and superintend the construction of the building. He made a plan of the entire building, called the working plan, and from which his estimates were made for the Commissioners, before a contract was made with the plaintiffs.

When this work was done he could have had no motive, but to sustain his professional character for accuracy and taste.

Mr. Rogers also drew a general plan of the building, showing its outlines and general appearance. From the proportions thus delineated, the experts called by the defendants made their estimates.

The first item of limestone in the walls of the building, McLaughlin & Baily estimate the cost at thirteen thousand dollars, while Rogers estimates it at seventeen thousand, eight hundred and twenty dollars. The latter sum being stated by the plaintiff's witness, and being higher in amount than defendants witnesses, it would seem to be entitled to greater weight, as Rogers had the best opportunity of making an accurate estimate.

The same remark applies to the brick work, which is estimated by Rogers at thirty-four thousand, nine hundred and seventy-five dollars, while the sum stated by Johnson and Morris was about twenty thousand dollars.

The sheet iron roofing, Mr. Rogers sets down at eleven thousand, nine hundred and eighty-three dollars, which is not objected to by defendants. The same may be said of the plastering, which Rogers states at seven thousand and twenty four dollars.

The carpenters work is estimated by Byefield at twenty-three thousand, three hundred and seventy-six dollars, whilst Rogers puts the cost at eighteen thousand, six hundred and twenty-nine dollars. You must decide between these estimates, by taking the one or the other, or by making an average, as you may think the evidence requires.

The bill for plumbing is set down by Rogers, at three thousand dollars, whilst Gibson and Borrowly estimate it at more than three times that amount. Mr. Rogers does not profess to be acquainted with that work, and admits that his opinion respecting it is not to be relied on.

Rogers estimates the painting and glazing at eight thousand four hundred and forty-seven dollars, whilst Hasbaugh, a professed painter and glazier, estimates the cost at ten thousand six hundred and eighteen dollars.

The heating apparatus is estimated by Byefields, at thirteen thousand nine hundred and forty-seven dollars; whilst Rogers puts down the sum of six thousand dollars.

Rogers estimates the cut stone at two hundred and eight thousand three hundred and sixteen dollars, and this is taken by both parties. The iron is estimated by the same witness, at one hundred and twenty-three thousand dollars.

Mr. Rogers says that the prices at which he made the estimate would have given to the plaintiffs, on both buildings, a profit of fifty thousand dollars. No estimates have been proved in regard to the jail, as the contract for that building was not sanctioned by the legislature, consequently it cannot be considered as a valid contract.

You will compare gentlemen the estimated cost of the building, with the contract price, and taking into view the profit on the court house, as may appear to be just, and from the sum thus made up, you will deduct the amount received by plaintiffs, after deducting from such amount the value of the materials furnished by the plaintiffs, and the work done by them on the foundation.

The jury found for the plaintiffs and assessed damages in their favor, amounting to the sum of forty-five thousand dollars. Judgment.

DAVIS, BROOKS & CO. v. WILLIAM F. CLEMSON.

Clemson, a citizen of Ohio, drew a bill on Suydam & Co., of New York, for their accommodation, and after indorsing it forwarded it to them.

They accepted the bill, and negotiated it with the plaintiffs, citizens of New York, for a usurious consideration, by the laws of New York.

An action being brought against the drawer, the usury was pleaded, under the laws of New York, which, for usury, avoids the contract.

Held that the laws of New York governed the contract, and that the assignment to the plaintiffs, being usurious, avoided the contract.

Messrs. *Stanbery & Hunter*, for plaintiffs.

Messrs. *Swayne &* —— for defendants.

OPINION OF THE COURT.

This action is brought on a bill of exchange dated 1st June, 1850, by Clemson, payable to his own order, on Suydam, Sage & Co., for five thousand dollars payable in four months, and indorsed by him.

Several special pleas were filed by the defendant, substantially the same. Among other things they set out that the cause of action in the different counts of the declaration are the same; that the bill was drawn for the accommodation of Suydam, Sage & Co., who were to pay it at maturity, of which the plaintiffs had notice; that they accepted the paper, and afterwards made a corrupt and usurious agreement with the plaintiffs to loan from them four thousand eight hundred sixty-nine dollars and ninety-nine cents, until October 4th, 1850, for the sum of one hundred and thirty dollars, and to receive the above bill accepted by Suydam, Sage & Co.; which sum so paid as interest was more than seven per cent. per annum on the sum loaned, in violation of the Statutes of New York, which declare all instruments void, founded on a usurious consideration.

To these pleas the plaintiff's filed a general demurrer.

As the demurrer admits the facts stated in the pleas, the law must be applied to the facts. The main stress of the argument by the plaintiffs counsel is, that the drawer of the bill who indorsed it, is a citizen of Ohio; and that the contract must be considered as governed by the laws of Ohio. It is admitted that the drawer and indorser, whether the same person or different persons, do not contract to pay the money in the place on which the bill is drawn; but only to gaurantee its acceptance and payment, in that place by the drawer. And it is also admitted that the liability of both the drawer and indorser arises, under the law of the place where, in legal contemplation, the bill was drawn or indorsed.

And it is also admitted, that where a valid instrument is created, untainted with usury, that a subsequent usurious negotiation of it, cannot be pleaded by the drawer in discharge of his obligation. That in such a case, the question of usury is limited between the indorser and the indorsee; but does not reach or taint the original instrument. There are authorities which do not go this length; but the weight of authority sustains the principles above stated; and they embrace the legal ground assumed by the plaintiffs' counsel. *Nichols v. Fearson et al* 7 *Peters* 110; *Munn v. Commission Co.* 18 *John Rep.* 55; *Lloyd v. Scott* 4 *Peters* 229; *Beaman v. Hess* 13 *John. Rep.* 52.

The bill in question was signed by Clemson and indorsed by him, and then it was transmitted to Suydam, Sage & Co., in New York, who accepted it, and by them it was offered to the plaintiffs of New York, who discounted it, reserving a rate of interest which, by the law of New York, was usurious.

This bill was blank paper when it was transmitted by Clemson to Suydam, Sage & Co., and after it was accepted by them, it was nothing more than blank paper. It was intended for the benefit of the acceptors, but thus far, there was no liability by the drawer, indorser or acceptors. No action could be sustained on it. It was then, in contemplation of law, no contract or bill of exchange. Until negotiated, it was, in effect, blank paper. It was susceptible of being made a valid bill by filling up the blanks, and passing it *bona fide* to a third party.

In *Smith v. Mingay* 1 *Maul & Selwyn* 87, It was held, that where a merchant in Ireland, sends to England certain bills of exchange, with blanks for the dates, the sums, the times of payment, and the names of the drawers, signed and indorsed by himself, with a request that his correspondent in England would fill up the blanks, who did so with a date at a place in Ireland, the bills were held to be Irish contracts. And Mr. Justice Bailey held in the same case, if the bills had been negotiated to an innocent indorsee, after the death of the drawer, his representatives would have been bound.

But if these Irish bills had been signed by the drawer for the accommodation of the acceptor, and they had been filled up and negotiated on a usurious consideration, could the usurious holder have recovered their amount from the drawer? These Irish bills were drawn for the benefit of the drawer, the drawees were his debtors or securities, and the bill was to pay the debt of the drawer. The transaction was *bona fide*, and altogether different from the one before us.

It is true no additional name was added to the paper, but that on principle can make no difference. The act of negotiation imparted to the bill validity, if it be a valid bill. Without this, the bill with the names upon it, was of no validity. It was not the signature of Clemson, or the signatures of the acceptors, but the loan of the money, on the credit of the bill, which could give effect to it. And here the question arises, whether that which was essential to give effect to the bill, did not enter into its inception. Whether that, without which the paper constituted no bill of exchange, does not constitute a part of it.

But it is argued by the plaintiffs that Suydam, Sage & Co., did not indorse the bill, and that they claim under the blank indorsement of Clemson. If the bill had been an effective instrument as between the parties, before it was negotiated, the argument would be unanswerable. But as its negotiation was essential to its vitality, the argument is without application to the case.

On principle, these positions would seem to be clear, and they are also clear on authority. "If a bill of exchange be drawn in consequence of an usurious agreement for discounting it, although the drawer to whose order it was payable was

40a

not privy to this agreement, still it is void in the hands of a *bona fide* indorser." 2 *Comp.* 599. In *Halt's N. P.*, Lord Ellenborough lays down the law, that a *bona fide* holder cannot recover upon a bill founded in usury; so neither can he recover upon a note where the payer's indorsement, through which he must claim, has been made by an usurious agreement. But if the first indorsement be valid, a subsequent usurious indorsement will not affect him; because such intermediate indorsement is not necessary to his title to sue the original parties to the note. *Floyd* v. *Scott*, 8 *Peters*, 229.

In *Nichols* v. *Freeman et al.* 7 *Peters* 106, the Court say: " It is necessary to bear in mind that we are not now called upon to consider a case occurring upon the transfer of a note which is, in its origin, a mere nominal contract, one on which, as the test is very properly established in the New York Courts, no cause of action arose between the original parties. The present is a case of greater difficulty." " It will hardly be contended that although the indorsement gave no cause of action against the indorser, yet it did operate to give a right of action against the maker of the note."

In the case of *Munn* v. *The Commission Co.* 15 *John Rep.* 55, the Court say: " if a bill or note be made for the purpose of raising money upon it, and it is discounted at a higher premium than the legal rate of interest, and where none of the parties whose names are on it, can, as between themselves, maintain a suit upon the bill when it becomes mature, provided it had not been discounted, that then such discounting of the bill would be usurious and the bill must be void."

The counsel for the plaintiffs admit, at least tacitly, that the negotiation of this bill was void under the laws of New York, by the argument that it is an Ohio contract, and is, consequently, governed by the laws of Ohio.

The legal obligation which arises against the defendant, whether as drawer or indorser, it is contended, is not that he shall pay the money positively, but that he will pay it, if the acceptors do not pay it at the maturity of the bill, provided payment shall be demanded and a legal protest made, and he shall be duly notified of the same.

There is no expression on the face of this contract, where the money was to be paid. In such an obligation, unless there was something in the negotiation of the instrument to change the effect of it, the place of payment is taken to be the domicil of the person bound. But on such a contract the party is liable wherever he shall be found. Where was the bill in question made and under what law? The plaintiffs who discounted it were citizens of New York, and so were Suydam Sage & Co. The latter were bound to pay the bill at maturity. That it was usurious and void, as to them, will not be controverted. And if this be so, how can a void act create a liability against the defendant, either as an accommodation drawer or indorser. As before shown, until the plaintiffs discounted the bill, it had no binding effect upon the defendant. And if by reason of the usury this discount imposed no obligation to pay on the acceptors, for whose benefit the bill was drawn, can it be binding on his sureties? If an instrument be void for usury as to one, it is so as to all; and any party may set up the defence. *Austin* v. *Tuttle,* 12 *Barbour* 360.

The case of *Andrews* v. *Pondard,* 13 *Peters* 65, arose on the following bill of exchange.

Exchange for $7,287 78.

New York, March 11, 1837.

Sixty days after date of this first of exchange, second of same tenor and date unpaid, pay to Messrs. Pond, Converse & Wadsworth, or order, seven thousand, two hundred and eighty-seven dollars, seventy-eight cents, negotiable and payable at the Bank of Mobile, value received, which place to the account of your obedient servant.

D. CARPENTER.

To Messrs. Sayre, Converse & Co.,
    Mobile, Alabama.

The bill was indorsed by Carpenter, the drawer, who, as well as the drawees were citizens of Alabama. The bill was drawn to pay a debt admitted to be due to H. M. Andrews & Co., of New York. But the amount stated in the bill, included a prior indebtment with ten per cent on it to cover exchange, and which appeared to have been done, to avoid the Statute of usury.

In their opinion, the Court say, "the defendants allege that the contract was not made in reference to the laws of either state, and was not intended to conform to either. That a rate of interest forbidden by the laws of New York, where the contract was made, was reserved on the debt actually due; and that it was concealed under the name of exchange, in order to evade the law. Now if this defence is true, and shall be so found by the jury, the question is not which law is to govern in executing the contract; but which is to decide the fate of a security taken upon usurious agreement, which neither will execute. Unquestionably, it must be the law of the State where the agreement was made and the instrument taken to secure its performance. A contract of this kind cannot stand on the same principles, with a *bona fide* agreement made in one place to be executed in another. In such cases the legal consequences of such an agreement, must be decided by the law of the place where the contract was made. If void there, it is void everywhere."

In that case it was argued by Mr. Webster, as the counsel in the case before us have argued, " that the contract is to be governed by the laws of the place where it was to be executed. The contract on the face of this bill of exchange expresses that it was to be executed elsewhere than where it was made. The parties entered into it with a view to its performance at another place. It is a foreign bill and of course is dated in one place, and in one State, and made payable in another."

In that case the usury was included in the body of the bill, but the bill was made payable in Alabama, and all the defendants were citizens of that state. It was an Alabama contract, in a much stronger point of view, than the one before us was an Ohio contract. The effect of usury in New York was to avoid the instrument; in Alabama, the interest only was avoided.

In the case under consideration, the bill, as between the parties was as blank paper, until it was negotiated to the plaintiffs on an usurious consideration. Could the plaintiffs sue the acceptors, who were and are citizens of New York? This will not be contended. They were citizens of New York, and acted under the laws of New York. They were the principals in the transaction, and the usury releases them from all liability on the bill.

Admit, that the imperfect bill was forwarded to the acceptors by the defendant to be filled up by them; to bind him must they not act in good faith; and must not the party who discounts the bill, act in good faith? Can the plaintiffs complain that they should be governed by the laws of their own State? In the defence, it is averred that they had notice, that the defendant was an accommodation drawer and indorser. He, therefore, can only be made responsible on strict principles of law.

If the bill had been a valid instrument, as between the parties to it; if an action could have been sustained against the acceptor by the drawer for non-payment, at maturity, and it had been negotiated *bona fide*, it is admitted, (the bill having been signed and indorsed in Ohio, from which facts the legal liability arises, on the failure of payment by the acceptors, so far as the defendant is concerned), it would have been an Ohio contract. But it is denied that any liability against the defendant can arise, he being an accommodation drawer and indorser, on an usurious negotiation of the bill, in the hands of the person who thus obtained it. It is void by the act under which it was negotiated. Not void in part, but in whole. Void not only as against the acceptors, for whose benefit it was negotiated, but also as against the accommodation drawer and indorser.

If the facts alleged in the pleas shall not be established before a jury, the rulings now made, will not apply.

Demurrer overruled.

SYLVANUS LATHROP v. WILLIAM STEWART.

Where a record is introduced collaterally as evidence, from a Court of general jurisdiction, and where, from the face of the record, it appeared the Court had jurisdiction, no evidence will be heard, to contradict the record.

A plea of fraud, generally, is not sufficient to admit of evidence in a bankrupt case, where the bankrupt had been engaged in an extensive commercial business.

The bankrupt, in such a case, is entitled to notice of the acts which are alleged to be fraudulent.

Mr. *Peck*, for plaintiff.
Mr. *Fox*, for defendant.

OPINION OF THE COURT.

This action is founded upon four bills of exchange, one for five thousand dollars, payable to plaintiff and accepted by defendant; a second for two thousand dollars, drawn by defendant on Shannon, indorsed by Church, Lathrop and Stockton; a third drawn by defendant and indorsed as above; and a fourth drawn and indorsed as the third bill.

The defendant pleaded a discharge under the bankrupt law.

The plaintiff replied, that the Court had no jurisdiction, as the bankrupt was neither a citizen or resident at Mobile, in Alabama, where the discharge was obtained. Issue joined on the replication.

The Court held that under this issue, parol evidence could not be received to contradict the record. The bankrupt Court had general jurisdiction in bankruptcy. On the face of the record, the Court appears to have had jurisdiction of the case; and as the record is introduced collaterally, it could not be impeached.

Evidence was then offered to show the accounts of the bankrupt, and his general dealing with his creditors. But the Court held that in this case a general plea of fraud was insufficient. That the specific acts which are alleged to be fraudulent must be stated, to give notice to the bankrupt, that he may be prepared to meet them. That without such notice, in a case so complicated as a bankruptcy must be, where the bankrupt had been engaged in a large commercial business, he could not be expected to be prepared to meet the fraud, unless reasonable notice of the facts relied upon to show it, were given.

The counsel for the defendant admitted, that the ground on which he principally relied to show fraud, involved the jurisdiction of the court. The Court, in order to admit the plea to be filed, discharged the jury and gave leave to the plaintiff to amend his pleadings. But as amended pleadings were not filed, at the close of the term, the Court entered a judgment of nonsuit, with leave for the defendant, at the ensuing regular term, to move to set it aside.

ZABULON PARKER v. THOMAS BAMKER.

When no answer is made to an alleged infringement of a patent, the charge is admitted.

One-fourth of the proceeds being estimated as the profits of the mill, the damages were estimated at that amount.

Mr. *Stanbery* for plaintiff.

This is an action for damages, by the plaintiff. for the infringement of his patent, in using his percussion water wheel for mills, &c. No plea being filed, the charge in the declaration was admitted. A witness being sworn, proved the use of the wheel three months in the year; that three thousand feet of plank would be sawed in a day, and he estimated one-fourth of the proceeds for the expense of the mill, one-fourth to keep the mill in repair, one-fourth for the hire of a sawyer, and the other fourth for profit, which amounted, in five years, to the sum of four hundred and sixty dollars, for which the jury found a verdict. Judgment.

Several other cases were decided on the same principle.

INDEX.

ABATEMENT.

A plea in abatement is not a waiver of process. *Halsey v. Hurd*, 14.

A proceeding in a State court by attachment, where a garnishee is summoned, cannot be set up in bar as abatement to a creditors bill. *Wilkinson v. Yate et al.*

ACKNOWLEDGEMENT.

By the laws of Illinois, when a married woman, who is a resident of the State, conveys her real property by deed, it is the acknowledgement which gives effect to it. *Lane v. Dolick*, 200.

The form of acknowledgement of her right of dower, different from that by which she transfers her estate. *Ib.*

ACTION.

In a case where an informer may prosecute, the government may sue also. *United States v. Bougher*, 277.

ADMIRALTY.

On a voyage from Ogdensburg to Chicago, the bill of lading promised to deliver the merchandise in good order, the dangers of navigation only excepted. Held, damages being shown, that the carrier must show it was within the exception of the bill of lading. *Hunt v. the Propeller Cleveland*, 76.

This being shown by facts, from which the exception can be fairly inferred, and the shipper failing to show that the damage might have been avoided, the carrier was held not liable. *Ib.*

It is proper, though not indispensable, to enter a protest after the accident. *Ib.*

In case of a collision between a steamer and sail vessel, in which the owners of the former libel the latter, the libelants must not only show fault in the latter, but all precautionary measures on their part. *Fashion v. Ward*, 152.

Allegations in pleading are admissions by the pleader, and need no proof, unless denied and put in issue. *Ib.*

The protest of the captain and crew, made the morning after the collision, when admitted in evidence, may be considered as evidence corroborative of the witnesses in court. *Ib.*

Two seamen being discharged from the steamer London, at the port of Detroit, made oath before a United States Commissioner, of the amount due them as wages, who certifies the same to the District Clerk; on which a summons was issued directed to the master of

ADMIRALTY.— *Continued.*

the vessel, to show cause why proceedings should not be instituted
against the vessel.

The principle objection to the process was, that the certificates on
which it was founded did not state the residence of the District
Judge, or that he was absent—held insufficient.

A decree in admiralty is the judgment of the court, on the subject in
controversy. *Fashion v. Ward*, 195.

The opinion of the judge on collateral matters is not a part of the
judgment. *Ib.*

When damage is sought in case of collision, and fault on both sides
is shown, or no fault of either, the libel is dismissed. *Ib.*

The act of Congress of 3d March 1848, requires a vessel on the Lake
at night to show, while on the starboard tack, a red light, and a
vessel having the wind free, a white light, and reflectors to the
lights are required. In a collision between a brig and Schooner—
the brig was close hauled on the wind—having a white light, this
was a violation of the act so as to preclude the brig from recovering a full indemnity. *George Porter v. Schooner Miranda*, 221.

There was some fault also in the schooner. The damages were
divided. *Ib.*

Great care is requisite when a vessel enters a harbor, especially
when there is wind, and vessels at anchor. *Ward v. Schooner
Dousman*, 28.

Apportionment of damages will not be made if the fault be doubtful. *Ib.*

A steamer is bound to avoid a collision when practicable. *Ib.*

The libellant must show the fault is chargeable on the boat complained
of. *Lucas v. Steamboat Thomas Swan*, 282.

A case of inevitable accident is no ground for an action. *Ib.*

Where there are faults on both sides, damages are divided. *Ib.*

AGENTS.

On an appeal in admiralty, from the district court, reasonable diligence should be used in prosecuting the appeal. *Neil v. Steamer
Illinois*, 418.

If the party delay to perfect the appeal for six months, and until a
day or two before the term of the Circuit Court, the appellee may
under the rule, notice the cause for a hearing, and the court will
require the appellant to take his depositions during the session of
the court, so as to come to a hearing. *Ib.*

At the home port of a vessel the local law must regulate the lien. *Ib.*

A purely maritime lien may arise in every 'port, under the maritime
jurisdiction, unless it be in the home port. *Ib.*

AGENTS.—*Continued.*

An action being brought against the defendant charging him with an abuse of his powers, as agent of the plaintiff, it is essential that the plaintiff should allege he had acted as agent. *Ætna Insurance Co. v. Sabins,* 398.

Unless he was authorized he could not bind the company, and any ratification of the company would excuse the defendant. *Ib.*

If the plaintiff ratified what had been done, it binds the company, though the agent had no power. *Ib.*

The conductor of a train of cars is bound to reasonable care for the passengers, and at cross roads, or where the tracks lie very near each other, more than an ordinary degree of care is requisite. *Ib.*

Any carelessness in loading a freight train of cars, or in not attending to the adjustment of a load of lumber by which an injury is done to a passenger on another train, will make the owners of the freight train responsible. *Ib.*

ALIEN.

By the common law an alien can take lands by purchase though not by descent. *Normers Loan Co. v. McKinney,* 5.

He may claim by grant or devise. *Ib.*

A title acquired by an alien is not divested until office found. *Ib.*

There is a close analogy between an alien and a corporation. *Ib.*

APPEALS IN ADMIRALTY.

If the appellant delay to protest his appeal, so that the record is filed a very short time before the court commences, the appellant may notice the cause for hearing or continue at his option. *Bachus v. Schooner Merango,* 499.

No one should be permitted to take advantage of his own remissness. *Ib.*

ASSUMPSIT.

Where the statute has run and a subsequent promise to pay is relied on, the action must be on the new promise. The original debt is not revived, and it is considered only as affording a good consideration on the new promise. *Kampshall v. Goodman,* 190.

BAIL.

A recognisance taken by a Commissioner must describe an offence punishable, or it is void. *United States v. Hand et al,* 274.

BANKS.

On the failure of a bank to pay the specie, it may be forced into liquidation under the laws of Ohio, and receivers are appointed to collect the debts and pay the liabilities of the bank. *Bank of Circleville v. Iglehart,* 560.

Banks.   Bills in Chancery.   Bills of Lading.   Chancery.   Collision.

BANKS.—*Continued.*

If there be a deficiency of assets and the stockholders are required to contribute pro rata, on the amount of stock they own, and to pay the whole amount if necessary, on such a decree an action of debt cannot be sustained. *Ib.*

To maintain an action of debt, the sum decreed must be certain, so as to require no further action of the court. *Ib.*

An action being brought on the decree, is subject to the condition expressed. *Ib.*

A suit in equity is sustainable to carry a decree into effect. *Ib.*

BILL IN CHANCERY.

On a demurrer to a bill being sustained, the court will give leave to amend the bill and time for answer. *Ketchum v. Driggs,* 14.

To restrain a creditors bill, an execution is not necessary unless required by statute, when the property cannot be reached at law. *Wilkinson v. Gale,* 16.

A citizen of Connecticut, being a stockholder, may file his bill for an injunction against the collection of an unconstitutional tax, and make the directors of the bank defendants, they having refused to take the necessary steps. *Woolsey v. Dodge, Treasurer,* 142.

An action of trespass is not an adequate remedy for the bank, when its funds are annually and unlawfully abstracted. *Ib.*

The State cannot be sued, its officer may not be responsible. *Ib.*

The courts of the Union follow the construction of the statutes of the State as established by its Supreme court. *Ib.*

All persons interested should be made parties to a bill to foreclose a mortgage. *Matcolm v. Smith,* 416.

This is indispensable when a party may be chargeable with any balance which the sale of the premises may not satisfy. *Ib.*

BILL OF LADING.

A bill of lading is conclusive to establish the articles shipped, unless fraud or mistake is shown. *Backus v. the Schooner Marengo,* 487.

Such an instrument has some of the characteristics of a bill of exchange. *Ib.*

Good faith in the agents of commerce is requisite. *Ib.*

CHANCERY.

Under the rules of court a bill is not amendable after replication is filed, unless the plaintiff shows the proposed amendment is material. *Ross et al v. Carpenter,* 352.

Such amendment will not be allowed to introduce a new party, where the party were known before the bill was filed. *Ib.*

COLLISION.

A steamer in entering a harbor must use great caution to avoid a col-

COMPACT.

A law of Indiana was passed declaring lands sold by the United States, within the State, should not be taxed until after the expiration of five years from the time of sale. In 1847 Congress passed a law taking off the restriction as to taxation before the year 1820. The act of Indiana remained unrepealed. Before the repeal of the law lands had been sold. *Held*, that such lands were exempt from taxation for five years from the sale. *Thompson v. Halton Treasurer*, 886.

CONSTITUTIONAL LAW.

A provision in a bank charter which declares, "that the bank shall pay a tax of six per cent. upon its dividends, after deducting ascertained expenses and losses, in lieu of all taxation whatever," is a contract the obligation of which the legislature cannot impair. *Woolsey v. Dodge*, 142.

CONSEQUENTIAL DAMAGES.

Consequential damages are often recovered, but they must be such as result from a failure to perform by one of the parties to the contract. But possible or probable profits cannot be the ground of increasing damages. *Chapin & Butts v. Norton et al*, 500.

In the course of a contract if accounts are presented and no objection made, it is too late afterwards to object. *Ib.*

CONTRACT.

A contract was entered into that defendant should take a stock farm and manage it for one third of the profits. Shortly after he took possession, he sold the stock on the farm, reserving to himself the homestead and a small part of the grounds, and he rented the residue of the farm. *Held*, that this was an abandonment of the contract. *Tibbatts & Wife v. Tibbatts*, 80.

Any modification or change of the contract after, by the husband without the consent of the wife, cannot bind the wife, the land being hers, after the death of her husband. *Ib.*

Where a contract was made for the purchase of wheat at Detroit to be delivered in the spring, on the opening of navigation, parol proof is admissible to show, at what time the payment is to be made. *Halsey v. Hurd*, 102.

On a failure to deliver the article at the time specified, the purchasers may claim, as damages, the difference between the contract price and the current price of the article. *Ib.*

The plaintiffs agreed with the Commissioners of Hamilton county to build for the county, upon the old court house lot in Cincinnati, a court house upon such place and of such materials as to them shall seem proper, which covered the entire lot.

CONTRACT.—*Continued.*

In the same contract they agreed to build a jail, on such lot or within certain limits, as the legislature might authorize. *Held*, that although the law contemplated all the buildings for the county should be placed on the court house lot, yet the contract for building the jail on another lot, is not illegal on the condition expressed. *Cook & Cook v. Commissioners of Hamilton county*, 112.

It was to be made binding by the action of the legislature. *Ib.*

The contracts to build the court house and jail were separate and distinct, although included in the same instrument. *Ib.*

To justify a party to put an end to a contract, the contractor must in effect abandon it. *Ib.*

Where two hundred thousand dollars were appropriated to construct county buildings, which must cost three times that sum, the appropriation imposes no limitation as to expenditures. *Ib.*

If in construction of a public work, it is provided that the engineer may put an end to the contract, if in his judgment the contractor does not act with the necessary vigor—the engineer is not responsible, though he may be mistaken in judgment. *Culbertson v. Ellis et al*, 248.

But if the engineer act corruptly he is responsible. *Ib.*

The declaration of forfeiture will prevent the contractor from the recovery of damages. *Ib.*

When a receipt is given in evidence to show the contract of affreightment, the whole document is in proof and one part cannot be separated from the other. *Butler v. Steamer Arrow*, 470.

After the voyage had been completed the clerk of a steamer sailing between Sandusky, Ohio, and Chatham, Canada, touching at Detroit and other ports, gave the following receipt to the owner of a horse lost:

Received of T. B. three dollars for transporting horse from Sandusky to Chatham. One dollar for the steamer Ploughboy, and two dollars for the steamer Arrow. The horse (by consent) transferred to the Ploughboy. *Ib.*

Parol evidence admitted to explain receipt. *Ib. Held*, steamboat not liable, the horse having been handed over to the Ploughboy.

Where a person has agreed to deliver a quantity of lumber at specified prices, and he fails to comply with his contract, the plaintiff is entitled to recover in damages the difference in price between the lumber contracted for, and the market price at the place of delivery. *Barnad v. Conger*, 497.

If the market price at the place of delivery was as low or lower, than the price agreed to be paid in the contract, the plaintiff will be entitled to no damages. *Ib.*

CONTRACT.— *Continued.*

The rule is that no damages can be recovered, where none has been sustained. *Ib.*

Under a contract made by complainants, with the defendants, that the former would purchase all the lumber sawed by the defendants, and complainant would furnish supplies, etc., which they afterwards refused to do, on which defendants abandoned the contract; held that where one party refuses to do a certain thing under the contract which was necessary to enable the other party to perform his part of the contract, he may abandon it. *Ib.*

And in such case the party first refusing is liable to the other for damages. *Ib.*

But such damages are limited to the immediate consequences resulting from the refusal to perform the contract, and not to probable profits. *Ib.*

A large amount of lumber being in the possession of the defaulting party, having repudiated the contract, he cannot claim the benefits under it. *Ib.*

But in selling the lumber he would be entitled to compensation. *Ib.*

CORPORATION.

A corporation in the State of New York, may hold land in the State of Michigan. *Farmers' Loan Co. v. McKinney,* 4.

This is a matter of comity. *Ib.*

COUNTY ORDERS.

Counties are established by law and need not be proved. *Lyall v. Lapeer county,* 446.

The revised statutes of Michigan of 1846, sec. 46, having provided that the county treasurer shall pay money on the order of the Board of Supervisors, countersigned by the Chairman and signed by the Clerk, an order in that form will be presumed correct, and the official act of the Supervisors. *Ib.*

Such an order is a county liability, drawn by one county officer on another, for payment out of county funds, and no presentment and demand are necessary. *Ib.*

The statute expressly authorizes such orders for county indebtments to be drawn by the Board of Supervisors, and does not prohibit their negotiability. *Ib.*

An action lies against the county upon such county orders for county indebtment, in the court of the United States. *Ib.*

COSTS.

There can be no taxation of costs except under the act of 1858. *Lyall v. Miller,* 422.

That law abolishes all previous laws on the subject, without any reservation. *Ib.*

2

DAMAGES.

In an action against a bridge company for the loss of a boat which struck the pier of a bridge, the court held, that the injury of the boat was to be ascertained by the hire of it during the time it was undergoing repairs, and the cost of repairs. *Jolly v. Terre Haute Company*, 238.

When a contract to build a court house was put an end to by the wrongful act of the superintendants, they are subject to an action for damages for the work done, and the materials purchased, also for the profit of the work. *Cook & Cook v. Commissioners of Hamilton county*, 512.

DEEDS, ACKNOWLEDGMENT OF.

A quit claim deed executed before title vested in the grantor, is not made good by a subsequent title. *Farmers' Loan & Trust Co. v. McKinney*, 8.

Such a deed transfers only the title of grantor. *Ib.*

The grantor's equity will be conveyed. *Ib.*

DEBTORS TO THE GOVERNMENT.

A State regulation that the estate of deceased persons shall be settled in the probate court, which shall appoint commissioners to adjust the claims against the estate, and prescribe the time within which such claims must be presented, and if not presented, shall be barred, is not obligatory on the federal government, in the collection of its debts. *United States v. Backus*, 448.

The amount claimed has been adjusted by the accounting department of the government, and must be collected under its own laws. *Ib.*

It has priority of claim, and cannot, therefore, do any injustice to general creditors by enforcing its claim. A law of a State which requires eighteen months before suit can be brought against executors, does not apply to a demand by the federal government. *Ib.*

If the act could be so construed, it would be in conflict with acts of Congress, and would, consequently, be inoperative. *Ib.*

DECLARATION.

A party which charges an agent with an abuse of his power, must allege in the declaration, that the individual was appointed as agent. *Ætna Insurance Co. v. Sabine*, 393.

DEMURRER.

A demurrer to a bill praying an injunction, must be decided before a motion for the injunction can be heard. *Ketchum v. Driggs*, 13.

A defective allegation of citizenship is a good ground of demurrer. *Ib.*

DEPOSITION.

The deposition of a witness who is at the place where the court is held, is not admissible if the witness be able to attend. *Weed v. Armstrong*, 44.

EVIDENCE.—*Continued.*

An instrument not denied by the pleading may be read as evidence as it appears on its face. *Benedict v. Maynard,* 21. *Pratt v. Willard,* 27.

When a record of a judgment of a State court is offered in evidence, in the Circuit Court, sitting within the State, it was received on the certificate of the clerk and seal of the court. *Brewster v. Spalding,* 24.

The confession of a silent partner, not known in the proceedings, may be given as evidence. *Ward v. Armstrong,* 44.

In a suit against a marshal and his sureties for moneys collected on executions, he cannot set up by way of offset, moneys disallowed on former accounts. *U. States v. Prentiss,* 65.

Proof of good character, ought to outweigh a presumption of stealing money from the mail, arising merely from the fact of association with one who was in possession of the money. *United States v. Poage,* 89.

To convict, a jury must find the defendant guilty beyond a reasonable doubt. *Ib.*

Where no time is fixed for payment, on a purchase of wheat, parol evidence is admissible. *Halsey v. Hurd,* 102.

An agreement that payment should be forwarded through the express, the payee incurs the risk of detention of the express by bad roads or high water. *Ib.*

Under the territorial government, the copy of a deed recorded is prima facie evidence of its execution. *Buckley's heirs v. Carlton,* 125.

But this presumption may be rebutted by facts and circumstances. *Ib.*

Where the acts of the grantor are inconsistent with the presumption that the deed was delivered, they may be weighed against the presumption. *Ib.*

If a letter written to a certain individual, was intended for him and also another person, and such other person is authorized to take the letter from the post office, and he does so take or receive it, there is no violation of the post office law. *United States v. Turner,* 128.

The person who writes a letter has a right to control its use. *Ib.*

Where a post master is charged with stealing a letter from the mail, to establish the charge the post masters on the route and at the office to which the letter was directed, should be examined. *United States v. Whitaker,* 342.

At the office where clerks or others opened the mail, they should be examined. *Ib.*

Parol evidence is not admissible to prove at what time a patent was applied for. *Wayne v. Winter,* 344.

Evidence.

FRAUD.

Conveyances by an insolvent is held prima facie void. *Walcott v. Almy and Wife*, 28.

Where the consideration passed from the grantor to the grantee, with the view to cover the property, it is void. *Ib.*

Fraud may be shown in procuring a patent at law, as the execution of a deed, if fraudulent, may be avoided at law. *Cooper v. Roberts*, 98.

But in neither case can fraud be alleged and proved at law, except in the issuing of the patent or the execution of the instrument. *Ib.*

An individual may, bona fide, convey his property in trust for the benefit of his creditors. *Fuller v. Ives*, 478.

But if previous to his assignment he has appropriated his funds, in the name of another, to delay and defraud his creditors, the court will set aside his assignment and his previous conveyances and fraudulent investments, and make them answerable to his creditors. *Ib.*

When an individual, having given acceptances to another with a view to his own indemnity, receives a large amount of property, which he applies to his own purposes, and leaves his acceptances unpaid, his acts are fraudulent. *Ib.*

FUGITIVES FROM LABOR.

See Slaves.

GRANTS.

A grant made by Congress to certain settlers in the village of Peoria, where buildings had been destroyed by a company of militia in the service of the United States, cannot be considered a gratuity. *Forsyth v. Ballance*, 562.

The grant, when made, referred back to the consideration, and fully recognized it. *Ib.*

The individual who made the settlement and whose property was destroyed, died before the grant was issued, though it was made by the act; the property descended to his heirs, and when the patent was issued, it was properly made to the legal representatives of the deceased. *Ib.*

Under the laws of Illinois this property was sold to pay the debts of the deceased, no objection being made, though notice by publication was given as the statute required. *Ib.*

When this proceeding is offered collaterally, it cannot be objected to, as the jurisdiction of the court which sanctioned it is undoubted. *Ib.*

The heirs being content, a stranger cannot object to the irregularity of the proceedings. *Ib.*

Indorser and indorsee.   Injunction.   Insurance.   Judiciary.   Indictment.

LIMITATION, STATUTE OF— *Continued.*

1. A clear and an unconditional acknowledgment of the debt, from which the law implies a promise to pay.
2. If the acknowledgment be conditional, the liability attaches under the conditions. *Ib.*

But if the acknowledgment be connected with any condition which shows there was no intention to pay the debt, it does not take the case out of the statute. *Ib.*

The action must be on the new promise; the indebtment is considered a sufficient consideration to support the promise. *Ib.*

The 8th section of the Revised Statute of the 3d March, 1845, of Illinois, requires three things to protect the possession: 1. The party must have entered upon the land in good faith, under color of title. 2. He must have been in possession for seven years before suit was brought. 3. He must have paid all taxes during that period. *Russel v. Barney*, 577.

Under the 9th section, two things only are required: 1. Color of title made in good faith. 2. He must have paid taxes for seven years on the land. *Ib.*

The above is an act of limitation. *Ib.*

The tenant can not claim in part under such section. *Ib.*

LUNATIC.

An individual is liable to punishment when he can discriminate right from wrong. *U. States v. Shultz*, 121.

And this can be best ascertained, not by any theory as to the mind, but by the acts of the party. *Ib.*

The concealment of the offense, endeavors to elude the officers of justice by an escape, a judicious use of the money stolen, all show a knowledge of the wrong. And this is the point to be ascertained when insanity is pleaded. *Ib.*

MILITARY RESERVES.

A military reserve may be abandoned by the government, when it becomes useless for public purposes; and by giving notice through the Secretary of the Interior, it may be considered as a part of the public lands, from which it was temporarily reserved. *United States v. Railroad Bridge*, 517.

Such lands having been surveyed and offered at public auction, may be opened for entry as other lands. *Ib.*

The reserve on Rock Island, though surveyed, never having been offered for sale at public auction, does not come technically within the act of 1852, authorizing Railroad Companies to locate their roads through the lands of the United States. *Ib.*

The act of 1819 only authorizes the rule of reservations which then existed. *Ib.*

MILITARY RESERVES— *Continued.*

By all the Western States, roads have been made through the lands of the United States. *Ib.*

This is the power of eminent domain, which the States may exercise. *Ib.*

It is essential to the welfare of the State. *Ib.*

MORTGAGE.

A mortgage having been given on certain articles of property to secure the payment of $1,500, a subsequent arrangement was made by the parties to deliver to the mortgagor the articles of property, on his giving security to sell the same at reasonable prices, and account to the mortgagee.

The security was given, and suit being brought, the defendant pleaded the original mortgage had been assigned to him. To this defendant demurred. Held, this plea was no answer to the declaration. *Harper v. Neff,* 890.

NEW TRIAL.

When a new trial is granted as a matter of right in the action of ejectment, the party can not bring a new suit in another Court. *Fraser v. Waller,* 11.

Where the evidence preponderates in favor of the verdict, the Court will not set it aside on the ground of testimony which impeaches a witness. *U. States v. Potter,* 182.

Where a jury return a sealed verdict, each juror may be asked, is, or is not, this his verdict. *U. States v. Potter,* 182.

ORDINANCE.

The whole legislation, from the ordinance of 1787 to the present time, shows that the Mississippi and its tributaries were intended to be free for navigation. *Columbus Insurance Co. v. Mertorius et al.,* 209.

PATENT RIGHTS.

The thing invented must be so clearly described, as to enable a person well skilled in the subject matter of the invention to construct or make it. *Allen v. Hunter,* 808.

In a matter of science, no man can be a fit expert, who does not understand the science involved. *Ib.*

And a jury in such a matter will give weight to the evidence as the witnesses may be competent to speak on the subject. *Ib.*

A specification of a chemical compound is not addressed to one ignorant of chemistry. *Ib.*

A specification must be construed according to the true import of the words used, rather than by their grammatical arrangement. *Ib.*

In a case of prior invention, a patent is not to be superseded, unless the thing patented was invented before the invention patented. *Ib.*

PATENT RIGHTS.—*Continued.*

Where reaping machines prior to the plaintiff's invention, had a grain divider or reel part similar to the plaintiff's the defendants may use the same without injuring the plaintiff's patent. *Ib.*

Plaintiff's invention of 1847 and 1853, was not a raker's seat, but it was the improvement of his machine, by which it was balanced and the shortening of the reel so that room was made for the raker's seat on the extended finger bar. *Ib.*

A patent for a combination of machinery is not infringed, if less than the entire combination is used. *Pitts & Pitts v. Wemple et al.* 550.

A combination is usually formed by using unknown processes or mechanical powers, in which case the invention consists in the union of those powers. *Ib.*

The constituent parts remain with the public as before the combination. *Ib.*

But the combination can not be used, though something be added to it. *Ib.*

An improvement of a combined machine, for which a patent may be obtained, gives no right to use the combined machine. *Ib.*

Nor under such circumstances, has the inventor of a combined machine the right to use the improvement. *Ib.*

The inventions of the original and improved machine, are separate and distinct. *Ib.*

PARTNERSHIP.

Partners can not distribute among themselves, any part of the stock in trade, to the injury of creditors. *Williamson v. Yale.*

But when a distribution is made with the assent of the creditors it is not fraudulent. *Ib.*

PERJURY.

A false swearing to obtain a pre-emptive right is made perjury by statute. *United States v. Stanley,* 409.

The person commencing an improvement has a right to continue it, and any one who interferes may be considered a trespasser. *Ib.*

But if a first occupant gives way to a second, and to him the right is granted, it is good against all the world, except the first occupant. *Ib.*

PLEADINGS.

The general issue admits the signature of the defendant, unless the plea be sworn to, by rule of court. *Benedict v. Maynard,* 21.

The affidavit will not be permitted when the cause is called for trial. *Ib.*

The declaration alleged that the defendant constructed piers in the channel of the Illinois river, which essentially obstructed naviga-

PLEADINGS.—*Continued*.

tion to the great injury of the plaintiff. The defendants pleaded that the piers were as authorized by an act of the legislature. Held, that the plea was bad. *Columbus Insurance Co. v. Customers*, 209.

A special plea which amounts to the general issue is demurrable. *Curtis v. Central Railroad*, 401.

A plea which states in bar to the plaintiff's demand, is not good, if the facts so stated do not constitute a bar. *Ib.*

Leave to file a supplemental answer to a bill of foreclosure, founded on a fact known to the party at the time the original answer was filed—refused.

A supplemental answer must embrace new matter discovered after the answer was filed. *Suydam v. Truesdale*, 459.

This is an application to the discretion of the court. *Ib.*

The rule as to parties in equity is not inflexible, and will not be enforced so as to do injustice. *Ib.*

POWER OF ATTORNEY.

A power of Attorney to authorize the conveyance of a deed, requires the same solemnities as the deed. *Farmers' Trust Co. v. McKinney*, 4.

PRACTICE.

A usage constitutes a rule of practice, although there be no written rule on the subject. *Curtis v. Central Railroad*, 401.

PRE-EMPTION.

If the first occupant of land give way to a second, who claims a right of pre-emption, his claim is good against all except the first occupant. *U. States v. Stanley*, 409.

If the first occupant abandon his right the right of the second can not be questioned. *Ib.*

PROCESS.

A strict compliance with the statute is required, when leaving a copy at defendant's residence is a service. *Halsey v. Hurd*, 14.

STATUTE OF A STATE.

Doubtful words in a statute, if not scientific or technical, are to be interpreted according to their familiar use and acceptation. *Fashion v. Wards*, 152.

SUB-TREASURY.

No bank under the sub-treasury law can become a depository of the public money. *United States v. City Bank*, 180.

The law prohibits such a deposit and inflicts a severe penalty on the officer who makes it. *Ib.*

But a state bank is not prohibited from transmitting drafts. *Ib.*

Where the money of the government is deposited in a bank, the illegality of the transaction is no bar to a recovery. *Ib.*

In such case the agent does not bind the government. *Ib.*

TAX.

The tax law of 1852, against banks, incorporated under the act of 1845, having been held to be unconstitutional, it can afford no justification to a collector of the tax on banks. *Woolsey v. Dodge*, 142.

A claim under a tax sale can only be sustained, by showing a substantial compliance with the statute. *Lamb's Heirs v. Gillett*, 365.

The deed of the auditor, is prima facie evidence under the statute. *Ib.*

The auditor's deed is prima facie evidence of the recitals of what is contained in it. *Ib.*

Land, exempted at the time of purchase from taxation by a law of the State, cannot be taxed until the limitation has expired. *Thompson v. Holton, Treasurer*, 286.

A tax can be just and equal on railroad corporations only, by taxing profits. *Paine et al. v. Wright, and Indiana & Bellefontaine Railroad*, 395.

TAX TITLE.

In a sale of land for taxes, any material act which the law requires, or which may prejudice the rights of the owner, will be fatal to the title of the claimant. *Ogden v. Harrington*, 418.

But mere technicalities which do not come within this rule, and can not prejudice the interest of the land-holder, do not vitiate the rule. *Ib.*

A payment of the money into the county treasury instead of the State treasury, or the treasury of the county, instead of the township, cannot effect the title. *Ib.*

The officer who pays or receives the money wrongfully, is liable to pay it over into the proper treasury. *Ib.*

SLAVES.

In an action for aiding and abetting slaves to escape, it must appear that the colored persons were slaves, and that this fact was known to the defendant. *Weimer v. Sloane*, 259.

The statute authorizes an arrest by the owner or his agents. *Ib.*

To make defendant liable, it must appear that he had notice or knowledge that the fugitives were slaves. *Ib.*

The test of the legality of an arrest, is the law, and not the opinion of defendant. *Ib.*

Any words or actions tending to effect an escape, and which lead to that result, are sufficient to implicate the defendant. *Ib.*

An intention to effect an escape must appear, but such intention may be inferred from the facts. *Ib.*

A party acting as counsel, for a fugitive slave, is protected from the consequences of his acts, so far only as they are within the proper limits of his professional duty. *Ib.*

WITNESS.

When witnesses contradict each other in a material fact, a jury will consider which of the witnesses, from the circumstances connected with the transaction, would be most likely to know and recollect the facts. *Able & Colt v. Rood & Rood,* 107.

A witness swearing that he thought a particular order was given, and to his belief was obeyed, is not contradicted by testimony positively averring that such order was not given. *Paskion v. Ward,* 152.

When the interest of a witness is equal, on both sides, he is competent. *Scott v. Plymouth,* 464.

Lightning Source UK Ltd.
Milton Keynes UK
UKHW020619120219
337137UK00005B/589/P